Lecture Notes in Computer S

Edited by G. Goos, J. Hartmanis and J. ᵥ

Springer

Berlin
Heidelberg
New York
Barcelona
Hong Kong
London
Milan
Paris
Singapore
Tokyo

Josef Kittler   Fabio Roli (Eds.)

Multiple Classifier Systems

Second International Workshop, MCS 2001
Cambridge, UK, July 2-4, 2001
Proceedings

 Springer

Series Editors

Gerhard Goos, Karlsruhe University, Germany
Juris Hartmanis, Cornell University, NY, USA
Jan van Leeuwen, Utrecht University, The Netherlands

Volume Editors

Josef Kittler
University of Surrey, Centre for Vision, Speech and Signal Processing
Guildford, Surrey GU2 7XH, UK
E-mail: j.kittler@eim.surrey.ac.uk

Fabio Roli
University of Cagliari, Department of Electrical and Electronic Engineering
Piazza d'Armi, 09123 Cagliari, Italy
E-mail: roli@diee.unica.it

Cataloging-in-Publication Data applied for

Die Deutsche Bibliothek - CIP-Einheitsaufnahme

Multiple classifier systems : second international workshop ; proceedings /
MCS 2001, Cambridge, UK, July 2 - 4, 2001. Josef Kittler ; Fabio Roli (ed.).
- Berlin ; Heidelberg ; New York ; Barcelona ; Hong Kong ; London ; Milan ;
Paris ; Singapore ; Tokyo : Springer, 2001
  (Lecture notes in computer science ; Vol. 2096)
  ISBN 3-540-42284-6

CR Subject Classification (1998): I.5, I.4, I.2.10, I.2, F.1

ISSN 0302-9743
ISBN 3-540-42284-6 Springer-Verlag Berlin Heidelberg New York

Springer-Verlag Berlin Heidelberg New York
a member of BertelsmannSpringer Science+Business Media GmbH

http://www.springer.de

© Springer-Verlag Berlin Heidelberg 2001
Printed in Germany

Typesetting: Camera-ready by author, data conversion by PTP-Berlin, Stefan Sossna
Printed on acid-free paper   SPIN: 10839435   06/3142   5 4 3 2 1 0

Foreword

Driven by the requirements of a large number of practical and commercially important applications, the last decade has witnessed considerable advances in pattern recognition. Better understanding of the design issues and new paradigms, such as the Support Vector Machine, have contributed to the development of improved methods of pattern classification. However, while any performance gains are welcome, and often extremely significant from the practical point of view, it is increasingly more challenging to reach the point of perfection as defined by the theoretical optimality of decision making in a given decision framework.

The asymptoticity of gains that can be made for a single classifier is a reflection of the fact that any particular design, regardless of how good it is, simply provides just one estimate of the optimal decision rule. This observation has motivated the recent interest in *Multiple Classifier Systems*, which aim to make use of several designs jointly to obtain a better estimate of the optimal decision boundary and thus improve the system performance. This volume contains the proceedings of the international workshop on Multiple Classifier Systems held at Robinson College, Cambridge, United Kingdom (July 2–4, 2001), which was organized to provide a forum for researchers in this subject area to exchange views and report their latest results.

Following its predecessor, Multiple Classifier Systems 2000 (Springer ISBN 3-540-67704-6), the particular aim of the MCS 2001 workshop was to bring together researchers from the diverse communities with interests in multiple classifiers: Machine Learning, Pattern Recognition, Neural Networks, and Statistics. This aim has been successfully accomplished, with this volume presenting 44 papers from the 4 different communities. The collection has been organized into thematic sessions dealing with bagging and boosting, MCS design methodology, ensemble classifiers, feature spaces for MCS, applications of MCS, one-class MCS and clustering, and, finally, combination strategies. It includes contributions from the invited speakers: Tin Ho (Lucent Technologies, USA), Nathan Intrator (Tel-Aviv University, Israel), and David Hand (Imperial College of Science and Technology London).

The workshop was sponsored by the University of Surrey, Guildford, United Kingdom and the University of Cagliari, Italy, and was co-sponsored by the International Association for Pattern Recognition through its Technical Committees TC1: Statistical Pattern Recognition techniques, and TC16: Algebraic and Discrete Mathematical Techniques in Pattern Recognition and Image Analysis, without whose support the workshop could not have taken place. Their financial assistance is gratefully acknowledged.

We also wish to convey our gratitude to all those who helped to organize MCS 2001. First of all our thanks are due to the members of the Scientific Committee who selected the best papers from a large number of submissions to create an excellent technical content. Jon Benediktsson played a particularly important role in this context in soliciting contributions for the special session on remote sensing. Last but not the least, special thanks are due to the members of the Organizing Committee for their selfless effort to make MCS 2001 successful. Notably, we would like to thank David Windridge for his contribution to the production of this volume, Giorgio Giacinto and Giorgio Fumera for maintaining the MCS 2001 website and to Terry Windeatt for compiling the workshop program.

Josef Kittler and Fabio Roli

April 2001

Workshop Chairs

J Kittler (University of Surrey, United Kingdom)
F Roli (University of Cagliari, Italy)

Scientific Committee

J A Benediktsson (Iceland)
H Bunke (Switzerland)
L P Cordella (Italy)
B V Dasarathy (USA)
R P W Duin (The Netherlands)
C Furlanello (Italy)
J Ghosh (USA)
T K Ho (USA)
S Impedovo (Italy)
N Intrator (Israel)
A K Jain (USA)
M Kamel (Canada)

L I Kuncheva (UK)
L Lam (Hong Kong)
D Landgrebe (USA)
D-S Lee (USA)
D Partridge (UK)
C Scagliola (Italy)
A J C Sharkey (UK)
S N Srihari (USA)
C Y Suen (Canada)
K Tumer (USA)
G Vernazza (Italy)
T Windeatt (UK)

Organizing Committee

G Fumera (University of Cagliari, Italy)
G Giacinto (University of Cagliari, Italy)
T Windeatt (University of Surrey, United Kingdom)
D Windridge (University of Surrey, United Kingdom)

Sponsored by

The University of Surrey
The University of Cagliari
The International Association for Pattern Recognition

Supported by

The University of Surrey
The University of Cagliari

Table of Contents

Ensemble Classifiers

Feature Spaces for MCS

MCS in Remote Sensing

One Class MCS and Clustering

Combination Strategies

Bagging and the Random Subspace Method for Redundant Feature Spaces

Marina Skurichina and Robert P.W.Duin

Pattern Recognition Group, Department of Applied Physics, Faculty of Applied Sciences,
Delft University of Technology, P.O. Box 5046, 2600GA Delft, The Netherlands
{marina, duin}@ph.tn.tudelft.nl

Abstract. The performance of a single weak classifier can be improved by using combining techniques such as bagging, boosting and the random subspace method. When applying them to linear discriminant analysis, it appears that they are useful in different situations. Their performance is strongly affected by the choice of the base classifier and the training sample size. As well, their usefulness depends on the data distribution. In this paper, on the example of the pseudo Fisher linear classifier, we study the effect of the redundancy in the data feature set on the performance of the random subspace method and bagging.

1   Introduction

In many applications of discriminant analysis, data often consist of a large number of measurements (features) with a relatively small number of observations (objects). In these circumstances, it may be difficult to construct a good single classification rule. Usually, a classifier, constructed on small training sets is biased and has a large variance. Consequently, such a classifier may be weak, having a poor performance [1]. One way to improve a weak classifier is to stabilize its decision, for instance, by regularization [2] or noise injection [3]. Another popular approach is to use a combined decision of many weak classifiers instead of a single classifier. The examples of such combining techniques are bagging [4], boosting [5] and the Random Subspace Method (RSM) [6], which are originally designed for decision trees.

When applying bagging and the RSM to Linear Discriminant Analysis (LDA), it was established that these techniques are useful in different situations. Their performance is strongly affected by the choice of the base classifier and the training sample size [7]. As well, it was noticed that their relative performance differs for different data sets. It was demonstrated that the problem complexity (feature efficiency, the length of class boundary etc.) affects the performance of combining techniques [8]. In particular, it was shown that the RSM performs relatively better when a discrimination power is distributed evenly over many features.

In this paper we study the effect of the redundancy in the feature set on the performance of bagging and the RSM. When data have many completely redundant noise features or many data features are highly correlated (many features contain the same information), the intrinsic (true) data dimensionality is smaller than the dimensionality of the feature space where data objects are described. The intrinsic data dimensionality is one of the important characteristics of the data set that may influence the performance of classifiers. Consequently, the redundancy in the data feature set (and the intrinsic data dimensionality) may affect the performance of the combining

J. Kittler and F. Roli (Eds.): MCS 2001, LNCS 2096, pp. 1–10, 2001.

techniques, as their performance depends on the training sample size referred to the data dimensionality. It is especially of interest for the RSM, where one constructs classifiers in random subspaces, because the number of informative features and the dimensionality of random subspaces should affect the performance of the RSM.

In order to study the effect of redundancy in the data feature set on the performance of bagging and the RSM (which are discussed in section 2), we consider two cases of the redundancy representation in the data feature set. In the first case, data have many completely redundant noise features. In the second case, the useful information is spread over many features while the data itself have a low intrinsic dimensionality. The used data sets representing a two-class problem are described in section 3. We perform our simulation study on the example of the Pseudo Fisher Linear Discriminant (PFLD) [9]. Using this classifier as a single classification rule is not recommended because it is weak for critical training sample sizes (when the number of training objects is comparable with the data dimensionality) (see Fig. 1). However, bagging and the RSM are just designed for weak classifiers. So the PFLD is very suitable to be used as a base classifier in these combining techniques when it is constructed on critical training sample sizes. Moreover, our previous study [7] has shown that bagging and the RSM are useful for the PFLD. The results of our simulation study of the effect of the redundancy in the data feature set on the performance of bagging and the RSM are discussed in section 4. Conclusions are summarized in section 5.

2   Bagging and the Random Subspace Method

In order to improve the performance of weak classifiers, a number of combining techniques can be used. Bagging and the RSM are two of them. They both modify the training data set by sampling either training objects (in bagging) or data features (in the RSM), build classifiers on these modified training sets and then combine them into a final decision. Usually the simple majority vote is used to get a final decision. However, the weighted majority vote used in boosting [5] is more preferable because it is more resistant to overtraining (when increasing the number B of combined classifiers) than other combining rules [10]. Therefore, we use the weighted majority vote in both studied combining techniques.

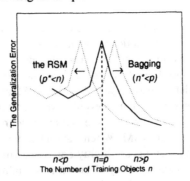

Fig. 1. The shifting effect of the *generalization error* (GE) of the PFLD for the RSM and bagging. In the RSM, the GE shifts with respect to the GE of the original classifier in the direction of the GE obtained on larger training sets. In bagging, the GE shifts with respect to the GE of the original classifier in the direction of the GE obtained on smaller training sets. (Here, n is the number of training objects and p is the data dimensionality.)

Bagging is proposed by Breiman [4] and based on bootstrapping [11] and aggregating concepts. By that, it incorporates benefits of both approaches. Bootstrapping is based on random sampling with replacement. Therefore, taking a bootstrap replicate $X^b = (X_1^b, X_2^b, ..., X_n^b)$ (the random selection with replacement) of the training set $X = (X_1, X_2, ..., X_n)$, one can sometimes avoid or get less misleading training objects in the bootstrap training set. Consequently, a classifier constructed on such a training set may have a better performance. Aggregating actually means combining classifiers. Often a combined classifier gives better results than individual classifiers. Therefore, bagging might be helpful to build better classifiers on training sample sets with misleaders. In bagging, bootstrapping and aggregating techniques are implemented in the following way.

1. Repeat for $b=1,2,...,B$.
   a) Take a bootstrap replicate X^b of the training data set X.
   b) Construct a classifier $C^b(x)$ (with a decision boundary $C^b(x) = 0$) on X^b.
   c) Compute combining weights $c_b = \frac{1}{2}\log\left(\frac{1-err_b}{err_b}\right)$, where $err_b = \frac{1}{n}\sum_{i=1}^{n} w_i^b \xi_i^b$
   and $\xi_i^b = \begin{cases} 0, & \text{if } X_i \text{ is classified correctly} \\ 1, & \text{otherwise} \end{cases}$.
2. Combine classifiers $C^b(x)$, $b=1,2,...,B$, by the weighted majority vote with weights c_b to a final decision rule $\beta(x) = \underset{y \in \{-1,1\}}{\arg\max} \sum_b \delta_{\text{sgn}(C^b(x)), y}$, where $\delta_{i,j} = \begin{cases} 1, & i = j; \\ 0, & i \neq j; \end{cases}$ is Kronecker symbol, $y \in \{-1, 1\}$ is a decision (class label) of the classifier.

Bootstrapping is most efficient when the training set is in order of the data dimensionality. By this, bagging is useful for linear classifiers constructed on critical training sample sizes, when they are unstable [12]. When bootstrapping the training set in bagging, in average only $1-1/e= 63.2\%$ of the training objects is used in each bootstrap replicate. In this way, the bootstrap sample is comparable with a smaller training set. So, the bagged classifier will have similar characteristics as the classifier built on the smaller training set. *The generalization error of the bagged classifier is shifted* with reference to the generalization error of the original classifier in the direction of the generalization error obtained on a smaller training set (see Fig. 1). Thus, *the performance of bagging depends on the training sample size related to the data dimensionality and on the small sample size properties of the base classifier.* It implies that, when applied to LDA, *bagging is useful for classifiers with a non-decreasing learning curve* (the dependency of the classification error as a function on the training sample size) *constructed on critical training sample sizes* [12].

The *Random Subspace Method* is the combining technique proposed by Ho [6]. In the RSM, one also samples the training data. However, the sampling is performed in the feature space. Let each training object $X_i = (x_{i1}, x_{i2}, ..., x_{ip})$ $(i=1,...,n)$ in the training sample set $X = (X_1, X_2, ..., X_n)$ be a p-dimensional vector, described by p features. In the RSM, one randomly selects $p^*<p$ features from the p-dimensional data set X. By this, one obtains the p^*-dimensional random subspace of the original p-dimensional feature space. So the modified training set $\tilde{X}^b = (\tilde{X}_1^b, \tilde{X}_2^b, ..., \tilde{X}_n^b)$ consists of p^*-dimensional training objects $\tilde{X}_i^b = (x_{i1}^b, x_{i2}^b, ..., x_{ip*}^b)$ $(i=1,...,n)$, where p^* components x_{ij}^b $(j=1,...,p^*)$ are randomly selected from p components x_{ij} $(j=1,...,p)$ of the training vector X_i (the selection is the same for each training vector). Then one constructs classifiers in the random subspaces $\tilde{X}^b$ and aggregates them b in the final decision rule. Namely, the RSM is organized in the following way.

1. Repeat for $b=1,2,...,B$.

   a) Select the $p*$ -dimensional random subspace $\tilde{X}^b$ from the original p-dimensional feature space X .

   b) Construct a classifier $C^b(x)$ (with a decision boundary $C^b(x) = 0$) in $\tilde{X}^b$.

   c) Compute combining weights $c_b = \frac{1}{2}\log\left(\frac{1 - err_b}{err_b}\right)$, where $err_b = \frac{1}{n}\sum_{i=1}^{n} w_i^b \xi_i^b$

   and $\xi_i^b = \begin{cases} 0, if\ X_i\ is\ classified\ correctly \\ 1, otherwise \end{cases}$.

2. Combine classifiers $C^b(x)$, $b=1,2,...,B$, by the weighted majority vote with weights c_b to a final decision rule $\beta(x) = \underset{y \in \{-1, 1\}}{argmax}\sum_b \delta_{sgn(C^b(x)), y}$, where $\delta_{i, j} = \begin{cases} 1, i = j; \\ 0, i \neq j; \end{cases}$ is Kronecker symbol, $y \in \{-1, 1\}$ is a decision (class label) of the classifier.

The RSM may benefit from both, using random subspaces for constructing the classifiers and aggregating the classifiers. In the case, when the number of training objects is relatively small as compared with the data dimensionality, by constructing classifiers in random subspaces one may solve the small sample size problem, because the training sample size relatively increases in random subspaces. When data have many redundant features, one may obtain better classifiers in random subspaces than in the original feature space. The combined decision of such classifiers may be superior to a single classifier constructed on the original training set in the complete feature space.

   The performance of the RSM is also affected by the training sample size and the small sample size properties of the base classier [7]. The subspace dimensionality is smaller than in the original feature space while the number of training objects remains the same. By this, the relative training sample size increases. Similar to bagging, *in the RSM, the final classifier will have a shifting effect of the generalization error* with respect to the generalization error of the original classifier (see Fig. 1). However, this shift will be in the opposite direction: in the direction of the generalization error obtained on larger training sample sizes. So *the RSM is useful for classifiers having a decreasing learning curve constructed on small and critical training sample sizes.*

   Thus, bagging and the RSM may be useful for linear classifiers constructed on critical training sample sizes. However, bagging is beneficial for linear classifiers with a non-decreasing learning curve, while the RSM is useful for linear classifiers having a decreasing learning curve. The PFLD is weak when it is constructed on critical training sample sizes, having a peak of the generalization error at point $n=p$ (see Fig. 1). By this, the learning curve of the PFLD increases for training sample sizes $n<p$, and decreases for $n>p$. Therefore, both, bagging and the RSM, may improve the performance of the single PFLD constructed on critical training sample sizes.

3   Data

In our experimental investigations we considered one artificial and five real data sets representing a two-class problem, which we have modified in order to get data sets having a high redundancy in the data feature space.

   The artificial data set used to obtain data with many redundant features is the *2-dimensional correlated Gaussian data* set constituted by two classes with equal covariance matrices. Each class consists of 500 vectors. The mean of the first class is zero for both features. The mean of the second class is equal to 3 for both features. The common covariance matrix is a diagonal matrix with a variance of 40 for the second feature and unit variance for the first feature. This data set is rotated by using a rotation matrix $R = \frac{\sqrt{2}}{2}\begin{bmatrix} 1 & -1 \\ 1 & 1 \end{bmatrix}$.

The real data sets, used to obtain highly redundant data sets, are taken from the UCI Repository [14]. They are the 34-dimensional *ionosphere* data set, the 8-dimensional *pima-diabetes* data set, the 60-dimensional *sonar* data set, the 30-dimensional *wdbc* data set and the 24-dimensional *german* data set.

In order to make these data sets highly redundant in the feature space, to each of them we added r completely redundant noise features distributed normally $N(0,10^{-4})$. Thus, we have obtained $p+r$-dimensional data sets with many completely redundant noise features (one way of the redundancy representation in the data feature set). Here, p is the dimensionality of the original data set. In order to obtain data sets where a useful information is spread over all $p+r$ features (other way of the redundancy representation in the feature set), we have rotated the data enriched by noise features. The rotation was performed in all $p+r$ dimensions by using a Hadamard matrix [15]. By this, we have obtained the data sets where the classification ability (discrimination power) is spread over all features.

Training sets are chosen randomly from a total data set. The remaining data are used for testing. All experiments are repeated 50 times on independent training sets. So all figures show the averaged results over 50 repetitions. The standard deviations of the mean generalization errors for the single and combined PFLD's are around 0.01 for each data set.

In bagging and the RSM, ensembles consist of 100 classifiers combined by the weighted majority vote in the final decision. The size $p*$ of random subspaces used in the RSM is 10.

4   The Effect of the Redundancy in the Data Feature Space

In order to study the effect of redundancy in the data feature set on the performance of bagging and the RSM, we have modified several data sets by artificially increasing their redundancy in the data feature set (see previous section). In order to investigate whether redundancy representation in the data feature space affects the performance of the combining techniques, we modify the original data sets in two different ways: 1) just adding r completely redundant noise features to the original p-dimensional data set (by this, a discrimination power is condensed in the subspace described by the original p-dimensional data set), 2) additionally rotating the data set in all $p+r$ dimensional space after injecting r completely redundant noise features to the original data set (by this, a discrimination power is spread over all $p+r$ features).

Fig. 2 shows learning curves of the single PFLD, bagging and the RSM for the 80-dimensional data sets ($p+r=80$). Fig. 3 represents the generalization errors versus the number of redundant noise features r when the training sample size is fixed to 40 objects per class (80 training objects in total). Left plots in Fig. 2 and 3 show the case when the classification ability is concentrated in p features. Right plots represent the case when the discrimination power is spread over all $p+r$ features. Figures show that both combining techniques are useful in highly redundant feature spaces. The RSM performs relatively better when the discrimination power is spread over many features than when it is condensed in few features (this coincides with results obtained by Ho for decision trees [8]). When all data features are informative, the increasing redundancy in the data feature set does not affect the performance of the RSM. This can be explained as follows. In order to construct good classifiers in random subspaces, it is important that each subspace would contain as much as possible useful information. This could be achieved only when information is "uniformly" spread over all features (it is especially important when small random subspaces are used in the RSM). If useful information is condensed in few features, many random subspaces will be "empty" of useful information, the classifiers constructed in them will be bad and may worsen the combined decision.

In contrast to the RSM, the performance of bagging is affected neither by the redundancy representation in the data feature set, nor by the increasing feature redundancy (it is affected by the data dimensionality referred to the training sample size). It happens because all features are kept in bagging when training objects are sampled. Rotation does not change the informativity of the bootstrap replicate of the

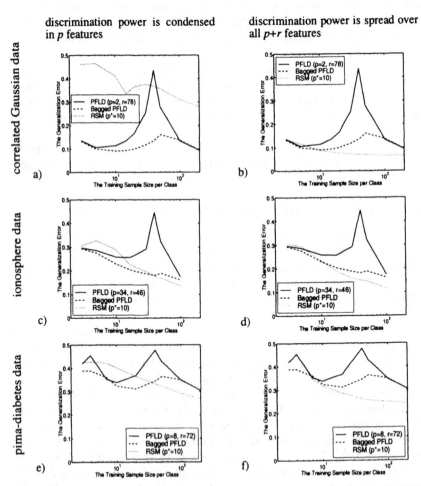

Fig. 2. Learning curves of the single PFLD, bagging and the RSM (p^*=10) for the 80-dimensional data sets ($p+r$=80). Left plots show the case when discrimination power is condensed in p features (data have r completely redundant noise features). Right plots show the case when discrimination power is spread over all features (after adding r redundant features to p-dimensional original data set, the data are rotated in all $p+r$=80 directions).

training set. Thus, bagging may perform better than the RSM for the highly redundant feature spaces when the discrimination power is condensed in few features and the training sample size is small. However, the RSM outperforms bagging when the discrimination power is distributed over all data features.

As well, besides the redundancy in the data feature set, other factors (e.g., the class overlap, the data distribution etc.) affect the performance of the PFLD, bagging and the RSM. Usually many factors act simultaneously, assisting and counteracting each other. Sometimes, some factors may have a stronger influence than the redundancy in the data feature set. For instance, the sonar data set represents time signals where the order of features jointly with their values are very important. When rotating this data set enriched by redundant noise features, some important information is lost. By this reason, the RSM performs worse on the rotated sonar data set than when no rotation is

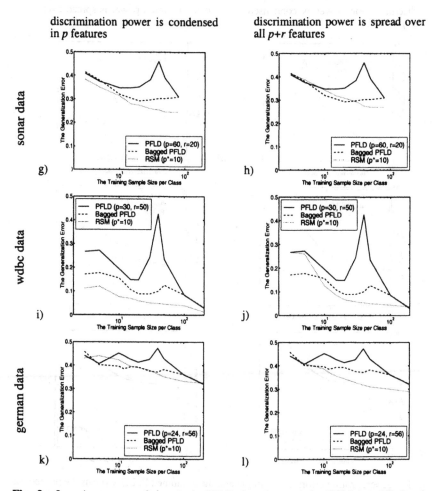

Fig. 2. Learning curves of the single PFLD, bagging and the RSM ($p*=10$) for the 80-dimensional data sets ($p+r=80$). Left plots show the case when discrimination power is condensed in p features (data have r completely redundant noise features). Right plots show the case when discrimination power is spread over all features (after adding r redundant features to p-dimensional original data set, the data are rotated in all $p+r=80$ directions).

performed (see Fig. 2g,h and Fig. 3g,h). Another example, where rotation does not improve the performance of the RSM, is the modified wdbc data set (see Fig. 2i,j and Fig. 3i,j). All features of the original data set are already strongly correlated and it has the largest Mahalanobis distance (d=14.652) among all considered data sets. It seems that rotation somewhat "worsens" the distribution of the useful information over the features. So the RSM performs worse on the rotated data set than when no rotation is performed.

5   Conclusions

Besides the training sample size related to the data dimensionality and the choice of the base classifier, *the efficiency of the combining techniques may depend on the level*

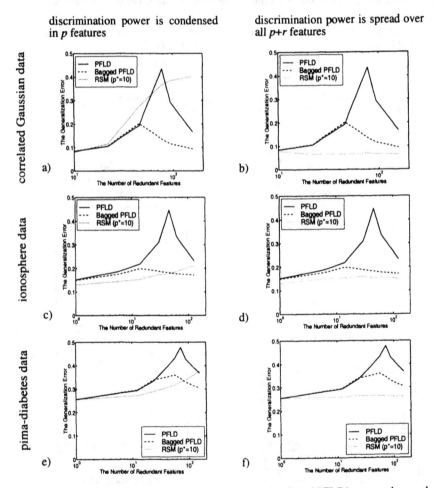

Fig. 3. The generalization errors of the single and the combined PFLD's versus the number of redundant noise features *r* added to the original *p*-dimensional data sets. Left plots show the case when a discrimination power is condensed in *p* features (data have *r* completely redundant noise features). Right plots represent the case when a discrimination power is spread over *p+r* features (after adding *r* redundant features to *p*-dimensional data set, the data are rotated in all *p+r* directions). 80 training objects are used to train the single and the combined classifiers.

of redundancy in the data feature set and on the way this redundancy is presented.

When applied to the Pseudo Fisher linear classifier, *the RSM performs relatively better when the classification ability* (discrimination power and also the redundancy) *is spread over many features* (i.e., for the data sets having many informative features) *than when the classification ability is condensed in few features* (i.e., for the data sets with many completely redundant noise features). *When the discrimination power is spread over all features, the RSM is resistant to the increasing redundancy in the data feature set.*

Unlike the RSM, *the performance of bagging,* when applied to the PFLD, *depends neither on the redundancy representation nor on the level of redundancy in the data*

discrimination power is condensed
in *p* features

discrimination power is spread over
all *p+r* features

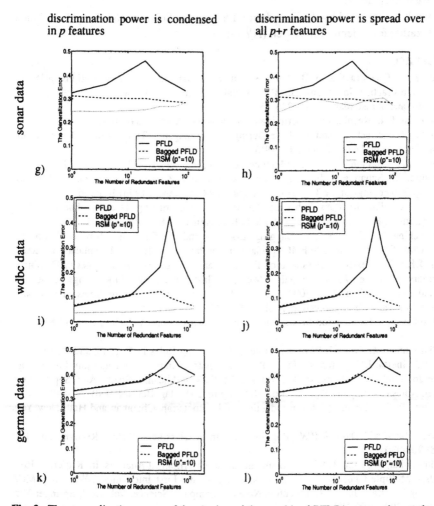

Fig. 3. The generalization errors of the single and the combined PFLD's versus the number of redundant noise features *r* added to the original *p*-dimensional data sets. Left plots show the case when a discrimination power is condensed in *p* features (data have *r* completely redundant noise features). Right plots represent the case when a discrimination power is spread over *p+r* features (after adding *r* redundant features to *p*-dimensional data set, the data are rotated in all *p+r* directions). 80 training objects are used to train the single and the combined classifiers.

feature set (it depends on the data dimensionality related to the training sample size). Therefore, *bagging may perform better than the RSM for the highly redundant feature spaces where the discrimination power is condensed in few features.* However, *when the discrimination power is spread over all features, the RSM outperforms bagging.*

The success of the combining techniques depends on many different factors that act simultaneously and may assist and counteract each other. However, notwithstanding the difficulty to study the influence of each factor independently of other ones, it is very important to understand what factors affect the performance of the combining techniques and in what way. Obviously, more study should be done in this direction.

Acknowledgment

This work is supported by the Foundation for Applied Sciences (STW) and the Dutch Organization for Scientific Research (NWO).

References

1. Jain, A.K., Chandrasekaran, B.: Dimensionality and Sample Size Considerations in Pattern Recognition Practice. In: Krishnaiah, P.R., Kanal, L.N. (eds.): Handbook of Statistics, Vol. 2. North-Holland, Amsterdam (1987) 835-855

2. Friedman, J.H.: Regularized Discriminant Analysis. JASA **84** (1989) 165-175

3. An, G.: The Effects of Adding Noise During Backpropagation Training on a Generalization Performance. Neural Computation **8** (1996) 643-674

4. Breiman, L.: Bagging predictors. Machine Learning Journal **24**(2) (1996) 123-140

5. Freund, Y., Schapire, R.E.: Experiments with a New Boosting Algorithm. In: Machine Learning: Proceedings of the Thirteenth International Conference (1996) 148-156

6. Ho, T.K.: The Random Subspace Method for Constructing Decision Forests. IEEE Transactions on Pattern Analysis and Machine Intelligence **20**(8) (1998) 832-844

7. Skurichina, M., Duin, R.P.W.: Bagging, Boosting and the Random Subspace Method for Linear Classifiers. Submitted to FMC special issue of Pattern Analysis and Applications (2001)

8. Ho, T.K.: Complexity of Classification Problems and Comparative Advantages of Combined Classifiers. In: Kittler, J., Roli, F. (eds.): Multiple Classifier Systems (Proceedings of the First International Workshop MCS 2000, Cagliari, Italy, June 2000). Lecture Notes in Computer Science, Vol. 1857, Springer-Verlag, Berlin (2000) 97-106

9. Fukunaga, K.: Introduction to Statistical Pattern Recognition. Academic Press (1990) 400-407

10. Skurichina, M., Duin, R.P.W.: The Role of Combining Rules in Bagging and Boosting. In Ferri, F.J., Inesta, J.M., Amin, A., Pudil, P. (eds): Advances in pattern recognition (Proceedings of the Joint Int. Workshops SSPR'2000 and SPR'2000, Alicante, Spain, Aug.-Sept. 2000). Lecture Notes in Computer Science, Vol. 1876, Springer-Verlag, Berlin (2000) 631-640

11. Efron, B., Tibshirani, R.: An Introduction to the Bootstrap. Chapman and Hall, New York (1993)

12. Skurichina, M., Duin, R.P.W.: Bagging for Linear Classifiers. Pattern Recognition **31**(7) (1998) 909-930

13. Skurichina, M., Duin, R.P.W.: Boosting in Linear Discriminant Analysis. In: Kittler, J., Roli, F. (eds.): Multiple Classifier Systems (Proceedings of the First International Workshop MCS 2000, Cagliari, Italy, June 2000). Lecture Notes in Computer Science, Vol. 1857, Springer-Verlag, Berlin (2000) 190-199

14. Blake, C.L., Merz, C.J.: UCI Repository of machine learning databases [http://www.ics.uci.edu/~mlearn/MLRepository.html]. Irvine, CA: University of California, Department of Information and Computer Science (1998)

15. Golomb, S.W., Baumert, L.D.: The Search for Hadamard Matrices, American Mathematics Monthly **70** (1963) 12-17

Performance Degradation in Boosting

Jeevani Wickramaratna, Sean Holden, and Bernard Buxton

Department of Computer Science, University College London,
Gower Street, London WC1E 6BT
{jeevaniw, s.holden, b.buxton}@cs.ucl.ac.uk

Abstract. AdaBoost boosts the performance of a weak learner by training a committee of weak learners which learn different features of the
training sample space with different emphasis and jointly perform classification or regression of each new data sample by a weighted cumulative
vote. We use RBF kernel classifiers to demonstrate that boosting a Strong
Learner generally contributes to performance degradation, and identify
three patterns of performance degradation due to three different strength
levels of the underlying learner. We demonstrate that boosting productivity increases, peaks and then falls as the strength of the underlying
learner increases. We highlight patterns of behaviour in the distribution
and argue that AdaBoost's characteristic of forcing the strong learner to
concentrate on the very hard samples or outliers with too much emphasis
is the cause of performance degradation in Strong Learner boosting. However, by boosting an underlying classifier of appropriately low strength,
we are able to boost the performance of the committee to achieve or
surpass the performance levels achievable by strengthening the individual classifier with parameter or model selection in many instances. We
conclude that, if the strength of the underlying learner approaches the
identified strength levels, it is possible to avoid performance degradation
and achieve high productivity in boosting by weakening the learner prior
to boosting ...

1   Introduction

Freund & Schapire's algorithm AdaBoost and its variants have been applied
extensively for boosting the performance of weak learners. However, boosting
tends to fail or degrade performance in some instances. Quinlan [5] first attracted
attention to performance degradation in his early experiments of boosting C4.5.
Freund & Schapire [1] record further results on performance degradation of C4.5.
In their recent work, Freund & Schapire [2] pose this as an open problem: can
we characterise or predict when boosting will fail in this manner?

We are strongly motivated to research the effects of the strength of the learner
on boosting performance, paying specific attention to instances of performance
degradation. This paper is an exposition of the effects of the strength of the
underlying learner on the performance of AdaBoost and a response to the open
problem posed by Freund & Shapire.

J. Kittler and F. Roli (Eds.): MCS 2001, LNCS 2096, pp. 11–21, 2001.

The learnability of a problem by a classifier is dependent on the inherent difficulty of the problem, the capacity of the classifier, and the size of the training dataset relative to the size of the problem. Given a learning problem posed by a training dataset and a test dataset of fixed size, we form a judgement on the strength of a learner of fixed capacity, based on how well it learns the original training data supported by how well it performs on the test data. Variation in learner strength is achieved by varying the capacity of the learner from one committee to another. To achieve a weaker classifier it is only necessary to vary a parameter or the kernel, so that the classifier gives a lower training accuracy and a lower test accuracy according to the given training and test datasets respectively.

We watch the annealing process variations as the strength of the learner increases from one committee to another. We watch the effects of the strength of the learner on the distribution and highlight very insightful patterns in its behaviour. The results highlight the influence of the strength of the learner on the boosting process at different levels of classifier strength. They highlight three different patterns of performance degradation depending on three different high-strength levels of the learner. From our results we argue that AdaBoost's characteristic of forcing an underlying strong learner to concentrate on a few hard-to-learn samples or outliers with too much emphasis is the probable cause of performance degradation in boosting. We observe that boosting a learner of moderate strength is optimally productive and often achieves performance levels that surpass the performance of the strengthened individual classifier. Hence, we conclude by proposing that a learner approaching the high strength levels identified on a given problem instance be weakened prior to boosting, to achieve optimal productivity and to lower the probability of performance degradation.

2   Background and the Experiments

AdaBoost: AdaBoost.M1 is used for boosting RBF classifiers on the two class classification problems Monks1, Monks2, Monks3, Poisonous Mushroom, Credit Scoring and Tic-Tac-Toe Endgame from the UCI data repository.

Training the Learner: A Radial Basis Function classifier is trained as the underlying learner with variations in its strength being achieved by changing the number K of kernels. K is an input parameter to the training algorithm and is allowed to take a value between 2 and N, the number of training samples. The first layer projects the input samples to the K dimensional feature space by using spherical Gaussian kernels. The K function centres are trained by K-means clustering of the input samples. The function widths are set to twice the mean distance between the function centres. The final layer optimises the input samples projected onto the feature space by linear optimisation of the sum-of-squares error, and the real valued output is thresholded to provide a binary classification. The training algorithm allows us to train an RBF classifier of desired complexity on the training dataset. Given K and T, the number of iterations, AdaBoost

Given: Training dataset: $(x_1, y_1), \ldots, (x_N, y_N)$
       Test dataset: $(x_1, y_1), \ldots, (x_M, y_M)$
          where $x_i \in X, y_i \in Y = \{-1, +1\}$
Initialise: $D_1(i) = \frac{1}{N}$
For $t = 1, \ldots, T$

- Train weak learner with fixed capacity according to distribution D_t
- If $(t = 1)$
    $\epsilon_{train} \leftarrow$ error on Training dataset
    $\epsilon_{test} \leftarrow$ error on Test dataset
    Classifier Strength $:= f(1 - \epsilon_{train}, 1 - \epsilon_{test})$
- Get weak hypothesis $h_t : X \rightarrow \{-1, +1\}$
    with error $\epsilon_t = Pr_{i-D_t}[h_t(x_i) \neq y_i]$
- Update
$$D_{t+1} = \frac{D_t(i)}{Z_t} \times \begin{cases} e^{-\alpha t} & , \text{if } h_t(x_i) = y_i \\ e^{\alpha t} & , \text{if } h_t(x_i) \neq y_i \end{cases}$$
  where Z_t is the normalisation factor chosen so that D_{t+1} is a distribution

Output Classifier Strength and the final hypothesis
    $H(x) = sign\left(\sum_{t=1}^{T} \alpha_t h_t(x)\right)$

Fig. 1. AdaBoost.M1 (Freund & Schapire) with a measure of the underlying classifier strength.

trains a committee of T RBF classifiers, each with approximately K number of kernels. A classifier is trained according to the distribution by sampling the training data according to the distribution with replacement.

It is noted that the classifier strength increases with K. The graphs of Fig.2 plot the performance of the learners against K.

The Strength of the Learner: The strength of the classifier is defined with respect to the problem instance given by a fixed dataset, not the unknown problem. Subsequent performance improvements are judged relative to the fixed dataset. The complexity of the classifiers for a particular AdaBoost run is also fixed, so that all the classifiers of a particular committee have same capacity.

Within this context, an intuitive measure of the strength of the classifier being boosted is formed, based primarily on its performance on the training samples and supported by its performance on the test samples. The training accuracy is an important measure of the strength of the classifier in boosting as the committee concentrates on reducing its training error in a greedy manner by AdaBoost's choice of the voting parameter α_t. [6] However, we find that the generalisation accuracy must also support its strength. A classifier showing 95% accuracy on the given training dataset and 95% accuracy on the given test dataset is clearly a strong learner of the problem instance. The RBF classifier with 25 function centres on the Tic-Tac-Toe dataset having approximately 90%

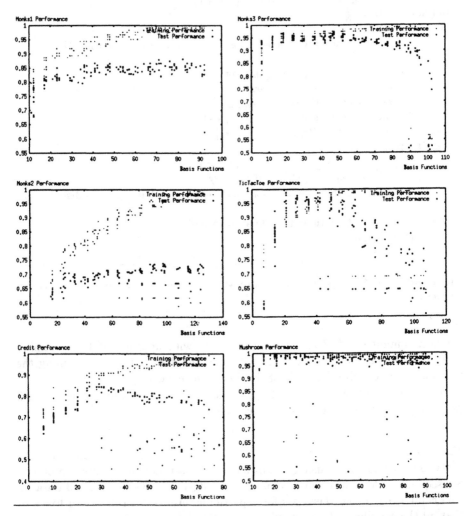

Fig. 2. RBF performance graphs for Monks1, Monks2, Credit, Monks3, Tic-Tac-Toe and Mushroom datasets. Performance on the training data (plotted in red dots) and on the test data (plotted in blue squares). The RBF classifier starts as a weak learner and becomes strong as the complexity increases for Monks1, Monks2, and Credit Scoring datasets. It is a strong learner of Monks3, Tic-Tac-Toe and Mushroom datasets. (Suboptimal classifiers are due to the inverted matrix in linear optimisation being near degenerate.)

training accuracy and 95% test accuracy is a significantly stronger learner than the RBF classifier with 30 function centres on the Monks1 dataset also having approximately 90% training accuracy, but only 82% test accuracy. However, a very high training accuracy (e.g. 94%) may be supported by a moderate test accuracy (e.g. 75%) and still show strong learner behaviour. Alternatively, when the test accuracy is very high (e.g. 97% for Tic-Tac-Toe) strong learner behaviour can start at classifiers with a lower training accuracy.

3   Boosting a Strong Learner Is Generally Counterproductive or Unproductive

As the strength of the classifier increases beyond approximately 90% (training accuracy above 90% and supported by high test performance), boosting consistently becomes counterproductive or unproductive. For the particular datasets the onset of unproductive or counterproductive boosting behaviour occurs when the base classifier is stronger than (approximately) the classifiers of Table 1. For all RBF classifiers stronger than these on the particular datasets, unproductive or counterproductive boosting behaviour is consistent.

Table 1. The classifier strength at which consistent unproductive or counterproductive behaviour starts for datasets tested

Dataset/Problem Title	Complexity	Training Performance	Test Performance	Behaviour
Monks1	47	92.5	85.0	Unproductive
Monks2	75	92.5	72	Unproductive
Credit Scoring	45	93.9	81.0	Unproductive
Monks3	18	93.0	93.0	Counterproductive
Tic-Tac-Toe Endgame	20	89.0	95.0	Counterproductive
Poisonous Mushroom	8 (lowest tested)	96.0	98.0	Counterproductive

It is noted that, in the case of unproductive behaviour, the high training accuracy is supported by a relatively modest test performance. Careful observation of the graphed distribution [3] indicates that a relatively small number of samples gets strongly highlighted and that their emphasis in the distribution keeps growing at the expense of the emphasis on the other samples throughout the boosting process, but never comes down. The low generalisation performance of the base classifier seems to contribute to AdaBoost's being unable to train a classifier in subsequent iterations that is capable of learning the highlighted very hard samples. This results in AdaBoost's being unable to affect either training or test error.

When a high training accuracy is supported by a high generalisation performance, AdaBoost is able to train hypotheses that learn the highly emphasised

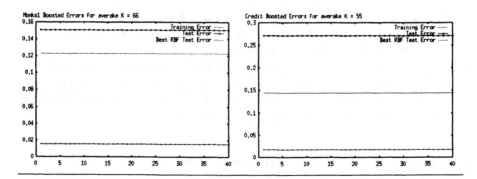

Fig. 3. Patterns of Performance Degradation I: Unproductive Boosting

hard samples. Then the training error drops to zero, but the test error continues to increase throughout. The distribution repeatedly highlights a very small number of samples very strongly; even though their weighting comes down with a good hypothesis that learns them, they are soon highlighted strongly again and again. [3] Hence too much emphasis is placed on the hard-to-learn outliers or the few very hard samples in the training data throughout, causing AdaBoost to continuously overfit the training data.

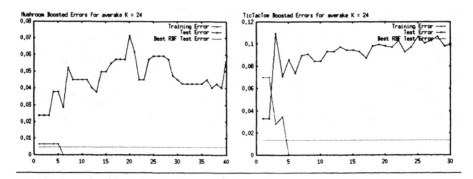

Fig. 4. Patterns of Performance Degradation II: Continuously Counterproductive Boosting

Onoda, Ratsch and Muller [4] conduct a theoretical analysis that confirms the conclusion drawn from our experimental results. They note: "when the annealing parameter $|\underline{b}|$ takes a very big value, AdaBoost type learning become a hard competition case: only the patterns with smallest margins (hardest samples) will get high weights; other patterns are effectively neglected in the learning process". This analysis confirms the conclusion drawn from our observations and leads us to conclude that too much emphasis placed on a few hard samples in the training dataset, and the neglect of important features of the other samples is the probable cause for performance degradation in strong learner boosting.

Counterproductive boosting results recorded by Freund and Schapire [1] on boosting C4.5 on Soybean-small, House-votes-84, Votes1 and Hypothyroid datasets all have very high test performances; the training accuracy is unknown. However, Freund and Schapire record a number of productive instances of boosting C4.5 where the generalisation performance is high; the training accuracy is unknown. The (unknown) training accuracy is a strong factor in our measure of learner strength. However, this warrants further investigation.

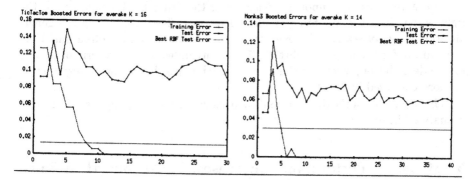

Fig. 5. Patterns of Performance Degradation III - Initially high degradation as the training error drops to zero, followed by a correction that is unable to compensate for the initial overfitting

4   Behaviour of the Distribution

The distribution over the training samples was graphed. Its careful observation gives an intuitive insight to the error reduction process.

When the classifier is very weak it highlights a large number of samples as hard and the weighting is distributed over a large number of samples. The distinction between weightings is small. There is a lot of activity in the distribution as the weightings change by small amounts over a large set of samples from iteration to iteration. Thus each iteration poses a large region in the feature space with little distinction among sample hardness, to be learned by a relatively weak classifier. This contributes to the slow error reduction process.

When the classifier is a moderate performer fewer samples are highlighted, allowing a classifier of moderate strength to focus on a moderate size region in the feature space. When they are learned, their weighting comes down allowing another moderate set to be highlighted. Their features are quickly learned to achieve very fast and optimal error reduction.

As the classifier gets even less weak, a smaller set of somewhat harder samples is highlighted. It takes a number of attempts to learn their features during which they remain highly emphasized with little activity. As soon as these samples are learned (noted by a strong performing hypothesis) their weighting comes down suddenly allowing a different small set to be highlighted; this activity generally coincides with a "step reduction" of the errors.

When the classifier is somewhat stronger, a few "significantly hard" samples are very strongly highlighted initially. In its attempt to learn the features of these few samples particular to the training data, AdaBoost seems forced to ignore the less hard but important low-highlighted samples (the weighting on the few very hard samples keep increasing at the cost of the others) and overfits the training dataset. Once they are learned, a correction process immediately follows, where AdaBoost relearns the important features of the other hard samples with the right emphasis (their weighting is allowed to rise), thereby reducing the generalization error somewhat. However, the subsequent reduction is often unable to compensate for the initial overfitting. This contributes to a third form of performance degradation, when the classifier strength is just below the strength levels of those discussed in 3.

The behaviour of the distribution when the underlying classifier is very strong is analysed in section 3.

5   Boosting Performance Increases, Peaks, and then Falls as the Strength of the Weak Learner Increases

Boosting performance graphs are taken for committees with decreasing levels of learner weakness for Monks1, Monks2 and Credit datasets. The decrease in weakness from one committee to the next is achieved by increasing the number of kernels K in the underlying classifier.

When the classifier is significantly weak the boosting process is slow and ridden with fluctuations. When the weakness of the classifier decreases to a certain level, AdaBoost achieves very fast and maximum error reduction.

AdaBoost is able to also boost the performance of a somewhat strong learner. A clear distinction of such a boosting instance is the "step reduction process" where the errors remain stable for a number of iterations and suddenly reduce by a significant amount.

AdaBoost's ability to boost the generalisation performance lessens as the RBF classifiers get stronger beyond a particular level. When the classifier's strength increases further, it overfits the training data and increases the generalization error by a significant amount as the training error rapidly drops to zero. After the training error has dropped to zero the generalization error resumes the reduction process. However, in many instances the subsequent reduction is unable to compensate for the initial overfitting. This shows a third pattern of performance degradation. The performance degradation graph recorded by Quinlan [5] in boosting C4.5 on the Colic dataset also demonstrates this behaviour. The test performance of the base C4.5 classifier is reported as 85.08%; the training accuracy is unknown.

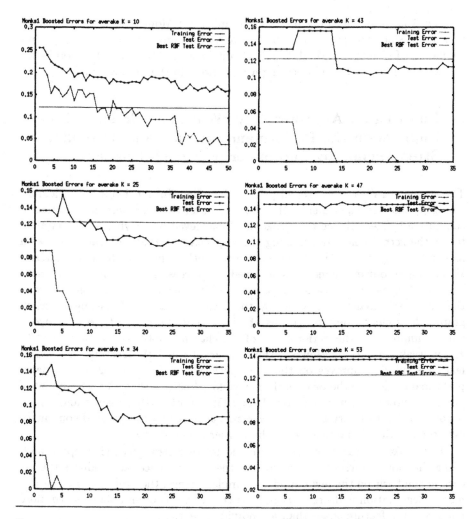

Fig. 6. Monks1 boosting for K=10,25,34,43,47,53. Error reduction is slow for very weak learner boosting. Boosting achieves very fast and optimal error reduction as the classifier weakness decreases. Initial overfitting effects and "step reduction" in errors shown as the weakness decreases further. Boosting becomes unproductive as the classifier becomes a Strong Learner. Detailed graphs in full paper [3]

When the strength of the classifier is very high the annealing behaviour is analysed in detail in section 3.

AdaBoost is hence optimally productive when the underlying classifier is moderately weak. It is slow and has low productivity when the learner is significantly weak. It is generally unproductive or counterproductive in boosting an already strong learner. If it is not possible to weaken a strong classifier to an appropriate level, it is better to train a good individual classifier by optimising on parameter and model selection.

The AdaBoost annealing process is graphed for Monks1 for RBF classifiers with increasing strength in Fig. 6. The annealing process follows a very similar pattern for datasets Monks2 and Credit Scoring. More detailed graphs for Monks1, Monks2 and Credit scoring are provided in the full paper [3].

6   Boosting an Appropriately Weakened Classifier Can Improve on the Performance of the Same Classifier Strengthened by Parameter or Model Selection

The strong classifier is weakened prior to boosting. In our definition of learner strength, and our experiments, the capacity of all the classifiers in a particular committee is fixed. Hence the weakening is achieved by varying a free parameter or the kernel (thereby changing this capacity), so that the learner shows a higher training error and a higher test error with respect to the same dataset. Weakening in our experiments is achieved by decreasing the number of kernels. The boosting performance of the weakened classifier is graphed together with the peak performance achievable by the classifier individually(straight line in graph). It is clear from the graphs of Fig. 6 that the boosted performance is able to improve on the performance of the classifier optimised with respect to K for weak learners of Monks1. (Further graphs in [3]) Boosting the weaker learner similarly improves on the peak performance for Monks2 and achieves performance close to the peak performance for Credit Scoring. A vast amount of published literature, in particular [1] and [5], report further results and analyses of significant performance improvements achieved by the boosted committee over the individual classifier when the learner is not strong.

The weakened learner causes AdaBoost to concentrate on the samples modelling the more representative regions in the feature space, and reduces the excessive emphasis on the few boundary samples. Hence, the probability of performance degradation is decreased, and the committee is often able to learn more regions in the feature space than an individual learner.

7   Conclusion

We have demonstrated that boosting an already strong learner is generally counterproductive, and that the boosting performance increases, peaks and then falls as the strength of the underlying weak learner increases. We have identified three patterns of performance degradation depending on three different identified strength levels of the underlying learner:

1. Unproductive boosting behaviour, when the base learner has high training accuracy supported by a modest test accuracy.
2. Continuously counterproductive boosting behaviour when the base learner has high training accuracy supported by a high test accuracy.

3. Initially highly counterproductive boosting behaviour followed by a slightly productive phase that is unable to compensate for the initial overfitting, when the base learner is just approaching the strength levels of instances discussed in 1 and 2.

We have highlighted patterns of behaviour in the distribution and have argued that performance degradation in boosting is due to:

1. An underlying strong learner
2. AdaBoost's characteristic of forcing the learner to concentrate on the very hard samples and outliers with too much emphasis when the learner is strong.

However, boosting a learner of appropriately low strength achieves good error reduction and, in some instances, improves on the peak performance the strengthened learner is capable of achieving by parameter or model selection. We have proposed therefore that, when the underlying learner approaches the Strong Learner strength levels identified, it is possible to avoid the probability of performance degradation and to achieve higher boosting productivity by weakening the learner. It is possible to weaken a kernel machine that is a Strong Learner by using a weaker kernel, decreasing the number of kernels or varying a free parameter, so that the learner has a higher training error and a higher test error with respect to the given dataset.

The proposed solution works by eliminating the first identified cause of performance degradation. Future work would address improving AdaBoost so that it curbs the excessive emphasis it places on the few extremely hard samples and outliers when the underlying learner is strong.

References

1. Freund, Yoav & Schapire, Robert E.: A Brief Introduction to Boosting. Proceedings of the Sixteenth International Joint Conference on Artificial intelligence.
2. Freund, Yoav & Schapire, Robert E.: Discussions of the paper "Arching Classifiers" by Leo Brieman. The Annals of Statistics, 26(3):824-832.
3. Wickramaratna, Holden & Buxton: Efects of the Strength of the Weak Learner in Boosting Kernel Machines. Submitted to the Journal of Machine Learning Research.
4. Onoda, T., Ratsch, G. & Muller, K.: An Asymptotic Analysis of AdaBoost in the Binary Classification Case. GMD FIRST Rudower Chaussee, Germany.
5. Quinlan, J.: Bagging, Boosting and C4.5. National Conference on Artificial Intelligence.
6. Schapire, Robert E.: Theoretical Views of Boosting and Applications. Proceedings of Algorithmic Learning Theory.

A Generalized Class of Boosting Algorithms Based on Recursive Decoding Models

Elizabeth Tapia, José C. González, and Julio Villena

Department of Telematics Engineering - Technical University of Madrid, Spain
{etapia, jcg, jvillena}@gsi.dit.upm.es

Abstract. A communication model for the Hypothesis Boosting (HB) problem is proposed. Under this model, AdaBoost algorithm can be viewed as a threshold decoding approach for a repetition code. Generalization of such decoding view under theory of theory of Recursive Error Correcting Codes allows the formulation of a generalized class of low-complexity learning algorithms applicable in high dimensional classification problems. In this paper, an instance of this approach suitable for High Dimensional Features Spaces (HDFS) is presented.

1 Introduction

Established Machine Learning boosting [1] theory assumes a low dimensional feature space setting. The extension of boosting to arbitrary HDFS is an area of potential interest [2] in fields like Information Retrieval. In this paper, we address the extension of the HB concept to HDFS by recalling common sense teaching-learning strategies and their similarity to the design of RECCs.

The remainder of the paper is organized as follows. Section 2 introduces a communication model for the HB problem and the interpretation of AdaBoost algorithm as an instance of APP threshold decoding. Section 3 introduces a generalized recursive learning approach in order to cope with complexity when constructing boosting algorithms in high dimensional spaces. Section 4 presents a first stage implementation suitable for high input domains through the Turbo_Learn algorithm. Finally, in Section 5 a summary and future work is presented.

2 Teaching and Learning Strategies

How must we teach and how can we learn? Both questions are essential in the design of ML algorithms. Consider a teaching through examples process for a target concept c belonging to a class $C : X \rightarrow \{-1,1\}$. Similarly, let WL be a weak learning from examples algorithm and let S be the training sample. Trivial repetition of the target concept may be considered as a simple teaching strategy in order to improve the WL performance.

Such strategy can be implemented by exposing S as many times as WL requires, reinforcing the presence of harder examples each time. In Machine Learning theory, the above teaching strategy is no more than the hypothesis-boosting concept. In the next section, we will show that the HB problem can be viewed the transmission of concepts through a noisy channel. Thus, under suitable (concept) channel-encoding, arbitrary small (learning) error rates can be achieved.

3   A Communication Model for HB

Transmission of information through a noisy channel requires channel-encoding [3] schemes. Let us consider the transmission of concepts c belonging to a target class $C: X \rightarrow \{0,1\}$ imbedded in some metric space R_ρ. Assume that transmission is intended with accuracy ε so that C can described by a set $A \subset R_\rho$ with $N_\varepsilon^R(C)$ elements (the set A being a minimal $\varepsilon - net$ for C under covering numbers theory [4] [5]). Following [6], for each $c \in C$ we can define a deterministic mapping $E: C \rightarrow B$, so that each concept can be represented by a bitstream $\mathbf{b} \in B$ with length n_B

$$n_B = H_\varepsilon^R(C) = \log_2 N_\varepsilon^R(C) \tag{1}$$

In order to transmit $c \in C$, E simply selects the integer $j \in \{1,....,N_\varepsilon^R(C)\}$ for which the ball $Ball(a_j, \varepsilon)$ with center in concept a_j and radio ε contains the target concept c. Similarly, we can define a decoding mapping $D: B \rightarrow R$ so that a received bitstream $\mathbf{b} \in B$ is mapped into a concept a_j being j the integer with bit representation sequence $\mathbf{b} \in B$. In communication terms, the mapping $E: C \rightarrow B$ can be modeled as a Discrete Memoryless Source (DMS) with output alphabet X, $|X| = N_\varepsilon^R(C)$. Let q be a DMS output distribution and let $H(X)$ be the entropy characterizing such DMS

$$p_U(a_k) = q_k \quad k = 1,.....,N_\varepsilon^R(C) \quad a_k \in X \tag{2}$$

Let us consider the transmission of information symbols from such source through a Discrete Memoryless Channel (DMC) [7] characterized by a finite capacity C_Π and resembling a *weak learner* behavior. Shannon's Noisy Coding theorem [8] states that reliable transmission of information through a noisy channel can be achieved by suitable channel encoding. Coding proceeds by transmission of arbitrary long T source sequences at a rate information symbol $r = \frac{k}{T}$ being k the number of information symbols in each $T - sequence$. In almost random encoding is performed at the transmitter side, then as $T \rightarrow \infty$, the bock error probability P_e can be bounded as follows

$$P_e \approx 2^{-T(C_\Pi - r)} \tag{3}$$

Whenever r is less than channel capacity C_Π, arbitrary small (learning) error rates can be achieved by the suitable introduction of parity redundant concepts. It should be note that for the learning case, r values are limited to $\frac{1}{T}$ ($k = 1$) if learning proceeds in a concept by concept fashion. For this case, the unique allowable linear block-coding scheme is a T - repetition code. Thus, in order to cope with learner limitations, a teacher would repeat the target concept T times, resembling the transmission of a codeword $\mathbf{t}$

$$\mathbf{t} = \underbrace{(c(x), \quad c(x), \quad ..., \quad c(x))}_{T-times} \tag{4}$$

Under the assumption of a weak learning algorithm with errors resembling a DMC channel, learning becomes a decoding problem on a received sequence $\mathbf{r}$

$$\mathbf{r} = (\ h_1\ (x\ ), h_2\ (x\ ), ...,\ h_T\ (x\ )\ ) \tag{5}$$

For binary transmitted and received concepts

$$\mathbf{r} = \mathbf{t} + \mathbf{e} \bmod 2 \tag{6}$$

The decoding problem is to give a good estimate $\mathbf{e}^{\cdot}$ for the error vector $\mathbf{e}$ under prior knowledge on channel behavior by means of probabilities $p_i = P(e_i = 1)$, $1 \le i \le T$, so that a final estimation $\mathbf{t}^* = \mathbf{r} + \mathbf{e}^{\cdot}$ can be assembled. Therefore, a suitable learning algorithm in some aspects should correlate the behavior of decoding schemes. From learning theory, we know that adaptation is a desirable feature for good generalization abilities and in fact, the same requirement applies for decoding algorithms when dealing with very noisy channels. In decoding terms, adaptation is equivalent to the application of APP (A Posteriori Probability) decoding techniques. In next section, we will analyze APP decoding methods for T -repetition codes. For sake of brevity, we refer the reader to original Massey´s doctoral dissertation [9] for background on APP methods.

3.1 Threshold Decoding for T – Repetition Codes

Let us consider a simple T -repetition code and the threshold-decoding estimation of the unique information bit. A T -repetition code naturally induces the following trivial set of parity check equations

$$A_t = e_1(x) - e_t(x) \qquad 2 \le t \le T \tag{7}$$

The above set is orthogonal on bit e_1 (in the APP sense for linear bock codes). Thus, we can estimate e_1 as follows

$$e_1^{\cdot} = \begin{cases} 1 & 2 \cdot \sum_{i=2}^{T} A_i \cdot \left[\log\left(\frac{1-p_i}{p_i} \right) \right] \succ \sum_{i=1}^{T} \log\left(\frac{1-p_i}{p_i} \right) \\ 0 & otherwise \end{cases} \tag{8}$$

The receiver will perform the following t_1^* estimates depending on the received value r_1. It can be shown that

$$
t_1^* \begin{cases} 0 & \sum_{i=1}^{T} (2r_i - 1)\left[\log\left(\frac{1-p_i}{p_i}\right)\right] \prec 0 \\ \\ 1 & \textit{otherwise} \end{cases}
\tag{9}
$$

Let us introduce a linear mapping $\phi(x) = 2x - 1$ between binary alphabets $A = \{0, 1\}$ and $A_{\mp} = \{-1, 1\}$. Then equation (9) can be expressed as

$$
c_1^* \begin{cases} -1 & \sum_{i=1}^{T} h_i\left[\log\left(\frac{1-p_i}{p_i}\right)\right] \prec 0 \\ \\ 1 & \textit{otherwise} \end{cases} \quad h_i \in A_{\mp}, \; 1 \le i \le T.
\tag{10}
$$

3.2 The Repetition of Concepts and APP-Threshold Decoding

Let us assume a teaching by repetition strategy over T units of time on fixed instance x through an additive DMC channel resembling a weak learner performance. Therefore, the learner can now implement APP decoding in its threshold-decoding form in order to arrive to a final decision. Assuming transmitted and received concepts with output domain $\{-1, 1\}$, we get

$$
c_1^*(x) \begin{cases} -1 & \sum_{i=1}^{T} h_i(x)\left[\log\left(\frac{1-p_i}{p_i}\right)\right] \prec 0 \\ \\ 1 & \textit{otherwise} \end{cases}
\tag{11}
$$

where each p_i is the probability that a received concept $h_i(x)$ is different from the transmitted concept $c_i(x)$, $1 \le i \le T$ i.e. the error probability achieved by the $i-th$ WL. Denoting $w_i = \log\left(\frac{1-p_i}{p_i}\right)$, for fixed x equation (12) is almost AdaBoost decision. However, two differences are observable. First, there is a factor $\frac{1}{2}$ difference between APP weighting factors w_i and those derived from AdaBoost. Though this fact does not affect the final decision, its presence can be explained [10] by the exponential cost function used in AdaBoost instead of a Log-likelihood criterion. The other difference is that computation of APP weighting factors w_i requires exact channel error probabilities. However, recall that in HB we always know the target concept at a finite set of sample points S so that we can provide a sample mean estimate $\hat{w}_i$ associated to each weak hypothesis $h_i(x)$ under distribution D_i for S as follows

$$\hat{w}_t = \frac{1}{2} \cdot \log \frac{E_{S-D_t}\ [c(x) = h_t(x)]}{E_{S-D_t}\ [c(x) \neq h_t(x)]}$$ (12)

Thus if we use (35) to estimate the weighting factors w_t required by the threshold decoding rule, the target learner will issue a final decision $h_f(\mathbf{x})$

$$h_f(x) = sign\left(\sum_{t=1}^{T} \hat{w}_t \cdot h_t(x)\right)$$ (13)

which is exactly the AdaBoost decision for discrete weak hypothesis with output domain $Y = \{-1, 1\}$. Concept repetition is a special case of general block concept-channel coding schemes. For AdaBoost like boosting algorithms, there is no way to construct an unbounded set of orthogonal parity checks equations for increasing T values. At some point dependency between distribution leads to significant correlation between errors so that no further improvements can be achieved. At this point, the best we can do is to adjust threshold coefficients i.e. „*the size of the weights is more important than the size of the network*" [11][12].

4   Learning by Diversity: Recursive Models

The decoding view for the HB problem explains simply the classic teaching by concept repetition strategy. In addition, it also suggests many unexplored teaching schemes. When learning classes which are too complex, it would be useful to think in some kind of target concept expansion so that any concept can be expressed and reconstructed from a fixed number of simple base concepts i.e. a *learning by diversity* model. Let $c(x)$ be a target concept admitting some kind of expansion

$$c(x) = Span(c_1(x),...c_k(x))$$ (14)

Then, a teaching strategy for a weak learner may be viewed as the transmission of a *frame* of base concepts over a noisy channel. Each concept codeword in the frame must be decoded first in order to reconstruct to whole target concept. For each *Span* definition, a particular learning algorithm would be obtained. A good example can be found in the ECOC [13] approach for M-class problems, where a M-valued target function is broken down into $k \succ \log_2 M$ binary base functions through an Error Correcting Output enCoding scheme (ECOC). Thus, the selected encoding scheme implicitly defines the components in the *Span* expansion whilst the Minimum Distance Hamming criterion defines the *Span*$^{-1}$ recombination function. An essential limitation in ECOC behavior is the increasing coding length requirement for better generalization performance and off course for growing M values. In fact, this is well known problem in coding theory, where the exchange between block-coding length and error rates has been largely treated. Coding theory has been able to find a promising solution for such problem under the theory of Recursive Error Correcting Codes so that alternative low-complexity ECOC extensions could be derived from them.

Definition 1: A bipartite graph is one in which the nodes can be partitioned in two different classes. An edge may connect nodes of distinct classes but there are no edges connecting nodes of the same class.

Definition 2: A Recursive Error Correcting Code (RECC) is a code constructed from a number of similar and simple component subcodes. A RECC in its simple form can be described by bipartite graphs known as Tanner graphs [14].

Let us consider a simple example (**Fig. 1**) of a RECC constructed from two parity check subcodes S_1 and S_2. Codewords in this simple RECC are all binary 6-tuples, which simultaneously verified parity restrictions imposed by each component subcode.

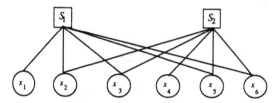

Fig. 1. Tanner graphs for a simple RECC built from two component subcodes

The main objective of defining codes in terms of component subcodes is to reduce decoding complexity. A RECC can be decoded by an ensemble of decoding processes, each one at a component subcode (check nodes in Tanner graph terms) and later exchange of information between them on bits (local variables in Tanner graph terms) they have in common. It should be note, that this decoding approach requires the implementation of local APP decoding methods, because these are the only methods that give us probabilistic estimation of code bits. For purposes of learning in high output domains, the set of code bits would define a set of binary weak learners with their corresponding error rates with communicating socket points at the component subcodes. The essential fact about Tanner graph representations is that they imply the existence of a message-passage mechanism between check nodes and local variables [15] and this is precisely what we need for the design of low-complexity learning algorithms in high dimensional spaces.

Now, let us consider the learning problem for target classes defined for HDFS. A common sense strategy would be to choose a *reduced and informative* number of features and teach through an associated *attribute-filtered version* of S. The problem with this strategy is the prior knowledge requirement. It may happen that we do not have such prior knowledge or even there is no reduced set of informative attributes. In such cases, an alternative strategy can still be applied. We can expose different, perhaps *random, attribute filtered versions* of S to a set of weak learners and then let them exchange information in order to encourage their common learning performance. It happens that this ML strategy can also be modeled by Tanner graphs under theory of RECCs.

4.1 Boosting Algorithms in HDFS

Let $C : X \to K$ a target class, the problem is to reduce learning complexity because of the number q of features in X. In the absence of prior knowledge about the relevant features, we may take the sample S and perform d Random Feature Filtering (RFF) steps over the set of feature vectors available in the training set S. We are thinking in a low density (with respect to q) binary random attribute filter matrix $H_{d \times q}$ characterized by the presence of k ones per row and j ones per column similar to parity matrix of a Low Density Parity Check Code (LDPC) code. [16][17]. The whole filtering process implemented by H over X can be modeled using a Tanner graph as it is shown in **Fig. 2**

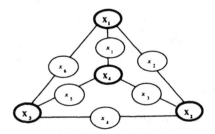

Fig. 2. RFF - $q = 6$, $d = 4$, $k = 3$, $j = 2$

The RFF process creates a set of input spaces $X_1, \ldots, X_d$, $|X_r| = k \prec\prec q$, $1 \le r \le d$. Therefore, from a sample S we can obtain a vector of samples S_H with components being RFF versions of S. Because of the underlying random and sparse structure of the diversity matrix H, the sample components in S_H may be assumed as being independent. The, we can apply a set of d supervised learning process so that each weak learning algorithm L_r over a sample S_r issues a weak hypothesis $h_r(x)$ $(r = 1, \ldots, d)$. As each learner sees only a fraction of the feature space X, its decisions suffer from some kind of distortion due to the filtering process.

4.2 Recursive Classifiers in HDFS

Assume that we have a teacher, a target concept and two different weak learners. Differences between learners arise because of their distinct criterions about the most important features defining a target concept. The same target concept is taught to each weak learner by concept repetition over d times. After the teacher has completed his class, each learner will be asked about the target concept. Both learners are allowed to exchange information before issuing a final decision. The first learner will issue a first decision after d units of time and then will help the second learner in order to improve its decision. The second learner will repeat the process and will help the first after d units of time... From the theory of RECCs, the proposed architecture is simplified learning version of a turbo coding scheme [18]. In **Fig. 3**, the proposed learning model is shown by a Tanner graph representation.

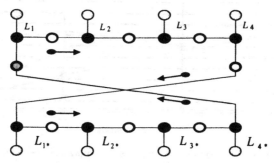

Fig. 3. Turbo_Learn exchange of information by means of a Tanner graph

Propagation of messages begins at the first graph from left to right until reaching check node L_4 and then continues to the second graph structure. This structure can be generalized using T parallel boosting units, thus defining the Turbo_Learn algorithm

---

Turbo_Learn Algorithm

Input: LDPC matrix H_{dxq}, $S / |S| = m$, weak learner WL, d, T

Initialization: $D_1^o(i) = \dfrac{1}{m}$, $1 \le i \le m$

For each $1 \le t \le T$, for each $1 \le r \le d$, do

$$h_r^t(x) = WL\left(D_r^{t-1}, S_r\right), \quad \text{Choose } \alpha_r^t \in R$$

$$D_r^{t+1}(i) = D_r^t(i) \cdot \frac{\exp\left(-\alpha_r^t \cdot y_i \cdot h_r^t(x_i)\right)}{Z_r^t}, \quad 1 \le i \le m$$

$$D_p^t(i) = D_r^{t+1}(i) \quad \text{being } p = (r+1) \bmod (d+1), \quad 1 \le i \le m$$

Output: $h_f(x) = sign\left(\displaystyle\sum_{t=1}^{T}\left(\sum_{r=1}^{d} \alpha_r^t \cdot h_r^t(x)\right)\right)$

End

Theorem 1: The training error ε in **Turbo_Learn** is at most $\displaystyle\prod_{t=1}^{T}\prod_{r=1}^{d} Z_r^t$.

Proof: The proof is almost the same as that in AdaBoost [1]. By unraveling the expression of $D_1^t(i)$ after T boosting steps.

To conclude, in **Fig. 4**, we present a representative **Turbo_Learn** test error response through the Vote dataset (UCI Repository of ML). We used methods in [19] to generate H matrixes and a Decision Stump algorithm as base learner.

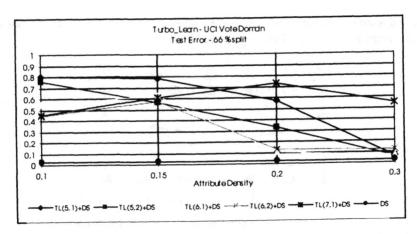

Fig. 4. : *Vote Domain* (binary problem, 16 attributes). *Turbo_Learn test error* for diversity d, T outer boosting steps and a Decision Stump weak learner – *TL (d, T)+DS*

The obtained response shows that boosting is achievable but it depends on the balance between diversity d and attribute density k/q. The latter parameter clearly regulates algorithm performance, because of its intrinsic effect in the independence assumption over samples. Furthermore, only a small number of outer boosting steps are required in order to improve overall learning.

5   Conclusions and Future Work

The main contribution of this work is the introduction of recursive coding related models for the analysis and design of practical boosting algorithms in high dimensional spaces. A number of directions for further work and research stand out. It is necessary to extend our toy-examples to high dimensional data and to analyze how random filtering parameters affect convergence properties. An important research line is the development of recursive decoding models for high M-classification problems as a generalization of the ECOC approach. It should be note that alternative binary boosting schemes could be constructed if we replace T-repetition block codes by convolutional schemes with rates $\frac{1}{T}$ i.e. the target concept and T-1 different parity concepts. It would be interesting to analyze the feasibility of this approach.

Acknowledgements. E. Tapia's work is supported by Argentinean FOMEC Grants and the National University of Rosario, Argentina.

References

1. Schapire, R. E., Singer, Y.: Improved Boosting Algorithms Using Confidence - rated Predictions. Machine Learning, Vol. 37, No. 3, 277–296 (1999)
2. Schapire, R. E., Singer Y.: BoosTexter: A Boosting Based System for Text Categorization. *Machine Learning*, Vol. 39, Numbers 2/3, May/June (2000)
3. Shannon, C.: A Mathematical Theory of Communication. The Bell System Technical Journal, Vol. XXVII, No. 3, 379 – 423 (1948)
4. Kolmogorov, A.N., Tihomirov, V. M.: ε - Entropy and ε -Capacity of Sets in Functional Spaces. *American Mathematical Society Translations*, Vol. 17, 277-364 (1961)
5. Donoho, D. L., Vetterli, M., De Vore, R., Daubechies, I.: Data Compresion and Harmonic Analysis. *IEEE Transactions on Information Theory*, Vol. 44, No. 6, 2435-2476 (1998)
6. Cohen, A., Dahmen, W., Daubechies, I., DeVore, R.: Tree Approximation and optimal encoding. *Institut für Geometrie und Praktische Mathematik, Bericht* Nr. 174, (1999)
7. Csiszár, I., Körner J.: Information Theory: Coding Theorems for Discrete Memoryless Systems. Academic Press, Inc. (London) LTD (1981)
8. Massey, J. L.: Shannon's proof of the noisy coding theorem. *Abstracts of Papers, IEEE International Symposium on Information Theory*, page 107 (1977)
9. Massey, J.: *Threshold Decoding*. Cambridge, MA: M.I.T. Press (1963)
10. Friedman, J., Hastie, T., Tibshirani R.: Additive Logistic Regression: a Statistical View of Boosting. (Tech. Report). Department of Statistics, Stanford University, California (1998)
11. Bartlett, P. L.: The Sample Complexity of Pattern Classification with Neural Networks: The Size of the Weights is More Important than the Size of the Network. *IEEE Transactions on Information Theory*, Vol. 44, No. 2, 525 – 536 (1998)
12. Schapire, R. E.; Freund, Y.; Bartlett, P. L., Lee, W. S.: Boosting the Margin: A New Explanation for the Effectiveness of Voting Methods. The Annals of Statistics, Vol. 26, No. 5, 1651–1686 (1998)
13. Dietterich, T., Bakiri, G.: Error-correcting output codes: A general method for improving multiclass inductive learning programs. *Proceedings of the Ninth National Conference on Artificial Intelligence (AAAI-91)*, 572-577, Anaheim, CA: AAAI Press (1991)
14. Tanner, M.: A recursive Approach to Low Complexity Error Correcting Codes. *IEEE Transactions on Information Theory*, Vol. IT-27, 533-547 (1981)
15. Kschischang, K., Frey, B.: Iterative decoding of compound codes by probability propagation in graphical models. *IEEE J. Sel. Areas Comm.*, Vol. 16 (2), 219-230 (1998)
16. Gallaguer, R. G.: Low Density Parity-Check Codes. Cambridge, Massachusetts: M.I.T. Press (1963)
17. Wiberg N.: *Codes and Decoding on General Graphs*. Doctoral Dissertation, Department of Electrical Engineering, Linköping University, Sweden (1996)
18. Berrou, C., Glavieux, A.: Near Optimum Error Correcting Coding and Decoding: Turbo Codes. *IEEE Transactions on Communications*, Vol. 44, No. 10, 1261-1271 (1996)
19. MacKay, D. J.: Good Error Correcting Codes based on Very Sparse Matrices. *IEEE Transactions on Information Theory*, Vol. 45, No. 2, 399-431 (1999)

Tuning Cost-Sensitive Boosting and Its Application to Melanoma Diagnosis

Stefano Merler, Cesare Furlanello, Barbara Larcher, and Andrea Sboner

ITC-irst,
38050 Trento, Italy
{merler,furlan,larcher,sboner}@itc.it
http://mpa.itc.it

Abstract. This paper investigates a methodology for effective model selection of cost-sensitive boosting algorithms. In many real situations, e.g. for automated medical diagnosis, it is crucial to tune the classification performance towards the sensitivity and specificity required by the user. To this purpose, for binary classification problems, we have designed a cost-sensitive variant of AdaBoost where (1) the model error function is weighted with separate costs for errors (false negative and false positives) in the two classes, and (2) the weights are updated differently for negatives and positives at each boosting step. Finally, (3) a practical search procedure allows to get into or as close as possible to the sensitivity and specificity constraints without an extensive tabulation of the ROC curve. This off-the-shelf methodology was applied for the automatic diagnosis of melanoma on a set of 152 skin lesions described by geometric and colorimetric features, out-performing, on the same data set, skilled dermatologists and a specialized automatic system based on a multiple classifier combination.

1 Introduction

In constructing a predictive classification tool for a real-world application, e.g. an automated diagnosis system, it is now well recognized that misclassification costs have to be incorporated into the learning process [1,12]. Still it is much less clear how to drive the system towards the optimal performance in terms of sensitivity and specificity, which are the measures typically required in the practical case. Given a good cost-sensitive algorithm, a particular choice of the costs will lead to build a model characterized by a pair of sensitivity and specificity values, e.g. a point on the ROC space. But very often the costs (e.g of a false negative or of a false positive in a binary medical classification problem) are estimated approximately, or at least less definitely of the minimum acceptable sensitivity and specificity rates, thus one is left with the doubt that modifying the costs might result more effective than improving the model in order to reach the minimum specified performance. Most likely, the learning procedure will also depend from the prior probabilities of the classes, thus adding training material at fixed costs will produce a model with different sensitivity and specificity. The

J. Kittler and F. Roli (Eds.): MCS 2001, LNCS 2096, pp. 32–42, 2001.

main question we want to address in this paper is thus how to develop a good cost-sensitive classification algorithm, which is independent as much as possible from cost availability and class imbalance, and which does not require dense sampling of the ROC curves for each training data set in order to satisfy or to go as close as possible to the performance constrains (in terms of sensitivity and specificity).

As a cost-sensitive algorithm, we will discuss in this paper a variant of the AdaBoost algorithm [8]: basic AdaBoost allows us to build systems with high accuracy (low misclassification error) and, although misclassification costs were not originally considered for the training phase, we can build a good cost-sensitive variant which separately optimize the margins for the two classes. In our variant, cost-sensitive boosting is achieved by (A) weighting the model error function with separate costs for false negative and false positives errors, and (B) updating the weights differently for negatives and positives at each boosting step.

Similar approaches have been described elsewhere. In particular, a cost-sensitive variant of AdaBoost was adopted for AdaCost [7]: based on the assumption that a misclassification cost factor has to be assigned for each training data, the weights are increased in case of misclassification or decreased otherwise according to a non negative function of the costs. A different model error function than in (A) is considered, as we focus on explicit weighting in terms of sensitivity and specificity. Karakoulas and Shawe-Taylor [11], have also introduced a similar approach based on misclassification costs constant for all the samples in a class. The procedure leads to increase the weights of false negatives more than false positives and, differently from our approach, to decrease the weights of true positives more than true negatives.

We have also included in our methodology a practical search procedure to get into, or as close as possible to, a target region in the sensitivity-specificity space. The aim is to wrap all of the cost-sensitive boosting learning cycle with a model selection procedure. For example, in the melanoma diagnosis problem, we will simulate the development of a model with sensitivity greater than 0.95 and specificity greater than .50 (a sensible request for assisting the screening of skin lesions). The search procedure allows us to satisfy for the first time the sensitivity and specificity constrains, without a tabulation of the whole curve in the ROC space. Our variant of AdaBoost allowed a remarkable improvement over previous results on the same data set obtained with a combination of classifiers specifically designed for the task [3]. An improvement was also found in the control of variability (standard deviation of error estimates). In the melanoma diagnosis application, our combined strategy resulted more effective than applying an external cost criterion to AdaBoost (as documented similarly in [14]).

The paper is organized as follows. The next Section 2 briefly introduces the classification problem which inspired our approach. Our cost-sensitive variant of AdaBoost, including the search procedure, is described in Section 3. The approach is evaluated on the melanoma data in Section 4. Section 5 concludes the paper.

2   The MEDS Melanoma Data

As described in [3], the MEDS data base is composed by 152 digital epilumines-cence microscopy images (D-ELM) of skin lesions, acquired at the Department of Dermatology of Santa Chiara Hospital, Trento. Image processing of D-ELM data produces 5 geometric-morphologic and 33 colorimetric features for each image, for a total of 38 features. D-ELM images and similar features were also used for automated classification in [2]. According to a subsequent histological analysis, the MEDS data base includes 42 malign lesions (melanomas: positive examples) and 110 naevi (negative examples). In [3], different classifiers and a panel of 8 dermatologists were compared reproducing a tele-dermatology set-up. For re-sult comparisons, we here use the same experimental structure of the previous study, consisting in a 10-fold cross validation for the estimates of sensitivity and specificity of the classification systems and of the physicians.

3   The SSTBoost Cost-Sensitive Procedure

3.1   AdaBoost and SSTBoost

Let us start with the basic Adaboost [8]. Given a training data set $L = \{(x_i, y_i)\}$, with $i = 1, ..., N$, where the x_i are input vectors (numerical, categorical or mixed) and the y_i are class labels taking values -1 or 1, the discrete Adaboost classifica-tion model is defined as the sign of an incremental linear combination of different realizations of a base classifier, each one trained on a weighted version of L, in-creasing the weights for the samples currently misclassified. Alternatively, if the base model does not accept internally weights, it can be trained over weighted bootstrap versions of L. The AdaBoost procedure for a combination H of T base classifiers is summarized in Box 1.

- Given $L = \{(x_i, y_i)\}_{i=1,...,N} \subset X \times \{-1, +1\}$
- Initialize $D_1(i) = 1/N$
- For $t = 1, ..., T$:
    1. Train the base classifier h using distribution D_t.
    2. Get hypothesis $h_t : X \rightarrow \{-1, +1\}$
    3. Compute model error $\epsilon_t = \sum_i D_t(i)\Theta[y_i h_t(x_i) = -1]$
       where $\Theta[P]$ returns 1 if predicate P = true, 0 otherwise.
    4. Choose $\alpha_t = \dfrac{1}{2} \ln \left(\dfrac{1 - \epsilon_t}{\epsilon_t} \right)$
    5. Update $D_{t+1}(i) = \dfrac{D_t(i)e^{-\alpha_t y_i h_t(x_i)}}{Z_t}$ where Z_t is a normalization factor chosen so that D_{t+1} will be a distribution
- Output the final hypothesis: $H(x) = sign \left(\displaystyle\sum_{t=1}^{T} \alpha_t h_t(x) \right)$

Box 1: The **AdaBoost** algorithm

- Given $L = \{(x_i, y_i)\}_{i=1,\ldots,N} \subset X \times \{-1, +1\}$
- Given cost parameter $w \in [0, 2]$
- Define $c_i = \begin{cases} w \text{ if } y_i = +1 \\ 2 - w \text{ if } y_i = -1 \end{cases}$
- Initialize $D_1(i) = 1/N$
- For $t = 1, \ldots, T$:
  1. Train base classifier h using distribution D_t.
  2. Get hypothesis $h_t : X \to \{-1, +1\}$
  3. Compute model error $\epsilon_t = (1 - Se)\pi_{+1}w + (1 - Sp)\pi_{-1}(2 - w)$
  4. Choose $\alpha_t = \dfrac{1}{2} \ln \left(\dfrac{1 - \epsilon_t}{\epsilon_t} \right)$
  5. Update $D_{t+1}(i) = \begin{cases} \dfrac{D_t(i)e^{-\alpha_t(2-c_i)}}{Z_t} \text{ if } y_i h_t(x_i) = +1 \\ \dfrac{D_t(i)e^{\alpha_t c_i}}{Z_t} \text{ if } y_i h_t(x_i) = -1 \end{cases}$

     where Z_t is a normalization factor chosen so that D_{t+1} will be a distribution
- Output the final hypothesis: $H_w(x) = sign \left(\displaystyle\sum_{t=1}^{T} \alpha_t h_t(x) \right)$

Box 2: The **SSTBoost** algorithm: internal learning procedures

To illustrate a typical situation, maximal decision trees implemented following the classic reference [4] can be considered as base classifiers h_t. In many applications, using unpruned trees not only avoids introducing an additional metaparameter (the regularization one) in the system: but also, maximal trees give overall optimal or suboptimal results with boosting when there is enough interaction between variables, as discussed in [5,9,10].

The definition of the model error ϵ in AdaBoost (Box 1) does not differentiate the costs of misclassification for training data from different classes. In Box 2 we introduce a variant of AdaBoost (Sensitivity-specificity Tuning Boosting: SSTBoost) which takes into account costs at two different levels. Firstly, given class priors π_i and costs (or losses) c_i of a misclassification for class $i \in \{-1, +1\}$, we propose to consider the following weighted version of the model error:

$$\epsilon = (1 - Se)\pi_{+1}c_{+1} + (1 - Sp)\pi_{-1}c_{-1}. \tag{1}$$

As discussed in [1], rather than considering separately the values of the two c_{-1} and c_{+1}, it is more convenient to consider the cost ratio $\frac{c_{+1}}{c_{-1}}$ or to impose a constraint $c_{+1} + c_{-1} = cost$. In a more complete view, imbalance between classes may also play an important function, not necessarily correlated with the cost ratio: in these cases one should consider the extended cost ratio $\frac{c_{+1}\pi_{+1}}{c_{-1}\pi_{-1}}$. We do not consider this extension in this paper. In Box 2, we introduce the cost parameter $w \in [0, 2]$ such that $c_{+1} = w$ and $c_{-1} = 2 - w$: clearly, $w = 1$ corresponds to the classical AdaBoost model, while values of $w > 1$ will increase contribution to error by misclassification of positive cases, and vice versa for $w < 1$. In particular, suppose $w > 1$: a greater weight α_t will be therefore assigned to the models with higher sensitivity.

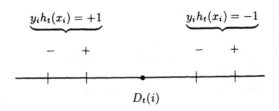

Fig. 1. Weight updates.

On a more local scale, Step 5 in Box 2 introduces a second variation to AdaBoost in the weight updating procedure. For $w > 1$, the weights of the misclassified positive samples will be increased more than those of misclassified negatives, and the weights of the correctly classified negative samples will be decreased more than those positive and correctly classified (Figure 1). In order to induce higher sensitivity, the procedure therefore puts more attention on the hardest positive examples. In terms of margin analysis, the result of the procedure is to increase the margin of the positive samples more than for the negative ones. According to the results in [13], it follows that the measure of confidence in the prediction is higher for the positive samples, i.e. for $w > 1$ the final SSTBoost model has been trained for generalizing with higher sensitivity.

   This property was tested on the MEDS melanoma data base: in the left panel of Figure 2, the cumulative margin distribution (data from both classes) is shown for three different values of the misclassification costs. For $w = 1$ (equivalent to the AdaBoost algorithm), we can see that the margins are approximately concentrated between 0.5 and 0.8. For values of w different from 1, a gap in the margin distribution is observed. In particular, for $w = 1.34375$ the cumulative distribution remains flat approximately from 0.3 to 0.8 (solid curve in the left panel of Figure 2). The right panel of Figure 2 clarifies how the gap is originated for this value of the cost parameter: training has aggressively increased the margin of the positive samples (always greater than 0.8), while the margin of the negative samples remains lower than 0.3.

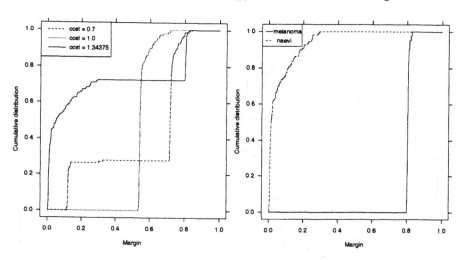

Fig. 2. Left panel: cumulative margin distribution for different values of the misclassification costs. For values of the misclassification cost w different from $+1$, a gap in the margin distribution is observable. Right panel: cumulative margin distribution of positive and negative samples for $w = 1.34375$.

3.2   The SSTBoost Search Procedure

The cost-sensitive procedure discussed in Section 3.1 supports the development of classification models H_w differently polarized towards sensitivity or specificity. We describe now a procedure for the automatic selection of an optimal cost parameter w^* in order to satisfy or to get as close as possible to admissible sensitivity and specificity constraints. The idea is to take advantage of the cost-sensitive learning variant described in Box 2 and at the same time to avoid a manual tuning of w or an extensive tabulation of the possible H_w in order to reach the minimal operative requirements. If A is a target region in the ROC space, i.e. A is a compact subset of $[0,1] \times [0,1]$, the constraints are satisfied for w^* such that $(1 - \widehat{Sp(w^*)}, \widehat{Se(w^*)}) \in A$, where $\widehat{Se(w)}$ and $\widehat{Sp(w)}$ are predictive estimates (e.g. from cross-validation over the training data L) of the sensitivity and specificity of the model H_w computed according to Box 2. The goal is then the minimization of the distance between the ROC curve and the compact set A, where the ROC curve is defined as $\phi_H : [0,2] \to \Re^2$

$$\phi_H(w) = (1 - \widehat{Sp(w)}, \widehat{Se(w)}). \tag{2}$$

The problem can be addressed as a minimization problem of a function of one real variable. Let $\Delta : [0,2] \to \Re^+$ be defined as

$$\Delta(w) = dist(\phi_H(w), A) = \min_{a \in A} \|\phi_H(w) - a\|. \tag{3}$$

- Given a target region A
- Set $w_1 = 1$, $w_{min} = 0$, $w_{max} = 2$
- Train $H_{w_1}(x)$ as in Box 2 and use cross-validation to estimate $\phi_H(w_1)$
- For $i = 1, ..., M$
  1. If $\phi_H(w_i) \in$ Failure Region
              Abort
     ElseIf $\phi_H(w_i) \in$ Low Specificity
              $w_{i+1} = 1/2(w_{max} - w_i)$
              $w_{min} = w_i$
     ElseIf $\phi_H(w_i) \in$ Low Sensitivity
              $w_{i+1} = 1/2(w_i - w_{min})$
              $w_{max} = w_i$
     ElseIf $\phi_H(w_i) \in A$
              Return $\tilde{w} = w_i$
     EndIf
  2. Train $H_{w_{i+1}}(x)$ and use cross-validation to estimate $\phi_H(w_{i+1})$
  EndFor

Box 3: The **SSTBoost** tuning procedure

The problem admits a solution, not necessarily unique: the possible optimal cost parameters are selected by $\tilde{w} = \mathrm{argmin}_w \Delta(w)$. In practice, constraints are likely to be of the type ($Se \geq a$ AND $Sp \geq b$). In this case, A is a rectangular subset and the two components of ϕ_H are increasing, so numerous search algorithms can be applied to quickly individuate an optimal cost parameter $\tilde{w}$. A simple but effective bisection method is described in Box 3. The algorithm fails when $\phi_H([0, 2]) \cap A = \emptyset$, otherwise one has to choose one of the w such that $\phi_H(w) \in A$ according to some super-optimality criterion, or just stopping at the first admissible $\tilde{w}$. It is clear that there are several effective alternatives for the search procedure, all leading to a fast convergence towards A, or at least as near to A as possible, particulary without strict hypotheses over the cost parameter. However, it must be taken into account that the $\phi_H(w)$ is only estimated (by cross-validation, in our example), and thus its smoothness is not necessarily assured. In case information about the c_i costs resulted available, as discussed in [1], the search can be constrained within a smaller interval $I \subset [0, 2]$. Finally, a non-euclidean distance may be considered for the *dist* function in Eq. 3.

4   Application to the Melanoma Data

We applied the procedure described in Boxes 2 and 3 to develop an effective model for early melanoma diagnosis. The goal was the development of a tool for supporting the discrimination between malign and benign lesions in accordance with application-specific constraints based on the MEDS data set described in Section 2. As the system was designed to support early diagnosis in a screening

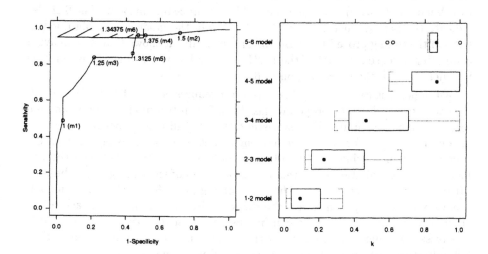

Fig. 3. Left panel: ROC curve for the SST boosting model applied to the melanoma MEDS data. The dashed rectangle represent the target region and the points over the curve indicate the value of the cost w during the optimization phase as described in Box 3. Right panel: distribution of the κ statistic for pairs (m_i, m_{i+1}) of models from the tuning procedure.

modality, it was required to recognize the maximum possible number of malign lesions, accepting a specificity of at least 0.5: in the real case, a non-expert clinician will perform the first visit, and all the patients with a suspect melanoma will be re-evaluated by a specialist. The target region A in the ROC space is therefore defined as $Se \geq 0.95$ and $1 - Sp \leq 0.5$. The target region corresponds to the shaded rectangle in the left panel of Figure 3. The ROC curve (estimated by

Table 1. For each classifier and combination of classifiers, sensitivity and specificity, with the standard deviation, are shown. The asterisk indicates results from [3].

Classifier	$Sens. \pm SD$	$Spec. \pm SD$
Discr. Ana.*	0.65 ± 0.30	0.83 ± 0.11
C4.5*	0.64 ± 0.28	0.84 ± 0.05
1-NN*	0.68 ± 0.30	0.90 ± 0.10
9-NN*	0.41 ± 0.25	0.96 ± 0.04
Discr. Ana. + C4.5 + 1-NN*	0.86 ± 0.32	0.64 ± 0.11
Discr. Ana. + C4.5 + 9-NN*	0.84 ± 0.32	0.71 ± 0.12
AdaBoost	0.49 ± 0.32	0.97 ± 0.04
th-AdaBoost	0.92 ± 0.12	0.70 ± 0.14
SSTBoost	0.97 ± 0.07	0.54 ± 0.18

cross-validation for different $H(w)$ models) is also plotted: the curve is obtained by tabulation of $\phi_H(w)$, following the SSTBoost procedure in Box2. The 6 circles indicate the performance for models $m1, \ldots, m6$: the models were obtained as steps of the tuning procedure in Box 3. This experiment shows that we can avoid computing a dense estimate of the ROC curve and leave the algorithm self-tune in order to reach the target region in 6 convergence steps.

An important issue in model selection procedures is to test the effective difference between different proposed classifiers. Given two models and a common test set, we can compute the κ statistic to test the difference between the two; for details, see [6]. For $\kappa = 0$ the agreement between classifiers equals that expected by chance, while $\kappa = 1$ indicates complete agreement between the two models. The distribution of κ statistic at each step of the tuning algorithm, i.e. $\kappa((m_i, m_{i+1})$ is shown in the right panel of Figure 3. For each pair of models (i.e. of pairs of cost parameters), the the κ statistic is computed on each of the 10 cross-validation test sets. It can be observed that diversity between models progressively reduces at each step: at the end, the median κ value is greater than 0.8 indicating very small changes in the model performance.

Table 1 summarizes performance results over the MEDS data set for classifiers developed in a previous study [3], and the different variants of AdaBoost studied in this paper, including SSTBoost. In [3], different classifiers were developed, and the most interesting results were obtained by combination. In particular, the performance closest to the constraints was obtained for a combination of Discriminant Analysis, C4.5 and Nearest Neighbors. That performance was comparable with the average over a panel of 8 expert dermatologists, on the same experimental conditions. The value for AdaBoost reported in Table 1 is clearly unbalanced towards specificity: however, a family of models was obtained from the AdaBoost models by thresholding the margin distributions for the two output classes and then choosing an optimal model th-AdaBoost as a function of the threshold. The performance for SSTBoost is also reported in Table 1 (see also Figure 3), and it indicates the overall best results. Not only was the target region A reached in only 6 steps, but also the model variability was very moderate in comparison with the other models developed in this and in the previous study. It is interesting to note that the improvement of SSTBoost over the th-AdaBoost seems to confirm the consideration on the differences between MetaCost architecture for boosting and AdaCost reported in [14]

5   Conclusions

This paper describes a methodology for automatically building a model with the required minimal performance in terms of sensitivity and specificity.

The introduction of a cost parameter w both within the estimated error function as well as within the weight updating of AdaBoost (as in [7]) allows us to effectively increase the margin of the predictions of one class with respect to the other. As a consequence, any admissible choice of this parameter leads to models characterized by different sensitivity-specificity pairs. We also indicate a procedure for selecting the optimal w, i.e. such that the corresponding model reaches or goes as close as possible to the target region defined in terms of required sensitivity and specificity. We have given only a basic example of a self-tuning procedure for cost-sensitive model selection: more elaborate search procedures may be considered within this approach.

Acknowledgments. The authors wish to thank B. Caprile (ITC-irst) for illuminating discussions on boosting magic, and S. Forti and C. Eccher (ITC-irst), M. Cristofolini and P. Bauer (Department of Dermatology, S. Chiara Hospital – Trento) for their significant collaboration on the melanoma diagnosis application.

References

1. N. Adams and D. Hand, "Classifier performance assessment," *Neural Computation*, vol. 12, no. 2, pp. 305–311, 2000.
2. L. Bischof, H. Talbot, E. Breen, D. Lovell, D. Chan, G. Stone, S. Menzies, A. Gutenev, and R. Caffin, "An automated melanoma diagnosis system," in *New Approaches in Medical Image Analysis* (B. Pham, M. Braun, A. Maeder, and M. Eckert, eds.), SPIE, 1999.
3. E. Blanzieri, C. Eccher, S. Forti, and A. Sboner, "Exploiting classifier combination for early melanoma diagnosis support," in *Proceedings of ECML-2000* (R. de Mantaras and E. Plaza, eds.), (Berlin), pp. 55–62, Springer-Verlag, 2000.
4. L. Breiman, J. Friedman, R. Olshen, and C. Stone, *Classification and Regression Trees*. Pacific Grove CA: Wadsworth and Brooks/Cole, 1984.
5. L. Breiman, "Combining predictors," in *Combining Artificial Neural Nets: Ensemble and Modular Multi-Net Systems* (A. Sharkey, ed.), (London), Springer-Verlag, 1999. pages 31–50.
6. T. Dietterich, "An experimental comparison of three methods for constructing ensembles of decision trees: bagging, boosting, and randomization," *Machine Learning*, vol. 40, no. 2, pp. 139–158, 2000.

7. W. Fan, S. Stolfo, J. Zhang, and P. Chan, "Adacost: Misclassification cost-sensitive boosting," in *Proceedings of ICML-99*, 1999.

8. Y. Freund and R. Schapire, "A decision-theoretic generalization of online learning and an application to boosting," *Journal of Computer and System Sciences*, vol. 55, no. 1, pp. 119–139, 1997.

9. J. Friedman, T. Hastie, and R. Tibshirani, "Additive logistic regression: a statistical view of boosting," tech. rep., Stanford University, 1999.

10. C. Furlanello and S. Merler, "Boosting of tree-based classifiers for predictive risk modeling in gis," in *Multiple Classifier Systems* (J. Kittler and F. Roli, eds.), vol. 1857, (Amsterdam), Springer, 2000. pages 220-229.

11. G. Karakoulas and J. Shawe-Taylor, "Optimizing classifiers for imbalanced training sets," in *Advances in Neural Information Processing Systems 11* (M. Kearns, S. Solla, and D. Cohn, eds.), MIT Press, 1999.

12. D. Margineantu and T. Dietterich, "Bootstrap methods for the cost-sensitive evaluation of classifiers," in *Proceedings of ICML-2000*, pp. 583–590, Morgan Kaufmann, 2000.

13. R. Schapire, Y. Freund, P. Bartlett, and W. Lee, "Boosting the margin: a new explanation for the effectiveness of voting methods," *The Annals of Statistics*, vol. 26, no. 5, pp. 1651–1686, 1998.

14. K. Ting, "A comparative study study of cost-sensitive boosting algorithms," in *Proceedings of ICML-2000* (M. Kaufmann, ed.), pp. 983–990, 2000.

Learning Classification RBF Networks by Boosting *

Juan J. Rodríguez Diez[1] and Carlos J. Alonso González[2]

[1] Lenguajes y Sistemas Informáticos, Universidad de Burgos, Spain,
jjrodriguez@ubu.es
[2] Grupo de Sistemas Inteligentes, Dpto. de Informática, Universidad de Valladolid,
Spain, calonso@infor.uva.es

Abstract. This work proposes a novel method for constructing RBF
networks, based on boosting. The task assigned to the base learner is to
select a RBF, while the boosting algorithm combines linearly the different
RBFs. For each iteration of boosting a new neuron is incorporated into
the network.

The method for selecting each RBF is based on randomly selecting several examples as the centers, considering the distances to these center as
attributes of the examples and selecting the best split on one of these
attributes. This selection of the best split is done in the same way than
in the construction of decision trees. The RBF is computed from the
center (attribute) and threshold selected.

This work is not about *using* RBFNs as base learners for boosting, but
about *constructing* RBFNs by boosting.

1 Introduction

This work is a follow-up of our research in boosting similarity literals for time
series classification [18]. In that work, following the good results of boosting
very simple classifiers (i.e., *stumps*) for several data sets [9], we proposed to use
similarity literals as base classifiers. The format of these literals were:

[not] <*distance*>_le(Example, Reference, Attributes, Value)

which is true if the <*distance*> between the Example considered and another
Reference example, restricted to the Attributes considered, is less or equal (_le)
than Value.

Normally, the parameter Attributes will include all the attributes of the examples, and it would be unnecessary. The reason for its inclusion is because for
several types of machine learning problems it is natural to group the attributes of
the examples. An important example is the case of multivariate time series. For
these problems, there are several series (e.g. x, y), and each series is composed

---

* This work has been supported by the Spanish CYCIT project TAP 99–0344 and the
"Junta de Castilla y León" project VA101/01

J. Kittler and F. Roli (Eds.): MCS 2001, LNCS 2096, pp. 43–52, 2001.

by several values (e.g. $x_1, \ldots x_n$). In this case it is interesting the possibility of using the distance between each series independently.

Each base classifier was only one literal, and their result was simply true or false. One of the improvements to the original ADABOOST algorithm is the use of confidence based predictions [22], where each base classifier also returns, for each example, a confidence (a real number) on its prediction.

A natural question is how to combine confidence based predictions with similarity literals. The first option was to consider a given literal as a boolean attribute and, using the methods of [22] for domain-partitioning weak classifiers, to assign a confidence value corresponding to the values true and false of the literal. Nevertheless, when using distance literals it is natural to use, somehow, the value of the distance for the current example, to the reference example, and the threshold value to obtain a confidence. In fact, an obvious option is a radial basis function. On the other hand, the result of ADABOOST is a linear combination of the predictions of the base classifiers, and if the base classifiers are RBFs, then the result of boosting is a RBF Network [15,16].

This work is also related with the methods for constructing RBFNs from decision trees [14]. These works share the idea of constructing the network from a symbolic machine learning method. For instance, the selection of each RBF is based on the one for the split of a node in a decision tree. A difference with that methods is that in the case of the decision trees there are two steps: first, constructing the symbolic classifier and second, "upgrading" it to a network. In our case, although there are also two parts, the base learner and the proper boosting method, they work in cooperation.

The rest of the paper is organized as follows. Section 2 describes the operation of the base learner. The concrete details of the boosting variant used are described in section 3. Section 5 presents experimental results when using this method. Finally, we give some concluding remarks in section 6.

2   The Base Classifiers

2.1   Literals Selection

The base learner works as follows. First, several examples are selected, randomly, as possible references. The number of reference examples considered (r) is a parameter, and even could be possible to use different number of positive and negative examples.

For each reference example, the distance to all the other training examples (e) is computed. The time necessary for this process is $e\,t(n)$, where $t(n)$ is the time necessary for calculating the distances between two examples with n attributes. In the case of the euclidean distance, $t(n) \in O(n)$.

Then the best threshold for the distances is computed in a similar way as done with decision trees. First, all the distances are sorted (time $e \lg e$). All the values are considered, from left to right, keeping into account the number and weight of positive and negative examples at the left from the current value. For each distance value it is computed the error of selecting this threshold. This can be done, for each value, in $O(1)$ because it only involve to calculate a function of the weight of positive and negative examples at the left and at the right of the threshold. For e distances the time necessary is $O(e)$, which is smaller than $O(e \lg e)$. Hence, the base learner requires a time of $re(t(n) + \lg e)$.

2.2 Assigning Confidences

Given a literal <*distance*>_le(Example, Reference, Attributes, Value), the RBF selected is

$$h(x) = 2\exp\left(-\left(\frac{d_A(x,c)}{t}\right)^2 \ln 2\right) - 1 \tag{1}$$

where x is the Example, c the Reference example, t the threshold Value and d_A the <*distance*> restricted to the Attributes A.

This function has the following properties:

- $h(c) = 1$
- $h(x) = 0$ if $d_A(x,c) = t$
- $-1 \le h(x) \le 1$, given $d_A(x,c) \ge 0$
- This function monotonically decreases as $d_A(x,c)$ increases

If the literal is negated, then the function is multiplied by -1. These functions are radial basis functions [15], and a linear combination of them is a RBFN.

3   Boosting

The combination of several classifiers, *ensembles*, is a natural way of increasing the accuracy with respect to the original classifiers. One of the most popular methods for creating ensembles is boosting [21], a family of methods, of which ADABOOST is the most prominent member. They work by assigning a weight to each example. Initially, all the examples have the same weight. In each iteration a base classifier is constructed, according to the distribution of weights. Afterward, the weight of each example is readjusted, based on the correctness of the class assigned to the example by the base classifier. The final result is obtained by weighted votes of the base classifiers.

The following sections give some details about the version of boosting used in this work.

3.1   Selecting α

In [22] several methods are proposed for selecting the weight (α) associated to each base classifier. The better value for α is obtained by minimizing

$$Z = \sum_i D(i)e^{-\alpha u_i}$$

Where $D(i)$ is the weight of the example x_i, $u_i = y_i h(x_i)$, $y_i \in \{-1, +1\}$ is the class of the example and $h(x_i)$ is the confidence given by the base classifier to the example. For the original ADABOOST, this expression is approximated, given $u_i \in [-1, +1]$, by

$$Z \leq \sum_i D(i) \left(\frac{1 + u_i}{2} e^{-\alpha} + \frac{1 - u_i}{2} e^{\alpha} \right)$$

And the minimum α for this expression was selected analytically. Nevertheless, they suggest that is possible to select other upper bounds, and we use

$$Z \leq \sum_{i:u_i \geq 0} D(i)(u_i e^{-\alpha} - u_i + 1) + \sum_{i:u_i < 0} D(i)(-u_i e^{+\alpha} + u_i + 1)$$

which gives a tighter approximation.

3.2   Multiclass Problems

There are several methods, which also deal with confidences, for extending ADABOOST to the multiclass case, such as ADABOOST.MH and AD-ABOOST.MR [22]. Nevertheless, our base classifiers are binary (stumps) and we cannot use, directly, the variants that use multiclass base classifiers.

On the other hand, ADABOOST.OC [20] can be used with any weak learner which can handle binary labeled data. It does not require that the weak learner can handle multilabeled data with high accuracy. The key idea is, in each round of the boosting algorithm, to select a subset of the set of labels, and train the binary weak learner with the examples labeled positive or negative depending if the original label of the example is or is not in the subset. Our implementation is based on a further variant of ADABOOST.OC, named ADABOOST.ECC [11], but dealing with confidence based predictions.

4   Running Example

This section shows a small example of the working of the method. The "control charts" data set has six classes: normal, cyclic, upward, downward, decreasing and increasing. The output codes version of the boosting algorithm selects a subset of the classes, e.g. decreasing, increasing and upward. The base learner selects a literal for discriminating between the classes in the subset and the rest of classes (i.e., normal, cyclic and downward). The literal selected is:

euclidean_le(Example, upward_55, 116.968937)

The argument Attributes is omitted, because all the attributes are used.

The confidence function, $h(x)$, assigned to this literal is given by Eq. 1. Using this confidence, the boosting algorithm i) calculates the weight, α, of this base classifier and ii) updates the weights of the example. The learning process consists of repeating these steps as many times as iterations.

The classification of an example x, consists of the repetition, for each base classifier of the following steps:

- The distance between the example x and the reference (upward_55) is calculated.
- A confidence $h(x)$ is calculated using Eq. 1
- For the classes in the corresponding subset (decreasing, increasing and upward), $\alpha h(x)$ is added to their weights. For the other classes, the quantity added is $-\alpha h(x)$

Finally, the class assigned to the example is the one with greater weight.

5   Experimental Validation

The characteristics of the data sets are summarized in table 1. The data sets waveform, waveform with noise [5,6], CBF (cylinder, bell and funnel) [19] and control charts [1,3] were already used in our work on boosting distance literals [18].

Table 1. Characteristics of the data sets

	Classes	Examples	Training / Test	Attributes
Waveform	3	5000	300 / 5000	21
Wave + noise	3	5000	300 / 5000	40
CBF	3	798	10-fold CV	128
Control charts	6	600	10-fold CV	60
Auslan	10	200	10-fold CV	8×30

Auslan is the Australian sign language, the language of the Australian deaf community. Instances of the signs were collected using an instrumented glove [12]. Each example is composed by 8 series The number of points in each example is variable, so they were reduced to 30 points (the series were divided in 30 segments along the time axis and the means of each segment were used as the values for the reduced series).

The experiments were performed using 100 iterations in boosting and with 20 reference examples (10 positive, 10 negative) in each iteration. For each data set, two distances were considered, the classical euclidean and dynamic time warping (DTW) [4], a distance designed for time series. For the data sets with an specified partition of training and test examples, the experiments were repeated 10 times. For the other data sets, 10-fold stratified cross-validation was used.

Table 2 and figure 1 resume the results. Comparing the results of euclidean and DTW, it is clear that the use of an adequate distance affects greatly the results of the classifier. The fact that euclidean is better than DTW for the waveform variants is due to the definition of these data sets. For them, all the randomness is in the vertical axis, and none in the horizontal (time) axis.

Comparing these results with our results using boosting literals [18] (which we considered then rather good), shows a very clear advantage for the new method. Nevertheless, two issues are relevant:

– The results of that work were obtained for all the data sets using cross validation, and in this work we use the specified partition when available.
– The number of iterations used in that work were 50, but in each iteration there were obtained as many literals as classes and in this one in each iteration only one literal (RBF)

Table 2. Experimental results.

Iterations:		10	20	30	40	50	60	70	80	90	100
Wave	Eucl.	17.17	14.99	14.26	14.00	13.85	13.69	13.65	13.54	13.51	13.50
	DTW	23.13	21.23	20.62	20.06	19.72	19.62	19.36	19.26	19.03	18.97
Wave	Eucl.	20.13	16.09	15.15	14.75	14.46	14.44	14.40	14.29	14.33	14.29
+ noise	DTW	26.59	25.26	24.73	24.01	23.69	23.60	23.52	23.15	22.99	22.89
CBF	Eucl.	9.49	8.00	6.89	6.89	6.88	6.50	6.74	6.00	6.00	6.00
	DTW	1.76	0.76	0.38	0.38	0.12	0.12	0.12	0.12	0.12	0.12
Control	Eucl.	38.17	8.50	8.50	7.67	7.50	8.00	5.50	6.17	4.83	4.17
charts	DTW	17.67	3.33	1.17	0.50	0.17	0.17	0.33	0.17	0.17	0.17
Iterations:		30	60	90	120	150	180	210	240	270	300
Auslan	Eucl.	11.00	5.50	3.50	3.50	3.00	3.00	3.00	2.50	2.50	2.50
	DTW	7.50	2.50	0.50	2.00	0.50	1.50	0.50	1.00	0.00	0.00

The Auslan data set was not used in [18]. This is the data set with the highest number of classes (10). Hence, we incremented the number of iterations for this data set, allowing up to 300 iterations. The result reported in [12] is an error of 2.50, using event extraction, event clustering and Naïve Bayes Classifiers.

Finally, an important detail is that we are not aware of better results for these data sets, even when some of them (waveform variants) are used very extensively in the literature. Table 3 shows results, from other authors, for these data sets.

Table 3. Results of other works for the data sets.

Data set	Result	Reference	Method
Wave	14.30	[23]	meta decision trees: decision trees, rules learner, nearest neighbor & naive Bayes
Wave + noise	>16.50	[2]	Boosting decision trees
CBF	1.90	[12]	event extraction, event clustering & decision trees
Auslan	2.50	[12]	event extraction, event clustering & Naïve Bayes

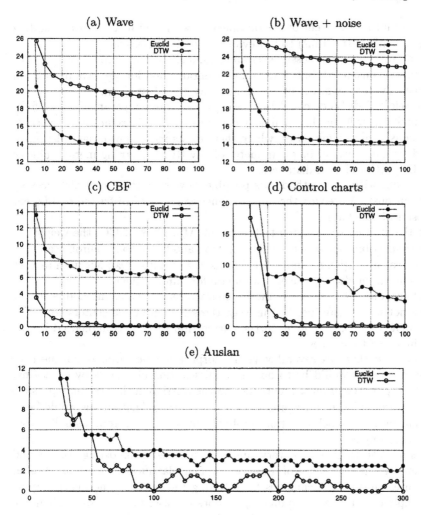

Fig. 1. Graphs of the results for the different data sets.

6 Discussion and Further Work

We have presented a novel method for learning RBFNs, based on boosting very simple classifiers. This classifiers are stumps of new attributes (distances to reference examples) of the examples. Finally, these stumps are converted to RBFs.

Some characteristics of the proposed method are:

- The method is nearly parameter-free. The only clear parameter is the number of iterations. Nevertheless, an interesting fact is that the classifiers (networks) obtained with a number of iterations are included (are sub networks) in the ones obtained with more iterations. Hence, it is possible i) to select only an initial fragment of the obtained network and ii) to continue adding base classifiers (neurons) to a previously obtained classifier.

- There are also other possible parameters, such as the number of reference examples considered, but in the experimental validation we have fixed them arbitrarily and we have not try, in any way, to adjust them.
- The selected distance could be considered as another parameter, but first, normally it will be the euclidean distance, with the exception of specific domains such as time series, where there exists more appropriate distances. And second, it would be a parameter of any RBFN learning method able of dealing with different distances.
- Note that with our method it is possible to work with several distances simultaneously. Moreover, the same distance can be used restricted to different subsets of attributes.
- For the multiclass case, due to the use of ADABOOST.ECC, the weights of the connections between the t RBF neuron and the output neurons can only take two values (i.e. α_t and $-\alpha_t$). This is clearly a disadvantage with respect to other methods, and a clear candidate for improvements.
- Perhaps, one of the most distinctive characteristics of this method is that it does not uses clustering. In this way, the selection of the centers considers the weights of the examples in the current iteration; it is influenced by the evolution of the process.
  In any case, there are several ways of incorporating clustering to our method. One possibility would be to do an initial selection of centers by clustering, and to apply the proposed method with the restriction that the only possible centers would be the ones preselected by clustering. Another one would be to do clustering for each iteration, probably, for efficiency, from a small subset of the examples.
- This method is, currently, very simple. It is based on boosting stumps and its implementation is one of the easiest among classification methods. It does not uses clustering techniques for selecting the centers. The mathematical concepts used are fairly simple, e.g. it does not uses matrices or gradients in any way. There is not feature selection or feature weighting, that is, all the attributes are considered with the same weight.

The results obtained for the data sets are clearly very competitive with the results we know for this data sets. The current method has its origin in a time series classification system, and the selection of the data sets is biased by this origin. An open question is to what extent our good results are due to the use of an specific distance for this domain.

The proposed method it is not based on any other method for learning RBFN, but it is clear that different combinations of this method with others are possible.

In [7], it is presented a method for constructing hybrid MLP and RBF networks. An interesting question is how to do, effectively, something similar with boosting. Especially, considering that boosting is well suited for combining different kinds of classifiers, as done in [17] with similarity and interval based literals.

The research on boosting has focused on classification, and this work follows this trend. On the other hand, RBFNs are frequently used for regression. Hence, it is interesting to consider the construction of regression RBFNs using one of the variants of ADABOOST for regression, such as ADABOOST.R [10] or EXPLEV [8].

References

[1] Robert J. Alcock and Yannis Manolopoulos. Time-series similarity queries employing a feature-based approach. In 7th *Hellenic Conference on Informatics*, Ioannina, Greece, 1999.

[2] Eric Bauer and Ron Kohavi. An empirical comparison of voting classification algorithms: Bagging, boosting and variants. *Machine Learning*, 36(1/2):105–139, 1999.

[3] Stephen D. Bay. The UCI KDD archive, 1999.

[4] D.J. Berndt and J. Clifford. Finding patterns in time series: a dynamic programming approach. In U.M. Fayyad, G. Piatetsky-Shapiro, P. Smyth, and R. Uthurusamy, editors, *Advances in Knowledge Discovery and Data Mining*, pages 229–248. AAAI Press /MIT Press, 1996.

[5] C.L. Blake and C.J. Merz. UCI repository of machine learning databases, 1998.

[6] L. Breiman, J.H. Friedman, A. Olshen, and C.J. Stone. *Classification and Regression Trees*. Chapman & Hall, New York, 1993.

[7] Shimon Cohen and Nathan Intrator. A hybrid projection based and radial basis function architecture. In Kittler and Roli [13], pages 147–156.

[8] Nigel Duffy and David Helmbold. Leveraging for regression. In *Computational Learning Theory: 13th Conference (COLT 2000)*, Stanford University, 2000.

[9] Y. Freund and R. Schapire. Experiments with a new boosting algorithm. In 13th *International Conference om Machine Learning (ICML-96)*, pages 148–156, Bari, Italy, 1996.

[10] Yoav Freund and Robert E. Scapire. A decision-theoretic generalization of online learning and an application to boosting. *Journal of Computer and System Sciences*, 55(1):119–139, August 1997.

[11] Venkatesan Guruswami and Amit Sahai. Multiclass learning, boosting, and error-correcting codes. In 12th *Annual Conference on Computational Learning Theory (COLT 1999)*. ACM, 1999.

[12] Mohammed W. Kadous. Learning comprehensible descriptions of multivariate time series. In Ivan Bratko and Saso Dzeroski, editors, 16th *International Conference of Machine Learning (ICML-99)*. Morgan Kaufmann, 1999.

[13] Josef Kittler and Fabio Roli, editors. *Multiple Classifier Systems: 1st International Workshop; MCS 2000*, volume 1857 of *Lecture Notes in Computer Science*. Springer, 2000.

[14] Miroslav Kubat. Decision trees can initialize radial-basis function networks. *IEEE Transactions on Neural Networks*, 9:813–821, 1998.

[15] Mark J. Orr. Introduction to radial basis function networks. Technical report, 1996. http://www.anc.ed.ac.uk/~mjo/papers/intro.ps.gz.

[16] Mark J. Orr. Recent advances in radial basis function networks. Technical report, 1999. http://www.anc.ed.ac.uk/~mjo/papers/recad.ps.gz.

[17] Juan J. Rodríguez, Carlos J. Alonso, and Henrik Boström. Learning first order logic time series classifiers: Rules and boosting. In Djamel A. Zighed, Jan Komorowski, and Jan Żytkow, editors, *Principles of Data Mining and Knowledge Discovery: 4th European Conference; PKDD 2000*, volume 1910 of *Lecture Notes in Artificial Intelligence*, pages 299–308. Springer, 2000.

[18] Juan J. Rodríguez Diez and Carlos J. Alonso González. Applying boosting to similarity literals for time series classification. In Kittler and Roli [13], pages 210–219.

[19] Naoki Saito. *Local Feature Extraction and Its Applications Using a Library of Bases*. PhD thesis, Department of Mathematics, Yale University, 1994.

[20] Robert E. Schapire. Using output codes to boost multiclass learning problems. In *14th International Conference on Machine Learning (ICML-97)*, pages 313–321, 1997.

[21] Robert E. Schapire. A brief introduction to boosting. In Thomas Dean, editor, *16th International Joint Conference on Artificial Intelligence (IJCAI-99)*, pages 1401–1406. Morgan Kaufmann, 1999.

[22] Robert E. Schapire and Yoram Singer. Improved boosting algorithms using confidence-rated predictions. In *11th Annual Conference on Computational Learning Theory (COLT 1998)*, pages 80–91. ACM, 1998.

[23] Ljupčo Todorovski and Sašo Džeroski. Combining multiple models with meta decision trees. In *Principles of Data Mining and Knowledge Discovery: 4th European Conference; PKDD 2000*, pages 54–64. Springer, 2000.

Data Complexity Analysis for Classifier Combination

Tin Kam Ho

Bell Laboratories, Lucent Technologies
700 Mountain Ave., 2C-425, Murray Hill, NJ 07974, USA

Abstract. Multiple classifier methods are effective solutions to difficult
pattern recognition problems. However, empirical successes and failures
have not been completely explained. Amid the excitement and confusion, uncertainty persists in the optimality of method choices for specific
problems due to strong data dependences of classifier performance. In
response to this, I propose that further exploration of the methodology
be guided by detailed descriptions of geometrical characteristics of data
and classifier models.

1 Introduction

Multiple classifier systems are often practical and effective solutions for difficult
pattern recognition tasks. The idea appeared in many names: hybrid methods,
decision combination, multiple experts, mixture of experts, classifier ensembles,
cooperative agents, opinion pool, sensor fusion, and more. In some areas it was
motivated by an empirical observation that specialized classifiers often excel in
different cases. In other areas it occurred naturally from the application context,
such as the need to employ a variety of sensor types which induces a natural
decomposition of the problem. There were also cases motivated by an attempt
to escape from the burden of making a commitment to some arbitrary initial
condition, such as the initial weights for a neural network. There were even hopes
that any sort of randomness introduced in classifier training would produce a
diverse collection that could perform better than a single element.

There are many ways to use more than one classifier in a single recognition
problem. A divide-and-conquer approach would isolate the types of input on
which each specific classifier performs well, and direct new input accordingly.
A sequential approach would use one classifier first, and invoke others only if
it fails to yield a decision with sufficient confidence. All these can be said to
be multiple classifier strategies, and have been explored to a certain extent.
However, motivated by the above mentioned factors, most combination research
focuses on applying all the available classifiers in parallel to the same input
and combining their decisions. Naturally one asks, what is gained and lost in a
parallel combination? When is it preferable to alternative approaches?

The trend of parallel combination of many classifiers deviates from, or even
follows an opposite philosophy of, the traditional selection approach in which one

J. Kittler and F. Roli (Eds.): MCS 2001, LNCS 2096, pp. 53–67, 2001.

evaluates the available classifiers against a representative sample and chooses the best one to use. Here, in essence, one abandons the attempt to find the best classifier, and instead, tries to use all the available ones in a smart way. This opposes the wisdom of economical design. But introducing needless classifiers is more than just harming efficiency. The agreement of two poor classifiers do not necessarily yield more correct decisions. And one can easily fall into a situation that the same training data are used to estimate an increasing and potentially infinite number of classifier parameters, which is not an unfamiliar trap.

As the idea prospered, many different proposals of combination emerged. It almost feels like we are simply bringing the fundamental pursuit to a different level. Instead of looking for the best set of features and the best classifier, now we look for the best set of classifiers and then the best combination method. One can imagine very soon we will be looking for the best set of combination methods and then the best way to use them all ... If we do not take the chance to review the fundamental problems arising from this challenge, we are bound to be driven into such an infinite recurrence, dragging along more and more complicated combination schemes and theories, and graduately losing insight into the original problem.

So, is classifier combination a well justified, systematic methodology, or is it a desperate attempt to make the most out of imperfect designs? What exactly is gained or lost in a combination effort? What has been achieved and what is still missing, and what should we do next? In this paper, I review the proposed methods and some of the challenges in related theories and practices, and suggest ways to further advance the methodology.

2 Difficulties in Combination Theories and Practices

The possibility, by now well supported by empirical evidences, of being able to go beyond the power of traditional classifiers is exciting. In pattern recognition, early discoveries that the combined accuracy of several classifiers can be better than that of each individual came as a surprise from experiments. Later studies revealed many alternative methods that can achieve similar effects. Proposed methods fall into two categories: (1) assume a given, fixed set of carefully designed and highly specialized classifiers, attempt to find an *optimal combination* of their decisions; and (2) assume a fixed decision combination function, *generate* a set of mutually complementary, generic classifiers that can be combined to achieve optimal accuracy. We will refer to combination strategies of the first kind as *decision optimization* methods and the second kind as *coverage optimization* methods. It is also possible to apply the decision optimization methods to classifiers generated with the aim of coverage optimization.

Decision Optimization

Often in pattern recognition practices, several classifiers can be designed for the same problem. Combining their decisions gives opportunities of improving accuracy or reliability. Choices of decision combination methods are dictated by several factors: what type of output the classifiers can produce, how many classes there are, and whether sufficient training data are available to tune the combination function. Table 1 summarizes the best known decision combination methods suitable under two contextual requirements.

Table 1. Decision combination methods

	Resolution of belief scores		
Trainable	binary or one of N decisions	ranked lists of classes	continuous prob. estimates or belief scores
No	majority, plurality vote	Borda count	sum, product rules
Yes	weighted vote	logistic regression	Bayes, Dempster-Shafer rules

The idea of employing multiple experts specialized for a given task in different aspects is probably as old as the history of human society. But such common wisdom does not necessarily and immediately apply in the context of pattern recognition, where concepts such as differences and cooperation have specific meanings. Behavior of classifiers can be mathematically characterized, and with accuracy being an objective measure of effectiveness, the benefits of any combination method can potentially be quantified. Reasons of having multiple sources of knowledge about an input pattern can be various, but whether they should be maintained in separate representations is never obvious.

Even less clear is whether one should integrate the separate representations and compare them under a single metric, or direct them to separate classifiers and defer the integration until after the classifiers have processed them. Regardless of the level where the integration is carried out, details of the integration procedure have to be stated in terms of a concise mathematical function and implemented in a well-defined algorithm. And early explorations show that there are vast differences in the effectiveness of different combination procedures.

Because of different contextual requirements, not all methods can be used with all problems. General performance claims about a particular combination strategy are thus difficult to make. Evaluation of the methods is further complicated by the fact that by and large only successful experiments are published, and it is difficult to find limits of a method's applicability. Nevertheless, it is obvious that very little can be tuned in the simple voting schemes, and in lack of sufficient training data, this may well be about all that can be done. With sophisticated output like estimates of posterior probabilities, other than the simple sum, product rules or Bayes schemes, more elaborated combination-level classifiers can be applied. However, for problems with a large number of classes, the availability of good estimates of posteriors is a very strong assumption. Without sufficient training data, the estimates given by the individual classifiers are inaccurate, and so are the estimates at the combination level. Thus, applying overly sophisticated combination methods is a dangerous game. The rank combining schemes weaken the requirement to only preferences which are always available as long as the classifiers compute any numerical similarity measure. For a very large number of classes and mixed type classifiers, this is an interesting middle ground. But the linear and uniform scale of the ranks may be too crude an approximation, and to simplify the model, the combinations may have to be restricted to only a small number of top ranks.

Hopes for a better understanding are placed on the development of good theories. But on the theory side, several problems persist. Most theoretical works suffer from failures to model various details in a classification problem.

In behavior sciences, methods for combining votings and rankings of alternative choices are referred to as *social choice functions* or *group consensus functions*. There, the focus is on obtaining a combined choice that best represents the voters' preferences. There is no notion of absolute *correctness* of the combined choice. The merit of a candidate in an election is solely determined by some specific characterization of voters' preferences. However, in classification, there is a true class associated with each input that is determined regardless of the combination mechanism. That makes a difference, since the combination function can be trained to optimize some objective accuracy measure. In classification, prior performance of the voters can also be evaluated against the objective truth, and based on such evaluation the combination function can be tuned. Some combination schemes such as regression make explicit use of these evaluations. Others that do not use such information carry an implicit assumption that the voters are competent to a certain extent and that the imposed characterization of the voters' preference is reasonable, either of which may not be correct.

Moreover, in the context of pattern recognition, the individual decisions of the voters are never independent. They are intrinsically linked by the fact that they are responses to the same input pattern. The degree of agreement of the individual decisions on the same input case, besides characterizing the amount of differences among the classifiers, is also a reflection of the relative difficulty of the case. These two effects must be modeled separately.

For combining estimates of posterior probabilities or belief scores represented in a normalized, continuous scale, Bayes decision theory and Dempster-Shafer's theory of evidence dominated. Prior performances of individual classifiers can be embedded into the combination function in the form of estimates of correctness probabilities conditioned on the individual decisions. Simpler combination rules that do not take into account the classifiers' prior performance were studied in [17], where a justification was given in support of the sum rule that chooses the class maximizing the sum of individual estimates of posterior probabilities. The justification is from the sum rule's relative insensitivity to local estimation errors when compared to the product rule. There are also other explored methods that essentially treat the belief scores given by the individuals as input features for a classifier at another level. These derive support from the classification principles. In statistics they are known as model-mix methods [20], justified by reducing the bias of the combined estimator.

Many attempts in modeling the performance of such combination schemes use some notion of complementariness among the component classifiers. But the precise definition of it is seldom given. A very common assumption is that the classifiers' decisions are statistically independent, in the sense that the probability of a joint decision equals the product of probabilities of each individual classifier's corresponding decision. But this is an imposed, very strong assumption which could be very far away from the truth. In a recognition system, classifier decisions are intrinsically correlated, as they respond to the same input. The correlation among the classifiers has to be *measured* from the data. Until measurements confirm the assumption of zero correlation, those theories dependent on it do not necessarily apply. This fact is well aware of at the level of feature representations, but is often neglected at the level of classifier decisions. Moreover, the correlation among different classifiers' decisions can vary from input to input. Decisions may be strongly corrected only on easy cases far from the class boundary. So even with the same set of classifiers, correlation of their decisions varies across problems and subproblems according to proportions of easy and hard cases. It is a theoretical challenge to model such detailed data dependency.

Coverage Optimization

A system using several classifiers may not be able to achieve the highest accuracy for a problem if there are cases for which none of the classifiers' decision is sufficiently close to being correct. Coverage optimization methods are called on to pursue the missing guarantee. There, the strategy is to *create* a set of classifiers, observing some specific notion of complementariness, such that they can yield a good final decision under the chosen combination function. Table 2 summarizes the better known coverage optimization methods and the training mechanism used to introduce complementariness between the components.

Table 2. Coverage optimization methods

Method	Training mechanism for introducing complementariness
perturbation	vary initial conditions or parameters of training process
stacking	train classifiers by nonoverlapping subsamples of training set
bagging	resample the training set by bootstrap replicates
boosting	resample the training set by weights evolving with accuracy
random subspaces	project training set to randomly chosen subspaces
stochastic discrimination	generate random kernels to measure coverage of training set
error correction output coding	force training on partial decision boundaries

Several methods introduce complementary strengths by training component classifiers on different subsamples of the training set. Despite many observed empirical successes, such training set subsampling methods are paradoxical. Weakening the individual classifiers by not training or equally weighing on all available data is said to help avoid overfitting. At an extreme, boosting cannot run on classifiers perfect for the training data, as there are no errors to train additional components. But the design is intended to make the entire system work well on the full training set. So do we want it or not that the classifiers perfectly adapt to the training data? If we want it, what is the point of deferring it to the level of decision combination? If we do not want it, what is the point of adding more and more components to improve accuracy on the full training set? Why should the full system treat the training set differently from the way followed by the component classifiers? If the training set is assumed to represent well the unseen cases, why would one believe that by sacrificing training set accuracy one can gain in testing set accuracy? If the feature space is small and the training sample is dense, the training set could overlap with the testing set perfectly. In such a case, what good will it do to deliberately sacrifice accuracy on the training set? On the other hand, without involving the generalization performance in the analysis, the argument that the methods can, eventually, do perfectly on the training set is useless – template matching can do the job, there is no reason to bother with such elaborated training procedures and sacrifices. Without a thorough understanding of how overfitting is avoided or controlled within the training process, there is no guarantee on the results, and empirical evidences do show that these methods do not always work.

Then there is the question of the form of the component classifiers. All these methods are known to work well with decision trees, though, details matter on the specific way data are split at each internal node. The much used notion of weak classifiers is not well defined. Fully split decision trees are very strong classifiers, though, pruned or forced shallow versions have been used to some success. With others, like linear discriminators, things are less clear. If the component classifiers are too weak, given the simple decision combination function involving weighted or unweighted averaging, the decisions of many bad classifiers can easily outweigh the good ones, especially in methods like boosting that focus more and more on the errors. And how about mixing in different types of classifiers?

Such fundamental issues are in the midst of confusion in several communities. In [18] Kleinberg offered a rigorous analysis of these issues, using a set-theoretic abstraction to remove all the algorithmic details of classifiers, feature extractors, and training procedures. It considers only the classifiers' decision regions in the form of point sets, called weak models, in the feature space. A collection of classifiers is thus just a sample into the power set of the feature space. If the sample satisfies a uniformity condition, i.e., if its coverage is unbiased to any local region of the feature space, then a symmetry is observed between two probabilities (w.r.t. the feature space and w.r.t. the power set respectively) of the same event that a point of a particular class is covered by a component of the sample. Then it is shown that discrimination between classes is possible as long as there is some minimum difference in each component's inclusion of points of different classes, which is trivial to satisfy. The symmetry translates such differences across different points in the space to differences among the models on a single point. Accuracy in classification is then governed by the law of large numbers. If the sample of weak models is large, the discriminant function, defined on the coverage of the models on a single point and the class-specific differences within each model, converges to poles distinct by class with diminishing variance. Moreover, it is proved that the combined system maintains the projectability of the weak models, i.e., if each model is thick enough with respect to the spatial continuity of the classes, estimates of the point inclusion probabilities from the training set are close to the true probabilities, then the combined system would retain the same goodness of approximation of the estimate, which will translate, by the symmetry, to accuracy in classifying unseen points.

The theory includes explicitly each of the three elements long believed to be important in pattern recognition: discrimination power, complementary information, and generalization ability. Here projectability of the weak models is a key element in the proof, and not an implicit side effect, as in several other theories attempted to explain the behavior of the coverage optimization methods. What is good about building the classifier on weak models instead of strong models? Because weak models are easier to obtain, and their smaller capacity subjects them less to sampling errors carried in small training sets [27] [28]. Why are many models needed? Because the method relies on the law of large numbers to reduce the variance of the discriminant on each single point. The uniformity condition specifies exactly what kind of correlation is needed among the individual models. Moreover, accuracy is not achieved by intentionally limiting the VC dimension of the complete system – the combination of many weak models can have very large VC dimension. It is a consequence of the symmetry relating probabilities in the two spaces, and the law of large numbers. It is a structural property of the topology. The theory succeeded in offering a complete explanation of the combined behavior of such simple classifiers. However, much remains to be explored in using it to predict the behavior of fewer but more sophisticated classifiers.

Combination theories must deal with the dilemma of choosing between a probabilistic view and a geometrical view of classification, or the difficulty of blending the two. Many theories model a classifiers' decision as a probabilistic event, and assume that decisions on each input are not related to decisions on others. However, in most application contexts, there is some geometrical continuity in the feature space, such that classifiers' decisions on neighboring points are likely to be similar. Some classifiers, such as decision trees, rely explicitly on this fact to partition the feature space into contiguous regions of the same class. But the notion of neighborhood is explictly used only in a few theories such as stochastic discrimination and consistent systems of inequalities [21]. Discussions on the optimal size of component decision trees barely touch on this, but are not followed through. Precise characterization of the problem geometry will involve descriptions of the fragmentation of the Bayes optimal decision regions, global or local linear separability, and convexity and smoothness of boundaries. Many of these depend the properties of a specific metric based on which the classifier operates. Better modeling of the geometrical behavior of classifiers is attempted in some neural network studies, where classifier training is seen as finding a good approximation to the desired decision boundary, but integration of such models with the probabilistic view is not complete.

The probabilistic view comes in because of the need to study a problem by random sampling due to the unavailability of complete data coverage. Then there is the issue of sampling density and training sample representativeness, which is intimately related to the classifier's generalization ability, and in turn to its accuracy. If the training sample densely covers all the relevant regions in the feature space, many classifiers, as long as they are trainable and expandable in capacity, will work perfectly, and then the competition among methods is more on representation and execution efficiency. Say, a decision tree may be preferable to nearest neighbors for efficiency reasons. So the difficulty of classification is mostly with sparse samples – and for this reason, all theories depending on assumptions of infinite samples are useless. Those relying on a vague definition of representativeness of the training samples is not much better, as quite typically such representativeness is not even parameterized by the sampling size *relative to the size of the underlying problem*.

There are vast differences due to sampling density. Consider a space where each point is randomly labeled as one of two classes. Whereas a dense sample may reveal the randomness to some extent, a two-point sample may suggest that the problem is linearly separable. With other less radical problems, sampling density affects the exact ways that isolated subclasses become connected and boundaries are constrained, much more than what can be captured in a collective description by a single count of points. Such problems can occur regardless of the dimensionality of the feature space, though they are more apparent in high-dimensional spaces where the decision boundary can vary with a larger degree of freedom. Observations of empirical evidences [7] [22] [23] suggested strongly that shortage of samples would ruin most promises from the classical approaches. This fact was addressed in many studies on error rate estimation as well [11] [16] [25].

Vapnik's capacity theory [27] [28] is among the first that directly faces the reality of small sample effects. It provides a link between the interacting effects of classifier geometry and training sample size. But the VC dimension theory is not constructive. It gives only a loose, worst case bound on the error rate given the geometrical characteristics of the classifier and the sample size. The difficulty in tightening the bounds is because of the distribution-free arguments [1] [2]. Nevertheless, as we have seen in the theory of stochastic discrimination, with a different characterization of training set representativeness, it is possible to show tighter error bounds without involving the VC dimension argument. Also, by using specific geometrical models matched to the problem, it is possible to overcome the infamous *curse of dimensionality* [4].

The theory is difficult because these factors interact with each other. With regard to the problem geometry, the classifier geometry, and the sampling and training processes, what exactly do we mean by saying that two or more classifiers are independent? How about other related concepts such as correlation, diversity, collinearity, coincidence, and equalization? What do they mean in each context where the decisions are represented as one out of many classes, as permutations of class preferences, or as continuous belief scores that are not necessarily probability estimates? Kleinberg's notion of uniformity offers a rigorous definition under the set-theoretic abstraction. How can this be generalized to other models of classifier decisions? The bias/variance decomposition [8] gives another way to relate geometry and probabilities, and has been used in analyzing decision boundaries of combined systems [26]. Though, many analyses are problematic due to inadequate assumptions on decision independence.

How can one relate local, point-wise measures of classification error and their correlation to collective measures over the entire training set? Say, if we observe two classifiers agreeing 99% of the time and differing for the rest, how much can we infer about the overall similarity of their decisions? And how likely is the agreement observed in a different problem? If all the agreed cases are correct decisions, simply because those cases are easy for both classifiers, can we tell anything about whether the classifiers decide by the same mechanism? Detailed studies on the patterns of correlation among the classifiers are necessary to answer these questions [10] [19].

As one compares different approaches of combination, and considers combination of combinations, there are a few more intriguing questions to ask:

- If one defers the final decision and uses the output of individual classifiers just as some scores describing the input, are those scores different in nature from the feature measurements on the input? Are there intrinsic differences between the mappings from the input to the representations given by a classifier or by a feature extractor?
- Is combination a necessity or a convenience? Is there some complementariness intrinsic to certain classifier training processes? Or is it just an easy way to derive a desired decision boundary?
- Are there any commonalities among all the combination approaches? If many of them are found to be similarly effective, are they essentially doing the same thing despite superficial differences?
- Does the hierarchy of combinations converge to a limit upon which one would have exhausted the knowledge contained in the training set, such that no further improvement in accuracy is possible?

3   Precise Characterization of Data Dependences of Performance

Many of the above questions are there because we do not yet have a detailed, scientific understanding of the classifier combination mechanisms. Theoretical explanations are often incomplete, or they have to stop at a level where the combinatorics defy detailed modeling. Many studies attempt to analyze classifier behavior for all possible problems and data distributions, which result inevitably in very weak performance bounds. On the other hand, empirical evidences are often very specific to particular applications, and are seldom systematically documented. Attempted comparative studies often stop on arriving at some collective accuracy measures. But trying a method on 100 published problems and counting how many it wins on does not mean much, because these problem may all be very similar in certain aspects and may not be typical in reality. On the other hand, we will never have a fair sample of realistic problems because of the ill-definition of the set. So what can we do?

If we have a way to characterize the problems in good relevance to classifier accuracy, we may hope to find certain rules relating those characteristics to the behavior of classifier or systems generated and combined in a specific way. Empirical observations of such relationships may point to opportunities for detailed analysis of underlying reasons.

Here I am advocating a realist's approach where selection of a classifier or a combination method is guided by characteristics of the data. And the data characteristics must include effects of the problem geometry and sampling density. Statements like "method X is of no help when the training sample is large ..." are overly simplifying. How large is large? An absolute number on the sample size means little without knowledge of the length of class boundary.

We need much more systematic ways to characterize the problems. We need a language to describe the problems in aspects more relevant to the actions of classifiers: i.e. not merely collective descriptors such as number of classes, number of samples, number of dimensions, etc. We need a better understanding of the geometry and topology of point sets in high dimensional spaces, preservation of such characteristics under feature transformations and sampling processes, and their interaction with the primitive geometrical models used in known classifiers. We need to measure or estimate the length and curvature of the class boundaries, fragmentation of the decision regions in terms of existence, size, and connectedness of subclasses, and the stability of these characteristics with respect to changes in sampling density. Some recent attempts are interesting starting points [3] [12] [13] [14] [24].

Characterization of Data Complexity

In reality, most practical classification problems arise from nonchaotic processes many of which can be described by an underlying physical model. Though the models may contain a stochastic component, there should still exist a significant structure in the resulting class distributions that differs from a random labeling of points. An analysis of such differences will provide us with a framework in which one can study the behavior of specific classifiers and combination methods.

Structured data differ from random labeling in that with random labeling there is no geometrical continuity or regularity based on which inferences can be made about labels of unseen points from the same source. On the other hand, automatic classification methodologies are based on the assumption that such learning is possible, to various degrees of difficulty.

Obviously one practical measure of problem difficulty is the error rate of a chosen classifier. However, since our eventual goal is to study behavior of classifiers, other measures should also be explored that are independent of such choices. Moreover, a problem can be difficult for different reasons. Certain problems are known to have nonzero Bayes error. There the classes are ambiguous either intrinsically or due to inadequate feature measurements. Others may have a complex class boundary and/or subclass structures. Sometimes high dimensionality of the feature space and sparseness of available samples are to be blamed.

Among the different reasons, the geometrical complexity of the class boundaries is probably most ready for detailed investigation. One can choose the class boundary to be the simplest (of minimum measure in the feature space) decision boundary that minimizes Bayes error. With a complete sample, the class boundary can be characterized by its Kolmogorov complexity. A problem is complex if it takes a long algorithm (possibly including an enumeration of all the points and their labels) to describe the class boundary. This aspect of difficulty is due to the nature of the problem and is unrelated to the sampling process. Kolmogorov complexity describes the absolute amount of information in a dataset, and is not algorithmically computable. By geometrical complexity one focuses on descriptions of regularities and irregularities contained in the dataset in terms of geometrical primitives. This would be sufficient for pattern recognition where classifiers can also be characterized by similar geometrical terms.

An incomplete or sparse sample adds another layer of difficulty to a discrimination problem, since an unseen point in the vicinity of some training points may share their class labels according to different generalization rules. In real world situations, often a problem becomes difficult because of a mixture of these two effects. Sampling density is more critical for an intrinsically complex problem than an intrinsically simple problem (e.g. a linearly separable problem with wide margins). If the sample is too sparse, an intrinsically complex problem may appear deceptively simple. Thus, in lack of a complete sample, such measures of the problem complexity have to be qualified by the representativeness of the training set.

Several measures of geometrical complexity were studied in [12], where it is shown that many real-world problems occupy a continuum between two extremes given by random labelings (the most difficult problems) and linearly separable problems (the easiest). Measures known to be useful fall into several groups, characterizing the linearity of decision boundaries, inter- and intra- class point proximity, overlap of class-specific convex hulls and their projections into subspaces, and existence and connectivity of subclasses. In addition, interesting characteristics of the datasets were observed from the behavior of two primitive classifiers, i.e, nearest neighbor and linear discriminant (obtained by linear programming minimizing sum of distances of error points to the separating hyperplane). Their error rates and measures of the intersection of their error points with the class-specific convex hulls give some hints to the problem geometry. Table 3 summarizes the definitions of these measures and the effects described by each. Details can be found in [12] and [13].

Some of these measures are correlated and can be indications of more fundamental geometrical or topological characteristics. Furthermore, sensitivity of

Table 3. Measures of geometrical complexity

Relevant effects	Measures
clustering and sphericity	% points with associated adherence subsets retained
inter versus intra class proximity	% points on boundary expressed as between-class edges in a minimum spanning tree
	error rate of nearest neighbor classifier
overlap of classes	maximum Fisher's discriminant ratio
	maximum (individual) feature efficiency
	ratio of average intra/inter class nearest neighbor distance
	volume of overlap region
linear separability	LP minimized sum of error distances
	error rate of linear classifier by LP
curvature of boundary	nonlinearity of linear classifier by LP
	nonlinearity of nearest neighbor classifier

these measures with respect to the sampling density is also important. This can potentially be estimated by repeating the measurements on subsamples of the given data set.

Coupling between Data Characteristics and Classifier Models

Once we find ways to characterize the problems, we can then ask the question: what type of problems does a particular classifier or combination method work for?

To investigate the optimality of match between a classifier or combination method and a given problem, one needs a detailed characterization of the geometrical structure of the decision regions given by the classifier, and the modifications introduced by the combination method. For example, decision trees splitting on single features divide the feature space into a set of hyper-rectangular cells within each classification remains invariant. Voting of two such trees further segments those cells into the cross-product of the two sets. How many of the boundary faces of neighboring cells are close to the class boundary depends on the geometry of the problem – whether the problem has axis-parallel, flat, or curved boundary surfaces, and disconnected subclasses, and to what extent.

An example is given in [13] where the performances of two decision forest constructors, namely, bagging and random subspaces, were studied along with several measures of problem geometry. Strong correlation was observed between the classifier accuracies and a measure of length of class boundaries as well as a measure of the thickness of class manifolds. Follow-up studies showed that both types of forests are capable of improving over a single tree for problems of various levels of complexity, i.e., improvements are observed in problems with very low, very high, and all intermediate single tree error rates. Neither works well when several conditions occur jointly: a very high fraction of boundary points (70% or above), a close to 1 ratio of intra/inter class nearest neighbor distances, a very low maximum Fisher's discriminant ratio (0.05 or below), and high nonlinearity of both nearest neighbor and linear classifiers (25% or above). For these cases a single tree performs poorly, nor will forest methods offer much help. Easier cases are those with relatively compact classes, i.e., when the pretopological measure is lower than 80%. For such cases improvements by forests over single trees are less significant. The geometrical measures also reveal comparative advantages of each type of forests. The subsampling method is preferable when the training set is very sparse relative to dimensionality, especially when coupled with a close-to-vanishing maximum Fisher's ratio (0.3 or below), and when the class boundary is highly nonlinear. Subspace forests perform better when the class boundary is smoother (both nearest neighbor and linear classifiers display low nonlinearity). If the training set is large relative to dimensionality, the subspace method is more preferable, even if the class distributions are long and thin. Rules similar to these may be observed in further studies.

Given a problem in a fixed feature space, is there a limit on how well an automatically trainable classifier can do? Recall that all such methods are based on certain particular geometrical primitives, such as convex regions, axis parallel cuts, rectangular boxes, Gaussian kernels, piecewise linear boundaries, etc. It needs to be established that such models will fit into arbitrary shaped decision regions with arbitrary degree of connectedness. At which point should we say that it is meaningless to continue training, and that any more improvement in accuracy will be from luck rather than effort? VC dimension theories give us a certain limit, but for certain classes of problems, by exploiting the structural regularities and matching them to appropriate classifiers, we should be able to do better than that. Knowledge on the structural regularity may not be sufficient to remove entirely the probabilistic nature of the estimates inherent in unseen data, but should help in reducing the level of uncertainty.

4   Conclusions

I reviewed some challenges in the theories and practices of combining parallel classifiers. Many open questions point to a lack of insight into the intriguing interactions of the geometric and probabilistic characteristics of a problem and the classifier models. A thorough understanding of such interactions holds the key to further improvements of the methods. An essential need in this direction is to find a better set of descriptors for the geometrical structure of a problem in the feature space and to describe the behavior of classifiers in corresponding terms. These descriptors can be used to categorize the real world problems and their subproblems or transformations, which would permit studies and prediction of the behavior of various classifiers and combination methods on a whole class of cases.

In addition, several methodological directions are also worth pursuing:

- Ingenious designs of feature extractors and similarity measures that can simplify the class boundary will continue to play an important role in real applications. Systematic searches with the same goal are even more interesting.

- Unsupervised learning will play an increasing role in the context of supervised learning. Clustering methods will be applied more extensively and systematically to better understand the geometry of the class boundaries and its sensitivity to sampling density. Others such as estimation of intrinsic and extrinsic dimensionalities of the classes or subclasses will also be helpful.
- More emphasis should be put on localized (or dynamically selected) classification methods. A blind application of everything to everything will prove to be inferior to localized methods. Systematic strategies should be developed to fine tune the classifiers to the characteristics of local regions and to associate them with corresponding input.
- Better understanding is needed to choose between deterministic and stochastic classifier generating methods. This will need a careful study of the exact role of randomization in various classifier or combination tuning processes and the corresponding geometrical effects.
- New methods can come from merging the decision optimization and coverage optimization strategies, such that collections of specialized classifiers can be enhanced by introducing additional components with enforced complementariness, and coverage optimization methods may use more sophisticated decision combination schemes.

By now, classifier combination has become a rich and exciting area with much proven success. It is my hope that these discussions can call for attention to some of the confusions and missing links in the methodology, and point out the more fruitful directions for further research. Some recent developments are already moving towards these directions. This is very encouraging.

References

1. L. Devroye, Any discrimination rule can have an arbitrarily bad probability of error for finite sample size, *IEEE Transactions on Pattern Analysis and Machine Intelligence*, **4**, 2, March 1982, 154-157.
2. L. Devroye, Automatic pattern recognition: a study of the probability of error, *IEEE Transactions on Pattern Analysis and Machine Intelligence*, **10**, 4, July 1988, 530-599.
3. R.P.W. Duin, Compactness and Complexity of Pattern Recognition Problems, in C. Perneel, eds., *Proc. Int. Symposium on Pattern Recognition, In Memoriam Pierre Devijver*, Royal Military Academy, Brussels, Feb 12, 1999, 124-128.
4. R.P.W. Duin, Classifiers in almost empty spaces, *Proceedings of the 15th International Conference on Pattern Recognition*, Barcelona, September 3-8, 2000, **II**, 1-7.
5. J.L. Engvall, A least upper bound for the average classification accuracy of multiple observers, *Pattern Recognition*, **12**, 415-419.
6. P.C. Fishburn, *The Theory of Social Choice*, Princeton University Press, Princeton, 1972.
7. K. Fukunaga, D.L. Kessell, Estimation of classification error, *IEEE Transactions on Computers*, **20**, 12, December 1971, 1521-1527.
8. S. Geman, E. Bienenstock, R. Doursat, Neural networks and the bias/variance dilemma, *Neural Computation*, **4**, 1992, 1-58.

9. D. Gernert, Distance or similarity measures which respect the internal structure of objects, *Methods of Operations Research*, **43**, 1981, 329-335.

10. G. Giacinto, F. Roli, A theoretical framework for dynamic classifier selection, *Proceedings of the 15th International Conference on Pattern Recognition*, Barcelona, September 3-8, 2000, **II**, 8-11.

11. D.J. Hand, Recent advances in error rate estimation, *Pattern Recognition Letters*, **4**, October 1986, 335-346.

12. T.K. Ho, M. Basu, Measuring the Complexity of Classification Problems, *Proceedings of the 15th International Conference on Pattern Recognition*, Barcelona, September 3-8, 2000, **II**, 43-47.

13. T.K. Ho, Complexity of classification problems and comparative advantages of combined classifiers, in J. Kittler, F. Roli, eds., *Multiple Classifier Systems*, Lecture Notes in Computer Science 1857, Springer, 2000, 97-106.

14. A. Hoekstra, R.P.W. Duin, On the nonlinearity of pattern classifiers, *Proc. of the 13th ICPR*, Vienna, August 1996, **D**271-275.

15. A.K. Jain, R.P.W. Duin, J. Mao, Statistical pattern recognition: A review, *IEEE Transactions on Pattern Analysis and Machine Intelligence*, **PAMI-22**, 1, January 2000, 4-37.

16. J. Kittler, P.A. Devijver, Statistical properties of error estimators in performance assessment of recognition systems, *IEEE Transactions on Pattern Analysis and Machine Intelligence*, **4**, 2, March 1982, 215-220.

17. J. Kittler, M. Hatef, R.P.W. Duin, J. Matas, On combining classifiers, *IEEE Transactions on Pattern Analysis and Machine Intelligence*, **PAMI-20**, 3, March 1998, 226-239.

18. E.M. Kleinberg, An overtraining-resistant stochastic modeling method for pattern recognition, *Annals of Statistics*, **4**, 6, December 1996, 2319-2349.

19. L.I. Kuncheva, C.J. Whitaker, C.A. Shipp, R.P.W. Duin, Is independence good for combining classifiers? *Proceedings of the 15th International Conference on Pattern Recognition*, Barcelona, September 3-8, 2000, **II**, 168-171.

20. M. LeBlanc, R. Tibshirani, Combining estimates in regression and classification, *Journal of the American Statistical Association*, **91**, 436, December 1996, 1641-1650.

21. V.D. Mazurov, A.I. Krivonogov, V.L. Kazantsev, Solving of Optimization and Identification Problems by the Committee Methods, *Pattern Recognition*, **20**, 4, 1987, 371-378.

22. S. Raudys, V. Pikelis, On dimensionality, sample size, classification error, and complexity of classification algorithm in pattern recognition, *IEEE Transactions on Pattern Analysis and Machine Intelligence*, **2**, 3, May 1980, 242-252.

23. S. Raudys, A.K. Jain, Small sample size effects in statistical pattern recognition: Recommendations for practitioners, *IEEE Transactions on Pattern Analysis and Machine Intelligence*, **13**, 3, 1991, 252-264.

24. S.Y. Sohn, Meta analysis of classification algorithms for pattern recognition, *IEEE Transactions on Pattern Analysis and Machine Intelligence*, **21**, 11, 1999, 1137-1144.

25. G.T. Toussaint, Bibliography on estimation of misclassification, *IEEE Transactions on Information Theory*, **20**, 4, July 1974, 472-479.

26. K. Tumer, J. Ghosh, Analysis of decision boundaries in linearly combined neural classifiers, *Pattern Recognition*, **29**, 1996, 341-348.

27. V. Vapnik, *Estimation of Dependences Based on Empirical Data*, Springer-Verlag, 1982.

28. V. Vapnik, *Statistical Learning Theory*, John Wiley & Sons, 1998.

Genetic Programming for Improved Receiver Operating Characteristics

W.B. Langdon and B.F. Buxton

Computer Science, University College, Gower Street, London, WC1E 6BT, UK
{W.Langdon,B.Buxton}@cs.ucl.ac.uk
http://www.cs.ucl.ac.uk/staff/W.Langdon, /staff/B.Buxton
Tel: +44 (0) 20 7679 4436, Fax: +44 (0) 20 7387 1397

Abstract. Genetic programming (GP) can automatically fuse given classifiers of diverse types to produce a combined classifier whose Receiver Operating Characteristics (ROC) are better than [Scott *et al.*1998b]'s "Maximum Realisable Receiver Operating Characteristics" (MRROC). I.e. better than their convex hull. This is demonstrated on a satellite image processing bench mark using Naive Bayes, Decision Trees (C4.5) and Clementine artificial neural networks.

1 Introduction

[Scott *et al.*1998b] has previously suggested the "Maximum Realisable Receiver Operating Characteristics" for a combination of classifiers is the convex hull of their individual ROCs. However the convex hull is not always the best that can be achieved [Yusoff *et al.*1998]. Previously we showed [Langdon and Buxton2001a, Langdon and Buxton2001b] in at least some cases better ROCs can be automatically produced. We extend [Langdon and Buxton2001b] to show, on the problems derived from those proposed by [Scott *et al.*1998b], that genetic programming can automatically fuse different classifiers trained on different data to yield a classifier whose ROC are better than the convex hull of the supplied classifier's ROCs.

Section 2 gives the back ground to data fusion and Sect. 3 summarises Scott's work. The three classifiers are described in Sect. 4, while Sect. 5 describes the satellite data. The genetic programming system and its results are given in Sects. 6 and 7. Finally we finish in Sects. 8 and 9 with a discussion and conclusions. Sections 2–6 (excluding Sects. 4.1 and 4.3) are similar to [Langdon and Buxton2001b] however the experimental work (Sect. 7 onwards) extends [Langdon and Buxton2001b] to consider fusing classifiers of very different types.

2 Background

There is considerable interest in automatic means of making large volumes of data intelligible to people. Arguably traditional sciences such as Astronomy, Biology and Chemistry and branches of Industry and Commerce can now generate

J. Kittler and F. Roli (Eds.): MCS 2001, LNCS 2096, pp. 68–77, 2001.
© Springer-Verlag Berlin Heidelberg 2001

data so cheaply that it far outstrips human resources to make sense of it. Increasingly scientists and Industry are turning to their computers not only to generate data but to try and make sense of it. Indeed the new science of Bioinformatics has arisen from the need for computer scientists and biologists to work together on tough, data rich problems, such as rendering protein sequence data useful. Of particular interest are the Pharmaceutical (drug discovery) and food preparation industries.

The terms Data Mining and Knowledge Discovery are commonly used for the problem of getting information out of data. There are two common aims: 1) to produce a summary of all or an interesting part of the available data 2) to find interesting subsets of the data buried within it. Of course these may overlap. In addition to traditional techniques, a large range of "intelligent" or "soft computing" techniques, such as artificial neural networks, decision tables, fuzzy logic, radial basis functions, inductive logic programming, support vector machines, are being increasingly used. Many of these techniques have been used in connection with evolutionary computation techniques such as genetic algorithms and genetic programming [Langdon1998].

We investigate ways of combining these and other classifiers with a view to producing one classifier which is better than each. Firstly we need to decide how we will measure the performance of a classifier. In practise when using any classifier a balance has to be chosen between missing positive examples and generating too many spurious alarms. Such a balancing act is not easy. Especially in the medical field where failing to detect a disease, such as cancer, has obvious consequences but raising false alarms (false positives) also has implications for patient well being. Receiver Operating Characteristics (ROC) curves allow us to show graphically the trade off each classifier makes between its "false positive rate" (false alarms) and its "true positive rate" [Swets et al.2000]. (The true positive rate is the fraction of all positive cases correctly classified. While the false positive rate is the fraction of negative cases incorrectly classified as positive). ROC curves are shown in Figs. 3 and 4. We treat each classifier as though it has a sensitivity parameter (e.g a threshold) which allows the classifier to be tuned. At the lowest sensitivity level the classifier produces no false alarms but detects no positive cases, i.e. the origin of the ROC. As the sensitivity is increased, the classifier detects more positive examples but may also start generating false alarms (false positives). Eventually the sensitivity may become so high that the classifier always claims each case is positive. This corresponds to both true positive and false positive rates being unity, i.e. the top right hand corner of the ROC. On average a classifier which simply makes random guesses will have an operating point somewhere on the line between the origin and 1,1 (cf. Fig. 1).

Naturally we want our classifiers to have ROC curves that come as close to a true positive rate of one and simultaneously a false positive rate of zero. In Sect. 6 we score each classifier by the area under its ROC curve. An ideal classifier has an area of one. We also require the given classifiers, not only to indicate which class they think a data point belongs to, but also how confident they are of this. Values near zero indicate the classifier is not sure, possibly because the data point lies near the classifier's decision boundary.

Arguably the well known "boosting" techniques combine classifiers to get a better one. However boosting is normally applied to only one classifier and produces improvements by iteratively retraining it. Here we will assume the classifiers we have are fixed, i.e. we do not wish to retrain them. Similarly boosting is normally applied by assuming the classifier is operated at a single sensitivity (e.g a single threshold value). This means on each retraining it produces a single pair of false positive and true positive rates. Which is a single point on the ROC rather than the curve we require.

3   "Maximum Realisable" ROC

Scott's Parcel system [Scott *et al.*1998b] followed on from work on using wrappers for feature subset selection [Kohavi and John1997] and the use of ROC hulls [Provost and Fawcett2001]. However [Scott *et al.*1998b] describe a method to create, from two existing classifiers, a new one whose ROC lie on a line connecting the ROC of its two components. This is done by choosing one or other of the component classifiers at random and using its result. E.g. if we need a classifier whose false positive rate vs. its true positive rate lies half way between the ROC points of classifiers A and B, then the Scott's composite classifier will randomly give the answer given by A half the time and that given by B the other half, see Fig. 1. (Of course persuading patients to accept such a random diagnose may not be straightforward).

The performance of the composite can be readily set to any point along the line simply by varying the ratio between the number of times one classifier is used relative to the other. Indeed this can be readily extended to any number of classifiers to fill the space between them. The better classifiers are those closer to the zero false positive axis or with a higher true positive rate. In other words the classifiers lying on the convex hull.

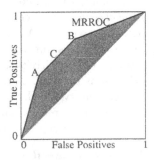

Fig. 1. Classifier C is created by choosing equally between the output of classifier A and classifier B. Any point in the shaded area can be created. The "Maximum Realisable ROC" is its convex hull (solid line).

Often classifiers have some variable threshold or tuning parameter whereby their trade off between false positives and true positives can be adjusted. This means their Receiver Operating Characteristics (ROC) are now a curve rather than a single point. We can apply Scott's random combination method to any set of points along the curve. So a "maximum realisable" ROC is the convex hull of the (single) classifier's ROC. Indeed, if the ROC curve is not convex, an improved classifier can easily be created from it [Scott et al.1998b]. The nice thing about the MRROC, is that it is always possible. But as we show it may be possible to do better.

4   Classifiers

4.1   C4.5

C4.5 [Quinlan1993], like the other classifiers, was extended to allow its use within our GP system. Each classifier takes a threshold parameter. To produce an ROC curve the threshold is varied from zero to one.

To use a classifier in GP we adopt the convention that non-negative values indicate the data is in the class. We also require the classifier to indicate its "confidence" in its answer. In our GP, it does this by the magnitude of the value it returns.

C4.5 was run with defaults setting to produce pruned trees containing "confidence" values Z0 and Z1. Normally the decision tree's final classification would depend on which of Z0 and Z1 was the bigger. When the threshold is 0.5, this is what GP returns. However if it is near 0, GP is more likely to return class 0. While if the threshold is near 1, GP is biased towards class 1. (In detail GP returns class 0 iff $(1 - \text{threshold})Z0 \geq \text{threshold } Z1$). This determines the sign of the value returned to the GP system. The magnitude is the C4.5 "confidence". This is $|Z0 - Z1|$.

4.2   Naive Bayes Classifiers

The Bayes [Ripley1996,Mitchell1997] approach attempts to estimate, from the training data, the probability of data being in each class. Its prediction is the class with the highest estimated probability. We extend it 1) to include a tuning parameter to bias its choice of class and 2) to make it return a confidence based upon the difference between the two probabilities.

If there is no training data for a given class/attribute value combination, we follow [Kohavi and Sommerfield1996, page 11] and estimate the probability based on assuming there was actually a count of 0.5. ([Mitchell1997] suggests a slightly different way of calculating the estimates).

A threshold T $(0 \leq T \leq 1)$, allows us to introduce a bias. That is if $(1 - T) \times P_{0,a}(E) < T \times P_{1,a}(E)$ then our Bayes classifier will predicts E is in class 1, otherwise 0. ($P_{c,a}(E)$ is the probability estimated from the training data, using attributes from the set a, that E is in class c). Finally we define the classifiers "confidence" to be $|P_{0,a}(E) - P_{1,a}(E)|$.

4.3   Artificial Neural Networks

We used the Clementine data mining tool to train an artificial neural network to model the training data. This model was then frozen and made available to genetic programming as a function with one argument.

The ANN model was trained using Clementine version 5.0 on 2956 training records. Each record had nine integer inputs (from the last of the four spectral bands, see next section) and an integer range output. The output was 0 or 1 depending on whether the pixel was "grey" or not (see next section). The defaults were used, i.e. quick training, prevention of over training (50%), sensitivity analysis and default stopping criterion for training. The model has one hidden layer of four nodes, whose performance Clementine estimates to be 72.32%. (Performance of ANN models for the first band to third bands were estimated at 83.78%, 71.36% and 65.90%).

The neural net model gives a continuous valued output. Values below 0.5 indicate class 0. For use in GP, we subtract 1.0 and add the threshold parameter. This means values below zero indicate class 0, while non-negative values indicate class 1. As usual the continuous threshold parameter allows us to tune the neural network to trade off false positive against true positives and so obtain a complete ROC curve rather than a single error rate. (A threshold of 0.5 indicates no bias, i.e. use the raw neural network). Notice that the "confidence" the GP sees is directly related to how far from the neural networks idle value (0.5) its output is.

5   Grey Landsat

The Landsat data comes from the Stalog project via the UCI machine learning repository[1]. The data is spilt into training (`sat.trn` 4425 records) and test (`sat.tst` 2000). Each record has 36 continuous attributes (8 bit integer values nominally in the range 0–255) and 6 way classification. (Classes 1, 2, 3, 4, 5 and 7). Following Scott [Scott *et al.*1998b], classes 3, 4 and 7 were combined into one (positive, grey) while 1, 2 and 5 became the negative examples (not-grey). `sat.tst` was kept for the holdout set.

The 36 data values represent intensity values for nine neighbouring pixels and four spectral bands (see Fig. 2). While the classification refers to just the central pixel. Since each pixel has eight neighbours and each may be in the dataset, data values appear multiple times in the data set. But when they do, they are presented as being different attributes each time. The data all come from a rectangular area approximately five miles wide. Each of the three types of classifiers is trained on data from one spectral band. (Naive Bayes - first band, C4.5 - second band, artificial neural network - last band).

After reducing to two classes, the continuous values in `sat.trn` were partitioned into bins before it was used by the Naive Bayes classifier. Following [Scott *et al.*1998a, page 8], we used entropy based discretisation

---

[1] `ftp://ftp.ics.uci.edu/pub/machine-learning-databases/statlog/satimage`

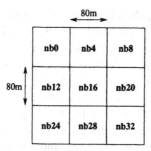

Fig. 2. Each record contains data from nine adjacent Landsat pixels. In these experiments, all of the Naive Bayes classifiers are trained on the first spectral band. There are two types of Naive Bayes classifiers, single attribute and those trained on pairs of attributes. All nine single attribute and all pairs of attributes 0, 4, 12, 16, 20 and 32 are available to GP. C4.5 was trained on nine attributes 1, 5, ... 33 (second band) while the ANN was trained on the fourth band (attributes 3, 7, ... 35).

[Kohavi and Sommerfield1996], implemented in MLC++ `discretize.exe`[2], with default parameters. (Giving between 4 and 7 bins per attribute). To avoid introducing bias, the holdout data (`sat.tst`) was partitioned using the same bin boundaries. `sat.trn` was randomly split into training (2956 records) and verification (1479) sets.

6   Genetic Programming Configuration

The genetic programming system is almost identical to that described in [Langdon and Buxton2001b]. The GP is set up to signal its prediction of the class of each data value in the same way as the classifiers. I.e. by returning a floating point value, whose sign indicates the class and whose magnitude indicates the "confidence". (Note confidence is not constrained to a particular range).

Following earlier work [Jacobs *et al.* 1991,Soule1999,Langdon1998] each GP individual is composed of five trees. Each of which is capable of acting as a classifier. The use of signed numbers makes it natural to combine classifiers by adding them. I.e. the classification of the "ensemble" is the sum of the answers given by the five trees. Should a single classifier be very confident about its answer this allows it to "out vote" all the others.

6.1   Function and Terminal Sets

The function set includes the four binary floating arithmetic operators (+, ×, − and protected division), maximum and minimum and absolute maximum and minimum. The latter two return the (signed) value of the largest, (or smallest) in absolute terms, of their inputs. IFLTE takes four arguments. If the first is

---

[2] http://www.sgi.com/Technology/mlc

less than or equal to the second, IFLTE returns the value of its third argument. Otherwise it returns the value of its fourth argument. INT returns the integer part of its argument, while FRAC(e) returns e - INT(e).

The classifiers are represented as floating point functions. Their threshold is supplied as their single argument. As described in Sect. 4.

The terminal T yields the current value of the threshold being applied to the classifier being evolved by GP. Finally the GP population was initially constructed from a number of floating point values. These constants do not change as the population evolves. However crossover and mutation do change which constants are used and in which parts of the program.

6.2   Fitness Function

Each new individual is tested on each training example with the threshold parameter (T) taking values from 0 to 1 every 0.1 (i.e. 11 values). So it is run 32516 times. For each threshold value the true positive rate is calculated. (The number of correct positive cases divided by the total number of positive cases). If a floating point exception occurs its answer is assumed to be wrong. Similarly its false positive rate is given by the no. of negative cases it gets wrong divided by the total no. of negative cases. It is possible to do worst than random guessing. When this happens, i.e. the true positive rate is less than the false positive rate, the sign of the output is reversed. This is common practise in classifiers.

Since a classifier can always achieve both a zero success rate and 100% false positive rate, the points (0,0) and (1,1) are always included. These plus the eleven true positive and false positive rates are plotted and the area under the convex hull is calculated. The area is the fitness of the individual GP program. Note the GP individual is not only rewarded for getting answers right but also for using the threshold parameter to get a range of high scores. Parameters are summarised in Table 1.

7   Results

The three types of classifier (C4.5, Naive Bayes and ANN) were made available to GP, singly, in pairs and finally all three together. I.e. seven experiments were run. (The 21 Naive Bayes classifiers are treated as a group, i.e. they are either all included or all excluded). In each run, GP's answer was chosen as the first occurrence of a program with the the largest ROC area (on the training data) found in the whole run. The ROC of these seven programs (on the holdout data) are plotted in Fig. 4 and tabulated in Table 2. In all seven cases GP automatically produced a classifier with better performance than those it was given. That is genetic programming fused classifiers of different types, trained on different data, to yield superior classifiers.

8   Over Fitting

We have taken some care to ensure our input classifiers do not over fit the training data. Similarly one needs to be careful when using GP to avoid over fitting. So far we have seen little evidence of over fitting. This may be related to the problems themselves or the choice of multiple tree programs or the absence of "bloat". The absence of bloat may be due to our choice of size fair crossover [Langdon2000] and a high mutation rate. Our intention is to evaluate this GP approach on more sophisticated classifiers and on harder problems. Here we expect it will be essential to ensure the classifiers GP uses do not over fit, however this may not be enough to ensure the GP does not.

Table 1.   Grey Landsat GP Parameters

Objective:	Evolve a function with Maximum Convex Hull Area
Function set:	INT FRAC Max Min MaxA MinA MUL ADD DIV SUB IFLTE C4.5 ANN (nb0 nb4 nb8 nb12 nb16 nb20 nb24 nb28 nb32 nb0,4 nb0,12 nb0,16 nb0,20 nb0,32 nb4,12 nb4,16 nb4,20 nb4,32 nb12,16 nb12,20 nb12,32 nb16,20 nb16,32 nb20,32)
Terminal set:	T 0 0.1 0.2 0.3 0.4 0.5 0.6 0.7 0.8 0.9 1
Fitness:	Area under convex hull of 11 ROC points on 2956 test points
Selection:	generational (non elitist), tournament size 7
Wrapper:	$\geq 0 \Rightarrow$ positive, negative otherwise
Pop Size:	500
No size or depth limits	
Initial pop:	ramped half-and-half (2:6) (half terminals are constants)
Parameters:	50% size fair crossover [Langdon2000], 50% mutation (point 22.5%, constants 22.5%, shrink 2.5% subtree 2.5%)
Termination:	generation 50

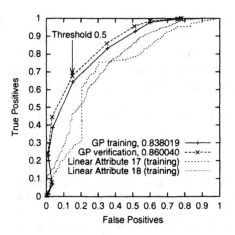

Fig. 3.   The ROC produced by GP (generation 50) using threshold values $0, 0.1, \ldots, 1.0$ on the Thyroid data. Details of the experiment are reported in [Langdon and Buxton2001b].

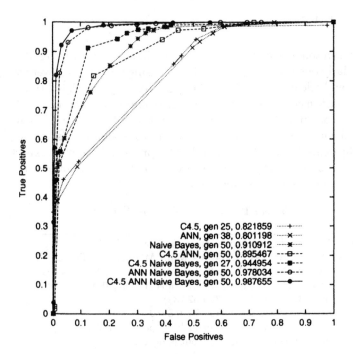

Fig. 4. The ROC produced by GP using seven combinations of classifiers on the Grey Landsat holdout data. The caption gives the area under the ROC (holdout) and the first generation to give the maximum area on the training data. (For simplicity only the convex hull of each classifier is plotted).

9   Conclusions

Previously [Langdon and Buxton2001a] we showed, using Scott's own bench marks, that genetic programming can do better than [Scott *et al.*1998b]'s MR-ROC [Langdon and Buxton2001b]. Here we have shown, GP can deal not only with different classifiers but with classifiers of different types, trained on different data. Genetic programming offers an automatic means of data fusion by evolving combined classifiers.

References

[Jacobs *et al.* 1991] Robert A. Jacobs, Michael I. Jordon, Steven J. Nowlan, and Geoffrey E. Hinton. Adaptive mixtures of local experts. *Neural Computation*, 3:79–87.

[Kohavi and John1997] Ron Kohavi and George H. John. Wrappers for feature subset selection. *Artificial Intelligence*, 97(1–2):273–323, 1997.

[Kohavi and Sommerfield1996] MLC++: Machine learning library in C++. Technical report, SGI. http://www.sgi.com/Technology/mlc/util/util.ps.

[Langdon and Buxton2001a] W. B. Langdon and B. F. Buxton. Evolving receiver operating characteristics for data fusion. In Julian F. Miller, *et. al.* editors, *Genetic Programming, Proceedings of EuroGP'2001, LNCS* 2038, pages 87–96. Springer-Verlag.

Table 2. Grey Landsat, Area under ROC on holdout set

		Given Classifiers			Genetic Programming	
			nb0,12	0.877244		
			nb0,16	0.880381		
			nb0,20	0.895346		
		nb0 0.873961	nb0,32	0.893585		
		nb4 0.883431	nb0,4	0.883431	ANN	0.801198
		nb8 0.886417	nb4,12	0.890616	C4.5	0.821859
ANN 0.764945		nb12 0.877244	nb4,16	0.888611	nb	0.910912
C4.5 0.74271		nb16 0.880381	nb4,20	0.89729	ANN + C4.5	0.895467
		nb20 0.895346	nb4,32	0.901857	ANN + nb	0.978034
		nb24 0.888831	nb12,16	0.888113	C4.5 + nb	0.944954
		nb28 0.8898	nb12,20	0.896233	all	0.987655
		nb32 0.893585	nb12,32	0.891777		
			nb16,20	0.901793		
			nb16,32	0.892662		
			nb20,32	0.900468		

[Langdon and Buxton2001b] W. B. Langdon and B. F. Buxton. Genetic programming for combining classifiers. In *GECCO'2001*. Morgan Kaufmann.

[Langdon1998] *Data Structures and Genetic Programming*, Kluwer.

[Langdon2000] William B. Langdon. Size fair and homologous tree genetic programming crossovers. *Genetic Programming And Evolvable Machines*, 1(1/2):95–119.

[Mitchell1997] Tom M. Mitchell. *Machine Learning*. McGraw-Hill, 1997.

[Provost and Fawcett2001] Foster Provost and Tom Fawcett. Robust classification for imprecise environments. *Machine Learning*, 42(3):203–231, 2001.

[Quinlan1993] *C4.5: Programs for Machine Learning*. Morgan Kaufmann.

[Ripley1996] *Pattern Recognition and Neural Networks*. Cambridge University Press.

[Scott et al.1998a] M. J. J. Scott, M. Niranjan, and R. W. Prager. Parcel: feature subset selection in variable cost domains. Technical Report CUED/F-INFENG/TR.323, Cambridge University Engineering Department, Trumpington Street, CB2 1PZ, UK.

[Scott et al.1998b] M. J. J. Scott, M. Niranjan, and R. W. Prager. Realisable classifiers: Improving operating performance on variable cost problems. In Paul H. Lewis and Mark S. Nixon, editors, *Ninth British Machine Vision Conference*, volume 1, pages 304–315, University of Southampton, UK, 14-17 September 1998.

[Soule1999] Terence Soule. Voting teams: A cooperative approach to non-typical problems using genetic programming. In Wolfgang Banzhaf, et. al. editors, *Proceedings of the Genetic and Evolutionary Computation Conference*, pages 916–922. Morgan Kaufmann.

[Swets et al.2000] John A. Swets, Robyn M. Dawes, and John Monahan. Better decisions through science. *Scientific American*, pages 70–75, October 2000.

[Yusoff et al.1998] Y. Yusoff, J. Kittler, and W. Christmas. Combining multiple experts for classifying shot changes in video sequences. In *IEEE International Conference on Multimedia Computing and Systems*, volume II, pages 700–704, Florence.

Methods for Designing Multiple Classifier Systems

Fabio Roli[1], Giorgio Giacinto[1], and Gianni Vernazza[2]

[1]Department of Electrical and Electronic Engineering, University of Cagliari
Piazza d'Armi, 09123, Cagliari, Italy
{roli,giacinto}@diee.unica.it,
[2]Dept. of Byophisical and Electronic Eng., University of Genoa
Via all'Opera Pia 11a, 16145, Genoa, Italy
vernazza@dibe.unige.it

Abstract. In the field of pattern recognition, multiple classifier systems based on the combination of outputs of a set of different classifiers have been proposed as a method for the development of high performance classification systems. In this paper, the problem of design of multiple classifier system is discussed. Six design methods based on the so-called "overproduce and choose" paradigm are described and compared by experiments. Although these design methods exhibited some interesting features, they do not guarantee to design the optimal multiple classifier system for the classification task at hand. Accordingly, the main conclusion of this paper is that the problem of the optimal MCS design still remains open.

1. Introduction

In the last decade, quite a lot of papers proposed the combination of multiple classifiers for designing high performance pattern classification systems [1, 2]. The rationale behind the growing interest in multiple classifier systems (MCSs) is the acknowledgement that the classical approach to designing a pattern recognition system that focuses on finding the best individual classifier has some serious drawbacks [3]. The main one being that it is very difficult to determine the best individual classifier for the classification task at hand, except when deep prior knowledge is available. In addition, the use of a single classifier does not allow the exploitation of the complementary discriminatory information that other classifiers may encapsulate.

Roughly speaking, MCS consists of an ensemble of different classification algorithms and a decision function for combining classifier outputs. Therefore, the design of MCSs involves two main phases: the design of the classifier ensemble, and the design of the combination function. Although this formulation of the design problem leads one to think that effective design should address both the phases, most of the design methods described in the literature focus only on the former one. In particular, methods that focus on the design of the classifier ensemble have tended to assume a fixed, simple decision combination function and aim to generate a set of mutually complementary classifiers that can be combined to achieve optimal accuracy [2]. A common approach to the generation of such classifier ensembles is to use some form of data "sampling" technique, such that each classifier is trained on a different

J. Kittler and F. Roli (Eds.): MCS 2001, LNCS 2096, pp. 78-87, 2001.

subset of the training data [4]. Alternatively, methods focused on the design of the combination function assume a given set of carefully designed classifiers and aim to find an optimal combination of classifier decisions. In order to perform such optimisation, a large set of combination functions of arbitrary complexity is available to the designer, ranging from simple voting rules through to "trainable" combination functions [2].

Although some design methods have proved to be very effective and some papers have investigated the comparative advantages of different methods [5], clear guidelines are not yet available for choosing the best design method for the classification task at hand. The designer of an MCS therefore has a toolbox containing quite a range of instruments for generating and combining classifiers. She/he may also design a myriad of different MCSs by coupling different techniques for creating classifier ensembles with different combination functions. However, the best MCS can only be determined by performance evaluation. Accordingly, some researchers proposed the so-called "overproduce and choose" paradigm (also called "test and select" approach [6]) in order to design the MCS most appropriate for the task at hand [7, 8, 9]. The basic idea is to produce an initial large set of "candidate" classifier ensembles, and then to select the sub-ensemble of classifiers that can be combined to achieve optimal accuracy. Typically, constraints and heuristic criteria are used in order to limit the computational complexity of the "choice" phase (e.g., the performances of a limited number of candidate ensembles are evaluated by a simple combination function like the majority voting rule [6, 7]).

In this paper, six design methods based on the overproduce and choose paradigm are described (Section 2). Two methods proposed in [7], and four methods developed by the authors (Section 2.3 and 2.4). The measures of classifier "diversity" used for MCS design are discussed in Section 2.2. The performances of such design methods were assessed and compared by experiment. Results are reported in Section 3. Conclusions are drawn in Section 4.

2. Design Methods Based on the Overproduce and Choose Paradigm

According to the overproduce and choose design paradigm, MCS design cycle can be subdivided into the following phases:

1) Ensemble Overproduction
2) Ensemble Choice

The overproduction design phase is aimed to produce a large set of candidate classifier ensembles. To this end, techniques like Bagging and Boosting that manipulate the training set can be adopted. Different classifiers can be also designed by using different initialisations of the respective learning parameters, using different classifier types and different classifier architectures. In practical applications, variations of the classifier parameters based on the designer expertise can provide very effective candidate classifiers [1,11].

The choice phase is aimed to select the subset of classifiers that can be combined to achieve optimal accuracy. It is easy to see that such optimal subset could be obtained by exhaustive enumeration, that is, by assessing on a validation set the classification accuracy provided by all possible subsets, and then choosing the subset exhibiting the best performance. Such performance evaluation should be performed with respect to a given combination function (e.g., the majority voting rule). Unfortunately, if N is the size of the set produced by the overproduction phase, the number of possible subsets is equal to $\sum_{i=1}^{N}\binom{N}{i}$. Therefore, different strategies have been proposed in order to limit the computational complexity of the choice phase. Although the choice phase usually assumes a given combination function for evaluating the performances of classifier ensembles, there is a strong interest for techniques that allow choosing effective classifier ensembles without assuming a specific combination rule. This can be seen via the analogy with the feature selection problem, where techniques for choosing those features that are most effective for preserving class separability have been developed. Accordingly, techniques for evaluating the degree of error diversity of classifiers forming an ensemble have been used for classifier selection purposes. We review some of these techniques in Section 2.2.

In the following, we shall assume that a large ensemble C made up of N classifiers was created by the overproduction phase:

$$C=\{c_1, c_2,\ldots,c_N\} \tag{1}$$

The goal of the choice phase is to select the subset C* of classifiers that can be combined to achieve optimal accuracy.

2.1 Methods Based on Heuristic Rules

Partridge and Yates proposed some techniques that exploit heuristic rules for choosing classifier ensembles [7]. One technique can be named "choose the best". It assumes an a priori fixed size n of the "optimal" subset C*. Then, selects from the set C the n classifiers with the highest classification accuracy to create the subset C*. The rationale behind such heuristic choice is that all the classifier subsets exhibit similar degrees of error diversity. Accordingly, the choice is based only on the accuracy value. The other choice technique proposed by Partridge and Yates can be named "choose the best in the class". For each classifier "class", it chooses the classifier exhibiting the highest accuracy. Therefore, a subset C* made up of three classifiers will be created if the initial set C is made up of classifiers belonging to three classifier types (e.g., the multilayer perceptron neural net, the k-nearest neighbours classifier, and the radial basis functions neural net). With respect to the previous rule, this heuristic rule takes also into account that classifiers belonging to different types should be more error independent than classifiers of the same type. It should be noted that the use of heuristic rules allows us to strongly reduce the computational complexity of the choice phase, because the evaluation of different classifier subsets is not required. On the other hand, the general validity of such heuristics is obviously not guaranteed.

2.2 Diversity Measures

As previously pointed out, several measures of error diversity for classifier ensembles have been proposed. Partridge and Yates proposed a measure named "within-set generalization diversity", or simply GD, that is computed as follows [7]:

$$GD = 1 - \frac{p(2 \text{ both fail})}{p(1 \text{ fails})} \qquad (2)$$

where p(2 both fail) indicates the probability that two randomly selected classifiers from the set C will both fail on a randomly selected input, and p(1 fails) indicates the probability that one randomly selected classifier will fail on a randomly selected input. GD takes values in the range [0,...,1] and provides a measure of the diversity of classifiers forming the ensemble.

Another diversity measure was proposed by Kuncheva et al. [10]. Let $X = \{X_1, X_2,...,X_M\}$ be a labelled data set. For each classifier c_i, we can design an M-dimensional output vector $O_i = [O_{1,i},...,O_{M,i}]$, such that $O_{j,i} = 1$, if c_i classifies correctly the pattern X_j, and 0, otherwise. Q statistics allow us to evaluate the diversity of two classifiers c_i and c_k:

$$Q_{i,k} = \frac{N^{11} N^{00} - N^{01} N^{10}}{N^{11} N^{00} + N^{01} N^{10}} \qquad (3)$$

where N^{ab} is the number of elements X_j of X for which $O_{j,i} = a$ and $O_{j,k} = b$. ($M = N^{00} + N^{01} + N^{10} + N^{11}$). Q varies between -1 an 1. Classifiers that tend to classify the same patterns correctly, that is, classifiers that are positively correlated, will have positive values of Q. Classifiers that make errors on different patters will exhibit negative values of Q. For statistically independent classifiers, $Q_{i,k} = 0$. The average Q computed over all the possible classifier couples is used for evaluating the diversity of a classifier ensemble.

Giacinto and Roli proposed a simple diversity measure, named "compound diversity", or simply CD, based on the compound error probability for two classifiers c_i and c_j [8]:

$$CD = 1 - \text{prob}(c_i \text{ fails}, c_j \text{ fails}) \qquad (4)$$

As for Q, the average CD computed over all the possible classifier couples is used for evaluating the diversity of a classifier ensemble.

It should be noted that the GD and CD measures are based on similar concepts.

As none of the above measures can be claimed to be the best, we used all of them in our design methods (Sections 2.3 and 2.4) and compared their performances (Section 3).

2.3 Methods Based on Search Algorithms

It is easy to see that search algorithms are the most natural way of implementing the choice phase required by the overproduce and choose design paradigm. Sharkey et al. proposed an exhaustive search algorithm based on the assumption that the number of candidate classifier ensembles is small [6]. In order to avoid the problem of exhaustive search, we developed three choice techniques based on search algorithms previously used for feature selection purposes (Sections 2.3.1 and 2.3.2), and for the solution of complex optimisation tasks (Section 2.3.3). All these search algorithms use an evaluation function for assessing the effectiveness of candidate ensembles. The above diversity measures and the accuracy value assessed by the majority voting rule have been used as evaluation functions. It should be remarked that the following search algorithms avoid exhaustive enumeration, but the selection of the optimal classifier ensemble is not guaranteed. It is worth noting that evaluation functions are computed with respect to a validation set in order to avoid "overfitting" problems

2.3.1 Forward Search

The choice phase based on the forward search algorithm starts by creating an ensemble made up of a single classifier (e.g., the classifier c_2). This initial classifier is usually chosen randomly. Alternatively, the classifier with the highest accuracy can be used. Then, single classifiers are added to c_2 to form subsets of two classifiers. If the subset made up of c_2 and c_3 exhibits the highest value of the evaluation function, one more classifier is added to such subset to form the subsets of three classifiers. Such an iterative process stops when all the subsets of size $k+1$ exhibit values of the evaluation function lower than the ones of size k. In this case, the subset of size k that exhibited the highest value of the evaluation function is selected.

2.3.2 Backward Search

In order to explain the developed search algorithms, let us use a simple example in which the set C created by the overproduction phase is made up of four classifiers. The backward search starts from the full classifier set. Then, eliminating one classifier from four, all possible subsets of three classifiers are created and their evaluation function values are assessed. If the subset made up of c_1, c_3, and c_4 exhibit the highest value, then it is selected and the subsets of two classifiers are obtained from this set by again eliminating one classifier. The iterative process stops when all the subsets of size k exhibit values of the evaluation function lower than the ones of size $k+1$. In such case, the subset of size $k+1$ that exhibited the highest value of the evaluation function is selected.

2.3.3 Tabu Search

The two previous algorithms stop the search process if the evaluation function decreases with respect to the previous step. As the evaluation function can exhibit a non-monotonic behaviour, it can be effective to continue the search process even if the evaluation function is decreasing. Tabu search is based on this concept. In addition, it implements both a forward and backward search strategy. The search starts from the full classifier set. At each step, adding and eliminating one classifier creates new subsets. Then, the subset that exhibits the highest value of the evaluation function is selected to create new subsets. It should be remarked that such subsets are selected even if the evaluation function is decreased with respect to the previous step. In order to avoid the creation of the same subsets in different search steps (i.e., in order to avoid "cycles" in the search process), a classifier added or eliminated cannot be selected for insertion/deletion for a certain number of search steps. Different stop criteria can be used. For example, the search can stop after a certain number of steps, and the best subset created during the search process is returned.

2.4 A Method Based on Clustering of Classifiers

We developed an approach to the choice phase that allows the identification of an effective subset of classifiers with limited computational effort. It is based on the hypothesis that set C created by the overproduction phase is made up of the union of M disjoint subsets C_i. In addition, we assumed that the compound error probability between any two classifiers belonging to the same subset is greater than the one between any two classifiers belonging to different subsets. It is easy to see that effective MCS members can be extracted from different subsets C_i, the more highly error-correlated the classifiers belonging to the same subset, the classifiers belonging to different subsets being error-independent. Therefore, under the hypotheses above, we defined a choice phase made up of two phases, namely the identification of the subsets C_i by clustering of classifiers, and the extraction of classifiers from different clusters in order to create an effective classifier ensemble C*. Classifiers have been clustered according to the CD measure (eq. 4, section 2.2) so that classifiers that make a large number of coincident errors are assigned to the same cluster, and classifiers that make few coincident errors assigned to different clusters. At each iteration of the clustering algorithm, one candidate ensembles C* is created by taking from each cluster the classifier that exhibits the maximum average distance from all other clusters. For each candidate ensemble C*, the classifiers are then combined by majority voting, and the ensemble with the highest performance is chosen. Further details on this design method can be found in [8,9].

3. Experimental Results

The Feltwell data set was used for our experiments. It consists of a set of multisensor remote-sensing images related to an agricultural area near the village of Feltwell (UK). Our experiments were carried out characterizing each pixel by a fifteen-element feature vector containing the brightness values in six optical bands and over nine radar channels. We selected 10944 pixels belonging to five agricultural classes and randomly subdivided them into a training set (5124 pixels), a validation set (528 pixels), and a test set (5238 pixels). We used a small validation set in order to simulate real cases where validation data are difficult to be obtained. A detailed description of this data set can be found in [11].

Our experiments mainly aimed to assess the performances of the proposed design methods (Sections 2.3 and 2.4) and to compare our methods with other design methods proposed in the literature (Section 2.1).

To this end, we performed different overproduction phases, thus creating different initial ensembles C (see equation 1). Such sets were created using different classifier types, namely, Multilayer Perceptrons (MLPs), Radial Basis Functions (RBF) neural networks, Probabilistic Neural Networks (PNNs), and the k-nearest neighbour classifier (k-nn). For each classifier type, ensembles were created by varying some design parameters (e.g., the network architecture, the initial random weights, the value of the "k" parameter for the k-nn classifier, and so on). In the following, we report the results relating to three initial sets C, here referred to as sets C^1, C^2, and C^3, generated by overproduction phases:

- set C^1 contains fifty MLPs. Five architectures with one or two hidden layers and different numbers of neurons per layer were used. For each architecture, ten training phases with different initial weights were performed. All the networks had fifteen input units and five output units as input features and data classes, respectively;

- set C^2 contains the same MLPs belonging to C^1 and fourteen k-nn classifiers. The k-nn classifiers were obtained by varying the value of the "k" parameter in the following two ranges: (15, 17, 19, 21, 23, 25, 27) and (75, 77, 79, 81, 83, 85, 87);

- set C^3 contains thirty MLPs, three k-nn classifiers, three RBF neural networks, and one PNN. For the RBF neural network, three different architectures were used.

3.1 Experiments with Set C^1

First of all, we evaluated the performances of the whole of set C^1, the best classifier in the ensemble, and those ensembles designed by the two methods based on heuristic rules (see Section 2.1). Such performances are reported in Table 1 in terms of percentage accuracy values, percentage rejection rates, and differences between accuracy and rejection values. The sizes of the selected ensembles are shown. The classifiers were always combined by the majority-voting rule. A pattern was rejected when a majority of classifiers assigning it to the same data class was not present. All values reported in Table 1 referred to the test set. For the method named "choose the best" (indicated with the term "Best" in Table 1), the performances of ensembles of size ranging from 3 through 15 were assessed. The size of the ensemble designed by the method named "choose the best in the class" method (indicated with the term "Best-class") is five, because five types of classifiers (namely, five types of net architectures) were used to create the ensemble C^1 (Section 2.1). For each ensemble, the value of the Generalisation Diversity measure (GD) is reported in order to show the degree of error diversity among the classifiers.

Table 1 shows that the design methods based on heuristic rules can provide some improvements with respect to the accuracy of the initial ensemble C^1 and the best classifier. However, such improvements are small. It should be noted that these design methods do not provide improvements in terms of error diversity as assessed by the GD measure. This can be explained by observing that such methods select classifiers on the basis of accuracy, and they do not take explicitly into account error diversity.

Table 2 reports results obtained by our design methods based on search algorithms (Section 2.3). The classifiers were always combined by the majority-voting rule. A pattern was rejected when a majority of classifiers assigning it to the same data class was not present. All values reported in Table 2 referred to the Feltwell test set. It should be noted that these design methods improve the error diversity, that is, the ensembles are characterised by GD values higher that the ones reported in Table 1. However, the improvements in accuracy with respect to the initial ensemble C^1 and the best classifier are similar to the ones provided by the methods based on heuristic rules.

Table 1. Performances of the whole set C^1, the best classifier in the ensemble, and the ones of the ensembles designed by two methods based on heuristic rules.

Ensemble	Size	Accuracy	Rejection	Accuracy – Rejection	GD
Initial set C^1	50	89.8357	1.2027	88.6330	0.2948
Best classifier	1	89.2516	0.0000	89.2516	N/A
Best	3	90.2565	0.2673	89.9892	0.2399
Best	5	90.4278	0.4773	89.9505	0.1937
Best	7	90.0134	0.4009	89.6125	0.1801
Best	9	90.0459	0.2673	89.7786	0.1783
Best	11	90.0747	0.3627	89.7120	0.1935
Best	13	89.9732	0.2291	89.7441	0.2008
Best	15	89.9712	0.4391	89.5321	0.2063
Best-class	5	89.9847	0.4964	89.4883	0.2617

Table 2. Performances of the ensembles generated by design methods based on search algorithms. The evaluation function used to guide the search is indicated within brackets.

Choice Method	Size	Accuracy	Rejection	Acc. - Rej.	GD
Initial set C^1	50	89.8357	1.2027	88.6330	0.2948
Best classifier	1	89.2516	0.0000	89.2516	N/A
Backward(GD)	3	89.9981	1.6991	88.2990	0.4752
Backward(CD)	3	90.4890	0.8400	89.6490	0.3573
Backward(Accuracy)	45	89.8517	0.8591	88.9926	0.2950
Backward(Q)	3	88.6901	0.7446	87.9455	0.4129
Forward_from_best(GD)	3	89.5669	0.8209	88.7460	0.4402
Forward_from_best(CD)	3	90.0499	0.6109	89.4390	0.3454
Forward_from_best(Accuracy)	11	90.3965	0.8018	89.5947	0.3274
Forward_from_best(Q)	3	88.2387	1.1455	87.0932	0.3942
Forward _random(GD)	3	89.0993	1.2218	87.8775	0.3958
Forward_random (CD)	7	90.2866	0.7446	89.5420	0.3346
Forward_random (Accuracy)	7	90.2420	0.6109	89.6311	0.2589
Forward_random (Q)	3	87.0609	0.5536	86.5073	0.3845
Tabu(GD)	3	89.9459	1.2600	88.6859	0.4613
Tabu(CD)	3	90.1425	0.8400	89.3025	0.3806
Tabu(Accuracy)	9	90.1156	0.9164	89.1992	0.3416
Tabu(Q)	3	89.8180	1.3746	88.4434	0.4826

Table 3 reports results obtained by our design method based on clustering of classifiers (Section 4.4). Conclusions similar to those for the design methods based on search algorithms can be drawn.

Table 3. Performances of the ensembles generated by design method based on clustering of classifiers. The evaluation function used to guide the search is indicated within brackets.

Choice Method	Size	Accuracy	Rejection	Acc. − Rej.	GD
Initial set C^1	50	89.8357	1.2027	88.6330	0.2948
Best classifier	1	89.2516	0.0000	89.2516	N/A
Cluster(CD)	7	90.5294	0.8209	89.7085	0.3193
Cluster(Q)	49	89.6592	0.8591	88.8001	0.2962
Cluster(GD)	9	89.6179	1.0691	88.5488	0.3788

It is worth noting that the performances of various design methods are slightly better than the ones of initial ensemble C^1 and the best classifier, but the differences are small. However, it should be noted that methods based on search algorithms and clustering of classifiers improve the error diversity of classifiers.

3.2 Experiments with Set C^2 and C^3

The same experiments previously described for set C^1 were performed for sets C^2 and C^3. For the sake of brevity, for each design method we report the average performances in terms of accuracy and error diversity values. Table 4 shows the average accuracy values and the average error diversity values (in terms of the GD measure) of different design methods applied to sets C^2 and C^3.

Table 4. For each design method, the average percentage accuracy value and the average error diversity value (in terms of the GD measure) are reported for the experiment with the set C^2 and for the experiment with the set C^3.

	Set C^2		Set C^3	
Choice Method	Accuracy	GD	Accuracy	GD
Initial set	90.4918	0.3170	89.4645	0.3819
Best classifier	90.0916	-	88.2016	-
Choose the best	90.1090	0.1989	91.1097	0.3279
Choose the best in the class	89.9847	0.2617	92.0613	0.4905
Backward	89.8945	0.3488	92.3871	0.5851
Forward from the best	89.9024	0.3400	93.2471	0.5917
Forward from random	89.7408	0.3270	91.5023	0.5969
Tabu	90.0931	0.3631	93.5092	0.6225
Clustering	89.9013	0.3410	92.1911	0.5383

With regard to the experiments performed on sets C^2 and C^3, the performances of various design methods are close to or better than those of the initial ensembles and the best classifier. Significant improvements were obtained for some of the experiments performed on set C^2.

4. Discussion and Conclusions

Although definitive conclusions cannot be drawn on the basis of the limited set of experiments above, some preliminary conclusions can be drawn. The overproduce and choose paradigm does guarantee optimal MCS design for the classification task at hand. In particular, no choice method can be claimed to be the best, because the superiority of one over the other depends on the classification task at hand. Accordingly, optimal MCS design is still an open issue. The main motivation behind the use of the overproduce and choose paradigm is that at present clear guidelines to choose the best design method for the classification task at hand are lacking. Thanks to this design paradigm it is possible to exploit the large set of tools developed to generate and combine classifiers. The designer can create a myriad of different MCSs by coupling different techniques to create classifier ensembles with different combination functions. Then, the most appropriate MCS can be selected by performance evaluation. It is worth noting that this approach is commonlyused in engineeringfields where optimal design methods are not available (e.g., software engineering). In addition, the overproduce and choose paradigm allows to create MCSs made up of small sets of classifiers. This is a very important feature for practical applications.

References

[1]   Xu, L., Krzyzak A., Suen C.Y.: Methods for combining multiple classifiers and their applications to handwriting recognition. IEEE Trans. on Systems, Man, and Cyb. 22 (1992) 418-435
[2]   Kittler J., Roli F. (eds.): Multiple Classifier Systems. Proc. of the First Int. Workshop MCS 2000. Lecture Notes in Computer Science, Vol. 1857. Springer-Verlag (2000)
[3]   Kittler J.: A framework for classifier fusion: is it still needed? In: Ferri F.J., Inesta J.M., Amin A., Pudil P. (eds.): Advances in Pattern Recognition. Proc. Int. Workshop SSPR&SPR 2000. Lectures Notes in Computer Science, Vol. 1876. Springer-Verlag (2000) 45-56
[4]   Breiman, L.: Bagging Predictors. Machine Learning 24 (1996) 123-140
[5]   Ho T.K.: Complexity of classification problems and comparative advantages of combined classifiers. In: Kittler J., Roli F. (eds.): Multiple Classifier Systems. Proc. of the First Int. Workshop MCS 2000. LNCS Vol. 1857 Springer-Verlag (2000) 97-106
[6]   Sharkey A.J.C., et al.: The "test and select" approach to ensemble combination. In: Kittler J., Roli F. (eds.): Multiple Classifier Systems. LNCS 1857. Springer-Verlag, (2000) 30-44
[7]   Partridge D., Yates W.B.: Engineering multiversion neural-net systems. Neural Computation 8 (1996) 869-893
[8]   Giacinto G., Roli F.: An approach to the automatic design of multiple classifier systems. Pattern Recognition Letters 22 (2001) 25-33
[9]   Giacinto G., Roli F.: Design of effective neural network ensembles for image classification purposes. to appear in Image and Vision Computing Journal (2001)
[10]   Kuncheva, L.I., et al.: Is independence good for combining classifiers?. Proc. of ICPR2000, 15th Int. Conf. on Pattern Recognition, Barcelona, Spain (2000), Vol. 2, 168-171
[11]   Giacinto G., Roli F., Bruzzone L.: Combination of Neural and Statistical Algorithms for Supervised Classification of Remote-Sensing Images. Pattern Recognition Letters 21 (2000) 385-397

Decision-Level Fusion in Fingerprint Verification

Salil Prabhakar and Anil K. Jain

Dept. of Comp. Sci. and Eng., Michigan State University, East Lansing, MI 48824

Abstract. A scheme is proposed for classifier combination at decision level which stresses the importance of classifier selection during combination. The proposed scheme is optimal (in the Neyman-Pearson sense) when sufficient data are available to obtain reasonable estimates of the join densities of classifier outputs. Four different fingerprint matching algorithms are combined using the proposed scheme to improve the accuracy of a fingerprint verification system. Experiments conducted on a large fingerprint database ($\sim$ 2,700 fingerprints) confirm the effectiveness of the proposed integration scheme. An overall matching performance increase of $\sim$ 3% is achieved. We further show that a combination of multiple impressions or multiple fingers improves the verification performance by more than 4% and 5%, respectively. Analysis of the results provide some insight into the various decision-level classifier combination strategies.

1 Introduction

A number of classifier combination strategies exist [1], [2], [3], however, a priori it is not known which combination strategy works better than the others and if so under what circumstances. In this paper we will restrict ourselves to a particular decision-level integration scenario where each classifier may select its own representation scheme and produces a confidence value as its output. A theoretical framework for combining classifiers in such a scenario has been developed by Kittler et al. [2]. However, the product rule for combination suggested in [2] implicitly assumes an independence of classifiers. The sum rule further assumes that the aposteriori probabilities computed by the respective classifiers do not deviate dramatically from the prior probabilities. The max rule, min rule, median rule, and majority vote rule have been shown to be special cases of the sum and the product rules. Making these assumptions simplifies the combination rule but does not guarantee optimal results and hinders the combination performance. We follow Kittler et al.'s framework without making any assumptions about the independence of various classifiers.

The contributions of this paper are two fold. Firstly, we propose a general system design for decision-level classifier fusion that uses the optimal Neyman-Pearson rule and outperforms the combination strategies based on the assumption of independence among the classifiers. Secondly, we propose a multi-modal biometric system design based on multiple fingerprint matchers. The use of the proposed combination strategy in combining multiple matchers significantly improves the overall accuracy of the fingerprint-based verification system. The

J. Kittler and F. Roli (Eds.): MCS 2001, LNCS 2096, pp. 88–98, 2001.

effectiveness of the proposed integration strategy is further demonstrated by building multi-modal biometric systems that combine two different impressions of the same finger or fingerprints of two different fingers.

2 Biometrics

The biometric verification problem can be formulated as follows. Let the stored biometric signal (template) of a person be represented as S and the acquired signal (input) for authentication be represented by I. Then the null and alternate hypotheses are:

$H_0 : I \neq S$, input fingerprint is not from the same finger as the template,

$H_1 : I = S$, input fingerprint is from the same finger as the template.

The associated decisions are as follows: D_0 : person is an imposter, and D_1 : person is genuine. The verification involves matching S and I using a similarity measure. If the matching score is less than some decision threshold T, then decide D_0, else decide D_1. Then, $FAR = P(D_1|w_0)$, and $FRR = P(D_0|w_1)$, where w_0 is the class with $H_0 = true$ and w_1 is the class with $H_1 = true$.

Several biometric systems have been designed and tested on large databases. However, in some applications with stringent performance requirement, no single biometric can meet the requirements due to inexact nature of sensing, feature extraction, and matching processes. This has generated interest in designing multimodal biometric systems. Multimodal biometric systems may work in one of the following five scenarios: (i) Multiple sensors: the information obtained from different sensors for the same biometric may be combined. For example, optical, ultrasound, and capacitance based sensors are available to capture fingerprints. (ii) Multiple biometric system: multiple biometrics such as fingerprint and face may be combined [2]. (iii) Multiple units of the same biometric: one image each from both the iris, or both hands, or ten fingerprints may be combined. (iv) Multiple instances of the same biometric: for example multiple impressions of the same finger may be combined. (v) Multiple representation and matching algorithms for the same input biometric signal: for example, combining different approaches to feature extraction and matching of fingerprints [4]. The first two scenarios require several sensors and are not cost effective. Scenarios (iii) causes inconvenience to the user in providing multiple cues and has a longer acquisition time. In scenario (iv), only a single input is acquired during verification and matched with several stored templates acquired during the one-time enrollment process. Thus, it is slightly better than scenario (iii). In our opinion, scenario (v) is the most cost-effective way to improve biometric system performance.

We propose to use a combination of four different fingerprint-based biometric systems where each system uses different feature extraction and/or matching algorithms to generate a matching score which can be interpreted as the confidence level of the matcher. These different matching scores are combined to obtain the lowest possible FRR for a given FAR. We also compare the performance of our integration strategy with the sum and the product rules [2]. Even though we propose and report results in scenarios (iii), (iv) and (v), our combination strategy could be used for scenarios (i) and (ii) as well.

3   Optimal Integration Strategy

Let us suppose that pattern Z is to be assigned to one of the two possible classes, w_0 and w_1. Let us assume that we have N classifiers, and the ith classifier outputs a single confidence value θ_i about class w_1 (the confidence for the class w_0 will be $1-\theta_i$), $i = 1, 2, .., N$. Let us assume that the prior probabilities for the two classes are equal. The classifier combination task can now be posed as an independent (from the original N classifier designs) classifier design problem with two classes and N features (θ_i, $i = 1, 2, .., N$).

3.1   Classifier Selection

It is a common practice in classifier combination to perform an extensive analysis of various combination strategies involving all the N available classifiers. In feature selection it is well known that the most informative d-element subset of N conditionally independent features is not necessarily the union of the d individually most informative features. Cover [5] argues that no non-exhaustive sequential d-element selection procedure is optimal, even for jointly normal features. He further showed that all possible probability of error ordering can occur among subsets of features subject to a monotonicity constraint. The statistical dependence among features causes further uncertainty in the d-element subset composed of the individually best features. One could argue that the combination strategy itself should pick out the classifiers that should be combined. However, we know in practice that the "curse of dimensionality" makes it difficult for a classifier to automatically delete less discriminative features [6]. Therefore, we propose a classifier selection scheme prior to classifier combination. We propose to use the *class separation* statistic [7] as the feature effectiveness criterion. This statistic, CS, measures how well the two classes (imposter and genuine, in our case) are separated with respect to the feature vector, X^d, in a d-dimensional space, R^d.

$$CS(X^d) = \int_{R^d} |p(X^d|w_0) - p(X^d|w_1)| dx, \qquad (1)$$

where $p(X^d|w_0)$ and $p(X^d|w_1)$ are the estimated distributions for the w_0 (imposter) and w_1 (genuine) classes, respectively. Note that $0 \leq CS \leq 2$.

We will use the class separation statistic to obtain the best feature subset using an exhaustive search of all possible $2^N - 1$ feature subsets.

3.2   Non-parametric Density Estimation

Once we have selected the subset containing d ($d \leq N$) features, we develop our combination strategy. We do not make any assumptions about the form of the distributions for the two classes and use non-parametric methods to estimate the two distributions. We use Parzen window density estimate to obtain the non-parametric distributions [8]. A Gaussian kernel was used and the window width was empirically determined.

3.3   Decision Strategy

We use the likelihood ratio $L = P(X^d|w_0)/P(X^d|w_1)$ to make the final decision for our two-class problem: Decide D_0 (person is an imposter) for low values of L; decide D_1 (person is genuine) for high values of L. If L is small, the data is more likely to come from class w_1; the likelihood ratio test rejects the null hypothesis for small values of the ratio. The Neyman-Pearson lemma states that this test is optimal, that is, among all the tests with a given significance level, α (FAR), the likelihood ratio test has the maximum power. For a specified α, λ is the smallest constant such that $P(L \leq \lambda) \leq \alpha$. The type II error, β (FRR), is given by $P(L > \lambda)$.

4   Matching Algorithms

We have developed four fingerprint verification systems which can be broadly classified into two categories: (i) minutiae-based, and (ii) filter-based. The three minutiae-based and one filter-based algorithms are summarized in this section.

4.1   Matcher *Hough*

The fingerprint matching problem can be regarded as template matching [10]: given two sets of minutia features, compute their matching score. The two main steps of the algorithm are: (1) Compute the transformation parameters δ_x, δ_y, θ, and s between the two images, where δ_x and δ_y are translations along x- and y- directions, respectively, θ is the rotation angle, and s is the scaling factor; (2) Align two sets of minutia points with the estimated parameters and count the matched pairs within a bounding box; (3) Repeat the previous two steps for the set of discretized allowed transformations. The transformation that results in the highest matching score is believed to be the correct one. The final matching score is scaled between 0 and 99. Details of the algorithm can be found in [10].

4.2   Matcher *String*

Each set of extracted minutia features is first converted into polar coordinates with respect to an anchor point. The two-dimensional (2D) minutia features are, therefore, reduced to a one-dimensional (1D) string by concatenating points in a increasing order of radial angel in polar coordinate. The string matching algorithm is applied to compute the edit distance between the two strings. The edit distance can be easily normalized and converted into a matching score. This algorithm [9] can be summarized as follows: (1) Rotation and translation are estimated by matching ridge segment (represented as planar curve) associated with each minutia in the input image with the ridge segment associated with each minutia in the template image. The rotation and translation that results in the maximum number of matched minutiae pairs within a bounding box is considered the correct transformation and the corresponding minutiae are labeled as anchor minutiae, $\mathcal{A}_1$ and $\mathcal{A}_2$, respectively. (2) Convert each set of minutia into a 1D string using polar coordinates anchored at $\mathcal{A}_1$ and $\mathcal{A}_2$, respectively; (3) Compute the edit distance between the two 1D strings. The matched pairs are retrieved based on the minimal edit distance between the two strings; (4) Output the normalized matching score which is the ratio of the number of matched-pairs and the number of minutiae points in the two sets.

4.3   Matcher *Dynamic*

This matching algorithm is a generalization of the above mentioned string algorithm. The transformation of a 2D pattern into a 1D pattern usually results in a loss of information. Chen and Jain [11] have shown that fingerprint matching using 2D dynamic time warping can be done as efficiently as 1D string editing while avoiding the above mentioned problems with algorithm *String*. The 2D dynamic time warping algorithm can be characterized by the following steps: (1) Estimate the rotation between the two sets of minutia features as in Step 1 of algorithm *String*; (2) Align the two minutia sets using the estimated parameters from Step 1; (3) Compute the maximal matched minutia pairs of the two minutia sets using 2D dynamic programming technique. The intuitive interpretation of this step is to warp one set of minutia to align with the other so that the number of matched minutiae is maximized; (4) Output the normalized matching score which is based on only those minutiae that lie within the overlapping region.

4.4   Matcher *Filter*

The four mains steps in the filter-based feature extraction algorithm are: (i) determine a reference point and region of interest for the fingerprint image. The reference point is taken to be the center point in a fingerprint which is defined as the point of maximum curvature of the ridges in a fingerprint. The region of interest is a circular area around the reference point. The algorithm rejects the fingerprint images for which the reference point could not be established. (ii) tessellate the region of interest. The region of interest is divided into sectors and the gray values in each sector are normalized to a constant mean and variance. (iii) filter the region of interest in eight different directions using a bank of Gabor filters (eight directions are required to completely capture the local ridge characteristics in a fingerprint while only four directions are required to capture the global configuration). Filtering produces a set of eight filtered images. (iv) compute the average absolute deviation from the mean (AAD) of gray values in individual sectors in each filtered image. AAD value in each sector quantifies the underlying ridge structures and is defined as a feature. A feature vector, which we call FingerCode, is the collection of all the features (for every sector) in each filtered image. Thus, the feature elements capture the local information and the ordered enumeration of the tessellation captures the invariant global relationships among the local patterns. The representation is invariant to translation of the image. It is assumed that the fingerprint is captured in an upright position and the rotation invariance is achieved by storing ten representations corresponding to the various rotations ($-45.0°$, $-45°$, $-33.75°$, $-22.5°$, $-11.25°$, $0°$, $11.25°$, $22.5°$, $33.75°$, $45.0°$) of the image. Euclidean distance is computed between the input representation and the ten templates to generate ten matching distances. Finally, the minimum of the ten distances is computed and inverted to give a matching score. The matching score is scaled between 0 and 99 and can be regarded as a confidence value of the matcher.

5   Experimental Results

Fingerprint images were collected in our laboratory from 167 subjects using an optical sensor manufactured by Digital Biometrics, Inc. (image size = 508×480, resolution = 500 *dpi*). A single impression each of the right index, right middle, left index, and left middle fingers for each subject was taken in that order. This process was then repeated to acquire a second impression. The fingerprint images were collected again from the same subjects after an interval of six weeks in a similar fashion. Thus, we have four impressions for each of the four fingers of a subject. This resulted in a total of $2,672$ ($167 \times 4 \times 4$) fingerprint images. We call this database MSU_DBI. A live feedback of the acquired image was provided and the subjects were guided in placing their fingers in the center of the sensor in an upright position. A total of 100 images (about 4% of the database) was removed from the MSU_DBI because the filter-based fingerprint matching algorithm rejected these images due to failure in locating the center or due to a poor quality of the images. We matched all the remaining $2,572$ fingerprint images with each other to obtain $3,306,306$ ($\frac{2572 \times 2571}{2}$) matchings and called the matchings genuine only if the pair are different impressions of the same finger. Thus, we have a total of $3,298,834$ ($3,306,306 - 7,472$) imposter and $7,472$ genuine matchings per matcher from this database. For the multiple matcher combination, we randomly selected half the imposter matching scores and half the genuine matching scores for training and the remaining samples for test. This process was repeated ten times to give ten different training sets and ten corresponding independent test sets. All performances will be reported in terms of *ROC* curves computed as an average from the ten *ROC* curves corresponding to the ten different training and test sets (two-fold cross validation repeated ten times). For the multiple impression and multiple finger combinations, the same database of $3,298,834$ imposter and $7,472$ genuine matchings computed using the *Dynamic* matcher was used.

The *ROC* curves computed from the test data for the four individual fingerprint matchers used in this study are shown in Figure 1. The class separation statistic computed from the training data was 1.88, 1.87, 1.85 and 1.76 for the algorithms *Dynamic*, *String*, *Filter*, and *Hough*, respectively, and is found to

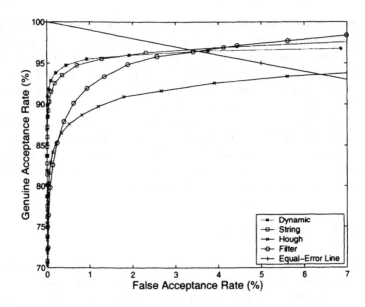

Fig. 1. Performance of individual fingerprint matchers.

Table 1. Combining two fingerprint matchers. CS is the class separation statistic. CS and ρ are computed from the training data. Ranks by ROC and ranks by $\Delta\ ROC$ are computed from the independent test data.

Combination	CS (rank)	rank by ROC	ρ	rank by $\Delta\ ROC$
String + Filter	1.95 (1)	1	0.52	2
Dynamic + Filter	1.95 (1)	2	0.56	3
String + Dynamic	1.94 (3)	2	0.82	3
Hough + Dynamic	1.93 (4)	4	0.80	6
Hough + Filter	1.91 (4)	6	0.53	1
Hough + String	1.90 (6)	5	0.83	5

be highly correlated to the matching performance on the independent test set. Figure 1 shows that matchers *Dynamic* and *String* are comparable, *Filter* is better than *Dynamic* and *String* at high *FAR*s and slightly worse at very low *FAR*s, and matcher *Hough* ranks the last.

First, we combine the matchers in pairs of two. To combine two fingerprint matchers, we estimate the two-dimensional genuine and imposter densities from the training data. The two-dimensional genuine density was computed using the Parzen density estimation method. The value of window width (h) was empirically determined to obtain a smooth density estimate and was set at 0.01. We used the same value of h for all the two-matcher combinations. As a comparison, the genuine density estimates obtained from the normalized histograms were extremely peaky due to unavailability of sufficient data (only about 3, 780 genuine matching scores were available in the training set to estimate a two-

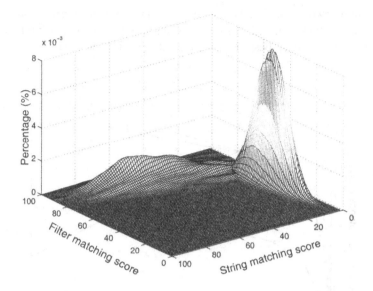

Fig. 2. Two-dimensional density estimates for the genuine and imposter classes for *String+Filter* combination. Genuine density was estimated using Parzen window ($h = 0.01$) estimator and the imposter density was estimated using normalized histograms.

dimensional distribution in $10,000$ (100×100) bins). However, for estimation of the two-dimensional imposter distribution, over 1.6 million matching scores were available. Hence, we estimated the two-dimensional imposter distribution by computing a normalized histogram using the following formula:

$$p(X^d|w_0) = \frac{1}{n} \sum_{j=1}^{n} \delta(X, X_j) \tag{2}$$

where δ is the delta function that equals 1 if the raw matching score vectors X and X_j are equal, 0 otherwise. Here n is the number of imposter matchings from the training data. The computation time for Parzen window density estimate depends on n and so, it is considerably larger than the normalized histogram method for large n. The estimates of the two-dimensional genuine and imposter densities thus computed for *String + Filter* combination are shown in Figure 2. The class separation statistic for all pairs of matcher combination is shown in the second column of Table 1; the number in parenthesis is the predicted ranking of the combination performance based on CS. The actual ranking of performance obtained from the independent test set is listed in the third column marked ROC for ROC curves). As can be seen, the predicted ranking is very close to the actual rankings on independent test data.

The following observations can be made from the two-matcher combinations:

- Classifier combination improvement is directly related to the "independence" (lower values of ρ) of the classifiers.

– Combining two weak classifiers results in a large performance improvement.
– Combining two strong classifiers results in a small performance improvement.
– The two individually best classifier do not form the best pair.

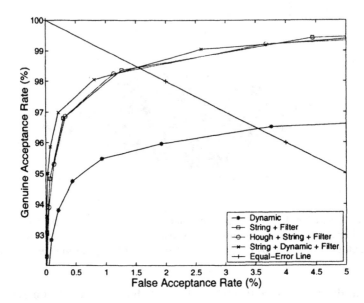

Fig. 3. The performance of the best individual matcher *Dynamic* is compared with the various combinations. The *String + Filter* is the best two-matcher combination and *String + Dynamic + Filter* is the best overall combination. Note that addition of the classifier *Hough* to the combination *String + Filter* results in a degradation of the performance.

Next, we combine the matchers in groups of three and then combine all the four matchers together. The class separation statistic is maximum (1.97) for the *String + Dynamic + Filter* combination. From the tests conducted on the independent data set, we make following observations (see Figure 3).

– Adding a classifier may actually degrade the performance of classifier combination. This degradation in performance is a consequence of lack of independent information provided by the classifier being added and finite size of the training and test database.
– Classifier selection based on a "goodness" statistic is a promising approach.
– Performance of combination is significantly better than the best individual matcher.

Among all the possible subsets of the four fingerprint matchers, the class separation statistic is maximum for *String + Dynamic + Filter* combination. Hence, our feature selection scheme selects this subset for the final combination and rejects the matcher *Hough*. This is consistent with the nature of the *Hough* algorithm, which is basically the linear pairing step in algorithms *String* and *Dynamic*, without the capability of dealing with elastic distortions. Therefore, *Hough* does not provide "independent" information with respect to *String* and *Dynamic*. The performance of the various matcher combinations on an independent test supports the prediction that *String + Dynamic + Filter* is the best combination. The proposed combination scheme either outperforms or matches the performance of the sum rule and outperforms the product rule in all the two- three- and four-matcher combinations because the proposed technique can produce a nonlinear complex decision boundary that is close to optimal.

The performance of the combined system is more than 3% better than the best individual matcher. The matcher combination takes about 0.02 seconds on an Sun Ultra 1 in the test phase. In an authentication system, this increase in time will have almost no effect on the verification time and the overall matching time is still bounded by the slowest individual matcher.

The performance improvement due to combination of two impressions of the same finger and the combination of two different fingers of the same person using the proposed strategy is 4% and 5%, respectively. The matcher *Dynamic* was used. The correlation coefficient between the two scores from two different impressions of the same finger is 0.42 and between two different fingers of the same person is 0.68 and is directly related to the improvement in the performance of combination. The *CS* for individual impressions is 1.84 and 1.87 respectively, and for the combination is 1.95. The *CS* for individual fingers is 1.87 and 1.86 respectively, and for the combination is 1.98. Combination of two impressions of the same finger or two fingers of the same person using the proposed combination strategy is extremely fast. Therefore, the overall verification time is same as the individual matcher *Dynamic*.

6   Conclusions and Discussions

We have presented a scheme for combining multiple matchers (classifiers) at decision-level in an optimal fashion. Our design emphasis is on classifier selection before arriving at the final combination. It was shown that one of the fingerprint matchers in the given pool of matchers is redundant and no performance improvement is achieved by utilizing this matcher. This matcher was identified and rejected by the matcher selection scheme. In case of a larger number of classifiers and relatively small training data, a classifier may actually degrade the performance when combined with other classifiers, and hence classifier selection is essential. We demonstrate that our combination scheme improves the performance of a fingerprint verification system by more than 3%. We also show that combining multiple instances of the same biometric or multiple units of the same biometric characteristics is a viable way to improve the verification system performance. We observe that independence among various classifiers is directly related to the improvement in performance of the combination.

References

1. A. K. Jain, R. P. W. Duin and J. Mao, "Statistical Pattern Recognition: A Review", *IEEE Transactions on Patt. Anal. and Machine Intell.*, Vol. 22, No. 1, pp. 4-37, 2000.
2. J. Kittler, M. Hatef, R. P. W. Duin, and J. Matas, "On Combining Classifiers", *IEEE Trans. on Patt. Anal. and Machine Intell.*, Vol. 20, No. 3, pp. 226-239, 1998.
3. T. K. Ho, J. J. Hull, and S. N. Srihari, "Decision Combination in Multiple Classifier Systems", *IEEE Trans. on Patt. Anal. and Machine Intell.*, Vol. 16, No. 1, pp. 66-75, 1994.
4. A. K. Jain, S. Prabhakar, and S. Chen, "Combining Multiple Matchers for a High Security Fingerprint Verification System", Pattern Recognition Letters, Vol 20, No. 11-13, pp. 1371-1379, November 1999.
5. T. M. Cover, "On the Possible Ordering in the Measurement Selection Problem", *IEEE Trans. on Systems, Man, and Cybernetics*, Vol. SMC-7, No. 9, pp. 657-661, 1977.
6. S. Raudys and A. K. Jain, "Small Sample Size Effects in Statistical Pattern Recognition: Recommendations for Practitioners", *IEEE Trans. on Patt. Anal. and Machine Intell.*, Vol. 13, No. 3, pp. 252-264, 1991.
7. I.-S. Oh, J.-S Lee, and C. Y. Suen, "Analysis of Class Separation and Combination of Class-Dependent Features for Handwriting Recognition", *IEEE Trans. Patt. Anal. and Machine Intell.*, Vol. 21, No. 10, pp. 1089-1094, 1999.
8. R. O. Duda, P. E. Hart, and D. G. Stork, Pattern Classification, 2nd Edition, John Wiley & Sons, November 2000.
9. A.K. Jain, L. Hong, S. Pankanti and R. Bolle, "An Identity Authentication System Using Fingerprints", *Proc. IEEE*, Vol. 85, No. 9, pp. 1365-1388, 1997.
10. N. K. Ratha, K. Karu, S. Chen, and A. K. Jain, "Real-time Matching System for Large Fingerprint Database", *IEEE Trans. on Patt. Anal. and Machine Intell.*, Vol. 18, No. 8, pp. 799-813, 1996.
11. S. Chen and A. K. Jain, "A Fingerprint Matching Algorithm Using Dynamic Programming", *Technical Report*, Department of Computer Science and Engineering, Michigan State University.
12. A. K. Jain, S. Prabhakar, L. Hong, and S. Pankanti, "Filterbank-based Fingerprint Matching", *IEEE Trans. on Image Proc.*, Vol. 9, No. 5, pp. 846-859, May 2000.

Genetic Algorithms for Multi-classifier System Configuration: A Case Study in Character Recognition

K. Sirlantzis, M.C. Fairhurst, and M.S. Hoque

Department of Electronics, University of Kent, Canterbury, Kent, CT2 7NT, UK.
{K.Sirlantzis, M.C.Fairhurst, msh4}@ukc.ac.uk

Abstract. We describe a multiple classifier system which incorporates an automatic self-configuration scheme based on genetic algorithms. Our main interest in this paper is focused on exploring the statistical properties of the resulting multi-expert configurations. To this end we initially test the proposed system on a series of tasks of increasing difficulty drawn from the domain of character recognition. We then proceed to investigate the performance of our system not only in comparison to that of its constituent classifiers, but also in comparison to an independent set of individually optimised classifiers. Our results illustrate that significant gains can be obtained by integrating a genetic algorithm based optimisation process into multi-classifier schemes both in the performance enhancement and in the reduction of its volatility, especially as the task domain becomes more complex.

1 Introduction

The comparative advantages offered by multiple classifier systems are, by now, well appreciated by the pattern recognition community [8], [2]. Although a significant number of theoretical and empirical studies have been published to date, determining the optimal selection of constituent members for any particular multi-expert scheme remains an open question. Additionally, taking into consideration the variety of task domains encountered and varying degrees of task complexity and information availability (as expressed by the training set sizes), optimal selection is not always straightforward. Normally, reconfiguration is needed, usually through laborious experimentation and intuition, each time the training set or the task domain is changed. Considerations about the diversity of the properties of different individual classifiers add further complications to the reconfiguration process. For example, the generalisation capacity of some classifiers can lead to saturation as the training set size increases, resulting in highly volatile performance. On the other hand, some classifiers require increased training set sizes to achieve acceptable levels of performance (a well known example in this category is the $k-$nearest neightbours classifier). Finally, the variability of performance for some types of classifier leads to a significant dependence on the variability (complexity) of the particular task domain, while others seem to be more versatile.

J. Kittler and F. Roli (Eds.): MCS 2001, LNCS 2096, pp. 99–108, 2001.

In the light of these considerations it seems necessary to incorporate into a multiple classifier system a mechanism which will systematically attempt to optimise the structure every time the domain or the amount of available information changes. Such a mechanism should have the following properties:

1. To be a global optimisation technique which has been shown to be successful in highly complex domains, such as the space of the possible configurations for a multiple classifier system given a pool of individual classifiers.
2. To be generic in the sense that there will be no need for recoding each time the application domain or the training set size changes.
3. To offer a straightforward way to express the problem of optimisation of the multiple classifier structure.

Among the large number of the optimisation processes available, genetic algorithms [7] present a highly desirable choice which successfully fulfill the above requirements. Furthermore, initial reports of the application of genetic algorithms to multi-classifier systems have shown promising results [14] and [9].

In this paper we present a multiple classifier system which incorporates an automatic self-configuration scheme based on genetic algorithms. Our main interest is focused on exploring the statistical properties of the resulting multi-classifier configurations. To this end we initially test the proposed system on a series of tasks of increasing difficulty drawn from the domain of character recognition. We then proceed to investigate the performance of our system, initially, in comparison to that of its constituent classifiers, and finally and most importantly, in comparison to an independent set of individually optimised classifiers. In the following we will briefly describe the fusion scheme, the individual classifiers, and the genetic algorithm used, and we will proceed to discuss further the findings of our experimental investigation.

2   The Fusion Scheme

In the present work we draw the candidate members of the multi-classifier scheme from a pool of 12 individual classifiers which belong to four different classes. We use a parallel combination strategy where the constituent classifiers provide crisp decisions and the final classification is performed by a majority voting scheme where ties are broken arbitrarily. Diversity of classifiers is ensured by the use of either different training parameters or different feature sets, as can be seen in the following description. The classes of experts chosen are the following:

Binary Weighted Scheme(BWS): This is a type of classifier which is based on simple n-tuple sampling [12]. Here, memory elements calculate a Boolean function based on the sampled n-tuples. The decisive training parameter in this case is the size n of the n-tuple used, which defines the quality and capacity of the resulting classifier. In our experiments we used sizes of 5 (BWS1), 6 (BWS2), and 7 (BWS3).

Frequency Weighted Scheme(FWS): This is similar to the previous class in its structure, but, in this case, the memory elements calculate the relative frequency of occurrence of the sampled features [12]. The important parameter is again the size of the n-tuple used. We used again sizes of 5 (FWS1), 6 (FWS2), and 7 (FWS3).

Moment-based Pattern Classifier(MPC): This is a statistical classifier which explores the possible cluster formation with respect to a distance measure calculated on the nth order mathematical moments derived from the binarised patterns [12]. Crucial parameters are the order of the mathematical moments and the distance metric used. Our experiments use 7th order moments and a Euclidean metric (MOM1), 6th order and Mahalanobis metric (MOM2), and 7th order and Mahalanobis metric (MOM3).

k-Nearest Neighbours Classifier(KNN): This algorithm is based on initially determining the k instances from the training samples that are closest in a Euclidean n-dimensional space to the pattern to be classified. The classification decision is chosen as the class to which the majority of these nearest neighbours belong [11]. The number of neighbours considered and the features sampled form the set of important training parameters for this class. In this work we used the 5th order mathematical moments of the binarised images as the feature space and the three classifiers obtained had 1 (KNN1), 3 (KNN2), and 5 (KNN3) effective nearest neighbours.

3   The Set of Optimised Experts

While it is common in the literature to compare the performance of a multiple classifier scheme to that of its constituent classifiers, we provide an additional test to examine the performance enhancement provided by our scheme. We used a set of individually trained classifiers which do not participate in the aforementioned pool. These have been optimised experimentally with respect to their effective parameters and the optimal training set size. The optimal performances achieved in each of the different task domains used in our experiments are presented in Table 5. This set of classifiers consists of two groups. To the first group belong classifiers from classes included in our pool of candidates for the combination scheme. These are a Frequency Weighted Scheme classifier (FWS) with an n-tuple size of 12 [4], and a Moment-based Pattern Classifier which uses up to 7th order mathematical moments of the patterns (indicated as MAXL in the Table, because it uses a Maximum Likelihood-based distance measure) [13]. It should be noted here that these were included to provide a basis for comparisons with optimised versions of the classifiers used in the combination scheme. To the second group belong classifiers which come from classes often reported to provide excellent performance in the task domain of character recognition and they consequently present a valid benchmark for the performance obtained by our scheme. These classifiers are the following:

Hidden Markov Model Classifier (HMM): This is a statistical classifier based on the simulation of the evolution of the states of a Markov Chain

[3]. Its optimisation parameters include the number of states used and the number of symbols observed in each state. For the results presented we used 12 to 16 states with 16 symbols per state.

Scanning n-tuple Classifier (SNT): This is an enhancement of the basic n-tuple based class which works on the contour shape of the image represented using a chain coding scheme [10]. Again the critical parameters are the size of the n-tuple and the number of n-tuples used. Here we used five 5-tuples.

Multilayer Perceptron (MLP): This is the well-known Artificial Neural Network architecture trained using Backpropagation Learning [15]. Essential parameter in this case is the number of hidden units. The MLP classifier we used had 40 hidden units.

Moving Window Classifier (MWC): This is again an n-tuple based scheme which utilizes the idea of a window scanning the binarised image to provide partial classification indexes which are finally combined to obtain the overall classification decision [5]. In this case the critical parameters include the n-tuple size and the size of the moving window. Our results are based on an MWC using a 21x13 (pixels) window and n-tuples with size 12.

4   Optimisation of the Configuration

In genetic algorithms the solution to an optimisation problem is achieved as follows [6]: First, an initial set of possible solutions (population) to the problem encoded as bit strings (called chromosomes) are generated, usually randomly. Then, successive populations of solutions are constructed by applying to the previous population a number of transformations (called genetic operations), depending on their quality (called fitness of the chromosomes) as solutions to the particular problem in hand. Finally, the above recursion is terminated when a prespecified criterion (e.g. a level of fitness or a number of iterations) is met. The most commonly used genetic operators are: a) "selection" which determines which chromosomes will be selected to reproduce, b) "crossover" which defines how the children will be created from the parents (i.e. which parts of the parent chromosomes will be used in the children's chromosomes), and mutation which attempts to infuse diversity into the population by randomly changing the value of randomly selected parts of chromosomes. The genetic operators we used are:

Selection: We used the so-called classical Tournament method [1] to select chromosomes for reproduction.
Crossover: We used a two point crossover operator.
Mutation: This was applied in conjunction to the crossover operator.

The choice of a relatively simple genetic algorithm was made in order to facilitate better interpretability and clarity of our results.

The search in the space of possible multi-classifier system configurations is naturally encoded in our case as 12-bit binary string, where every bit represents an individual classifier with the value of 1 indicating participation in the combination scheme and 0 the opposite event. An exhaustive search in the set of all possible combinations involves excessively high computational time and load. The fitness function is, also, naturally defined as the recognition rate on an unknown evaluation set, as follows:

$$Fitness = (Correctly\ classified\ patterns)\ /\ (All\ tested\ patterns)\,.$$

It should be noted here that performing the optimisation based on the recognition rate over the training set, instead of an unknown evaluation set, although a perfectly valid procedure, would not provide a fitness measure which would reflect the property we are interested in, namely the generalisation ability of the resulting classifier system.

5 Experiments and Discussion

The two databases we used reflect our main aim in this work which is to explore the properties of the genetic algorithm generated multi-expert schemes in a range of tasks with varying complexity and level of available information. Each of the databases consists of 34 classes of pre-segmented characters (numerals 0-9, and upper case letters A-Z, without differentiation between the pairs 0/O and 1/I). The first database (D1) corresponds to machine-printed characters extracted from post codes on envelopes in the UK mail. The second (D2) corresponds to handwritten characters. In each database every class has 300 samples provided at a resolution of 16x24 pixels.

The experimental procedure adopted was as follows:

1. The samples in each class for each database were randomly divided into three disjoint sets to form a training set, an evaluation set, and a testing set. While the sizes of the evaluation and test sets were kept constant at 50 samples to enable comparisons, there were three sizes of training sets used (50, 100, and 200) in order to test for the effect of providing additional information.
2. The individual classifiers were trained.
3. The genetic algorithm was applied to the pool of trained classifiers. The population had a size of ten configurations and the genetic algorithm ran for 5 generations with a probability of crossover 0.85, and a mutation probability of 0.08. The two best individual configurations (chromosomes) were always copied to the next population to ensure that no deterioration in the performance will occur. The final configuration obtained is labelled Genetic in the Tables presented below.
4. Two alternative configuration schemes were constructed for comparisons, the first consisting of all the classifiers available (denoted Comb1 in our Tables) and the second consisting only of the individual classifiers that achieved a recognition rate above 50% on the evaluation set (indicated as Comb2).
5. Finally, all resulting solutions were tested on the disjoint test set.

The above process was repeated 10 times with different random starting points in each case, for each one of the different training set sizes, and for each of the databases. The same experiments were repeated for both databases first using only a 10 class problem (the numerals) and then the whole of the available

Table 1. Recognition rate statistics (%) in Database D1 (10 classes).

	Training set size					
	$n = 50$		$n = 100$		$n = 200$	
	Mean	Std	Mean	Std	Mean	Std
BWS1	98.52	0.6941	98.86	0.3134	98.74	0.3658
BWS2	98.42	0.6070	99.04	0.5060	99.02	0.3938
BWS3	*98.66	0.4904	*99.14	0.4006	*99.14	0.2836
FWS1	94.26	1.2438	95.36	1.0741	94.84	0.7763
FWS2	94.72	1.0881	95.20	1.1035	94.86	0.8996
FWS3	95.08	1.0963	95.84	1.1108	95.30	0.7846
MOM1	57.66	2.8814	57.52	1.7943	56.82	1.8606
MOM2	96.18	0.7685	96.84	0.7531	97.30	0.7958
MOM3	95.54	0.9383	96.82	0.7743	97.48	0.6613
KNN1	83.16	2.2426	86.94	1.2580	87.92	1.3506
KNN2	84.06	2.4295	87.72	1.2479	88.44	1.4261
KNN3	85.12	2.6553	88.30	1.3004	89.16	0.9652
Comb1	98.40	0.7424	98.92	0.5594	98.66	0.3893
Comb2	98.40	0.7424	98.92	0.5594	98.66	0.3893
Genetic	98.60	0.8273	99.46	0.1897	99.64	0.2633

34 classes (digits and upper case letters) to form a sequence of increasingly difficult problems. Our results represent the averaged performance of these 10 runs in each of these cases (indicated as Mean in Tables 1–4). To examine the variability of these performances with respect to different training set sizes and on different task domains we calculated, also, the standard deviations based on these 10 runs (indicated as Std in the Tables).

An initial inspection of the Mean recognition rates presented reveals that the configurations found by the genetic algorithm-based optimisation (indicated Genetic) are consistently better than the best individual classifier in the pool (indicated by * in the Tables). Also, in every case, these configurations outperform the two alternative combination schemes proposed (denoted Comb1 and Comb2 in the Tables). Additional examination of the same Tables show that in most cases the variability of the performance of the genetic algorithm proposed configurations is smaller than the variability of the performances of the individual classifiers and the alternative combination schemes examined here.

We can now examine the properties of the genetic algorithm-generated solutions as we move from less to more additional information availability (as expressed by the training set sizes) for each of the task domains (machine-printed to handwritten character recognition). Clearly, for the easiest tasks (database D1, Tables 1, 3) as the training set size increases the variability of the performances decreases in most of the cases. However, the same is not true for the most difficult tasks (database D2, Tables 2, 4) where the variability inherent in the data sets is higher.

Two important observations can be made here. First, some of the individual classifiers show signs of saturation in their generalisation capacity, presenting

Table 2. Recognition rate statistics (%) in Database D2 (10 classes).

	Training set size					
	$n = 50$		$n = 100$		$n = 200$	
	Mean	Std	Mean	Std	Mean	Std
BWS1	85.86	1.3201	84.04	1.3978	80.66	4.3595
BWS2	87.88	1.8861	87.18	1.3315	86.14	2.7746
BWS3	*87.98	1.4093	*89.06	0.7058	89.26	2.6399
FWS1	79.60	1.9956	79.64	1.6406	81.20	1.3367
FWS2	80.38	2.3953	80.16	1.4010	81.70	1.5384
FWS3	79.58	1.8390	80.60	1.3728	82.74	0.8435
MOM1	44.52	1.7106	43.70	2.2652	44.44	1.9039
MOM2	81.20	2.0000	84.54	1.7815	87.76	1.6487
MOM3	83.08	1.1555	86.58	1.8023	*89.84	1.9202
KNN1	59.14	2.0807	63.98	2.7397	72.66	6.7192
KNN2	60.44	2.0887	65.98	2.5094	74.08	6.0282
KNN3	62.82	2.1301	67.40	2.5820	75.56	5.2492
Comb1	89.54	1.3167	89.68	1.2621	92.68	2.8146
Comb2	90.00	1.4996	90.26	1.0458	93.06	2.8799
Genetic	91.00	1.4453	93.94	1.1664	96.60	0.8641

higher standard deviations as the training set size increases. Typical examples are the three BWS classifiers, which in contrast to the FWS classifiers, present a constant or even decreased mean recognition rate but gradually increasing standard deviations. Second, some of the classifiers reveal their high dependence on the training set size and their sensitivity to the variability in the data set. A typical example in this case is the KNN classifiers, for which, while the performance increases with the training set size, its variability increases as well. As a general observation we can see that all the combination schemes examined help to reduce the variability in performance as expressed by the standard deviations. However, it is easily realised that additional benefit is gained, in terms of improving the stability of the observed performance, by the configurations produced by the genetic algorithm scheme, as we move to the more complex task domains (handwritten characters with 34 class problem). It is important, also, to note that in all our experiments the average number of classifiers chosen by the optimisation process to participate in the final solutions ranged from six (6) to eight (8). This suggests that, additional to the improvements in the performance, the genetic algorithm based optimisation can offer savings in the computational load required.

Finally, we can move to the second principal question to be addressed, the comparative performance of the genetic algorithm generated solutions with respect to a set of independently optimised individual classifiers. The performances of the latter are presented in the top part of Table 5, while in the bottom part we present the minimum and maximum (indicated MINPOOL and MAXPOOL respectively) of the performances achieved by the classifiers participating in the pool for the configuration optimisation, in the corresponding cases (training set

Table 3. Recognition rate statistics (%) in Database D1 (34 classes).

	Training set size					
	$n = 50$		$n = 100$		$n = 200$	
	Mean	Std	Mean	Std	Mean	Std
BWS1	96.73	2.0048	97.50	0.3825	97.73	0.5227
BWS2	*97.04	1.9933	98.04	0.2882	98.47	0.3620
BWS3	96.98	1.9212	*98.24	0.2958	*98.67	0.3236
FWS1	92.38	2.0258	93.11	0.7614	92.81	0.3344
FWS2	92.59	1.8017	93.31	0.8430	93.23	0.3892
FWS3	92.82	2.2611	93.41	0.4878	93.62	0.4216
MOM1	38.85	0.7966	39.32	1.0287	39.85	0.8448
MOM2	89.62	3.3977	93.45	1.3382	94.94	0.6031
MOM3	90.90	2.8450	94.68	1.4398	96.11	0.8181
KNN1	66.42	0.9642	70.88	1.9108	76.35	3.7481
KNN2	67.95	1.0895	72.30	1.7867	77.66	3.6160
KNN3	69.25	1.1210	73.88	1.7251	78.81	3.4442
Comb1	96.95	2.0733	97.77	0.4509	98.45	0.6438
Comb2	97.15	1.9927	97.96	0.4225	98.60	0.6551
Genetic	97.48	1.8923	98.82	0.4205	99.18	0.5735

size 200). It is easy to observe that the former outperform the latter, as in most cases the best performance of the classifiers in the pool (MAXPOOL) is worst than the worst obtained by the optimised group. In the top part of Table 6, we present the improvement in performances achieved by the genetic algorithm-based configurations, expressed as differences between the average recognition rates of the genetic algorithm produced solutions and the best individual classifier in the pool (the negative signs indicate deterioration in performance). The bottom part of the same Table (row 4) presents the corresponding performance differences between the genetically produced solutions and the best classifier in the optimised group. It is not difficult to see that the performance enhancement achieved by the solutions generated genetically increases significantly as the available information increases but, most importantly, also as we move towards more complex task domains.

6   Conclusions

This paper has presented a multiple classifier system which incorporates an automatic self-configuration scheme based on genetic algorithms, and has further investigated some of its statistical properties in a range of tasks of increasing difficulty drawn from the domain of character recognition. Our main questions in this study were the relative stability of the performance of the proposed scheme and the possible performance enhancement that can be achieved, not only with respect to the participating individual classifiers, but also with respect to a diverse group of classifiers which were individually and independently optimised for the tasks in hand. Our findings strongly suggest, in compliance with, and in

Table 4. Recognition rate statistics (%) in Database D2 (34 classes).

	Training set size					
	$n = 50$		$n = 100$		$n = 200$	
	Mean	Std	Mean	Std	Mean	Std
BWS1	70.81	2.1925	68.32	3.8472	63.15	7.0037
BWS2	73.74	1.7536	73.42	3.6810	71.25	7.2861
BWS3	*75.29	1.3351	75.85	3.4415	76.48	6.6236
FWS1	58.12	1.9307	58.67	1.3238	59.39	1.7851
FWS2	59.65	1.4496	59.57	1.8719	59.91	1.7291
FWS3	59.75	2.2004	60.14	2.1262	60.33	2.0437
MOM1	26.69	1.2419	26.55	0.8637	26.84	0.6899
MOM2	69.11	1.7130	74.24	2.2711	76.44	2.0000
MOM3	70.38	1.6733	*76.71	2.5400	*79.55	2.3024
KNN1	40.38	4.1742	44.43	6.1929	50.28	14.9791
KNN2	41.56	4.2913	45.84	6.1871	52.19	14.3573
KNN3	43.54	4.1489	47.72	5.6984	54.30	13.4194
Comb1	77.58	1.6930	79.98	3.8026	80.62	6.0651
Comb2	79.85	1.7335	81.84	2.8193	82.61	5.2548
Genetic	81.67	1.8372	85.73	1.4009	91.38	3.4990

addition to, previously reported results, that the comparative benefits that can be gained by integrating a genetic algorithm-based optimisation scheme into the multiple classifier system, are significant and increase as the available information on a specific problem domain increases. The most important observation, however, is that the benefits of this approach to classifier design increase substantially as task complexity increases.

Acknowledgement. The authors gratefully acknowledge the support of the UK Engineering and Physical Sciences Research Council.

References

1. A. Brindle, *Genetic algorithms for function optimization.* Included in TCGA Tech. Report No. 91002, University of Alabama, Tuscaloosa, AL 35487, USA (Report authors: R. E. Smith, D. E. Goldberg and J. A. Earickson).
2. T.G. Dietterich. Machine Learning Research: Four Current Directions. *AI Magazine*, 18(4):97–136, 1997.
3. A.J. Elms and J. Illingworth. Combination of HMMs for the representation of printed characters in noisy document images. *Image and Vision Computing*, 13(5):385–392, 1995.
4. M.C. Fairhurst and T.J. Stonham. A classification system for alphanumeric characters based on learning network techniques. *Digital Processes,*, 2:321–339, 1976.
5. M.C. Fairhurst and M.S. Hoque. Moving window classifier: approach to off-line image recognition. *Ellectronics Letters*, 36(7):628–630, 2000.
6. D.E. Goldberg. *Genetic Algorithms in Search, Optimization, and Machine Learning.* Addison-Wesley Publishing Company, Inc., 1989.

Table 5. Average performance (%) of the optimised individual classifiers and the minimum and maximum performance of the classifiers in the pool of candidates.

	10 classes		34 classes	
	D1	D2	D1	D2
FWS	99.1	91.1	98.5	80.0
HMM	97.9	89.1	96.3	81.2
SNT	99.5	*95.8	98.2	*89.3
MAXL	96.1	90.5	94.1	80.0
MLP	98.3	92.2	96.3	81.1
MWC	*99.7	94.4	*99.2	85.5
MINPOOL	56.82	44.44	39.85	26.84
MAXPOOL	99.14	89.84	98.67	79.55

Table 6. Improvements in recognition rate (%)

Training set size	10 classes		34 classes	
	D1	D2	D1	D2
$n = 50$	−0.06	3.02	0.44	6.38
$n = 100$	0.32	4.88	0.58	9.02
$n = 200$	0.50	6.76	0.51	11.83
$n = 200$	−0.06	0.80	−0.02	2.08

7. J.H. Holland. *Adaption in Natural and Artificial Systems.* University of Michigan Press, Ann Arbor, 1975.
8. J. Kittler, M. Hatef, R.P.W. Duin, and J. Matas. On combining classifiers. *IEEE Transactions on Pattern Analysis and Machine Intelligence*, 20(3):226–239, 1998.
9. L.I. Kuncheva and L.C. Jain. Designing classifier fusion systems by genetic algorithms. *IEEE Transactions on Evolutionary Computation*, 4(4):327–336, 2000.
10. S. Lucas. Can scanning n-tuple classifiers be improved by pre-transforming training data? In *IEE Workshop on Handwriting Analysis and Recognition - A European Perspective (Ref. No 1996/165)*, pages 4/1–6, IEE, UK, 1996.
11. D. Michie, D.J. Spiegelhalter, and C.C. Taylor. *Machine Learning, Neural and Statistical Classification.* Ellis Horwood Series in Artificial Intelligence. Ellis Horwood Ltd, London, 1994.
12. A.F.R. Rahman and M.C. Fairhurst. An evaluation of multi-expert configurations for recognition of handwritten numerals. *Pattern Recog.*, 31(9):1255–1273, 1998.
13. A.F.R. Rahman and M.C. Fairhurst. Machine-printed character recognition revisited: Re-application of recent advances in handwritten character recognition research. *Special Issue on Document Image Processing and Multimedia Environments, Image & Vision Computing*, 16(12-13):819–842, 1998.
14. A.F.R. Rahman and M.C. Fairhurst. Automatic self-configuration of a novel multiple-expert classifier using a genetic algorithm. In *Proc. Int. Conf. on Image Processing and Applications (IPA'99)*, volume 1, pages 57–61, 1999.
15. D.E. Rumelhart, G.E. Hinton, and R.J. Williams. *Learning internal representations by error propagation, in Parallel Distributed Processing*, volume 1, pages 318–362. MIT Press, Cambridge, MA, 1986. D.E. Rumelhart and J.L. McClelland(Eds.).

Combined Classification of Handwritten Digits Using the 'Virtual Test Sample Method'

Jörg Dahmen, Daniel Keysers, and Hermann Ney

Lehrstuhl für Informatik VI, Computer Science Department
RWTH Aachen - University of Technology
D-52056 Aachen, Germany
{dahmen, keysers, ney}@informatik.rwth-aachen.de

Abstract. In this paper, we present a combined classification approach called the 'virtual test sample method'. Contrary to classifier combination, where the outputs of a number of classifiers are used to come to a combined decision for a given observation, we use multiple instances generated from the original observation and a single classifier to compute a combined decision. In our experiments, the virtual test sample method is used to improve the performance of a statistical classifier based on Gaussian mixture densities. We show that this approach has some desirable theoretical properties and performs very well, especially when combined with the use of invariant distance measures. In the experiments conducted throughout this work, we obtained an excellent error rate of 2.2% on the original US Postal Service task.

1 Introduction

In this paper, we present a combined classification approach called the 'virtual test sample method' (VTS), which is based on the idea of using a single classifier to classify a set of observations which are known to belong to the same class. This approach is somewhat contrary to the common idea of classifier combination, where the outputs of different classifiers are combined to come to a final decision for a given observation. In our approach, a number of instances is created from the original observation using prior knowledge about the classification task. For example, in handwritten digit recognition, invariance to image shifts and other affine transformations plays an important role. Thus, VTS can be considered a counterpart of the common creation of virtual training data ('perturbation of the training data'). In the experiments, it is used to improve the performance of a Bayesian classifier based on Gaussian mixture densities. We show that using VTS not only yields state-of-the-art results on the well known US Postal Service handwritten digit recognition task (USPS), but that it also has some desirable theoretical properties.

In the next section, we describe the US Postal Service database used in our experiments and present some state-of-the-art results that were reported on this database in the last years. In Section 3, we briefly discuss the idea of classifier combination and one particular classifier combination scheme, namely the very

J. Kittler and F. Roli (Eds.): MCS 2001, LNCS 2096, pp. 109–118, 2001.

popular sum rule. In Section 4, the VTS method is presented and its theoretical properties are discussed. In Section 5, the statistical classifier we used in our experiments (in combination with VTS) is described. In this context, we will also discuss possibilities to incorporate invariances into the classifier which go beyond the use of virtual test samples. This is done by creating virtual training data and by using an invariant distance measure called tangent distance, which was proposed by Simard in 1993 [14]. After presenting some experimental results in Section 6, the paper is ended by drawing some conclusions and giving an outlook to future work in Section 7.

2   The US Postal Service Task & Feature Analysis

The USPS database (`ftp://ftp.kyb.tuebingen.mpg.de/pub/bs/data/`) is a well known handwritten digit recognition task. It contains 7,291 training examples and 2,007 test examples. The digits are isolated and represented as 16×16 pixels sized grayscale images (see Figure 1). Making use of 'appearance based pattern recognition', we interpret each pixel as a feature in our experiments, resulting in 256-dimensional feature vectors. Because of this rather high-dimensional feature space, we optionally apply a linear discriminant analysis (LDA, [5]) for feature reduction. As the maximum number of features that can be extracted by applying the LDA to a K-class problem is $K - 1$, we create four pseudoclasses for each USPS digit class by training a mixture with four densities using the algorithms described in Section 5. Thus, the resulting feature vectors are 39-dimensional [2]. One of the advantages of USPS is that many recognition results have been reported by various research groups throughout the last years. Because of that, a meaningful comparison of the different classifiers is possible, with some results given in Tab. 1. Error rates marked with an asterisk were obtained using a modified USPS training set, which – resulting in restricted comparability – was extended by adding 2,418 machine printed digits.

3   The Idea of Classifier Combination

The idea of classifier combination the following: Given a particular pattern recognition problem, the goal is usually to implement a system which achieves the best possible recognition results on unseen data. Thus, in many cases, a variety of pattern recognition approaches is evaluated and the one performing best is

Fig. 1. Example images taken from USPS.

Table 1. Results reported on USPS.

Author	Method	Error [%]
Simard[+] 1993	Human Performance	2.5
Vapnik 1995	Decision Tree C4.5	16.2
Freund & Schapire 1996	AdaBoost & Nearest Neighbour	*6.4
Simard[+] 1998	Five-Layer Neural Net	4.2
Schölkopf 1997	Support Vectors	4.0
Schölkopf[+] 1998	Invariant Support Vectors	3.0
Drucker[+] 1993	Boosted Neural Net	*2.6
Simard[+] 1993	Tangent Distance & Nearest Neighbour	*2.5
This work:	Gaussian Mixtures, Invariances	2.2

*: 2418 machine printed digits were added to the training set

chosen to solve the task. Unfortunately – in that approach – all other systems that have been developed are useless. In opposite to this, the idea of classifier combination is to use all classifiers $C_m, m = 1, ..., M$ for classification and to come to a final decision by combining the outputs in a suitable way (cp. Fig. 2). In the last years, many combination approaches have been considered, among them the product rule, the sum rule, or the median rule, where in some cases the 'vote' of a classifier is weighted according to its performance on the training set (i.e. boosting methods). Note that if such combination rules should be meaningful, the outputs of the classifiers must be normalized. Thus, we assume that - given the observation $x \in \mathbb{R}^D$ - each classifier C_m computes posterior probabilities $p_m(k|x)$ for each class $k = 1, ..., K$, which are normalized in the sense that $\sum_{k=1}^{K} p(k|x) = 1$. It should be noted that – for instance – the outputs of an artificial neural net approximate such posterior probabilities [10], assuming that a sufficient amount of training data is available. Thus, normalization comes for free in many applications.

For a single classifier, the Bayesian decision rule can be used for classification:

$$x \mapsto r(x) = \operatorname*{argmax}_{k} \{p(k|x)\} = \operatorname*{argmax}_{k} \left\{ \frac{p(k) \cdot p(x|k)}{\sum_{k'=1}^{K} p(k') \cdot p(x|k')} \right\}, \quad (1)$$

where $p(k)$ is the prior probability of class k and $p(x|k)$ is the class conditional probability for the observation x given class k. Note that the denominator of Eq. (1) is independent of k and can be neglected for classification purposes. If different classifiers C_m are available (computing posterior probabilities $p_m(k|x)$) the final decision can – for instance – be obtained using the sum rule

$$x \mapsto r(x) = \operatorname*{argmax}_{k} \left\{ \sum_{m=1}^{M} p_m(k|x) \right\}. \quad (2)$$

Although Eq. (2) is widely accepted to yield state-of-the-art results in many applications, KITTLER assumed in his derivation of the sum rule that the posterior probabilities $p_m(k|x)$ computed by the different classifiers do not differ much from the prior probabilities $p(k)$ [9]. In other words, the derivation of

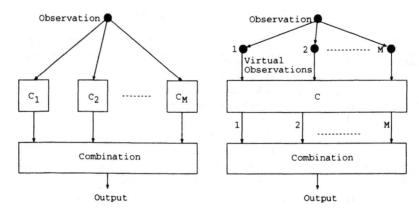

Fig. 2. Classifier combination (left) vs. the virtual test sample method (right).

the sum rule for classifier combination is based on the strong assumption that the features extracted from the data contain no discriminatory information. Interestingly, KITTLER also observed that the good performance of the sum rule could possibly be explained by its error tolerance: Using the sum rule, errors in estimating the real (and therefore usually unknown) posterior probabilities are dampened, while for instance in the case of the product rule, these estimation errors are amplified [9].

If no set of classifiers exists for combination, techniques like 'bagging' [1] or 'boosting' [13] exist, which generate a variety of classifiers using different subsets (bagging) respectively differently weighted versions of the training data (boosting) for training. Here, it is assumed that the classifiers are 'instable', i.e. that modifications of the training set have a significant impact on the resulting classifier. Otherwise, combination of the resulting classifiers would be pointless.

4   The Virtual Test Sample Method

The basic idea of the virtual test sample method is to create a number of 'virtual test samples' starting from the original observation, to classify each of these separately using a single classifier C and to suitably combine these decisions to a final decision for the original observation (cp. Fig. 2). In handwritten digit recognition, invariance to affine transformations is usually desired, but generally speaking all transformations respecting class membership can be considered here. Thus, given the observation x, we can create virtual test samples $x(\alpha) = t(x, \alpha)$, $\alpha \in \mathcal{M}$, with $M = |\mathcal{M}|$, where $t(x, \alpha)$ is a transformation with parameters $\alpha \in \mathbb{R}^L$. In the experiments, ± 1 pixel shifts were applied, i.e. $M = 9$ (eight shifts and the original image). As an image cannot be shifted into different directions at the same time, the resulting 'events' $x(\alpha)$, $\alpha \in \mathcal{M}$ can be regarded as being mutually exclusive and a final decision can be computed as follows:

$$x \longmapsto r(x) \;\; = \;\; \underset{k}{\operatorname{argmax}} \{p(k|x)\}$$

$$= \operatorname*{argmax}_{k} \left\{ \sum_{\alpha \in \mathcal{M}} p(k, \alpha | x) \right\}$$

$$= \operatorname*{argmax}_{k} \left\{ \sum_{\alpha \in \mathcal{M}} p(\alpha | x) \cdot p(k | x, \alpha) \right\}$$

$$\stackrel{model}{=} \operatorname*{argmax}_{k} \left\{ \sum_{\alpha \in \mathcal{M}} p(\alpha) \cdot p(k | x(\alpha)) \right\} \tag{3}$$

Here, the simultaneous occurrence of an observation x and a parameter vector $\alpha \in \mathbb{R}^{L}$ is modeled by the virtual test sample $x(\alpha)$, i.e. by applying the respective transformation to the observation. Furthermore, α is assumed to be independent of x. Thus, to come to a final decision for the original observation, we only have to add the posterior probabilities $p(k | x(\alpha))$, weighted with the prior probabilities $p(\alpha)$ of the transformation parameters. In the experiments conducted throughout this work - if nothing else is said - these transformation parameters are assumed to be uniformly distributed. Thus, the prior probabilities $p(\alpha)$ can be neglected for classification purposes and Eq. (3) reduces to

$$x \longmapsto r(x) = \operatorname*{argmax}_{k} \left\{ \sum_{\alpha \in \mathcal{M}} p(k | x(\alpha)) \right\} \tag{4}$$

The only assumption needed here is the mutual exclusiveness of the virtual test samples. As each of these is the result of applying a unique transformation to the given observation, this assumption seems reasonable. This 'virtual test sample method' has a number of desirable properties:

Computational Complexity:
The computational complexity of the VTS recognition step is the same as that of classifier combination. Yet, only one classifier has to be trained in the VTS training phase, which is especially important for statistical classifiers, where the training step is computationally expensive in many cases.

Theoretical Basis:
In contrast to the derivation of the sum rule in the framework of classifier combination, VTS sum rule is straightforward to derive, with the assumption of mutual exclusiveness of the $x(\alpha)$ sounding reasonable.

Increased Transformation Tolerance/ Invariance:
Obviously, invariance properties with respect to the transformations used for virtual test data creation are incorporated into the classifier.

Ease of Implementation & Effectiveness:
Assuming a suitable normalization of the classifier's output, VTS is very simple to embed into an existing classifier. Furthermore, using VTS significantly reduced the error rates in the experiments conducted throughout this work. For real-time applications, VTS is straightforward to parallelize (just like classifier combination), as it is inherently parallel.

Applicable together with Classifier Combination:
In principle, VTS and classifier combination can be used at the same time. Doing so, our best VTS result could in fact be slightly improved (cp. Section 7).

Incorporation of Prior Knowledge about Transformation Probabilities:
Finally, it is possible to incorporate prior knowledge into VTS classification via an appropriate choice of the probabilities $p(\alpha)$ (our model) respectively $p(\alpha|x)$. For instance, in a statistical framework as the one presented in the next section, these probabilities could be learned from the training data.

5   The Statistical Classifier

In this section, we describe the statistical classifier which we used in combination with the VTS method in our experiments. To classify an observation $x \in \mathbb{R}^D$, we use the Bayesian decision rule as given in Eq. (1), which is known to minimize the number of expected classification errors in the case that the true distributions $p(k)$ and $p(x|k)$ are known. Naturally, as these are unknown in most practical applications, we have to choose models for them and learn the respective parameters using the training data. In the experiments, we choose $p(k) = \frac{1}{K}$, $k = 1, ..., K$, and model the class conditional probabilities $p(x|k)$ using Gaussian mixture densities (GMD) (see Eq. (6)) respectively Gaussian kernel densities (GKD). In order to keep the number of free model parameters small (and thus allow for reliable parameter estimation), we make use of a globally pooled covariance matrix

$$\Sigma = \sum_{k=1}^{K} \sum_{i=1}^{I_k} \frac{N_{ki}}{N} \cdot \Sigma_{ki}, \tag{5}$$

where Σ_{ki} is the covariance matrix of component density i of class k and N_{ki} is the number of observations that are assigned to that particular density. Thus, we obtain the following expression for the class conditional probabilities:

$$p(x|k) = \sum_{i=1}^{I_k} c_{ki} \cdot \mathcal{N}(x|\mu_{ki}, \Sigma), \tag{6}$$

where I_k is the number of component densities used to model class k, c_{ki} are weight coefficients (with $c_{ki} > 0$ and $\sum_{i=1}^{I_k} c_{ki} = 1$, which is necessary to ensure that $p(x|k)$ is a probability density function) and μ_{ki} is the mean vector of component density i of class k. Furthermore, we only use a diagonal covariance matrix, i.e. a variance vector. Note that this does not lead to a loss of information, since a Gaussian mixture of that form can still approximate any density function with arbitrary precision. Maximum likelihood parameter estimation is now done using the Expectation-Maximization algorithm [3]. Concerning Gaussian kernel densities it should be pointed out that these can be regarded an extreme case of a Gaussian mixture, where each reference sample x_n defines a Gaussian normal distribution $\mathcal{N}(x|x_n, \Sigma)$ [8].

Note that the approach presented above is only invariant with respect to transformations that are present in the training data. In the following, we therefore briefly describe two possibilities to enhance the invariance properties of the statistical classifier that go beyond the usage of VTS.

5.1 Creation of Virtual Training Data

A typical drawback of statistical classifiers is their need for a large amount of training data, which is not always available. A common solution for this problem is the creation of virtual training data. Here, just like for the VTS method, ± 1 pixel shifts were chosen, resulting in $9 \cdot 7{,}291 = 65{,}619$ reference samples.

5.2 Incorporating Invariant Distance Measures

Another way to incorporate invariances is to use invariant probability density functions or - equivalently - invariant distance measures [7]. Here, we choose tangent distance (TD), which proved to be especially effective for optical character recognition. In [14], the authors observed that reasonably small transformations of certain objects (like digits) do not affect class membership. Simple distance measures like Euclidean or Mahalanobis distance do not account for this and are very sensitive to transformations like translations or rotations. When an image x of size $I \times J$ is transformed (e.g. scaled and rotated) with a transformation $t(x, \alpha)$ which depends on L parameters $\alpha \in \mathbb{R}^L$ (e.g. the scaling factor and the rotation angle), the set of all transformed images $M_x = \{t(x, \alpha) : \alpha \in \mathbb{R}^L\} \subset \mathbb{R}^{I \times J}$ is a manifold of at most L dimensions. The distance between two images can now be defined as the minimum distance between their according manifolds, being truly invariant with respect to the L transformations regarded. Unfortunately, computation of this distance is a hard optimization problem and the manifolds needed have no analytic expression in general. Therefore, small transformations of an image x are approximated by a tangent subspace $\hat{M}_x$ to the manifold M_x at the point x. Those transformations can be obtained by adding to x a linear combination of the vectors $x_l, l = 1, ..., L$ that span the tangent subspace. Thus, we obtain as a first-order approximation of M_x:

$$\hat{M}_x = \left\{ x + \sum_{l=1}^{L} \alpha_l \cdot x_l : \alpha \in \mathbb{R}^L \right\} \subset \mathbb{R}^{I \times J} \tag{7}$$

Now, the single sided TD $D_T(x, \mu)$ between two images x and μ is defined as

$$D_T(x, \mu) = \min_{\alpha} \left\{ \left\| x + \sum_{l=1}^{L} \alpha_l \cdot x_l - \mu \right\|^2 \right\} \tag{8}$$

The tangent vectors x_l can be computed using finite differences between the original image x and a small transformation of x [14]. Furthermore, a double sided TD can also be defined by approximating M_x and M_μ. In the experiments, we computed seven tangent vectors for translations (2), rotation, scaling, axis

$$\frac{1}{16} \begin{array}{|ccc|} \hline 1 & 2 & 1 \\ 2 & 4 & 2 \\ 1 & 2 & 1 \\ \hline \end{array}$$

Fig. 3. Prior probabilities $p(\alpha)$ chosen for image shifts in the experiments. For example, the prior probability for the original (i.e. unchanged) image is $(4/16) = 0.25$.

deformations (2) and line thickness as proposed by Simard [14]. Given that the tangent vectors are orthogonal, Eq. (8) can be solved efficiently by computing

$$D_T(x, \mu) = \|x - \mu\|^2 - \sum_{l=1}^{L} \frac{[(x - \mu)^t \cdot x_l]^2}{\|x_l\|^2} \tag{9}$$

The combination of TD with virtual data creation makes sense, as TD is only approximately invariant with respect to the transformations considered. Thus, creating virtual training data yields a better approximation of the original manifold, as the virtual training images lie exactly on it.

For the calculation of the Mahalanobis distance, the observation x and the references μ_{ki} are replaced by the optimal tangent approximations $x(\alpha_{opt})$ respectively $\mu_{ki}(\alpha_{opt})$ in the TD experiments. When calculating single sided TD, the tangents are applied on the side of the references. Note that TD can also be used to compute a 'tangent covariance matrix', which is defined as the empirical covariance matrix of all possible tangent approximations of the references [2]. Further information on a probabilistic interpretation of TD is given in [7].

6 Results

The experiments were started by applying the statistical approach described in Section 5 to the high-dimensional USPS data, using different combinations of virtual training and test data. In Tab. 2, the notation 'a-b' indicates that we increased the number of training samples by a factor of a and that of the test samples by a factor of b. Thus, $b=9$ indicates the use of VTS. As can be seen, VTS significantly reduces the error rate on USPS from 8.0% to 6.6% (without virtual training data) respectively from 6.4% to 6.0% (with virtual training data). These error rates can be further reduced by applying an LDA. Thus, the best error rate decreases from 6.0% to 3.4%, which is mainly because parameter estimation is more reliable in this rather low-dimensional feature space. Note that in this case, applying VTS reduced the 9-1 error rate from 4.5% to 3.4%, being a relative improvement of 24.4%. This error rate could be slightly improved to 3.3% by assuming a Gaussian distribution for the prior probabilities $p(\alpha)$, resulting in the template depicted in Figure 3. As a key experiment, we boosted the statistical classifier based on 39 LDA features using AdaBoost.M1 [6] for $M = 10$. Indeed, we were able to reduce the 9-1 error rate from 4.5% to 4.2%, yet VTS - by reducing the error rate from 4.5% to 3.4% - significantly outperformed AdaBoost on this particular dataset.

In another experiment, we investigated on the use of TD in combination with VTS. These experiments were performed in the high-dimensional feature space

Table 2. USPS results for Mahalanobis/ tangent distance, with/ without LDA.

Method:	Error rate [%]			
	1-1	1-9	9-1	9-9
GMD,	8.0	6.6	6.4	6.0
GMD, LDA,	6.7	5.9	4.5	3.4
GMD, tangent distance	3.9	3.6	3.4	2.9
GKD, tangent distance	3.0	2.6	2.5	2.4

(no LDA), as TD in its basic form is defined on images (although it can also be defined on arbitrary feature spaces, where the tangent vectors are learned from the data itself [7]). Using single sided TD, the best error rate could be reduced from 3.4% for the LDA based statistical classifier to 2.9% (using single sided TD and about 1,000 normal distributions per class). This error rate could be further reduced to 2.7% by using double sided TD. Replacing the mixture density approach by kernel densities, the VTS error rate was reduced to 2.4%. In these experiments, standard deviations were used instead of diagonal covariance matrices. Finally, by combining the outputs of five VTS based kernel density classifiers (using different norms in the distance calculations and different kinds of training data multiplication), the error rate could be further reduced to 2.2%. To make sure that these good results are not the result of overfitting, we also applied our best kernel density based USPS classifier (error rate 2.4%) to the well known MNIST task without further parameter tuning, obtaining a state-of-the-art result of 1.0% (1.3% without VTS). Although this result is not the best known on MNIST (the best error rate of 0.7% was reported by DRUCKER in [4]), it shows that the algorithms presented here generalize well.

7 Conclusions & Outlook

In this paper, we presented a combined classification approach called the 'virtual test sample method', which is based on using a single classifier in combination with artificially created test samples. Thus, it can be regarded as a counterpart to the creation of virtual training data, which is a common approach in pattern recognition. We showed that the proposed method is straightforward to justify and has some desirable properties, among them the possible incorporation of prior knowledge and the fact that only a single classifier has to be trained. In our experiments, the approach was used to improve the performance of a statistical classifier based on the use of Gaussian mixture densities in the context of the Bayesian decision rule. The results obtained on the well known US Postal Service task are state-of-the-art, especially when the virtual test sample method is combined with the incorporation of invariances into the classifier, which was done by using SIMARD's tangent distance and resulted in an error rate of 2.2%. Finally, the approach seems to generalize well, as a state-of-the-art error rate of 1.0% was also obtained on the MNIST handwritten digit task. Besides developing better models for the probabilities $p(\alpha)$ respectively $p(\alpha|x)$ considered in the virtual test sample method, future work will also include investigating its effectiveness in other pattern recognition domains.

Acknowledgement. The authors wish to thank the student researchers Mark Oliver Güld and Ralf Perrey for implementing parts of the methods and conducting some of the experiments described in this paper.

References

1. Breiman, L.: Bagging Predictors. Technical Report 421, Department of Statistics, University of California at Berkeley, 1994.
2. Dahmen, J., Keysers, D., Ney, H., Güld, M.: Statistical Image Object Recognition using Mixture Densities. Journal of Mathematical Imaging and Vision, Vol. 14, No. 3, Kluwer Academic Publishers, pp. 285-296, May 2001.
3. Dempster A., Laird, N., Rubin, D.: Maximum Likelihood from Incomplete Data via the EM Algorithm. Journal of the Royal Statistical Society, 39(B), pp. 1–38, 1977.
4. Drucker, H., Schapire, R., Simard, P.: Boosting Performance in Neural Networks. Int. Journal of Pattern Recognition and Artificial Intelligence, Vol. 7, No. 4, pp. 705–719, 1993.
5. Duda, R., Hart, P.: Pattern Classification and Scene Analysis. John Wiley & Sons, 1973.
6. Freund, Y., Schapire, R.: Experiments with a New Boosting Algorithm. 13th Int. Conference on Machine Learning, Bari, Italy, pp. 148-156, July 1996.
7. Keysers, D., Dahmen, J., Ney, H.: A Probabilistic View on Tangent Distance. 22nd Symposium German Association for Pattern Recognition (DAGM), Kiel, Germany, pp. 107-114, 2000.
8. Keysers, D., Dahmen, J., Theiner, T., Ney, H.: Experiments with an Extended Tangent Distance. 15th Int. Conference on Pattern Recognition, Barcelona, Spain, Vol. 2, pp. 38-42, September 2000.
9. Kittler, J.: On Combining Classifiers. IEEE Transactions on Pattern Analysis and Machine Intelligence, Vol. 20, No. 3, pp. 226–239, March 1998.
10. Ney, H.: On the Probabilistic Interpretation of Neural Network Classifiers and Discriminative Training Criteria, IEEE Transactions on Pattern Analysis and Machine Intelligence, Vol. 17, No. 2, pp. 107–119, February 1995.
11. Schölkopf, B.: Support Vector Learning. Oldenbourg Verlag, Munich, 1997.
12. Schölkopf, B., Simard, P., Smola, A., Vapnik, V.: Prior Knowledge in Support Vector Kernels. Advances in Neural Information Processing Systems 10, MIT Press, Cambridge, MA, pp. 640–646, 1998.
13. Schapire, R., Freund, Y., Bartlett, P., Lee, W.: Boosting the Margin: A New Explanation for the Effectiveness of Voting Methods. The Annals of Statistics, Vol. 26, No. 5, pp. 1651–1686, 1998.
14. Simard, P., Le Cun, Y., Denker, J.: Efficient Pattern Recognition using a New Transformation Distance. Advances in Neural Information Processing Systems 5, Morgan Kaufmann, San Mateo CA, pp. 50–58, 1993.
15. Simard, P., Le Cun, Y., Denker, J., Victorri, B.: Transformation Invariance in Pattern Recognition – Tangent Distance and Tangent Propagation. Lecture Notes in Computer Science, Vol. 1524, Springer, pp. 239–274, 1998.
16. Vapnik, V.: The Nature of Statistical Learning Theory, Springer, New York, pp. 142-143, 1995.

Averaging Weak Classifiers

Dechang Chen[1] and Jian Liu[2]

[1] University of Wisconsin, Green Bay, WI 54311, USA
chend@uwgb.edu
[2] University of Minnesota, Minneapolis, MN 55455, USA
jliu@cs.umn.edu

Abstract. We present a learning algorithm for two-class pattern recognition. It is based on combining a large number of weak classifiers. The weak classifiers are produced independently with diversity. And they are combined through a weighted average, weighted exponentially with respect to their apparent errors on the training data. Experimental results are also given.

1 Introduction

"Averaging" has been a useful technique for constructing ensembles. Well known examples are bagging [1], Bayesian averaging [12], and Stochastic Discrimination (SD) [10]. A recent paper [5] also uses this technique.

"Weak classifiers" generated by using the training data set first appeared in [8]. In the literature there is a considerable amount of research work using the idea of weak classifiers to form strong classifiers. See, for example, [2], [3], [6], [7], [9] and [10]. In [2], [9] and [10], weak classifiers are obtained by finite unions of rectangular regions in the feature space and they are combined through the average of the base random variables. In [3], weak classifiers are obtained by finite unions of rectangular regions and they are combined by majority vote. In [7], weak classifiers are linear classifiers, generated by random selections of hyperplanes, and they are combined by majority vote. In [6], multiple trees are constructed systematically by pseudorandomly selecting subsets of components of the feature vectors, and the combination is done through majority vote for fully split trees. The combined results from the methods cited above are often remarkable.

In this paper we present a binary classification learning algorithm by producing a number of weak classifiers from SD and combining them through a weighted average employed in [5]. The motivation to use weak classifiers from SD is that they are computationally cheap and easy to obtain. We use the "averaging" method in [5] to combine weak classifiers simply because it has several appealing properties. First, predictions of final classifiers from this method are stable and reliable. Second, the method has the potential that the final classifier may significantly outperform the best among the set of weak classifiers. The work presented in this paper can be viewed as not only an application of

J. Kittler and F. Roli (Eds.): MCS 2001, LNCS 2096, pp. 119–125, 2001.

weak classifiers from SD, but also an implementation of the algorithm carefully studied in [5].

This paper is organized as follows. Section 2 describes the algorithm. Section 3 presents some experimental results. Our conclusion is given in Section 4.

2   The Algorithm

In this section, we present our algorithm for binary classification. First we show how to produce weak classifiers. And then we show how to combine them to form a strong classifier.

2.1   Weak Classifiers

Consider the standard two-class pattern recognition problem. We have a training set of independently and identically distributed observations: $(\mathbf{x}_1, y_1)$, $\cdots$, $(\mathbf{x}_n, y_n)$, where $\mathbf{x}_i$ is a feature vector of dimension p, belonging to the feature space F, and $y_i \in \{1, 2\}$ is a class label. Alternatively, we may write the training set as $\mathbf{TR} = \{TR_1, TR_2\}$, where TR_k is a given random sample from class k for $k = 1, 2$.

Based on the training data set $\mathbf{TR} = \{TR_1, TR_2\}$, we can produce a sequence of weak classifiers using the rectangular regions ([2]). A rectangular region in R^p is a set of points $(x_1, x_2, \ldots, x_p)$ such that $a_i \leq x_i \leq b_i$ for $i = 1, \ldots, p$, where a_i and b_i are real numbers. For simplicity, a rectangular region is denoted by $\prod_{i=1}^p (a_i, b_i)$.

Suppose κ is a fixed natural number and $\lambda (\lambda \geq 1)$, ρ $(0 < \rho < 1)$, and β $(0 < \beta < 1)$ are fixed real numbers. Let $\Re_1$ be the smallest rectangular region containing $\mathbf{TR}$. Let $\Re$ be the rectangular region (in R^p) such that $\Re$ and $\Re_1$ have the same center, $\Re$ is similar to $\Re_1$ and the "width" of $\Re$ along the x_i-axis is λ times the corresponding width of $\Re_1$. Suppose that $\Re = \prod_{i=1}^p (L_i, U_i)$. Inside $\Re$, one randomly chooses a training feature vector $q = (q_1, \cdots, q_p)$ and numbers l_i and u_i such that $L_i \leq l_i \leq q_i \leq u_i \leq U_i$ and $u_i - l_i \geq \rho(U_i - L_i)$ for $i = 1, \ldots, p$. Form a rectangular region $R = \prod_{i=1}^p (l_i, u_i)$. For any subsets T_a and T_b of F, let $r(T_a, T_b)$ denote the ratio of the number of common feature vectors in T_a and T_b and the number of feature vectors in T_b. For example, if T_b contains 5 feature vectors and T_a and T_b have 3 feature vectors in common, then $r(T_a, T_b) = 3/5 = 0.6$. An S is a *weak classifier* if S is a union of κ rectangular regions R's constructed above which satisfies $|r(S, TR_1) - r(S, TR_2)| \geq \beta$.

A classification rule ϕ is a map from the feature space F to $\{1, 2\}$, the set of class labels. A weak classifier S gives a classification rule ϕ_S as follows. Given $\mathbf{x} \in F$, if $r(S, TR_1) > r(S, TR_2)$, $\phi_S(\mathbf{x}) = 1$ for any $\mathbf{x} \in S$ and $\phi_S(\mathbf{x}) = 2$ for any $\mathbf{x} \in S^c$; if $r(S, TR_2) > r(S, TR_1)$, $\phi_S(\mathbf{x}) = 2$ for any $\mathbf{x} \in S$ and $\phi_S(\mathbf{x}) = 1$ for any $\mathbf{x} \in S^c$. For convenience, ϕ_S is also called a weak classifier. The error rate on $\mathbf{TR}$ of a weak classifier S or ϕ_S can be close to 0.5. Thus a weak classifier may be very weak in terms of classification error.

In this paper, we use as weak classifiers the finite unions of rectangular regions defined previously. From the theoretical point of view, weak classifiers may be formed by using other geometric objects such as spheres and half-planes. One key in constructing weak classifiers is that each weak classifier should be topologically "thick." A "thicker" weak classifier contains more training feature vectors than a "thinner" one. In this paper, λ, ρ, and κ are used to determine the "thickness" of weak classifiers. In the theory of Kleinberg's SD, other important concepts related to weak classifiers include *enrichment* and *uniformity*. The effect of enrichment is picked up by β. Uniformity is not discussed in this paper since it seems that the empirical log ratio l (See Section 2.2) does not require this. For the discussion on various aspects of weak classifiers, we refer the readers to [8], [9], and [11].

2.2 Combining Weak Classifiers

Suppose that there is a sequence of weak classifiers $S_1, \cdots, S_t$, which are produced independently. Correspondingly we may rewrite this sequence of weak classifiers as $\phi_1, \cdots, \phi_t$, where $\phi_k = \phi_{S_k}$ for $k = 1, \cdots, t$. It is seen that $\phi_1, \cdots, \phi_t$ are also diverse. Here diversity is used to indicate the following: if t is large, then for any feature point $\mathbf{x}$ the probability is very high that there exist a pair ϕ_i and ϕ_j such that they make different errors in classifying $\mathbf{x}$. To combine these weak classifiers, one can use the *empirical log ratio* in [5]. For each weak classifier ϕ, denote by $\epsilon(\phi)$ the apparent error of ϕ on the training data, and define a weight $w(\phi) = e^{-\eta\epsilon(\phi)}$ where η is a positive constant. For a new feature vector $\mathbf{x}$, the value of the prediction function based on $\phi_1, \cdots, \phi_t$ is the value of the empirical log ratio:

$$l(\mathbf{x}) = \frac{1}{\eta} \ln \left(\frac{\Sigma_{\phi,\, \phi(\mathbf{x})=1} w(\phi)}{\Sigma_{\phi,\, \phi(\mathbf{x})=2} w(\phi)} \right).$$

Also following [5], we define the classification rule as follows. Let Δ be a non-negative constant. Given $\mathbf{x} \in F$, classify $\mathbf{x}$ into class 1 if $l(\mathbf{x}) > \Delta$, classify $\mathbf{x}$ into class 2 if $l(\mathbf{x}) < -\Delta$, and the status of $\mathbf{x}$ is "no prediction" if $\Delta \leq l(\mathbf{x}) \leq -\Delta$. "No prediction" means that the information is insufficient to make a classification.

Denote the above classification rule by AWC, short for *Averaging Weak Classifiers*. Clearly a natural question is: what performance can one expect AWC to achieve? From [5], we see that the generalization error of AWC is close to that of the best ϕ in the sequence $\phi_1, \cdots, \phi_t$. [5] also points out that in some cases AWC may significantly outperform the best ϕ among $\phi_1, \cdots, \phi_t$. For example, let us consider the following scenario. Imagine one has a sequence of classifiers $\phi_1, \cdots, \phi_t$, where ϕ_i's are not necessarily weak classifiers as defined in Section 2.1. Suppose that from this sequence there is one ϕ^* such that $\epsilon(\phi^*) = 1/10$, and that $\epsilon(\phi) = 1/5$ for each $\phi \in \{\phi_1, \cdots, \phi_t\} - \{\phi^*\}$. Also suppose that for each $\mathbf{x}$, the fraction of $\phi \in \{\phi_1, \cdots, \phi_t\} - \{\phi^*\}$ giving the right label is approximately

3/4. Let $\eta = 1$. Then if $\phi(\mathbf{x}) = 1$, which is the correct label for $\mathbf{x}$, we have

$$l(\mathbf{x}) \approx \ln \left(\frac{e^{-1/10} + (3/4)(t-1)e^{-1/5}}{(1/4)(t-1)e^{-1/5}} \right) = \ln \left(3 + \frac{4e^{1/10}}{t-1} \right) \approx \ln 3$$

as t is large. Similarly, if $\phi(\mathbf{x}) = 2$, which is the correct label for $\mathbf{x}$, $l(\mathbf{x}) \approx -\ln \left(3 + \frac{4e^{1/10}}{t-1} \right) \approx -\ln 3$ as t is large. If $\phi(\mathbf{x}) = 1$, which is a wrong label for $\mathbf{x}$, $l(\mathbf{x}) \approx \ln \left(\frac{1}{3} + \frac{4e^{1/10}}{3(t-1)} \right) \approx -\ln 3$ as t is large. And if $\phi(\mathbf{x}) = 2$, which is a wrong label for $\mathbf{x}$, $l(\mathbf{x}) \approx -\ln \left(\frac{1}{3} + \frac{4e^{1/10}}{3(t-1)} \right) \approx \ln 3$ as t is large. The above simply shows that if t is large enough, AWC (for $\eta = 1$) classifies all the feature points correctly. In this example, the classifiers are averaged almost uniformly. [5] states that if in some cases there are more ϕ's with low error rates, the balance between the two sets becomes more delicate. This explains why we produce weak classifiers and then put them into the empirical log ratio l. Suppose we have a sequence of weak classifiers $\phi_1, \cdots, \phi_t$. Let S_l denote a set of ϕ's with low apparent error rates and S_l^c denote the set of all the remaining ϕ's. Then our hope is that as t is large the balance between S_l and S_l^c will make AWC a classification rule with a good generalization performance.

To conclude this section, we summarize our binary classification algorithm as follows.

1. Given λ, ρ, κ, and β, generate t weak classifiers $S_1, \cdots, S_t$. Set $\phi_k = \phi_{S_k}$ for $k = 1, \cdots, t$.
2. Given η, calculate the weights $w(\phi_1) = e^{-\eta\epsilon(\phi_1)}, \cdots, w(\phi_t) = e^{-\eta\epsilon(\phi_t)}$.
3. For any $\mathbf{x}$, calculate the prediction value $l(\mathbf{x})$. Classify $\mathbf{x}$ with given Δ.

3   Experimental Results

In this section, we report the experimental results on classifying feature vectors from several problems. In example 1 a simulated dataset was used. The datasets in examples 2–4 were taken from the UCI Machine Learning Depository. The choices of the parameters of our learning algorithm were made as follows. In order to compare our results with those available in the literature, we set $\Delta = 0$ in our algorithm so that "no prediction" actually did not occur and all the test points were classified. Also before the experiments we fixed $\eta = 10$.

Note that ρ, λ, and κ together determine the "thickness" of each weak classifier. For convenience we fixed $\rho = 0.3$ and tuned λ and κ. (Note that β tells us that a weak classifier covers the two classes of feature vectors in the training set differently. Therefore, to a certain degree, β contains the information about the accuracy of each weak classifier.) Tuning λ, κ and β was done through 10-fold cross-validation for examples $2-4$ or the usual training/test procedure for the simulated data in example 1. This tuning process consisted of two steps. In step 1, we conduced a coarse tuning. We considered $\lambda \in [1.0, 2.0]$, $\kappa \in \{2, \cdots, 30\}$, and $\beta \in [0.1, 0.9]$. We ran AWC ($t = 200$) for each choice of λ, κ and β by looping over the ranges with a step size of 0.1, 2, and 0.1 for λ, κ, and β, respectively. For example 1, we selected the combination of λ, κ and β corresponding to the best performance on the test dataset. For examples 2-4, we selected the combination of λ, κ, and β corresponding to the best averaged test performance. Denote the selected parameters by λ_0, κ_0, and β_0. In step 2, we conducted a fine tuning. We considered new ranges of λ, κ and β centered at λ_0, κ_0, and β_0, respectively. The length of each range was set to be half of that in step 1. An obvious truncating was done if the new range would extend beyond the range in step 1. We ran AWC (again $t = 200$) for each choice of λ, κ and β by looping over the ranges with a step size of 0.05, 1, and 0.05 for λ, κ, and β respectively. As in step 1, we chose the combination of λ, κ and β corresponding to the best test performance as the fine tuning result. Denote the selected parameters by λ_1, κ_1, and β_1. These values were used with the actual runs of the experiments.

With all the known parameters, we ran AWC to estimate the test error rates. For each necessary run, $t = 1000$ weak classifiers were produced.

Example 1 (Two normal populations with equal covariance matrix)
Consider two distributions $N(\mu_1, I)$ (class 1) and $N(\mu_2, I)$ (class 2), where I is the 2×2 identity matrix, μ_1 is the vector $(1.5, 0)'$, and μ_2 is the vector $(0, 0)'$. Both of the prior class probabilities π_1 (for class 1) and π_2 (for class 2) are equal to $1/2$. The training set contains 400 points from each class, and test set contains 1000 points from each class. The averaged results over ten such independently drawn training/test set combinations were used to estimate the error rates. Parameter values from the tuning process are $\lambda = 1.05$, $\kappa = 5$, and $\beta = 0.40$. The averaged test error from the "averaging" method described in this paper is 23.3% . As a comparison, the linear discriminant rule yields a test error 23.2%.

Example 2 (Breast cancer)
The dataset was taken from the UCI Machine Learning Depository. The data came from Dr. William H. Wolberg, University of Wisconsin Hospitals, Madison ([14]). The dataset contains 699 points in the nine-dimensional space R^9, coming from two classes: benign (458 cases) and malignant (241 cases). We used (from the tuning) $\lambda = 1.05$, $\kappa = 3$, and $\beta = 0.85$. The test error based on 10-fold cross-validation is 3.8%.

Example 3 (Diabetes)
The data were gathered among the Pima Indians by the National Institute of Diabetes and Digestive and Kidney Diseases ([13]). The dataset contains 768 points in the eight-dimensional space R^8. There are two classes: tested positive (268 cases) and negative (500 cases). We used $\lambda = 1.00$, $\kappa = 4$, and $\beta = 0.30$. The test error based on 10-fold cross-validation is 25.2%.

Example 4 (Hepatitis)
The data were from Gail Gong at Carnegie Mellon University. The dataset contains 155 points with dimension 19. There are two classes: die (32 cases) and

live (123 cases). We used $\lambda = 1.50$, $\kappa = 20$, and $\beta = 0.30$. The test error based on 10-fold cross-validation is 17.3%.

Table 1 presents the results for our runs, as well as for other "weak learning algorithms." We used the same notations as in [10]. In the table, the results of the first nine columns are from [4]. Specifically, FIA, FID, and C45 represent three learning algorithms FindAttrTest, FindDecRule, and Quinlan's C4.5, respectively. Their boosted versions are denoted by ABO, DBO, and 5BO, respectively. And Their bagged versions are denoted by ABA, DBA, and 5BA, respectively. The tenth column (SDK) reports the results of Stochastic Discrimination from [10]. Our results from averaging weak classifiers are given in the last column. From the table, we can see that the test errors of AWC obtained in examples 2-4 are comparable to the best results.

Table 1. Test error rates. The first nine columns contain the results of FindAttrTest, FindDecRule, C4.5, and their boosted and bagged versions from Freund and Schapire, the 10th column (SDK) contains the results of Stochastic Discrimination from Kleinberg, and the last column reports the results of the method of averaging weak classifiers.

dataset	FIA	ABO	ABA	FID	DBO	DBA	C45	5BO	5BA	SDK	AWC
breast cancer	8.4	4.4	6.7	8.1	4.1	5.3	5.0	3.3	3.2	2.6	3.8
diabetes	26.1	24.4	26.1	27.8	25.3	26.4	28.4	25.7	24.4	25.5	25.2
hepatitis	19.7	18.6	16.8	21.6	18.0	20.1	21.2	16.3	17.5	16.2	17.3

The above examples are merely used to demonstrate the effectiveness of the method presented in this paper. We have not tried to find the best setting of the parameters λ, ρ, κ, and β. Although the tuning process proposed above (when ρ is fixed) often works, it is in no way the best procedure. As better methods are found to pick up the parameters, the classification results will definitely be improved. AWC has also been applied to many other binary classification problems. Experiments show that classification results depend on the parameters and that carefully tuned parameters often lead to excellent results.

4 Conclusion

Combination of classifiers is a rich research area in pattern recognition. In this article, we combine an arbitrary number of weak classifiers through a weighted average. Experimental results show that the ensemble constructed this way is comparably accurate in classifying feature vectors and overfitting does not occur for the ensemble.

References

1. Breiman, L. (1996). Bagging predictors. *Machine Learning*, 24 (2), pp. 123–140.

2. Chen, D. and Cheng, X. (2000, a). A simple implementation of the stochastic discrimination for pattern recognition. In *Proc. Joint IAPR International Workshops SSPR 2000 and SPR 2000* (Francesc J. Ferri, José M. Iñesta, et al., eds.), Alicante, Spain, Springer LNCS-1876, pp. 882–887.

3. Chen, D. and Cheng, X. (2000, b). Majority vote based on weak classifiers. *2000 5th International Conference on Signal Processing Proceedings,* Beijing, China, vol. 3, pp. 1560–1562.

4. Freund, Y. and Schapire, R. E. (1996). Experiments with a new boosting algorithm. *Proc. 13th Int'l Conf. Machine Learning,* pp. 148-156.

5. Freund, Y., Mansour, Y., Schapire, R. E. (2001). Why averaging classifiers can protect against overfitting. In *Proceedings of the Eighth International Workshop on Artificial Intelligence and Statistics.*

6. Ho, T. K. (1998). The random subspace method for constructing decision forests. *IEEE Trans. Pattern Analysis and Machine Intelligence,* vol. 20, no. 8, pp. 832–844.

7. Ji, C. and Ma, S. (1997). Combinations of weak classifiers. *IEEE Trans. Neural Networks,* vol. 8, no. 1, pp. 32–42.

8. Kleinberg, E. M. (1990). Stochastic discrimination. *Annals of Math. and Artificial Intelligence,* 1, pp. 207–239.

9. Kleinberg, E. M. (1996). An overtraining-resistant stochastic modeling method for pattern recognition. *Annals of Statistics,* 24, pp. 2319–2349.

10. Kleinberg, E. M. (2000, a). On the algorithmic implementation of stochastic discrimination. *IEEE Transactions on Pattern Analysis and Machine Intelligence,* vol. 22, No. 5, pp. 473–490.

11. Kleinberg, E. M. (2000, b). A mathematically rigorous foundation for supervised learning. *Proc. First Int'l Workshop on Multiple Classifier Systems,* Cagliari, Italy, pp. 67–76.

12. MacKay, D. J. C. (1991). *Bayesian Methods for Adaptive Models,* Ph.D. thesis, California Institute of Technology.

13. Smith, J., Everhart, J., Dickson, W., Knowler, W., & Johannes, R. (1988). Using the ADAP learning algorithm to forecast the onset of diabetes mellitus. In *Proceedings of the Symposium on Computer Applications and Medical Care,* IEEE Computer Society Press, pp. 261–265.

14. Wolberg, W. H. & Mangasarian, O. L. (1990). Multisurface method of pattern separation for medical diagnosis applied to breast cytology. Proceedings of the National Academy of Sciences, U.S.A., Volume 87, pp. 9193 –9196.

Mixing a Symbolic and a Subsymbolic Expert to Improve Carcinogenicity Prediction of Aromatic Compounds

Giuseppina Gini,[1] Marco Lorenzini[1], Emilio Benfenati[2], Raffaella Brambilla[2], and Luca Malvé[2]

[1] Dept of Electronics and Information, Politecnico di Milano,
piazza L. da Vinci 3", 20133 Milano, Italy
gini@elet.polimi.it
[2] Dept. of Environmental Health Sciences,
Istituto di Ricerche Famacologiche "Mario Negri",
Via Eritrea 62, 20157 Milano, Italy Milano, Italy
benfenati@marionegri.it

Abstract. One approach to deal with real complex systems is to use two or more techniques in order to combine their different strengths and overcome each other's weakness to generate hybrid solutions. In this project we pointed out the needs of an improved system in toxicology prediction. An architecture able to satisfy these needs has been developed. The main tools we integrated are rules and ANN. We defined chemical structures of fragments responsible for carcinogenicity according to human experts. After them we developed specialized rules to recognize these fragments into a given chemical and to assess their toxicity. In practice the rule-based expert associates a category to each fragment found, then a category to the molecule. Furthermore, we developed an ANN-based expert that uses molecular descriptors in input and predicts carcinogenicity as a numerical value. Finally we added a classifier program to combine the results obtained from the two previous experts into a single predictive class of carcinogenicity to man.

1 Introduction

The goal to predict carcinogenicity is a challenging one, in consideration of the social and economical importance of the problem. Chemicals are responsible for many tumors, and industry is required to take into account carcinogenicity of the chemicals used and produced. However, the experimental tests on chemicals last for years, are costly and require the use of animals, with the consequent ethical problems. Considering the importance of the goal, it is interesting to continue the attempts to improve computerized systems to predict carcinogenicity. So far the most popular programs have been expert systems [1] (ES). In many cases they look for the presence of toxic residues in the molecule, as in [2]. More recently neural networks (ANN) have been used [3], and inductive learning [4].

In the present study we tried a new approach, combining different systems in hybrid architecture. We developed an ES able to recognize toxic residues predicting a class of toxicity. Furthermore, we used ANN with molecular descriptors as input to provide

J. Kittler and F. Roli (Eds.): MCS 2001, LNCS 2096, pp. 126–135, 2001.

a different prediction of toxicity. Finally, we used a symbolic rule induction program to merge the information from the two sources.

2 Definition of the Phenomenon to Be Modeled: Carcinogenicity

Cancer is not a single disease. Furthermore, each single cancer involves a complex sequence of events. The complexity of the phenomenon means that experimental data are not precise, and in some cases contradictory. Most of the experiments are done on animals. Extrapolation of results from animals to humans is complicated also because in animal experiments high doses are used, while humans are generally exposed to low doses.

Carcinogens are listed in classes by national and international agencies. The International Agency on Research on Cancer (IARC) considers four classes: the compounds which have been recognized as carcinogenic to man are in *class 1*, the compounds which are not carcinogenic (only a few compounds) are in *class 4*, the other compounds are split in three classes of different degree of uncertainty: probably or possibly carcinogenic to man (*class 2A and 2B*), not classifiable as their carcinogenicity to humans (*class 3* - the most numerous one, characterized by the highest uncertainty). This classification combines, in the evaluation of carcinogenicity, the experimental evidences with the amount of epidemiological knowledge available.

A different approach has been introduced by Gold and colleagues [5]. They developed a numerical data set that contains standardized and reviewed results for carcinogenicity for more than 1200 chemicals. The cancerogenicity data on rat and mouse are expressed in term of the parameter TD50, which is the chronic dose rate, which would give half of the animals tumors within some standard experiment time. The huge amount of data and the quantitative homogeneous evaluation represented two important advantages.

Both kinds of characterization have been used: categorical (as the IARC) and continuous (as the Gold data set), the first with the residue approach, the second with the ANN. We extended its applicability to man using a symbolic rule induction program. To do this, for the training of this module we used the IARC classification.

In the area of toxicity prediction QSAR (Quantitative Structure Activity Relationships) and SAR (Structure Activity Relationships) models are common. They are based on the evidence that the structure of a molecule is responsible of its activity, and that biological data about the mechanisms are not a must to predict the outcome. Generally SAR models for carcinogenicity are only able to classify in two classes: positive or negative, while QSAR models give a real value for the toxicity.

Usually QSAR are methods to assess drugs; the challenge is to use them to predict toxicity values for large classes of chemicals and for complex phenomena as cancer.

3 Our Residue Approach

Many toxicologists consider the presence of given fragments in the molecule as an indication of potential carcinogenicity.

For instance, Ashby and Paton [6] listed many toxic residues responsible for adverse activity. CompuDrug at the end of the eighties started from this approach and encoded into its ES, called HazardExpert, the behaviour of selected residues based on a report by the U.S. Environmental Protection Agency. To enhance the efficiency of the system, there are built-in modules, which predict the dissociation constant (pKa) and the distribution coefficient (log$P$). These can be used to predict the bioabsorption and accumulation of xenobiotics in living organisms, which have already been predicted, in addition to oncogenicity, mutagenicity, teratogenicity, irritation, sensitization, immunotoxicity and neurotoxicity. HazardExpert examines the compound itself as well as potential metabolites, based on modules providing for generation of potential metabolites. We made an accuracy test on HazardExpert in 1995 in the European project EST, and we found ways to improve it [7].

Sanderson and Earnshaw [8] used the rules *if..then* introducing a series of substructures known to be toxic in the rule base of a system called DEREK (Deductive Estimation of Risk from Existing Knowledge), that then recognizes any such residues in the compound examined. DEREK makes qualitative rather than quantitative predictions. It looks for previously characterized toxicophores that are highlighted in the display and their toxic activity associated. The presence of several toxicophores in the molecule means there are more risks, but whether the risks are additive or not is decided by the user. also DEREK takes into account physicochemical properties such as log$P$ and pKa. There are several toxicological endpoints including mutagenicity, carcinogenicity, skin sensitization, irritation, reproductive effects, neurotoxicity and others.

3.1 Definitions of Rules of Ar-N Compounds

We studied this topic for aromatic amines and related compounds; in particular, we considered all the aromatic compounds with at least a nitrogen linked to the aromatic ring (Ar-N compounds), that contain a large number of chemicals, many of them carcinogens. The Ar-N group is divisible into 10 chemical classes further split into some subclasses, as shown in Table 1.

While classes are defined only considering the presence of a chemical group characterizing the Ar-N bond, subclasses are bounded by the following criteria:
1. presence of the same atom or substituent or chemical structure in a fixed position relative to the Ar-N bond,
2. implementation convenience: in order to reduce memory needs and accelerate the computer search;
3. toxicological affinity of chemicals in terms of TD50 values, target tissue and/or IARC class.

The structure for implementing this knowledge is a two-level structure, as illustrated in Fig. 1.

Table 1. Ar-N compounds divided into classes and subclasses.

1) PRIMARY AMINES
a- Monocyclic aromatic primary amines
b- Pentaatomic heteroaromatic primary amines
c- Hexaatomic heteroaromatic primary amines
d- Biphenyl primary amines
e- Di- and triphenylmethane amines and analogues
f- 4- and 4,4'-Stilbenes
g- 2-aminofluorene and analogues
h- Condensed polycyclic primary aromatic amines 1
i- Condensed polycyclic primary aromatic amines 2

2) NITROCOMPOUNDS
a- Monocyclic aromatic nitro compounds
b- 2-nitro-5-furyl
c- Thio- and azo-pentaatomic nitro compounds
d- Condensed polycyclic nitro compounds 1
e- Condensed polycyclic nitro compounds 2
f- Miscellaneous nitro compounds

3) AZOCOMPOUNDS
a- Dibenzo azo compounds
b- 1-naphtho azo compounds
c- 2-naphtho azo compounds

4) HYDRAZINES
a- Hydrazines 1
b- Hydrazines 2

5) SECONDARY AMINES
a- Aromatic secondary aliphatic amines
b- Diphenyl secondary amines
c- Carbazole
d- Solfonic secondary amines
e- Purines

6) AMIDES
a- Monocyclic aromatic amides
b- Biphenyl amides
c- 2-acetylaminofluorene derivatives
d- Pentaatomic heteroaromatic amides
e- Hexaatomic heteroaromatic amides

7) TERTIARY AMINES
a- Monocyclic aromatic tertiary amines
b- Di- and triphenylmethane tertiary amines
c- N,N-dihydroxyethyl tertiary amines
d- Nitrogen mustards
e- Pentaatomic heterocyclic tertiary amines

8) C-NITROSOCOMPOUNDS

9) N-NITROSOCOMPOUNDS

10) ISOCYANATES

For each subclass a first level structure, which identifies the chemical fragment common to each residue belonging to the subclass, has been individuated. The second level structures specify each residue. Two corresponding inhibition levels have been introduced for situations where the found fragment has no effect.

- *First level*: identifies the structure of the nitrogen fragment characterizing the class and the aromatics structures bonded to that group.
- *First inhibition level*: it solves the problem of compounds that, even if related to the structure of the subclass, are not carcinogens or have been ascribed to another subclass.
- *Second level*: the second search level permits the identification of a specific compound or small groups of compounds that refer to the same subclass but differ for some specific elements bound to the nitrogen group and/or to the aromatic structure, and suspected to be involved in the carcinogenicity process.
- *Second inhibition level*: this second inhibition level is useful to exclude a specific compound or a small group of compounds.

First Level Structure:
1-Naphtho azocompounds.

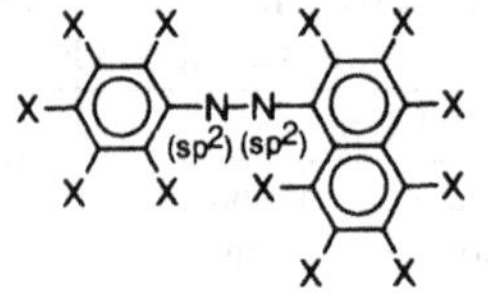

First Level Inhibition.

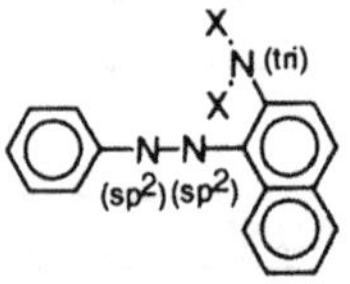

Second Level Structure:
Bensub-1NA residue

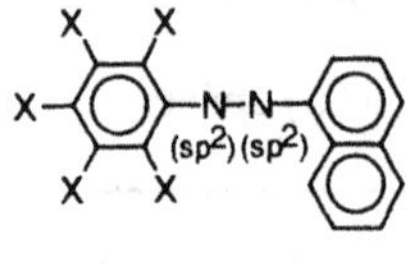

Second Level Inhibition

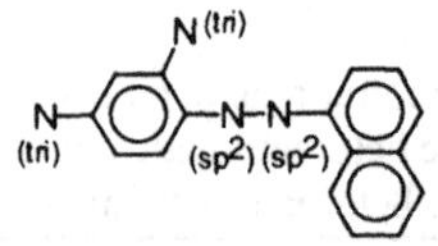

Fig. 1 . Example of structure levels. The Figure shows the structure to search at the first and second levels and the relevant inhibitions.

Each fragment is associated with a category expressing the level of toxicity. Our system reports the highest level obtained and the residue responsible; if more than a

toxic residue is present, the program selects the most active. We defined five "carcinogenicity levels", using three parameters:
- the TD50 of the molecules [5];
- the level of carcinogenicity ascribed to the fragment contained in the molecule (averaging the evaluation for each fragment on all molecules containing the substructure);
- the classification or the evidence of carcinogenicity given by the databases IARC, IRIS, HSDB, NTP, RTECS.
The COSMIC format has been chosen to describe the molecules; it uses atom hybridization instead of information on atomic bonds, with two positive consequences:

- All bonds are equals. The chemical information is hidden in the nodes and so the search algorithm is easier.
- Hydrogens are left out. The molecular graph is smaller and so the search is faster.

3.2. Internal Representation

Graph theory was used to represent the chemical structures. They are stored as adjacency lists: given the *node i*, the nodes in the list *I* contain atoms that are adjacent to vertex *i* as shown in Figure 2.

3.3 Search Method

The search of a fragment in a molecule is a *subgraph isomorphism problem*. A graph G_α is *isomorphic* to a subgraph of a graph G_β if and only if there is a one to one correspondence between the node sets of this subgraph and those of G_α that preserves adjacency. The computational complexity of this problem is, in general, NP-Complete [9]. The search operation has been divided into two parts: the first search level is performed by finding all possible isomorphisms between the structure considered and the molecule, with the Ullmann's algorithm [9], modified to manage hydrogens and wildcards. After finding a first level structure, the second part of the search procedure checks positive and negative conditions, using a backtracking technique. If a second level structure and no inhibition are found, a residue is considered found.

4   The ANN-Based Prediction

Backpropagation neural network [10] has been adopted in this study to implement the quantitative prediction of carcinogenicity; more details are in [11].
From the Gold's database 104 molecules presenting an aromatic ring and a nitrogen linked to the aromatic ring have been chosen. We computed molecular descriptors of six main groups (physico-chemical, geometric, topological, electrostatic, quantum-chemical and thermodynamic); from the initial set of 34 descriptors a selection was necessary in order to avoid an excessive time for training the network. Principal

component analysis (PCA) has been used for the selection, building a final set of 13 descriptors (molecular weight, HOMO, LUMO, dipole moment, polarizability, Balaban, ChiV3 and flexibility indices, logD at pH 2 and pH 10, third principal axis of inertia, ellipsoidal volume, electrotopological sum).

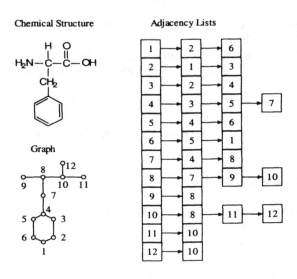

Fig. 2 The implementation through the adjacency lists.

The parameter TD50 reported by Gold et al. [11] has been adopted for the output. The output has been derived from a transformation of the TD50 according to the following formula:

$$output = Log\,(MW*1000/TD50)$$

Data were scaled between 0 and 1. The output has been also scaled accordingly. The scaling was based on the training set. Validation set was scaled on the basis of scaling of the training set.

All simulations were performed using MBP v 1.1 [10], initialing the weight with the SCAWI technique, and using the acceleration factors. Each network has been trained starting from 100 points random in the space, in order to minimize the probability of converging towards local minima.

For validation the N/2-fold-crossvalidation has been used. MSE and R^2_{cv} resulting from 10000 iterations of the back-propagation ANN, using different numbers of internal neurons, showed best results using four or seven hidden neurons: R^2_{cv} was in both cases 0.691.

The presence of outliers in the set has been supposed and investigated; 12 molecules were identified as outliers and removed. Results after outliers removal showed clear improvement in the R^2_{cv} which became 0.824 (with 4 hidden neurons). The majority (9 out of 12) of the outliers is molecules for which the experimental results were not statistically significant and an arbitrary 10^{31} value was given by Gold.

5 Combining the Two Predictions into the Hybrid System

The results we obtained from the two parts of the prediction should now be combined. In the present study we added a third module dedicated to the classification. Given the output of the residues research, and the expected TD50, we wanted to extrapolate a combined prediction of the human carcinogenicity.

We split some classes of the IARC classification according to the following criteria:
- to define 5 classes, 1 to 5, from lower to higher risks, based on the TD50 values;
- to check the presence of each residue in the molecules under study;
- to give to each residue a toxicity class obtained as the mean of the toxicity of the molecules where it was found;
- to assign to the molecule the maximum toxicity obtained from the residues and ANN module.

We built classification trees from examples, using different tree construction programs:

- C4.5 [12] which makes use of the maximization of the entropy gain, and builds hyper-rectangular in the attribute space;
- CART, which builds binary trees [13];
- OC1 [14], that uses a random perturbation of parameters to escape from local minima.

The training set has been prepared with all molecules and two attributes each, TD50 (predicted by BNN) and the carcinogenicity category predicted by the residue module. Performances using the leave-one-out are in Table 2.

Table 2. Results obtained with tree induction systems (accuracy %)

	C4.5	CART	OC1
Training	93.3	88.5	90.2
Validation	81.9	85.5	82.8

6 Discussion and Conclusions

Results in Table 2 show the accuracy (the ratio between the sum of correct assignments and the total compounds) show promising possibilities. The integration of the two approaches improved the performances of the individual methods.

Very few comparisons have been made of different ES in toxicology. Most of the papers presented by the authors of the different ES claim good predictions, often better than 90%. Omenn [15] reported the results of predictions on 44 chemicals made by some human experts and different computer programs. Table 3 compares the results with the ES and the best human results. This indicates that for the time being no ES can do better than a good human expert.

A particular problem is the nature and evaluation of the information. In several cases experts pay special attention to some data and overlook others, because they know from experience which data are most reliable. Sometimes their experience is concentrated on certain aspects of the problem. As a consequence, different experts will give different answers.

Table 3.- ES and human experts predictions for toxicology of 44 chemicals

Expert	Accuracy	Percentage
Human experts	30/40	75
DEREK	22/37	59
TOPKAT	14/24	58
COMPACT	19/35	54
CASE	17/35	49

For this reason to assess the reliability of predictive models we must rely on internal evaluation, mainly on leave-one-out. The best we can expect is to be able to correctly predict a new external set, as we will try in the future.

In the attempt to overcome the limitation of attribute-based learning, some programs learn first-order predicate logic. Given background knowledge (expressed as predicates, positive examples, and negative examples) the ILP system is able to construct a predicate logic formula H such as all the positive examples can be logically derived from the background formulas and H, and no negative example can be logically derived.

The main work in ILP is the predictive toxicology challenge, which aims at constructing a SAR model based on data from NTP (National Toxicology Program). The NTP produced the PTE data sets, based on the study of about 300 compounds, to be used as training set, and the definition of small tests sets (30 compounds). For all molecules the carcinogenicity is available, expressed as yes/not. The data set presents a mix of chemicals (both organic and inorganic as representative of 19 millions); some chemical classes are not represented, some known biological mechanism is not represented.

In [16] a report of the submissions to the challenge is shown. In the models, presented by 9 laboratories, the best estimated accuracy is 0.87 for a stocastic system, on the outcome of 23 of the 30 molecules. The other models range from 0.78 o 0.48. The approach based on ILP reached 0.78.

Our research confirms the feasibility of an ANN for carcinogenicity for several chemical classes, which exhibit their activity according to different mechanisms. A valuable characteristic of our ANN is that it seems to correctly predict carcinogenic compounds; unfortunately, it is less accurate in the prediction of non-active compounds. It is likely that ANN alone cannot solve all the problems linked with carcinogenicity prediction. A classical example is the case of ortho- and para-anisidine that have very similar descriptors values, but one of the compounds is carcinogenic, while the other not. In this case an approach based on the residues can distinguish the two chemicals.

An advantage of our architecture, which evolved from a previous work on fitotoxicity [17] is that the output is not simply a classification into two classes of activity: carcinogenic or not, as in several programs predicting toxicity. Our system gives a quantitative prediction of the activity, and also a classification similar to IARC.

Moreover, we do bot need biological data to predict carcinogenicity. A key advantage of programs based on the simple chemical structure is that they do not require the synthesis of the chemical to be tested and biological experiments in order to make prediction. However, in the hybrid architecture we defined it is easy to introduce in the rule induction program other inputs, such as results from mutagenicity tests.

Acknowledgements. The European Union contracts COMET and IMAGETOX.

References

1. Benfenati, E., and Gini, G.:Computational predictive programs (expert systems) in toxicology, Toxicology, vol.119 (1997).213-225,.
2. HazardExpert, version 3.0. Compudrug Chemistry Ltd, Budapest, Hungary.
3. Benigni R. and Richard, A.M.: QSARS of mutagens and carcinogens: two case studies illustrating problems in the construction of models for noncongeneric chemicals, Mutation Res., vol.371 (1996).29-46.
4. Lee, Y., Buchanan, B. G., Mattison, D. M., Klopman, G., and Rosenkranz, H. S.: Learning rules to predict rodent carcinogenicity of non-genotoxic chemicals. Mutation Res., vol. 328 (1995) 127-149.
5. URL: http://sciweb.lib.umn.edu/s&e/chem.htm.
6. Ashby, J., and Paton, D.: The influence of chemical structure on the extent and sites of carcinogenesis for 522 rodent carcinogens and 55 different human carcinogens exposures. Mutation Res. 286 (1993) 3-74.
7. Darvas, F., Papp, A., Allerdyce, A., Benfenati, E., Tichy, M., Sobb, N., Citti, A., Gini, G.: Overview of Different Artificial Intelligence Approaches Combined with a Deductive Logic-based Expert System for Predicting Chemical Toxicity. In Gini and Katritzky (eds) AAAI Spring Symposium on Predictive Toxicology, SS-99-01, AAAI Press, Menlo Park, California (1999) 94-99.
8. Sanderson, D.M., and Earnshaw, C.G.: Computer prediction of possible toxic action from chemical structure; the DEREK system. Human and Experimental Toxicology 10 (1991) 261-273.
9. Ullmann, J. R.: An algorithm for subgraph isomorphisms. Journal of ACM, Vol. 23 - 1 (1976) 31-42.
10. Anguita, D.: Matrix Back Propagation v. 1.1 User Manual, Genova, Italy (1993).
11. Gini, G., Benfenati, E., Lorenzini, M., Bruschi, M., Grasso, P.: Predictive Carci-nogenicity: a Model for Aromatic Compounds, with Nitrogen-containing Substituents, Based on Molecular Descriptors Using an Artificial Neural Network. J of Chem Inf and Comp Sciences, 39 (1999) 1076-1080.
12. Quinlan, J.R.: C4.5 Programs for Machine Learning. Morgan Kaufmann Publishers Inc.: San Mateo, CA (1993).
13. Breiman, L., Friedman, J.H., Olshen, R.A., and Stone, C.J.: Classification and regression trees. Wadsworth: Belmont, CA (1984).
14. Murthy, S. K., Kasif, S. and Salzberg, S.: A system for induction of obliques decision trees. J. of Artificial Intelligence Research, vol.2 (1994).
15. Omenn, G.S.: Assessing the risk assessment paradigm. Toxicology 102 (1995) 23-28.
16. Srinivasan, A., King, R. D., Bristol, D. W.: An assessment of submissions made to the predictive toxicology evaluation challenge. Proc.IJCAI 1999 (1999) 270-275.
17. Gini, G., Benfenati, E., Testaguzza, V., Todeschini, R.: Hytex (Hybrid Toxicology Expert System): Architecture and implementation of a multi-domain hybrid expert system for toxicology. Chemometrics and intelligent laboratory systems 43 (1998) 135-145.

Multiple Classifier Systems Based on Interpretable Linear Classifiers

David J. Hand, Niall M. Adams, and Mark G. Kelly

Department of Mathematics, Imperial College, London, SW7 2BZ, UK
{d.j.hand,n.adams,m.g.kelly}@ic.ac.uk

Abstract. Multiple classifier systems fall into two types: classifier combination systems and classifier choice systems. The former aggregate component systems to produce an overall classification, while the latter choose between component systems to decide which classification rule to use. We illustrate each type applied in a real context where practical constraints limit the type of base classifier which can be used. In particular, our context – that of credit scoring – favours the use of simple interpretable, especially linear, forms. Simple measures of classification performance are just one way of measuring the suitability of classification rules in this context.

Keywords: logistic regression, perceptron, support vector machines, product models

1 Introduction

This paper argues that there are two kinds of multiple classifier system, which we shall call *classifier combination systems* and *classifier choice* systems. Classifier combination systems combine the predictions from multiple classifiers to yield a single class prediction. In contrast, classifier choice systems select a single classifier from a set of potential candidate classifiers, choosing one which is best suited to classify the target point, where 'best' is defined in some appropriate sense. We shall further argue that, although classifier combination systems are the most common kind of 'multiple classifier system', in a deeper sense it is inappropriate to regard them as multiple classifier systems, and that the name might better be reserved for classifier choice systems. We illustrate these ideas with systems we have developed in the context of a particular practical domain — that of credit scoring in retail banking.

The illustrations presented in the paper are motivated by the following observation: *much work on classifier design goes too far*. In particular, a colossal effort has been expended by the research community on developing classification rules which have as small an (out of sample) error rate as possible. This is inappropriate for several reasons. Firstly, as argued in Hand [1], error rate is seldom of real interest in practical problems. Secondly, almost all of the assessment of classification rules is based on the assumption that future points to be classified are obtained from the same distribution as the design set. The very choice of

J. Kittler and F. Roli (Eds.): MCS 2001, LNCS 2096, pp. 136–147, 2001.

the word 'future' here suggests that often this is a false assumption: populations change and evolve over time. Thus the distribution from which future points are drawn is unlikely to be exactly the same as that from which the design set was drawn - and the difference is likely to increase over time. (For a discussion and illustration of this see Kelly *et al* [2]). The implication of this is that it is pointless refining the performance of a classification rule beyond a certain point: by the time it is used in practice, the problem may have changed so that other sources of uncertainty and variation far outweigh the gain in accuracy resulting from refining the rule. Thirdly, in many real problems (not all) there is intrinsic arbitrariness in the definitions of the classes. For example, Kelly *et al* [3] and Kelly and Hand [4] describe situations when the classes are defined in terms of thresholds on an underlying continuum – and where the threshold is a human choice. The arbitrariness of the definitions, and the possibility that one might want to change them, means that refining the classification rule to match one particular definition very well may be wasted effort. More generally than these reasons, there is also the point that a simple focus on error rate (or any other specific measure of *performance* for that matter) is one-sided: there are many other aspects to a good rule, including features such as interpretability (the machine learning community has generally put more emphasis on this than has the statistics community – perhaps leading to classification rules such as rule-based methods which are more attractive in real applications), speed, and the readiness with which the 'reasoning' underlying the classification may be explained to a non-experts (in human commercial applications there are sometimes legal requirements for this, but more generally such facility expedites good customer relations). There are also special circumstances affecting applications of classification rules. Indeed it is possible that, when looked at closely, every situation is rather different from every other. An example of such a special circumstance arises in building rules to predict the classes objects will fall into in the future if one never discovers the true class of those one assigns to class 1 (say). This arises, for example, in any situation where the classifier is used to decide which cases to investigate (e.g. tax investigations, medical investigation, etc.)

Motivated by these points, we describe some approaches to multiple classifier systems below which deliberately constrain the model to take simple forms. This does not mean that the models are not complicated – they are multiple classifier systems, after all – but just that the final decision is based on a simple form. We illustrate such ideas for both classifier combination systems and classifier choice systems.

The body of this paper is divided into two main sections. The first deals with classifier combination systems, and the second with classifier choice systems. In each case we give an informal background description of the basic ideas, and then illustrate how some of our work fits into each framework.

2   Classifier Combination Systems

2.1   Background

The simplest approach to combining classifiers is to take a maximum vote of the predicted classes from each of several distinct and separately estimated classifiers. There are two distinct possibilities here. Firstly, the classifiers could each be of a different kind – for example, one could be a tree classifier, one a neural network, one a nearest neighbour classifier, and so on. The hope would be that the combined classifier could steal the strength of the strongest individual one - but note that the overall classifier is a combination of the individual results. This is in contrast to systems described in Section 3.1, which partition the space of predictor variables into regions such that the 'best' individual classifier is used in each region.

The second possibility is that the classifiers would all be of the same form: for example, they might all be tree classifiers, or simple regression classifiers applied to different subsets of the data - as in bagging (Breiman [5]). With this approach, the way in which the individual classifiers are generated yields a 'weighting' across the classifier space - including many classifiers similar to a particular one is equivalent to weighting that one heavily. This observation leads us onto the first extension of the basic voting method: instead of simply counting the predictions, evaluate a weighted sum (an 'average' over the weight distribution) of predicted classes from each of several distinct and separately estimated classifiers. We conjecture that statisticians tend to think in terms of weighted combinations of constituent classifiers, while computer scientists tend to think of voting systems.

The key question here, of course, is that of what weights to use. This has been investigated by many researchers. Empirical approaches based on performance of the individual classifiers are one possibility. It is also possible to cast this problem into a formal Bayesian framework – and this has proved a popular approach to combining tree classifiers (where it is sometimes seen as an alternative to pruning). See, for example, Buntine [6] and Oliver and Hand [7]. Indeed, there are stronger links to Bayesian statistics here, via work on combining the opinions of experts (all we have to do is regard the individual classification rules as 'experts') – see, for example, Genest and McConway [8].

Despite all that, the phenomenon known as the *flat maximum effect* (von Winterfeldt and Edwards [9] ; Hand [1]) suggests that often the use of equal weights will be almost as effective as 'optimal' weights. Indeed, Kittler and Duin [10] reported precisely this: 'A surprising outcome of the comparative study was that the combination rule developed under the most restrictive assumptions – the sum rule – and its derivatives consistently outperformed other classifier combinations schemes. To explain this empirical finding, we investigated the sensitivity of the various schemes to estimation errors. The sensitivity analysis has shown that the sum rule is most resilient to estimation errors.'

Much of the above also applies to another extension of the weighted class predictions from different rules. This is to average the predicted 'probabilities'

rather than the predicted classes. Suppose that the jth classification rule estimates the probability of belonging to class 1 (say two classes for simplicity),
$p(1|\mathbf{x})$ by $\hat{p_j}(1|\mathbf{x})$. Then its error is $e_j(\mathbf{x}) = \hat{p_j}(1|\mathbf{x}) - p(1|\mathbf{x})$. It follows that the
expected squared error of a weighted sum with weights w_j is

$$E\left[\left\{\sum_j w_j e_j(\mathbf{x})\right\}^2\right] = \int \left\{\sum_j w_j e_j(\mathbf{x})\right\}^2 f(\mathbf{x})dx.$$

With a little standard algebra this can be rewritten as $w'\mathbf{C}w + (w'E(e))^2$, where
$\mathbf{C}$ is the covariance matrix of the errors. If $E(e) = 0$ then (imposing the constraint $w'w = 1$), the set of weights which minimise this are the components of
the eigenvector of $\mathbf{C}$ corresponding to the smallest eigenvalue. These ideas can
be applied more generally, and do not require the e to be defined in terms of
differences between probabilities and their estimates. They could, for example,
be in terms of error rates.

A more elaborate extension is to relax the requirement that the component
classifiers are estimated separately. That is, given that we know that the classifiers are to be combined, perhaps we could optimise the parameters of the individuals in the context of using the others as well. This is similar to the distinction
between using a combination of simple linear regressions and using a multiple
regression. An example of this strategy is given in Mertens and Hand [11] and
we give a further example below. Of course, estimation of such models is much
more laborious than when the individual parameters are estimated separately.
The usual approach is an iterative one cycling between the different components
(if this is arranged in such a way that the criterion decreases monotonically, then
convergence is guaranteed by the monotone convergence theorem).

Up until this point we have assumed that the individual 'base' classifiers are
combined through a *linear* combination. Relaxing this leads to our next extension, in which the outputs of each classifier (estimated probabilities of belonging
to each class, or a predicted class, for example) are used as input to a higher order
classifier, where this need not be a simple linear combination classifier, but could
be arbitrarily complex. This is the principle underlying Wolpert's idea of *stacked
generalisation* (Wolpert [12]). Of course, as soon as we do this, we see (another
generalisation) that it is unnecessarily constraining to require the components
to be *classifiers*. They are really simply feature extractors. This means that they
need not be chosen to predict probabilities of class membership but could be more
elaborate feature extractors. Perhaps, if estimated separately, then it might be
an effective strategy to let them each be classifiers, but if estimated simultaneously this might not be so good. This extension is why we think it is misleading
to think of such systems as 'multiple classifier systems': the components need
not be classifiers at all. At this point, of course, we have described what essentially takes place in neural networks, projection pursuit regression, generalised
additive models, boosting (which is really a type of generalised additive model
– see Friedman *et al* [13]) and other highly flexible modern classification tools.

2.2 Product Classifier

In Section 1 we remarked that often criteria other than mere classification performance was crucial. The work described here arose in a context in which a strong historical preference had been placed on simple linear classification rules based on categorised variables – 'front end' credit scoring in the retail banking sector (Hand and Henley [14]). This emphasis is a consequence of the ready interpretability and the ease of explanation of such rules to those with limited statistical expertise. One consequence is a large base of software which uses such rules in this sector, along with a very large base of user expertise and familiarity with such rules. We should note parenthetically here that front end credit scoring describes situations in which one might be called upon to justify the decision to a lay person – hence the desire for simplicity. In contrast, in back end scoring (fraud detection is an illustration) systems of arbitrary complexity can be used.

Models of the kind we are concerned with may be written as

$$\hat{y} = \text{logit}(p(0|\mathbf{z})) = \sum_{i=1}^{p} a_i \tag{1}$$

where the summation is over the variables, and where a_i takes a value which depends on the category of the ith variable into which the case to be classified falls.

The earliest models of this kind are naive Bayes models (Hand and Yu [15] , in which the a_i parameters are obtained by combining values estimated separately for each of the classes. As shown in Hand and Adams [16] and Hand [17], however, more powerful models result if the parameters of the logit transformation of the class probabilities are estimated directly – a logistic regression on dummy variables defined by the categorisation. Because of the nonlinear transformation implicit in the categorisation of the variables prior to fitting the model, the decision surfaces in such a model can be quite complicated, and are certainly not constrained to be linear. On the other hand, they remain simple. While an attractive feature of such models, this simplicity does raise the question of whether they could be made even more powerful without too much sacrifice of the notion of the combination of contributions from each variable. We explored this in the classifier combination system described below.

Since models of the form in (1) are so widespread in the retail credit industry, we wanted to retain this form as our base classifier. We also wanted our classifier combination system to be simple enough to explain to bank employees who may not have a numerate background. This meant that, for example, a model averaging approach was not acceptable.

We eventually settled on models which use structures of the form (1) as factors in a product form. Thus a simple two component model will take the form

$$\hat{y} = \sum_{i=1}^{p} a_i \sum_{i=1}^{p} b_i \tag{2}$$

Given the parameters of the model (the a_i and b_i) the predictions from the model are obtained by using the standard bank software to obtain the components of (2), and these are simply multiplied together. Both of these steps are thus simple and, more importantly, the overall process is only slightly more complicated than those used at present (based on a single linear combination).

The parameters of this model could be estimated separately, as described in Section 2.1, and as is the case with most classifier combination systems. However, the real gains of this system are likely to manifest themselves when the parameters of each component are estimated in the context of each other component – when the model is treated as a whole. We have developed a simple iterative parameter estimation procedure (Hand and Kelly [18]). We used this model to make predictions about whether applicants for current accounts would turn out to be good or bad risks (defined in a formal operational way, which cannot be publicly stated for commercial reasons). That is, we have a two class problem, with the true class being discovered by following the customers over time. One of the distinguishing features of problems of this kind in the retail credit context is that the proportion of bad customers is often low (the classes are 'unbalanced'): in this case 3.76%.

Another feature, and one which is crucial and which illustrates the points about assessing classification rules made in the opening section, is that one does not observe the outcome for all cases. The classifier is essentially being used as a screening instrument, and one only follows up and observed those applicants one accepts (the predicted 'goods'). This means that criteria such as error rate simply cannot be calculated – apart from any doubts one might have about the issue of regarding the two kinds of misclassification as equally serious. For such problems, we have argued (Hand [19]) that the most appropriate criterion is *bad rate amongst accepts*, and that this is best displayed as a plot of bad rate amongst accept against the accept rate, so that the choice of operating point can be made on the basis of as much information as possible.

A further complication arises from the fact that the classes in problems of this kind are often poorly separated. This means that there is often little difference between classifiers, and that what difference there is can easily be swamped by random variation, especially if (relatively) small data sets are being used for the estimation. On the other hand, a little difference matters in a context where a small reduction in number of 'bads' accepted can translate into millions of pounds. In the present illustration, we were provided with a sample of 10,000 observations. We split this randomly into a design set and test set 200 times, estimating both a basic logistic model and simple product model of form (2), and averaged the results.

The results of using the logistic model (upper curve throughout figure) and the two factor product model are shown in Figure 1. The differences here are of sufficient size to be significant in the banking context. For example, with an accept rate of 90% (typical for this application), the product classifier has a bad rate amongst accepts 0.26% below that of the logistic model. This translates into an 8.87% reduction in the bad rate among the accepts compared with the logistic model (an improvement which has been described as 'massive').

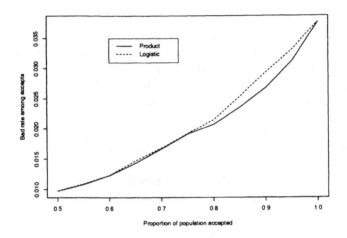

Fig. 1. Logistic model and product classifier on current account data

3   Classifier Choice Systems

3.1   Background

Classifier choice systems are systems of classifiers in which only one component of the system is chosen to actually make the classification. Obviously, a different component may be chosen for each point (or else it would reduce to choosing just one classifier from a set of classifiers during the system's construction). Once again, one might choose the component classifiers to have different forms or one could choose them to have the same form (but with different parameters). We discuss the latter approach in more detail in Section 3.2.

Multiple classifier systems of this form may be thought of as partitioning the measurement space during training, so that a particular ('the best') classifier relates to each cell of the partition. The nature of the partitioning will depend on the nature of the component classifiers: linear classifiers will lead to piecewise linear surfaces separating the regions. In general, a local performance estimate could be made, possibly, but not necessarily, at each design set point, during construction.

A different approach to classifier choice systems has been suggested by Scott [20] and Provost and Fawcett [21]. This arose from the observation that different classifiers are best at different operating points. Figure 2 shows a schematic diagram of the ROC curves for two classifiers (see Hand [1] for a discussion of these). As the operating point of a problem changes, so the performance of a classifier is given by the corresponding point on its ROC curve. However, when a system of classifiers is used, the best possible performance is given by points on the convex hull of the ROC curves. Thus, in the figure, given the two classifiers illustrated there, for operating points between A and B, neither classifier alone can achieve performance on the line connecting A and B, but taken together such performance can be achieved. In particular, for (1-specificity) values between A and B, best performance is obtained by choosing between the rules at random – yielding an overall classifier with performance which lies on the straight line connecting A and B. That is, a randomly chosen proportion α of points are classified by one classifier and a proportion $1 - \alpha$ by the other, with $0 < \alpha < 1$. This is a 'random choice' classifier system.

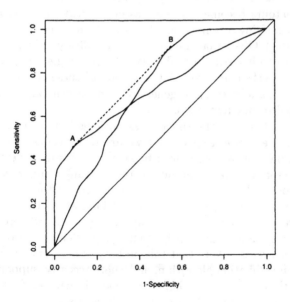

Fig. 2. A random choice classifier system

3.2   Cost Specific Classifiers

We are again concerned with situations in which we need, for external reasons, to adopt a classifier of simple form, and we will assume (again we are motivated by the credit scoring environment) that we will use a linear classifier. In general, this simple form will mean that the model is misspecified – it would be a rare situation in which the true probability of belonging to class 0, say, did follow a logistic model exactly. This implies that there are places, in predictor space, where the model does not match the underlying conditional distribution $p(0|\mathbf{x})$. In particular, there are places (presumably most places) where the contours of the model will not lie along the true contours (which may be curved, unlike those of a logistic model, or may have different directions in different parts of the $\mathbf{x}$ space, even if they are linear).

The majority of comparative studies of classification rules use error rate as the measure of performance. This assumes that the costs of the two (we restrict this discussion to two classes) types of misclassification are equally serious. From this it follows that the optimum rule is based on comparing an estimated probability with the contour $p(0|\mathbf{x}) = 1/2$. This contour is the crucial one for classification when the costs are assumed equal. If, on the other hand, different costs are used, then different contours become relevant - as noted in Adams and Hand [22], if the cost of misclassifying a point from class i is c_i, then the relevant contour is $p(0|\mathbf{x}) = c_1/(c_0 + c_1)$. Given that the contours are unlikely to be parallel, and are thus unlikely both to be estimated effectively by the single misspecified logistic regression model, performance with at least one of these sets of costs will be poor. Of course, this applies more generally, and, in general, different models will be best suited to different costs.

A single model (such as the single classical logistic model) is obtained by aggregating over the entire $\mathbf{x}$ space, but we are really concerned with a more local interpretation. All we really need to know, to classify a new object with measurement vector $\mathbf{x}$, is on what side of the relevant contour it lies. In particular, we do not need accurate estimates for $p(0|\mathbf{x})$ for the new point. When we aggregate, we are distorting the contour of interest by those which we are not interested in. We are ending up with an average of the (differently oriented or shaped) contours, and it is unlikely that the particular one of interest will coincide with this average. Note that this problem is overcome in methods such as the perceptron estimation algorithm, and, more recently, support vector machines, because they are more fundamentally local in nature. They concentrate on the decision surface (the contour of interest) and its vicinity, and are not led astray by the averaging with other contours.

We have experimented with local logistic models which iteratively reweight the design sets points, favouring those near to the current estimate of the relevant contour. This has a flavour similar to that of boosting, except that we choose a single logistic model, best suited to the costs concerned, rather than taking a weighted average of all the models constructed. Adams and Hand [22,23], have described how difficult it is to choose a set of costs accurately. For this reason, rather than producing a single model, we find a set of models, covering the range of cost ratios. That is, we present a set of models from which one is chosen – hence the description of this approach as a classifier cost system.

To illustrate the ideas, Figure 3 shows simulated data in which 1000 points are uniformly distributed over the unit square, and where the contours of the probability of belonging to class 0 are straight lines radiating symmetrically outwards from the origin (at the bottom left of the figure). That is, each of the 1000 points were assigned to class 0 (denoted by a cross) or class 1 (denoted by a circle) with a probability determined by these contours. Logistic regression, with true decision surface at $p(0|\mathbf{x}) = 0.5$, leads to the (correct) estimated decision surface given by the continuous diagonal line in the figure. (In fact the contour shown differs slightly from the true one, which stretches from $(0, 0)$ to $(1, 1)$, because of sampling variation.) All the other estimated contours arising from this model are parallel to this diagonal line, but shifted up or down. In particular, the estimated contour corresponding to $p(0|\mathbf{x}) = 0.8$ lies in the upper triangle and thus crosses the true contour, which has a steeper slope. That is, all contours except the 0.5 one have the wrong slope. This inaccuracy has arisen because the estimate of the 0.8 contour has the same orientation as the others, an average over all of them, despite the fact that the true contours have different slopes.

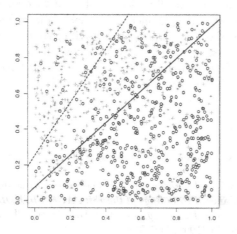

Fig. 3. Simulated data illustrating cost specific classification rules

To construct a cost specific classifier for the 0.8 contour, we estimated the probability of belonging to class 0 using nearest neighbour methods and dis-

carded all points with estimates less than 0.7 or greater than 0.9. We then built
a logistic regression model using only the remaining points. This led to the 0.8
contour shown as a broken line in Figure 3. This is much closer to the true
orientation for the 0.8 contour.

These ideas are not restricted to models such as logistic regression, which is
obviously a global model, but apply more generally to any model which estimates
parameters according to global rather than local goodness of fit or predictive ability. For example, the standard k-nearest neighbour classifier is based on a single
choice of k, obtained by cross-validated error rate or some more sophisticated
method. But this single choice of k is an 'optimal' value aggregated over the
whole space, and ignores the fact that different values may be best in different
regions - and that the region which matters for the problem at hand will depend
on the costs. This is true even for sophisticated Bayesian methods of averaging
over k (eg. Holmes and Adams [24]).

4   Discussion

Multiple classifier systems have attracted much interest because of their potential
for combining component classifiers to yield overall performance better than that
of any component. However, practical problems often have other features and
restrictions, beyond issues of simple classifier performance, and the adaptability
and flexibility of multiple classifier systems means that they can be effective
at meeting these requirements. We have illustrated by describing two multiple
classifier systems based on simple linear classifiers – a form which arose from the
practical constraints of the domain we are studying. We have found it convenient
to divide multiple classifier systems into two types, those which aggregate the
components and those which choose between them, and have illustrated one of
each kind.

References

[1]   Hand, D.J.: *Construction and Assessment of Classification Rules*. Chichester: Wi-
      ley (1997)
[2]   Kelly, M.G., Hand, D.J., Adams, N.M.: The impact of changing populations on
      classifier performance. *Proceedings of the Fifth ACM SIGKDD International Con-
      ference on Knowledge Discovery and Data Mining*, ed. Chaudhuri, S., Madigan,
      D., New York: ACM (1999) 367–371
[3]   Kelly, M.G., Hand, D.J., Adams, N.M.: Defining the goals to optimise data mining
      performance. *Proceedings of the Fourth ACM SIGKDD International Conference
      on Knowledge Discovery and Data Mining*, ed. Agrawal, R., Stolorz, P., Piatetsky-
      Shapiro, G., Menlo Park: AAAI Press (1998) 234–238
[4]   Kelly, M.G., Hand, D.J.: Credit scoring with uncertain class definitions. *IMA
      Journal of Mathematics Applied in Business and Industry* 10 (1998) 331–345
[5]   Breiman, L.: Bagging predictors. *Machine Learning* 24 (1996) 123–140
[6]   Buntine, W.L.: Learning in classification trees. *Statistics and Computing* 2 (1992)
      63–73 1992

[7] Oliver, J.J., Hand, D.J.: Averaging over decision trees. *Journal of Classification,* **13** (1996) 281–297

[8] Genest, C., McConway, K.J.: Allocating the weights in the linear opinion pool. *Journal of Forecasting* **9** (1990) 53–73

[9] von Winterfeld, D., Edwards, D.: Costs and payoffs in perceptual research. *Psychological Bulletin* **91** (1982) 213–217

[10] Kittler, J., Duin, R.P.W.: Combining classifiers. *Proceedings of the International Conference on Pattern Recognition,* IEEE (1996) 897–900

[11] Mertens, B.J.A, Hand, D.J.: Adjusted estimation for the combination of classifiers. *Intelligent Data Analysis* **4** (2000) 165–179

[12] Wolpert, D.H.: Stacked generalisation. *Neural Networks* **5** (1992) 241–259

[13] Friedman, J., Hastie, T., Tibshirani, R.: Additive logistic regression: a statistical view of boosting. *Annals of Statistics* **28** (2000) 337–374

[14] Hand, D.J., Henley, W.E.: Statistical classification methods in consumer credit scoring: a review. *Journal of the Royal Statistical Society, Series A* **169** (1997) 523–541

[15] Hand, D.J., Yu, K.: Idiot's Bayes – not so stupid after all? To appear in *International Statistical Review* (2001)

[16] Hand, D.J., Adams,N.M.: Defining attributes for scorecard construction. *Journal of Applied Statistics* **27** (2000) 527–540

[17] Hand, D.J.: Modelling consumer credit risk. Submitted to *IMA Journal of Management Mathematics* (2000)

[18] Hand, D.J., Kelly, M.G.: Superscorecards. Technical Report, Department of Mathematics, Imperial College, London.

[19] Hand, D.J.: How and why to choose a better scorecard. Technical Report, Department of Mathematics, Imperial College, London.

[20] Scott, M.J.: *PARCEL: feature selection in variable cost domains.* Doctoral dissertation, Engineering Department, Cambridge University, UK (1999)

[21] Provost, F.J., Fawcett, T.: Robust classification systems for imprecise environments. *Proceedings of the Fifteenth National Conference on Artificial Intelligence,* Madison, WI: AAAI press (1998) 706–713

[22] Adams, N.M., Hand D.J.: Comparing classifiers when the misallocation costs are uncertain. *Pattern Recognition* **32** (1999) 1139–1147

[23] Adams, N.M., Hand D.J.: Improving the practice of classifier performance assessment. *Neural Computation* **12** (2000) 300–311

[24] Holmes, C.C.,Adams, N.M.: A probabilistic nearest neighbor method for statistical pattern recognition. *Journal of the Royal Statistical Society, Series, B* (2001) in press

Least Squares and Estimation Measures via Error Correcting Output Code

Reza Ghaderi and Terry Windeatt

Centre for Vision, Speech and Signal Processing (CVSSP)
University of Surrey, Guildford, Surrey, GU2 5XH, U.K.
R.Ghaderi,T.Windeatt@eim.surrey.ac.uk

Abstract. It is known that the Error Correcting Output Code (ECOC) technique can improve generalisation for problems involving more than two classes. ECOC uses a strategy based on calculating distance to a class label in order to classify a pattern. However in some applications other kinds of information such as individual class probabilities can be useful. Least Squares(LS) is an alternative combination strategy to the standard distance based measure used in ECOC, but the effect of code specifications like the size of code or distance between labels has not been investigated in LS-ECOC framework. In this paper we consider constraints on choice of code matrix and express the relationship between final variance and local variance. Experiments on artificial and real data demonstrate that classification performance with LS can be comparable to the original distance based approach.

1 Introduction

Use of Error Correcting Output Codes (ECOC) for decomposing a multi-class problem into a set of complementary two class problems is a well established method in many applications [1,2,4,5,6,7,8,9,10,11,12,13,15,16,17,18]. When first suggested ECOC was based on the idea of using error-correcting codes as class labels, so that individual classification errors propagated from a set of binary classifiers can potentially be corrected [4]. For a two-class problem, classification errors can be one of two types, either predicted class w_1 for target class w_2 or predicted class w_2 for target class w_1.

In the ECOC method, a $k \times b$ binary code word matrix Z has one row (code word) for each of k classes, with each column defining one of b sub-problems that use a different labelling. Specifically, for the jth sub-problem, a training pattern with target class w_i ($i = 1...k$) is re-labelled as class w_1 if $Z_{ij} = x$ and as class w_2 if $Z_{ij} = \bar{x}$ (where x is a binary variable, typically zero or one). One way of looking at the re-labelling is to consider the k classes as being arranged into two super-classes. The original ECOC combining strategy uses a simple distance measure (L1 norm) which is calculated with respect to real-valued classifier outputs to determine the closest code word and assigns a test pattern accordingly. If the code word matrix satisfies suitable constraints, this strategy is identical to the Bayesian decision rule [17,16]. A problem with imposing constraints on code

J. Kittler and F. Roli (Eds.): MCS 2001, LNCS 2096, pp. 148–157, 2001.
© Springer-Verlag Berlin Heidelberg 2001

words is that the generation process becomes very complex, but fortunately these constraints are approximated by random codes providing b is large enough [9].

Despite improvements in generalisation for many problems that have been reported for ECOC, there is some discussion as to why it works well. A long random code appears to perform as well or better than a code designed for its error-correcting properties [9]. Attempts have been made to develop a theory for ensemble classifiers in terms of bias/variance and margin [8], but so far these ideas have not provided a convincing explaination for ECOC. A practical approach to determining source of effectiveness of ECOC is to look at variants of the ECOC strategy to see how they perform. This is also useful if we want to extend ECOC to deal with applications for which it would be desirable to understand ECOC features as estimation measures.

In this paper we look at an alternative ECOC combination strategy based on Least Squares (LS-ECOC), which was investigated in [11] and extended by incorporating ridged regression when b is small [8]. Recovering individual class probabilities from super-class probabilities is easily accomplished by matrix inversion when the individual probability estimates are exact and columns of ECOC matrix are arranged in "one-per-class" structure. In practice, estimates are not perfect and a natural choice for attempting to recover probabilities is Least Squares. However the effect of the code on performance of LS-ECOC has not been investigated in the way that it has for ECOC.

In Sect. 2 we determine, for Least Squares combining, the required form of the ECOC matrix such that errors in super-class probabilities (local experts) and individual class probabilities are jointly minimised. In Sect. 3 we find the relationship between final variance and the variance of expert's error as a function of number of columns b and distance between rows of ECOC matrix for equidistance codes. Experimental results in Sect. 4 demonstrate the effect of code selection on classification performance in comparison with original distance-based approach.

2   ECOC and LS-ECOC

Decomposition of a multi-class classification problem into binary sub-problems in ECOC can be interpreted as a transformation between spaces from the original output q to p, given in matrix form by

$$p = Z^T.q \tag{1}$$

Having the estimation of posterior probability $\hat{p}_j$ of super-classes (provided by jth expert), this matrix equation can be solved to find an estimation of class membership probabilities $\hat{q}$. However, Z^T is not a square matrix in general, and so does not have an inverse. Furthermore base classifiers will not produce correct probabilities, and the error can be represented by

$$\hat{p}_j = \sum_{i=1}^{k} Z_{ij}.q_i + \epsilon_{p_j} \qquad j = 1...b \tag{2}$$

A natural unbiased solution to equation (1) is based on using the method of least squares which means finding $\hat{q}$ which minimises a cost function such as

$$R_p = \sum_{j=1}^{b} \epsilon_{\hat{p}_j}^2 = \sum_{j=1}^{b} (\hat{p}_j - p_j)^2 = \sum_{j=1}^{b} (\hat{p}_j - \sum_{i=1}^{k} Z_{ij}.q_i)^2 \qquad (3)$$

The optimum point is given by

$$q^* = (Z.Z^T)^{-1}.Z.\hat{p} \qquad (4)$$

For the solution of equation (4) to exist, ZZ^T must be non-singular. If all elements of the ith row in Z are zero ($z_{il} = 0$ *for any* l), or if two rows (or columns) are equal, ZZ^T is singular. Also these conditions are not meaningful for the decomposition, so when the code is generated we make sure that they do not occur. In summary, having a precise estimation of p (Bayesian binary experts), we will find q precisely, but in the presence of noise the sensitivity of solution to the code matrix Z could be important.

3   Error and Code Selection

Any Z satisfying equation (3) will minimise R_p, but we may like to find a Z that will also minimise the sum square error of q (R_q). Now from (3)

$$R_p = \hat{p}^T \hat{p} - 2\hat{p}^T.p + p^T p \qquad (5)$$

and using equation (1)

$$R_p = \hat{q}^T.ZZ^T.\hat{q} - 2\hat{q}^T.ZZ^T.q + q^T.ZZ^T.q \qquad (6)$$

If we let $ZZ^T = m.I$, where I is the identity matrix and m a positive integer

$$R_p = m.I.(\hat{q}^T.\hat{q} - 2\hat{q}^T.q + q^T.q) = m.I.R_q$$

However this corresponds to the one-per-class case since it implies that $Z = I$, which means Z has no error-correcting capability.

Consider the case that ZZ^T can be written in the form

$$ZZ^T = \begin{bmatrix} n & m & \cdots & m \\ m & n & \cdots & m \\ \multicolumn{4}{c}{\cdots\cdots\cdots\cdots} \\ m & m & \cdots & n \end{bmatrix} \qquad (7)$$

Using the fact that $ZZ^T.q$ is a vector whose elements can be written in the form $(n - m)q_i + m$ equation (6) can be written as

$$R_p = -2(n-m).\hat{q}^T\hat{q} + m - 2(n-m).\hat{q}^T q - 2m(n-m).q^T q + m - 2\hat{q}^T.ZZ^T.q$$

so that

$$R_p = (n - m).R_q \qquad (8)$$

Therefore from equation (8), if Z is in the form given by equation (7), both R_q and R_p can be minimised simultaneously.

3.1   Equi-Distance Code

Furthermore, consider the situation that Z is an equi-distance code, so that $\sum_{l=1}^{b} |Z_{il} - Z_{jl}| = 2d$ for any pair i, j. Since Hamming Distance between pair i, j is the sum of the number of ones in row i and row j minus number of common ones between i, j we may write

$$\sum_{l=1}^{b} Z_{il} + \sum_{l=1}^{b} Z_{jl} - 2 \sum_{l=1}^{b} Z_{il}.Z_{jl} = 2d \tag{9}$$

similar equations can be written for pair i, k and pair j, k

$$\sum_{l=1}^{b} Z_{il} + \sum_{l=1}^{b} Z_{kl} - 2 \sum_{l=1}^{b} Z_{il}.Z_{kl} = 2d \tag{10}$$

$$\sum_{l=1}^{b} Z_{jl} + \sum_{l=1}^{b} Z_{kl} - 2 \sum_{l=1}^{b} Z_{jl}.Z_{kl} = 2d \tag{11}$$

From equations (9), (10),(11) after re-arranging

$$\sum_{l=1}^{b} Z_{il}.Z_{jl} = \sum_{l=1}^{b} Z_{kl}.Z_{jl} = \sum_{l=1}^{b} Z_{kl}.Z_{il} = m \tag{12}$$

where m is number of common bits in code word, and

$$\sum_{l=1}^{b} Z_{il} = \sum_{l=1}^{b} Z_{kl} = \sum_{l=1}^{b} Z_{jl} = n \tag{13}$$

where n is the number of ones in each row

Therefore if Z is an equi-distance matrix, the number of ones in different rows are the same, and the number of common ones between any pair of rows is equal. But a matrix Z of the form satisfying (7) will have the property of equation (13) and (12) and will minimise both R_p and R_q simultaneously, since

$$ZZ^T = \sum_{l=1}^{b} Z_{il}Z_{lj}^T = \sum_{l=1}^{b} Z_{il}Z_{jl} = \begin{cases} n \text{ if i=j} \\ m \text{ otherwise} \end{cases}$$

3.2   Variance and Bias

For ZZ^T of the form (7) the inverse is given by

$$C = (ZZ^T)^{-1} = \begin{bmatrix} c_1 & c_2 & \cdots & c_2 \\ c_2 & c_1 & \cdots & c_2 \\ \cdots & \cdots & \cdots & \cdots \\ c_2 & c_2 & \cdots & c_1 \end{bmatrix} \tag{14}$$

where c_1 and c_2 can be expressed in terms of m, n, k

$$c_1 = \frac{n + (k-1).m}{n^2 + (k-2).m.n - (k-1).m^2} \tag{15}$$

$$c_2 = \frac{-m}{n^2 + (k-2).m.n - (k-1).m^2} \tag{16}$$

From equation (4)

$$\hat{q} = \begin{bmatrix} c_1 & c_2 & \cdots & c_2 \\ c_2 & c_1 & \cdots & c_2 \\ & \cdots\cdots\cdots & \\ c_2 & c_2 & \cdots & c_1 \end{bmatrix} Z \begin{bmatrix} \hat{p}_1 \\ \hat{p}_2 \\ .. \\ \hat{p}_b \end{bmatrix}$$

We assume that individual classifers have same variance of error σ_p, and that the covariance of expert's error between any pair is simply $\rho.\sigma_p$, Then from using equation (13), the final variance can be written

$$\sigma_q = (c_1 - (k-1)c_2)^2.n.\sigma_p(1 + (n-1)\rho) \tag{17}$$

From equations (15) and (16), and knowing that $d = n - m$ (equation (9)) and that for any row of an equi-distance code $b = m + n$, equation (17) can be written as

$$\sigma_q = \frac{(b-d)^3(1 + (b-d-1)\rho)}{((1-2k)d^2 + kbd)^2}\sigma_p \tag{18}$$

Equation (18) tells us that final variance increases with correlation among experts. Although (18) is not a simple formula, with some simplification we can understand how d and b affect σ_q. If we consider the case of $\rho = 0$ for simplicity

$$\sigma_q = \frac{n^3}{(knd - (k-1)d^2)^2}.\sigma_p$$

so that σ_q increases with n, for fixed d. Also σ_q is reduced if d is increased for fixed n. In other words if we use longer words so that b is increased then m should also be increased to keep n fixed.

To determine effect of bias, suppose that local experts provide $\hat{p} + \delta$ where δ is the bias. From equation (3), R_p with bias is given by

$$\sum_{j=1}^{b}(\hat{p}_j + \delta - p_j)^2 = \sum_{j=1}^{b}(\hat{p}_j^2 + \delta^2 + p_j^2 + 2\hat{p}_j\delta - 2p_j\delta)$$

In most applications $\delta^2 \simeq 0$, and if $\hat{p}$ is an acceptable estimation, $\delta(\hat{p} - p)$ is small. Therefore R_p is not sensitive to bias.

4 Experimental Results

4.1 Artificial Data

We test our ideas on an artificial benchmark in which we can find the result of Bayesian classifier as reference and visualise the decision boundaries to show the behaviour of ECOC. It is helpful for understanding the behaviour of composite system in mimicking the Bayesian classifier.

Consider five groups of two dimensional random vectors having normal distribution as: $p(x|c_i) = \frac{1}{2\pi\sigma_i^2} exp[\frac{||x-\mu_i||^2}{-2\sigma_i^2}]$ for $i = 1, 2, ..., 5$ with parameters given in table 1.

Table 1. Distribution parameters of data used in artificial benchmark

class	c_1	c_2	c_3	c_4	c_5
μ_i(mean)	[0,0]	[3,0]	[0,5]	[7,0]	[0,9]
σ_i^2(variance)	1	4	9	25	64

Having a set of patterns consisting of equal number of patterns from each group, our goal is to classify them. Our base classifiers are not made by training, but using the parameters from table 1 we will just find the posterior probability of class (or super-class) membership for each sample. Using equal number of patterns from each group for test set(equal prior probability for classes); Bayesian decision rule says: $assign$ $x \to w_i$ if $P(w_i|x) = ArgMax_i(P(c_i|x))$. $P(c_i|x)$ is the posterior probability of class membership for class c_i, and can be found by the Bayesian formula: $P(c_i|x) = \frac{p(x|c_i)P(c_i)}{p(x)}$, in which $P(c_i)$ is the prior probability of class i and $p(x)$ is the same for all classes. So the decision rule can be changed: $assign$ $x \to c_i$ if $p(x|c_i) = ArgMax_i(p(x|c))$

To simulate the behaviour of the system, Gaussian and uniform random data are added to the output of experts. For a fair comparison between different methods, the noise for each code matrix is produced once and used in all combining methods. To find a code with desired properties, we have used BCH method[14], followed by selecting rows using properties (12) and (13). Columns with all zeros or ones have been removed, as explained in Sect. 3.

The following code matrices are used in this experiment ($k = 5$):
C1: a $k \times k$ unitary code(one per class)
C2: a $k \times 7$ matrix with randomly chosen binary elements
C3: a $k \times 7$ BCH code (minimum distance of 3, non-equal)
C4: a $k \times 7$ BCH code with equal distance of 4
C5: a $k \times 15$ matrix with randomly chosen elements
C6: a $k \times 15$ BCH code with equal distance of 8
C7: a $k \times 31$ BCH code with equal distance of 16

Adding Gaussian noise with variance of 0.5 and zero bias, the classification rate of the Bayesian classifier is 71.82% and with zero variance and 0.5 bias it is 72.08%, The rates of matching (representing how close the Bayes rate is approximated) for original ECOC and LS-ECOC are presented in table 2.

Table 2. Matching rate (% Bayesian) for ECOC and LS-ECOC with added noise

Code	Exp 1	Exp 2	Exp 3	Exp 4	Exp 5	Exp 6
C1	100.00	100.00	57.66	57.74	100.00	100.00
C2	97.56	100.00	65.74	59.98	53.88	86.88
C3	97.30	100.00	66.40	60.30	83.06	81.52
C4	100.00	100.00	69.04	69.04	98.64	98.64
C5	97.08	100.00	78.72	76.02	87.50	88.30
C6	100.00	100.00	82.78	82.78	100.00	100.00
C7	100.00	100.00	89.50	89.50	100.00	100.00

Exp 1: ECOC with no noise
Exp 2: LS-ECOC with no noise
Exp 3: ECOC with Gausian noise (Bias=0, Variance=.5)
Exp 4: LS-ECOC with Gausian noise (Bias=0, Variance=.5)
Exp 5: ECOC with Gausian noise (Bias=.5, Variance=0)
Exp 6: LS-ECOC with Gausian noise (Bias=.5, Variance=0)

From table 2:

1. Without noise, the performance of LS-ECOC for codes with unequal distance between rows is better than ECOC (Exp 1 and 2).
2. In noisy data
   a) For equi-distance codes(C1,C4,C6,C7) original ECOC and LS -ECOC have similar performance (Exp. 3,4 and 5,6).
   b) For codes with unequal distance, ECOC is better in variance reduction (Exp. 3 and 4) while LS-ECOC has better performance for added bias (Exp. 5 and 6). It seems reasonable that for added bias the distance measurement in ECOC is adversely affected since the number of ones in code word labels is different. On the other hand, LS-ECOC is less sensitive to bias as predicted in Sect. 3.
3. For longer random codes (C5), it can be expected that on average the number of ones in rows is similar and therefore there will be less difference in the ability of ECOC and LS-ECOC in handling bias and variance (Exp. 3,4 and 5,6).

4.2   Real Data

We tested Codes C1-C6 on real data for problems from [3] The base classifier is an MLP trained by BackPropagation with fixed learning rate, momentum and number of training epochs. The number of hidden nodes of MLP, number of training and test patterns and number of classes for the problems are shown in table 3. We also compared ECOC and LS-ECOC with Centroid-ECOC [8], which is identical to ECOC except distance is calculated to centroid of classes rather than to code word label. The mean and standard deviation of classification rates for ten independent runs are given in tables 4 and 5.

From tables 4 and 5:

1. The combining srategy (ECOC, Cent-ECOC, LS-ECOC) appears to have little impact, except for codes C2, C3 with LS.
2. In all datasets for 7-bit code, equi-distant is best (C2,C3,C4).
3. Longer codes perform better. However for the 15-bit code, random is better for two datasets, while equidistant is better for the other two.

Table 3. Specification of problems, showing nunber of problems, number of train and test patterns, and number of MLP hidden nodes

Database	Class (Num)	Train (Num)	Test (Num)	Nodes (Num)
zoo	7	50	51	1
car	4	50	1678	1
vehicle	4	350	496	5
satellite	6	1000	5435	2

Table 4. Mean and Std classification rate for ECOC, LS-ECOC and Centroid-ECOC on zoo and car data base.

code	ECOC(zoo)	Cent(zoo)	Lsqu(zoo)	ECOC(car)	Cent(car)	Lsqu(car)
C1	89.54	89.54	89.54	72.15	72.15	72.15
	5.99	5.99	5.99	4.83	4.83	4.83
C2	77.78	77.78	43.14	73.60	73.60	72.63
	13.91	13.91	6.79	0.93	0.93	1.21
C3	88.89	88.89	84.97	72.96	72.96	71.99
	6.30	6.30	2.26	3.62	3.62	2.79
C4	86.27	86.27	86.27	74.16	74.16	74.16
	8.98	8.98	8.98	3.70	3.70	3.70
C5	94.77	94.77	94.12	74.33	74.33	74.55
	2.99	2.99	3.39	2.35	2.35	2.39
C6	93.46	93.46	93.46	72.79	72.79	72.79
	2.99	2.99	2.99	2.65	2.65	2.65

Table 5. Mean and Std classification rate for ECOC, LS-ECOC and Centroid-ECOC on vehicle and satellite data base.

code	ECOC(veh)	Cent(veh)	Lsqu(veh)	ECOC(sat)	Cent(sat)	Lsqu(sat)
C1	62.77	62.77	62.77	65.05	65.05	65.05
	8.65	8.65	8.65	17.29	17.29	17.29
C2	66.94	66.94	61.22	80.29	80.29	23.91
	4.42	4.42	5.54	6.915	6.915	2.30
C3	53.02	53.02	57.12	70.06	70.06	62.67
	14.90	14.90	15.33	10.42	10.42	6.96
C4	69.15	69.15	69.15	69.48	69.48	69.48
	5.62	5.62	5.62	3.88	3.88	3.88
C5	73.32	73.32	73.72	77.74	77.74	77.74
	2.78	2.78	3.82	4.31	4.31	4.98
C6	75.34	75.34	75.34	80.43	80.43	80.43
	1.81	1.81	1.81	1.73	1.73	1.73

5   Discussion and Conclusion

We have demonstrated theoretically and practically that LS-ECOC used with equi-distant code words may give better performance, at least for shorter codes. However as length of code word was increased no performance advantage was apparent when comparing ECOC with LS-ECOC. Results on real data confirmed that any theoretical advantage of LS-ECOC is not necessarily realised in practice if longer codes are used. Comparison of three combining strategies ECOC, LS-ECOC and Centroid-ECOC suggest that the combination strategy does not play a major role in improving performance. This result lends support to the finding of others [9] that the error-correcting capability of a designed code may not be a significant aspect of the ECOC method, at least with respect to the combining strategies considered here.

In order to apply ECOC to situations where super-class probabilities are not suitable measures by themselves, we conclude that it may be useful to look at variants of ECOC. Least Squares represents an alternative combining strategy for ECOC that can give comparable classification results to the original distance-based strategy. If individual class probabilities are required, LS-ECOC provides a method of recovering them.

References

1. E. Alpaydin and E. Mayoraz. Learning error-correcting output codes from data. In *Proceeding of ICANN'99*, Edinburgh, U.K., September 1999. //www.cmpe.boun.edu.tr/ ethem/.
2. A. Berger. Error-correcting output coding for text classification. In *Proccedings of IJCAI'99*, Stockholm, Sweden, 1999. http://proxy3.nj.nec.com/did/8956.

3. C.L. Blake and C.J. Merz. UCI repository of machine learning databases. University of California, Irvine, Dept. of Information and Computer Sciences, 1998. http://www.ics.uci.edu/~mlearn/MLRepository.html.
4. T.G Dietterich and G. Bakiri. Error-correcting output codes: A general method for improving multiclass inductive learning programs. In *Proceedings of the Ninth National Conference on Artificial Intelligence (AAAI-91)*, pages 572–577. AAAI Press, 1991.
5. T.G. Dietterich and G Bakiri. Solving multi-class learning problems via error-correcting output codes. *Journal of Artificial Intelligence Research*, 2:263–286, 1995.
6. R. Ghaderi and T. Windeatt. Circular ecoc, a theoretical and experimental analysis. In *International Conference of Pattern Recognition(ICPR2000)*, pages 203–206, Barcelona,Spain, September 2000.
7. R. Ghaderi and T Windeatt. Viewpoints of error correcting output coding in classification task. In *The 7th Electrical and electronic Engineering seminar of Iranian students in Europ.*, Manchester U.K, May 2000.
8. G. James. *Majority Vote Classifiers: Theory and Applications*. PhD thesis, Dept. of Statistics, Univ. of Stanford, May 1998. http://www-stat.stanford.edu/ gareth/.
9. G. James and T. Hastie. The error coding method and PICT's. *Computational and Graphical Statistics*, 7:377–387, 1998.
10. E.B. Kong and T.G. Diettrich. Error-correcting output coding correct bias and variance. In *12th Int. Conf. of Machine Learning*, pages 313–321, San Fransisco, 1995. Morgan Kaufmann.
11. E.B. Kong and T.G. Diettrich. Probability estimation via error-correcting output coding. In *Int. Conf. of Artificial Inteligence and soft computing*, Banff,Canada, 1997. http://www.cs.orst.edu/ tgd/cv/pubs.html.
12. F. Leisch and K. Hornik. Combining neural networks voting classifiers and error correcting output codes. In I. Frolla and A. Plakove, editors, *MEASURMENT 97*, pages 266–269, Smolenice, Slovakia, May 1997.
13. F Masulli and G Valentini. Effectiveness of error correcting output codes in multiclass learning problems. In J.Kittler and F.Roli, editors, *Multiple Classifier Systems, MCS2000*, pages 107–116, Cagliari, Italy, 2000. Springer Lecture Notes in Computer Science.
14. W.W. Peterson and JR. Weldon. *Error-Correcting Codes*. MIT press, Cambridge,MA, 1972.
15. R.E. Schapire. Using output codes to boost multiclass learning problems. In *14th International Conf. on Machine Learning*, pages 313–321. Morgan Kaufman, 1997.
16. T. Windeatt and R. Ghaderi. Binary codes for multi-class decision combining. In *14th Annual International Conference of Society of Photo-Optical Instrumentation Engineers (SPIE)*, volume 4051, pages 23–34, Florida,USA, April 2000.
17. T. Windeatt and R. Ghaderi. Multi-class learning and ecoc sensitivity. *Electronics Letters*, 36(19), September 2000.
18. T. Windeatt and R. Ghaderi. Binary labelling and decision level fusion. *Information fusion, to be published*, 2001.

Dependence among Codeword Bits Errors in ECOC Learning Machines: An Experimental Analysis

Francesco Masulli[1,2] and Giorgio Valentini[1,2]

[1] DISI - Dipartimento di Informatica e Scienze dell'Informazione
Università di Genova, via Dodecaneso 35, 16146 Genova, Italia
[2] Istituto Nazionale per la Fisica della Materia
via Dodecaneso 33, 16146 Genova, Italia
{masulli, valenti}@disi.unige.it

Abstract. One of the main factors affecting the effectiveness of ECOC methods for classification is the dependence among the errors of the computed codeword bits. We present an extensive experimental work for evaluating the dependence among output errors of the decomposition unit of ECOC learning machines. In particular, we compare the dependence between ECOC Multi Layer Perceptrons (ECOC *monolithic*), made up by a single *MLP*, and ECOC ensembles made up by a set of independent and parallel dichotomizers (ECOC *PND*), using measures based on mutual information. In this way we can analyze the relations between performances, design and dependence among output errors in ECOC learning machines. Results quantitatively show that the dependence among computed codeword bits is significantly smaller for ECOC *PND*, pointing out that ensembles of independent dichotomizers are better suited for implementing ECOC classification methods.

1 Introduction

Error Correcting Output Coding (ECOC) [4] is a two-stage Output Coding (OC) decomposition method [10,8] that has been successfully applied to several classification problem [2,5]. In its first stage it decomposes a multiclass classification problem in a set of two-class subproblems, and in a second stage recomposes the original problem combining them to achieve the class label.

ECOC methods present several open problems such us the tradeoff between error recovering capabilities and learnability of the dichotomies induced by the decomposition scheme [1]. A connected problem is the analysis of the relation between codeword length and performances [5], while the selection of optimal dichotomic learning machines and the design of optimal codes for a given multiclass problem are other open questions subject to active research [3].

Another problem tackled by different works [7,6] is the relation between performances of ECOC and dependence among output errors. In the framework of coding theory Peterson [12] has shown that the error recovering capabilities of

J. Kittler and F. Roli (Eds.): MCS 2001, LNCS 2096, pp. 158–167, 2001.

ECOC codes hold if there is a low dependence among codeword bits. In particular, in a previous work [8] we qualitatively identify the dependence among output errors as one of the factors affecting the effectiveness of ECOC decomposition methods. In that work we outlined that we would expect an higher dependence among codeword bits in *monolithic Error Correcting Output Coding* [4,8] (ECOC *monolithic* for short) compared with *ECOC Parallel Non linear Dichotomizers (PND)* [8] (ECOC *PND* for short) learning machines, considering that ECOC *monolithic* share the same hidden layer of a single *MLP*, while *PND* dichotomizers, implemented by a separate *MLP* for each codeword bit, have their own layer of hidden units, specialized for a specific dichotomic task.

The aim of this work is to *quantitatively* test if the dependence among output errors between ECOC *monolithic* and ECOC *PND* is significantly different. In particular, we perform an extensive experimentation for comparing the dependence among output errors of the decomposition unit of ECOC *monolithic* and ECOC *PND* using measures based on mutual information [9], in order to evaluate if a low dependence among output errors is related to better classification performances.

The paper is structured as follows. In the next section we summarize the main characteristics of the measures based on mutual information we propose for evaluating the dependence among output errors in learning machines. Sect. 3 presents the experimental setup, the results and the discussion about the quantitative comparison of dependence among output errors between ECOC *monolithic* and ECOC *PND* learning machines. The conclusions summarize the main results and the incoming developments of this work.

2   Mutual Information Based Measures of Dependence among Output Errors

In this section we present a brief overview of the mutual information based measures for evaluating the dependence among output errors in learning machines. A more detailed discussion can be found in [9].

The main idea behind the evaluation of dependence among output errors of learning machines through mutual information based measures consists in interpreting the dependence among the outputs as the common information shared among them. Mutual information takes into account the marginal and joint probability distributions of the output errors, measuring in a sense the information shared among them. Using standard statistical measures such as the covariance or the coefficient of correlation we estimate only the linear relation between output errors. Conversely, a suitable measure of dependence must evaluate directly the probability distribution of the output errors in order to properly evaluate the stochastic independence between random variables. Mutual information, being a special case of the Kullback-Leibler divergence between two distributions, measures the matching between the joint density distribution and the product of the marginal density distribution of the output errors. If we a have a complete matching, the mutual information is 0 and the output errors are independent, otherwise higher is the value of the mutual information between output errors, higher will be the dependence between them.

The first measure based on mutual information we define is the *mutual information error* I_E:

$$I_E(e_1, \dots, e_l) = \sum_{j_1=1}^{b} \cdots \sum_{j_l=1}^{b} p(e_{1j_1}, \dots, e_{lj_l}) \log \left(\frac{p(e_{1j_1}, \dots, e_{lj_l})}{p(e_{1j_1}) \cdots p(e_{lj_l})} \right) \quad (1)$$

where $p(e_{1j_1}, \dots, e_{lj_l})$ is the *discrete joint probability distribution* among all the l output errors and $p(e_{ij_i})$ is the *discrete probability distribution* of the ith output error, with $i \in \{1, \dots, l\}$ and with the $j_i \in \{1, \dots, b\}$ corresponding to the discretization of the output errors in b intervals. The mutual information error (eq. 1) expresses the dependence among all output errors of a learning machine. If it is equal to 0 then the distributions of the output errors are statistically independent. It expresses also how are similar the probability distribution of the output errors.

Considering the outputs of a learning machine correct if their errors are below a certain threshold, i.e if $\forall i$, $e_i < \delta$, $\delta > 0$, we define the *mutual information specific error* I_{SE}:

$$I_{SE}(e_1, \dots, e_l) = \sum_{\mathcal{J}} p(e_{1j_1}, \dots, e_{lj_l}) \log \left(\frac{p(e_{1j_1}, \dots, e_{lj_l})}{p(e_{1j_1}) \cdots p(e_{lj_l})} \right) \quad (2)$$

where

$$\mathcal{J} = \left\{ [j_1, \dots j_l] | \exists (j_v, j_w) | (j_v \neq 1) \wedge (j_w \neq 1) \right\}$$

with $v, w \in \{1 \dots l\}$. This measure takes into account the output errors only when two or more errors spring from the output, disregarding all cases with no errors or with only one error. For evaluating the dependence among specific pairs of output errors, we introduce the *pairwise mutual information error matrix* R composed by the elements $I_E(e_i, e_j) = [R_{ij}]$ and the *pairwise mutual information specific error matrix* S, composed by the elements $I_{SE}(e_i, e_j) = [S_{ij}]$. We then define also two other global indices: the *pairwise mutual information error matrix index* Φ_R:

$$\Phi_R = \sum_{i=1}^{l} \sum_{j=1}^{l} I_E(e_i, e_j) \quad (3)$$

and the *pairwise mutual information specific error matrix index* Φ_S:

$$\Phi_S = \sum_{i=1}^{l} \sum_{j=1}^{l} I_{SE}(e_i, e_j) \quad (4)$$

These indices measure the sum of the the mutual information error and the mutual information specific error between all the output pairs of the learning machines, and in this sense can be regarded as global measures of dependence

Table 1. Main features of the data sets.

Data set	Number of attributes	Number of classes	Number of training samples	Number of testing samples
d5	3	5	30000	30000
glass	9	6	214	10-fold cross-val
letter	16	26	16000	4000
optdigits	64	10	3823	1797

between output errors. Note that these indices (Eq. 3 and 4) are not equivalent to the corresponding Eq. 1 and 2 of the mutual information among all output errors: Eq. 3 and 4 consider only the mutual information between pairs of output errors, while Eq. 1 and 2 consider the overall mutual information among all output errors.

These mutual information related quantities can be used to compare the dependence of the output errors among different learning machines on the same learning problem, using, of course, the same data sets.

3   Experimental Results

In this section we present a *quantitative* comparison of the dependence among output errors of the decomposition   unit of ECOC *monolithic* and ECOC *PND* learning machines, and we analyze the relations between performances, design and dependence among output errors. For this purpose we experimentally compare the mutual information error I_E, the mutual information specific error I_{SE} and the pairwise indices Φ_R and Φ_R (Sect. 2) of the ECOC *monolithic* and *PND* learning machines using different data sets.

3.1   Experimental Setup

We have used four different data sets: the first one, $d5$ [1] is generated by NEU-RObjects [13], a set of C++ library classes for neural networks development, and the other three, *glass, letter* and *optdigits* are from the UCI machine learning repository of Irvine [11]. The synthetic data set $d5$ is made up by five three-dimensional classes, each composed by two normal distributed disjoint clusters of data. The main characteristics of the data sets are shown in Tab. 1.

In order to perform training and testing of the considered learning machines, we have applied multiple runs of different random initializations of weights using a single pair of training and testing data sets and *k-fold cross validation* methods. The results are summarized in Tab.2: errors on the test set are expressed as percent rates, and for each data set the minimum (min), average (mean), and standard deviation (stdev) of the error is given. We have used, both for training

---

[1] $d5$ is on line available at ftp://ftp.disi.unige.it/person/ValentiniG/Data.

the learning machines and for evaluating the dependence among the output errors the software library *NEURObjects* [13].

We have compared the dependence among output errors of ECOC *monolithic* and ECOC *PND* learning machines varying the structure (number of hidden units), the number of discretization intervals of the output errors, and the values of δ (Sect. 2) that define the notion of "correctness" of the outputs.

3.2   Results and Discussion

In this section we present the results of the comparison of I_E and I_{SE} among all outputs, of the Φ_R and Φ_S pairwise indices and the comparison of R and S matrices.

In Fig. 1 we compare I_E and I_{SE} among all output errors of the *monolithic* and ECOC *PND* learning machines on the data sets *d5* and *glass*. On the axes are represented the computed I_E (Fig. 1 a and b) and I_{SE} (Fig. 1 c and d) values. Each point corresponds to a different triplet number of hidden units, number of intervals and values of δ. We point out that all points are above the dotted line, showing that both I_E (Fig. 1 a and b) and I_{SE} (Fig. 1 c and d) are greater for ECOC *monolithic* respect to ECOC *PND*, no matter the structure, the number of intervals and the δ values used. Fig. 2 shows that on all the data sets about all the points are above the dotted line, i.e. all the values of Φ_R are greater for ECOC *monolithic* compared with ECOC *PND*. Similar results hold also considering the Φ_S index. The examination of the pairwise mutual information error matrices can provide us with information about the dependence of specific pairs of output errors. The S and R matrices are represented as triangular matrices, without the diagonal, because they are symmetric and the elements on the diagonal are the entropy of output errors.

Comparing the mutual information   matrices of ECOC *monolithic* and *PND* learning machines, we find that about all the pairwise mutual information errors are higher in ECOC *monolithic*: on the d5 data set no element of the R matrix is higher for *PND* and only 1 of 21 is higher considering the S matrix; on optdigits only 3 of 91 both for R and S matrices are higher, and no element of the 435 composing the triangular matrices R and S is higher for *PND* on letter data set.

Table 2. Performance of ECOC monolithic and ECOC *PND* ensemble on four data sets (percent error rates).

	ECOC monolithic			ECOC *PND* ensemble		
Data set	min	mean	stdev	min	mean	stdev
d5	13.27	18.31	6.44	11.91	12.34	0.74
glass	33.18	36.17	4.54	30.37	32.05	1.77
letter	4.95	6.55	1.91	3.05	3.24	0.24
optdigits	2.61	3.08	0.47	1.89	1.95	0.10

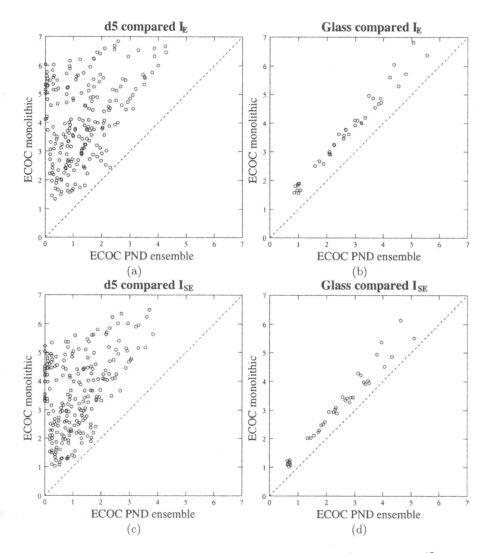

Fig. 1. Compared mutual information error I_E and mutual information specific error I_{SE} among all outputs between ECOC *monolithic* and *PND* learning machines on d5 (a)(c) and glass (b)(d) data sets.

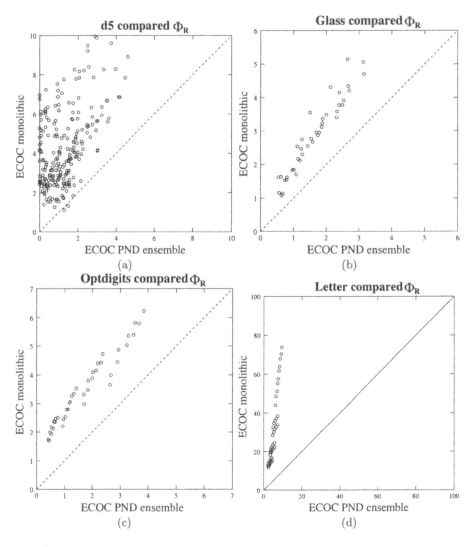

Fig. 2. Compared mutual information error matrix indices Φ_R between ECOC *monolithic* and *PND* learning machines on d5 (a), glass (b), optdigits (c) and letter (d) data sets.

Fig. 3 shows the relations between error rates and mutual information based measures I_E and I_{SE} considering the $d5$ data set. Both I_E and I_{SE} curves of ECOC PND ensemble lie below the corresponding curves of ECOC $monolithic$ learning machines: These figures confirm that the dependence among output errors is smaller for ECOC PND. It is worth noting that, as expected, I_E and I_{SE} grow with error rates, but their values are mostly related to a specific learning machine architecture.

We have seen that all the results relative to the mutual information error I_E and the mutual information specific error I_{SE} among all the outputs on the data sets $d5$ and $glass$ show greater values for ECOC $monolithic$ respect to ECOC PND (Fig. 1). These results are confirmed by the evaluation of the mutual information error matrix indices Φ_R and Φ_S (Fig. 2), concerning also the $optdigits$ and $letter$ data sets. The analysis of the pairwise mutual information matrices R and S converges on showing that also about all the I_E and I_{SE} values between each pair of output errors are greater for ECOC $monolithic$ learning machines. Moreover, applying the $mutual\ information\ error\ t\text{-}test$ [9] for evaluating the significance of the differences between the I_E and I_{SE} values of the two ECOC learning machines, we have verified that in almost all the comparisons we have registered a significant difference with a degree of confidence of 95%.

Consequently the experimental results on the selected data sets confirm that ECOC Parallel Non linear Dichotomizers show a lower dependence among the output errors of their decomposition unit compared with the output errors of the corresponding ECOC $monolithic$ multi layer perceptron.

4   Conclusions

In this paper, we have compared the dependence among output errors between ECOC $monolithic\ MLP$ and ECOC PND learning machines using measures based on mutual information.

The measurements of the mutual information error I_E, the mutual information specific error I_{SE} and the mutual information error matrix indices Φ_R and Φ_S show that ECOC PND have a lower dependence among the output errors of their decomposition unit compared with the output errors of the corresponding ECOC $monolithic\ MLP$. Hence ECOC PND ensembles appear more suited to exploit the error recovering capabilities of ECOC methods, whose effectiveness depends on the independence among codeword bits errors [12,8].

The observed difference in the dependence among output errors is related to the different design of the two learning machines and in particular to the design of the decomposition unit. Our experimentation suggests that a low dependence can be achieved implementing the decomposition unit through an ensemble of parallel and independent dichotomizers, such as the dichotomic $MLPs$ proposed in our experimentation, or other suitable dichotomizers such as decision trees or support vector machines.

An ongoing development of this work consists in quantitatively studying how boosting methods can increase the diversity among the dichotomizers and

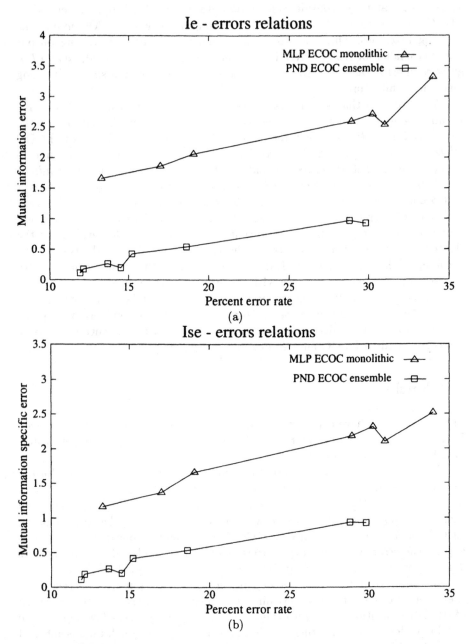

Fig. 3. Relations error rates - mutual information error I_E (a) and error rates - mutual information specific error I_{SE} (b) in ECOC *monolithic* and *PND* learning machines on the d5 data set.

the independence among output errors in ECOC learning machines, using the proposed measures based on mutual information, and extending them to evaluate the diversity between the base learners.

Acknowledgments. We would like to thank the anonymous reviewers for their comments and suggestions. This work has been partially funded by Progetto finalizzato CNR-MADESS II, INFM and University of Genova.

References

1. E.L. Allwein, R.E. Schapire, and Y. Singer. Reducing multiclass to binary: a unifying approach for margin classifiers. In *Proc. ICML'2000, The Seventeenth International Conference on Machine Learning*, 2000.
2. A. Berger. Error correcting output coding for text classification. In *IJCAI'99: Workshop on machine learning for information filtering*, 1999.
3. Y. Crammer and Y. Singer. On the learnability and design of output codes for multiclass problems. In *Proceedings of the Thirteenth Annual Conference on Computational Learning Theory*, pages 35-46, 2000.
4. T.G. Dietterich and G. Bakiri. Solving multiclass learning problems via error-correcting output codes. *Journal of Artificial Intelligence Research*, (2):263–286, 1995.
5. R. Ghani. Using error correcting output codes for text classification. In *ICML 2000: Proceedings of the 17th International Conference on Machine Learning*, pages 303–310, San Francisco, US, 2000. Morgan Kaufmann Publishers.
6. V. Guruswami and A. Sahai. Multiclass learning, boosting, and error-correcting codes. In *Proc. of the Twelfth Annual Conference on Computational Learning Theory*, pages 145–155. ACM Press, 1999.
7. E. Kong and T.G. Dietterich. Error - correcting output coding correct bias and variance. In *The XII International Conference on Machine Learning*, pages 313–321, San Francisco, CA, 1995. Morgan Kauffman.
8. F. Masulli and G. Valentini. Effectiveness of error correcting output codes in multiclass learning problems. In *Lecture Notes in Computer Science*, volume 1857, pages 107–116. Springer-Verlag, Berlin, Heidelberg, 2000.
9. F. Masulli and G. Valentini. Mutual information methods for evaluating dependence among outputs in learning machines. Technical Report TR-01-02, DISI - Dipartimento di Informatica e Scienze dell' Informazione - Università di Genova, 2001. ftp://ftp.disi.unige.it/person/ValentiniG/papers/TR-01-02.ps.gz.
10. E. Mayoraz and M. Moreira. On the decomposition of polychotomies into dichotomies. In *The XIV International Conference on Machine Learning*, pages 219–226, Nashville, TN, July 1997.
11. C.J. Merz and P.M. Murphy. UCI repository of machine learning databases, 1998. www.ics.uci.edu/mlearn/MLRepository.html.
12. W.W. Peterson and E.J.Jr. Weldon. *Error correcting codes*. MIT Press, Cambridge, MA, 1972.
13. G. Valentini and F. Masulli. NEURObjects, a set of library classes for neural networks development. In *Proceedings of IIA'99 and SOCO'99*, pages 184–190, Millet, Canada, 1999. ICSC Academic Press.

Information Analysis of Multiple Classifier Fusion[*]

Jiří Grim[1], Josef Kittler[2], Pavel Pudil[1], and Petr Somol[1]

[1] Institute of Information Theory and Automation,
P.O.BOX 18, CZ-18208 Prague 8, Czech Republic,
{grim, pudil,somol}@utia.cas.cz
[2] School of Electronic Engineering, Information Technology and Mathematics,
University of Surrey, Guildford GU2 5XH, United Kingdom

Abstract. We consider a general scheme of parallel classifier combinations in the framework of statistical pattern recognition. Each statistical classifier defines a set of output variables in terms of a posteriori probabilities, i.e. it is used as a feature extractor. Unlike usual combining schemes the output vectors of classifiers are combined in parallel. The statistical Shannon information is used as a criterion to compare different combining schemes from the point of view of the theoretically available decision information. By means of relatively simple arguments we derive a theoretical hierarchy between different schemes of classifier fusion in terms of information inequalities.

1 Introduction

A natural way to solve practical problems of pattern recognition is to try different classification methods, parameters and feature subsets with the aim to achieve the best performance. However, as different classifiers frequently make different recognition errors, it is often useful to combine multiple classifiers in order to improve the final recognition accuracy. In the last few years various combination methods were proposed by different authors (cf. [12,13] for extensive references).

The most widely used approach typically combines the classifier outputs directly by means of simple combining rules or functions. It relates to techniques like majority vote, threshold voting, averaged Bayes classifier, different linear combinations of a posteriori probabilities, maximum and minimum rules, product rule (cf. e.g. [11,6,14]) and also more complex combining tools like fuzzy logic or Dempster-Shafer theory of evidence (cf. e.g. [9,10,15]).

Another approach makes use of classifiers as feature extractors. The extracted features (e.g. a posteriori probabilities) are used simultaneously in parallel to define a new decision problem (cf. [16,18,7,8]). Instead of a simple combining function the new features are evaluated by a classifier again (e.g. by a neural network) to realize the compound classification. This approach is capable of very

[*] Supported by the grant No. 402/01/0981 of the Czech Grant Agency and partially by the Complex research project No. K1019101 of the Czech Academy of Sciences.

J. Kittler and F. Roli (Eds.): MCS 2001, LNCS 2096, pp. 168–177, 2001.
© Springer-Verlag Berlin Heidelberg 2001

general solutions but the potential advantages are achieved at the expense of the lost simplicity of the combining rules.

In the present paper we consider a general scheme corresponding to the last type of parallel classifier combinations in the framework of statistical pattern recognition. In particular we assume that each statistical classifier defines a set of output variables in terms of a posteriori probabilities which are simply used in parallel as features. We use the term parallel classifier fusion to emphasize the difference with the combining functions.

The standard criterion to measure the quality of classifier combination techniques is the recognition accuracy. In this paper we use the statistical Shannon information to compare different combining schemes as it is more sensitive than the classification error and easily applicable. By means of relatively simple facts we derive a theoretical hierarchy between basic schemes of classifier fusion in terms of information inequalities. The results have general validity but their meaning is rather theoretical since the compared decision information is only theoretically available in the new compound feature space.

In Section 2 we describe the framework of statistical pattern recognition and introduce the basic concept of information preserving transform. In Section 3 we discuss the information properties of imprecise classifiers and show how the information loss of practical solutions can be reduced by the parallel fusion (Sec. 4). In Sec. 5 we compare the parallel classifier fusion with a method based on general combining rules. The obtained hierarchy of different methods of multiple classifier fusion is discussed in Sec. 6 and finally summarized in the Conclusion (Sec. 7).

2   Information Preserving Transform

Considering the framework of statistical pattern recognition we assume in this paper that some N-dimensional binary observations x have to be classified into one of mutually exclusive classes $\omega \in \Omega$:

$$x = (x_1, \ldots, x_N) \in \mathcal{X}, \quad \mathcal{X} = \{0,1\}^N, \quad \Omega = \{\omega_1, \ldots, \omega_K\}.$$

The observations $x \in \mathcal{X}$ are supposed to occur randomly according to some a priori probabilities $p(\omega)$ and class-conditional probability distributions

$$P(x|\omega)p(\omega), \quad x \in \mathcal{X}, \quad \omega \in \Omega. \tag{1}$$

Given the probabilistic description of classes, we can compute for any input vector x the a posteriori probabilities

$$p(\omega|x) = \frac{P(x|\omega)p(\omega)}{P(x)}, \quad P(x) = \sum_{\omega \in \Omega} P(x|\omega)p(\omega), \quad x \in \mathcal{X} \tag{2}$$

where $P(x)$ is the unconditional joint probability distribution of x. The a posteriori probabilities $p(\omega|x)$ contain all statistical information about the set of classes Ω given $x \in \mathcal{X}$ and can be easily used to classify uniquely the input vector x, if necessary.

For the sake of information analysis let us consider the following vector transform T of the original decision problem defined on the input space $\mathcal{X}$:

$$T : \mathcal{X} \to \mathcal{Y}, \quad \mathcal{Y} \subset R^K, \quad y = T(x) = (T_1(x), \ldots, T_K(x)) \in \mathcal{Y} \qquad (3)$$

$$y_k = T_k(x) = \varphi(p(\omega_k|x)), \quad x \in \mathcal{X}, \quad k = 1, \ldots, K. \qquad (4)$$

where φ is any bijective function. Let us remark that there are strong arguments to specify the function φ as logarithm in connection with neural networks [2,4].

The transform (3), (4) naturally induces a partition of the space $\mathcal{X}$

$$S = \{S_y, y \in \mathcal{Y}\}, \quad S_y = \{x \in \mathcal{X} : T(x) = y\}, \quad \bigcup_{y \in \mathcal{Y}} S_y = \mathcal{X} \qquad (5)$$

and transforms the original distributions $P_{\mathcal{X}}, P_{\mathcal{X}|\omega}$ on the input space $\mathcal{X}$ to the distributions $Q_{\mathcal{Y}}, Q_{\mathcal{Y}|\omega}$ on $\mathcal{Y}$:

$$Q_{\mathcal{Y}}(y) = \sum_{x \in S_y} P_{\mathcal{X}}(x) = P_{\mathcal{X}}(S_y), \quad y \in \mathcal{Y}, \qquad (6)$$

$$Q_{\mathcal{Y}|\omega}(y|\omega) = \sum_{x \in S_y} P_{\mathcal{X}|\omega}(x|\omega) = P_{\mathcal{X}|\omega}(S_y|\omega), \quad \omega \in \Omega. \qquad (7)$$

Throughout the paper we use, whenever tolerable, the more simple notation

$$P(x) = P_{\mathcal{X}}(x), \quad P(x|\omega) = P_{\mathcal{X}|\omega}(x|\omega), \quad Q(y) = Q_{\mathcal{Y}}(y), \quad Q(y|\omega) = Q_{\mathcal{Y}|\omega}(y|\omega).$$

In analogy with (2) we can write

$$p(\omega|y) = \frac{Q(y|\omega)p(\omega)}{Q(y)}, \quad \omega \in \Omega, \quad y \in \mathcal{Y}. \qquad (8)$$

It is well known that, from the point of view of classification error, the a posteriori probabilities represent optimal features (cf. [1]). Moreover, it has been shown that the transform defined by Eqs. (4) preserves the statistical decision information and minimizes the entropy of the output space (cf. [2,17]). In particular, if we introduce the following notation for the unconditional and conditional Shannon entropies

$$H(p_\Omega) = \sum_{\omega \in \Omega} -p(\omega) \log p(\omega), \quad H(p_{\Omega|x}) = \sum_{\omega \in \Omega} -p(\omega|x) \log p(\omega|x), \qquad (9)$$

$$H(p_\Omega|P_{\mathcal{X}}) = \sum_{x \in \mathcal{X}} P(x) H(p_{\Omega|x}), \quad H(p_\Omega|Q_{\mathcal{Y}}) = \sum_{y \in \mathcal{Y}} Q(y) H(p_{\Omega|y}), \qquad (10)$$

then we can write

$$I(P_{\mathcal{X}}, p_\Omega) = H(p_\Omega) - H(p_\Omega|P_{\mathcal{X}}) = H(p_\Omega) - H(p_\Omega|Q_{\mathcal{Y}}) = I(Q_{\mathcal{Y}}, p_\Omega). \qquad (11)$$

Let us recall that

$$S_y = \{x \in \mathcal{X} : T(x) = y\} = \{x \in \mathcal{X} : p(\omega_k|x) = \varphi^{-1}(y_k),\ k = 1, \ldots, K\} \quad (12)$$

and therefore the distributions $p_{\Omega|x}$ are identical for all $x \in S_y$. Thus, in view of the definition (8), we can write for any $\omega \in \Omega, y \in \mathcal{Y}$ and for all $x \in S_y$:

$$p(\omega|y) = \frac{Q(y|\omega)p(\omega)}{Q(y)} = \frac{P(S_y|\omega)p(\omega)}{P(S_y)} = \sum_{x \in S_y} \frac{P(x)}{P(S_y)} p(\omega|x) = p(\omega|x). \quad (13)$$

Consequently, we obtain equation

$$H(p_\Omega|Q_\mathcal{Y}) = \sum_{y \in \mathcal{Y}} P(S_y) H(p_{\Omega|y}) = \sum_{y \in \mathcal{Y}} \sum_{x \in S_y} P(x) H(p_{\Omega|x}) = H(p_\Omega|P_\mathcal{X}) \quad (14)$$

which implies Eq. (11). In words, the transform T preserves the statistical Shannon information $I(P_\mathcal{X}, p_\Omega)$ about p_Ω contained in $P_\mathcal{X}$ (cf. [2,17]).

3   Information Loss Caused by Imprecise Classifiers

Let $P_{\mathcal{X}|\omega}^{(i)}$ be some estimates of the unknown conditional probability distributions $P_{\mathcal{X}|\omega}$ obtained e.g. in I different computational experiments:

$$\{P_{\mathcal{X}|\omega}^{(i)}, \omega \in \Omega\},\ i \in \mathcal{I},\ \mathcal{I} = \{1, \ldots, I\}. \quad (15)$$

We denote $p^{(i)}(\omega|x)$ the a posteriori probabilities which can be computed from the estimated distributions

$$p^{(i)}(\omega|x) = \frac{P^{(i)}(x|\omega)p(\omega)}{P^{(i)}(x)},\quad P^{(i)}(x) = \sum_{\omega \in \Omega} P^{(i)}(x|\omega)p(\omega),\quad x \in \mathcal{X}. \quad (16)$$

Here and in the following Sections we assume the a priori probabilities $p(\omega)$ to be known and fixed. In analogy with (3),(4) we define

$$T^{(i)} : \mathcal{X} \to \mathcal{Y}^{(i)},\quad \mathcal{Y}^{(i)} \subset R^K,\quad y^{(i)} = T^{(i)}(x) = (T_1^{(i)}(x), \ldots, T_K^{(i)}(x)) \in \mathcal{Y}^{(i)},$$

$$y_k^{(i)} = T_k^{(i)}(x) = \varphi(p^{(i)}(\omega_k|x)),\quad x \in \mathcal{X},\quad k = 1, \ldots, K,\quad (i \in \mathcal{I}). \quad (17)$$

Again, the transform $T^{(i)}$ induces a partition of the input space $\mathcal{X}$:

$$\mathcal{S}^{(i)} = \{S_{y^{(i)}}, y^{(i)} \in \mathcal{Y}^{(i)}\},\quad S_{y^{(i)}} = \{x \in \mathcal{X} : T^{(i)}(x) = y^{(i)}\} \quad (18)$$

and transforms the original true probability distributions $P_\mathcal{X}, P_{\mathcal{X}|\omega}$ on $\mathcal{X}$ to the corresponding distributions $Q_{\mathcal{Y}^{(i)}}^{(i)}, Q_{\mathcal{Y}^{(i)}|\omega}^{(i)}$ on $\mathcal{Y}$ (cf. (6), (7)):

$$Q_{\mathcal{Y}^{(i)}}^{(i)}(y^{(i)}) = P_\mathcal{X}(S_{y^{(i)}}),\quad Q_{\mathcal{Y}^{(i)}|\omega}^{(i)}(y^{(i)}|\omega) = P_{\mathcal{X}|\omega}(S_{y^{(i)}}|\omega),\quad y^{(i)} \in \mathcal{Y}^{(i)}. \quad (19)$$

In analogy with (13) we can write for any $\omega \in \Omega$ and $\boldsymbol{y}^{(i)} \in \mathcal{Y}^{(i)}$:

$$p(\omega|\boldsymbol{y}^{(i)}) = p(\omega|S_{y^{(i)}}) = \frac{P(S_{y^{(i)}}|\omega)p(\omega)}{P(S_{y^{(i)}})} = \sum_{x \in S_{y^{(i)}}} \frac{P(\boldsymbol{x})}{P(S_{y^{(i)}})} p(\omega|\boldsymbol{x}). \qquad (20)$$

However, unlike Eq. (13), the probabilities $p(\omega|\boldsymbol{x})$ need not be identical for all $\boldsymbol{x} \in S_{y^{(i)}}$ because the partition $S^{(i)}$ derives from the estimated distributions $P_{\mathcal{X}|\omega}^{(i)}$ which may differ from the unknown true distributions $P_{\mathcal{X}|\omega}$. Thus, for some $S_{y^{(i)}} \in S^{(i)}$, there may be different vectors $\boldsymbol{x}, \boldsymbol{x}' \in S_{y^{(i)}}$ such that $p(\omega|\boldsymbol{x}) \neq p(\omega|\boldsymbol{x}')$ for some $\omega \in \Omega$. Consequently, we can write the following general Jensen's inequality for the convex function $\xi \log \xi$:

$$- p(\omega|S_{y^{(i)}}) \log p(\omega|S_{y^{(i)}}) \geq \sum_{x \in S_{y^{(i)}}} \frac{P(\boldsymbol{x})}{P(S_{y^{(i)}})} [-p(\omega|\boldsymbol{x}) \log p(\omega|\boldsymbol{x})]. \qquad (21)$$

Multiplying the inequality (21) by $P(S_{y^{(i)}})$ and summing through $\omega \in \Omega$ and $\boldsymbol{y}^{(i)} \in \mathcal{Y}^{(i)}$ we obtain the following inequality for conditional entropies

$$H(p_\Omega|Q_{y^{(i)}}^{(i)}) = \sum_{y^{(i)} \in \mathcal{Y}^{(i)}} Q^{(i)}(\boldsymbol{y}^{(i)}) H(p_{\Omega|y^{(i)}}) \geq \sum_{x \in \mathcal{X}} P(\boldsymbol{x}) H(p_{\Omega|x}) = H(p_\Omega|P_\mathcal{X}). \qquad (22)$$

In view of Eq. $H(p_\Omega|P_\mathcal{X}) = H(p_\Omega|Q_y)$ (cf. (14)) it follows that

$$I(P_\mathcal{X}, p_\Omega) = I(Q_y, p_\Omega) \geq I(Q_{y^{(i)}}^{(i)}, p_\Omega), \quad (i \in \mathcal{I}). \qquad (23)$$

Thus, if the true probabilistic description $P_{\mathcal{X}|\omega}, \omega \in \Omega$ is unknown and we are given only some estimated distribution $P_{\mathcal{X}|\omega}^{(i)}$, then we may expect the transform $T^{(i)}$ to be accompanied with some information loss. In other words, as it is well known, the extracted features $y_k^{(i)}(\boldsymbol{x})$ usually contain only a part of the original decision information.

Remark 4.1 It should be emphasized at this point that there is an important difference between the present concept of information analysis and a practical problem of pattern recognition. In a practical situation we would use the estimated conditional distributions $P_{\mathcal{X}|\omega}^{(i)}$ to compute a posteriori probabilities $p^{(i)}(\omega|\boldsymbol{x})$ and finally the decision $d^{(i)}(\boldsymbol{x}) \in \Omega$ given an input observation $\boldsymbol{x} \in \mathcal{X}$. However, in case of the above information analysis, we use the estimated distributions $P_{\mathcal{X}|\omega}^{(i)}$ only to define the related transform (feature extractor) $T^{(i)}$. The resulting information inequality (23) compares the original "complete" decision information $I(Q_y, p_\Omega)$ and the theoretically available information content $I(Q_{y^{(i)}}^{(i)}, p_\Omega)$ of the new features $y_k^{(i)}$ (cf. (17)). Note that the true statistical properties of the new features expressed by the distributions $Q_{y^{(i)}|\omega}^{(i)}, Q_{y^{(i)}}^{(i)}$ cannot be deduced from the estimated conditional distributions $P_{\mathcal{X}|\omega}^{(i)}$. It would be necessary to estimate them again from the training data. This remark applies in analogous way to all transforms considered in the following Sections.

4   Parallel Classifier Fusion

The inequality (23) suggests possible information loss which may occur in practical solutions. One possibility to reduce this information loss is to fuse multiple classifiers in parallel. In particular, considering multiple estimates (15) of the unknown conditional distributions $P_{\mathcal{X}|\omega}, \omega \in \Omega$ we can use the corresponding transforms $\boldsymbol{T}^{(i)}, i \in \mathcal{I}$, (cf. (17)) simultaneously to define a compound transform $\tilde{\boldsymbol{T}}$:

$$\tilde{\boldsymbol{T}} : \mathcal{X} \to \tilde{\mathcal{Y}}, \quad \tilde{\mathcal{Y}} \subset R^{IK}, \quad \tilde{\boldsymbol{y}} = (\boldsymbol{y}^{(1)}, \boldsymbol{y}^{(2)}, \dots, \boldsymbol{y}^{(I)}) = \tilde{\boldsymbol{T}}(\boldsymbol{x}),$$

$$\tilde{\boldsymbol{y}} = \tilde{\boldsymbol{T}}(\boldsymbol{x}) = (T_1^{(1)}(\boldsymbol{x}), \dots, T_K^{(1)}(\boldsymbol{x}), \dots, T_1^{(I)}(\boldsymbol{x}), \dots, T_K^{(I)}(\boldsymbol{x})) \in \tilde{\mathcal{Y}} \qquad (24)$$

$$y_k^{(i)} = T_k^{(i)}(\boldsymbol{x}) = \varphi(p^{(i)}(\omega_k|\boldsymbol{x})), \quad \boldsymbol{x} \in \mathcal{X}, \quad k = 1, \dots, K, \quad i \in \mathcal{I}. \qquad (25)$$

In this sense the joint transform $\tilde{\boldsymbol{T}}$ can be viewed as a parallel fusion of the transforms $\boldsymbol{T}^{(1)}, \boldsymbol{T}^{(2)}, \dots, \boldsymbol{T}^{(I)}$. Again, the transform $\tilde{\boldsymbol{T}}$ induces the corresponding partition of the input space $\mathcal{X}$:

$$\tilde{S} = \{S_{\tilde{\boldsymbol{y}}}, \tilde{\boldsymbol{y}} \in \tilde{\mathcal{Y}}\}, \quad S_{\tilde{\boldsymbol{y}}} = \{\boldsymbol{x} \in \mathcal{X} : \tilde{\boldsymbol{T}}(\boldsymbol{x}) = \tilde{\boldsymbol{y}}\} \qquad (26)$$

and generates the transformed distributions $\tilde{Q}_{\tilde{\boldsymbol{y}}}, \tilde{Q}_{\tilde{\boldsymbol{y}}|\omega}$ on $\tilde{\mathcal{Y}}$:

$$\tilde{Q}_{\tilde{\boldsymbol{y}}}(\tilde{\boldsymbol{y}}) = P_{\mathcal{X}}(S_{\tilde{\boldsymbol{y}}}), \quad \tilde{Q}_{\tilde{\boldsymbol{y}}|\omega}(\tilde{\boldsymbol{y}}|\omega) = P_{\mathcal{X}|\omega}(S_{\tilde{\boldsymbol{y}}}|\omega), \quad \tilde{\boldsymbol{y}} \in \tilde{\mathcal{Y}}, \quad \omega \in \Omega. \qquad (27)$$

It is easy to see (cf. (18)) that the partition $\tilde{S}$ of $\mathcal{X}$ can be obtained by intersecting the sets of the partitions $S^{(1)}, S^{(2)}, \dots, S^{(I)}$:

$$S_{\tilde{\boldsymbol{y}}} = \{\boldsymbol{x} \in \mathcal{X} : \boldsymbol{T}^{(i)}(\boldsymbol{x}) = \boldsymbol{y}^{(i)}, i \in \mathcal{I}\} \quad \Rightarrow \quad S_{\tilde{\boldsymbol{y}}} = \bigcap_{i \in \mathcal{I}} S_{\boldsymbol{y}^{(i)}}, \qquad (28)$$

and therefore the partition $\tilde{S}$ is a refinement of any of the partitions $S^{(i)}, i \in \mathcal{I}$. Now we prove the following simple Lemma:

Lemma 4.1 Let $Q_y, Q_{y|\omega}$ be discrete probability distributions defined by the partition S (cf. (6),(7)) and $\bar{Q}_{\bar{y}}, \bar{Q}_{\bar{y}|\omega}$ discrete probability distributions defined by the partition $\bar{S}$:

$$\bar{Q}_{\bar{y}}(\bar{\boldsymbol{y}}) = P_{\mathcal{X}}(S_{\bar{\boldsymbol{y}}}), \quad \bar{Q}_{\bar{y}|\omega}(\bar{\boldsymbol{y}}|\omega) = P_{\mathcal{X}|\omega}(S_{\bar{\boldsymbol{y}}}|\omega), \quad \bar{\boldsymbol{y}} \in \bar{\mathcal{Y}}, \quad \omega \in \Omega. \qquad (29)$$

Further let S be a refinement of the partition $\bar{S}$. Then the statistical decision information about p_Ω contained in Q_y is greater or equal to that contained in $\bar{Q}_{\bar{y}}$, i.e. we can write the inequality

$$I(Q_y, p_\Omega) \geq I(\bar{Q}_{\bar{y}}, p_\Omega). \qquad (30)$$

Proof. We use notation (cf. (6),(7) and (29))

$$p(\omega|\boldsymbol{y}) = \frac{P(S_y|\omega)p(\omega)}{P(S_y)}, \quad p(\omega|\bar{\boldsymbol{y}}) = \frac{P(S_{\bar{y}}|\omega)p(\omega)}{P(S_{\bar{y}})} \qquad (31)$$

and recall that for any two subsets $S_y \in \mathcal{S}, S_{\bar{y}} \in \bar{\mathcal{S}}$ it holds that either $S_y \subset S_{\bar{y}}$ or their intersection is empty: $S_y \cap S_{\bar{y}} = \emptyset$. It follows that we can write for any $\bar{y} \in \bar{\mathcal{Y}}$

$$p(\omega|\bar{y}) = \sum_{y \in \mathcal{Y}} \frac{P(S_y \cap S_{\bar{y}})}{P(S_{\bar{y}})} \frac{P(S_y|\omega)p(\omega)}{P(S_y)} = \sum_{y \in \mathcal{Y}} \frac{P(S_y \cap S_{\bar{y}})}{P(S_{\bar{y}})} p(\omega|y). \qquad (32)$$

Applying Jensen's inequality to the function $-\xi \log \xi$ and considering (32) we obtain

$$- p(\omega|\bar{y}) \log p(\omega|\bar{y}) \geq \sum_{y \in \mathcal{Y}} \frac{P(S_y \cap S_{\bar{y}})}{P(S_{\bar{y}})} [-p(\omega|y) \log p(\omega|y)]. \qquad (33)$$

Further, multiplying the inequality (33) by $P(S_{\bar{y}})$ and summing through $\omega \in \Omega$ and $\bar{y} \in \bar{\mathcal{Y}}$, we obtain the following inequality for conditional entropies

$$H(p_\Omega|\bar{Q}_{\bar{y}}) = \sum_{\bar{y} \in \bar{\mathcal{Y}}} \bar{Q}(\bar{y}) H(p_{\Omega|\bar{y}}) \geq \sum_{y \in \mathcal{Y}} Q(y) H(p_{\Omega|y}) \qquad (34)$$

which implies the inequality (30). •

Consequently, since the partition $\tilde{\mathcal{S}}$ is a refinement of any of the partitions $\mathcal{S}^{(i)}, i \in \mathcal{I}$, Lemma 4.1 implies the following information inequality

$$I(\tilde{Q}_{\bar{y}}, p_\Omega) \geq I(Q^{(i)}_{y^{(i)}}, p_\Omega), \quad i \in \mathcal{I}. \qquad (35)$$

We can conclude that, expectedly, the classifier fusion represented by the compound transform $\tilde{T}$ preserves more decision information than any of the component transforms $T^{(i)}$. Let us remark, however, that the dimension of the feature space $\tilde{\mathcal{Y}}$ produced by $\tilde{T}$ is I-times higher than those of $\mathcal{Y}^{(i)}$. This computational aspect of the considered form of classifier fusion will be discussed later in Sec. 6.

5   Combining Functions

Now we return to the most widely used classifier combination scheme based on simple combining functions or combining rules. In particular we assume that the a posteriori distributions $p^{(i)}_{\Omega|x}, i \in \mathcal{I}$ computed by different statistical classifiers are transformed to a single K-dimensional output vector by means of some combining functions. We denote by $\hat{T}$ the resulting transform

$$\hat{T} : \mathcal{X} \to \hat{\mathcal{Y}}, \quad \hat{\mathcal{Y}} \subset R^K, \quad \hat{y} = \hat{T}(x) = (\hat{T}_1(x), \dots, \hat{T}_K(x)) \in \hat{\mathcal{Y}},$$

$$\hat{y}_k = \hat{T}_k(x) = \Phi_k(p^{(1)}_{\Omega|x}, p^{(2)}_{\Omega|x}, \dots, p^{(I)}_{\Omega|x}), \quad x \in \mathcal{X}, \quad k = 1, \dots, K \qquad (36)$$

whereby $\Phi_k : R^{IK} \to R$ are arbitrary mappings which uniquely define the output variables $\hat{y}_k$ as a function of the a posteriori distributions $p^{(i)}_{\Omega|x}, i \in \mathcal{I}$. Let us note that, in this way, we can express in a unified manner various combining rules for a posteriori distributions like average, median, product, weighted average and others. More generally, the mapping Φ_k may be described e.g. by a simple procedure and, in this way, we can formally describe different voting schemes like majority voting, weighted voting, etc.

If we define the partition of $\mathcal{X}$ induced by the transform $\hat{T}$

$$\hat{S} = \{S_{\hat{y}}, \hat{y} \in \hat{\mathcal{Y}}\}, \quad S_{\hat{y}} = \{x \in \mathcal{X} : \hat{T}(x) = \hat{y}\} \tag{37}$$

we can see that, for any particular type of the mappings Φ_k, the partition $\tilde{S}$ of Sec. 4 is a refinement of the partition $\hat{S}$. To verify this property of $\hat{S}$ we recall that the a posteriori distributions $p_{\Omega|x}^{(i)}$ are identical for any $x \in C$, $C \in \tilde{S}$ (cf. (25),(26)). Consequently, in view of the definition (36), we obtain identical vectors $\hat{y} = \hat{T}(x)$ for all $x \in C$ and therefore $C \subset S_{\hat{y}}$. In other words, for each subset $C \in \tilde{S}$ there is a subset $S_{\hat{y}} \in \hat{S}$ such that $C \subset S_{\hat{y}}$, i.e. the partition $\tilde{S}$ is a refinement of the partition $\hat{S}$. If we denote $\hat{Q}_{\hat{y}}, \hat{Q}_{\hat{y}|\omega}$ the transformed distributions on $\hat{\mathcal{Y}}$ defined by the partition $\hat{S}$:

$$\hat{Q}_{\hat{y}}(\hat{y}) = P_{\mathcal{X}}(S_{\hat{y}}), \quad \hat{Q}_{\hat{y}|\omega}(\hat{y}|\omega) = P_{\mathcal{X}|\omega}(S_{\hat{y}}|\omega), \quad \hat{y} \in \hat{\mathcal{Y}}, \quad \omega \in \Omega \tag{38}$$

then we can write the information inequality (cf. Lemma 4.1):

$$I(\tilde{Q}_{\tilde{y}}, p_\Omega) \geq I(\hat{Q}_{\hat{y}}, p_\Omega). \tag{39}$$

We can conclude that, expectedly, the classifier fusion represented by the compound transform $\tilde{T}$ preserves more decision information than any transform of the type $\hat{T}$ based on the combining functions (36).

6   Discussion

Summarizing the inequalities derived in the above Sections we recall that the transform $T(x)$ (cf. (3), (4)) based on the true probability distributions $P_{\mathcal{X}|\omega}$ is information preserving in the sense of Eq. (11). Section 3 describes a practical situation when only some estimates $P_{\mathcal{X}|\omega}^{(i)}$ of the true conditional distributions are available. We have shown that the transform $T^{(i)}$ defined by means of the estimated distributions $P_{\mathcal{X}|\omega}^{(i)}$ may be accompanied with some information loss, as expressed by the inequalities (cf. (23))

$$I(Q_y, p_\Omega) \geq I(Q_{y^{(i)}}^{(i)}, p_\Omega), \quad i \in \mathcal{I}. \tag{40}$$

The potential information loss (40) can be partly avoided by combining classifiers. In particular, by parallel fusion of the transforms $T^{(i)}, i \in \mathcal{I}$, we obtain the compound transform $\tilde{T}$ and the corresponding transformed distribution $\tilde{Q}_{\tilde{y}}$ satisfies the inequality (35). Consequently, as the general inequality (40) can be proved for the distribution $\tilde{Q}_{\tilde{y}}$ without any change, we can write

$$I(Q_y, p_\Omega) \geq I(\tilde{Q}_{\tilde{y}}, p_\Omega) \geq I(Q_{y^{(i)}}^{(i)}, p_\Omega), \quad i \in \mathcal{I}. \tag{41}$$

In other words, the compound transform $\tilde{T}$ preserves more decision information than any of the component transforms $T^{(i)}$ but the dimension of the feature space $\tilde{\mathcal{Y}}$ produced by $\tilde{T}$ is I-times higher than the dimension of each of the subspaces $\mathcal{Y}^{(i)}$.

In view of the inequality (cf. (39))

$$I(\tilde{Q}_{\tilde{y}}, p_\Omega) \geq I(\hat{Q}_{\hat{y}}, p_\Omega) \tag{42}$$

the parallel classifier fusion preserves more decision information than various methods based on combining functions. However, it should be emphasized that the inequality (42) compares the decision information theoretically available by means of parallel classifier fusion and by using combining functions respectively. Moreover, the information advantage of parallel fusion is achieved at the expense of the lost simplicity of the combining rules. In order to exploit the available decision information it would be necessary to design a new classifier in the high-dimensional feature space $\tilde{\mathcal{Y}}$. On the other hand, in the feature space $\hat{\mathcal{Y}}$ of the combined classifier a large portion of the decision information may be lost irreversibly.

Let us remark finally that inequalities analogous to (41) can be obtained in connection with probabilistic neural networks (PNN) when the estimated conditional distributions $P^{(i)}_{\mathcal{X}|\omega}$ have the form of distribution mixtures [5]. For each PNN$^{(i)}$ we have a transform defined in terms of component distributions [3] which preserves more decision information about p_Ω than the corresponding transform $T^{(i)}$. Again, the underlying information loss connected with the individual neural networks can be reduced by means of parallel fusion. It can be shown that, theoretically, the parallel fusion of PNN is potentially more efficient that the classifier fusion of Section 4.

7   Conclusion

For the sake of information analysis we consider a general scheme of parallel classifier combinations in the framework of statistical pattern recognition. Formally each classifier defines a set of output variables (features) in terms of the estimated a posteriori probabilities. The extracted features are used in parallel to define a new higher-level decision problem. By means of relatively simple facts we derived a hierarchy between different schemes of classifier fusion in terms of information inequalities. In particular, we have shown that the parallel fusion of classifiers is potentially more efficient than the frequently used techniques based on simple combining rules or functions. However the potential advantages are achieved at the expense of the lost simplicity of the combining functions and of the increased dimension of the new feature space. Thus, unlike combining functions, the most informative parallel combining schemes would require to design a new classifier in a high-dimensional feature space.

References

1. Fukunaga K., Ando S.: The optimum nonlinear features for a scatter criterion and discriminant analysis. In Proc. ICPR 1976, pp 50-54.
2. Grim J.: Design of multilayer neural networks by information preserving transforms. In E. Pessa M.P. Penna A. Montesanto (Eds.), Proceedings of the Third European Congress on System Science, Roma: Edizzioni Kappa, 1996, pp 977-982.
3. Grim J., Kittler J., Pudil P., Somol P.: Combining multiple classifiers in probabilistic neural networks. In Multiple Classifier Systems, Kittler J., Roli F., (Eds.), Springer, 2000, pp 157 - 166.
4. Grim J., Pudil P.: On virtually binary nature of probabilistic neural networks. In: Advances in Pattern Recognition, Sydney, August 11 - 13, 1998), A. Amin, D. Dori, P. Pudil, H. Freeman (Eds.), pp. 765 - 774, Springer: New York, Berlin, 1998.
5. Grim J., Pudil P., Somol P.: Recognition of handwritten numerals by structural probabilistic neural networks. In Proceedings of the Second ICSC Symposium on Neural Computation, Berlin, 2000. (Bothe H., Rojas R. eds.). ICSC, Wetaskiwin, 2000, pp 528-534.
6. Hansen L.K., Salamon P.: Neural network ensembles, IEEE Transactions on Pattern Analysis and Machine Intelligence 1990; 12(10):993- 1001.
7. Huang Y.S., Suen C.Y.: A method of combining multiple classifiers - a neural network approach. In Proc. 12th IAPR Int. Conf. on Pattern Recognition and Computer Vision, Los Alamitos: IEEE Comp. Soc. Press., 1994, pp 473-475.
8. Huang Y.S., Suen C.Y.: Combination of multiple experts for the recognition of unconstrained handwritten numerals. IEEE Transactions on Pattern Analysis and Machine Intelligence 1995; 17(1):90-94.
9. Cho S.B., Kim J.H.: Combining multiple neural networks by fuzzy integral for robust classification, IEEE Transactions on Systems Man and Cybernetics 1995; 25(2):380-384.
10. Cho S.B., Kim J.H.: Multiple network fusion using fuzzy logic, IEEE Transactions on Neural Networks 1995; 6(2):497-501.
11. Chuanyi Ji, Sheng Ma.: Combinations of weak classifiers. IEEE Transactions on Neural Networks, 8(1): 32-42.
12. Kittler J.: Combining classifiers: A theoretical framework. Pattern Analysis and Applications 1998; 1:18–27.
13. Kittler J., Duin R.P.W., Hatef M., Matas J.: On combining classifiers. IEEE Transactions on Pattern Analysis and Machine Intelligence 1998; 20(3):226–239.
14. Lam L., Suen C.Y.: A theoretical analysis of the application of majority voting to pattern recognition. In Proc. 12th IAPR Int. Conf. on Pattern Recognition and Computer Vision, Los Alamitos: IEEE Comp. Soc. Press., 1994, pp 418-420.
15. Rogova G.: Combining the results of several neural network classifiers, Neural Networks 1994; 7(5):777-781.
16. Soulie F.F., Vinnet E., Lamy B.: Multi-Modular Neural Network Architectures: Applications in Optical Character and Human Face Recognition, Int. Journal of Pattern Recognition and Artificial Intelligence, Vol. 5, No. 4, pp 721-755, 1993.
17. Vajda I., Grim J.: About the maximum information and maximum likelihood principles in neural networks. Kybernetika 1998; 34(4):485-494.
18. Wolpert D.H.: Stacked generalization. Neural Networks, Vol. 5, No. 2, pp 241-260, 1992.

Limiting the Number of Trees in Random Forests

Patrice Latinne[1], Olivier Debeir[2], and Christine Decaestecker[3]

[1] IRIDIA Laboratory, Université Libre de Bruxelles,
50, avenue Franklin Roosevelt cp 196/06
B-1050 Brussels, Belgium
platinne@ulb.ac.be
http://www.ulb.ac.be/polytech/march
[2] Information and Decision Systems, Université Libre de Bruxelles
50, avenue Franklin Roosevelt cp 165/57
B-1050 Brussels, Belgium
odebeir@ulb.ac.be
[3] Laboratory of Histopathology , Université Libre de Bruxelles,
808, route de Lennik cp 620
B-1070 Brussels, Belgium
cdecaes@ulb.ac.be

Abstract. The aim of this paper is to propose a simple procedure that *a priori* determines a minimum number of classifiers to combine in order to obtain a prediction accuracy level similar to the one obtained with the combination of larger ensembles. The procedure is based on the McNemar non-parametric test of significance. Knowing a priori the minimum size of the classifier ensemble giving the best prediction accuracy, constitutes a gain for time and memory costs especially for huge data bases and real-time applications. Here we applied this procedure to four multiple classifier systems with C4.5 decision tree (Breiman's Bagging, Ho's Random subspaces, their combination we labeled 'Bagfs', and Breiman's Random forests) and five large benchmark data bases. It is worth noticing that the proposed procedure may easily be extended to other base learning algorithms than a decision tree as well. The experimental results showed that it is possible to limit significantly the number of trees. We also showed that the minimum number of trees required for obtaining the best prediction accuracy may vary from one classifier combination method to another.

1   Introduction

Many methods have been proposed for combining multiple decision trees to improve prediction accuracy [4,6,8,10,12,13,22]). These classifiers are *weakened* to commit errors in a different way so that their combination can correct the mistakes an individual makes [1,11,19,21]. The main experimental studies quoted above applied *systematic* methods to combine hundreds of classifiers and then did not limit *a priori* the number of trees to combine.

J. Kittler and F. Roli (Eds.): MCS 2001, LNCS 2096, pp. 178–187, 2001.

As far as we know, optimizing the number of classifiers to combine is an open question in the literature about the improvements of MCSs' design. This number has to be large enough to create diversity among the predictions but it may exist a number beyond which the prediction accuracy remains the same or even decreases with respect to a given criterion. Giacento and Roli [9] proposed to select among a large set of classifiers an optimal subset of both diverse and accurate classifiers of different types (neural and statistical classifiers) .

This approach combines both a systematic design and an 'overproduce-and-choose' strategy which is a problem simpler than generating accurate and diverse classifiers 'directly'. Here we propose a simple procedure based on a direct non-parametric test of comparison, the McNemar test. The procedure systematically determines a minimum number of weakened classifiers to combine for a given data base. It does not require the overproduction of classifiers and does not select better classifiers than others with respect to a given criterion such as proposed by Giacento and Roli's approach. We mean that, once the procedure has been applied, it may be possible to improve the MCS design again with other post-treatments based on the selection of 'good' classifiers for instance.

Nevertheless, to assess the performance of the proposed procedure, we built a large number of weakened decision trees to show that it may not be required to grow random forests to significantly improve prediction accuracy. We applied the procedure to four multiple classifier systems based on C4.5 decision tree: Breiman's Bagging [4], Ho's Random Subspaces [10], their combination in a same model labeled 'Bagfs' [13] and Breiman's Random forests [6]. We assessed the procedure's performances on five large benchmark databases. Indeed, the proposed procedure based on the McNemar test is practically useful for huge data bases or real-time applications for which it has already been successfully applied. It actually allows to reduce memory and time requirements which may be strong criteria for the real-world application of MCSs. The experimental results showed that the use of the McNemar test enables to limit the number of trees for each method significantly. We also observed that the minimal number of trees required for maximum accuracy may vary so that a good trade-off between prediction accuracy and tree requirements of an MCS may be found.

The paper is organized as follows. The random forests are described in Section 2. Then the McNemar test of significance and the procedure for limiting the numbers of classifiers are explained in Section 3. The data bases to which the multiple classifier systems are applied are detailed in Section 4 and the experimental framework in Section 5. We discuss the results in Section 6 before the conclusion (Section 7) and the references.

2   Random Forests

To illustrate our idea of limiting the number of classifiers, we selected four ways of building weakened decision forests: (1) bootstrap aggregating ('Bagging',[4, 16]) (2) Random subspace method (or 'MFS' for Multiple Feature Subsets,[10,

2]) (3) the combination of Bagging with Random subspace ('Bagfs', [14]) and (4) Random Forest ('Bagrf', [6]).

Bagging consists of building B bootstrap replicates of an original data set and of using these to run a learning algorithm. Ross Quinlan [16] has validated the Bagging method with C4.5 decision tree inducer.

The Random subspace method consists of training a given number of classifiers (B), with each having as its input a given proportion of features (k) picked *randomly* from the original set of f features with or without replacement. Ho [10] proposed this approach for decision trees. Bay [2] applied a very similar approach, labeled 'MFS', to nearest neighbors. This method was performed here by using the original feature set only (i.e. without expanding the feature vector with combination functions of features) and by selecting randomly a proportion of features *without* replacement. In the rest of the paper, we will refer to this weakening method by the label 'MFS'.

We showed on benchmark data bases in [13] that combining Bagging and MFS in the same architecture ('Bagfs') could improve prediction accuracy. In [13], the Bagfs' architecture had two levels of decision (A 'nested' level for each bootstrap between all its MFS and a 'final' level between all bootstraps). Here, we applied a simpler architecture with only one level of decision (See also [14]). We generated B bootstrap replicates of the learning set (The same ones used to apply the bagging method). In each replicate we independently sampled a subset of f' features, randomly selected from amongst the f initial ones without replacement (the same ones used to apply 'MFS'). We denoted $k = f'/f$ as the proportion of features in these B subsets. The proposed architecture has thus two parameters, B and k, to be set.

The proportion of features in each subspace, denoted k_{opt} in Table 1, of MFS and Bagfs was optimized by performing a nested stratified 10-fold crossvalidation (as more detailed in [13]). It's worth noticing that we obtained the same f_{opt} for both MFS and Bagfs.

Breiman's Random forest method (we labeled 'Bagrf', [6]) consists of creating B bootstrap replicates of the learning set. For each replicate, a feature subset to split on is randomly selected (without replacement) at each node of the tree. According to Breiman's method, we fixed the size of these random subsets, denoted F in Table 1, to be the first integer less than $\log_2(f) + 1$, where f is the number of features.

A common feature of all methods is that they combine predictions by means of the plurality vote. Moreover, Bagging, MFS and Bagfs can be applied to any learning algorithms that are *unstable* for training modifications (e.g. decision trees, artificial neural networks) and feature set modification (e.g. decision trees, nearest neighbours) while Bagrf is specific to decision trees.

We tested each method with respect to Ross Quinlan's C4.5 decision tree Release 8 ([15]) with its default parameter values and its pruning method (all the decision trees were pruned except for Bagrf, as specified in its original formulation).

3   McNemar Test of Significance

3.1   General Background

In this paper, we use the McNemar test [20,17,18] as a direct method for testing whether two sets of predictions differ significantly among themselves. Given the two algorithms A and B, this test compares the number of examples misclassified by A, but not by B (labeled M_{ab}), with the number of examples misclassified by B, but not by A (labeled M_{ba}). In the case that $M_{ab} + M_{ba} \geq 20$, if the null hypothesis H_0 is true (i.e.,if there is no difference between the algorithms' predictions), then the statistics X^2 (equation 1) can be considered as following an χ^2 distribution (with 1 degree of freedom).

$$X^2 = \frac{(|M_{ab} - M_{ba}| - 1)^2}{M_{ab} + M_{ba}} \sim \chi^2_{1,0.95} \tag{1}$$

The hypothesis H_0 is rejected if X^2 is greater than $\chi^2_{1,0.05} = 3.841459$ (significance level $p < 0.05$). In this case, the algorithms have significantly different levels of performance. If condition $M_{ab} + M_{ba} \geq 20$ is not satisfied, the approximation of the statistical distribution cannot be used and the *exact test* described in [17] has to be performed. As this happened rarely in our experimental design, in these cases, we preferred to accept the hypothesis that the two algorithms have the same performance.

Moreover, different studies (see for instance [7,18]) showed that this non-parametric test is also preferred to parametric ones (such as the commonly used t-test) because no assumption is required and it is independent of any evaluation measurement (error rate, kappa degree of agreement, ...). Dietterich [7] also showed that McNemar has a low type I error (the probability of incorrectly detecting a difference when no difference exists) and concluded that it is one of the more acceptable tests among the most common ones if the algorithms can only be executed once.

3.2   Limiting the Number of Classifiers

When creating multiple classifier systems such as the random forests described in Section 2, we may overproduce an arbitrary large number, B, of voting classifiers. In this paper, the question is how to limit the number of classifiers to produce while being as accurate as the same MCS combining a larger number of classifiers.

We applied McNemar test of significance as described in Section 3.1 between two sets of predictions from two MCSs that differ only by their number of classifiers. Let us denote $\mathcal{L}$ a learning set and $\mathcal{T} = \{(\mathbf{x}, y)\}$ a data set independent from $\mathcal{L}$. Let $\mathcal{C}_m = \{\widehat{y} = vote\{\varphi^{(k)}(\mathbf{x}, \mathcal{L}), k = 1, \dots, m\}\}$ be the prediction set of m voting classifiers. The classifiers $\varphi^{(k)}$ are built so that the classifier predictions are diverse and on an equal footing in terms of voting i.e. no classifier is a priori better than another with respect to any criterion (e.g. as it is the case here by building multiple random decision trees, see Section 2).

The proposed procedure consists of comparing the prediction set C_m to C_n, with $n > m$, with respect to the McNemar test. Either the set of classifiers used to obtain predictions C_n is completely independent from the one that predicts C_m, or it contains all or part of the m classifiers that predicts C_m. We showed that this does not change our conclusion as it will be detailed in Section 6.

The McNemar test gives an answer d with a significance level $p < 0.05$:

$$d(m, n) = \begin{cases} 1 & \text{if } H_0 \text{ rejected } and\ M_{mn} > M_{nm} \\ -1 & \text{if } H_0 \text{ rejected } and\ M_{nm} > M_{mn} \\ 0 & \text{if the two prediction sets do not differ} \end{cases}$$

If $d(m, n) = 1$, then we conclude that combining n classifiers gives a higher level of performance than combining m classifiers with respect to McNemar test. So we should carry on the procedure with a higher number of classifiers than n.

If $d(m, n) = -1$, we should stop the procedure and use m classifiers only. It may only appear rarely since increasing the number of voting classifiers should not degrade the prediction accuracy significantly. As a matter of fact, this case never appears in our experiments.

If $d(m, n) = 0$, then combining m weakened classifiers does not significantly differ from combining n classifiers and we may keep $\{\varphi^{(k)}(\mathbf{x}, \mathcal{L}), k =, 1 \ldots, m\}$ as the multiple classifier system with the minimal number of classifiers, $m^* = m$, that limits the number of classifiers to combine.

4   Material

We applied Bagging, MFS, Bagfs and Bagrf to 5 large data bases (see Table 1). Four of these were downloaded from the UCI Machine Learning repository [3], i.e. satimage, image segmentation ('image'), letter and DNA. We also included the artificial data base 'ringnorm' used by Breiman in [5]. All these data bases have no missing values. Notice that for DNA, we gave Bagrf's parameter F a higher value since the one obtained by the original computation ($F = 7$, see Section 2) led to a low prediction accuracy.

Table 1. Databases used to perform the classification tasks.

Data set	Learning Set Size	#Feat. Cont/nominal	# Classes	f_{opt}	F
ringnorm *	7400	20/0	2	8	5
satimage	6435	36/0	6	18	6
image	2310	18/0	7	7	5
DNA	3186	0/60	3	36	20
letter *	20000	16/0	26	7	5

* : databases where the examples are equi-distributed across the classes.

5   Experimental Design

In the present paper, we investigated the benefit of using the McNemar test of significance as described in Section 3 to determine m^*, the minimum number of classifiers to combine for a given multiple classifier system on a given data set. We illustrated this procedure on four multiple classifier systems described in Section 2, namely Bagging, Random subspaces ('MFS'), Bagfs and another Random forest, 'Bagrf', applied to five data bases (as detailed in Section 4). For each of these MCSs, we *overproduced* $B = 200$ weakened decision trees. We split each data base in 3 stratified folds, a learning set $\mathcal{L}$, a validation set $\mathcal{V}$ and a testing set $\mathcal{T}$. Evaluations and comparisons of the MCSs were made on the basis of these 3 folds and we validated our approach by permuting the role played by each fold. $\mathcal{L}$ is used as the learning set to build 200 weakened decision trees. $\mathcal{V}$ is used to apply the McNemar test between the prediction set resulting from the vote of m classifiers ($m = 1 \ldots 200$) and the prediction set of the vote of n classifiers ($n > m$). Finally, we kept $\mathcal{T}$ for testing independently the procedure predictions.

Using the validation set $\mathcal{V}$, we obtained the table $D_v = d_v(m, n)$, $m, n = 1, \ldots, 200$ (subscript v is used for results carried out on the basis of the validation set $\mathcal{V}$). Once D_v is so computed, we extracted the recommended m_v^* as explained in Section 3.2. Then the remaining data set, $\mathcal{T}$, is used to determine $D = d(m, n)$ and extract m^* in order to assess the proposed procedure on the independent testing set. For each classification task and each MCS, we are then able to compare m^* to m_v^* and thus to appreciate the quality of the predicted value m_v^*.

6   Results and Discussion

On Figure 1, for each method and each data base, each dot represents $d(m, n)$, the result of McNemar test that compares the prediction set of a m-classifier system (on a row) with the prediction of a n-classifier system (on a column) ($m, n = 1..200$). Each figure is symmetrical and composed of a bright and dark region. The dark region means that the compared architectures differ significantly with respect to McNemar. The bright region means that the compared architectures do not differ significantly. These results showed that a threshold appeared distinctly between the two regions 'differ' or 'differ not significantly'. So the proposed procedure based on McNemar test led to the determination of m_v^*, a significantly lower number of classifiers on most data bases than the total of 200 classifiers overproduced for each MCS.

Table 2 shows the results' summary of the experimental design for each multiple classifier system and each data base. This table indicates in bold and in brackets each m_v^* computed as detailed above. We also give the percentage of good classification obtained with each m_v^* to compare the performance of each MCS on the same data base.

The results obtained on the remaining independent testing set from the global data base, m^*, showed that this number was always close to the predicted value

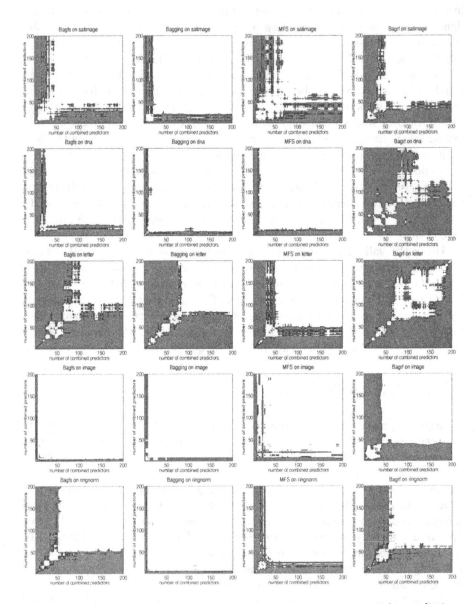

Fig. 1. Experimental results. Influence of the number of trees on the predictions with respect to McNemar test

m_v^* (most of the time equal or even lower). In the too optimistic but rare cases where $m_v^* < m^*$, we observed that the difference was never larger than 10. Nevertheless, the results showed that by performing this procedure, we obtained a drastic decrease of the number of classifiers required to obtain the same level of performance than MCSs combining 200 classifiers. We also observed in Table 2 that

- Bagfs systematically exhibited a better prediction accuracy and a lower m_v^* than Bagrf with respect to McNemar test.
- By increasing the number of classifiers, Bagfs always exhibited significantly better performance than Bagging with respect to McNemar test.
- To obtain the same level of accuracy than MFS, Bagfs required less classifiers on satimage and image. On the other data bases, Bagfs exhibited significantly better results than MFS (with respect to McNemar) but it required more classifiers.

Table 2. Experimental Results. Performance in terms of the prediction accuracy (%), minimum recommended number of trees with respect to McNemar in bold and in brackets.

	C4.5	Bag	MFS	Bagfs	Bagrf
ringnorm	89.3	94.0	97.7	98.4	96.2
		(10)	(30)	(50)	(60)
satimage	84.0	88.2	89.8	89.6	89.1
		(20)	(70)	(50)	(50)
image	93.6	96.1	96.2	96.0	94.5
		(10)	(50)	(10)	(40)
DNA	86.5	89.5	90.0	91.5	89.8
		(20)	(20)	(30)	(130)
letter	81.4	88.6	90.4	91.6	89.0
		(90)	(50)	(110)	(200)

In the present paper, we systematically *overproduced* classifiers (200) to assess the method's performance. The results obtained on each data base with each MCS let us suggest that we could incrementally increase the number of classifiers by step of 10 classifiers and perform the direct test of McNemar at each step *instead*. Furthermore, this approach of the MCS' design would combine a limited number of classifiers, m_v^*, (i.e. predicted on a reduced validation set independent from the learning set) without any *significant* loss of accuracy and applied to a large data set of unknown cases. This question is especially interesting for huge data bases and real-time applications working on other base learning algorithms slower than decision trees (e.g. neural networks) to obtain a gain in time and memory costs.

7   Conclusion

We suggested a simple procedure based on the direct test of McNemar to limit the number of classifiers to combine in a multiple classifier system. The procedure compares the set of predictions of a MCS with a given number of classifers with the prediction set of the same MCS with a higher number of classifiers. If the prediction sets do not differ with respect to McNemar test, we concluded that the smallest number of classifiers is enough to obtain the same level of accuracy with respect to McNemar test.

Experimental results showed on four different MCSs applied to C4.5 decision tree and cross-validations on five large benchmark data bases, that it may be possible to select *a priori* a minimum number of classifiers which, once combined with the plurality voting rule, offered the same level of performance than larger numbers of trees with respect to the McNemar test. Moreover, we showed that a sharp threshold appeared between the region where the prediction sets 'differ' and the one where the prediction sets 'do not differ significantly' with respect to McNemar test.

Furthermore, we suggested a way to improve the design of a MCS without overproducing classifiers. It consists of incrementally adding new classifiers to the existing ensemble and comparing by means of a cross-validation the predictions of the resulting ensemble to the one with less classifiers.

Finally, we proposed a simple approach in this paper to improve the design of a multiple classifier system that consisted of limiting the number of classifiers to combine without a loss of prediction accuracy (with respect to a direct statistical test of comparison, McNemar) but with a gain in memory and time costs that may be significant for huge data bases and real-time applications.

Acknowledgements. Patrice Latinne and Olivier Debeir are supported by a grant under an ARC (Action de Recherche Concertée) programme of the Communauté Française de Belgique. Christine Decaestecker is a Research Associate with the 'F.N.R.S' (Belgian National Scientific Research Fund).

The authors also thank the anonymous reviewers for their pertinent and constructive remarks.

References

1. Ali and Pazzani. Error reduction through learning multiple descriptions. *Machine Learning*, 24:173–202, 1996.
2. Stephen D. Bay. Nearest neighbor classification from multiple feature subsets. In *Proceedings of the International Conference on Machine Learning*, Madison, Wisc., 1998. Morgan Kaufmann Publishers.
3. C. Blake, E. Keogh, and C.J. Merz. Uci repository of machine learning databases. [http://www.ics.uci.edu/ mlearn/MLRepository.html]. Irvine, CA: University of California, Department of Information and Computer Science, 1998.
4. Leo Breiman. Bagging predictors. *Machine Learning*. 24, 1996.
5. Leo Breiman. Arcing classifiers. *Annals of statistics*, 26:801–849, 1998.

6. Leo Breiman. Random forests - random features. Technical Report 567, Statistics Department, University of California, Berkeley, CA 94720, september 1999.
7. T.G. Dietterich. Approximate statistical tests for comparing supervised classification learning algorithms. *Neural Computation*, 10:1895–1923, 1998.
8. T.G. Dietterich. An experimental comparison of three methods for constructing ensembles of decision trees : bagging, boosting and randomization. *Machine Learning*, 40:139–157, 2000.
9. Giorgio Giacento and Fabio Roli. An approach to the automatic design of multiple classifier systems. *Pattern recognition letters*, 22:25–33, 2001.
10. T.K. Ho. the random subspace method for constructing decision forests. *IEEE Trans. Pattern Analysis and Machine Intelligence*, 20:832–844, 1998.
11. Ji and Ma. Combinations of weak classifiers. *IEEE Trans. Neural Network*, 7(1):32–42, 1997.
12. Ron Kohavi and Clayton Kunz. Option decision trees with majority votes. In *Proceedings of the Fourtheeth International Conference on Machine Learning*, pages 161–169, San Francisco, CA, 1997. Morgan Kaufmann.
13. Patrice Latinne, Olivier Debeir, and Christine Decaestecker. Different ways of weakening decision trees and their impact on classification accuracy. In *Proc. of the 1st International Workshop of Multiple Classifier System*, pages 200–210, Cagliari, Italy, 2000. Springer (Lecture Notes in Computer Sciences; Vol. 1857).
14. Patrice Latinne, Olivier Debeir, and Christine Decaestecker. Mixing bagging and multiple feature subsets to improve classification accuracy of decision tree combination. In *Proc. of the Tenth Belgian-Dutch Conference on Machine Learning Benelearn'00*, pages 15–22, Tilburg University, 2000. Ed. Ad Feelders.
15. J.R. Quinlan. *C4.5 : Programs For Machine Learning.* Morgan Kaufmann Publishers, San Mateo, California, 1993.
16. J.R. Quinlan. Bagging, boosting, and c4.5. In *Proceedings of the Thirteenth National Conference on Artificial Intelligence*, pages 725–730, 1996.
17. Bernard Rosner. *Fundamentals of Biostatistics.* Duxbury Press (ITP), Belmont, CA, USA, 4th edition, 1995.
18. Steven Salzberg. On comparing classifiers : Pitfalls to avoid and a recommended approach. *Data Mining and knowledge discovery*, 1:317–327, 1997.
19. R.E. Schapire. The strength of weak learnability. *Machine Learning*, 5:197–227, 1990.
20. S. Siegel and N.J. Castellan. *Nonparametric Statistics for the behavioral sciences.* McGraw-Hill, second edition, 1988.
21. K. Tumer and J. Ghosh. Classifier combining : analytical results and implications. In *Proceedings of the National Conference on Artificial Intelligence*, Portland, OR, 1996.
22. Zijian Zheng. Generating classifier committees by stochastically selecting both attributes and training examples. In *Proceedings of the 5th Pacific Rim International Conferences on Artificial Intelligence (PRICAI'98)*, pages 12–23. Berlin: Springer-Verlag, 1998.

Learning-Data Selection Mechanism through Neural Networks Ensemble

Pitoyo Hartono and Shuji Hashimoto

Department of Applied Physics, Waseda University
{hartono,shuji}@shalab.phys.waseda.ac.jp

Abstract. In this paper we propose a model of neural networks ensemble consisting of a number of MLPs, that deals with an imperfect learning supervisor that occasionally produces incorrect teacher signals. It is known that a conventional unitary neural network will not learn optimally from this kind of supervisor. We consider that the imperfect supervisor generates two kinds of input-output relations, the correct relation and the incorrect one. The learning characteristics of the proposed model allows the ensemble to automatically train one of its members to learn only from the correct input-output relation, producing a neural network that can to some extent tolerate the imperfection of the supervisor.

1   Introduction

In recent years a number of multi-net models have been introduced [1]. One of them is the Mixture of Experts (ME) [2,3,4,5,6], which is a combination of a number of Multi-layer Perceptrons (MLP) with a gating network. The objective of this model is to decompose a given task, and allocate different experts to deal with different sub-tasks. ME successfully solved problems that are difficult for unitary neural networks. An ensemble model with similar objective was also proposed more recently [7,8]. Unlike ME, there are also neural networks ensemble models that train their modules on the whole task and combine the outputs to achieve better generalization. The methods of generating neural networks ensemble and their advantages compared to a unitary neural network have been explained in [9,10,11,12,13,14]. All of the multi-net models described above showed better performance than conventional unitary neural networks, but they were designed based on the assumption that the tasks/environments that have to be solved are stationary, which means that the dynamics that regulate the input and output are fixed over time. In real world problems, there are possibilities that the neural network has to deal with data originated from different sources with different dynamics. The multi-net models described above will fail to deal with this kind of "switching dynamics" problem because it is impossible for them to map the same inputs to different outputs. To deal with a switching dynamics problem, an ensemble model that can train each of the members to recognize a particular dynamic through competition was proposed in [15,16,17]. We have also proposed a model of neural networks ensemble with

J. Kittler and F. Roli (Eds.): MCS 2001, LNCS 2096, pp. 188–197, 2001.
© Springer-Verlag Berlin Heidelberg 2001

a switching mechanism that allows simultaneous learning for all the ensemble's members while automatically selecting one member that is considered to be the most suitable for a particular input-output relation (environment) and allocating different members for different environments [18,19]. In this paper we applied the proposed ensemble model in a situation where the neural network has to learn from an imperfect supervisor that occasionally produces erroneous teacher signals. An imperfect supervisor is a supervisor which stochastically produces two kinds of input-output relations(dynamics), the correct input-output relation and the erroneous one. We are dealing with a condition in which during the learning process the supervisor adopts "the correct dynamics" most of the time but occasionally switches its dynamics to erroneous ones. Because our proposed ensemble can train each of its members with different input-output relations, it can be expected that one of the ensemble's members will learn the correct input-output relation while the erroneous one will be absorbed by others, so that a neural network that is not contaminated by the incorrect data produced by the imperfect supervisor can be generated.

2   Problem Specification

Suppose we have a training set,

$$D = \{(X(1), d(1)), \cdots, (X(n), d(n))\} \tag{1}$$

$X \in R^{N_{in}}$ is the input vector and $d \in \{0, 1\}^{N_{out}}$ is the desired output vector. N_{in}, N_{out} are the dimensions of the input and output vectors, respectively. In this paper we considered an imperfect supervisor who occasionally gives erroneous desired output with a certain probability. The behavior can be written as

$$P(d^{true}(i)|X(i)) = 1 - \epsilon$$
$$P(d^{true}(i)|X(i)) = \epsilon \tag{2}$$
$$0 \leq \epsilon \leq 1,$$

where $P(d|x)$ is the conditional probability that the supervisor produces d as teacher signal for input X, and ϵ is the error rate. d^{true} and d^{false} are the correct and erroneous teacher signal respectively.

In this paper we are dealing with problems that require binary outputs, so the erroneous teacher signal is not cause by additive noise to the correct one, but by misclassification of the supervisor. We focus our attention to classification problem where the teacher signal is represented by a set of bits, only one of which has the value of 1 to denote a certain class. The erroneous teacher signal is a teacher signal that relates a given input to an incorrect class.

Our objective is to train a neural network that can achieve,

$$y(X(i)) \approx d^{true}(X(i)) \tag{3}$$

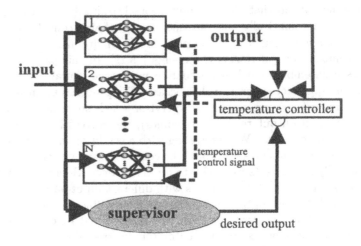

Fig. 1. Neural networks ensemble

$y(X(i))$ denotes the output of the neural network given input $X(i)$. However, presented with an imperfect supervisor defined above, a conventional unitary neural network will produce output according to Eq. 4, which does not satisfy our objective.

$$y(x(i)) \approx E[d|X(i)]$$
$$E[d|X(i)] = (1 - \epsilon)d^{true} + \epsilon d^{false}, \tag{4}$$

where $E[d|X(i)]$ denotes the expectation of teacher signal d given input X.

3   Neural Networks Ensemble

The structure of the proposed ensemble is shown in Fig.1. The ensemble consists of a number of independent multi-layer perceptrons (MLP), which we call members. Each member has an identical number of input neurons and output neurons, but because we want each member to specialize on different input-output relations , they are diversified by setting different numbers of middle neurons for each of them. In the learning process, an input coming into the ensemble is directed to the input layers of all members and simultaneously and independently processed by them. Each member will automatically decide whether to learn from the training set or to discard it. The data selection through competition between the members is governed by the temperature control mechanism explained in Section 4.

The output of the neurons in the middle layer is described as follows,

$$y_m^{i,mid} = \frac{1}{1 + exp(-u_m^{i,mid})} \tag{5}$$

$$u_m^{i,mid} = \sum_{n=1}^{N_{in}} w_{nm}^{i,mid} x_n + \theta_m^{i,mid},$$

where, $y_m^{i,mid}$, $u_m^{i,mid}$ and $\theta_m^{i,mid}$ are the output, potential and threshold value of the m-th middle neuron in the i-th member, respectively. $w_{nm}^{i,mid}$ is the connection weight between the n-th neuron in the input layer and the m-th neuron in the middle layer of the i-th member, x_n is the n-th element of the input vector, while N_{in} is the dimension of the input vector.

The output of the neuron in the output layer is described as follows,

$$y_k^{i,out} = \frac{1}{exp(-\frac{u_k^{i,out}}{T_i})} \tag{6}$$

$$u_k^{i,out} = \sum_{m=1}^{N_{mid}^i} w_{mk}^{i,out} y_m^{i,mid} + \theta_m^{i,out},$$

where $y_k^{i,out}$, $u_k^{i,out}$, $\theta_k^{i,out}$ are the output, potential and threshold value of the k-th member, respectively. $w_{mk}^{i,out}$ is the connection weight between the m-th neuron in the middle layer and k-th neuron in the output layer of the i-th member, while N_{mid}^i is the number of middle neurons in the i-th member. T_i is the temperature of the i-th member.

It is clear that when T_i is high, the output neurons in the i-th member will always produce responses close to 0.5 regardless of their potentials. Because for problems requiring binary answers, 0.5 is a value without any significance, a member with high temperature is defined as an inactive member.

Adopting backpropagation learning method [20] for each member, the weight correction between the m-th middle neuron and the k-th output neuron of the i-th member, $\Delta w_{mk}^{i,out}$ can be written as,

$$\Delta w_{mk}^{i,out} = \frac{1}{T_i} y_m^{i,mid} \delta_k^{out} \tag{7}$$

$$\delta_k^{out} = (d_k - y_k^{i,out}) y_k^{i,out} (1 - y_k^{i,out})$$

d_k is the k-th element of the teacher signal. From Eq. 7, if temperature T_i is sufficiently large, then the weight correction will be insignificant, and consequently the weight corrections between neurons in the input layer and ones in the middle layers will be insignificant, because the correction can be written as follows,

$$\Delta w_{nm}^{i,mid} = \frac{1}{T_i} x_n y_m^{i,mid} (1 - y_m^{i,mid}) \delta_m^{mid} \tag{8}$$

$$\delta_m^{mid} = \sum_{k=1}^{N_{out}} w_{mk}^{i,out} \delta_k^{out}$$

From Eqs. 7 and 8, we can see that if a member decides to discard a training pattern, then it can increase its temperature so that the member will not be influenced by the training pattern. This is the basic idea on how the ensemble can produce a member that selects only the correct learning data, thus minimizing the effect of an imperfect supervisor. The temperature control mechanism controls the temperatures of all members based on their performance for a given learning pattern.

The correction of connection weight vector in the i-th member is expressed as follows,

$$W^i(t+1) = W^i(t) + \eta \triangle W^i(t) + \kappa \triangle W^i(t-1) \tag{9}$$

$W^i(t)$ and $\triangle W^i(t)$ are the weight vector and correction vector of the i-th member at time t, respectively. η and κ are the learning rate and momentum, respectively.

Because we focus on binary problems, the continuous output of each member should be rounded by a stepping function defined as follows,

$$\begin{aligned} s(x) &= 1 \quad x \geq 0.5 + \beta \\ &= 0.5 \quad for \quad 0.5 - \beta < x < 0.5 + \beta \\ &= 0 \quad for \quad x \leq 0.5 - \beta \end{aligned} \tag{10}$$

The value of 0.5 is adopted in the stepping function because we consider values in the vicinity of 0.5 as ambiguous for binary problems, they can be interpreted as "don't know" in classification problems.

4   Temperature Control Mechanism

The temperature control mechanism is introduced to enable the ensemble to allocate a given training pattern to the most appropriate member. The basic idea is to reward members that perform relatively well with respect to the given training pattern by decreasing their temperatures, so that they may learn further from the training pattern, and to punish members that perform badly by increasing their temperatures. Adopting this idea, from a particular member's point of view, that member is allowed to select training data that suit its specialty. The performance of the i-th member is measured by its relative error τ^i defines as,

$$\tau^i = \frac{\sum_{k=1}^{N_{out}} (d_k - y_k^{i,out})^2}{\sum_{j=1}^{M} \sum_{k=1}^{N_{out}} (d_k - y_k^{j,out})^2}, \tag{11}$$

where d_k, $y_k^{i,out}$, M and N_{out} are the k-th element of the teacher signal, response of the k-th neuron in the output layer of the i-th member, the number of members in the ensemble and the number of output neurons which is shared by all the members, respectively. A small relative error shows the good performance of the member, and a big relative error indicates the opposite. Furthermore, it is favorable that a member with the lowest temperature dominates the rest, so a member that performs well should also punish the others by increasing their temperatures, and members with low performances should surrender their rights to learn by decreasing others' temperatures. The temperature correction is executed for every learning iteration according to,

$$T_i(t+1) = T_i(t) + \Delta T_i(t) - C \tag{12}$$

$$\Delta T_i(t) = -p^{self}(1 - M\tau^i) + p^{cross} \sum_{j \neq i}^{M} (1 - M\tau^j),$$

where p^{self}, p^{cross} and C are positive self-penalty, cross-penalty and cooldown constants, respectively.

The first term in Eq. 12 is the self-penalty term, which will increase a particular member's temperature if the performance of that member is below average, and decrease it if the performance is better than average. The second term is the cross-penalty term, which is the cumulative penalty or reward from other members. When all the members have identical performances (no particular winner), learning chances have to be given to all members. In this case, the cool-down constant acts as a catalyst to prevent deadlock in the learning competition. We limit temperature value between T_{min} and T_{max} according to,

$$
\begin{aligned}
T_i(t+1) &= T_{max} \ \ if \ \ T_i(t) + \Delta T_i(t) - C > T_{max} \\
T_i(t+1) &= T_{min} \ \ if \ \ T_i(t) + \Delta T_i(t) - C < T_{min} \\
& 0 < T_{min} < T_{max}
\end{aligned}
\tag{13}
$$

For binary problems, it is clear that a member that performed well regarding the correct input-output relation of the supervisor, will perform badly whenever the supervisor gives an erroneous learning pattern, causing its temperature to rise, blocking the member from learning that training pattern. The temperature control mechanism allows each member to automatically select learning-data that are relevant to the member's expertise. The characteristic of the imperfect supervisor shown in Eq. 2 ensures that although the supervisor is imperfect, in general it generates correct teacher signals, so at the end of the learning process we can extract a winner from the ensemble by selecting the member that is active most of the time, because it is a member that benefits most from the learning process. This is done by selecting a member that has the lowest average temperature over the learning process.

5   Experiment

In this experiment, the proposed ensemble model is applied to Iris Classification problem [21]. In this problem, the neural network has to classify an Iris flower to one of three classes (Iris-Setosa, Iris-Versicolor, Iris-Virginica), based on the length and width of the flower's sepal and petal.

In this experiment, each member of the ensemble has 4 input neurons and 3 output neurons. In the output layer, Iris-Setosa is represented by "100", Iris-Versicolor by "010" and Iris-Virginica by "001"

An error in teacher signal is generated by flipping the "1" bit to "0" and randomly flipping one of the two "0" bits to "1".

We used a three-membered ensemble, with 8,9,10 middle neurons respectively. The parameter settings for this experiment are shown in Table 1.

Table 1. Parameter Settings

Parameter	Value
Learning Rate	0.3
Momentum	0.1
Self-Penalty	100
Cross-Penalty	10
Cooldown	30
T_{max}	200
T_{min}	1

60 Iris data sets are provided (20 for each respective class), learning iteration is set to 20000 in which a training pattern is chosen randomly each time. After the learning process, the winner is tested using 60 data that were not used in the learning process to evaluate its classification accuracy. The accuracy of the ensemble's winner (represented by "win") when the supervisor is imperfect is shown in Fig. 2. For comparison, we also tested each member's accuracy, provided that the member was trained independently (represented by "sgl8", "sgl9","sgl10"). The accuracy of a particular member, A is defined as follows,

$$A = 1 - \frac{1}{N_p} \sum_{i=1}^{N_p} dif(O(X(i)), d^{true}(X(i)) \tag{14}$$
$$O(X(i)) = s(y^{out}(X(i)))$$
$$dif(a,b) = 1 \ for \ a \neq b$$
$$= 0 \ otherwise,$$

where $y^{out}(X(i))$ and $d^{true}(X(i))$ are the output vector of the neural network and the correction teacher signal given input $X(i)$, respectively. N_p is the number of test patterns.

We also compared the classification accuracy of the ensemble's winner with another ensemble system which averages the independently trained members' outputs as follows,

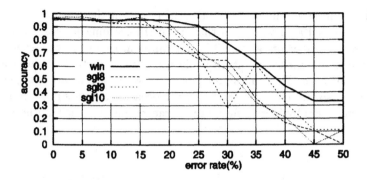

Fig. 2. Performance Comparison (Winner-Unitary MLPs)

$$O^{avr}(X) = s(\frac{1}{M} \sum_{j=1}^{M} y^j(X)) \qquad (15)$$

O^{avr} is the output of the average system(shown by "avr" in Fig. 3), y^j is the output of the j-th member, $s()$ is the stepping function defined in Eq. 10 and M shows the number of members. Figs. 2 and 3 show that the winner classifies better in wider range of error rate compared with conventional unitary MLPs and average system. It will be reasonable to use the proposed ensemble model when we do not have any information concerning the supervisor's reliability.

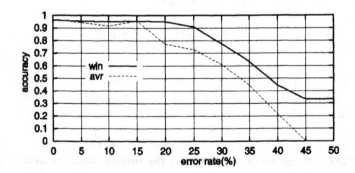

Fig. 3. Performance Comparison (Winner-Average system)

Figure 4 shows the temperatures of the ensemble's members during the training process. The left graph shows the members' temperatures when the error rate is 0%, in which the temperature of the member with 10 middle neurons converged to the T_{min} after a number of learning iterations while the temperatures of the rest of the members converged to T_{max}, while the right one shows the members' temperatures when the error rate is 10%. This implies that the member with

10 middle neurons dominated the other members in the learning process and should be selected as a winner in the end of the learning process. In the right graph in which the error rate is 10%, the temperature of the winner fluctuates around the minimum temperature while the others' fluctuate around a much higher temperature. This fluctuation is caused by the erroneous data generated by the supervisor which forces the winner to occasionally pass its domination to the other members by increasing its temperature and decreasing others'.

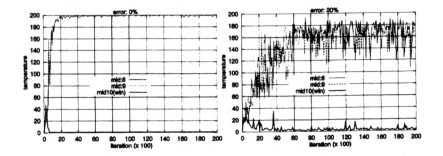

Fig. 4. Temperature during training

6   Conclusion and Future Works

We have proposed a model of neural networks ensemble that allows its members to automatically select learning data. The characteristics of the temperature control mechanism allow us to obtain a member that learns only from the correct learning data generated by an imperfect supervisor, assuming that in general the supervisor behaves correctly. The ability of automatic selection of the correct learning data is useful, because the strict requirement of having to provide a neural network with perfect training data can be eased, implying that we have more freedom in designing learning data. The toleration of the existence of erroneous learning data to some extent will support the broader usage of neural networks in real world problems in which the help of human experts for data selection is not cost-efficient, or in complicated problems where even human experts commit errors. In the future we are considering the application of the proposed ensemble in on-line training system, fault-tolerant systems, medical diagnosis support systems, etc. In this paper our focus was on binary problems, in the future we plan to refine the ensemble model so that it can deal with regression problems.

References

1. Sharkey, A.: On Combining Artificial Neural Nets. Connection Science **8(3 & 4)** (1996) 299–313
2. Jacobs, R.A., Jordan, M., Nowlan, S., Hinton, G.: Adaptive Mixture of Local Experts. Neural Computation **3** (1991) 79–87
3. Jacobs, R.A., Jordan, M.: A Competitive Modular Connectionists Architecture. Advances in Neural Information Processing Systems **3** (1991) 767–773
4. Nowlan, S., Hiton, G.: Evaluation of Adaptive Mixture of Competing Experts. Advances in Neural Information Processing Systems **3** (1991) 774–780
5. Jordan, M., Jacobs, R.: Hierarchical Mixture of Experts and the EM Algorithm. Neural Computation **6** (1994) 181–214
6. Jacobs, R.: Computational Studies of the Development of Functionally Specialized Neural Modules. Trends in Cognitive Sciences **3** (1999) 31–38
7. Liu, Y., Yao, X.: A Cooperative Ensemble Learning System. Proc. Int. Joint Conference on Neural Networks 1998 (1998) 2202-2207
8. Liu, Y., Yao, X.: Simultaneous Training of Negatively Correlated Neural Networks in an Ensemble. IEEE Trans. Systems, Man, Cybernetics B **29(6)** (1999) 716–725
9. Sharkey, A., Sharkey, N.: Diversity, Selection, and Ensemble of Artificial Neural Nets. Proc. Neural Network and Their Applications 1997 (1997) 205–212
10. Baxt, W.: Improving the Accuracy of an Artificial Neural Network Using Multiple Differently Trained Networks. Neural Computation **4** (1992) 772–780
11. Hansen, L., Salomon, P.: Neural Networks Ensemble. IEEE Trans. Pattern Analysis and Machine Intelligence **12(8)** (1990) 993-1001
12. Rosen, B.: Ensemble Learning Using Decorralated Neural Networks. Connection Science **8(3 & 4)** (1996) 373-383
13. Tumer, K., Gosh, J.: Error Correlation and Error Reduction in Ensemble Classifier. Connection Science **8(3 & 4)** (1996) 383-404
14. Geman, S., Bienenstock, E., Doursat, R.: Neural Networks and the BiasVariance Dillema. Neural Computation **4** (1992) 1–58
15. Müller, K-R., Kohlmorgen, J., Pawelzik, K.: Segmentation and Identification of Switching Dynamics with Competing Neural Networks. Proc. Int. Conference on Neural Information Processing 1994 (1994) 213–218
16. Müller, K-R., Kohlmorgen, J., Pawelzik, K.: Analysis of Switcing Dynamics with Competing Neural Networks. IEICE Trans. Fundamentals **E78-A(10)** (1995) 1306-1314
17. Pawelzik, K., Kohlmorgen, J., Müller, K-R. : Annealed Competition of Experts for a Segmentation and Classification of Switching Dynamics. Neural Computation **8** (1996) 304–356
18. Hartono, P., Hashimoto, S.: Ensemble of Neural Network with Temperature Control. Proc. Int. Joint Conference on Neural Networks 1999 (1999) 4073–4078
19. Hartono, P., Hashimoto, S.: Temperature Switching in Neural Network Ensemble. Journal of Signal Processing **4(5)** (2000) 395–402
20. Rumelhart, D., McClelland, J.: Learning Internal Representation by Error Propagation. Parallel Distributed Processing **1**, MIT Press (1996) 318–362
21. Fisher, R: The Use of Multiple Measurement in Toxanomic Problems. Annals of Eugenic (1936) 179-188

A Multi-SVM Classification System

Dimitrios S. Frossyniotis and Andreas Stafylopatis

National Technical University of Athens
Department of Electrical and Computer Engineering
Zographou 157 73, Athens, Greece
dfros@cslab.ntua.gr,andreas@cs.ntua.gr

Abstract. It has been shown by several researchers that multi-classifier systems can result in effective solutions to difficult tasks. In this work, we propose a multi-classifier system based on both supervised and unsupervised learning. According to the principle of *"divide-and-conquer"*, the input space is partitioned into overlapping subspaces and Support Vector Machines (SVMs) are subsequently used to solve the respective classification subtasks. Finally, the decisions of the individual SVMs are appropriately combined to obtain the final classification decision. We used the Fuzzy c-means (FCM) method for input space partitioning and we considered a scheme for combining the decisions of the SVMs based on a probabilistic interpretation. Compared to single SVMs, the multi-SVM classification system exhibits promising accuracy performance on well-known data sets.

1 Introduction

Multi-classifier systems have been recently used with great success in difficult pattern recognition problems. A major issue in the design of multiple classifier systems concerns whether individual learners are *correlated* or *independent*. The first alternative is usually applied to multistage approaches (such as boosting techniques [1,2,3,4]), whereby specialized classifiers are serially constructed to deal with data points missclassified in previous stages. In particular, the approach described in [4] concerns the application of boosting to speed up the training of Support Vector Machines (SVMs). The second alternative advocates the idea of using a committee of classifiers which are trained independently (in parallel) on the available training patterns, and combining their decisions to produce the final decision of the system. The latter combination can be based on two general strategies, namely *selection* or *fusion*. In the case of selection, one or more classifiers are nominated "local experts" in some region of the feature space (which is appropriately divided into regions), based on their classification "expertise" in that region [5], whereas fusion assumes that all classifiers have equal expertise over the whole feature space. A variety of techniques have been applied to implement classifier fusion by combining the outputs of multiple classifiers [6, 7,8,9,10].

J. Kittler and F. Roli (Eds.): MCS 2001, LNCS 2096, pp. 198–207, 2001.

In the case of multiple independent classifiers, several schemes can be adopted regarding the generation of appropriate training sets. The whole set can be used by all classifiers [11,12] or multiple versions can be formed as bootstrap replicates [13]. Another approach is to partition the training set into smaller disjoint subsets but with proportional distribution of examples of each class [11,14].

The present work follows a different approach based on partitioning of the original training data set into subsets and the subsequent use of individual classifiers for solving the respective learning subtasks. A key feature of the method is that the training subsets represent non-disjoint regions that result from input-space clustering. Thus, SVMs are assigned to overlapping regions from the beginning and acquire their specialization through training with data sets that are representative of the regions. This partitioning approach produces a set of correlated "specialized" classifiers which attack a complex problem by applying the divide-and-conquer principle.

In the next section, we address the issue of data partitioning based on unsupervised learning with the fuzzy c-means method. Section 3 describes the multi-classifier system and the scheme for combining SVMs decisions. Experimental results for the evaluation of the proposed method are presented in Section 4 and conclusions are presented in Section 5.

2   Partitioning of the Data Set

Consider a data set D having N patterns $\vec{x}^i$ where $\vec{x}^i \in R^d$, $i = 1, \ldots, N$. The first stage of the proposed classification technique consists of partitioning the original data set $D = \{\vec{x}^1, \ldots, \vec{x}^N\}$ using clustering techniques to identify natural groupings. As a result of clustering, a number of training subsets $D_1, D_2, \ldots, D_M$ are generated from the set D. The clustering technique tested in this work is briefly described in the following subsection.

2.1   Fuzzy C-Means Clustering

Fuzzy c-means (FCM) [15] is a data clustering technique in which a data sample belongs to all clusters with a membership degree. FCM partitions the data set into M fuzzy clusters (where M is specified in advance), and provides the center of each cluster. Clustering is usually based on the Euclidean distance:

$$d^2(\vec{x}, \vec{\mu}) = \sum_{j=1}^{d} (x_j - \mu_j)^2 \tag{1}$$

where $\vec{x} \in R^d$ is a training sample and $\vec{\mu} \in R^d$ corresponds to a cluster center. The FCM algorithm provides fuzzy partitioning, so that a given data point $\vec{x}$ belongs to cluster j (with center $\vec{\mu}_j$) with membership degree u_j varying between 0 and 1:

$$u_j = \frac{1}{\sum_{k=1}^{M} \frac{d(\vec{x}, \vec{\mu}_j)}{d(\vec{x}, \vec{\mu}_k)}}, \quad j = 1, \ldots, M \tag{2}$$

The membership degrees are normalized in the sense that, for every pattern,

$$\sum_{j=1}^{M} u_j = 1, \tag{3}$$

Starting from arbitrary initial positions for cluster centers, and by iteratively updating cluster centers and membership degrees using e.q. (1) and (2) for each training point $\vec{x}^i, i = 1, \ldots, N$, the algorithm moves the cluster centers to sensible locations within the data set. This iteration is based on minimizing an objective function J that represents the distance from any given data point to a cluster center weighted by the data point's membership degree.

$$J(\vec{\mu}_1, \ldots, \vec{\mu}_M) = \sum_{i=1}^{N} \sum_{j=1}^{M} \left(u_{ij}^m d^2(\vec{x}^i, \vec{\mu}_j) \right), \tag{4}$$

where $m \in [1, \infty)$ is a weighting exponent.

The main drawbacks of this algorithm is that its performance depends on the initial cluster centers and that the number of clusters is predefined by the user. Therefore, it is required to run the FCM algorithm several times, each time with a different number of clusters to discover the number of clusters that results in best performance of the classification system.

2.2   Training Sets Generation

Following fuzzy clustering we can specify the degree (varying between 0 and 1) with which a data point belongs to each cluster. Let $\vec{x}$ be an input data point with its corresponding membership degree u_j to cluster j. To create M non-disjoint training sets corresponding to the M clusters we perform the following steps for each data point $\vec{x}$:

1. If $u_J \geq u_j$, $\forall j = 1, \ldots, M$, then the data point $\vec{x}$ is assigned to the training set D_J.
2. For every $j = 1, \ldots, M$, $j \neq J$, a random number q is generated according to a uniform distribution in the interval $(0, 1)$ and the data point $\vec{x}$ is assigned to the training set D_j if $q < u_j$.

Therefore, the data point $\vec{x}$ is assigned deterministically to the training set corresponding to the cluster with maximum membership for that point and is assigned probabilistically to each of the remaining training sets (with probability equal to the degree of membership to the respective cluster).

Figure 1 displays non-disjoint training sets that result from the fuzzy c-means clustering method applied to the well-known Clouds data set considering three clusters. The three cluster centers are represented as big circles and the patterns of each training set are represented as crosses, circles and stars respectively. We can also observe a degree of overlapping between the training sets, as some patterns belong to two or three training sets simultaneously. The correlation between the data sets has a beneficial impact increasing the robustness of the multi-SVM classification system.

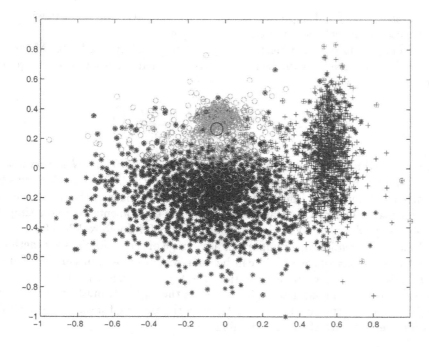

Fig. 1. Training sets corresponding to three-cluster partition of the Clouds data set using the fuzzy c-means algorithm.

3   The Multi-classifier System

Support Vector Machines (SVMs) is a learning paradigm based on the work of V. Vapnick [16] and his team (AT&T Bell Labs). The support vector algorithm applies the Structural Risk Minimization principle to construct rules that exhibit good generalization abilities. In doing so, they extract a small subset of the training data called the "*support vectors*" [16,17,18,19].

In what concerns the classification modules of the proposed multi-classifier system, the primary idea is to train a Support Vector Machine for each group of patterns D_j generated through the partitioning of the original data set D. In this sense, each classifier learns a subspace of the problem domain and becomes a "local expert" for the corresponding subdomain.

3.1   Training of Individual SVMs

The idea of a support vector machine is based on the following two operations:

1. Nonlinear mapping of an input vector into a high-dimensional feature space that is hidden from both the input and the output.
2. Construction of an optimal hyperplane for separating the above features.

For details on the SVM approach we refer to the literature. In the following we briefly discuss the options adopted in our implementation.

Each individual classifier has been implemented as a Support Vector Machine using radial basis functions as the nonlinear transformations from the input space to the feature space:

$$f(\vec{x}) = sign\left(\sum_{i=1}^{N} a_i \, exp\left\{-\frac{|\vec{x} - \vec{x}^i|^2}{\sigma^2}\right\}\right)$$

$$(5)$$

Here σ is a width parameter defined a priori and a_i , $i = 1, \ldots, N$ are parameters (Lagrange multipliers) determined optimally by the SVM algorithm, which permits us to construct a decision surface that is nonlinear in the input space, but its image is linear in the feature space. For our experiments we used a simple easy-to-use package for SVM classification: OSU SVM Toolbox 2.00 [20].

As already mentioned, an important advantage of the multi-classifier method is that the training of each SVM can be done separately and in parallel. Thus, in the case of a parallel implementation, the total training time of the system equals the worst training time achieved among the SVMs. It must be noted that this total training time cannot be greater than the training time of a single SVM classifier dealing with the entire training set.

3.2   Combination of Decisions

As described above, the original training data set D is partitioned into M (non-disjoint) subsets, and M classifiers are trained, one for each subset. Consider a new input vector $\vec{x}$ which belongs to one of c classes. Given the vector $\vec{x}$, a class label C_j , $j = 1, \ldots, M$, is produced by each SVM_j, and the membership degree u_j of the vector $\vec{x}$ to the respective cluster j is computed. To obtain the final classification decision, the decisions of the individual SVMs are combined in a probabilistic way.

A usual approach to obtain the classification of $\vec{x}$ is to compute the probability $P(k \mid \vec{x})$ $(k = 1, \ldots, c)$ that pattern $\vec{x}$ belongs to class k and select the class C with the maximum $P(C \mid \vec{x})$ as the final decision following the Bayes rule.

We have adopted the latter approach, where the probability $P(k \mid \vec{x})$ is computed as follows:

$$P(k \mid \vec{x}) = \sum_{j=1}^{M} u_j I(C_j = k)$$

$$(6)$$

Here $I(z)$ is an indicator function, i.e. $I(z) = 1$ if $z = $ true, otherwise $I(z) = 0$. The above equation states that the class probability $P(k \mid \vec{x})$ results as the sum of the weights u_j of the classifiers that suggest class k. It is easy to check that $\sum_{k=1}^{c} P(k \mid \vec{x}) = 1$. It must be noted that the combination method (6) is general since it considers the class label suggested by each classifier and not the numerical output vectors. Consequently, the method can also be used with other types of classifiers, eg. decision trees or neural networks.

4   Experimental Results

In this section, we present performance results from the use of the proposed classification system using the FCM algorithm for data partitioning and the previously described scheme for combining classifier decisions. Four well-known data sets were used in our experiments, as shown in Table 1.

Table 1. Summary of the data sets.

Dataset	Cases	Classes	Features Continuous	Discrete
Clouds	5000	2	2	-
Diabetes	768	2	9	-
Segmentation	2310	7	19	-
Phoneme	5404	2	5	-

For each data set, ten experiments were performed with random splits of the data into training and test sets of fixed sized. The *min*, *mean* and *max* errors were calculated from these ten trials. For each experiment, each individual SVM was trained several times with different values for σ and the regularization parameter C of the SVM algorithm. The best outcome of the trials according to the training error and the number of support vectors was used when testing the combination scheme. The obtained results show that the proposed multi-SVM classification system outperforms several methods reported in the literature for the Clouds data set [7,21], the Diabetes data set [1,2,8,22,23], the Segmentation data set [2] and the Phoneme data set [7,12,21]. It should be noted however, that since the partitioning of the data may or may not be the same as in our case, this comparison should be considered as rather indicative.

4.1   The Clouds Data

The Clouds artificial data from the ELENA project [21] are two-dimensional with two a priori equally probable classes. There are 5000 examples in the data set, 2500 in each class (50%). The theoretical error is 9.66%.

Table 2. The Clouds data set: Test set error (%) comparative results.

Clouds data set			
Classifier	min	mean	max
Multi-SVM	9.4	**9.99**	10.9
SVM	9.9	**11.02**	11.9

In our experiments, we used 4000 patterns for training and 1000 patterns for testing the system, respectively. For the FCM algorithm, we obtained the best results by splitting the original training data set into three subsets. As a result of clustering, three SVM classifiers combined in our system. The testing results for the multi-SVM classification system are shown in Table 2. For comparison, results from using a single SVM classifier are also shown in Table 2.

The classification error obtained with the multi-SVM system is quite close to the theoretical one; therefore, any further improvement can hardly be achieved.

4.2   The Diabetes Data

The Diabetes set from the UCI data set repository [24] contains 768 8-dimensional data belonging to two classes. In our experiments, we used 600 patterns for training and 168 patterns for testing the system. For the FCM algorithm, we obtained the best results by splitting the original training data set into three subsets. As a result of clustering, three SVM classifiers combined in our system. The testing results for the multi-SVM classification system are shown in Table 3. For comparison, results from using a single SVM classifier are also shown in Table 3.

Table 3. The Diabetes data set: Test set error (%) comparative results.

Diabetes data set			
Classifier	min	mean	max
Multi-SVM	16.67	**21.13**	25.6
SVM	17.26	**22.86**	26.79

It must also be noted that this data set contains some known outliers, that affect the construction of the clusters and eventually the classification performance of the system.

4.3   The Image Segmentation Data

The Image Segmentation data set from the UCI data set repository [24] contains 2310 19-dimensional examples belonging to 7 classes. We used 1500 patterns for training and 810 patterns for testing the system. For the FCM algorithm, we obtained the best results by splitting the original training data set into four subsets. As a result of clustering, four SVM classifiers combined in our system. The testing results for the multi-SVM classification system are shown in Table 4. For comparison, results from using a single SVM classifier are also shown in Table 4.

In our experiments, we preprocessed the Image Segmentation data set by applying principal component analysis (PCA). In addition, the size of the input

Table 4. The Segmentation data set: Test set error (%) comparative results.

Segmentation data set			
Classifier	min	mean	max
Multi-SVM	6.3	**7.1**	8.02
SVM	6.67	**7.38**	8.15

vectors was reduced to a 7-dimensional space by retaining only those components which contribute more than a specified fraction (defined 0.009) of the total variation in the data set.

4.4 The Phoneme Data

The Phoneme dataset from the ELENA project [21] contains 5404 5-dimensional data belonging to two classes. In our experiments, we used 4500 patterns for training and 904 patterns for testing the system. For the FCM algorithm, we obtained the best results by splitting the original training data set into two subsets. As a result of clustering, two SVM classifiers combined in our system. The testing results for the multi-SVM classification system are shown in Table 5. For comparison, results from using a single SVM classifier are also shown in Table 5.

Table 5. The Phoneme data set: Test set error (%) comparative results.

Phoneme data set			
Classifier	min	mean	max
Multi-SVM	8.85	**9.73**	10.4
SVM	8.63	**10.25**	10.95

5   Conclusions

In this work, we present and test a multi-SVM classification system that is based on both unsupervised and supervised learning methods. To build the classification system, first the original training set is divided into overlapping subsets by applying a clustering technique. Then, an individual SVM is trained on every defined subset. To obtain the classification of a new pattern, the decisions of the SVMs are appropriately combined. An important strength of the proposed classification approach is that it does not depend on the type of the classifier, therefore, it is quite general and applicable to a wide class of models including neural networks and other classification techniques. The learning method offers the advantages of the *"divide-and-conquer"* framework, i.e., smaller classification models may be employed that can be trained in parallel on smaller (and usually easier to discriminate) training sets.

We have applied the fuzzy c-means algorithm for data clustering and considered a combination of the decisions of multiple SVMs based on a probabilistic interpretation. The resulting approach has been tested on different benchmark data sets exhibiting very promising performance. The main conclusion that can be drawn from the experimental results is that, as expected, the multi-SVM system exhibits better performance between 0.3% and 1.7% on (four) datasets of different size and number of classes than a single SVM classifier. An important result that occasionally came up during data partitioning in our study, was the creation of training sets with examples of a single class. Thus, there was no need of training a classifier for these data sets.

The multi-classifier methodology implemented in this work is quite general allowing the implementation and testing of other techniques both in the clustering and the classification module.

References

1. R. Maclin and D. Opitz. An empirical evaluation of bagging and boosting. In *Proceedings of the Fourteenth National Conference on Artificial Intelligence*, pages 546–551, 1997.
2. Y. Freund and R.E. Schapire. Experiments with a new boosting algorithm. In *Proceedings of the Thirteenth International Conference on Machine Learning*, pages 148–156, 1996.
3. R. Avnimelech and N. Intrator. Boosted mixture of experts: an ensemble learning scheme. *Neural computation*, 11(2):483–497, 1999.
4. D. Pavlov, J. Mao, and B. Dom. Scaling-up support vector machines using boosting algorithm. In *Proceedings of the 15th International Conference on Pattern Recognition (ICPR2000)*, volume 2, pages 219–222, Barcelona, Spain, September 2000.
5. L. Kuncheva. Clustering-and-selection model for classifier combination. In *Proceedings of the 4th International Conference on Knowledge-based Intelligent Engineering Systems (KES'2000)*, Brighton, UK, 2000.
6. E. Alpaydin. Techniques for combining multiple learners. In *Proceedings of Engineering of Intelligent Systems*, volume 2, pages 6–12. ICSC Press, 1998.
7. A. Vericas, A. Lipnickas, K. Malmqvist, M. Bacauskiene, and A. Gelzinis. Soft combination of neural classifiers: A comparative study. *Pattern Recognition Letters*, (20):430–441, 1999.
8. K. Tumer and J. Ghosh. Order statistics combiners for neural classifiers. In *Proceedings of the World Congress on Neural Networks*, pages I:31–34, Washington D.C., 1995. INNS Press.
9. A.J.C. Sharkey. *Combining Artificial Neural Nets: Ensemble and Modular Multi-Net Systems*. Springer Press, 1999.
10. M.I. Jordan and R.A. Jacobs. Hierarchical mixtures of experts and the em algorithm. *Neural Computation*, (6):181–214, 1994.
11. E. Alpaydin. Voting over multiple condensed nearest neighbor subsets. *Artificial Intelligence Review*, 11:115–132, 1997.

12. L. Kuncheva. Combining classifiers by clustering, selection and decision templates. Technical report, University of Wales, UK, 2000.

13. L. Breiman. Bagging predictors. Technical Report 421, Department of Statistics, University of California, Berkeley, 1994.

14. P.K. Chan and S.J. Stolfo. A comparative evaluation of voting and meta-learning on partitioned data. In *Proceedings of the Twelfth International Machine Learning Conference*, San Mateo,CA, 1995. Morgan Kaufmann.

15. J.C. Bezdek. *Pattern Recognition with Fuzzy Objective Function Algorithms*. Plenum Press, New York, 1981.

16. V. Vapnik. *The Nature of Statistical Learning Theory*. Springer-Verlag, New York, 1995.

17. Y. Cherkassky and F. Mulier. *Learning from Data - Concepts, Theory and Methods*. John Wiley & Sons. New York, 1998.

18. C. J. C. Burges. A tutorial on support vector machines for pattern recognition. *Data Mining and Knowledge Discovery*, 2(2):955–974, 1998.

19. B. Schölkopf, C.J.C. Burges, and V. Vapnik. Extracting support data for a given task. In U.M. Fayyad and R. Uthurusamy, editors, *Proceedings, First International Conference on Knowledge Discovery & Data Mining*. AAAI Press, Menlo Park, 1995.

20. OSU SVM Toolbox 2.00. [http://eewww.eng.ohio-state.edu/~maj/osu-svm/].

21. ESPRIT Basic Research Project ELENA (no. 6891). [ftp://ftp.dice.ucl.ac.be/pub/neural-nets/ELENA/databases], 1995.

22. R. Herbrich and J. Weston. Adaptive margin support vector machines for classification learning. In *Proceedings of the Ninth International Conference on Artificial Neural Networks*, pages 880–885, 1999.

23. Y.-J. Lee and O.L. Mangasarian. SSVM: A smooth support vector machine for classification. Technical Report 99-02, Data Mining Institute, 1999.

24. UCI Machine Learning Databases Repository, University of California-Irvine, Department of Information and Computer Science. [ftp://ftp.ics.edu/pub/machine-learning-databases].

Automatic Classification of Clustered Microcalcifications by a Multiple Classifier System

P. Foggia[1], C. Sansone[1], F. Tortorella[2], and M. Vento[1]

[1]Dipartimento di Informatica e Sistemistica
Università degli Studi di Napoli "Federico II"
via Claudio, 21 80125 Napoli – Italy
{foggiapa,carlosan,vento}@unina.it,

[2]Dipartimento di Automazione, Elettromagnetismo,
Ingegneria dell'Informazione e Matematica Industriale
Università degli Studi di Cassino
via G. di Biasio, 43 03043 Cassino – Italy
tortorella@unicas.it

Abstract. Mammography is a not invasive diagnostic technique widely used for early detection of breast cancer. One of the main indicants of cancer is the presence of microcalcifications, i.e. small calcium accumulations, often grouped into clusters. Automatic detection and recognition of malignant clusters of microcalcifications are very difficult because of the small size of the microcalcifications and of the poor quality of the mammographic images. Up to now, mainly two kinds of approaches have been proposed to tackle this problem: those performing the classification by looking at the features of single microcalcifications and those based on the classifications of clusters, which in turn use features characterizing the spatial distribution of the microcalcification in the breast. In this paper we propose a novel approach for recognizing malignant clusters, based on a Multiple Classifier System (MCS) which uses simultaneously the evidences obtainable from the classification of the single microcalcifications and from the classification of the cluster considered as a whole. The approach has been tested on a standard database of 40 mammographic images and revealed very effective with respect to the single experts.

1. Introduction

Mammography is a radiological screening technique which makes it possible to detect lesions in the breast using low doses of radiation. At present, it represents the only not invasive diagnostic technique which allows the diagnosis of a breast cancer at a very early stage, when it is still possible to successfully attack the disease with a suitable therapy.

A visual clue of breast cancer particularly meaningful is the presence of clusters of microcalcifications [1]. Microcalcifications are tiny granular deposits of calcium that appear on the mammogram as small bright spots. Their size ranges from about

J. Kittler and F. Roli (Eds.): MCS 2001, LNCS 2096, pp. 208–217, 2001.

0.1 mm to 0.7 mm, while their shape is sometimes irregular. Besides being arranged into clusters, microcalcifications can appear isolated and spread over the breast tissue, but in this case they are not indication of a possible cancer. However, even in the case of clustered microcalcifications their nature is not necessarily malignant, and thus the radiologist must carefully analyze the mammogram to decide if the appearance of the cluster suggests a malignant case. Such decision is taken on the basis of some properties (shape, size, distribution, etc.) related to both the single microcalcifications [2] and the whole cluster [3].

A computer aided analysis could be very useful to the radiologist both for prompting suspect cases and for helping in the diagnostic decision as a "second reading" [4], especially in the case of a mass screening. Such a tool should improve both the *sensitivity* of the diagnosis, i.e. the accuracy in recognizing all the malignant cases and its *specificity*, i.e. the ability to avoid erroneous recognition of benign clusters as malignant.

In the recent past, many approaches have been proposed for the automatic detection and recognition of clusters of microcalcifications (e.g. see [5]). Up to now, most of the research efforts in this field have been devoted to the detection of microcalcifications, which is an inherently complex problem because of the low resolution and very low contrast of mammograms. The main approach currently used is based on the wavelet transform [6]; other proposed methods rely on Gaussian filtering, artificial neural networks, texture analysis, mathematical morphology and fuzzy logic.

On the other hand, methods explicitly devoted to the classification phase are very few and mainly focused on the analysis of the single microcalcifications [7]. Additional information attainable by examining the cluster is usually not considered, although in several cases it has proven to be essential for a correct diagnosis.

In this paper we propose a novel approach for the automatic classification of clusters of microcalcifications, based on the adoption of a Multiple Classifier System (MCS). The proposed system employs two classifiers, one for classifying single microcalcifications and the other for classifying the cluster as a whole. The responses of both the classifiers, together with their estimated reliability, are used by a combination stage to take the final decision. The assumption underlying this approach is that the collective decision taken on the basis of the responses of an ensemble of classifiers is less likely to be in error than the decision made by any of the individual classifiers, if these latter can provide complementary discriminative information [8,9]. The proposed method has been experimented with a standard database of mammograms. Since the focus of this work is on the combining scheme, for the classifiers we have adopted two sets of relatively simple features found in the literature. The results obtained confirmed the effectiveness of the MCS, whose performance resulted better than each of the composing experts.

2. The Proposed Method

As previously said, the automatic recognition of malignant clusters of microcalcifications is a classification task quite difficult because of the low quality of the input images. So, even the most sophisticated segmentation methods can extract the microcalcifications with seriously distorted shapes. These distortions make the successive feature selection phase very critical. Various feature sets have been proposed up to now, based, among others, on shape analysis [10] or texture analysis [5]. Experiments on real images highlighted advantages and disadvantages of these feature sets when used singularly, but none of them resulted definitely optimal.

A different approach for the classification stage is to consider the whole cluster instead of the single microcalcifications, since the distribution of the microcalcifications within the breast tissue is recognized as another meaningful clue for the final diagnosis [3]. In this case, the features to be employed describe the shape of the cluster and other parameters characterizing the distribution of microcalcifications within it. These features give good results in situations where microcalcifications are heavily distorted in their shape, as long as the cluster they belong to is clearly identifiable. Unfortunately, this approach becomes unreliable when the cluster is weakly described, i.e. when the total number of microcalcifications forming the cluster is low.

These considerations suggest to suitably employ, in the classification stage, both the different approaches, using a MCS which will effectively exploit the complementary evidence coming from the two diverse classifiers. In next subsection we will introduce the architecture of such system.

2.1 System Architecture

The first processing task in a system for the automatic recognition of malignant microcalcifications consists in detecting the microcalcifications and grouping them in clusters. This task can be carried out by adopting one of the many methods proposed up to now in the specialized literature. As the present paper is mainly concerned with the classification issues, we consider as our starting point an image in which the microcalcifications have already been detected and grouped into clusters (see fig. 1). At this point, the problems of feature extraction and classification can be faced. For the sake of clarity, we will use hereon the term *expert* to denote a system composed by a classifier and the corresponding feature extractor. According to this terminology, we can say that the whole MCS is composed of two different experts: the first one (μC-Expert) is devised for the classification of the single microcalcifications, while the second one (**Cluster Expert**) looks at the entire cluster.

To classify a cluster containing N_μ microcalcifications, each microcalcification is classified by the μC-Expert, while the cluster, considered as a whole, is classified by the Cluster Expert. The final classification decision is obtained by collecting their responses and applying a suitable decision scheme based on the evaluation of the reliability of each classification.

Both the considered experts employ the same classification model, i.e. a Multi-Layer Perceptron (MLP) with a sigmoidal activation function. It is made by a three layers fully connected network, containing 25 neurons in the hidden layer, 2 output neurons (associated with the benign and the malignant class) and a number of nodes in the input layer depending on the size of the feature vector employed. Both the classifiers have been trained with the standard Back Propagation algorithm, adopting a costant learning rate η equal to 0.5.

In the next subsections we will describe in more detail the features used by the two types of expert and the rules that determine the combiner final decision.

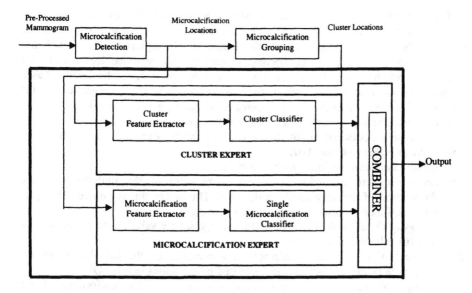

Fig. 1. : The architecture of the proposed Multi-Classifier System (MCS).

2.2 The μC-Expert Features

Since the main goal of this paper is to evaluate the benefits introduced by the use of a MCS we have avoided the definition of new features, preferring the adoption of features already known in the literature.

The μC-Expert uses four features based on the shape of the microcalcifications and eight on its texture properties. This choice is based on the experimental evidence that the more irregular the shape of the calcification, the higher the risk of breast cancer. In particular, benign cases are characterized by round microcalcifications with smooth border and uniform shapes, while clusters having microcalcifications with irregular border and with various sizes and shapes are typically malignant [3]. On this basis, we have adopted the following four features, based on the analysis of the shape:

S1. *compactness*: evaluated as the ratio between the area of the microcalcification and the square of the perimeter of its border;

S2. *roughness*: it is a measure of the irregularity of the border. It is defined in [10] as the standard deviation of the square distance of the points of the border from the center of the microcalcification;

S3. *border gradient strenght*: it is an estimate of the intensity gradient measured on the points of the border of the microcalcification;

S4. *local contrast*: it is a measure of the average difference between the intensity of the points belonging to the microcalcification and the intensity of the points belonging to the background.

These features are evaluated on an Area of Interest (AOI), made of a square box of 17×17 pixels centered on the centroid of the microcalcification.

The reason for using an additional set of features based on the texture properties is twofold. First, in this way we have a characterization of the tissue surrounding the microcalcification and (indirectly) of the underlying biological process which has produced the microcalcification. Second, in case the shape based features are not completely reliable (because of the low quality of the image), the texture based features can provide further information to decide about the malignancy of the microcalcification. The used texture features are the ones proposed in [5]:

T1. *energy in the AOI*: the average square intensity in the AOI;

T2. *energy in the background*: the average square intensity in the background;

T3. *average intensity in the AOI*;

T4. *standard deviation of the intensity in the AOI*;

T5. *entropy of the 1st order histogram*: a measure of the uniformity of the distribution of the gray levels in the AOI. The higher this parameter, the more uniform the distribution of gray levels in the AOI;

T6. *energy of the 2nd order histogram*: the average square value of the co-occurrence matrix evaluated on the AOI;

T7. *contrast of the 2nd order histogram*: a measure of the distribution of the difference among the gray levels exhibited by the points in the AOI;

T8. *entropy of the 2nd order histogram*: a measure of the uniformity of the distribution of the values in the co-occurrence matrix.

2.3 The Cluster Expert Features

The choice of effective cluster features presents the same problems we have highlighted in the previous sections. However, experiments made by several research groups have shown that three meaningful clues to distinguish benign from malignant clusters could be the shape of the cluster, the distribution of the microcalcifications within the clusters and the uniformity of their shapes.

As regards the shape, malignant clusters are typically quite elongated, while benign clusters are more round. The only notable exception is given by the clusters created by intraductal microcalcifications which show an extreme ellipticity even though they are benign. An adequate measure of the ellipticity can be obtained by evaluating the ratio between the major and the minor axis of the ellipse of inertia of the cluster.

The second type of feature we employ concerns the distribution of the microcalcifications within the cluster. We consider both the mass distribution and the spatial distribution of the microcalcifications, since malignant clusters show a much higher density of microcalcifications with respect to the benign clusters.

The third group of features is based on the presence of microcalcifications with irregular and non uniform shapes. Information about the distribution of shape features S1 and S2 on the microcalcifications belonging to the cluster can be very helpful. In fact, the more irregular and the less uniform the shapes of the microcalcifications, the more likely a malignant cluster. On the basis of the considerations made, we have adopted the following features for the Cluster Expert:

C1. ratio between the major and the minor axis of the ellipse of inertia of the cluster;

C2. mass density of the whole cluster;

C3. average mass of the microcalcifications;

C4. standard deviation of the masses of the microcalcifications;

C5. average distance among the centroids of microcalcifications and the centroid of the cluster;
C6. standard deviation of the distances among the centroids microcalcifications and the centroid of the cluster;
C7. average of the compactness;
C8. standard deviation of the compactness;
C9. average of the roughness;
C10. standard deviation of the roughness.

3. The Combination Scheme

In the literature different combination criteria have been proposed up to now [8,9]. The most popular ones are those based on statistical methods, evidence theory or heuristic approaches. In all such proposals the number of confidence degrees coming from the classifiers involved in the MCS is fixed.

In our case, though the number of classifiers is fixed (one Cluster Expert and one μC Expert), the number of confidence degrees to be combined is not fixed, because the μC Expert is activated once for each microcalcification contained in the cluster, ranging from few instances to more than 100. This leads to two problems: first, the unique confidence degree coming from the Cluster Expert has to be combined with a variable number of confidence degrees coming from the μC Expert. Second, the relative significance of the single expert changes with the number of the microcalcifications. In fact, while the reliability of the μC expert is not affected by the number of microcalcifications, most of the cluster features become unreliable when the microcalcifications are very few.

As regards the first point, if N_μ is the total number of microcalcifications in the cluster we are considering, we have N_μ outputs coming from the μC expert applied to each of the microcalcifications in the cluster: let us call $\left(O_m^{(i)}, O_b^{(i)}\right)$, with i=1.. N_μ, the two output values provided by the μC expert when classifying the i-th microcalcification for the malignant and the benign class. In order to elicit two overall confidence degrees, whose values are homogeneous with the outputs of the Cluster Expert (which range from 0 to 1), a first solution is to count the microcalcifications classified as malignant and benign and normalizing such numbers with respect to N_μ. In other words, if M is the number of microcalcifications for which $O_m^{(i)} > O_b^{(i)}$, the estimated confidence degrees (K_m, K_b) are given by:

$$K_m = \frac{M}{N_\mu} \qquad K_b = \frac{N_\mu - M}{N_\mu}$$

Unfortunately, while such estimate is very reliable for high values of N_μ, it does not work well when the cluster contains a small number of microcalcifications. For this reason, we have also considered another estimate (A_m, A_b) which provides the desired confidence degrees by averaging the outputs produced by the μC Expert:

$$A_m = \frac{1}{N_\mu} \sum_{i=1}^{N_\mu} O_m^{(i)} \qquad A_b = \frac{1}{N_\mu} \sum_{i=1}^{N_\mu} O_b^{(i)}$$

Note that also for the proposed estimates we find the same dependence on N_μ that we highlighted for the Cluster Expert. To overcome this problem, the most suitable combining scheme is the "Weighted Voting" rule, according to which the "vote" (i.e. the output) of each expert is weighted by the estimated significance associated to the expert; all the votes are finally collected and the input sample is assigned to the class for which the sum of the votes is the highest. However, in our case, the weights of the different contributions coming from the cluster and from the microcalcifications cannot be fixed, but must vary as a function of N_μ. As a result, we obtain the two-stage combining scheme described in Fig. 2.

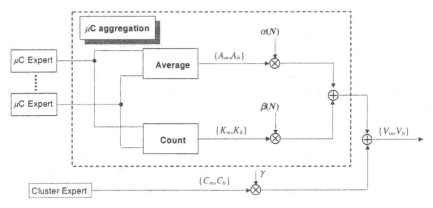

Fig. 2. The adopted two-stage combining scheme.

The first stage (hereon called *μC aggregation*) collects the classification decisions coming from the *μC* Expert applied to all the microcalcifications of the input cluster and evaluates the two couples of confidence degrees (A_m, A_b) and (K_m, K_b). These ones are successively weighted by two weight functions $\alpha(N_\mu)$ and $\beta(N_\mu)$. Both the functions are linear on N_μ, but with different slopes: $\alpha(N_\mu)$ is increasing while $\beta(N_\mu)$ is decreasing.

The weighted values coming from the *μC* aggregation are finally combined with the outputs coming from the Cluster Expert, weighted by a constant γ. In conclusion the final confidence degrees, said V_m and V_b, are obtained in the following way:

$$V_m = \alpha(N_{\mu C}) \cdot A_m + \beta(N_{\mu C}) \cdot K_m + \gamma \cdot C_m$$
$$V_b = \alpha(N_{\mu C}) \cdot A_b + \beta(N_{\mu C}) \cdot K_b + \gamma \cdot C_b$$

The parameters of the weight functions and γ are evaluated by means of an optimization phase whose details are given in the following section. As a result, two particular values of N are determined such that the highest weight is given to the pair (A_m, A_b) for $N < N_0$ and to the pair (K_m, K_b) for $N > N_1$; thus, in these two intervals, the contribution coming from the for *μC*-Experts is prevailing with respect to the Cluster Experts. This is consistent with the experimental evidence that the cluster features are not very reliable with a low number of microcalcifications, while, for clusters with many microcalcifications, the combined outputs of the μC-Experts are more accurate.

4. Experimental Results

For testing our approach we have used a public database (available at the site http://figment.csee.usf.edu/) of 40 mammographies containing 72 malignant clusters and 30 benign ones, with 1792 malignant and 331 benign microcalcifications. Images were provided by courtesy of the National Expert and Training Centre for Breast Cancer Screening and the Department of Radiology at the University of Nijmegen, the Netherlands. All images are 2048 by 2048 and use 12 bits per pixel of gray level information. Some preprocessing was performed to convert the images to a 8 bit/pixel format using an adaptive noise equalisation described in [11].

The database has revealed to be a severe test bed for our approach, since the dimensions of the microcalcifications were typically very small. Moreover, the low number of clusters makes very difficult the learning of experts based on neural classifiers. For this reason, we have adopted a *leave-one-out* approach for our experiments. With this method, the learning of the classifiers was performed with a training set containing 101 clusters, while the one remaining cluster was used as a test sample. More precisely, for each trial, the 90% of the training set was actually used for training the neural networks, while the 10% (randomly extracted) was employed to estimate the optimal parameters for the weight functions $\alpha(N_\mu)$ and $\beta(N_\mu)$. In this way, the classification is repeated until all cluster have been used once as a test sample.

In order to evaluate the diagnostic ability of the MCS in recognizing malignant clusters, we have employed the *Receiver Operating Characteristic* curve (*ROC* curve) [12]. This is a graph obtained by calculating the sensitivity and specificity for every operating point and plotting *sensitivity* (estimated as the true positive rate, or TP rate, i. e. the ratio of actual benign cases among the cases classified as positive) against $(1 - specificity)$ (estimated as the false positive rate, or FP rate, i. e. the ratio of malignant cases among the cases classified as positive). A diagnostic system that perfectly discriminates between the two classes would yield a curve that coincides with the left and top sides of the plot. A test that is completely useless would give a straight line from the bottom left corner to the top right corner. In practice, there is always some overlap in the two classes, so the curve will lie between these extremes.

For evaluating the ROC curve of the MCS we have used the ROCKIT 0.9B package, developed by Metz and his research group at the Department of Radiology of the University of Chicago. This software is designed to fit binormal ROC curves to both continuously-distributed and ordinal category diagnostic test results, on the basis of a maximum-likelihood estimate [13].

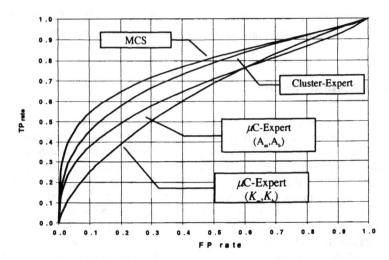

Fig. 3.   The ROC curves of the single experts and of the whole MES.

The ROC curves obtained for the MCS and the single experts from the tests on the data set described above are shown in fig. 3. It is possible to note that the MCS provides a discriminative performance sensibly better than the single experts: in fact, its ROC curve is at the left and over the curves of the experts. Among them, the Cluster Expert has the best performance, while the two aggregations realized on the μC-Expert give quite similar results.

To have a quantitative evaluation of the performance of the MCS and its componing experts, we have also evaluated the area under the respective ROC curves. This parameter provides a global assessment of the performance of the test (sometimes called diagnostic accuracy) and is equal to the probability that a random malignant sample has a higher value of the measurement (in our case, of the malignant output of the classifier) than a random benign sample. More precisely, this probability is 0.5 for an uninformative diagnostic system, while equals 1.0 for a perfectly discriminative diagnostic system. In particular, the optimal parameters for the weight functions have been estimated by maximizing this parameter.

The obtained values are shown in table 1. Also in this case, the MCS reveals to be better than the componing experts. In particular, while there is some improvement with respect the Cluster Expert, the difference with the μC-Expert is very high. It is worth noting that, even though its performance is not very good, the μC-Expert contribute is very helpful to enhance the discriminative ability of the MCS.

Table 1. The measures of the areas under the curves presented in fig. 3.

	Cluster Expert	μC-Expert (A_m, A_h)	μC-Expert (K_m, K_h)	MCS
Area under the ROC curve	0.71	0.67	0.57	0.79

5. Conclusions

In this paper we have presented a novel method for classifying clusters of microcalcifications, which is based on a Multiple Classifier approach in order to exploit the evidence coming both from single microcalcifications and from the cluster as a whole. An experimental analysis performed on a standard database has shown the effectiveness of the approach with respect to single classifier systems.

References

[1]   W.A. Murphy, K. DeSchryver-Kecskemeti, "Isolated clustered microcalcifications in the breast: radiologic-pathologic correlation", *Radiology*, vol. 127, pp. 335-341, 1978.

[2]   M. Lanyi, *Diagnosis and differential diagnosis of breast calcifications*, Springer-Verlag, New York, 1986.

[3]   B. de Lafontan, J.P. Daures, B. Salicru, F. Eynius, J. Mihura, P. Rouanet, J.L. Lamarque, A. Naja, H. Pujol, "Isolated Clustered Microcalcifications: Diagnostic Value of Mammography—Series of 400 Cases with Surgical Verification", *Radiology*, vol. 190, pp. 479-483, 1994.

[4]   E.D. Pisano, F. Shtern "Image processing and Computer Aided Diagnosis in digital mammography: A clinical perspective", *Int. Journal of Pattern Recognition and Artificial Intelligence*, vol. 7, no. 6, pp. 1493-1503, 1993.

[5]   A.P. Dhawan, Y. Chitre, C. Kaiser-Bonasso, M. Moskowitz, "Analysis of Mammographic Microcalcifications Using Gray-Level Image Structure Features", *IEEE Trans. on Medical Imaging*, vol. 15, no. 3, pp. 246-259, 1996.

[6]   M.J.Lado, P.G. Tahoces, A.J. Méndez, M. Souto, J.J. Vidal, "A Wavelet-based Algorithm for Detecting Clustered Microcalcifications in Digital Mammograms", *Medical Physics*, vol. 26, no. 7, pp. 1294-1305, 1999.

[7]   S.S. Buchbinder, I.S. Leichter, P.N. Bamberger, B. Novak, R. Lederman, S. Fields, D.J. Behar, "Analysis of Clustered Microcalcifications by Using a Single Numeric Classifier Extracted from Mammographic Digital Images", *Academic Radiology*, vol. 5, no. 11, pp. 779-784, 1998.

[8]   T.K Ho, J.J. Hull, S. Shrihari, "Decision Combination in Multiple Classifier Systems", *IEEE Trans. on Pattern Analysis and Machine Intelligence*, vol 16, no.1, pp.66-75, 1994.

[9]   J. Kittler, "A Framework for Classifier Fusion: Is It Still Needed ?", in F.J. Ferri, J.M. Iñesta, A. Amin, P. Pudil (eds.), *Advances in Pattern Recognition*, Lecture Notes in Computer Science 1876, pp. 45-56, Springer, Berlin, 2000.

[10] L. Shen, R.M. Rangayyan, J.E.L. Desautels, "Application of Shape Analysis to Mammographic Calcifications", *IEEE Trans. on Medical Imaging*, vol. 13, no. 2, pp. 234-253, 1994.

[11] N. Karssemeijer, "Adaptive Noise Equalization and Recognition of Microcalcification Clusters in Mammograms", *Int. Journal of Pattern Recognition and Artificial Intelligence*, vol. 7, no. 6, pp. 1357-1376, 1993.

[12] C.E. Metz, "ROC methodology in radiologic imaging", *Investigative Radiology*, vol. 21, pp. 720-733, 1986.

[13] C.E. Metz, B.A. Herman, J-H. Shen, "Maximum-likelihood estimation of receiver operating characteristic (ROC) curves from continuously-distributed data", *Statistics in Medicine*, vol. 17, no. 9, pp. 1033-53.

Feature Weighted Ensemble Classifiers –
A Modified Decision Scheme

Thomas Martini Jørgensen[1] and Christian Linneberg[1,2]

[1]Risø National Laboratory, P.O. Box 49, DK-4000 Roskilde, Denmark
thomas.martini@risoe.dk
[2]Intellix A/S, H.C. Ørsteds vej 4, DK-1879 Frederiksberg, Denmark
cli@intellix.com

Abstract. In order to determine the output from an aggregated classifier a number of methods exists. A common approach is to apply the majority-voting scheme. If the performance of the classifiers can be ranked in some intelligent way, the voting process can be modified by assigning individual weights to each of the ensemble members. For some base classifiers, like decision trees, a given node or leaf is activated if the input lies within a well-defined region in input space. In other words, each leaf-node can be considered as defining a given feature in input space. In this paper, we present a method for adjusting the voting process of an ensemble by assigning individual weights to this set of features, implying that different nodes of the same decision tree can contribute differently to the overall voting process. By using a randomised "look-up technique" for the training examples the weights used in the decision process is determined using a perceptron-like learning rule. We present results obtained by applying such a technique to bagged ensembles of C4.5 trees and to the so-called PERT classifier, which is an ensemble of highly randomised decision trees. The proposed technique is compared to the majority-voting scheme on a number of data sets.

1   Introduction

Combining multiple classifiers to obtain improved performance by now is a technique widely used [1]. Using an ensemble classifier [2] it is possible to reduce the mean error rate over that of the individual classifiers and often the ensemble outperforms even the strongest individual member of the ensemble. Ideally, one wants to combine independent classifiers, but as it is often impossible to obtain independent classifiers, the aim of ensemble training algorithms is to create classifiers with low inter-correlation and moderate individual strengths.

During the last decade, a number of methods for growing ensemble classifiers has been proposed, most widely known is the techniques denoted as boosting [3], bagging [4] and randomisation [5]. Both bagging and boosting perturb the learning process from one ensemble member to the next by using individual training sets obtained by resampling the original training set. In addition to this, boosting also assign weights to the individual classifiers. The randomisation techniques operate by having one or more randomisation steps integrated into the model building process. For a general discussion of these and other techniques, see e.g. [6,7].

J. Kittler and F. Roli (Eds.): MCS 2001, LNCS 2096, pp. 218–227, 2001.

The outputs of a given ensemble member is often scaled so that the values can be considered as estimates of the posterior likelihoods of a given class given the input example and the trained model. Alternatively, one may only pay attention to the class that obtains the largest output. Depending on these interpretations, a number of schemes exist for combining the classifiers. If the errors made by individual classifiers to a large degree are uncorrelated, product rules for combining the probability estimates can be used. A more robust scheme is to have each classifier vote on just one class and then apply a simple majority rule for deciding the winner. The simple majority rule can be modified to put different weights on different members, which of course implies that some sensible quality measure must be used to rank the performance of the individual classifiers. Such decision rules are all fixed. Alternatively, one can train a decision model by using all the outputs of the individual classifiers as input to a classification model [8].

A theoretical analysis of the n-tuple classifier [9], which is an ensemble-based classifier, revealed that for this classifier the majority-voting rule, which is conventionally used, often could be a bad choice. As a result the decision border has to be adapted to the specific set of ensemble members, and a method for obtaining an adequate decision border for a voting ensemble was recently derived [9,10]. The principle behind the modified decision scheme is to assign different weighting schemes (including biases) to each of the possible output scores. It turns out that in many situations (especially with highly randomised ensembles) a simple adaptation of the decision border in what we denote "score space" can improve the performance of the ensemble. Accordingly, an initial decision border (normally corresponding to the majority voting scheme) is adjusted by considering the individual score points as acting with forces on the border. In the present paper, we extend this idea. If it is beneficial to adjust the weightings of the class votes, then it may also be advantageous to adjust the influence of the features leading to the class-scores. Instead of having the score points act with forces on the decision border we use the opposite approach of having a given decision border act on the individual score points. In the case of decision trees, this implies that different leaves of a single tree will contribute differently to the overall voting process. Especially in cases where the ensemble building process is based on a large degree of randomisation, the quality of the different substructures of a decision tree with respect to separating the classes can vary quite a lot. Breiman has shown that the use of ensembles of randomised decision trees corresponds to performing a kernel operation over the input space [11]. The method presented below can be seen as adapting this kernel to the individual look-up paths, which the examples traverse on their way through the "decision forest".

Below we describe an algorithm that can be applied to modify the score values obtained for each example. In addition we present results obtained by applying the technique on a number of data sets using respectively a bagged ensemble of C4.5 classifiers and the so-called PERT ensemble classifier (Perfect Random Tree) [12,13].

2   Non-optimality of the Majority Voting Scheme

Consider a classification problem specified by a set of m training examples, $\{(\mathbf{x}_1, y_1), (\mathbf{x}_2, y_2), \ldots (\mathbf{x}_m, y_m)\}$, where $\mathbf{x}_i$ define the input vector and y_i is the corresponding class label. The set of all input vectors x_i is denoted X. In the case of a voting scheme, a single classifier trained on X performs a mapping from the input-space to a binary-valued output space, $I \to B$. Usually, the output takes the form of a one-in-n encoding of the output class. By creating a voted ensemble, the overall transformation can be seen as a transformation from input to output via an intermediate score space, $I \to S \to B$. The class scores are simply the average (or sum) of the output vectors obtained from the individual classifiers.

As mentioned in the introduction, the majority-voting scheme will not always be an adequate choice for combining voting classifiers. This will especially be true if the training distribution is highly skewed over the classes or if the spread of the classes in input space is highly different. Correspondingly, a modification of the decision scheme is needed [10]. In [14] it is shown that the scheme developed for adjusting the decision border for the n-tuple classifier also can be useful for other types of ensemble based classifiers, especially highly randomised ones such as the PERT classifier [12,13]. In the next sections, we will briefly review the procedure described in [10].

2.1   Modified Decision Border

The method used to adjust the decision border in score space [10] can be explained as follows. After training an ensemble of classifiers, the ensemble is used to classify a set of validation examples. Preferably, the scores are obtained using leave-one-out cross-validation, hence reducing the need for a separate validation set (it is simple to perform a leave-one-out classification when using the n-tuple classifier [15]). Figure 1 illustrates a case where inspection of the distribution of score values obtained on a validation set reveals that the error rate could be lowered by using another decision border than that corresponding to the majority-vote decision. One way for handling this problem could be to train another classifier to separate the examples in score space, e.g. using a Support Vector Machine [16,17]. A simple approach is to restrict the decision border to a line, and then use a force-field analogy to adjust the line parameters [10]. This technique has been applied to the case shown in Figure 1. As illustrated in Figure 2 the gained performance on the validation set generalises well to the test set.

2.2   Adaptive Feature Weighting

For a decision tree, there will in general be several leaf nodes that all result in the same output. The "activation" of these leaf nodes, however, is caused by different input values that belong to different regions in the input space. The method of changing the decision border as outlined above treats all scores obtained on a given class equivalently – it is not possible to separate two examples having identical scores no matter how the border is modified. If we instead allow the individual score values to be modified it may be possible to solve such conflicts, and at the same time we could adapt to a given decision border.

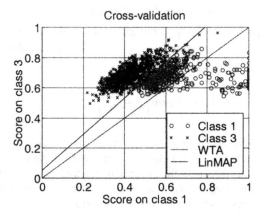

Fig. 1. Score values in score space between two of the three classes in the DNA data set. The majority-voting scheme (WTA) is not optimal to separate the classes. A new border (LinMAP) is made to optimise the performance on the validation set

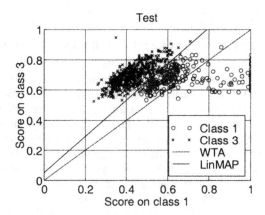

Fig. 2. Application of the initial and adjusted border depicted in Fig. 1 on the test set. The misclassification between the two classes shown decreases from 23% to 7%

In order to be able to modify the score values we propose to assign a set of weights (one for each class) to each leaf node of all the decision trees that make up a given ensemble. The values in score-space are now defined, not as the average of the votes on the individual classes, but as the sum (or average) of the class weights of the activated leaf nodes. By adjusting the weights, it is therefore possible to change the score values resulting from a given input, effectively moving the examples to other locations in score-space. How should we then control these movements? We suggest using the opposite of the above-described scheme: Instead of changing the location of the decision border caused by forces from the examples, we look at the opposite forces. A force from the majority-vote decision line now influences each example causing the examples to move in score-space.

Let $\mathbf{w}_{j,i}$ denote the weight vector of the i'th leaf node in the j'th tree. For short, we denote the weight vector being activated in the j'th tree by an example $\mathbf{x}$ as $\mathbf{w}_{j,\mathbf{x}}$. $\mathbf{w}_{j,i}$ contains scalar weights, $w_{j,i,c}$, for each class c. When classifying an example, the output of the ensemble is found as

$$\hat{y} = f(\mathbf{x}) = \underset{c}{\arg\max}\left(\sum_j w_{j,\mathbf{x},c}\right). \tag{1}$$

Each leaf is normally assigned a specific class label, given as the most frequent class within the training examples falling into the leaf. In the proposed scheme, the weights are initialised to zero with the exception that the weight corresponding to the class label of the leaf is assigned the value one. With this choice of initialised values, the initial output corresponds to a majority vote decision.

Besides reducing the number of errors on a validation set the adjustment scheme should also attempt to ensure a certain margin between the score on the true class and the closest competitor. One such scheme for adjusting the weights is listed in Figure 3. In order to adjust the weights, it is needed to use a set of examples $\mathbf{X}_{Adj}$ with known class labels. However, in order to model the score values that will be obtained on examples not used for building the decision trees it is important that the set $\mathbf{X}_{Adj}$ somehow deviate from the training data set. Still it might be a good idea that $\mathbf{X}_{Adj}$ also contains the examples used for training the trees. One possibility for having separate examples reserved for the weight adjustment procedure is to reserve a part of the training examples for this adjustment set. However, it would often be desirable if all available training examples could be used for building the individual classifiers. This is possible if the examples used for adjustment are based on adding small but varying amounts of noise to the training examples (i.e. training with jitter). We have both tried this concept as well as using a separate part of the training set for adjustment. The noise we use is additive Gaussian noise. The standard deviation for the noise is chosen as a fraction (between one and ten percent) of the deviation calculated for the input variables in the total training set.

When applying the weight adjustment scheme the ensemble of decision trees can be interpreted as an advanced feature extractor, see Figs. 4 and 5. Training the weights then corresponds to detecting and weighting the combinations that in an adequate way can discriminate between the classes in question.

The suggested method is applicable for ensembles of any classifier where the output can be related to a specific activation pattern. In the following section, we present results of applying the weighting scheme to the PERT classifier and to bagged ensembles of C4.5 trees.

```
For all  x_i ∈ X_Adj ,
   ŷ_i = f(x_i)  or  ŷ_i = f(x_i + n) // n is a noise vector
   c_r = argmax ( Σ w_j,x_i,c )  // Runner up class
         c≠ŷ_i     j
   //Adjust examples within a given margin t
   if | Σ w_j,x_i,c_r − Σ w_j,x_i,ŷ_i | < t ,
        j              j
      For all trees,
         //Increase weight on the true class
         w_j,x_i,y_i = w_j,x_i,y_i + Δw
         if  ŷ ≠ y_i ,
            //Decrease weight on false winner
            w_j,x_i,ŷ = w_j,x_i,ŷ − Δw
         else
            //Decrease weight on runner up class
            w_j,x_i,c_r = w_j,x_i,c_r − Δw
         end if
      next tree
next
```

Fig. 3. Adjustment scheme for determining the weights. The threshold t determines the margin region in score space where examples will influence the weight adjustment.

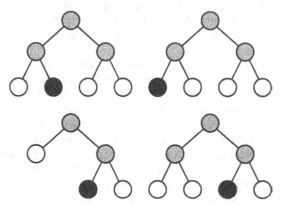

Fig. 4. Ensemble of four decision trees. The white and black nodes are inactive and active leaf nodes respectively

Fig. 5. Binary activation pattern corresponding to the ensemble depicted in Fig 4

3   Results

In order to investigate the proposed weighting scheme, we have implemented and tested the algorithm on two types of ensemble based classifiers. The classifiers have then been applied to a number of data sets from the UCI repository [18], the Statlog project [19] and an artificial data set described by Breiman [4].

Table 1 lists the preliminary results of the proposed scheme. The "voted" column corresponds to the error-rate of the unweighted ensemble, other results are given after 15 iterations. A noise level of 0.01 specifies that the noise contribution to a given input variable is drawn from a normal distribution having a standard deviation being 100 times smaller than the standard deviation measured for the input variable in question. For the runs having a noise level of zero, only 70% of the training examples were used to build the trees, but all training examples were used to adjust the weights. All results are obtained as the average error rate over 10 runs. For each run, the data sets are randomly split into training and test sets, the sizes of which are listed in Table 1. For C4.5, bagging is used to create the ensembles. In the case of PERT the randomisation takes place within the model construction itself, and it is therefore not necessary to apply a technique like bagging. An ensemble size of 100 trees is used for all experiments, but it should be noted that for several of the data sets the performances could be improved by using more classifiers in the ensembles. The threshold level determining the desired margin (see Figure 3) is set to 70% of the maximum number of votes that can be obtained using the majority rule. The size used for Δw was 0.1, see Figure 3.

It can be observed that the weight adjustment scheme in the case of PERT leads to an essential performance improvement on Cut20, DNA, BelgianII and the Ringnorm data sets. Smaller improvements are obtained on the BelgianI data set as well as on the Sonar and the Vowel data sets. For C4.5, improvements can be observed on BelgianII, Cut20, Image, Ringnorm, Vehicle and Vowel. The very large improvements on PERT takes place on exactly those data sets, where PERT performs poorly compared to the C4.5 ensemble. It is also noted that the strategy of leaving an amount of the training examples aside when training the trees and not using jitter is sometimes better than using all examples for building the trees.

Figs. 6 and 7 illustrates how the error rates evolve over the adjustment iterations. On the Liver data set, the weight adjustment is leading to overfitting, which might be caused by having too few examples in the training set. For the case shown in Fig. 6 the overfitting can actually be revealed during the training phase by using an artificial validation set, obtained by adding noise to the training examples. Unfortunately, this approach for observing whether overfitting occurs is not always working.

Table 1. Test error rates of ensemble based classifiers on a number of problems

Data set	Train/test examples	PERT Voted	PERT weighted, noise level 0	PERT weighted, noise level 0.01	PERT weighted, noise level 0.05	PERT weighted, noise level 0.10	C4.5 Voted	C4.5 weighted, noise level 0	C4.5 weighted, noise level 0.01	C4.5 weighted, noise level 0.05	C4.5 weighted, noise level 0.10
Belgiani	1250/ 1250	3.5 ±0.5	2.9 ±0.5	3.1 ±0.4	3.1 ±0.4	3.0 ±0.4	2.5 ±0.5	2.6 ±0.4	2.5 ±0.4	2.4 ±0.4	2.3 ±0.6
Belgianii	2000/ 1000	7.3 ±0.5	4.3 ±0.7	4.7 ±0.8	4.3 ±0.8	4.3 ±0.9	1.9 ±0.4	1.7 ±0.5	1.6 ±0.5	1.7 ±0.5	1.6 ±0.4
Cut20	11220/ 7480	3.8 ±0.2	2.6 ±0.2	2.8 ±0.1	2.5 ±0.1	2.8 ±0.1	2.7 ±0.2	2.5 ±0.2	2.4 ±0.2	2.4 ±0.2	2.4 ±0.2
DNA	2000/ 1187	27.5 ±2.1	10.4 ±1.0	10.9 ±1.3	10.8 ±0.9	10.5 ±1.0	6.0 ±1.0	5.5 ±0.8	5.8 ±0.8	5.8 ±0.8	5.8 ±0.8
Image	2079/ 231	2.5 ±0.8	2.4 ±0.7	1.8 ±0.6	2.1 ±0.8	2.5 ±1.1	2.6 ±1.0	2.8 ±1.2	2.4 ±1.2	2.1 ±1.0	2.1 ±0.9
Ionosphere	315/ 16	7.6 ±3.9	3.9 ±3.0	6.1 ±3.7	7.5 ±3.7	4.7 ±3.5	7.2 ±4.0	7.2 ±3.8	7.8 ±3.4	6.7 ±3.5	7.2 ±3.5
Liver	310/ 35	25.6 ±6.2	31.4 ±10.2	31.4 ±6.2	30.6 ±7.5	32.3 ±6.3	27.9 ±7.8	30.6 ±10.2	30.3 ±7.6	28 ±6.4	28.3 ±7.1
Ringnorm	300/ 6800	11.1 ±1.9	5.8 ±0.4	6.0 ±0.6	6.0 ±0.6	7.1 ±0.6	9.5 ±1.8	7.5 ±1.2	7.8 ±1.8	7.3 ±1.8	7.1 ±1.8
Sonar	187/ 21	11.4 ±5.6	11.5 ±5.3	7.6 ±5.6	7.6 ±4.6	7.6 ±4.0	18.1 ±8.3	19.5 ±8.8	17.6 ±9.3	15.7 ±8.7	15.7 ±8.7
Vehicle	761/ 85	27.1 ±4.8	28.5 ±5.7	25.9 ±4.3	24.5 ±3.2	26.2 ±4.2	24.0 ±4.9	21.9 ±4.5	21.1 ±3.7	22.5 ±0.5	20.8 ±4.4
Vowel	891/ 99	2.2 ±1.6	1.3 ±1.0	1.4 ±1.4	1.4 ±1.4	2.0 ±1.0	8.3 ±3.0	8.1 ±2.3	4.9 ±2.4	4.3 ±1.8	4.4 ±2.2
Votes	391/ 44	3.6 ±2.7	4.1 ±3.5	3.4 ±2.7	3.2 ±2.9	3.2 ±2.4	5.0 ±2.6	5.5 ±3.0	5.7 ±2.9	5.7 ±2.9	5.7 ±2.9

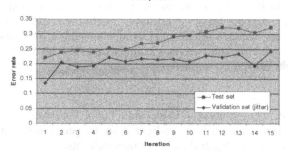

Fig. 6. Error rates versus number of iterations for the liver data set applied to the PERT ensemble. On this problem, the method leads to overfitting

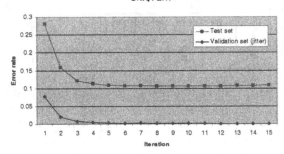

Fig. 7. Error rates versus number of iterations for the PERT classifier applied to the DNA data set

4   Discussion

In the present paper, we have investigated the effect of introducing individual weighting of the features specified by the leaves of a decision tree. Introducing such weights will influence the decision process of the whole ensemble in a local manner. The potential benefit from a theoretical point of view is the possibility of increasing the modelling capability of ensembles. A drawback is the fact that the individual weights have to be estimated partly from examples that differ from the examples that are used when building the individual classifiers. The approach taken here for dealing with this problem is to extract further examples from the training set by applying jitter. For adjusting the weights, we have applied a perceptron learning rule. In the present study, we have simply used a specific number of adjustment iterations, but due to the large number of weights we are faced with the risk of overfitting. Early stopping is one (too) simple way for handling this problem.

The preliminary results presented in this work shows that under certain circumstances it can be highly beneficial to use the suggested weighting scheme, while in other cases, it might lead to overfitting. Overfitting is more likely to happen for the small data sets. Future work should investigate methods for finding the proper amounts of noise to add to the training examples and look for improved ways for adjusting the weight values.

Acknowledgement. The authors wish to thank Louis Wehenkel at Université de Liége and Reza Nakhaeizadeh at Daimler-Benz, Ulm, for permission to use and report results on respectively, the BelgianII and the Cut20 data sets.

References

1. Kittler, J. and Roli, F. (eds.): Multiple Classifier Systems, First International Workshop, MCS 2000, Cagliari, Italy, June 2000. Proceedings, Berlin: Springer, (2000)
2. Hansen, L.K. and Salamon P.: Neural Network Ensembles *IEEE Transactions on Pattern Analysis and Machine Intelligence*, vol. 12, (1990) 993-1001
3. Freund, Y. and Schapire, R.E.; A decision-theoretic generalization of on-line learning and an application to boosting *Journal of Computer and System Sciences*, vol. 55, (1997) 119-139
4. Breiman, L.: Bagging Predictors *Machine Learning*, vol. 24, (1996) 123-140
5. Dietterich, T.G. and Kong, E.B.: Machine Learning Bias, Statistical Bias, and Statistical Variance of Decision Tree Algorithms, technical report, Department of Computer Science, Oregon State University. (1995)
6. Dietterich, T.G.: An experimental comparison of three methods for constructing ensembles of decision trees: bagging, boosting, and randomization *Machine Learning*, vol. 40, (2000) 139-157
7 Dietterich, T.G.: Ensemble Methods in Machine Learning. In: Kittler, J. and Roli, F. (eds.): Multiple Classifier Systems, First International Workshop. Lecture Notes in Computer Science. Vol 1857. Springer Verlag. New York. (2000) 1-15
8. Duin, R.P.W. and Tax, D.M.J.: Experiments with classifier combining rules. In: Kittler, J. and Roli, F. (eds.): Multiple Classifier Systems, First International Workshop. Lecture Notes in Computer Science. Vol 1857. Springer Verlag. New York. (2000) 16-29
9. Jørgensen, T.M. and Linneberg, C.: Theoretical Analysis and Improved Decision Criteria for the n-Tuple Classifier *IEEE Transactions on Pattern Analysis and Machine Intelligence*, vol. 21, (1999) 336-347
10. Jørgensen, T.M. and Linneberg, C.: Boosting the performance of weightless neural networks by using a post-processing transformation of the output scores, International Joint Conference on Neural Networks. IEEE. Washington, DC. (1999) paper no 126
11. Breiman, L: Some infinite theory for predictor ensembles, Technical report no 577, University of California. Berkerley, California. (2000)
12. Cutler, A. and Zhao, G.: Fast Classification Using Perfect Random Trees, Technical report no 5/99/99, Department of Mathematics and Statistics, Utah State University. (1999)
13. Cutler, A and Zhao, G.: Voting Perfect Random Trees, Technical report no 5/00/100, Department of Mathematics and Statistics, Utah State University. (2000)
14. Linneberg, C. and Jørgensen, T.M.; Improved Decision Scheme for Ensembles of Randomised Decision Trees *submitted for publication* (2001)
15. Jørgensen, T.M., Christensen, S.S. and Liisberg, C.: Crossvalidation and information measures for RAM based neural networks. In: Austin, J. (ed.): *RAM-Based Neural Networks*, Singapore: World Scientific, (1998) 78-88.
16. Burges, C.J.C.: A Tutorial on Support Vector Machines for pattern Recognition *Data Mining and Knowledge Discovery*, vol. 2, (1998) 121-167
17. Vapnik, V.: *The Nature of Statistical Learning Theory*, New York: Springer-Verlag, (1995)
18. Blake, C.L. and Merz, C.J.: *UCI Repository of machine learning databases* http://www.ics.uci.edu/~mlearn/MLRepository.html, Irvine, CA: University of California, Department of Information and Computer Science, (1998)
19. Michie, D., Spiegelhalter, D.J. and Tayler, C.C.: Machine Learning, Neural and Statistical Classification, Out of print, available at http://www.amsta.leeds.ac.uk/~charles/statlog/ Prentice-Hall, (1994)

Feature Subsets for Classifier Combination: An Enumerative Experiment

Ludmila I. Kuncheva and Christopher J. Whitaker

School of Informatics, University of Wales, Bangor
Bangor, Gwynedd, LL57 1UT, United Kingdom
{l.i.kuncheva,c.j.whitaker}@bangor.ac.uk

Abstract. A classifier team is used in preference to a single classifier in the expectation it will be more accurate. Here we study the potential for improvement in classifier teams designed by the feature subspace method: the set of features is partitioned and each subset is used by one classifier in the team. All partitions of a set of 10 features into 3 subsets containing $\langle 4, 4, 2 \rangle$ features and $\langle 4, 3, 3 \rangle$ features, are enumerated and nine combination schemes are applied on the three classifiers. We look at the distribution and the extremes of the improvement (or failure); the chances of the team outperforming the single best classifier if the feature space is partitioned at random; the relationship between the spread of the individual classifier accuracy and the team accuracy; and the combination schemes performance.

1 Introduction

We examine by an enumerative experiment what the support is for the intuition that a team of classifiers performs better than the single best classifier in the team. The feature subspace method has been used: we partition the set of features into subsets where each subset is used by one classifier in the team. Using different feature subsets has been recognized as a promising team design method, especially in text recognition [12,15] and speech recognition [1]. Kittler et al. [6, 7] derive a series of theoretical results based on the assumption that the individual classifiers use conditionally independent subsets of features. Sometimes the features are naturally grouped and this suggests which of them should be used together. For example, Duin and coauthors [3] (and earlier [13]) study classifier fusion methods for recognizing handwritten numerals by using 6 types of different features sets: Fourier coefficients, profile correlation, Karhunen-Loève coefficients, pixel averages in 2×3 windows, Zernike moments and morphological features. Random sampling from the feature set for designing the individual classifiers has been studied in [2,4,11]. A genetic algorithm for partitioning the feature space is proposed in [8,10].

Here we offer an exhaustive experimental study with $L = 3$ classifiers and a data set with $n = 10$ features enumerating all partitions of the feature set into $\langle 4, 4, 2 \rangle$ and $\langle 4, 3, 3 \rangle$ features. Let P_t be the accuracy of the team, P_b be the

J. Kittler and F. Roli (Eds.): MCS 2001, LNCS 2096, pp. 228–237, 2001.

best (maximal) individual accuracy, and P_w be the worst (minimal) individual accuracy.

We seek answers to the following questions:

1. How is $P_t - P_b$ distributed and what are the maximal and the minimal possible values for different combination schemes?
2. How likely is an improvement ($P_t - Pb > 0$) if we pick a random partition of the set of features?
3. Is the team accuracy P_t related to the range $P_b - P_w$ of individual accuracies?
4. How do the combination schemes compare with respect to the answers to the previous three questions?

Section 2 details the combination methods used, so that they be reproducible from the text. Section 3 contains the results of our experiment and the conclusion section offers the answers to the above questions.

2   Combination Methods

Let $\mathcal{D} = \{D_1, D_2, \ldots, D_L\}$ be a set of classifiers and $\Omega = \{\omega_1, \ldots, \omega_c\}$ be a set of class labels. Each classifier gets as its input a feature vector $\mathbf{x} \in \Re^n$. The classifier output is a c-dimensional vector $D_i(\mathbf{x}) = [d_{i,1}(\mathbf{x}), \ldots, d_{i,c}(\mathbf{x})]^T$ where $d_{i,j}(\mathbf{x})$ is the degree of "support" given by classifier D_i to the hypothesis that $\mathbf{x}$ comes from class ω_j, $j = 1, \ldots, c$. Without loss of generality we can restrict $d_{i,j}(\mathbf{x})$ within the interval $[0, 1]$, $i = 1, \ldots, L$, $j = 1, \ldots, c$, and call the classifier outputs "soft labels". Most often $d_{i,j}(\mathbf{x})$ is an estimate of the posterior probability $P(\omega_i|\mathbf{x})$.

Combining classifiers means we combine the L classifier outputs $D_1(\mathbf{x}), \ldots, D_L(\mathbf{x})$ to get a soft label for $\mathbf{x}$, denoted $D(\mathbf{x}) = [\mu_1(\mathbf{x}), \ldots, \mu_c(\mathbf{x})]^T$.

If a crisp class label of $\mathbf{x}$ is needed, we can use the maximum membership rule: Assign $\mathbf{x}$ to class ω_s iff,

$$d_{i,s}(\mathbf{x}) \geq d_{i,j}(\mathbf{x}) \;\; \forall j = 1, \ldots, c. \quad \text{for individual crisp labels}$$
$$\mu_s(\mathbf{x}) \geq \mu_t(\mathbf{x}), \;\; \forall t = 1, \ldots, c. \quad \text{for the final crisp label.} \quad (1)$$

Ties are resolved arbitrarily. The minimum-error classifier is recovered from (1) when $\mu_i(\mathbf{x}) = P(\omega_i|\mathbf{x})$.

2.1   Majority Vote, Maximum, Minimum, Average, Product

For the majority vote combination (MAJ), the class label assigned to $\mathbf{x}$ is the one that is most represented in the set of L class labels $D_1(\mathbf{x}), \ldots, D_L(\mathbf{x})$. For the remaining simple combination methods,

$$\mu_j(\mathbf{x}) = \mathcal{O}\left(d_{1,j}(\mathbf{x}), \ldots, d_{L,j}(\mathbf{x})\right), \;\; j = 1, \ldots, c. \quad (2)$$

where $\mathcal{O}$ is the respective operation (maximum (MAX), minimum (MIN), average (AVR) or product (PRO)).

2.2 Naive Bayes (NB)

This scheme assumes that the classifiers are mutually independent (this is the reason we use the name "naive"); Xu et al. [15] and others call it *Bayes* combination. For each classifier D_i, a $c \times c$ confusion matrix CM^i is calculated by applying D_i to the training data set. The (k, s)th entry of this matrix, $cm^i_{k,s}$ is the number of elements of the data set whose true class label was ω_k, and were assigned by D_i to class ω_s. By $cm^i_{\cdot,s}$ we denote the total number of elements labeled by D_i into class ω_s (the sum of the sth column of CM^i). Using $cm^i_{\cdot,s}$, a $c \times c$ label matrix LM^i is computed, whose (k, s)th entry $lm^i_{k,s}$ is an estimate of the probability that the true label is ω_k given that D_i assigns crisp class label s.

$$lm^i_{k,s} = \hat{P}\left(\omega_k|D_i(\mathbf{x}) = \omega_s\right) = \frac{cm^i_{k,s}}{cm^i_{\cdot,s}}, \qquad (3)$$

Considering the label matrix for D_i, LM^i, associated with ω_s is a *soft label vector*
$[\hat{P}\left(\omega_1|D_i(\mathbf{x}) = \omega_s\right), \ldots, \hat{P}\left(\omega_c|D_i(\mathbf{x}) = \omega_s\right)]^T$, which is the sth column of the matrix. Let $s_1, \ldots, s_L$ be the crisp class labels assigned to $\mathbf{x}$ by classifiers $D_1, \ldots, D_L$, respectively. Then, by the independence assumption, the estimate of the probability that the true class label is ω_j, is calculated by

$$\mu_j(\mathbf{x}) = \prod_{j=1}^{L} \hat{P}\left(\omega_j|D_i(\mathbf{x}) = s_i\right) = \prod_{i=1}^{L} lm^i_{j,s_i}, \quad j = 1, \ldots, c. \qquad (4)$$

2.3 Behavior-Knowledge Space (BKS)

Let again $(s_1, \ldots, s_L) \in \Omega^L$ be the crisp class labels assigned to $\mathbf{x}$ by classifiers $D_1, \ldots, D_L$, respectively. Every possible combination of class labels is an index regarded as a cell in a look-up table (BKS table)[5]. The table is designed using a labeled data set $\mathbf{Z}$. Each $\mathbf{z}_j \in \mathbf{Z}$ is placed in the cell indexed by $D_1(\mathbf{z}_j), \ldots, D_L(\mathbf{z}_j)$. The number of elements in each cell are tallied and the most representative class label is selected for this cell. Ties are resolved arbitrarily and the empty cells are labeled appropriately (e.g., at random or by majority, if applicable). After the table has been designed, the BKS method labels an $\mathbf{x} \in \Re^n$ to the class of the cell indexed by $D_1(\mathbf{x}), \ldots, D_L(\mathbf{x})$.

2.4 Wernecke's Method (WER)

The model is similar to the BKS. The difference is that in constructing the table, Wernecke [14] considers the 95 % confidence intervals of the frequencies in each cell. If there is overlap between the intervals, the L confusion matrices are used to identify the "least wrong" classifier among the L members of the team. First, L estimates of the probability $P(error$ and $D_i(\mathbf{x}) = s_i)$ are calculated. Then the classifier with the smallest probability is nominated for labeling the cell. For an $\mathbf{x} \in \Re^n$, the cell is identified by the labels assigned by $D_1, \ldots, D_L$ and then either the cell label is recovered or the label of the nominated classifier is taken as the label of **x**.

2.5 Decision Templates (DT)

The classifier outputs can be conveniently organized in a **decision profile** as the following matrix [9]

$$DP(\mathbf{x}) = \begin{bmatrix} d_{1,1}(\mathbf{x}) & \dots & d_{1,j}(\mathbf{x}) & \dots & d_{1,c}(\mathbf{x}) \\ \dots \\ d_{i,1}(\mathbf{x}) & \dots & d_{i,j}(\mathbf{x}) & \dots & d_{i,c}(\mathbf{x}) \\ \dots \\ d_{L,1}(\mathbf{x}) & \dots & d_{L,j}(\mathbf{x}) & \dots & d_{L,c}(\mathbf{x}) \end{bmatrix}. \tag{5}$$

Using decision templates (DT) for combining classifiers is proposed in [9]. Given L (trained) classifiers in $\mathcal{D}$, c decision templates are calculated from the data, one per class.

$$DT_i = \frac{1}{N_i} \sum_{\substack{z_j \in \omega_i \\ z_j \in Z}} DP(\mathbf{z}_j), \quad i = 1, \dots, c. \tag{6}$$

DT_i can be regarded as the expected $DP(\mathbf{x})$ for class ω_i. The support for the class offered by the combination of the L classifiers, $\mu_i(\mathbf{x})$ is then found using a measure of *similarity* between the current $DP(\mathbf{x})$ and DT_i, e.g.,

$$d_E(DP(\mathbf{x}), DT_i) = \sum_{j=1}^{c} \sum_{k=1}^{L} (d_{k,j}(\mathbf{x}) - dt_i(k,j))^2, \tag{7}$$

where $dt_i(k,j)$ is the k,j-th entry in decision template DT_i. Here we use Euclidean distance for calculating the similarity but other measures can also be applied.

3 The Experiment

We used the Wisconsin Diagnostic Breast Cancer data base[1] taken from the UCI Repository of Machine Learning Database[2]. The set consists of 569 patient vectors with features computed from a digitized image of a fine needle aspirate of a breast mass. They describe characteristics of the cell nuclei present in the image. The objects are grouped into two classes: benign and malignant. Out of the original 30 features we used the first 10; these were the means of the relevant variables calculated in the image. The study was confined to 10 variables for two reasons: to enable a reasonable enumerative experiment and to enhance

---

[1] Created by Dr. William H. Wolberg, W. Nick Street and Olvi L. Mangasarian, University of Wisconsin

[2] http://www.ics.uci.edu/ mlearn/MLRepository.html

variability in classifier performance. The data set was split randomly into two, halves, one being used for training and one for testing.

We considered $L = 3$ classifiers. All partitions of the 10-element feature set into $\langle 4, 4, 2 \rangle$ (3150 partitions) and $\langle 4, 3, 3 \rangle$ (4200 partitions) were generated. For each partition, three classifiers were built, one on each subset of features. Two simple classifier models were tried: the linear and the quadratic classifier, leading to 4 sets of experiments:

1. $\langle 4, 4, 2 \rangle$ with linear classifiers;
2. $\langle 4, 4, 2 \rangle$ with quadratic classifiers;
3. $\langle 4, 3, 3 \rangle$ with linear classifiers;
4. $\langle 4, 3, 3 \rangle$ with quadratic classifiers.

To answer the four questions in the Introduction,

1. The minimal and the maximal values of the differences between the accuracy of the team and the best individual accuracy $(P_t - P_b)$ for the 9 combination schemes are shown in Table 1. We denote by P_{ia} the individual average of the team. The bar above P denotes the mean value over all generated teams for the respective experiment. Example histograms of $P_{AVR} - P_b$ and $P_{AVR} - P_w$ are given in Figure 1.

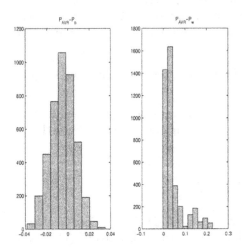

Fig. 1. Histograms illustrating the distribution of the improvement for the Average aggregation method, experiment $\langle 4, 3, 3 \rangle$ and quadratic individual classifiers.

2. Given in Table 1 are the fraction of cases when $P_t > P_b$ (the probability that the team is better than the single best classifier) and also the fraction when $P_t < P_w$ (the team is worse than the worst classifier). As an illustration, Figure 2 (left) plots the accuracy of the Decision Template combination,

Table 1. Results from the 4 experiments: 2 partitions × 2 classifier models.

$\langle 4, 4, 2 \rangle$
linear classifiers
$\bar{P}_w = 83.60 \%$
$\bar{P}_{ia} = 87.62 \%$
$\bar{P}_b = 90.43 \%$

Comb. sch.	min $P_t - P_b$ (in %)	max $P_t - P_b$ (in %)	% better single best	% worse single worst	Corr with $P_b - P_w$ (in %)
MAJ	-3.51	2.81	32.13	0.13	3.46
NB	-3.51	3.16	42.03	0.06	8.42
BKS	-8.42	3.16	31.40	2.22	18.52
WER	-5.96	3.51	36.86	1.87	16.29
MAX	-4.56	3.51	37.21	0	-42.08
MIN	-4.56	3.51	37.21	0	-42.08
AVR	-4.21	3.51	46.67	0	-18.68
PRO	-4.21	2.81	44.38	0.13	-19.17
DT	-2.11	4.21	79.62	0	- 0.54

$\langle 4, 4, 2 \rangle$
quadratic classifiers
$\bar{P}_w = 85.35 \%$
$\bar{P}_{ia} = 89.01 \%$
$\bar{P}_b = 91.55 \%$

Comb. sch.	min $P_t - P_b$ (in %)	max $P_t - P_b$ (in %)	% better single best	% worse single worst	Corr with $P_b - P_w$ (in %)
MAJ	-3.86	2.46	18.67	0.25	-6.53
NB	-3.86	2.46	18.79	0.25	-2.51
BKS	-4.21	2.46	21.56	1.59	6.39
WER	-4.21	3.16	19.21	1.24	7.18
MAX	-3.16	2.81	29.71	0.25	-3.37
MIN	-3.16	2.81	29.71	0.25	-3.37
AVR	-3.16	2.81	27.87	0.06	2.18
PRO	-3.16	2.46	28.00	0.25	0.20
DT	-2.81	2.46	35.75	0.25	4.98

$\langle 4, 3, 3 \rangle$
linear classifiers
$\bar{P}_w = 87.72 \%$
$\bar{P}_{ia} = 90.46 \%$
$\bar{P}_b = 92.42 \%$

Comb. sch.	min $P_t - P_b$ (in %)	max $P_t - P_b$ (in %)	% better single best	% worse single worst	Corr with $P_b - P_w$ (in %)
MAJ	-3.86	2.46	41.10	0	-17.16
NB	-3.86	2.46	39.29	0	-19.06
BKS	-7.72	2.46	20.26	3.26	-12.80
WER	-7.02	2.46	19.17	2.88	-17.53
MAX	-3.16	3.51	59.86	0	-58.55
MIN	-3.16	3.51	59.86	0	-58.55
AVR	-2.81	3.51	68.29	0	-33.07
PRO	-2.81	3.16	64.81	0	-41.23
DT	-1.75	4.21	86.67	0	-45.18

$\langle 4, 3, 3 \rangle$
quadratic classifiers
$\bar{P}_w = 88.43 \%$
$\bar{P}_{ia} = 91.17 \%$
$\bar{P}_b = 93.29 \%$

Comb. sch.	min $P_t - P_b$ (in %)	max $P_t - P_b$ (in %)	% better single best	% worse single worst	Corr with $P_b - P_w$ (in %)
MAJ	-4.56	3.16	26.90	0.19	-18.31
NB	-4.56	3.16	26.90	0.19	-18.17
BKS	-5.96	3.51	24.24	3.55	-1.62
WER	-5.61	3.16	20.64	4.33	-0.52
MAX	-3.86	2.81	20.38	1.29	-9.21
MIN	-3.86	2.81	20.38	1.29	-9.21
AVR	-3.86	3.51	28.14	0.14	-2.51
PRO	-3.51	2.81	17.62	0.95	-1.16
DT	-3.86	3.16	23.48	0.43	-16.94

P_{DT} and the single best accuracy P_b versus the (sorted by P_{DT}) number of splits for experiment # 3.

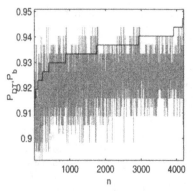

Sorted P_{DT} (the black line) and P_b (the grey line) for experiment $\langle 4,3,3 \rangle$ and linear individual classifiers. $P_{DT} > P_b$ in 86.7 % of the cases.

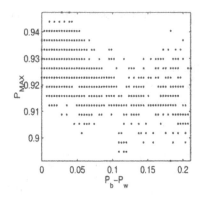

Scatterplot of P_{MAX} versus $P_b - P_w$ for $\langle 4,3,3 \rangle$ and linear individual classifiers. The correlation between the two is -0.59.

Fig. 2. Illustration of the results

3. The last columns in the subtables in Table 1 show the correlation between $P_b - P_w$ and P_t. Figure 2 (right) displays an example of the relationship between P_{DT} and $P_b - P_w$.
4. A Two-way ANOVA was run to estimate whether there is a significant difference between the 9 combination schemes. The test found significant differences between the means of the team accuracies computed by the 9 schemes. The means with the 95 % confidence intervals from the $\langle 4,4,2 \rangle$ experiments are shown in Figure 3 and from the $\langle 4,3,3 \rangle$ experiments, in Figure 4.

4   Conclusions

1. *How is $P_t - P_b$ distributed and what are the maximal and the minimal possible values for different combination schemes?*
The difference between the team accuracy and the best individual shows a stable pattern. In all experiments the accuracy increases by a few per cent. The maximum of the $\max(P_t - Pb)$ in Table 1 is the Decision Template combination method with 4.21 % for linear classifiers for both $\langle 4,4,2 \rangle$ and $\langle 4,3,3 \rangle$. All minimal values of $P_t - P_b$ are negative indicating that there is no combination scheme (at least not among the studied ones) that *guarantees* improvement over the single best classifier. The combination schemes with the worst negative result are the BKS and the Wernecke's method (up to -8.42 % for BKS). BKS is known

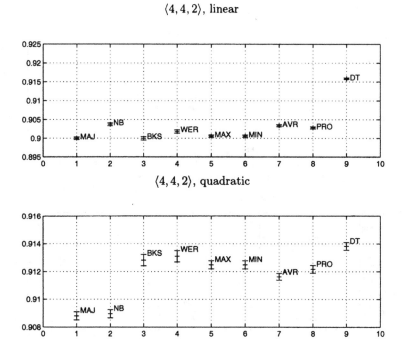

Fig. 3. Means and the 95 % confidence intervals for experiment $\langle 4, 4, 2 \rangle$.

for being prone to overtraining, so the result is not surprising. In general, the classification accuracy of the individual classifiers is around 90 %, so we cannot expect substantial improvement from the combination. The differences have approximately normal distributions for all combination schemes, a typical example is shown in the left plot in Figure 1. Results much worse than the single worst classifier are unlikely, as shown in the penultimate columns in Table 1 to which have very small (often zero) values. However, the distribution is not normal as is shown by the typical example in the right plot in Figure 1.

2. How likely is an improvement ($P_t - Pb > 0$) if we pick a random partition of the set of features?
The numerical answers to this question are given in the fourth column of the subtables in Table 1 for the experiments we carried out. However, we cannot offer a clear-cut conclusion. A persistent pattern is that the percentage getting an improvement over the single best dramatically depends on the quality of the individual classifiers. For the (weak) linear models, the improvement is more often encountered whereas for the quadratic models the chance for improvements are halved. For example, the DT combination has a chance of about 85 % (Table 1, bottom left subtable) to improve on the single best linear classifier if the feature set is split randomly into subsets of 4, 3, and 3 features. For the same

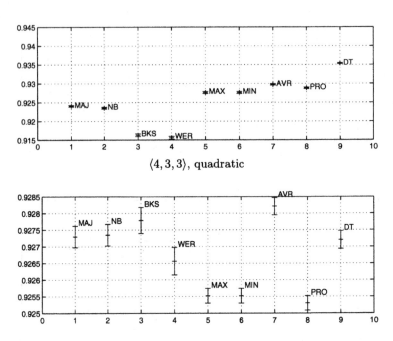

Fig. 4. Means and the 95 % confidence intervals for experiment $\langle 4, 3, 3 \rangle$.

split, when quadratic classifiers are used, none of the schemes has more than about 30 % chance for improvement (Table 1, bottom right subtable).

Perhaps we can conjecture that this chance depends on the problem (how complex it is), the classifier model (weak or strong), the number of features used per classifier, and more factors which we did not examine here, e.g., the number of classifiers L.

3. *Is the team accuracy P_t related to the range $P_b - P_w$ of individual accuracies?* The correlation coefficients, and the scatterplot in Figure 2 (right) do not indicate an unequivocal relationship. As the correlation coefficients tend to be small by absolute value, there is little evidence that the more similar the individual accuracies the higher the improvement.

4. *How do the combination schemes compare with respect to the answers to the previous three questions?*
Again, the combination schemes exhibit variable performance, and this shows that: (a) there is no "best" combination for all scenarios, and (b) building a classifier team that outperforms the single best individual is a delicate job. Based on our results, we nominate the Decision Templates as the most successful combination scheme in our experiments.

References

1. K. Chen, L. Wang, and H. Chi. Methods of combining multiple classifiers with different features and their applications to text-independent speaker identification. *International Journal on Pattern Recognition and Artificial Intelligence*, 11(3):417–445, 1997.
2. T.G. Dietterich. Ensemble methods in machine learning. In J. Kittler and F. Roli, editors, *Multiple Classifier Systems*, volume 1857 of *Lecture Notes in Computer Science*, pages 1–15, Cagliari, Italy, 2000. Springer.
3. R.P.W. Duin and D.M.J. Tax. Experiments with classifier combination rules. In J. Kittler and F. Roli, editors, *Multiple Classifier Systems*, volume 1857 of *Lecture Notes in Computer Science*, pages 16–29, Cagliari, Italy, 2000. Springer.
4. T.K. Ho. The random space method for constructing decision forests. *IEEE Transactions on Pattern Analysis and Machine Intelligence*, 20(8):832–844, 1998.
5. Y.S. Huang and C.Y. Suen. A method of combining multiple experts for the recognition of unconstrained handwritten numerals. *IEEE Transactions on Pattern Analysis and Machine Intelligence*, 17:90–93, 1995.
6. J. Kittler, M. Hatef, R.P.W. Duin, and J. Matas. On combining classifiers. *IEEE Transactions on Pattern Analysis and Machine Intelligence*, 20(3):226–239, 1998.
7. J. Kittler, A. Hojjatoleslami, and T. Windeatt. Strategies for combining classifiers employing shared and distinct representations. *Pattern Recognition Letters*, 18:1373–1377, 1997.
8. L.I. Kuncheva. Genetic algorithm for feature selection for parallel classifiers. *Information Processing Letters*, 46:163–168, 1993.
9. L.I. Kuncheva, J.C. Bezdek, and R.P.W. Duin. Decision templates for multiple classifier fusion: an experimental comparison. *Pattern Recognition*, 34(2):299–314, 2001.
10. L.I Kuncheva and L.C. Jain. Designing classifier fusion systems by genetic algorithms. *IEEE Transactions on Evolutionary Computation*, 4(4):327–336, 2000.
11. P. Latinne, O. Debeir, and C. Decaestecker. Different ways of weakening decision trees and their impact on classification accuracy of dt combination. In J. Kittler and F. Roli, editors, *Multiple Classifier Systems*, volume 1857 of *Lecture Notes in Computer Science*, pages 230–239, Cagliari, Italy, 2000. Springer.
12. H.-S. Park and S.-W. Lee. Off-line recognition of large-set handwritten characters with multiple hidden Markov models. *Pattern Recognition*, 29(2):231–244, 1996.
13. M. van Breukelen, R.P.W Duin, D.M.J. Tax, and J.E. den Hartog. Combining classifiers for the recognition of handwritten digits. In *I-st IAPR TC1 Workshop on Statistical Techniques in Pattern Recognition*, pages 13–18, Prague, Czech Republic, 1997.
14. K.-D. Wernecke. A coupling procedure for discrimination of mixed data. *Biometrics*, 48:497–506, 1992.
15. L. Xu, A. Krzyzak, and C.Y. Suen. Methods of combining multiple classifiers and their application to handwriting recognition. *IEEE Transactions on Systems, Man, and Cybernetics*, 22:418–435, 1992.

Input Decimation Ensembles: Decorrelation through Dimensionality Reduction

Nikunj C. Oza[1] and Kagan Tumer[2]

[1] Computer Science Division
University of California
Berkeley, CA 94720-1776, USA
oza@cs.berkeley.edu
[2] Computational Sciences Division
NASA Ames Research Center
Mail Stop 269-3
Moffett Field, CA 94035-1000, USA
kagan@ptolemy.arc.nasa.gov

Abstract. Using an ensemble of classifiers instead of a single classifier has been shown to improve generalization performance in many machine learning problems [4, 16]. However, the extent of such improvement depends greatly on the amount of correlation among the errors of the base classifiers [1,14]. As such, reducing those correlations while keeping the base classifiers' performance levels high is a promising research topic. In this paper, we describe *input decimation*, a method that decouples the base classifiers by training them with different subsets of the input features. In past work [15], we showed the theoretical benefits of input decimation and presented its application to a handful of real data sets. In this paper, we provide a systematic study of input decimation on synthetic data sets and analyze how the interaction between correlation and performance in base classifiers affects ensemble performance.

1 Introduction

Using an ensemble of classifiers instead of a single classifier has been repeatedly shown to improve generalization performance in many machine learning problems [4, 16]. It is well-known that, in order to obtain such improvement, one needs to simultaneously maintain a reasonable level of performance in the base classifiers that constitute the ensemble and reduce their correlations. There are many ensemble methods that actively promote diversity (i.e., lower correlations in the outputs) among their base classifiers. Bagging [4], boosting [7], and cross-validation partitioning [9, 14] generate diverse base classifiers by training with different subsets of the training set. Error-correcting output codes [5] generate new training sets with different class labels and use these different training sets to generate base classifiers. Merz [10] use Principal Component Analysis [8] to measure the correlations among the base models and combine them accordingly. Dietterich [6] combines decision trees in which each test is chosen at random among the 20 best tests.

J. Kittler and F. Roli (Eds.): MCS 2001, LNCS 2096, pp. 238–247, 2001.
© Springer-Verlag Berlin Heidelberg 2001

Most work in this field, however, focuses on pattern-level selection (e.g., Bagging, Boosting). **Input Decimation (ID)** on the other hand is a feature selection method that generates different subsets of the input features for each of the classifiers in the ensemble. By training each base classifier with a different feature subset, the correlations among the base classifiers are reduced. (Note that input decimation can be used in conjunction with pattern-based ensemble methods such as bagging and boosting, as discussed in Section 3.) Input decimation is different from most other dimensionality reduction methods that are widely used, including PCA, in that it generates different feature subsets for different classifiers. On the other hand, PCA aims to maximize the variability among the newly constructed features, but makes no provisions on how that variability is related to class information (see [11] for details).

In this work we explore using class information to reduce the dimensionality of the feature space presented to each base classifier. While strong ensemble performance was expected, input decimation also provided improvements in the base classifiers by pruning *irrelevant* features, thereby simplifying the learning problem faced by each base classifier. Consequently, Input Decimated Ensembles (IDEs) significantly outperformed both base classifiers trained on the full feature space as well as ensembles of such classifiers. In the next section we briefly highlight the need for correlation reduction in ensembles. We then present the input decimation algorithm, along with results on synthetic data sets.

2   Correlation and Ensemble Performance

In this article we focus on classifiers that model the *a posteriori* probabilities of the output classes. Such algorithms include Bayesian methods [3], and properly trained feed forward neural networks such as Multi-Layer Perceptrons (MLPs) [12]. We can model the ith output of such a classifier as follows (details of this derivation are in [13, 14]):

$$f_i(x) = P(C_i|x) + \eta_i(x),$$

where $P(C_i|x)$ is the posterior probability of the ith class given instance x, and $\eta_i(x)$ is the error associated with the ith output. Given an input x, if we have one classifier, we classify x as being in the class i whose value $f_i(x)$ is largest.

Instead, if we use an ensemble that calculates the arithmetic average over the outputs of N classifiers $f_i^m(x)$, $m \in \{1, \ldots, N\}$, then $P(C_i|x)$ is given by:

$$f_i^{ave}(x) = \frac{1}{N} \sum_{m=1}^{N} f_i^m(x) = P(C_i|x) + \bar{\eta}_i(x), \tag{1}$$

where:

$$\bar{\eta}_i(x) = \frac{1}{N} \sum_{m=1}^{N} \eta_i^m(x)$$

and $\eta_i^m(x)$ is the error associated with the ith output of the mth classifier.

Now, the variance of $\bar{\eta}_i(x)$ is given by [14]:

$$\sigma_{\bar{\eta}_i}^2 = \frac{1}{N^2} \sum_{m=1}^{N} \sigma_{\eta_i^m(x)}^2 + \frac{1}{N^2} \sum_{m=1}^{N} \sum_{l \neq m} cov(\eta_i^l(x), \eta_i^m(x)).$$

If we express the covariances in terms of the correlations ($cov(x, y) = corr(x, y)\sigma_x\sigma_y$), assume the same variance $\sigma_{\eta_i}^2$ across classifiers, and use the average correlation factor among classifiers, δ_i, given by

$$\delta_i = \frac{1}{N(N-1)} \sum_{m=1}^{N} \sum_{l \neq m} corr(\eta_i^l(x), \eta_i^m(x)), \tag{2}$$

then the variance becomes:

$$\sigma_{\bar{\eta}_i}^2 = \frac{1}{N}\sigma_{\eta_i(x)}^2 + \frac{N-1}{N}\delta_i\sigma_{\eta_i(x)}^2 = \frac{1 + \delta_i(N-1)}{N}\sigma_{\eta_i(x)}^2. \tag{3}$$

Based on this variance, we can compute the variance of the decision boundary and, generalizing this result to the classifier error, we obtain the relationship between the model error (beyond the Bayes error) of the ensemble (E_{model}^{ave})and that of an individual classifier (E_{model}^{ave}) [13, 14]:

$$E_{model}^{ave} = \left(\frac{1 + \delta(N-1)}{N}\right)E_{model} \tag{4}$$

where

$$\delta = \sum_{i=1}^{L} P_i\delta_i \tag{5}$$

and P_i is the prior probability of class i.

Equation 4 quantifies the connection between error reduction and the correlation among the errors of the base classifiers. This result leads us to seek to reduce the correlation among classifiers prior to using them in an ensemble. In the next section we present the input decimation concept which merges dimensionality reduction and correlation reduction to provide classifier ensembles.

3   The Input Decimated Ensembles

Input decimation decouples the classifiers by exposing them to different aspects of the same data by selecting features most correlated with a particular class. ID trains L classifiers, one corresponding to each class in an L-class problem[1]. For each classifier, the method selects a user-determined number of the input

---

[1] More generally, one trains nL classifiers where n is an integer.

features having the highest absolute correlation to the presence or absence of the corresponding class[2]. The objective is to "weed" out input features that do not carry strong discriminating information for a particular class, and thereby reduce the dimensionality of the feature space to facilitate the learning process.

Let the training set take the following form:

$$\{(\mathbf{x_1}, \mathbf{y_1}), (\mathbf{x_2}, \mathbf{y_2}), \ldots, (\mathbf{x_m}, \mathbf{y_m})\},$$

where m is the number of training examples. Each $\mathbf{x_i}$ has $\|FS\|$ elements (where FS is the set of input features) representing the values of the input features in example i. Each $\mathbf{y_i}$ represents the class using a distributed encoding, i.e., it has L elements, where L is the number of classes, $y_{il} = 1$ if example i is an instance of class l and $y_{il} = 0$ if example i is not an instance of class l. In this study our base classifiers consist of MLPs trained with the backpropagation algorithm[3].

Given such a data set, and a base classifier learning algorithm, input decimated ensembles operate as follows:

- For each class $l \in \{1, 2, \ldots, L\}$,
    1. Compute the absolute value of the correlation between each feature j ($\mathbf{x_{ij}}$ for all patterns i) and the output for class l ($\mathbf{y_{il}}$ for all patterns i).
    2. Select the n_l features having the highest absolute correlation, resulting in new feature set FS_l. One can either predetermine n_l based on prior information about the data set, or learn the value to optimizes performance.
    3. Construct a new training set by retaining only those elements of the $\mathbf{x_i}$'s corresponding to the features FS_l and all the outputs.
    4. Call the base classifier learning algorithm on this new training set. Call the resulting classifier f^l.

Given a new example x, we classify it as follows:

- For each class $k \in \{1, 2, \ldots, L\}$, calculate $f_k^{ave}(x) = \frac{1}{L} \sum_{l=1}^{L} f_k^l(x)$, by presenting the proper feature sets (FS_l) to each of the L classifiers.
- Return the class $K = argmax_k f_k^{ave}(x)$.

Fundamentally, input decimation seeks to reduce the correlations among individual classifiers by using different subsets of input features, while methods such as bagging and boosting attempt to do so by choosing different subsets of training patterns. These facts imply that input decimation is orthogonal to pattern-based methods such as bagging and boosting, i.e., one can use input decimation in conjunction with pattern-based methods, and directly comparing

---

[2] Note that this method requires the problem to have at least three classes. In a two-class problem, features strongly correlated with one class will be strongly anti-correlated with the other class, so the same features would be chosen for both classifiers.

[3] In principle, any learning algorithm that estimates the a posteriori class probabilities can be used.

input decimation to bagging or boosting serves little purpose. Rather one should compare input decimated ensembles to original ensembles (which is done here) or input decimated, *bagged* ensembles to bagging alone (which we are currently investigating).

4   Experimental Results

In this section, we present the results of input decimation on synthetic datasets. As discussed above, our base classifiers are multi-layer perceptrons. In this work all such classifiers contain a single hidden layer and the learning rate, momentum term, and number of hidden units were experimentally determined[4].

As a standard against which to compare our input decimation results, we also trained a classifier on the full feature set (referred to as the "original single classifier") and separately trained L copies of the same classifier and incorporated them into an averaging ensemble (referred to as the "original ensemble"). As anticipated, the original ensemble often performs significantly better than each of its base classifiers. Comparing input-decimated ensembles with these original ensembles isolates the benefits of removing input features from the base classifiers. Because PCA is a standard dimensionality reduction method, we also compare input decimated ensembles to PCA ensembles (i.e., ensembles where each constituent classifier was trained on a preselected set of the principal components of the feature space).

In these experiments, we used the following three synthetic datasets:

- Set 1:
  - Three classes–one unimodal Gaussian per class.
  - 300 training patterns and 150 test patterns–100 training and 50 test patterns per class.
  - 100 features per pattern where there are:
    * 10 relevant features per class–each class's instances are generated from a multivariate normal distribution in 10 independent dimensions distributed as $N(40, 5^2)$. There are no dimensions in common among the three classes. Therefore, there are 30 relevant features. For instances of each class, the 20 features that are relevant to the other two classes are distributed as $U[-100, 100]$.[5]
    * 70 irrelevant features–distributed as $U[-100, 100]$.
- Set 2: Same as Set 1, except that only 50 irrelevant features were added to the 30 relevant features, for a total of 80 features in the dataset.
- Set 3: Same as Set 1, except that there is overlap among the relevant features for each class (e.g., classes have three relevant features in common).

---

[4] We experimented on a single neural network with all input features by trying learning rates and momentum terms in increments of 0.05 and hidden units in increments of 5 until the performance began to decline.

[5] Clearly, because of this, all 30 features have some relevance to all three classes; however, the 10 features used to generate each class's instances are clearly substantially more relevant than the other 20 features.

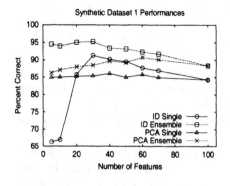

Fig. 1. Dataset 1 Performances   **Fig. 2.** Dataset 1 Correlations

In dataset 1 there is an abundance of features that are irrelevant for the classification task. This data set was chosen to represent large data mining problems where the algorithms may get swamped by irrelevant data. Dataset 2 has fewer irrelevant features and was chosen to illustrate the performance of input decimation as a function of irrelevant information present in the feature space. By reducing the amount of noise in the feature space, the problem is subtly modified: selecting the relevant features is now easier, but the effect of removing the irrelevant features on the base classifiers' performance is reduced. Finally, dataset 3 was chosen to have overlap among the features relevant to each class. This provides a more difficult problem where the base classifiers are now *forced* to select some common features, reducing the potential for correlation reduction.

4.1   Synthetic Set 1

Figures 1 and 2 present the classification accuracies and base classifier correlations, respectively as a function of the number of inputs (which are either the number of selected principal components or the number of features selected for each base classifier through input decimation). The original single classifier and original ensemble use all the input features[6]. The points for the maximum number of features (e.g., 100 features in this dataset), always represent the performance of the original classifier/ensemble.

An important observation that is apparent from these results is that neither PCA ensembles nor PCA base classifiers are particularly sensitive to the number of inputs. The correlations among the base classifiers reinforce this conclusion. Fewer input features in PCA means the base classifiers are more correlated since they all share the same principal features. Note however, that input decimated base classifiers have little correlation for small numbers of features, increasing correlation up to 30 features, and decreasing correlation after that. The base classifiers' average performance follows a similar pattern. Interestingly though,

---

[6] The base classifier used was an MLP with a single hidden layer consisting of 95 units, trained using a learning rate of 0.2 and a momentum term of 0.5.

input decimated ensembles are not adversely affected by the poor performance of the base classifiers (e.g., input decimated ensembles with 5 features outperformed input decimated ensembles with 50 features while base classifiers with 5 features gave significantly worse results than base classifiers with 50 features).

In cases where more than 30 features were used, the performance of the ensemble declined with the addition of additional features, i.e., as more and more irrelevant features were included. However, all the input decimation ensembles provided statistically significant improvements over the original ensembles and PCA ensembles.

The single decimated classifiers with 20 and more features outperformed the original single classifier. This perhaps surprising result (as one might have expected only the ensemble performance to improve when using subsets of the features) is mainly due to the simplification of the learning tasks, which allows the classifiers to learn the mapping more efficiently.

Interestingly, the average correlation among classifiers does not decrease until a very small number of features remain. We attribute this to the removal of noise—removing noise increases the amount of information shared between the base classifiers. Indeed, the correlation increases steadily as features are removed until we reach 30 features (which corresponds to the actual number of relevant features). After that point, removing features reduces the correlation and the individual classifier performances. However, the ensemble performance still remains high. This experiment clearly shows a typical trade-off in ensemble learning: one can either increase individual classifier performance (as for input decimation with more than 30 features) or reduce the correlation among classifiers (as for input decimation with less than 20 features) to improve ensemble performance.

4.2   Synthetic Set 2

Figures 3 and 4 present the classification accuracies and base classifier correlations, respectively, for the second data set which is obtained by reducing the number of irrelevant features (from 70 to 50) from the first dataset[7]. The decimated ensembles with 5 and 70 features marginally outperformed the original ensemble and PCA-based ensemble, while the remaining ones performed significantly better. Note that, just as it was for the first data set, the input decimated single classifiers with 20 or more features outperformed the single original classifier. This demonstrates that if the feature set is noisy (an assumption that almost always holds in the real world) improvements are achieved through dimensionality reduction alone.

4.3   Synthetic Set 3

Figures 5 and 6 present the results for the third data set, which is similar to the first dataset except that there is overlap among the relevant features for the

---

[7] The single classifier used was an MLP with a single hidden layer consisting of 65 units, trained using a learning rate of 0.2 and a momentum term of 0.5.

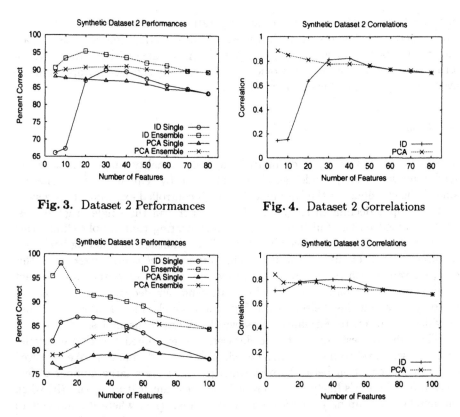

Fig. 3. Dataset 2 Performances

Fig. 4. Dataset 2 Correlations

Fig. 5. Dataset 3 Performances

Fig. 6. Dataset 3 Correlations

classes.[8] Because of this overlap, this feature set has fewer total relevant features and thus it constitutes a more difficult problem (as indicated by comparing the results on the full feature classifiers and ensembles on this dataset to the previous ones).

Note that the correlations in this data set remained fairly constant across the board. Unlike results shown in Figure 2, input decimation did not reduce correlations dramatically for small feature sets. This is mainly caused by the "coupling" among the features (i.e., the presence of features that are essential to many classes due to the overlap).

In spite of these difficulties, input decimation ensembles perform extremely well. Indeed, they significantly outperform both the original ensemble and PCA ensembles on all but a few subsets where they only provide marginal improvements. Furthermore the input-decimated single classifiers also outperform their original and PCA counterparts for all but the 60 and 70 feature subsets. This is particularly heartening since this feature set is a more representative abstraction

---

[8] The single classifier used was an MLP with a single hidden layer consisting of 95 units, trained using a learning rate of 0.2 and a momentum term of 0.5.

of real data sets (data sets with "clean" separation among classes are quite rare). This experiment demonstrates that when there is overlap among classes, class information becomes particularly relevant. PCA operates without this vital information, therefore it cannot provide any statistically significant improvements over the original classifiers and ensembles.

5   Discussion

This paper discusses input decimation, a dimensionality reduction-based ensemble method that provides good generalization by reducing the correlations among the classifiers in the ensemble. Through controlled experiments, we show that the input decimated single classifiers outperform the single original classifiers (trained on the full feature set), demonstrating that simply eliminating irrelevant features can improve performance[9]. In addition, eliminating irrelevant features in each of many classifiers using *different relevance criteria* (in this case, relevance with respect to different classes) yields significant improvement in ensemble performance, as seen by comparing our decimated ensembles to the original ensembles. Selecting the features using class label information also provides significant performance gains over PCA-based ensembles.[10]

Through our tests on synthetic datasets, we examined the characteristics that datasets need to have to fully benefit from input decimation. We observed that input decimation performs best when (i) there are a large number of features (i.e., where it's likely that there will be irrelevant features); and (ii) when the number of training examples is relatively small (i.e., where it's difficult to properly learn all the parameters in a classifier based on the full feature set). In both cases, by removing the extraneous features, input decimation reduces noise and thereby reduces the number of training examples needed to produce a meaningful model (i.e., alleviating the curse of dimensionality). Our synthetic datasets were generated using multivariate distributions where the feature values were generated independently. We plan to generate synthetic datasets with dependencies among the features to see how they affect our method.

Note that input decimation shares the central aim of generating a diverse pool of classifiers for the ensemble with many methods, and most notably with bagging. However, by focusing on the input features rather than the input patterns, input decimation focuses on a different "axis" of correlation reduction than does bagging. Consequently, input decimation is orthogonal to bagging, and one can use input decimation in conjunction with bagging.

A final observation is that input decimation works well *in spite* of our rather crude method of feature selection (i.e., using statistical correlation of each feature individually with each class). One reason why this simple method succeeds

---

[9] Although this result is perplexing from an information theory perspective, it is consistent with learning theory: by removing features we simplify the learning task and thus allow the base classifiers to reach their "peak" performance.

[10] Furthermore, IDEs also outperform random feature subset selection [2, 17] on real datasets [15].

is that we have greatly simplified the relevance criterion: unlike other feature selection methods that consider the discriminatory ability across all classes, we only consider the relevance of the features to a *single* class. This typically causes each classifier in the ensemble to get a different subset of features, leading to the superior performance we have demonstrated. Nevertheless, we are currently extending this work in three directions: considering cross-correlations among the features; investigating mutual information-based relevance criteria; and incorporating global relevance into the selection process.

Acknowledgments. Part of this work was done while Nikunj Oza was visiting NASA Ames Research Center.

References

1. K.M. Ali and M.J. Pazzani. On the link between error correlation and error reduction in decision tree ensembles. Technical Report 95-38, Department of Information and Computer Science, University of California, Irvine, 1995.
2. S.D. Bay. Combining nearest neighbor classifiers through multiple feature subsets. In *Proc. 15th ICML*, pages 415–425. Morgan Kaufmann, 1998.
3. J. O. Berger. *Statistical Decision Theory and Bayesian Analysis.* (2nd Ed.), Springer, New York, 1985.
4. L. Breiman. Bagging predictors. *Machine Learning*, 24(2):123–140, 1996.
5. T.G. Dietterich and G. Bakiri. Solving multiclass learning problems via error-correcting output codes. *Journal of AI Research*, 2:263–286, 1995.
6. Thomas G. Dietterich. An experimental comparison of three methods for constructing ensembles of decision trees: Bagging, boosting, and randomization. *Machine Learning*, 40:139–158, Aug. 2000.
7. Y. Freund and R. Schapire. Experiments with a new boosting algorithm. In *Proc. 13th ICML*, pages 148–156, Bari, Italy, 1996. Morgan Kaufmann.
8. I.T. Jolliffe. *Principal Component Analysis*. Springer-Verlag, 1986.
9. A. Krogh and J. Vedelsby. Neural network ensembles, cross validation and active learning. In G. Tesauro, D.S. Touretzky, and T.K. Leen, editors, *Advances in Neural Information Processing Systems-7*, pages 231–238. M.I.T. Press, 1995.
10. C.J. Merz. *Classification and Regression by Combining Models*. PhD thesis, University of California, Irvine, Irvine, CA, May 1998.
11. N.C. Oza and K. Tumer. Dimensionality reduction through classifier ensembles. Technical Report NASA-ARC-IC-1999-126, NASA Ames Research Center, 1999.
12. M.D. Richard and R.P. Lippmann. Neural network classifiers estimate Bayesian a posteriori probabilities. *Neural Computation*, 3(4):461–483, 1991.
13. K. Tumer and J. Ghosh. Analysis of decision boundaries in linearly combined neural classifiers. Pattern Recognition, 29(2):341–348, February 1996.
14. K. Tumer and J. Ghosh. Error correlation and error reduction in ensemble classifiers. *Connection Science, Special Issue on Combining Artificial Neural Networks: Ensemble Approaches*, 8(3 & 4):385–404, 1996.
15. K. Tumer and N.C. Oza. Decimated input ensembles for improved generalization. In *Proc. of the Int. Joint Conf. on Neural Networks (IJCNN-99)*, 1999.
16. D. H. Wolpert. Stacked generalization. *Neural Networks*, 5:241–259, 1992.
17. Z. Zheng and G.I. Webb. Stochastic attribute selection committees. In *Proc. of the 11th Australian Joint Conf. on AI (AI'98)*, pages 321–332, 1998.

Classifier Combination as a Tomographic Process

D. Windridge and J. Kittler

Dept. of Electronic and Electrical Engineering,
University of Surrey, Guildford, Surrey, GU2 7XH, U.K.
{D.Windridge,J.Kittler}@surrey.ac.uk

Abstract. A mathematical analogy between the process of multiple expert fusion and the tomographic reconstruction of Radon integral data is outlined for the specific instance of the combination of classifiers containing discrete data sets. Within this metaphor all conventional methods of classifier combination come, to a greater or lesser degree, to resemble the unfiltered back-projection of the constituent classifiers' probability density functions: an implicit attempt to reconstruct the PDF of the composite pattern space. In these probabilistic terms, the combination of classifiers with *identical* feature-sets correspondingly constitutes an attempt at morphological manipulation of the composite pattern-space PDF. A consideration of the separate benefits of combination along these dualistic lines eventually leads to an optimal strategy for classifier combination under arbitrary conditions.

1 Introduction

We present a metaphor for classifier combination in terms of the apparently unrelated process of the reconstruction of Radon integral data via tomographic means. By interpreting the combination of classifiers with *distinct* feature sets as the implicit reconstruction of the composite pattern space probability density function (PDF) of the entire space of features, we can begin to envisage the problem in geometric terms, and, ultimately (although beyond the scope of this paper) propose an optimal approach both to this, and later to the more general, problem of non-distinct feature sets [cf 5].

2 Context of Analysis

We specify as follows our prior assumptions in relation to conventional combinatorial schemes (generalising later to a less constricting set of assumptions):

1. It is assumed, at least initially, that the selection of features is decided through classifier preference, and that this is accomplished via the straightforward omission of superfluous dimensions as appropriate.
2. For simplicity, it shall (at least at the outset) be assumed that the set of classifiers operate on only one feature individually, and that these are distinct (though note that the former is not a prerequisite of the method).

J. Kittler and F. Roli (Eds.): MCS 2001, LNCS 2096, pp. 248–258, 2001.

Evidence that the stronger of these two assumptions, the latter, is reasonably representative of the usual situation comes from [1], wherein features selected *within* a combinatorial context are consistently shown to favour the allocation of distinct feature sets to the constituent classifiers.

3. We shall consider that the construction of a classifier is the equivalent of estimating the PDFs $p(x_{\mathcal{N}(1,i)}, x_{\mathcal{N}(2,i)} \ldots x_{\mathcal{N}(k_i,i)} | \omega_i)$ $\forall i$, where $\mathcal{N}(x,y)$ is the final set of feature dimensions passed from the feature selection algorithm for class y (the cardinality of which, k_i, we will initially set to unity for every class identified by the feature selector: ie $k_i = 1$ $\forall i$).

4. It is assumed that in any reasonable feature selection regime the total set of features employed by the various classifiers exhausts the classification information available in the pattern space (ie, the remaining dimensions contribute only a stochastic noise component to the individual clusters).

Given assumption 3 above (that individual classifiers may be regarded as PDFs) and further, that pattern vectors corresponding to a particular class may be regarded as deriving from an n-dimensional probability distribution, then the process of feature selection may be envisaged as an integration over the dimensions redundant to that particular classification scheme (the discarding of superfluous dimensions being, in effect, the linear projection of a higher dimensional space onto a lower one, ultimately a 1-dimensional space in the above framework). That is, for n-dimensional pattern data of class i:

$$p(x_k|\omega_i)dx_k = \left[\int_{-\infty}^{+\infty} \underbrace{\cdots}_{n-1} \int_{-\infty}^{+\infty} p(\boldsymbol{X}|\omega_i)dx_1 \ldots \right.$$

$$\left. \ldots dx_{k-1}dx_{k+1} \ldots dx_n \right].dx_k \tag{1}$$

with $\boldsymbol{X} = (x_1, x_2, \ldots, x_n)$

Because of condition 4 above (a good approximation when a range of classifiers is assumed), we shall consider that the pattern vector effectively terminates at index j, where $j \leq n$ is the total number of features (and also classifiers, given condition 3). That is, $\boldsymbol{X} = (x_1, x_2, \ldots, x_j)$ now represents the extent of the pattern vector dimensionality. In the integral analogy, the remaining dimensions that are integrated over in equation 1 serve to reduce the stochastic component of the joint PDF by virtue of the increased bin count attributable to each of the pattern vector indices.

3   The Radon Transformation

Now, it is the basis of our thesis that we may regard equation 1 as the j-dimension analogue of the Radon transform (essentially the mathematical equivalent of the physical measurements taken within a tomographic imaging regime), an assertion that we shall make explicit in section 5 after having found a method for extending the inverse Radon transform to an arbitrarily large dimensionality.

The conventional Radon transform, however, is defined in terms of the two-dimensional function $f(x, y)$ as follows; (after [2])

$$R(s, \theta)[f(x, y)] = \int_{-\infty}^{+\infty} \int_{-\infty}^{+\infty} f(x, y)\delta(s - x\cos\theta - y\sin\theta)dx\, dy$$

$$(= g(s, \theta)) \qquad (2)$$

where s may be regarded as a perpendicular distance to a line in (x,y) space, and θ the angle that that line subtends in relation to the x axis. $R(s, \theta)$ is then an integral over $f(x, y)$ along the line specified.

As a first approximation to inverting the Radon transform and reconstructing the original data $f(x, y)$, we might apply the Hilbert Space adjoint operator of $R(s, \theta)$, the so-called back-projection operator:

$$R^*[R(s, \theta)](\boldsymbol{x}) = \int_S R(\boldsymbol{\theta}, \boldsymbol{\theta} \cdot \boldsymbol{x})d\theta \qquad (3)$$

with $\boldsymbol{x} = (x, y), \boldsymbol{\theta} = (\cos\theta, \sin\theta)$

To appreciate how this operates, consider first the following identity written in terms of the arbitrary function v, where $V = R^*v$:

$$\int_S \int_s v(\theta, \boldsymbol{x} \cdot \boldsymbol{\theta} - s)g(\theta, s)ds\, d\theta$$

$$= \int_S \int_s v(\theta, \boldsymbol{x} \cdot \boldsymbol{\theta} - s) \int_{\mathcal{R}'^2} f(\boldsymbol{x}')\delta(s - \boldsymbol{x}' \cdot \boldsymbol{\theta})d^2x'\, dsd\theta$$

$$= \int_S \int_{R'^2} v(\theta, \boldsymbol{x} \cdot \boldsymbol{\theta} - \boldsymbol{x}' \cdot \boldsymbol{\theta})f(\boldsymbol{x}')d^2x'd\theta$$

(eliminating s)

$$= \int_{\mathcal{R}'^2} \left[\int_S v(\theta, (\boldsymbol{x} - \boldsymbol{x}') \cdot \boldsymbol{\theta})d\theta \right] f(\boldsymbol{x}')d^2x'$$

$$= \int_{\mathcal{R}'^2} V(\boldsymbol{x} - \boldsymbol{x}')f(\boldsymbol{x}')d^2x'$$

(via the definition of V [= R*v])

$$= V \star f \qquad (4)$$

The first term in the above may be symbolically written $R^*(v \star g)$, where it is understood that the convolution is with respect to the length variable and not the angular term in g. Hence, we have that $V \star f = R^*(v \star g)$.

We may describe the relationship between V and v in terms of their Fourier transforms. Consider first the two-dimensional transform of V:

$$F(\boldsymbol{k})[V(\boldsymbol{x})] = (2\pi)^{-1} \int_{\mathcal{R}^2} e^{-i\boldsymbol{x} \cdot \boldsymbol{k}} V(\boldsymbol{x})d^2x \qquad (5)$$

$$= (2\pi)^{-1} \int_{\mathcal{R}^2} e^{-i\boldsymbol{x} \cdot \boldsymbol{k}} \int_S v(\theta, \boldsymbol{x} \cdot \boldsymbol{\theta})d^2x\, d\theta$$

(by substitution)

$$= (2\pi)^{-1} \int_S \int_{\mathcal{R}^2} e^{-i\boldsymbol{x}\cdot\boldsymbol{k}} v(\theta, \boldsymbol{x}\cdot\boldsymbol{\theta}) d^2x \, d\theta$$

We now consider a slice through this transform along the direction θ. This may be accomplished in the above by substituting in the delta function $\delta(\boldsymbol{k}-\sigma\boldsymbol{\theta})$ within the θ integral (ie coupling the variables $\boldsymbol{k}$ and $\boldsymbol{\theta}$) and transforming it to a $\boldsymbol{k}$ space integral via the corresponding transformation $d\boldsymbol{k} \to \sigma d\theta$ (σ is a positive real number):

$$F(\sigma\boldsymbol{\theta})[V(\boldsymbol{x})]$$

$$= (2\pi)^{-1} \int_S \int_{\mathcal{R}^2} e^{-i\boldsymbol{x}\cdot\boldsymbol{k}} v(\theta, \boldsymbol{x}\cdot\boldsymbol{\theta}) d^2x \, \delta(\boldsymbol{k}-\sigma\boldsymbol{\theta}) d\theta$$

$$= (2\pi)^{-1} \int_S \int_{\mathcal{R}^2} e^{-i\boldsymbol{x}\cdot\boldsymbol{k}} v(\theta, \boldsymbol{x}\cdot\boldsymbol{\theta}) d^2x \, \delta(\boldsymbol{k}-\sigma\boldsymbol{\theta}) d\boldsymbol{k}\sigma^{-1}$$

$$= (2\pi)^{-1} \int_{\mathcal{R}^2} e^{-i\sigma\boldsymbol{x}\cdot\boldsymbol{\theta}} v(\theta, \boldsymbol{x}\cdot\boldsymbol{\theta}) d^2x\sigma^{-1}$$

We have also that $d(\boldsymbol{x}\cdot\boldsymbol{\theta}) = d\boldsymbol{x}\cdot\boldsymbol{\theta}$ for constant $\boldsymbol{\theta}$. Thus:

$$F(\sigma\boldsymbol{\theta})[V(\boldsymbol{x})]$$

$$= (2\pi)^{-1} \int_{\mathcal{R}^2} e^{-i\sigma\boldsymbol{x}\cdot\boldsymbol{\theta}} v(\theta, \boldsymbol{x}\cdot\boldsymbol{\theta}) d(\boldsymbol{x}\cdot\boldsymbol{\theta})(\sigma|\boldsymbol{\theta}|)^{-1}$$

$$= (2\pi)^{-1} \int_{\mathcal{R}^2} e^{-i\sigma z} v(\theta, z) dz(\sigma|\boldsymbol{\theta}|)^{-1}$$

(where $z = \boldsymbol{x}\cdot\boldsymbol{\theta}$)

The z dependent terms now form a Fourier transform with respect to the second variable in v. Hence, we may write the above in the following form to elucidate the precise relation between V and v in Fourier terms:

$$F(\sigma\boldsymbol{\theta})[V(\boldsymbol{x})] = (2\pi)^{-1} F_z(\sigma)[v(\theta, z)](\sigma|\boldsymbol{\theta}|)^{-1} \tag{6}$$

The effect of the back-projection operator on the Radon transform of f may then be appreciated, via a consideration of equation 4, by setting v to be a Dirac delta function in s (corresponding to an identity operation within the convolution). The V corresponding to this v may then be deduced by inserting the Fourier transform of the delta function (unity throughout f-space) into the above equation. Hence, we see that the effect of applying the back-projection operator to the Radon transformed f function is the equivalent of convolving f with the inverse Fourier-transformed remainder:

$$f_{\text{recovered}}(x, y) = f_{\text{original}} * F^{-1}(s^{-1}) \tag{7}$$

In terms of the tomographic analogy, we retrieve a "blurred" version of the original data. In fact, the object of tomography is exactly the reverse of this process: we seek to obtain a v function such that it is V that approaches the form of the delta function: that is, transforming the RHS of equation 4 into f alone. In this instance, we may regard the v function as a "filtering operator" that serves to remove morphology attributable to the sampling geometry rather than the original data, which is then hence applied to the Radon data at a stage prior to inversion via the back projection operator.

We shall in section 5 set out to show that the summation method of classifier combination (which is representative of many more generalised combination approaches under certain conditions, such as very limited class information within the individual classifiers) is, in effect, the equivalent of applying the backprojection operator immediately to the classifier PDFs (which in our analogy are to be considered Radon transforms), without any attempt to apply prior filtering (ie, setting v to the delta function in equation 4). It is then via this observation that we ultimately hope to improve on the combination process, achieving an optimal, or near optimal solution to the inversion problem by finding an appropriate filter, v, albeit in the context of probability theory.

Prior to setting out this correspondence we shall first extend the method to the j-dimensions required of our pattern vector, and illustrate how the mechanics of the Radon reconstruction might be applied within the current context.

4 N-Dimensional Generalisation of the Radon Transform

We can show that there exists [cf 5] a discretised $(n-1)$-to-n-dimensional generalisation of both the inverse Radon transformation and deblurring mechanisms, which, to take the three dimensional instance of the latter for the two-angular-sample spaces implicit in the probabilistic geometry of feature selection, has the form:

$$
\begin{aligned}
&A\sum\nolimits_{l_{\alpha\beta}=-q}^{q} v_{\Omega}(\boldsymbol{x}\cdot\boldsymbol{\theta}_{\alpha\beta0} - s_{\alpha\beta l})R(\boldsymbol{\theta}_{\alpha\beta0}, s_{\alpha\beta l}) \; + \\
&A\sum\nolimits_{l'_{\alpha\beta}=-q}^{q} v_{\Omega}(\boldsymbol{x}\cdot\boldsymbol{\theta}_{\alpha\beta1} - s_{\alpha\beta l'})R(\boldsymbol{\theta}_{\alpha\beta1}, s_{\alpha\beta l'}) \; + \\
&A\sum\nolimits_{l''_{\gamma\beta}=-q}^{q} v_{\Omega}(\boldsymbol{x}\cdot\boldsymbol{\theta}_{\gamma\beta1} - s_{\gamma\beta l''})R(\boldsymbol{\theta}_{\gamma\beta1}, s_{\gamma\beta l''}) \\
&\forall\, \alpha, \beta : \alpha, \beta \in \mathcal{I}; \alpha \neq \beta; 0 < \alpha, \beta < n,
\end{aligned}
\tag{8}
$$

(the subscript Ω appended here to indicate a bandwidth limitation attributable to the very low number of angular Radon samples implied by the orthogonal nature of the feature space integrations: cf [5] for a full specification of this term, and a description of its implication for the maximal information content of the reconstructed space).

The Greek subscripts are then feature labels, and the numeric subscripts are the angular sample indices within the (hyper)-plane specified by the feature indices: detailed derivation of the value of the multiplication constant, A, and the trivial normalising assumptions required in allocating the *same A* to each convolution are referred to [5].

We can therefore demonstrate that the *unfiltered* volumetric inverse Radon transformation (that is, the three-dimensional back-projection operator applied to the two-dimensional "facet" integrals obtained from the feature selection process) therefore constitutes a linear summation of the form:

$$A[R(\boldsymbol{\theta}_{\alpha\beta0}, \boldsymbol{x} \cdot \boldsymbol{\theta}_{\alpha\beta0}) + R(\boldsymbol{\theta}_{\alpha\beta1}, \boldsymbol{x} \cdot \boldsymbol{\theta}_{\alpha\beta1}) + R(\boldsymbol{\theta}_{\gamma\beta0}, \boldsymbol{x} \cdot \boldsymbol{\theta}_{\gamma\beta0})] \tag{9}$$

When generalised to an $(n-1)$-to-n dimensional inverse Radon transformation this formula can then be applied recursively to generate the full N-dimensional pattern-space PDF from component classifier feature-spaces of arbitrarily small dimensionality (equal to unity in our case, given the specifications at the outset), the recursion retaining this linearity of summation for both the inverse Radon transformation and geometry-filtering procedures.

5   Correspondence with Classifier Combination Theory

Having obtained a form (or rather, a *method*) for n-dimensional inverse Radon transformation, we are now in a position to make the correspondence with classifier combination theory more formal. That is, we shall seek to encompass the various extant combinatorial decision theories within the tomographic framework that we have developed over the preceding sections, and show that they represent, within certain probabilistic bounds, an imperfect approximation to the *unfiltered* inverse Radon transformation.

We will firstly, however, demonstrate how we might explicitly substitute probabilistic terms into equation 8, and therefore, by extension, the complete n-dimensional inverse Radon transformation. We have initially then to establish exactly what is meant in geometrical terms by the Radon forms upon which equation 8 is constructed. It is helpful in this endeavour to, at least initially, eliminate the complication of the pre-filtering convolution represented by v, and therefore we consider only equation 9.

However, recall from equation 2 that:

$$R(\theta, s)[f(x_1', x_2')]$$
$$= \int_{-\infty}^{+\infty} \int_{-\infty}^{+\infty} f(x_1', x_2')\delta(s - x_1' \cos\theta - x_2' \sin\theta)dx_1' \, dx_2'$$
$$(= g(s, \theta)) \tag{10}$$

Now, in explicitly making the feature geometry congruent with the Radon geometry, we also have that;

$$\cos\boldsymbol{\theta}_{x_2} = \sin\boldsymbol{\theta}_{x_1} = 0$$
$$\text{and}$$
$$\cos\boldsymbol{\theta}_{x_1} = \sin\boldsymbol{\theta}_{x_2} = 1. \tag{11}$$

(θ now being measured in relation to the x_1 axis)

Thus, for example, picking an ordinate at random:

$$R(\theta_{x_1}, x_1) = \int_{-\infty}^{+\infty} \int_{-\infty}^{+\infty} f(x_1, x_2)\delta(x_1 - x_1')dx_1' \, dx_2'$$

$$= \int_{-\infty}^{+\infty} f(x_1, x_2') \, dx_2'$$

$$= \int_{-\infty}^{+\infty} f(x_1, x_2) \, dx_2 \tag{12}$$

and similarly for x_2, x_3

Now, a rational extension of the nomenclature of equation 1 would allow us to write:

$$p(x_1, x_2|\omega_i)dx_k \tag{13}$$

$$= \int_{-\infty}^{+\infty} \underbrace{\cdots}_{n-2} \int_{-\infty}^{+\infty} p(X|\omega_i)dx_3 \ldots dx_R.dx_1 dx_2$$

(and similarly for the remaining pairs of basis vector combinations)

We, of course, still have that:

$$p(x_1|\omega_i)dx_k$$

$$= \int_{-\infty}^{+\infty} \underbrace{\cdots}_{n-1} \int_{-\infty}^{+\infty} p(X|\omega_i)dx_2 \ldots dx_R.dx_1$$

$$= \int_{-\infty}^{+\infty} p(x_1, x_2|\omega_i)dx_2 \tag{14}$$

Thus, by setting the equivalence $f(x_1, x_2) \equiv p(x_1, x_2|\omega_i)$, we find by direct substitution into equation 12 that we may state that:

$$R(\theta_{x_1}, x_1) = \int_{-\infty}^{+\infty} f(x_1, x_2) \, dx_2 = p(x_1|\omega_i) \tag{15}$$

and similarly for the remaining numeric subscripts.

Hence, in consequence, we may simply restate the unfiltered two-to-three dimensional inverse Radon transformation in the more transparent form:

$$A[p(x_1|\omega_i) + p(x_2|\omega_i) + p(x_2|\omega_i)] \tag{16}$$

Moreover, we can again go further and extend this approach to the recursive methodology of the n-dimensional inverse Radon transformation, in which case we find, in the most general terms, that the unfiltered n-dimensional inverse

Radon transformation will have the form: (declining explicit calculation of the various normalising constants corresponding to A in the above, this being a relatively complex undertaking, and not in any case required in the context of the decision making schemes within which the method will ultimately be applied [see later])

$$A'[\sum_{\text{all } k} p(x_k|\omega_i)] \quad , \tag{17}$$

which clearly comes to resemble the Sum Rule decision making scheme (a correspondence we shall make formal later).

The substitution of probabilistic terms into the generalised inverse Radon transformation having thus been rendered explicit, it is now an elementary matter to substitute the previously omitted filtering function v_Ω back into equation 17 (the various subscript redundancies induced by an appropriate selection of the coordinate system above applying equally to the variable s in equation 8), most particularly since the set of filtering convolutions will remain additive in relation to their correspondant $p(x_k|\omega_i)$ functions throughout the recursive increment in dimensionality, and will therefore readily generalise to a composite n-dimensional filtering function. (We omit a discussion of its specific form since this is entirely dependent on the choice of v_Ω).

Having transcribed the inverse Radon transform into purely probabilistic terms and eliminated any residual geometric aspects of the problem, we may now turn to an investigation of how the n-dimensional reconstruction relates to the decision making process implicit within every regime of classifier combination.

As a preliminary to this endeavour, we must firstly ensure that there exist comparable pattern vectors for each class PDF (such not necessarily being the case for feature sets constructed on a class-by-class basis, as within our approach). That is, we shall need to ensure that:

$$p(x_{R_i(1)}, \ldots, x_{R_i(j_{k,i})}|\omega_k) = p(x_{l_k}, \ldots, x_{u_k}|\omega_k) \ \forall i, k \tag{18}$$

where u_k and l_k are, respectively, the highest and lowest feature indices of the various feature sets involved in the combination, and $j_{k,i}$ is the cardinality of the feature set corresponding to the kth class and ith classifier: $R_i(n_{k,i})$ is then the nth highest feature index in the feature set presented to the ith classifier for computation of class PDF number k.

This may be straightforwardly accomplished by the inclusion of null vector components, such that:

$$p(x_{t \notin R_i(j_{k,i})}|\omega_k) = 1 \ \forall t, i, k \tag{19}$$

implicitly setting l_k to 1 and u_k to N, thereby allowing a universal approach for each class index, k

Now, we have via the Bayes decision rule (ie that we:

assign $\mathbf{X} \to \omega_j$ if

$$p(\omega_j | x_1, \ldots x_N) = \max_k p(\omega_j | x_1, \ldots x_N), \tag{20}$$

given;

$$p(\omega_k x_1, \ldots x_N) = \frac{p(x_1, \ldots, x_N | \omega_k) p(\omega_k)}{p(x_1, \ldots, x_N)} \tag{21}$$

), that our decision rule for unfiltered N-dimensional inverse Radon PDF reconstruction is:

assign $\boldsymbol{X} \to \omega_j$ if

$$p(\omega_j | x_1, \ldots x_N) = \max_k \left[\frac{\sum_{i=1}^{N} p(x_i | \omega_k) p(\omega_k)}{p(x_1, \ldots, x_N)} \right] \tag{22}$$

(from equation 17)

The more familiar decision rules, however, may be derived solely via probabilistic constraints on the Bayes decision rule. For instance, suppose that we impose the condition that $x_1, \ldots, x_N$ are independent random variables (such that:

$$p(x_1, \ldots, x_N | \omega_k) = \prod_{i=1}^{N} p(x_i | \omega_k) \tag{23}$$

), then we obtain the decision rule:

assign $\boldsymbol{X} \to \omega_j$ if

$$p(\omega_j | x_1, \ldots x_N) = \max_k \left[\frac{\prod_{i=1}^{R} p(x_i | \omega_k) p(\omega_k)}{p(x_1, \ldots, x_R)} \right] \tag{24}$$

That is, we obtain the classical "Product Rule".

If we impose the further constraint that:

$$p(\omega_k | x_i) = p(\omega_k)[1 + \delta f(\omega_k, x_i)] , \tag{25}$$

with $\delta f(\omega_k, x_i)$ an infinitesimal function (in effect, imposing a high degree of "overlap" amongst amongst the total set of class PDFs, or, equivalently, a ubiquitous class membership ambiguity), and apply this directly to the Bayes theorem for single vectors then we can demonstrate [5] that we obtain the classical "Sum Rule" decision scheme:

assign $\boldsymbol{X} \to \omega_j$ if

$$p(\omega_j | x_1, \ldots x_N) = \max_k \left[\frac{\sum_{i=1}^{R} p(\omega_k)}{p(x_1, \ldots, x_R)} \right] \tag{26}$$

This, however, is identical to our original decision rule for the unfiltered inverse Radon transformation. Hence, we may state that the unfiltered inverse

Radon PDF reconstruction is, within a Bayesian decision-making context, the equivalent of the Sum Rule decision making scheme under the specified probabilistic constraints, and will thus produce near-optimal results only when the two conditions are satisfied (ie that the pattern vector components are statistically independent, and that there exists a high class membership ambiguity owing to similar PDF morphologies). The unfiltered inverse Radon decision making scheme then recreates the Product Rule under the less constrictive (and therefore more common) condition of a high class membership ambiguity alone, a condition, however, which must still presuppose very major constraints on the N-dimensional PDF morphology if the equality is to hold.

Very many other classical combination rules are derived from combinations of these preconditions (see [3]) and thus come to resemble, to some degree, the unfiltered inverse transform. Without exception, however, they will all impose very considerable constraints on the implied N-dimensional PDF reconstruction. When viewed in this morphological regard, it is clear that the lack of universal application of classical methods of combination, however effective they may be within their typical domains of application, is (by an inversion of the above process) attributable to these implicit constrictions on the reconstructive process, to which these methods have been shown to offer an approximation. The only way in which we can free ourselves of these restrictions (on the assumption that we have obtained error-free PDFs [see later]) is then to apply the *filtered* inverse Radon transform in its entirety, since this inherently neither assumes nor imposes any morphological (and therefore probabilistic) constraints on the final N-dimensional PDF, other than those already implicit in the original PDF data.

On information-theoretic grounds this would therefore represent an optimal solution to the implied problem of N-dimensional PDF reconstruction, it being apparent, by an inversion of the arguments above, that at least one aspect of every method of classifier combination is in some (not necessarily immediately obvious) way, the implicit recovery of an N-dimensional PDF.

To be fully confident of this conclusion, we would have to consider whether the above argument is modified by the fact that the various classifier PDFs, in consequence of having been derived from a finite set of stochastically distributed pattern data points, would invariably, to some extent, deviate from the "true" (if only hypothetically existent) probability density functions. In fact a detailed analysis (see [5]) shows the method to exhibit a robustness to estimation error similar to that of the Sum Rule, which it has come to so closely resemble, the Sum Rule being the previously optimal combination scheme in this regard: see Kittler *et al* 1997. [4]

6   Prospect and Summary

We have thus far considered tomographic reconstruction theory only in terms of distinct feature sets: the contrary situation must be addressed if we are to arrive at a universal perspective of classifier combination. Before embarking on an investigation of this we should, however, reiterate just how exceptional it is to find overlapping feature sets amongst the classifiers within a combination when feature selection is explicitly carried out within a combinatorial context (see [1]).

There would appear, then, to be an apparent double aspect to the functionality of conventional classifier combination, one facet of which may be considered, to the extent that the feature spaces are overlapping, the refinement of PDF morphology to improve classification performance (such as via weighted averaging), and therefore a form of classification in its own right, and the other being that of tomographic reconstruction, in so far as the feature sets belonging to the classifiers within the combination are distinct. Classical techniques of combination have tended to conflate these two disparate aspects through not having made a rigorous distinction between those classifier combinations that, in effect, act as a single classifier and those combinations that may be considered to act on entirely distinct orthogonal projections of a single PDF encompassing the whole of the N-dimensional pattern space. We, in contrast, would find it necessary, in seeking an optimal solution to the combination problem, to make this distinction completely formal. Explicitly separating the two, however, involves reverting to a stage prior to combination, and addressing the nature of the feature selection process itself. Thus we find we must take a unified perspective on the apparently separate issues of feature selection and classifier combination if we are to fully exploit the potential of the tomographic metaphor in attaining an optimal solution to the problem. Full details of just such an approach are set out in [5].

It is fully intended that, besides the publication of this completely inclusive methodology, the findings in relation to an experimental implementation of the tomographic combination technique will form the basis of a future series of papers.

Acknowledgement. This research was carried out at the University of Surrey, UK, supported by, and within the framework of, EPSRC research grant number GR/M61320.

References

1. D. Windridge, J. Kittler, "Combined Classifier Optimisation via Feature Selection", Proceedings "Advances in Pattern Recognition", Joint IAPR International Workshops SSPR 2000 and SPR 2000 Alicante, Spain, August 30 - September 1, 2000, Lecture Notes in Computer Science.VOL. 1876
2. F. Natterer, Proceedings "State of the Art in Numerical Analysis", York, April 1-4, 1996.
3. J. Kittler, M. Hatef, R.P.W. Duin, and J. Matas, Combining classifiers, Proc. 13th ICPR, Vienna, pp. 897, August, 1996.
4. J. Kittler, "Improving Recognition Rates by Classifier Combination: A Review", 1st IAPR TC1 Workshop on Statistical Techniques in Pattern Recognition, 205-210, June 1997
5. Windridge D., "An Optimal Solution to the Problem of Multiple Expert Fusion", Technical Report VSSP-TR-5/2000, CVSSP, Dept. of E.E., University of Surrey, England, 2000

A Robust Multiple Classifier System for a Partially Unsupervised Updating of Land-Cover Maps

Lorenzo Bruzzone and Roberto Cossu

DICA - University of Trento, Via Mesiano, 77
I-38050, Trento, Italy
{lorenzo.bruzzone, roberto.cossu}@ing.unitn.it

Abstract. We propose a system for a regular updating of land-cover maps based on the use of temporal series of remote sensing images. Such a system is composed of an ensemble of partially unsupervised classifiers integrated in a multiple classifier architecture. The updating problem is formulated under the complex constraint that for some images of the considered multitemporal series no ground-truth information is available. With respect to the authors' previous works on this topic [1-3], the novel contribution of this paper consists in: i) developing partially unsupervised classification algorithms defined in the framework of a cascade-classifier approach; ii) defining a specific strategy for the generation of an ensemble of classifiers, which exploits the peculiarities of the cascade-classifier approach. These novel aspects result in the definition of more robust and accurate classification systems.

1. Introduction

One of the major problems in geographical information systems (GIS) consists in defining strategies and procedures for a regular updating land-cover maps stored in system databases. This crucial task can be carried out by using remote-sensing images regularly acquired on the specific area considered by space-born sensors. However, despite the production of a land-cover map for a given area can be easily performed by using standard supervised classification algorithms [4], the temporal updating of these maps is a more complex and challenging problem. The most critical problem concerns the availability of ground-truth information. In many cases, it is not possible to rely on training data for all the images necessary to ensure an updating of land-cover maps as frequent as required by applications. This prevents all the remote-sensed images acquired on the investigated area from being analysed by supervised classification techniques.

In previous work [1-3], the aforementioned topic has been addressed by considering different aspects of the problem. Firstly, partially unsupervised classification methodologies able to update parameters of an already trained classifier, on the basis of the distribution of a new image, have been proposed [2-3]. These methodologies formulate the problem of the unsupervised retraining of classifiers in the framework of a mixture estimation problem solved with the expectation-maximisation (EM) algorithm. Secondly, in order to increase the robustness and accuracy of the resulting

J. Kittler and F. Roli (Eds.): MCS 2001, LNCS 2096, pp. 259–268, 2001.

classification system, the use of a multiple classifier architecture has been proposed [1].

In this paper we go a step ahead in improving features of the proposed system. In particular, we integrate the partially unsupervised classification problem of each classification technique in the context of a cascade-classifier approach. This allows one to exploit the temporal correlation between images to increase the effectiveness of the partially unsupervised classification process. Consequently, the resulting classifiers improve their global performances, without significantly increasing the classification time. Another issue addressed in this paper concerns the definition of the multiple-classifier architecture in presence of cascade-classifier approaches. In fact, using cascade classifiers results in the possibility of defining a new simple strategy for making up an ensemble of classification algorithms.

The paper is organised in six sections. Section 2 reports the formulation of the problem and describes the general architecture of the system. Section 3 presents the partially unsupervised classification problem in the framework of a cascade-classifier approach for both the ML and RBF neural networks classification algorithms. Section 4 addresses the problem of defining suitable ensembles of cascade classifiers. Experimental results are reported in Section 5. Discussion and conclusion are drawn in Section 6.

2. Formulation of the Problem and Description of the General Architecture of the System

2.1 Formulation of the Problem and Simplifying Assumptions

Let $\mathbf{X}_1 = \left\{x_1^1, x_2^1, ..., x_{I \times J}^1\right\}$ and $\mathbf{X}_2 = \left\{x_1^2, x_2^2, ..., x_{I \times J}^2\right\}$ denote two multispectral images of dimensions $I \times J$ acquired in the area under analysis at the time t_1 and t_2, respectively. Let x_j^1 and x_j^2 be the feature vectors associated with the j-th pixel of the images, and $\Omega = \left\{\omega_1, \omega_2, ..., \omega_C\right\}$ be the set of C land-cover classes that characterise the geographical area considered at both t_1 and t_2. Let l_j^2 be the classification label of the j-th pixel at the time t_2. Finally, let X_1 and X_2 be two multivariate random variables representing the pixel values (i.e., the feature vector values) in $\mathbf{X}_1$ and $\mathbf{X}_2$, respectively.

In the formulation of the proposed approach, we make the following assumptions: i) the same set Ω of C land-cover classes characterise the area considered over time (only the spatial distributions of such classes are supposed to vary); ii) a reliable training set $\mathbf{Y}_1$ for the image $\mathbf{X}_1$ acquired at t_1 is available; iii) a training set $\mathbf{Y}_2$ for the image $\mathbf{X}_2$ acquired at t_2 is not available.

In the aforementioned assumptions, the proposed system aims at carrying out a robust and accurate classification of $\mathbf{X}_2$ by exploiting the image $\mathbf{X}_1$, the training set

Y_1, the image X_2 as well as the temporal correlation between classes at t_1 and t_2 (readers can refer to [1-3] for a discussion on the assumptions considered).

2.2 System Architecture

The proposed system is based on a multiple classifier architecture composed of N different classification algorithms. The choice of this kind of architecture is due to the complexity of the problem addressed. In particular, the intrinsic complexity of the partially unsupervised classification problem results in classifiers that are less reliable and accurate than the corresponding supervised ones, especially for complex data sets. Therefore, by taking into account that generally ensembles of classifiers are more accurate and robust than the individual classifiers that make them up [5], we expect that a multiple-classifier approach increases the reliability and accuracy of the global classification system. A further step in the direction of improving the performances of the system consists in the choice of implementing each classification algorithm of the ensemble in the framework of a cascade-classifier approach. This point will be described and discussed in Section 3.

The classification results provided by the members of the considered pool of cascade classifiers are combined by using classical unsupervised multiple-classifier strategies [6-7]. In particular, in this paper we consider two widely used combination procedures: the *Majority Voting* and the *Bayesian Combination*.

3.   Partially Unsupervised Classification Techniques: A Cascade-Classifier Approach

The standard supervised cascade-classifier approach (proposed by Swain in 1978 [8]) exploits the correlation between multitemporal images in order to increase the classification accuracy in cases in which training data are available for all the images considered. In our approach, we extend the application of the standard supervised cascade-classifier approach to partially unsupervised classification problems.

The cascade-classifier decision strategy associates a generic pixel x_j^2 of the image X_2 with a land-cover class according to the following decision rule [8]:

$$l_j^2 = \omega_m \in \Omega \quad \text{if and only if}$$
$$P\left(\omega_m / x_j^1, x_j^2\right) = \max_{\omega_k \in \Omega}\left\{P\left(\omega_k / x_j^1, x_j^2\right)\right\} \tag{1}$$

where $P\left(\omega_k / x_j^1, x_j^2\right)$ is the value of the probability that the j-th pixel of the images belongs to the class ω_k at t_2, given the observations x_j^1 and x_j^2. Under the conventional assumption of class-conditional independence [8-9], the above decision rule can be rewritten as:

$$l_j^2 = \omega_m \in \Omega \qquad \text{if and only if}$$

$$\sum_{n=1}^{C} p\left(x_j^1 / \omega_n\right) p\left(x_j^2 / \omega_m\right) P\left(\omega_n, \omega_m\right) =$$

$$\max_{\omega_k \in \Omega}\left\{\sum_{n=1}^{C} p\left(x_j^1 / \omega_n\right) p\left(x_j^2 / \omega_k\right) P\left(\omega_n, \omega_k\right)\right\}$$

(2)

where $p\left(x_j^i / \omega_k\right)$ is the value of the conditional density function for the pixel x_j^i, given the class $\omega_k \in \Omega$, and $P\left(\omega_n, \omega_k\right)$ is the prior joint probability of the pair of classes (ω_n, ω_k). The latter term takes into account the temporal correlation between the two images.

We propose to integrate the partially unsupervised classification problem of the image $\mathbf{X}_2$ in the context of the above-described classification rule. Since the $\mathbf{Y}_2$ training set is not available, the density functions of classes at the time t_1 (i.e. $p(X_1 / \omega_n)$, $\omega_n \in \Omega$) are the only statistical terms of (2) that we can estimate in a supervised way. This means that, in order to accomplish the classification task, we must estimate both the density functions of classes at t_2 ($p(X_2 / \omega_k)$, $\omega_k \in \Omega$) and the joint class probabilities ($P\left(\omega_n, \omega_k\right)$, $\omega_n, \omega_k \in \Omega$) in an unsupervised way. It is worth noting that usually the estimation of $p(X_i / \omega_n)$ ($\omega_n \in \Omega$, $i=1,2$) involves the computation of a parameter vector ϑ. The number and nature of the vector components depends on the specific classifier used.

To carry out the unsupervised estimation process, we propose to adopt an estimation procedure based on the observation that, under the assumption of class-conditional independence over time, the joint density function of the images $\mathbf{X}_1$ and $\mathbf{X}_2$ ($p(X_1, X_2)$) can be described as a mixture density with C×C components (as many components as the possible pair of classes):

$$p\left(X_1, X_2\right) \cong \sum_{n=1}^{C} \sum_{m=1}^{C} p\left(X_1 / \omega_n\right) p\left(X_2 / \omega_m\right) P\left(\omega_n, \omega_m\right).$$

(3)

In this context, the estimation of the above terms becomes a mixture density estimation problem, which can be solved by applying the EM algorithm [10-12].

The specific procedure to be adopted for accomplishing the estimation process depends on the technique considered for carrying out the cascade classification, and in particular, on the vector of parameters ϑ required by the classifier. The possibility of establishing a relationship between the classifier parameters and the statistical terms involved in (2) is a basic constraint that each classification technique should satisfy in order to permit the use of (2). According to this requirement, we choose two suitable classification methods. The former is a parametric approach, based on the maximum-likelihood (ML) classifier [4]; the latter consists of a non-parametric technique based on radial basis function (RBF) neural networks [13]. The specific procedures for the partially unsupervised estimation of the parameters of ML and RBF classifiers are described in the following two sub-sections.

3.1 Maximum-Likelihood Cascade Classifier

Let us consider the problem of partially unsupervised cascade classification in the framework of ML classifiers. For simplicity, let us assume that the probability density function of each class can be described by a Gaussian distribution (i.e. by a mean vector μ and a covariance matrix Σ). Under this common assumption (widely adopted for multispectral image classification problems), the parameter vector of the classifier ϑ consists of the following components:

$$\vartheta = \left[\mu_1^2, \Sigma_1^2, P(\omega_1, \omega_1), ..., \mu_C^2, \Sigma_C^2, P(\omega_C, \omega_C) \right] \; . \tag{4}$$

By applying the EM algorithm we can derive the following iterative equations to estimate the parameters necessary to accomplish the cascade-classification process [3]:

$$\left[\mu_m^2 \right]^{t+1} = \frac{\sum_{j=1}^{I \times J} \left\{ \sum_{n=1}^{C} P^t\left(\omega_n, \omega_m / x_j^1, x_j^2 \right) \right\} x_j^2}{\sum_{j=1}^{I \times J} \left\{ \sum_{n=1}^{C} P^t\left(\omega_n, \omega_m / x_j^1, x_j^2 \right) \right\}} \tag{5}$$

$$\left[\Sigma_m^2 \right]^{t+1} = \frac{\sum_{j=1}^{I \times J} \left\{ \sum_{n=1}^{C} P^t\left(\omega_n, \omega_m / x_j^1, x_j^2 \right) \right\} \left\| x_j^2 - \left[\mu_m^2 \right]^t \right\|^2}{\sum_{j=1}^{I \times J} \left\{ \sum_{n=1}^{C} P^t\left(\omega_n, \omega_m / x_j^1, x_j^2 \right) \right\}} \tag{6}$$

$$P\left(\omega_n, \omega_m \right)^{t+1} = \frac{\sum_{j=1}^{I \times J} P^t\left(\omega_n, \omega_m / x_j^1, x_j^2 \right)}{I \times J} \tag{7}$$

where, the superscripts t and $t+1$ refer to the values of the parameters at the current and next iterations, respectively. The estimates of the parameters obtained at convergence and those achieved by the classical supervised procedure are then substituted into (2) in order to derive the required classification map.

Concerning the initialization of the considered statistical terms, we refer the reader to [3].

3.2   RBF Neural Network Cascade Classifier

The problem of partially unsupervised cascade classification with RBF neural networks is significantly more complex than the one associated with the ML parametric classifier. The increased complexity mainly depends on the non-parametric nature of RBF neural networks. In this context, the joint density function of the images X_1 and X_2 ($p(X_1, X_2)$) is described by a mixture composed of K and Q Gaussian kernels at t_1 and t_2, respectively (both K and Q are greater than C). Consequently equation (3) can be rewritten as:

$$p(X_1, X_2) \cong \sum_{n=1}^{C} \sum_{m=1}^{C} \sum_{k=1}^{K} \sum_{q=1}^{Q} p(X_1 / \varphi_k) p(X_2 / \varphi_q) P(\varphi_k, \varphi_q) P(\omega_n, \omega_m / \varphi_k, \varphi_q) .$$

(8)

Each gaussian function φ_i is described by its mean vector μ_i and by a width parameter σ_i. Consequently, the parameter vector of the classifier ϑ is composed of the following terms:

$$\vartheta = \left[\mu_1^2, \Sigma_1^2, ..., \mu_Q^2, \Sigma_Q^2, P(\varphi_1^1, \varphi_1^2), ..., P(\varphi_K^1, \varphi_Q^2), P(\omega_1, \omega_1 / \varphi_1, \varphi_1), ..., P(\omega_C, \omega_C / \varphi_K, \varphi_Q) \right] .$$

(9)

By applying the EM algorithm we can derive the following iterative equations to estimate the required parameters:

$$\left[\mu_q^2 \right]^{t+1} = \frac{\sum_{j=1}^{I \times J} \left\{ \sum_{k=1}^{K} P'(\varphi_k, \varphi_q / x_j^1, x_j^2) \right\} x_j^2}{\sum_{j=1}^{I \times J} \left\{ \sum_{k=1}^{K} P'(\varphi_k, \varphi_q / x_j^1, x_j^2) \right\}}$$

(10)

$$\left[\sigma_q^2 \right]^{t+1} = \frac{\sum_{j=1}^{I \times J} \left\{ \sum_{k=1}^{K} P'(\varphi_k, \varphi_q / x_j^1, x_j^2) \right\} \left\| x_j^2 - \left[\mu_q^2 \right]' \right\|^2}{I \times J \times d}$$

(11)

$$P(\varphi_k, \varphi_q)^{t+1} = \frac{\sum_{j=1}^{I \times J} P'(\varphi_k, \varphi_q / x_j^1, x_j^2)}{I \times J}$$

(12)

where d is the dimensionality of the input space, and the superscripts t and $t+1$ refer to the values of the parameters at the current and next iterations, respectively. Although the parameters μ_q^2, σ_q^2 $P(\varphi_k, \varphi_q)$ of the vector ϑ can be estimated in a fully unsupervised way, the estimation of the joint conditional probabilities $P(\omega_n, \omega_m / \varphi_k, \varphi_q)$ requires additional information. In this context, we propose to exploit some of the information obtained at the convergence from the ML cascade classifier. In particular, a set $\hat{Y}_2$ of pixels, composed of the patterns that are most likely correctly categorized by the ML cascade classifier, is used for the initialization of the $P(\omega_n, \omega_m / \varphi_k, \varphi_q)$ conditional probabilities. Let $Y_{l,n}$ be the pixels of the training set Y_l that belong to land-cover class ω_n. Similarly, let $\hat{Y}_{2,m}$ be the sub-set of pixels of $\hat{Y}_2$ categorized by the ML cascade classifier as belonging to class ω_m. The iterative equation to be used for estimating the joint probabilities $P(\omega_n, \omega_m / \varphi_k, \varphi_q)$ is the following:

$$P^{l+1}\left(\omega_n,\omega_m/\varphi_k,\varphi_q\right)=\frac{\displaystyle\sum_{x_i^1\in Y_{1,n}}\sum_{x_j^2\in \hat{Y}_{2,m}} P^l\left(\varphi_k,\varphi_q/x_j^1,x_j^2\right)}{\displaystyle\sum_{x_i^1\in Y_1}\sum_{x_j^2\in \hat{Y}_2} P^l\left(\varphi_k,\varphi_q/x_j^1,x_j^2\right)}+$$

$$+\frac{\displaystyle\sum_{x_i^1\in Y_{1,n}}\sum_{x_j^2\in \hat{Y}_2}\sum_{i=1}^{C} P^l\left(\omega_i,\omega_m/\varphi_k,\varphi_q\right)P^l\left(\varphi_k,\varphi_q/x_j^1,x_j^2\right)}{\displaystyle\sum_{x_i^1\in Y_1}\sum_{x_j^2\notin \hat{Y}_2} P^l\left(\varphi_k,\varphi_q/x_j^1,x_j^2\right)}+$$

$$+\frac{\displaystyle\sum_{x_i^1\in Y_1}\sum_{x_j^2\in \hat{Y}_{2,m}}\sum_{i=1}^{C} P^l\left(\omega_n,\omega_i/\varphi_k,\varphi_q\right)P^l\left(\varphi_k,\varphi_q/x_j^1,x_j^2\right)}{\displaystyle\sum_{x_i^1\in Y_1}\sum_{x_j^2\in \hat{Y}_2} P^l\left(\varphi_k,\varphi_q/x_j^1,x_j^2\right)}. \tag{13}$$

As for the previous cascade classifier based on the ML technique, the estimates of the parameters obtained at convergence and those achieved by the classical supervised procedure are then used to accomplish the cascade classification.

4.   A Strategy for Generating Ensembles of Cascade-Classifier Algorithms

The selection of the pool of classifiers to be integrated into the multiple-classifier architecture is an important and critical task. In the literature, several different strategies for defining the classifier ensemble have been proposed [6-7], [14-15]. From a theoretical view point, a necessary and sufficient condition for an ensemble of classifiers to be more accurate than any of its individual members is that classifiers are accurate and diverse [16]. In our case, we can control only the second condition, since no training set is available to verify the first one. However, it is reasonable to assume that the majority of unsupervised cascade classifiers of the ensemble are sufficiently accurate. The main issue that remains to be solved for the definition of the ensemble concerns the capability of different classifiers to incur in uncorrelated errors. In our system, the choice of both parametric (ML) and a non-parametric (RBF) classifiers guarantees the use of two classification algorithms based on significantly different principles. For this reason, we expect these classifiers incur in quite uncorrelated errors. However, two classification algorithms are not sufficient to define an effective multiple classifier architecture. This issue is more critical in our specific problem, where we cannot test the accuracy of each member of the ensemble. Therefore, the probability that the partially unsupervised estimation procedures result in classifiers affected by a significant error rate is higher than in the standard supervised case. Consequently, to increase the reliability of the system, we need to generate a pool of N classifiers, with N>2. According to the literature, we can define different RBF architectures in order to define different classification algorithms for the ensemble [17]. However, since we are dealing with cascade-classifier approaches, we propose to use an alternative, deterministic, and simple strategy for defining the ensemble. This strategy is based on our classifier peculiarities. In particular, in the case of cascade classifiers, one set of key parameters estimated in the partially unsupervised process is composed of the joint class probabilities $P(\omega_n, \omega_k)$, which are associated with the temporal correlation between classes. The different classifiers (i.e. ML and RBF) perform different estimations of the aforementioned probabilities, on the basis of the different classification and estimation principles. For this reason, we propose to introduce in the ensemble classifiers obtained by exchanging the estimates of the prior joint probabilities of classes performed by different algorithms. In this way, we merge the parameters estimated with different procedures in order to obtain different classifier configurations. In our case, given an ML and an RBF cascade classifiers, this strategy results in an ensemble composed of the two "original" classifiers and two additional ML and RBF algorithms obtained by exchanging the prior joint probabilities estimated in a partially unsupervised way by the original classifiers. This involves a multiple classifier architecture composed of four classifiers. It is possible to further increase the number of classifiers by extending the aforementioned procedure to a case with more RBF neural network architectures.

5.   Experimental Results

To assess the effectiveness of the proposed approach, different experiments were carried out on a data set made up of two multispectral images acquired by the Thematic Mapper (TM) sensor of the Landsat 5 satellite. The selected test site was a section (412×382 pixels) of a scene including Lake Mulargias on the Island of Sardinia, Italy. The two images used in the experiments were acquired in September 1995 (t_1) and July 1996 (t_2). The available ground truth was used to derive a training set and a test set for each image. Five land-cover classes (i.e., urban area, forest, pasture, water, vineyard), which characterise the test site at the above-mentioned dates, were considered (see [2] for a detailed description of the data set composition). To carry out the experiments, we assumed that only the training set associated with the image acquired in September 1995 was available.

An ML and an RBF neural network cascade classifiers (with 50 hidden neurons) were applied to the September 1995 and July 1996 images. For the ML classifier, the assumption of Gaussian distributions was made for the density functions of classes (this was a reasonable assumption, as we considered TM images). In order to exploit the non-parametric characteristic of the RBF neural classifier, 5 texture features based on the Gray-Level Co-occurence matrix [18] were given as input to this classifier in addition to the 6 TM channels. From the considered ML and RBF cascade classifiers, other two classifiers were generated by exchanging the prior joint probabilities of classes according to the strategy described in Section 4. The classification accuracies exhibited by the four considered partially unsupervised cascade classifiers on the July 1996 test set are reported in Table 1.

Table 1. Classification accuracy exhibited by the four partially unsupervised cascade classifiers included in the proposed multiple classifier architecture (July 1996 test set)

Land cover class	Classification accuracy (%)			
	ML	RBF	ML with joint probabilities computed by RBF	RBF with joint probabilities computed by ML
Pasture	87.6	97.8	85.9	96.5
Forest	97.4	96.0	97.4	96.4
Urban area	94.4	97.9	94.2	97.7
Water	100.0	100.0	100.0	100.0
Vineyard	64.9	83.0	62.3	88.1
Overall	92.6	97.3	91.8	97.2

At this point, the four classifiers were combined by using both the majority voting and the Bayesian combination strategies. The overall accuracies obtained are given in Table 2, where the accuracies exhibited by the multiple classifier system proposed in [1] are also reported. By a comparison of Table 1 and 2, one can conclude that the classification accuracies provided by the considered ensemble of partially unsupervised cascade classifiers are higher than both those obtained by the single classifiers composing the ensemble and those yielded by our previous system.

6.   Conclusions

In this paper a multiple-classifier system for a partially unsupervised updating of land-cover maps has been proposed. The main features of the proposed system are the following: i) capability to exploit temporal correlation between multitemporal images; ii) capability to consider multisensor/multisource data in the process of updating of land-cover maps (thanks to the availability of non-parametric classification algorithms in the ensemble); iii) capability to easily define the multiple-classifier architecture to be adopted. In the experiments we carried out, the proposed multiple classifier system revealed effective, providing classification accuracies higher that those exhibited by both the single partially unsupervised cascade classifiers composing the ensemble and the classification system presented in [1].

The future developments of this work are now addressed in two different directions: i) to extend the partially unsupervised cascade-classification approach to other kind of

Table 2. Overall classification accuracies exhibited by the proposed multiple classifier system and by the system presented in [1]

Proposed system		System proposed in [1]	
Bayesian combination	Majority rule	Bayesian combination	Majority rule
98.0%	97.8%	96.5%	96.4%

classification techniques; ii) to study from a theoretical perspective the problem of the ensemble definition in presence of cascade-classification algorithms.

References

1. Bruzzone, L., Cossu, R., Fernàndez Prieto, D.: Combining parametric and non-parametric classifiers for an unsupervised updating of land-cover maps. Proc. of the First International Workshop on Multiple Classifier Systems, Cagliari, Italy (2000) 290-299.
2. Bruzzone, L., Fernàndez Prieto, D.: Unsupervised retraining of a maximum-likelihood classifier for the analysis of multitemporal remote-sensing images. IEEE Transactions on Geoscience and Remote Sensing **39** (2001), in press.
3. Bruzzone, L., Fernàndez Prieto, D.: A partially unsupervised approach to the automatic classification of multitemporal remote sensing images. Proc. of the First International Workshop on Pattern Recognition in Remote Sensing, Andorra, (2000) 62-66.
4. Richards. J. A.: Remote sensing digital image analysis, 2nd edn. Springer-Verlag, New York (1993).
5. Kittler, J., Hojjatoleslami, A., Windeatt, T.: Strategies for combining classifiers employing shared and distinct pattern representations, Pattern Recognition Letters **18** (1997) 1373-1377.
6. Lam, L., Suen, C. Y.: Application of majority voting to pattern recognition: An analysis of its behavior and performance. IEEE Transactions on System, man and Cybernetics **27** (1997) 553-568.
7. Kittler, J., Hatef, M., Duin, R.P.W., Mates, J.: On combining classifiers. IEEE Transactions on pattern Analysis and machine Inteligence **20** (1998) 126-239.
8. Swain, P.H.: Bayesian classification in time-varying environment. IEEE Transactions on System, man and Cybernetics **8** (1978) 880-883.
9. Bruzzone, L., Serpico, S.B.: An iterative technique for the detection of land-cover transitions in multitemporal remote-sensing images. IEEE Transactions on Geoscience and Remote Sensing **35** (1997), 858-867.
10. Dempster, A. P., Laird, N.M., Rubin, D.B.: Maximum likelihood from incomplete data via the EM algorithm. Journal of Royal Statistic. Soc. **39** (1977) 1-38.
11. Shahshahani B.M., Landgrebe, D.: The effect of unlabeled samples in reducing the small sample size problem and mitigating the Hughes phenomenon. IEEE Transactions on Geoscience and Remote-Sensing. **32** (1994) 1087-1095.
12. Bruzzone, L., Fernàndez Prieto, D., Serpico, S. B.: A neural statistical approach to multitemporal and multisource remote-sensing image classification. IEEE Transactions on Geoscience and Remote Sensing **37** (1999) 1350-1359.
13. Bruzzone, L., Fernàndez Prieto, D.: A technique for the selection of kernel-function parameters in RBF neural networks for classification of remote-sensing images. IEEE Transactions on Geoscience and Remote-Sensing **37** (1999) 1179-1184.
14. Benediktsson, J. A., Swain, P. H.: Consensus theoretic classification methods. IEEE Transactions on Systems, Man and Cybernetics, **22** (1992) 688-704.
15. Benediktsson, J. A., Sveinsson, J. R., Ersoy, O. K., Swain, P. H.: Parallel consensual neural Networks. IEEE Transactions on Neural Networks **8** (1997) 54-64.
16. Dietterich T.G.: Ensemble methods in machine learning. Proc. of the First International Workshop on Multiple Classifier Systems, Cagliari, Italy (2000) 1-15.
17. Sharkey, A.J.C., Sharkey, N.E., Gerecke, U., Chandroth, G.O.: The "test and select" approach to ensemble combination. Proc. of the First International Workshop on Multiple Classifier Systems, Cagliari, Italy (2000) 30-44.
18. Haralick R. M., Shanmugan K., and Dinstein I.: Textural features for image classification. IEEE Transactions on System, man and Cybernetics **3** (1993) 610-621.

Combining Supervised Remote Sensing Image Classifiers Based on Individual Class Performances

Paul C. Smits

Space Applications Institute, Joint Research Centre, TP262, I-21020 Ispra (VA), Italy
paul.smits@jrc.it

Abstract. This article focuses on the use of multiple classifier systems (MCSs) based on dynamic classifier selection. Four implementation strategies of MCSs are compared: majority voting, belief networks, and two designs based on dynamic classifier selection. Experimental results indicate that the direction taken by Woods *et al.* [1] is the best alternative for remote sensing applications for which the classifier-dependent posterior distributions are unknown.

1 Introduction

In remote sensing image data interpretation, there are two main categories of error. The first category is the labeling inconsistencies, which regards the representativeness of the training (and test) data and is due to mixed pixels (class overlap), transition zones, dynamic zones, within-class variability (covariance), limited training data, and topographic shading, just to name a few. In fact, it is due to these factors that the supervised classification of remote sensing images distinguishes itself from many other pattern recognition application domains: the physical parameters with which ground information is collected is often fundamentally different from the physical parameters collected by the sensor. For instance, when a human observer collects ground information for multspectral, hyperspectral, or microwave imagery, criteria are used that are not optimized for the natural clusters that characterize the data. This type of error is difficult to quantify.

The second type of error, the classification-induced error, can be reduced using carefully defined classes and number of classes, classification schemes, and the choice of the feature vector.

The subjectivity inherent in the training and testing of remote sensing image classifiers is widely recognized [2],[3]. The subjectivity is further amplified by the fact that training and test data are expensive, which poses limits on the quantity and sometimes on the quality of the training data.

Nowadays, classifiers are understood well enough to reproduce virtually any decision space in the feature space of a data set, reducing considerably the influence of the classification induced error. In this paper it is maintained that the main power of the application of Multiple Classifier Systems (MCSs) to remote sensing image classification is to reduce the influence of the first type of error mentioned above, namely the

J. Kittler and F. Roli (Eds.): MCS 2001, LNCS 2096, pp. 269–278, 2001.

labeling inconsistencies. It should be noted that if the classes separate well in the feature space, all classifiers should return the same result, and applying an MCS is not likely to be of any benefit.

The are two basic approaches to MCS design [1]: classifier fusion and dynamic classifier selection. The former approach combines in parallel the outputs of the classifiers in order to achieve some kind of "group consensus." The latter attempts to predict which single classifier is most likely to be correct for a given sample.

Many realizations of MCSs exploit the posterior probability of the classifiers rather than the classification results themselves. Examples include the consensus theory which uses the source-specific posterior probability [4], and the combination of the Bayesian average [5],[6].

In operational remote sensing, Bayesian classification methods are not frequently used, and a-posteriori probabilities are often rough estimations [4]. Huang and Suen [7] argue that the research on classifiers that output a unique class label indicating that this class has the highest probability to which the object belongs, will become most important in handwriting recognition. We feel that a similar statement would hold good for the field of remote sensing.

In this article the attention is focused on the category of MCSs that allow to combine different classification results and their respective confusion matrices, however without precise knowledge about the classifier-specific posterior probability. The aim of this article is to investigate the thesis that for remote sensing applications, MCSs using individual class performances are the most appropriate if no estimates of the a-posteriori probability are available. The novelty of the article is that it compares four different MCS design strategies using publicly available remote sensing data sets. The MCSs compared are based on: 1) the majority rule; 2) belief functions; 3) dynamic classifier selection by simple partitioning (DCS-SP); and 4) dynamic classifier selection by local accuracy (DCS-LA).

This paper is organized as follows. Section 2 focuses on previous work done in the field of MCSs based on individual classifier behavior, and explains briefly the four MCSs mentioned in the previous paragraph. Section 3 reports results on real-world data. Section 4 provides a discussion and draws the conclusions based on the experiments.

For more generic reviews on multiple classifier systems and combining classifiers the reader is referred to [8] and [9].

2 MCSs Based on Individual Classifier Behavior

Let Z be the object to be assigned to one of the M possible classes $\{\omega_1,...,\omega_M\}$. Assume that we have K classifiers each representing the given object by a feature vector $\overline{X}_k$, $k = 1, ..., K$. The output of classifier k assigned to feature vector $\overline{X}_k$ is denoted by $C_k(\overline{X}_k)$. In the measurement space each class ω_m is modeled by the probability density function $p(\overline{X}_k \mid \omega_m)$ and its *a-priori* probability of occurrence is denoted by $P(\omega_m)$.

It is widely agreed that the best possible way to assign class labels is according to the Bayesian theory [10]. This holds good for individual classifiers as well as for MCSs. Given the measurements $\overline{X}_k$, $k = 1, ..., K$, the object should be assigned to class ω_m, provided the a posteriori probability of that interpretation is maximum:

$$P\left(\theta = \omega_n \mid \overline{X}_1, ..., \overline{X}_K\right) = \max_m \left\{P\left(\theta = \omega_m \mid \overline{X}_1, ..., \overline{X}_K\right)\right\} \Rightarrow \theta \rightarrow \omega_n \tag{1}$$

The underlying hypothesis of using individual classifier behavior in the MCS design is that every classifier has characteristics justifying its participation in the MCS. If a for the data set under analysis very good classifier is applied (e.g., one based on the maximum a-posteriori [MAP] criterion with appropriate knowledge built-in) in combination with mediocre classifier (e.g., a minimum distance to class mean [MD] criterion), the result of the MCS is not likely to improve the MAP criterion.

The most straightforward way of exploiting the individual class performances of the combined classifiers is by means of dynamic classifier selection. Based on some method of partitioning the input samples, it is predicted which single classifier is most likely to be correct for a given sample. An example is partitioning by the set of individual classifier decisions [7], which we will refer to as dynamic classifier selection by simple partitioning (DCS-SP). In this case the feature space is partitioned based on the global performance of a classifier on the individual classes.

Another important means of MCS design exploiting the knowledge of the decisions made by classifiers on individual classes is based on belief functions. Belief functions often derive this knowledge from the confusion matrix computed from the training data [8]. Let $P\left(\theta = \omega_m \mid C_k\left(\overline{X}_k\right)\right)$ be the probabilities estimated from the confusion matrix. Then the belief function for class label ω_n becomes:

$$bel\left(\theta = \omega_n\right) = \eta \prod_{k=1}^{K} P\left(\theta = \omega_m \mid C_k\left(\overline{X}_k\right)\right) \tag{2}$$

where η is a normalizing constant ensuring that $\sum_{m=1}^{M} bel\left(\theta = \omega_m\right) = 1$. Then the MCS assigns the class label with the highest belief value.

In [1], an MCS is presented that uses estimates of each individual classifier's local accuracy in small regions of feature space surrounding an unknown test sample. The method, called Dynamic Classifier Selection by Local Accuracy (DCS-LA), considers only the output of the most locally accurate classifier. The local regions are defined in terms of the K-nearest neighbors in the training data. The best results were obtained by using the percentage of the local class accuracy as performance measure.

In the next section the performance of the different MCSs described above will be compared. Table 1 summarizes the MCSs.

Table 1. Overview of the MCSs used in the experiments.

MCS short name	Description	References
Majority rule	MCS based on the simple majority rule	Giacinto *et al.* [6]
Belief function	Based on belief functions created from the confusion matrix (from training set); implements equation (2)	Xu *et al.* [8]
DCS-SP	Dynamic Classifier Selection by Simple Partitioning. Uses the average class accuracy to assign each classifier to a class (see table 2)	Huang and Suen [7]
DCS-LA	Checks the individual class assignment of the 10 nearest samples, and selects the output of the locally most accurate classifier.	Woods *et al.* [1]

3 Experiments

The main aim of the experiments is to evaluate the different design strategies based on dynamic classifier selection and to compare these approaches to the much-used MCSs based on majority voting, and on belief functions.

Two publicly available data sets are used. Data set A is a multi-sensor, multi-spectral data set, and data set B is a hyperspectral data set. For each data set, different statistical classifiers are defined and combined in the different MCSs design strategies.

The performance of all classifiers and MCSs are measured by three parameters: the minimum accuracy, the maximum accuracy, and the kappa value.

3.1 Data Set A

3.1.1 Data Set Description
Data set A consists of Airborne Thematic Mapper imagery, co-registered with NASA/JPL synthetic aperture radar imagery, acquired over the agricultural area of Feltwell (UK). The images, 15 in total, are filtered and normalized. The set was first used in [11] and [12], and later in [6]. The data set contains training and test pixels (5124 and 5820 pixels, respectively). In the following, the different bands of this data set are identified by the letter b (band) and an index.

3.1.2 Classifier Definition
Four classifiers are build, all based on statistical image models and therefore with the lowest possible design complexity. Classifiers A.1-A.4 relate to data set A.. *Classifier A.1*: Maximum likelihood (ML) classifier. The features used in classifier A.1 are selected by a feature subset selection based on the ML criterion and a maximum allowed

mean error on the training data of 0.10 [13]. The feature subset selection based on the training pixels of data set A resulted in a feature vector of four features: $\overline{X}_i^{A.1} = [b_{12} \quad b_6 \quad b_5 \quad b_2]_i^T$, where $\overline{X}_i^{A.1}$ is the feature vector for classifier 1 at pixel i, b denotes the indexed band number, and T the transpose. *Classifier A.2*: Maximum likelihood (ML) classifier. The features used in classifier A.2 are selected by a feature subset selection based on the criterion proposed by Fukunaga ([15], equation 10.5); a maximum of five features was allowed. With these constraints, the feature subset selection based on the training pixels of data set A resulted in the feature $\overline{X}_i^{A.2} = [b_6 \quad b_{11} \quad b_3 \quad b_5 \quad b_{14}]_i^T$, where $\overline{X}_i^{A.2}$ is the feature vector for classifier A.2 at pixel i. *Classifier A.3*: Minimum distance to class mean (MD) classifier. The features used in classifier A.3 are selected by a feature subset selection based on the divergence criterion [15]; again, a maximum of five features was allowed. Based on the training data in data set A, this resulted in the feature subset $\overline{X}_i^{A.3} = [b_{13} \quad b_{15} \quad b_7 \quad b_8 \quad b_{14}]_i^T$, where $\overline{X}_i^{A.3}$ is the feature vector for classifier A.3 at pixel i. *Classifier A.4*: Classifier A.4 is based on maximum a-posteriori probability (MAP) implemented in a Markov random field (MRF) framework, as described in [16]. The features used in this classifier are the same as those used in classifier 1: $\overline{X}_i^{A.4} = [b_{12} \quad b_6 \quad b_5 \quad b_2]_i^T$, i.e., the image model is identical to the class conditional density functions defined by the ML approach. The settings of the MRF-MAP approach are: $\beta = 2.5$, a second order neighborhood system is used for the definition of the clique interactions, and a stochastic energy optimization is used with 300 iterations.

3.1.3 Definition of the MCSs

Table 1 summarizes the MCSs that have been implemented and tested. The Belief functions are created based on the confusion matrices of the individual classifiers applied to the training data set.

The DCS-SP approach is implemented based on the best classifier for each class. Table 2 gives an overview the classifier selected for each of the five classes, based on the classifier performance on the training data. Note that classifier A.1 is never selected in this approach.

For the DCS-LA algorithm, the Euclidean distance metric has been used. Note that the DCS-LA algorithm is applied only when classifiers do not agree. The number of nearest neighbors that are used in the DFC-LA algorithm is 10 [1].

3.1.4 Results

Table 3 reports the performances of the four individual classifiers on data set A. The MRF-MAP approach gives the best results in terms of maximum accuracy and kappa value. Table 4 shows the confusion matrix for classifier 4. It is interesting to note that, although relatively simple statistical classifiers have been used (the design complexity [6] was 1 for all classifiers), good results have been obtained. Three of the four classifiers on data set A have a maximum accuracy higher than the best classifier in [6].

Table 2. Example of the selection of best classifier for each partition for use in the DCS-SP approach, based on the training class accuracies of data set A.

Class 1		Class 2		Class 3		Class 4		Class 5	
P(O in 1|C1=1)	0.94	P(O in 2|C1=2)	0.84	P(O in 3|C1=3)	0.65	P(O in 4|C1=4)	0.92	P(O in 5|C1=5)	0.89
P(O in 1|C2=1)	0.95	P(O in 2|C2=2)	0.82	P(O in 3|C2=3)	0.71	P(O in 4|C2=4)	0.92	P(O in 5|C2=5)	0.92
P(O in 1|C3=1)	0.76	P(O in 2|C3=2)	0.33	P(O in |C3=3)	0.28	P(O in 4|C3=4)	0.76	P(O in 5|C3=5)	0.54
P(O in 1|C4=1)	0.92	P(O in 2|C4=2)	0.85	P(O in 3|C4=3)	0.62	P(O in 4|C4=4)	0.93	P(O in 5|C4=5)	0.93

Table 3. Summary of the test set accuracies (user's accuracies) and kappa values of the four classifiers. The best performances of data set A the are underlined.

Classifier	Minimum accuracy (%)	Maximum accuracy (%)	Kappa
A.1	70.4	94.9	0.860
A.2	76.6	94.9	0.865
A.3	16.1	70.8	0.446
A.4	69.5	96.4	0.868

Table 5 summarizes the results of the MCSs. The DCS-SP method outperforms the other MCSs in terms of maximum accuracy, but its minimum accuracy and kappa value are outperformed by the DCS-LA approach. Note that both the majority rule and the DCS-LA approaches outperform the minimum accuracy and kappa value of the MRF-MAP labeling. Comparing the confusion matrix of the DCS-LA result (Table 6) with the confusion matrix of the best individual classifier (Table 4), one can see that the user's accuracy of the weakest class (class 3) is improved by more than 10 points. From the results on data set A we may conclude that the DCS-LA approach is the best for the combination of classifiers A.1-A.4.

Table 4. Confusion matrix of classifier A.4 (MRF-MAP on data set A).

	1.	2.	3.	4.	5.	Sum	User's accuracy
Class 1.	1945	45	4	22	1	2017	96.4
Class 2.	24	1160	166	5	0	1355	85.6
Class 3.	21	90	381	56	0	548	69.5
Class 4.	34	17	8	783	35	877	89.3
Class 5.	30	13	0	9	911	963	94.6
Sum	2054	1325	559	875	947	5760	
Prod. accuracy	94.7	87.6	68.2	89.5	96.2		

Table 5. The performances of the MCSs on the test set A.

MCS	min. accuracy [%]	max. accuracy [%]	Kappa [.]
Majority rule	76.6	95.3	0.870
Belief functions	59.7	95.1	0.853
DCS-SP	69.9	95.9	0.861
DCS-LA	81.4	95.1	0.873

Table 6. Confusion matrix of the DCS-LA result, based on input from classifiers A.1-A.4.

	1.	2.	3.	4.	5.	Sum	User's accuracy
Class 1.	1919	55	3	34	6	2017	95.1
Class 2.	8	1175	162	7	3	1355	86.7
Class 3.	20	23	446	57	2	548	81.4
Class 4.	31	21	8	785	32	877	89.5
Class 5.	36	20	0	29	878	963	91.2
Sum	2014	1294	619	912	921	5760	
Producer's accuracy	95.3	90.8	72.1	86.1	95.3		

3.2 Data Set B

3.2.1 Data Set Description

Data set B is the hyperspectral data set that comes with the documentation of the publicly available application software MultiSpec [17]. It consists of 220 bands, and the ground truth samples of 16 classes. For the experiments reported here, the ground truth samples have been split in a training and a test set.

3.2.2 Classifier Definition

Classifier B.1: Maximum likelihood (ML) classifier. The features used in classifier B.1 are selected by a feature subset selection based on the ML criterion and a maximum allowed mean error on the training data of 0.15. This feature subset selection, based on the training pixels of data set B, resulted in a feature vector of 14 features, corresponding to bands 143, 168, 29, 71, 35, 16, 42, 198, 31, 60, 20, 123, 133, and 131. *Classifier B.2*: Maximum likelihood (ML) classifier. The features used in classifier B.2 are selected by a feature subset selection based on the criterion proposed by Fukunaga ([16], equation 10.5); a maximum of 13 features was allowed. With these constraints, the feature subset selection based on the training pixels of data set B resulted in a feature vector with bands 167, 10, 102, 140, 181, 41, 52, 37, 122, 17, 60, 29, 142. *Classifier B.3*: Like classifier A.4, classifier B.4 is based on the MRF-MAP approach. The features used in this classifier are the same as those used in classifier B.1. The settings of the MRF-MAP approach are: $\beta = 2.5$, a second order neighbourhood system is used for the definition of the clique interactions, and a stochastic energy optimization is used with 300 iterations.

3.2.3 Definition of the MCSs

On data set B, the two best MCSs identified in subsection 3.1 are compared: the majority voting approach, and the DCS-LA approach (see Table 1). Both MCSs use the three classifiers B.1-B3.

Like the DCS-LA used on classifiers A.1-A.4, the DCS-LA uses 10 samples to determine the locally most accurate classifier.

3.2.4 Results Set B

Table 7 reports the performances of the four individual classifiers on data set B. Also here, the MRF-MAP approach gives the best results.

Table 8 summarizes the results of the MCS based on the majority rule and on the DCS-LA approach.

In the case of data set B the minimum accuracy does not change when combining the classifiers. This is due to the very low number of test pixels available for class 9 (see also the confusion matrix in Table 9). For data set B the kappa value is considered more relevant.

Table 7. Summary of the test set user's accuracies and kappa values of the four classifiers defined for data set B. The best performances of data set B are underlined.

Classifier	Minimum accuracy (%)	Maximum accuracy (%)	Kappa
B.1	33.3	100.0	0.765
B.2	33.3	99.3	0.715
B.3	33.3	100.0	0.877

Table 8. The performances of the MCSs on the test set B based on B.1, B.2, and B.3. The DCS-LA computes the distance measure from the bands that are used in B.1-B.3.

MCS	min. accuracy [%]	max. accuracy [%]	Kappa [.]
Majority rule	33.3	100.0	0.829
DCS-LA 220	33.3	100.0	0.847

4 Discussion and Conclusions

MCSs are used to approach better an ideal Bayesian classifier than the individual classifiers applied separately. It is widely agreed upon that Bayesian, MAP labeling of images provides the most powerful approach to image analysis currently available [10]. The only way in which this approach can be improved is by incorporating application-specific, prior knowledge into the analysis problem. This knowledge can take various forms, and the use of data fusion principles that incorporate existing and previously computed information with newly acquired data in a Bayesian framework seems to be the most promising direction to continue.

Here, it is felt that MCS have the potential to approach the MAP approach in absence of precise prior knowledge. In this paper MCS design strategies based on majority voting, belief networks, DCS-SP, and DCS-LA were compared. The experiments reported in this paper indicate that the DCS-LA described by Woods *et al.* [1] is the preferred one among the tested MCS design strategies. However, better benchmarking is desired to confirm these findings.

Also, it should be noted that DCS-LA needs about 12 minutes for the Feltwell data set on a 450 MHz personal computer, against less than a second for Majority rule or the Belief networks. Users should therefore be aware that the improvement in accuracy may have a considerable price in terms of computing time.

Acknowledgements. The Feltwell data set (data set A) was kindly made available by Prof. F. Roli, University of Cagliari, Italy, and can be downloaded as the Electronic Annex of [6], and from the web page Geoscience and Remote Sensing Society's Data Fusion Committee (http://www.dfc-grss.org). The hyperspectral data set B is publicly available online via http://dynamo.ecn.purdue.edu/~biehl/MultiSpec/. Part of the results have been generated with the freely available software application program Resima (http://www.resima.com/).

Table 9. Confusion matrix of the DCS-LA result, based on input from classifiers B.1, B.2, B.3.

Class	1	2	3	4	5	6	7	8	9	10	11	12	13	14	15	16	Total	Accuracy
1	12	0	0	0	0	0	0	11	0	0	0	0	0	0	0	0	23	52
2	0	447	46	4	1	0	0	0	0	36	67	7	0	0	0	1	609	73
3	3	11	361	42	0	0	0	0	0	0	6	22	0	0	0	0	445	81
4	0	2	5	87	0	0	0	0	0	0	1	0	0	0	0	0	95	92
5	7	0	0	0	245	0	0	0	0	0	0	1	0	0	3	0	256	96
6	0	0	0	0	4	322	0	0	0	1	0	0	0	2	11	0	340	95
7	0	0	0	0	1	0	11	6	0	0	0	0	0	0	0	0	18	61
8	0	0	0	0	0	0	0	294	0	0	0	0	0	0	0	0	294	100
9	0	0	0	1	1	0	0	0	2	0	0	0	0	0	2	0	6	33
10	2	9	4	1	1	1	0	0	0	313	53	2	0	0	0	0	386	81
11	5	45	11	0	6	0	0	0	0	9	1033	125	0	0	1	0	1235	84
12	0	3	5	9	2	0	0	0	0	3	4	272	0	0	0	2	300	91
13	0	0	0	0	0	0	0	0	0	0	0	0	120	0	0	0	120	100
14	0	0	0	0	2	0	0	0	0	0	0	0	0	761	38	0	801	95
15	4	0	0	0	2	3	0	0	0	0	1	2	1	1	29	181	224	81
16	0	3	0	0	0	0	0	0	0	0	1	4	0	0	1	39	48	81
T.	33	520	432	144	265	326	11	311	2	363	1167	434	121	792	237	42		
A.	36	86	84	60	93	99	100	95	100	86	89	63	99	96	76	93		

Interested readers may contact the author for the software (Visual C++ project) that implements the MCSs discussed in this paper.

References

1. Woods K., Kevin Bowyer, W.P. Kegelmeyer, "Combination of Multiple Classifiers Using Local Accuracy Estimates", IEEE Trans. PAMI, vol. 19, no. 4, April 1997, pp. 405-410.
2. R. A. Schowengerdt, Remote Sensing - Models and methods for image processing, Academic Press, 1997.
3. Smits P.C., S.G. Dellepiane, and R. Schowengerdt, 1999. "Quality assessment of image classification algorithms for land-cover mapping: a review and a proposal for a cost-based approach," Int. Journal of Remote Sensing, 20 (8), pp. 1461-1486.
4. J.A. Benediktsson and I. Kanellopoulos, 1999. "Classification of multisource and hyperspectral data based on decision fusion". IEEE Transactions on Geoscience and Remote Sensing, Vol. 37, No. 3, May 1999, pp. 1367-1377.
5. Kittler, J., A. Hojjatoleslami, T. Windeatt, 1997. "Strategies for combining classifiers employing shared and distinct pattern representations," Pattern Recognition Letters, 18, pp. 1373-1377.
6. Giacinto G., F. Roli and L. Bruzzone, 2000. "Combination of neural and statistical algorithms for supervised classification of remote-sensing images," Pattern Recognition Letters, 21 (5) pp. 385-397. Electronic Annex on-line. http://www.elsevier.nl/locate/patrec.
7. Huang, Y.S., and Suen, C.Y, 1995. A method of combining multiple experts for the recognition of unconstraint handwritten numerals. IEEE Trans. Pattern Anal. Machine Intell., 17 (1), 90-94.
8. L. Xu, A. Kryzak, and C.Y. Suen, "Methods of combining multiple classifiers and their applications to handwriting recognition," IEEE Trans. Systems, Man, and Cybernetics, vol. 22, no. 3, pp. 418-435, May/June 1992.
9. Ho, T.K., Hull, J.J., Srihari, S.N., 1994. Decision combination in multiple classifier systems. IEEE Trans. Pattern Anal. Machine Intell. 16 (1), 66-75.
10. Oliver C. and S. Quegan 1998. " Understanding Synthetic Aperture Radar Images". SciTech Publishing .
12. Serpico S.B., L. Bruzzone and F. Roli, 1996. "An experimental comparison of neural and statistical non-parametric algorithms for supervised classification of remote-sensing images," Pattern Recognition Letters, 17 (13), pp. 1331-1341.
13. Smits P.C., 2000. "On the concepts of relevance and sufficiency in feature subset selection." In: Proceedings of the first workshop on Pattern Recognition in Remote Sensing. Andorra, Sept. 2000.
14. Smits P.C., A. Annoni, 2000. "Cost-based feature subset selection for interactive image analysis," In: Proceedings of the International Conference on Pattern Recognition (ICPR) 2000, Barcelona. IEEE Computer Society Press, pp. 386-389.
15. Fukunaga K. Introduction to statistical pattern recognition, 2nd edition. New York: Academic, 1990.
16. Rignot E. and R. Chellappa, 1993. "Maximum a posteriori classification of multifrequency, multilook, synthetic aperture radar intensity data," J. Opt. Soc. Am. A, vol. 10, no. 4, pp. 573-582.
17. The hyperspectral data set. Online. http://dynamo.ecn.purdue.edu/~biehl/MultiSpec/.

Boosting, Bagging, and Consensus Based Classification of Multisource Remote Sensing Data

Gunnar Jakob Briem, Jon Atli Benediktsson, and Johannes R. Sveinsson

Department of Electrical and Computer Engineering, University of Iceland
Hjardarhagi 2-6, 107 Reykjavik, Iceland.
{gjb,benedikt,sveinsso}@hi.is

Abstract. The need to optimize the classification accuracy of remotely sensed imagery has led to an increasing use of Earth observation data with different characteristics collected from a variety of sensors from different parts of the electromagnetic spectrum. Combining multisource data is believed to offer enhanced capabilities for the classification of target surfaces. In the paper several single and multiple classifiers which are appropriate for classification of multisource remote sensing and geographic data are considered. The focus is on multiple classifiers: bagging algorithms, boosting algorithms, and consensus theoretic classifiers. These multiple classifiers have different characteristics. The performance of the algorithms in terms of accuracies is compared for a multisource remote sensing and geographic data set.

1 Introduction

Traditionally, in pattern recognition, a single classifier is used to determine which class a given pattern belongs to. In many cases, classification accuracy can be improved by using an ensemble of classifiers in the classification. In such a case it is possible to have the individual classifiers support each other in making a decision. The aim is to determine an effective combination method which uses the benefits of each classifier but avoids the weaknesses.

In this paper, three multiple classifiers are investigated in terms of classification of multisource remote sensing and geographic data. The paper is organized as follows. First, multiclassifier systems are discussed with a special emphasis on the recently proposed bagging and boosting algorithms, and statistical consensus theory. Experimental results for a multisource remote sensing and geographic data set are given in Section 3. Finally, conclusions are drawn.

2 Multiclassifier Systems

Several methods have been proposed to combine multiple classifiers [1-3]. Wolpert [1] introduced the general method of stacked generalization where outputs from classifiers are combined in a weighted sum with weights which are

J. Kittler and F. Roli (Eds.): MCS 2001, LNCS 2096, pp. 279–288, 2001.
© Springer-Verlag Berlin Heidelberg 2001

based on the individual performance of the classifiers. Tumer and Gosh [2] have also shown that substantial improvements can be achieved in difficult pattern recognition problems by combining or integrating the outputs of multiple classifiers. Benediktsson *et al.* combined classifiers using neural networks [4-5] and improved their overall accuracies as compared to the best results of the single classifiers involved in the classification.

Multiclassifier systems [6-7] have been used since the sixties. Currently, two of the most used multiclassification approaches are boosting [8-9] and bagging [10]. Both these approaches are based on manipulating training samples. In contrast statistical consensus theory is based on independence between data sources and uses all the training data only once. All three approaches are discussed briefly below.

2.1   Boosting

Boosting is a general method which is used to increase the accuracy of any classifier. Several versions of boosting have been proposed but we will concentrate on AdaBoost [9] which was proposed in 1995. In particular, we will use the AdaBoost.M1 method which can be used on classification problem with more than two classes. A version of the AdaBoost algorithm is shown below.

Input: A training set S with m samples, base classifier $\mathcal{I}$ and number of classifiers T.

1. $S_1 = S$ and weight$(x_j) = 1$ for $j = 1 \ldots m$ $(x \in S_1)$
2. For $i = 1$ to $T\{$
3. $\qquad C_i = \mathcal{I}(S_i)$
4. $\qquad \epsilon_i = \frac{1}{m} \sum_{x_j \in S_i : C_i(x_j) \neq y_j} \text{weight}(x_j)$
5. $\qquad$ If $\epsilon_i > 0.5$, abort!
6. $\qquad \beta_i = \epsilon_i/(1 - \epsilon_i)$
7. $\qquad$ For each $x_j \in S_i\{$ if $C_i(x_j) = y_j$ then weight$(x_j) = $ weight$(x_j) \cdot \beta_i\}$.
8. $\qquad$ Norm weights such that the total weight of S_i is m.
9. $\}$

10. $C^*(x) = \arg\max_{y \in Y} \sum_{i:C_i(x)=y} \log \frac{1}{\beta_i}$

Output: The multiple classifier C^*.

In the beginning of AdaBoost, all patterns have the same weight and the classifier C_1 is the same as the base classifier. If the classification error is greater than 0.5, then the method does not work. Then, the procedure is usually stopped (in failure). A demand is therefore made on the minimum accuracy of the base classifier, which can be of considerable disadvantage in multiclass problems. Iteration by iteration, the weight of the samples which are correctly classified goes down. Therefore, the algorithm starts concentrating on the difficult samples. At the end of the procedure, T weighted training sets and T base classifiers have been generated.

The main advantage of AdaBoost is that in many cases it increases the over-all accuracy of the classification. Many practical classification problems include samples which are not equally difficult to classify and AdaBoost is suitable for such problems. AdaBoost tends to exhibit virtually no overfitting when the data is noiseless. Other advantages of boosting include that the algorithm has a ten-dency to reduce both the variance and the bias of the classification. On the other hand, AdaBoost is computationally more demanding than other simpler meth-ods. Therefore, it is dependent on the classification problem whether it is more valuable to get increased classification accuracy or to obtain a simple and fast classifier. Another problem with AdaBoost is that it usually does not perform well in terms of accuracies when there is noise in the data.

2.2   Bagging

Bagging is an abbreviation of *bootstrap aggregating*. Bootstrap methods are based on randomly and uniformly collecting m samples with replacement from a sample set of size m. The bagging algorithm was proposed in 1994 [10] and con-structs many different bags by performing bootstrapping iteratively, classifying each bag, and computing some type of an average of the classifications of each sample via a vote. Bagging is in some ways similar to boosting since both meth-ods design a collection of classifiers and combine their conclusions with a vote. However, the methods are different, e.g. because bagging always uses resampling instead of reweighting, it does not change the distribution of the samples (does not weight them) and all classes in the bagging algorithm have equal weights during the voting. It is also noteworthy that bagging can be done in parallel, i.e., it is possible to design all the bags at once. On the other hand boosting is always done in series, and each sample set is based on the latest weights. The bagging algorithm can be written as:

> **Input:** A training set S with m samples, base classifier $\mathcal{I}$ and number of bootstrapped sets T.
> 1. For $i = 1$ to $T\{$
> 2. S_i = bootstrapped bag from S
> 3. $C_i = \mathcal{I}(S_i)$
> 4. $\}$
>
> 5. $C^*(x) = \arg\max\limits_{y \in Y} \sum\limits_{i:C_i(x)=y} 1$
>
> **Output:** The multiple classifier C^*.

From the above it can be seen that bagging is a very simple algorithm. A simple majority vote is used, but if more than one class jointly receives the maximum number of votes, then the winner is selected using some simple mechanism, e.g. random selection. For a particular bag S_i the probability that a sample from S is selected at least once in m tries is $1 - (1 - 1/m)^m$. For a large m the probability is approximately $1 - 1/e \approx 0.632$ indicating that each bag only includes about 63.2% of the samples in S. If the base classifier is unstable, that is, when a small change in training samples can result in a large change in classification

accuracy, then bagging can improve the classification accuracy significantly. If
the base classifier is stable, like e.g., k-NN classifier, then bagging can reduce the
classification accuracy because each classifier receives less of the training data.

The main advantage of the bagging algorithm is that it can increase the
classification accuracy significantly if the base classifier is well selected. The
bagging algorithm is also not very sensitive to noise in the data. The algorithm
uses the instability of its base classifier in order to improve the classification
accuracy. Therefore, it is of great importance to select the base classifier carefully.
This is also the case for boosting since it is sensitive to small changes in the
input signal. Bagging reduces the variance of the classification (just as boosting
does) but in contrast to boosting bagging has little effect on the bias of the
classification.

2.3   Consensus Theory

Consensus theory is not based on manipulating the training data like bagging and
boosting. Consensus theory [4,11] involves general procedures with the goal of
combining single probability distributions to summarize estimates from multiple
experts with the assumption that the experts make decisions based on Bayesian
decision theory. The combination formula obtained is called a consensus rule. The
consensus rules are used in classification by applying a maximum rule, i.e., the
summarized estimate is obtained for all the information classes and the pattern
X is assigned to the class with the highest summarized estimate. Probably, the
most commonly used consensus rule is the linear opinion pool (LOP) which is
based on a weighted linear combination of the posterior probabilities from each
data source. Another consensus rule, the logarithmic opinion pool (LOGP), is
based on the weighted product of the posterior probabilities. The LOGP differs
from the LOP in that it is unimodal and less dispersed. Also, the LOGP treats
the data sources independently.

The weighting schemes in consensus theory should reflect the goodness of
the input data. The simplest approach is to give all the data sources equal
weights. Also, reliability measures which rank the data sources according to
their goodness can be used as a bases for *heuristic weighting* [4]. Furthermore,
the weights can be chosen to not only weight the individual sources but also the
individual classes. For such a scheme both linear and nonlinear optimization can
be used.

3   Experimental Results

The multiple classifiers (bagging, boosting, and consensus theoretic classifiers)
were compared in experiments. The data used in the experiments, the Anderson
River data set, are a multisource remote sensing and geographic data set made
available by the Canada Centre for Remote Sensing (CCRS) [12]. This data set
is very difficult to classify [4].

Six data sources were used:

Table 1. Training and Test Samples for Information Classes in the Experiment on the Anderson River Data.

Class #	Information Class	Training Size	Test Size
1	Douglas Fir (31-40m)	971	1250
2	Douglas Fir (21-30m)	551	817
3	Douglas Fir + Other Species(31-40m)	548	701
4	Douglas Fir + Lodgepole Pine (21-30m)	542	705
5	Hemlock + Cedar (31-40m)	317	405
6	Forest Clearings	1260	1625
	Total	4189	5503

1. Airborne Multispectral Scanner (AMSS) with 11 spectral data channels (10 channels from 380 to 1100 nm and 1 channel from 8 to 14 μm).
2. Steep Mode Synthetic Aperture Radar (SAR) with 4 data channels (X-HH, X-HV, L-HH, L-HV).
3. Shallow Mode SAR with 4 data channels (X-HH, X-HV, L-HH, L-HV).
4. Elevation data (1 data channel, where elevation in meters = 61.996 + 7.2266 * pixel value).
5. Slope data (1 data channel, where slope in degrees = pixel value).
6. Aspect data (1 data channel, where aspect in degrees = 2 * pixel value).

There are 19 information classes in the ground reference map provided by CCRS. In the experiments, only the six largest ones were used, as listed in Table 1. Here, training samples were selected uniformly, giving 10% of the total sample size. All other known samples were then used as test samples. To obtain baseline results for the multiple classifiers, several single classifiers were applied to the data. Two conventional statistical methods were used to classify the data: the MED and the Gaussian maximum likelihood method (ML) [13]. A conjugate gradient backpropagation (CGBP) algorithm [4] with two and three layers was also trained on the data with different numbers of hidden neurons (0, 15, 30, and 45 hidden neurons). Each version of the CGBP network was trained six times with different initializations and the overall average accuracies were computed in each case. This was also compared to the base classifiers which were used for bagging and boosting. These base classifiers were a decision table [14] and the j48 decision tree [15] which is a version of the C4.5 decision tree [16], frequently used in pattern recognition. The results of these classifications are shown in Tables 2 (training) and 3 (test).

In Tables 2 and 3, the conventional classification methods, the MED and ML showed different characteristics. The MED was not acceptable in terms of classification accuracies, but the ML accuracies were relatively good, especially considering that the data are clearly not Gaussian [12]. The j48 method outperformed all methods in terms of both training and test accuracies and achieved an overall accuracy for test data of 70.8%. The test accuracy of the decision table was somewhat lower than that of the CGBP neural network which achieved a test accuracy of 68.8%.

Table 2. Training Accuracies in Percentage for the Single Classifiers Applied to the Anderson River Data Set.

Method	Class 1	Class 2	Class 3	Class 4	Class 5	Class 6	Average Accuracy	Overall Accuracy
MED	40.4	8.9	47.6	67.7	42.3	72.4	46.6	50.5
ML	54.6	31.6	87.8	90.9	81.4	73.3	69.9	68.2
Decision Table	78.7	59.3	76.8	70.8	75.7	83.4	74.1	76.1
j48	93.9	91.5	93.8	93.9	96.2	97.0	94.4	94.7
CGBP (30 hidden neurons)	72.2	34.4	67.2	74.6	79.2	83.1	68.4	70.7
Number of Samples	971	551	548	542	317	1260		4189

Table 3. Test Accuracies in Percentage for the Single Classifiers Applied to the Anderson River Data Set.

Method	Class 1	Class 2	Class 3	Class 4	Class 5	Class 6	Average Accuracy	Overall Accuracy
MED	39.7	8.9	48.4	70.2	46.0	71.7	47.5	50.8
ML	50.8	27.7	84.5	81.9	73.8	72.0	64.3	65.1
Decision Table	73.8	42.4	66.5	61.7	72.8	77.0	65.7	67.5
j48	71.2	47.4	69.2	72.3	74.8	81.2	69.4	70.8
CGBP (30 hidden neurons)	71.9	29.3	67.5	73.8	79.3	82.4	67.4	68.8
Number of Samples	1250	817	701	705	405	1625		5503

3.1   Consensus Theory

For the LOP and LOGP six data classes (corresponding to the information classes in Table 1) were defined in each data source. The AMSS and SAR data sources were modeled to be Gaussian but the topographic data sources were modeled by Parzen density estimation with Gaussian kernels. For the non-linear versions, two and three layer CGBP neural networks were utilized with different numbers of hidden neurons (0, 15, 25, 35, and 45 hidden neurons). As in experiment 1, the neural networks were trained six times with different initializations. Then, the average of these six experiments was computed. The overall classification accuracies for the different consensus theoretic methods are summarized in Tables 4 (training) and 5 (test). In the tables the average result for the best

Table 4. Training Accuracies in Percentage for the Consensus Theoretic Classifiers Applied to the Anderson River Data Set.

Method	Class 1	Class 2	Class 3	Class 4	Class 5	Class 6	Average Accuracy	Overall Accuracy
LOP (equal weights)	49.6	0.0	0.0	51.5	0.0	94.9	32.7	47.6
LOP (heuristic weights)	68.2	0.0	0.0	73.1	24.3	89.4	42.5	54.0
LOP (optimal linear weights)	69.8	42.7	81.20	77.5	70.4	78.9	70.1	71.5
LOP (optimized with CGBP)	69.0	45.0	81.3	76.9	85.0	78.4	72.6	71.8
LOGP (equal weights)	68.7	28.1	79.6	78.8	81.7	74.3	68.5	68.8
LOGP (heuristic weights)	68.9	33.2	78.5	79.5	75.7	75.8	68.6	69.4
LOGP (optimal linear weights)	71.9	40.3	79.7	75.1	82.0	79.1	71.4	72.1
LOGP (optimized with CGBP)	81.2	56.0	84.3	88.7	91.7	86.4	81.4	81.6
Number of Samples	971	551	548	542	317	1260		4189

Table 5. Test Accuracies in Percentage for the Consensus Theoretic Classifiers Applied to the Anderson River Data Set.

Method	Class 1	Class 2	Class 3	Class 4	Class 5	Class 6	Average Accuracy	Overall Accuracy
LOP (equal weights)	49.8	0.0	0.0	50.4	0.0	95.3	32.6	45.8
LOP (heuristic weights)	68.9	0.0	0.0	73.1	20.8	89.3	42.0	53.9
LOP (optimal linear weights)	66.4	34.3	78.5	74.8	72.6	79.5	67.7	68.6
LOP (optimized with CGBP)	67.1	36.7	77.3	75.1	83.4	77.6	69.5	69.2
LOGP (equal weights)	67.9	23.1	77.8	77.5	81.2	73.7	66.9	66.4
LOGP (heuristic weights)	69.0	31.8	75.9	78.6	75.6	75.1	67.6	68.6
LOGP (optimal linear weights)	68.6	32.4	75.2	71.2	81.7	80.1	68.2	68.7
LOGP (optimized with CGBP)	75.4	43.1	76.9	79.5	87.2	82.1	74.0	74.1
Number of Samples	1250	817	701	705	405	1625		5503

implementation of the methods which are based on the neural networks is shown in each case. The following heuristic weights were used for the LOP: AMSS: 1.0, SAR Steep Mode Data: 0.8, SAR Shallow Mode Data: 0.8, Elevation data: 1.0, Slope data: 1.0, and Aspect data: 1.0. The heuristic weights for the LOGP were: AMSS: 1.0, SAR Steep Mode Data: 1.0, SAR Shallow Mode Data: 1.0, Elevation data: 0.0, Slope data: 0.0, and Aspect data: 0.0. A pseudo inverse method [4] was used as the optimal linear weighting for the consensus theoretic methods.

From the results in Tables 4 and 5 it is clear that the LOGP optimized with a neural network outperformed all other consensus theoretic methods in terms of overall and average training and test accuracies. It is noteworthy that the CGBP optimization increased the overall accuracies of the equally weighted LOGP by approximately 12% (training) and 6% (test), and the LOGP with non-linearly optimized weights outperformed easily the best single stage neural network classifiers both in terms of training and test accuracies. In contrast, the CGBP optimized LOP only gave comparable results to the single stage CGBP with 30 hidden neurons. However, the best CGBP optimized LOP results were achieved with 0 hidden neurons where the best CGBP optimized LOGP results were reached with 45 hidden neurons. These results are not surprising. The LOP is a linear combination of posterior probabilities but the LOGP is non-linear.

3.2 Bagging

Both bagging and boosting were run using the WEKA software provided by the University of Waikato, New Zealand [15]. In the case of bagging, 100 iterations were selected for the j48, and 30 iterations for the decision table. In both cases, the maximum test accuracy for the given base classifier seemed to have been reached. The results for bagging are shown in Tables 6 (training) and 7 (test). As can be seen from these tables, the bagging algorithm improved on the best training or test results given by LOGP when the j48 base classifier is used. This result comes as no surprise since decision tree classifiers are typical unstable classifiers which should perform well in classification by the bagging algorithm. Bagging based on the decision table does almost as well in terms of test accuracies, and in fact, slightly better than j48 after 30 iterations.

Table 6. Training Accuracies in Percentage for the the Bagging Method Applied to the Anderson River Data Set.

Base Classifier	Class 1	Class 2	Class 3	Class 4	Class 5	Class 6	Average Accuracy	Overall Accuracy
Decision Table	97.6	91.5	97.6	96.9	100.0	99.0	97.1	97.3
j48	98.7	96.2	97.4	98.3	99.4	99.3	98.2	98.4
Number of Samples	971	551	548	542	317	1260		4189

Table 7. Test Accuracies in Percentage for the Bagging Method Applied to the Anderson River Data Set.

Method	Class 1	Class 2	Class 3	Class 4	Class 5	Class 6	Average Accuracy	Overall Accuracy
Decision Table	80.7	48.2	82.9	77.3	89.6	85.5	77.4	77.8
j48	80.0	51.2	81.3	79.6	86.4	87.5	77.7	78.5
Number of Samples	1250	817	701	705	405	1625		5503

3.3 Boosting

For boosting, the Adaboost.M1, with 100 iterations for j48 was selected. After 19 iterations the boosting of the decision table aborted. This demonstrates how strict the demand for 50% accuracy is for multiclass problems. The results for the Adaboost.M1 are shown in Tables 8 (training) and 9 (test). As can be seen from these results, the Adaboost.M1 algorithm improved on the results given by bagging in the case of the j48 classifier, but not the decision table. The j48 base classifier results are outstanding. These results are the best accuracies achieved for the whole experiment. It is of interest to note that the best test accuracies were achieved 95 iterations after the training accuracy reached 100%.

Table 8. Training Accuracies in Percentage for the AdaBoost.M1 Method Applied to the Anderson River Data Set.

Base Classifier	Class 1	Class 2	Class 3	Class 4	Class 5	Class 6	Average Accuracy	Overall Accuracy
Decision Table	99.5	97.3	99.1	99.3	99.4	99.7	99.0	99.2
j48	100.0	100.0	100.0	100.0	100.0	100.0	100.0	100.0
Number of Samples	971	551	548	542	317	1260		4189

4 Conclusions

In this paper, three multiple classification schemes were looked at. All three schemes worked well and outperformed several single classifiers in terms of accuracies. Therefore, the results presented here demonstrate that multiple classification methods can be considered desirable alternatives to conventional classification methods when multisource remote sensing data are classified. In particular,

Table 9. Test Accuracies in Percentage for the AdaBoost.M1 Method Applied to the Anderson River Data Set.

Base Classifier	Class 1	Class 2	Class 3	Class 4	Class 5	Class 6	Average Accuracy	Overall Accuracy
Decision Table	77.3	51.7	73.9	75.0	83.7	85.4	74.5	75.6
j48	83.0	54.2	81.9	81.4	88.9	88.9	79.7	80.6
Number of Samples	1250	817	701	705	405	1625		5503

the AdaBoost.M1 method performed well when a j48 decision tree was used as its base classifier, and was the most accurate classifier both in terms of training and test accuracies. The AdaBoost.M1 did not demonstrate overtraining although it achieved 100% training accuracy. The simpler bagging algorithm performed better than AdaBoost.M1 in the case of the decision table base classifier, where the AdaBoost.M1 aborted after only 19 iterations. Bagging doesn't suffer from the restriction of needing at least 50% accuracy and has the further advantage of needing not as much computational resources as the other methods. The LOGP consensus theoretic classifier performed well in experiments. Consensus theoretic classifiers have the potential of being more accurate than conventional multivariate methods in classification of multisource data since a convenient multivariate model is not generally available for such data. Also, consensus theory overcomes two of the problems with the conventional maximum likelihood method. First, using a subset of the data for individual data sources lightens the computational burden of a multivariate statistical classifier. Secondly, a smaller feature set helps in providing better statistics for the individual data sources, when a limited number of training samples is available.

Acknowledgements. This research is supported in part by the Icelandic Research Council, and the Research Fund of the University of Iceland. The Anderson River SAR/MSS data set was acquired, preprocessed, and loaned by the Canada Centre for Remote Sensing, Department of Energy Mines, and Resources, of the Government of Canada.

References

1. Wolpert, D. H.: Stacked generalization. Neural Networks **5** (1992) 241-259.
2. Tumer, K., Ghosh, J.: Analysis of decision boundaries in linearly combined neural classifiers. Pattern Recognition **29** (1996) 341-348.
3. Hansen, L. K., Salamon, P.: Neural network ensembles, IEEE Transactions on Pattern Analysis and Machine Intelligence **12** (1990) 993-1001.
4. Benediktsson, J.A. Sveinsson, J.R., Swain, P.H.: Hybrid consensus theoretic classification. IEEE Transactions on Geoscience and Remote Sensing. **35** (1997) 833-843.
5. Benediktsson, J.A., Sveinsson, J.R., Ersoy, O.K., Swain, P.H.: Parallel Consensual Neural Networks. IEEE Transactions on Neural Networks. **8** (1997) 54-65.
6. Ho, T.K.: A Theory of Multiple Classifier Systems And Its Application to Visual Word Recognition, PhD dissertation, State University of New York at Buffalo (1992).

7. Wilson, S.W., and D.E. Goldberg: A Critical Review of Classifier Systems, Proceedings of the Third International Conference on Genetic Algorithms, Morgan Kaufmann, Palo Alto (1989).
8. Schapire, R.E.: A Brief Introduction to Boosting, Proceedings of the Sixteenth International Joint Conference on Artificial Intelligence (1999).
9. Freund, Y., and R.E. Schapire: Experiments with a New Boosting Algorithm, Machine Learning: Proceedings of the Thirteenth International Conference (1996).
10. Breiman, L.: Bagging Predictors, Technical Report No. 421, September 1994, Department of Statistics, University of California, Berkeley, California 94720.
11. Benediktsson, J.A., Swain, P.H.: Consensus theoretic classification methods. IEEE Transactions on Systems Man and Cybernetics. 22 (1992) 688-704.
12. D.G. Goodenough, M. Goldberg, G. Plunkett and J. Zelek, "The CCRS SAR/MSS Anderson River Data Set," *IEEE Transactions on Geoscience and Remote Sensing*, 25 (1987) 360-367.
13. Richards, J.A., Jia, X.: Remote Sensing Digital Image Analysis, An Introduction. Third, Revised and Enlarged Edition. Springer-Verlag, Berlin (1999).
14. Kohavi, R.: The Power of Decision Tables, Proceedings of the European Conference on Machine Learning (ECML), (1995).
15. Witten, I.H. et al: Weka 3.2 – Machine Learning Software in Java, http://www.cs.waikato.ac.nz/~ml/weka/ (2001).
16. Quinlan, J.R.: C4.5, Programs for Machine Learning, Morgan Kaufmann, San Francisco (1993).

Solar Wind Data Analysis Using Self-Organizing Hierarchical Neural Network Classifiers

S.A. Dolenko, Y.V. Orlov, I.G. Persiantsev, J.S. Shugai,
A.V. Dmitriev, A.V. Suvorova, and I.S. Veselovsky

Nuclear Physics Institute, Moscow State University, Vorobjovy gory,
Moscow, 119899, Russia
E-mail: yvo@radio-msu.net

Abstract. Recently, we have proposed an algorithm for construction of a hierarchy of neural network classifiers based on a modification of error backpropagation. It combines supervised learning with self-organization. Recursive use of the algorithm results in creation of compact and computationally effective self-organized structures of neural classifiers. The algorithm is applicable for unsupervised analysis of both static objects and dynamic objects, described by time series. In the latter case, the algorithm performs segmentation of the analyzed time-series into parts characterized by different types of dynamics. The algorithm has been successfully tested on pseudo-chaotic maps. In this paper the above algorithm is applied to Solar wind data analysis. Preliminary results indicate that new structural classes in the Solar wind could be distinguished aside from the traditional two- and three-state concepts.

1 Introduction

Hierarchical approach is often used in complex classification tasks, splitting a complex problem into a number of more simple ones. Recently, the algorithm for construction of a hierarchy of neural network classifiers (HNNC) was suggested [1]. The underlying idea of the algorithm is to use erroneous classifications during neural network (NN) training, for determination of classes that are „similar" in some sense. Such „similar" classes (in fact, the classes that can not be separated by NN) form a cluster of classes, simplifying the classification task at a given level of hierarchy. At the next level of hierarchy, another NN may be used for separation of classes assigned to this cluster.

The above algorithm is applicable for classification of static objects in a straightforward manner. The same algorithm may be expanded for the analysis of dynamic objects, described by time series with switching dynamics. It is assumed that the analyzed dynamic object possesses the following features:

- It has several unknown types of dynamics, while there is no *a priori* information about the types themselves and about the number of such types;
- At each moment the object is described by only one type of dynamics;
- Switching between the types of dynamics can occur at arbitrary time moments;

J. Kittler and F. Roli (Eds.): MCS 2001, LNCS 2096, pp. 289–298, 2001.
© Springer-Verlag Berlin Heidelberg 2001

- The duration of switching is negligible in comparison with the intervals between switching.

The task of time series analysis within the approach developed is to perform unsupervised segmentation of the analyzed time-series into parts characterized by different types of dynamics. Such analysis may help to determine both the actual number of dynamics types and the moments of dynamics switching. In spite of the above limiting assumptions, this model may potentially match numerous practical problems, say, EEG analysis in medicine, continuous speech segmentation, stock market analysis, etc.

In this paper, the algorithm is applied to the analysis of plasma processes in the Earth magnetosphere and in interplanetary space, and the first results of Solar wind data analysis using the HNNC algorithm are presented.

2 Statement of the Problem

Space physics data include information about hourly averaged magnitudes of interplanetary magnetic field, and about velocity, density, and temperature of Solar wind, measured on the Earth orbit. Many original papers, reviews and books are describing different types and morphological characteristics of the Solar wind (e.g., [3]). Historically, the first classification attempts were based on the empirical findings of the "quiet" and "perturbed" solar wind states, "fast" and "slow" streams, "hot" and "cold" plasma, "low" and "high" density, etc. Later, some correlations appeared more clearly between different solar wind parameters and states. Though many authors advocate the concept of the solar wind as „a two-state phenomenon", this classification is approximately valid only for the "unperturbed" quasistationary situations and can be often and strongly violated by the solar activity processes. Because of this, in the more recent literature three characteristic types of Solar Wind are discussed. The "third" class statistically is much less pronounced, and all three types are often overlapped in the statistical sense.

The solar activity develops with time in a complicated manner that is not completely understood and investigated. The corresponding classification of regimes and transitions between them is far from being established and belongs to the most important and interesting tasks of the current studies. The problem is very complicated because of the nonlocal, nonlinear, nonstationary and highly structured multi-scale nature of the solar activity driven by different energy, momentum and mass transport processes. Dozens of different regimes can be indicated theoretically, but their identification in observations is not easy because of the turbulent character of the processes in the solar wind.

From practical point of view, the most interesting phenomena are temporal dynamics of Solar wind, and some processes during interaction of the Earth magnetosphere with Solar wind (global deformation of magnetosphere, magnetic storms, etc). In this context, Solar wind dynamics analysis by the HNNC algorithm may be useful for detection of its characteristic types.

3   Description of the HNNC Algorithm

Multi-layer perceptron (MLP) is frequently used for solving classification and recognition tasks. In practice, the most critical problems of MLP training are unknown optimal number of hidden neurons and possibility of sticking in a local minimum. Typical solution is to repeat training several times. However, MLP training is computationally expensive. Taking into account that hidden layer size required for solving complex tasks may be large enough, even a single re-training of MLP may become unacceptably long.

The algorithm presented here pretends to solve (or facilitate at least) the above problems. It is based on a modification of error backpropagation training of MLP.

Let us consider the process of MLP training as simultaneous feature extraction in the hidden layer and decoding of these features in the output layer. For the simplest MLP architecture, the number of extracted features may be considered to be proportional to the number of neurons in the hidden layer. Then, a small number of neurons in the hidden layer may lead to the situation, when correct recognition of all initial classes will be impossible, and some classes will be considered „similar". Thus, the MLP architecture may be used to join classes into groups on the basis of some features.

The suggested algorithm for MLP training consists of three stages.

At the first stage, the desired output for all patterns from j-th class consists of 1 for j-th output neuron and of 0 for all other neurons, and training is performed using usual error back-propagation method.

The second stage is invoked every T training epochs. At this moment, the algorithm performs analysis of statistics of MLP's answers on the training set. One of possible methods of analysis is based on patterns "voting", and it is implemented as follows. Let us denote number of classes as C, i-th class as C_i, the amplitude of k-th output neuron as Y_k, and voting threshold as V. The pattern "votes" for belonging to class j if j=argmax(Y_i, i=1,...C) and if $Y_j>V$. The value of V is set either *a priori*, or using some objective indicator of network answers confidence.

Then a simple majority voting is done within each class. If the number of patterns that voted for belonging to C_j is greater than half of number of patterns in C_i, then all representatives of C_i are considered belonging to C_j. In fact, this procedure results in formation of groups of classes that are not separable by a given NN.

At the third stage, the desired output for each class is modified according to the voting results, and the training proceeds.

The stages training - voting - modification are repeated until the classes cease to join and until the recognition error reaches acceptable level. This procedure results in clustering the input data and, at the same time, in formation of the classifier that supports exactly that clustering.

The above feature is critical for the HNNC algorithm. The structure of a HNNC is not chosen *a priori*. Its construction starts from the base node. Each node is implemented as a MLP and is trained using the above procedure. All initial classes joined into one group form a separate branch of the tree. After creation of the base node, the same procedure is used for each branch. Within a node, each of the initial classes assigned to the corresponding branch of the tree is again considered as a separate class. The process is repeated until each branch contains one initial class.

By varying algorithm parameters (MLP hidden layer size H, learning rate r, momentum m, period T of analysis of answers statistics, and voting threshold V), it is possible to change the resulting number of classes in each node, thus controlling topology of the hierarchical tree constructed.

Some shortcoming of the algorithm is the dependence of the resulting structure on initialization of MLP weights, as discriminative features extracted during the process of HNNC construction depend on starting point. Nevertheless, such dependence does not necessarily result in poor performance of the HNNC constructed.

The algorithm performance has been tested on different real-world problems of classification of static patterns (printed letters, textures, spectrograms of isolated words and vowels), and the algorithm has demonstrated high efficiency [2]. For a well-known benchmark task of speaker-independent recognition of 11 steady state English vowels [4], the best recognition rate of the HNNC (H=1, r=0.01, m=0.9, T=1, V=0.2) on the test set was 58%. At the same time, the best recognition rate for a single MLP (H=60, r=0.01, m=0.9) was about 52%. Total number of weights in the HNNC mentioned above was equivalent to that of MLP with 7 hidden neurons. The same HNNC applied to the test set corrupted by 20% white noise outperformed all the MLPs tested, slightly degrading to recognition rate of 54%.

4 Time Series Analysis Using HNNC Algorithm

The underlying idea of using the algorithm for time-series analysis is the following [2]. The time-series is divided into segments of equal length, and dynamics describing each such segment is considered to be fixed. Under the assumption that switching between different types of dynamics is instant and rather rare, each segment is at first considered belonging to a separate class with its own dynamics.

Next, the HNNC algorithm is applied to the analyzed time-series. As the result, any segment of a time series may be reassigned to another class. Due to the ability of the algorithm to join similar classes, segments with similar or the same types of dynamics are attributed to the same class. This assignment is done without any *a priori* information.

In fact, the task of time series analysis is not a classification task, but an unsupervised segmentation. In such statement, the process of HNNC creation continues until no further classes separation is possible. A group of classes is considered non-separable if none of these classes can be separated from other classes in the group with recognition rate on train set better than 75%.

Some papers (e.g., [5]) describe neural network approaches to the analysis of time series with switching dynamics. However, in these approaches the number of neural networks is set in advance, so the whole structure of networks is non-adaptive. Also, the networks work in parallel instead of hierarchical organization.

Recently, the HNNC algorithm was tested on the model task of unsupervised segmentation of time series constructed using pseudo-chaotic maps [6]. Four well-known pseudo-chaotic sequences were used for time series generation:

logistic map: $f(x)=4x(1-x)$ for $x \in [0, 1]$;

tent map: $f(x)=2x$ for $x \in [0, 0.5)$, and $f(x)=2(1-x)$ for $x \in [0.5, 1]$;

double logistic map, and double tent map (latter two are produced by recursion of logistic map and tent map, respectively).

These sequences alternated, producing from 25 to 100 points each, while the total size of a training set made from 1000 to 2000 points, depending on the statement of the experiment. The algorithm was tested in different conditions, particularly, with unbalanced classes, when some chaotic maps produced much more points than other maps (1:27 in the worst case). Input pattern was formed of 5 sequential points from a time series, with the rightmost point of the window determining what class the pattern belonged to. Parameters settings were H=20-40; r=0.01-0.5; m=0.9; T=10; V=0.2. Usually, larger values of H and r were used at the first level of hierarchy. Typical HNNC consisted of 2-3 levels of hierarchy, separating segments of different dynamics with recognition rate 96-99% on train set, and about 85% on test set. For comparison, MLP with 4 classes (H=25, r=0.01, m=0.9) was trained using *a priori* information about model data (what is not available in practice). Recognition rate was about 95% on train set, and about 88% on test set. The results have shown that the HNNC algorithm was promising for time series segmentation and analysis.

5 Solar Wind Data Analysis

5.1 Data Preparation

Multi-factor statistical analysis of Solar activity dynamics and of Solar wind parameters presented by hourly averaged time series, was done recently [7]. According to this analysis, the characteristic time scale of dynamics that is going to be discovered by the developed algorithm, is equal to 27 days.

Time series data analyzed by the proposed algorithm, consisted of hourly averaged magnitudes of Solar Wind velocity during the period of March 1974-March 1975 (8760 points), taken from [8]. Due to substantial gaps in data (about 20% of points), a special procedure of gap filling was used. First, the gaps were filled linearly with some additive noise, and log10 of the resulting time series was calculated. Second, coefficients of wavelet transformation Daubechies-4 [9] over 512 points (i.e. 512 hours, constituting about 3 weeks) were found, and inverse wavelet transformation with rejection of coefficients lower than 30% of maximal was done. Filtered curve was smoothed by averaging over 6 hours, and moving average over 128 hours was subtracted. The resulting time series is presented in Fig.1.

In order to obtain compact representation of the analyzed time series dynamics, the first 4 coefficients of wavelet transformation Daubechies-4 were calculated over 128 points (128 hours, constituting about 5 days). These coefficients along with their 13 lags (taken with step 48 hours) formed 56 inputs for NN. Maximal lag was 624 hours, and the size of time window during analysis was about 27 days.

Solar wind data (as many other practical tasks) has no expert segmentation, so no test set is available. Nevertheless, recognition rate on train set still describes the segmentation quality. Let us denote i-th segment of a time series as S_i, and assume that a segment S_i was assigned to class C_k. In a sense, classification of patterns from S_i into C_k may be considered as a „correct" one, and the recognition rate is the number of patterns from S_i that were classified into C_k, divided by total number of patterns in

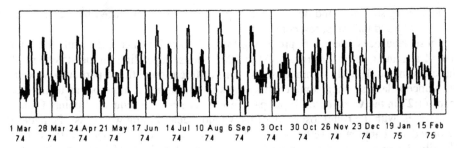

Fig. 1. Solar wind velocity, logarithmic scale (8760 hourly averaged points, March 74 – March 75). Distance between vertical lines is 648 hours (27 days, one period of Sun rotation).

S_i. Results presented below were calculated on train set. For the same reason (no expert segmentation) no comparison with a single MLP was done.

5.2 Results

In the first experiment, the time series was divided into 14 segments 648 points each (segment length corresponded to 27 days). Each segment was associated with one of the initial classes. Thus, the base network had 56 inputs and 14 outputs.

The HNNC constructed in this experiment is shown in Fig. 2. The algorithm segmented the analyzed time series into 7 groups (7 terminal nodes in Fig.2). Fig.3 presents the resulting segmentation of the time series. It shows the number of group each point was assigned to vs time, with groups numbered as follows: group #1 - segments 2, 6; group #2 - segments 8, 12; group #3 - segments 3, 7; group #4 - segments 1, 11; group #5 - segments 5, 10; group #6 - segments 4, 13, 14; group #7 - segment 9.

Unstable segmentation in group #3 (3 and 7 segments, see Fig.3), apparently, may be explained by the fact that these segments correspond to transition processes in studied dynamics (remind, that one of the basic assumptions of the algorithm is instant switching from one type of dynamics to another).

Possible solutions for this problem may be, first, expansion of the algorithm for the case of smooth drift between dynamics types, second, taking alternative information into account (e.g. Solar wind density and temperature), and third, decrease of segment length. In order to verify the latter supposition, further experiments were performed with the time series divided into 27 segments 324 points each. Thus, the base network had 56 inputs and 27 outputs.

The HNNC obtained in one of the experiments is shown in Fig. 4. All nodes of this HNNC were built using the parameters H=2, m=0.9, T=10, V=0.2. The value of learning rate was r=0.5 for the base node, and r=0.1 for all other nodes.

The algorithm segmented the analyzed time series into 5 groups. Groups were numbered as follows: group #1 - segments 1, 3, 11, 15, 21, 23; group #2 - segments 2, 10, 20, 22; group #3 - segments 4, 6, 7, 8, 12, 13, 16, 17, 24, 25, 27; group #4 - segments 5, 9, 14, 19, 26; group #5 - segment 18. Bottom chart in Fig.5 presents the

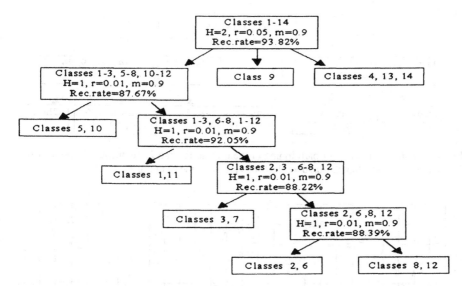

Fig. 2. HNNC constructed for partitioning of the time series into 14 segments 648 points each. Each node of the HNNC contains the list of numbers of segments assigned to this node. Each non-terminal node contains also the parameters used during its training (T=10, V=0.2 were used for all nodes), and recognition rate, which was calculated only for the segments assigned to this node. Overall recognition rate was 83.66%.

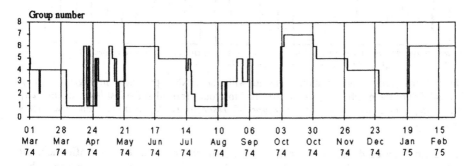

Fig. 3. The time series segmentation obtained with the HNNC presented in Fig.2. Vertical lines denote segments boundaries.

resulting segmentation of the time series. It is clearly seen that the segmentation is substantially more stable than in Fig.3, confirming our hypothesis that the segment length was too large in the first experiment.

Top chart in Fig.5 gives another view on the same segmentation. The number of patterns assigned by the HNNC to each of 5 groups, was calculated within a moving window of 100 points width. Resulting 5 curves (each curve amplitude ranges from 0 to 100) may be treated as confidence of the HNNC in its decision regarding the type

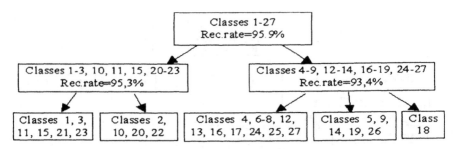

Fig. 4. HNNC constructed for partitioning of the time series into 27 segments 324 points each. Overall recognition rate was 90.96%. Notations are the same as in Fig.2.

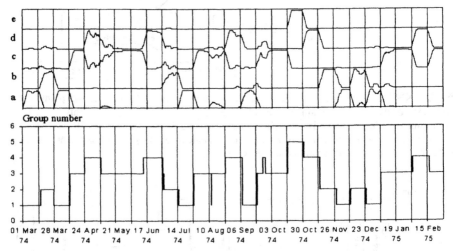

Fig. 5. Time series segmentation obtained with the HNNC presented in Fig.4 *(bottom)*. Dependence of the number of patterns assigned to groups formed at the last level of hierarchy vs time *(top; curves a-e correspond to groups 1-5, respectively)*. Vertical lines denote segments boundaries.

of the time series dynamics at a given time. In the case of 100% confidence, all patterns within a window should be assigned to a single group. One can see rather confident answers of the HNNC in most segments. However, the HNNC confidence within segments 5, 6, and 13 decreases substantially. It is interesting to note that these segments correspond to the ones where unstable segmentation in the previous experiment was obtained.

The HNNC constructed in this experiment is more balanced and more symmetric than the HNNC in Fig.2, and overall recognition rate is higher (90.96%).

The stability of segmentation results was also investigated. The HNNC algorithm was used for the same time series and with the same parameters as for HNNC in Fig.4, but with another weights initialization. Overall recognition rate of the constructed HNNC was 92.14%, and the segmentation obtained was very similar to the one in Fig.5. Apparently, it may demonstrate that the algorithm produces rather stable results, and that the segmentation obtained reflects some inherent features of the analyzed time series.

Analysis of typical waveforms in each of the groups obtained (cf. Fig.1 and Fig.5) gives rise to the hypothesis that groups #1 and #2 correspond to the periods of „quiet" Solar wind (these periods are characterized by evident transitions from maximal magnitudes to minimal ones); groups #3 and #4 correspond to the periods of „perturbed" Solar wind (these periods include numerous peaks of intermediate magnitudes). Group #5 (segment 18) corresponds to the untypical situation, when Solar wind velocity changed in a narrow range of magnitudes.

Obviously, we may treat each group number as a number of current state of the dynamic system. Let us denote sequences of states by numbers of corresponding groups, e.g. «1-3» denotes transition from state #1 to state #3. Then, several sequences of states of different length may be detected in the segmentation (Fig. 5, bottom chart), repeating with the step of half a year (one of well-known Solar cycles). The length of such sequences ranges from 2 segments (sequence «1-3», segments 3-4 and 15-16), to 3 segments (sequence «4-2-1», segments 9-11 and 19-21), and even 5 segments (sequence «2-1-3-3-5», segments 10-14 and 22-26). Our hypothesis is that the HNNC algorithm not only permits to detect different types of dynamics, but also may help to reveal rather long sequences of transitions from one type of dynamics to another.

On the basis of earlier investigations [7], we may suggest some interpretation of the transitions between groups recognized by the HNNC (Fig. 5). There could be additional structural elements and classes in Solar wind morphology aside from the simplified two- and three-state concept. The hypothesis is that the groups found reflect global asymmetry of the Solar wind emerging from its different sources in the corona. Namely, we suppose that the solar wind from northern and from southern coronal holes had different parameters during the period of time in 1974-1975. To verify this hypothesis, the polarity and geometry of the heliospheric magnetic field should be included in further analysis.

6 Conclusion

This paper presents the preliminary results of Solar Wind data analysis using hierarchical neural network classifiers (HNNC). The HNNC algorithm is based on a modification of error backpropagation combining supervised learning with self-organization. Recursive use of the algorithm builds a hierarchical tree during the process of training, resulting in creation of a self-organized structure of neural classifiers. The HNNC algorithm was expanded for the analysis of dynamic objects, described by time series with switching dynamics. The task of time series analysis within the approach developed is to perform unsupervised segmentation of the analyzed time-series into parts characterized by different types of dynamics.

In this paper, the algorithm is applied to the analysis of hourly averaged velocity of Solar Wind. We suppose that the segmentation obtained reflects some inherent features of the analyzed time series, distinguishing periods of „perturbed" and „quiet" Solar wind. The algorithm permits to detect different types of dynamics and may help to reveal rather long sequences of transitions between types of dynamics. Preliminary results indicate that new structural classes in the Solar wind could be distinguished aside from the traditional two- and three-state concepts.

Future development of the algorithm includes its expansion for the analysis of a more complex case of smooth drift between dynamics types.

This work was supported in part by RFBR (Russian Foundation for Basic Research) (grant number 01-01-00925).

References

1. Dolenko, S.A., Orlov, Yu.V., Persiantsev, I.G., Shugai, Ju.S., Eremin, E.K.: The Perceptron-Based Hierarchical Structure of Classifiers Constructed by the Adaptive Method. Pattern Recognition and Image Analysis, 7 (1997) 18-22
2. Dolenko, S.A., Orlov, Yu.V., Persiantsev, I.G., Shugai, Ju.S.: Construction of Hierarchical Neural Classifiers by Self-Organizing Error Back-Propagation. In: Heiss, M. (ed.): Proc. Int. ICSC/IFAC Symposium on Neural Computation, Vienna, Austria. ICSC Academic Press International Computer Science Conventions Canada/Switzerland (1998) 113-116
3. Burlaga, L.F.: Interplanetary Hydrodynamics. Oxford University Press (1995)
4. ftp://svr-ftp.eng.cam.ac.uk/pub/comp.speech/data/
5. Kehagias, A., Petridis, V.: Time-Series Segmentation Using Predictive Modular Neural Networks. Neural Computation 9 (1997) 1691-1709
6. Dolenko, S.A., Orlov, Yu.V., Persiantsev, I.G., Shugai, Ju.S.: Time Series Analysis Using Hierarchical Neural Network Classifiers. In: Wang, Paul P. (ed.): Proc.5th Joint Conf. on Information Sciences, Feb 27 - Mar 3, 2000, Atlantic City, NJ USA, Vol. 1. Association for Intelligent Machinery, Inc. (2000) 908-911
7. Dmitriev, A.V., Suvorova, A.V., Veselovsky, I.S.: Solar Wind and Interplanetary Magnetic Field Parameters at the Earth's Orbit During Three Solar Cycles. Physics and Chemistry of the Earth, Part C, 25 (2000) 125-128
8. http://nccdc.gsfc.nasa.gov/omniweb/form/omniweb_retriever.html
9. Strang, G., Nguyen, T.: Wavelets and Filter Banks. Wellesley - Cambridge Press (1996)

Combining One-Class Classifiers

David M.J. Tax and Robert P.W. Duin

Pattern Recognition Group, Delft University of Technology
{davidt,bob}@ph.tn.tudelft.nl

Abstract. In the problem of one-class classification target objects should be distinguished from outlier objects. In this problem it is assumed that only information of the target class is available while nothing is known about the outlier class. Like standard two-class classifiers, one-class classifiers hardly ever fit the data distribution perfectly. Using only the best classifier and discarding the classifiers with poorer performance might waste valuable information. To improve performance the results of different classifiers (which may differ in complexity or training algorithm) can be combined. This can not only increase the performance but it can also increase the robustness of the classification. Because for one-class classifiers only information of one of the classes is present, combining one-class classifiers is more difficult. In this paper we investigate if and how one-class classifiers can be combined best in a handwritten digit recognition problem.

1 Introduction

The goal of the Data Description (or One-Class Classification [10]) is to distinguish between a set of target objects and all other possible objects (per definition considered outlier objects). It is mainly used to detect new objects that resemble a known set of objects. When a new object does not resemble the data, it is likely to be an outlier or a novelty. When it is accepted by the data description, it can be used with higher confidence in a subsequent classification.

Different methods have been developed to make a data description. In most cases the probability density of the target set is modeled [12]. This requires a large number of samples to overcome the curse of dimensionality [4]. Other techniques than estimating a probability density estimate exist. It is possible to use the distance ρ to model or just to estimate the boundary around the class without estimating a probability density. A neural network can be restricted to form a closed decision surface [10], various forms of vector quantization [3] are possible and recently a method based on the Support Vector Classifier, the Support Vector Data Description [13] was proposed.

As in the normal classification problems, one classifier hardly ever captures all characteristics of the data. Combining classifiers can therefore be considered. Commonly a combined decision is obtained by just averaging the estimated posterior probabilities. This simple algorithm already gives very good results [11]. This is somewhat surprising, especially considering the fact that averaging of

J. Kittler and F. Roli (Eds.): MCS 2001, LNCS 2096, pp. 299–308, 2001.

the posterior probabilities is not based on some solid (Bayesian) foundation. When the Bayes theorem is adopted for the combination of different classifiers, a product combination rule automatically appears under the assumption of independence: the outputs of the individual classifiers are multiplied and then normalized (this is also called a logarithmic opinion pool [1]).

One-class classifiers cannot provide posterior probabilities for target objects, because information on the outlier data is not available. When a uniform distribution over the feature space is assumed, posterior probability can be estimated when the target class probability is found. When a one-class classifier does not estimate a density, its output should be mapped to a probability before it can be combined with other classifiers. In this paper we investigate the influence of the feature sets (are they dependent or not) and the type of one-class classifiers for the best choice of the combination rule.

2   Theory

We assume that we have data objects $\mathbf{x}_i, i = 1...N$, which are represented in several feature spaces $X_k, k = 1...R$. Each object can be a target object, labeled ω_T, or an outlier object ω_O (although during the training of one-class classifiers we assume example outlier objects are not available). In each feature space different one-class classifiers are trained. In [7] and in [8] a theoretical framework for combining (estimated posterior probabilities from) normal classifiers is developed. For different types of combination rules derivations are obtained. When classifiers are applied on (almost) identical data representations $X_1 = X_2 = ... = X_R$, the classifiers estimate the same class posterior probability $p(\omega_j|\mathbf{x}^k)$, potentially suffering from the same noise in the data. To suppress the errors in these estimates and the overfitting by the individual classifiers, the classifier outputs may be averaged. This results in the mean combination rule:

$$f_j(\mathbf{x}^1, ..., \mathbf{x}^R) = \frac{1}{R} \sum_{k=1}^{R} f_j^k(\mathbf{x}^k) \tag{1}$$

where j indexes the target and outlier class.

On the other hand, when independent data representations X_i are available, classifier outcomes should be multiplied to gain maximally from the independent representations. This results in the product combination rule:

$$f_j(\mathbf{x}^1, ..., \mathbf{x}^R) = \frac{\prod_{k=1}^{R} f_j^k(\mathbf{x}^k)}{\sum_{j'} \prod_{k=1}^{R} f_{j'}^k(\mathbf{x}^k)} \tag{2}$$

2.1   One-Class Classifiers

One-class classifiers are trained to accept data from the target class and to reject outlier data. We can distinguish two types of one-class classifiers. The first type are the density estimators, which just estimate the target class probability density $p(\mathbf{x}|\omega_T)$. In this paper we use a normal density, a mixture of Gaussians and the Parzen density estimation.

The second type of methods fit a model to the data and compute the distance $\rho_T(\mathbf{x})$ to this model. Here we will use four simple models, the support vector data description [14], k-means clustering, k-center method [15] and an auto-encoder neural network [6]. Here a descriptive model is fitted to the data and the resemblance (or distance) to this model is used. In the SVDD a hypersphere is put around the data. By applying the kernel trick (analogous to the support vector classifier) the model becomes more flexible to follow the characteristics in the data. Instead of the target density the distance to the center of the hyper sphere is used. In the k-means and k-center method the data is clustered, and the distance to the nearest prototype is used. Finally in the auto-encoder network the network is trained to represent the input pattern at the output layer. The network contains one bottleneck layer to force it to learn a (nonlinear) subspace through the data. The reconstruction error of the object in the output layer is used as distance to the model.

2.2   Posterior Probabilities for One-Class Classifiers

To make an accept/reject decision in all the one-class methods, a threshold should be set on the estimated probability or distance. A principled way for setting this threshold is to supply the fraction of the target set f_T which should be accepted. This defines the threshold:

$$\theta_{f_T} : \int I(p(\mathbf{x}|\omega_T) \geq \theta_{f_T})d\mathbf{x} = f_T \tag{3}$$

where $I()$ is the indicator function. In this paper it is assumed that for all methods the threshold is put such that f_T of the target data is accepted ($f_T = 0.9$).

When one-class classifiers are to be combined based on posterior probabilities, Bayes rule should be used to compute $p(\omega_T|\mathbf{x})$ from $p(\mathbf{x}|\omega_T)$:

$$p(\omega_T|\mathbf{x}) = \frac{p(\mathbf{x}|\omega_T)p(\omega_T)}{p(\mathbf{x})} = \frac{p(\mathbf{x}|\omega_T)p(\omega_T)}{p(\mathbf{x}|\omega_T)p(\omega_T) + p(\mathbf{x}|\omega_O)p(\omega_O)} \tag{4}$$

Because the outlier distribution $p(\mathbf{x}|\omega_O)$ is unknown, and even the prior probabilities $p(\omega_T)$ and $p(\omega_O)$ are very hard to estimate, equation (4) cannot be used directly. The problem is solved when an outlier distribution is assumed. When $p(\mathbf{x}|\omega_O)$ is independent of $\mathbf{x}$, i.e. it is an uniform distribution in the area of the feature space that we are considering, $p(\mathbf{x}|\omega_T)$ can be used instead of $p(\omega_T|\mathbf{x})$.

Regardless of the fact if a one-class classifier estimates a density or a reconstruction error (distance), for all types the chance of accepting and rejecting a target object, $p(\text{acc }\mathbf{x}|\omega_T)$ and $p(\text{rej }\mathbf{x}|\omega_T)$, are available. Then $p(\omega_T|\mathbf{x})$ is approximated by just two values, f_T and $1-f_T$. The binary outputs of the one-class methods can be replaced by these probabilities. Using just the binary output (accept or reject) the different one-class methods can only be combined by majority voting.

When the more advanced combining rules are required (equations (1) or (2)) $p(\mathbf{x}|\omega_T)$ should be available and a distance or resemblance $\rho(\mathbf{x}|\omega_T)$ should be transformed to a resemblance. Therefore some heuristic mapping has to be applied. One possible transformation is:

$$\tilde{P}(\mathbf{x}|\omega_T) = \exp\left(-\rho(\mathbf{x}|\omega_T)/s\right) \tag{5}$$

(which models a Gaussian distribution around the model if $\rho(\mathbf{x}|\omega_T)$ is a squared distance). The scale parameter s can be fitted to the distribution of $\rho(\mathbf{x}|\omega_T)$. Furthermore it has the advantage that the probability is always bounded between 0 and 1.

2.3   OC Combining Rules

Given a set of R posterior probability estimates, the following set of combining rules can be defined:

First the *mean vote*, which combines the binary (0-1) output labels:

$$y_{mv}(\mathbf{x}) = \frac{1}{R}\sum_{k=1}^{R} I(P_k(\mathbf{x}|\omega_T) \geq \theta_k) \tag{6}$$

Here θ_k is the threshold for method k. When the heuristic method for computing a probability $P_k(\mathbf{x}|\omega_T)$ from a distance $\rho(\mathbf{x}|\omega_T)$ has to be used (equation (5)), the original threshold for the method should also be mapped. For a threshold of 0.5 this rule becomes a majority vote in a two class problem.

The second combining rule is the *mean weighted vote*, where the weighting by $f_{T,k}$ and $1 - f_{T,k}$ is introduced. Here $f_{T,k}$ is the fraction of the target class that is accepted by method k.

$$y_{mwv}(\mathbf{x}) = \frac{1}{R}\sum_{k=1}^{R} \left(f_{T,k}I(P_k(\mathbf{x}|\omega_T) \geq \theta_k) + (1 - f_{T,k})I(P_k(\mathbf{x}|\omega_T) < \theta_k)\right) \tag{7}$$

This is a smoothed version of the previous version, but it gives identical results when a threshold of 0.5 is applied.

The third is the *product of the weighted votes*:

$$y_{pwv}(\mathbf{x}) = \frac{1}{Z}\prod_{k=1}^{R} f_{T,k}I(P_k(\mathbf{x}|\omega_T) \geq \theta_k) \tag{8}$$

with$Z = \prod_{k=1}^{R} f_{T,k}I(P_k(\mathbf{x}|\omega_T) \geq \theta_k) + \prod_{k=1}^{R}(1 - f_{T,k})I(P_k(\mathbf{x}|\omega_T) < \theta_k)$
Finally the *mean of the estimated probabilities*:

$$y_{mp}(\mathbf{x}) = \frac{1}{R}\sum_{k=1}^{R} P_k(\mathbf{x}|\omega_T) \tag{9}$$

and the *product combination of the probabilities*:

$$y_{pp}(\mathbf{x}) = \frac{\prod_k P_k(\mathbf{x}|\omega_T)}{\prod_k P_k(\mathbf{x}|\omega_T) + \prod_k P_k(\mathbf{x}|\omega_O)} \tag{10}$$

Here we will use the approximation that the outliers are uniformly distributed $P_k(\mathbf{x}|\omega_O) = \theta_T$. All these combining rules will be compared in a real world one-class problem in the next section.

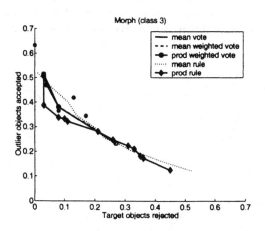

Fig. 1. ROC curves of the five combining rules. Individual classifiers are shown by stars.

2.4   Error

For the evaluation of one-class classifiers and the combination rules, we consider the Receiver-Operating Characteristic curve (ROC curve). It gives the target acceptance and outlier rejection rates for varying threshold values. Note that for estimating the outlier rejection rate, we need example outlier objects. An example is shown in figure 1. Here the results for four individual classifiers trained on one identical feature set and five combination rules are shown. Because each classifier is trained for a 10% target rejection rate, the method is optimized for just one point on the ROC curve (ideally on the vertical line with 10% target rejection rate). These points indicated by the thick dot. The 2-dimensional curves are the ROC curves of the combining rules. The product combination rule performs best here, because for the same fraction of target objects rejected, less outlier objects are accepted than by other methods.

To make comparisons between classifiers a 1-dimensional error is derived from this curve. This is called the Area Under the Curve (AUC) [2], and it measures the total error integrated over (in principle) all threshold values. Because we are mainly interested in situations where we accept large fractions of the target set, we use threshold values with a target rejection rate from 0.05 to 0.5. Although each classifier is optimized to reject 10% of the target data, during the evaluation of the combination rules, this complete range over the ROC curve is considered.

2.5 Difference Mean and Product Rule

In the combination of normal classifiers it appears that often the more robust average combination rule is to be preferred. Here extreme posterior probability estimates are averaged out. In one-class classification only the target class is modeled and a low uniform distribution is assumed for the outlier class. This makes this classification problem asymmetric and extreme target class estimates are not cancelled by extreme outlier estimates.

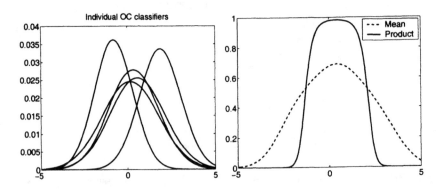

Fig. 2. (Left) Five target probability density estimates which should be combined. (Right) Combination of the five target probability density estimates

In figure 2 five one-class classifiers are shown for an artificial 1-dimensional problem with data normally distributed round the origin (with unit variance). Due to some atypical training samples two of the classifiers are somewhat remote from the other three. In figure 2 the resulting estimates by the product and mean combination rules are shown. The mean combination covers a broad domain in feature space, while the product rule has restricted range. Especially in high dimensional spaces this extra area will cover a large volume and potentially a large number of outliers.

This effect is observable in figure 1. For target rejection rates less than 20% the product combination rule accepts less outlier objects than the mean combination, or other combination rules. This indicates that the covered volume is less than for the other combining rules.

3   Experiments

We will apply the combining rules to one-class classifiers trained on a handwritten digits dataset [5]. This dataset consists of six feature sets: profile features,

Table 1. Results of all the individual classifiers on class 3. Results are multiplied by 100 and averaged over 10 runs. The number between brackets indicates the standard deviation of the outcome.

	profile	Fourier	KL	morph	pixel	Zernike
Gauss	2.98 (1.33)	3.37 (0.88)	1.34 (0.77)	10.76 (0.80)	0.45 (0.34)	6.23 (1.32)
MoG	3.46 (2.17)	3.34 (0.75)	1.66 (1.50)	11.17 (0.82)	0.43 (0.33)	6.60 (1.27)
Parzen	2.26 (0.89)	2.50 (0.73)	0.52 (0.35)	11.03 (0.84)	0.28 (0.27)	3.97 (1.52)
svdd	7.84 (2.51)	3.75 (3.63)	5.13 (2.49)	17.60 (3.48)	1.53 (1.12)	13.07 (3.59)
kmeans	4.17 (1.84)	2.64 (2.04)	1.07 (0.47)	12.56 (1.48)	0.49 (0.23)	8.40 (4.39)
kcenter	4.16 (1.23)	3.78 (3.57)	1.63 (0.77)	17.17 (3.79)	0.74 (0.29)	7.71 (1.65)
autoenc	8.67 (3.93)	3.52 (2.93)	1.93 (1.00)	13.21 (0.80)	0.89 (0.57)	9.99 (2.15)

Fourier features, Karhunen-Loève features, some morphological features, pixel features and Zernike features extracted from the scanned handwritten digits. For the one-class combining problem one class (digit class 3) of handwritten digits is described by the data descriptions and distinguished from all other classes. One hundred training objects are drawn from the target class (no negative examples are used). For testing again 100 objects per class, now both target and outlier classes, are used. This gives thus a total of 100 target and 900 outlier objects. All feature sets are mapped by PCA to retain 90% of the variance in the data. After the PCA all features are scaled to zero mean and unit variance.

All one-class classifiers contain some magic parameters. In the normal distribution the covariance matrix is regularized by $\Sigma' = \Sigma + \lambda \mathbf{1}$ to make inversion of the matrix possible (where λ is taken as small as possible to make inversion possible, most often $\lambda = 1 \cdot 10^{-3}$). The number of clusters in the mixture of Gaussians, the k-means and k-center methods are 5, 10 and 10 respectively. The number of units in the bottleneck layer in the autoencoder network is 5 and the SVDD is trained to reject 10% of the target data. Finally, the width parameter in the Parzen density is optimized using maximum likelihood optimization [9].

In table 1 the AUC-errors of the individual methods are shown for the different feature sets. The first three methods are density estimators, the other four are distance based methods. Different classifiers give different performances, and in most cases the Parzen density estimator performs best. Only for the most difficult dataset, the Morphological dataset the normal distribution performs better (on average). The best individual classifier is the Parzen density estimator, while the easiest dataset to classify is the pixel dataset. Apparently the pixel training set is a representative sample from the true distribution and the number of training objects is sufficient to do a proper density estimation by a Parzen density estimation. Finally note that in some cases the variance is very large!

In table 2 the AUC errors are shown for target class 3 when different classifiers are combined on the same dataset. In the top part of the table the three density methods are combined, the normal density, the mixture of Gaussians and the Parzen density estimation. In these cases the output of the methods do not require any mapping to probabilities. The results show that the product

Table 2. Results of the combination of classifiers by the five combination rules on class 3. Numbers in bold indicate an improvement over the best individual classifier.

	Combining 3 density methods					
	profile	Fourier	KL	morph	pixel	Zernike
mv	5.61 (1.29)	11.12 (11.93)	6.84 (13.44)	15.59 (0.99)	23.61 (22.56)	8.03 (1.22)
mwv	5.61 (1.29)	11.12 (11.93)	6.84 (13.44)	15.59 (0.99)	23.61 (22.56)	8.03 (1.22)
pwv	5.61 (1.29)	11.12 (11.93)	6.84 (13.44)	15.59 (0.99)	23.61 (22.56)	8.03 (1.22)
mp	3.00 (1.33)	3.37 (0.89)	1.35 (0.76)	10.85 (0.84)	0.45 (0.34)	6.23 (1.32)
pp	2.72 (1.25)	2.60 (0.62)	0.89 (0.54)	10.92 (0.81)	0.30 (0.30)	4.84 (1.61)
	Combining distance methods					
	profile	Fourier	KL	morph	pixel	Zernike
mv	4.23 (1.19)	3.78 (2.71)	1.53 (0.55)	13.51 (0.99)	6.16 (13.68)	**7.03 (2.05)**
mwv	4.33 (1.30)	3.78 (2.70)	1.52 (0.55)	13.45 (1.06)	6.18 (13.68)	**7.16 (2.36)**
pwv	**4.14 (1.19)**	3.81 (2.73)	1.48 (0.53)	13.54 (1.03)	6.15 (13.69)	**6.93 (1.99)**
mp	5.71 (1.55)	2.67 (2.13)	1.42 (1.21)	12.86 (1.63)	**0.48 (0.27)**	7.81 (2.92)
pp	**3.63 (0.81)**	**2.62 (2.07)**	1.14 (0.59)	**11.96 (1.06)**	**0.48 (0.27)**	**6.71 (2.31)**
	Combining all methods					
	profile	Fourier	KL	morph	pixel	Zernike
mv1	3.42 (1.18)	5.83 (1.09)	1.19 (0.26)	12.33 (0.65)	1.48 (0.68)	5.96 (1.65)
mwv	3.42 (1.16)	5.84 (1.09)	1.31 (0.58)	12.30 (0.67)	1.47 (0.68)	5.96 (1.62)
pwv	3.44 (1.15)	5.83 (1.10)	1.22 (0.30)	12.34 (0.65)	1.48 (0.68)	6.15 (1.96)
mp	3.23 (0.99)	4.57 (1.83)	1.23 (0.78)	12.29 (1.74)	0.75 (0.56)	7.41 (2.80)
pp	2.55 (0.55)	3.35 (0.73)	0.86 (0.42)	12.12 (1.87)	0.64 (0.71)	4.79 (0.96)

combination rule is a very good combining rule. When the three density methods would estimate approximately the same probability, the mean combination would give a more robust estimate. The fact that the density models vary much, combined with the effect that the mean combination rule tends to increase the estimated target class volume (see section 2.5), causes somewhat worse results than the product combination rule.

In none of the cases the combination rules achieve an improvement over the best individual performances of the one-class classifiers. But in most cases the product combination rule comes close. Only in one case the mean combination rule improves the product combination rule. Furthermore, the first three combination rules are often significantly worse than the last two, indicating that approximating the probabilities by one value is insufficient. Differences between these three rules are very small. They have an averaging behavior and often do not approach the best individual performance.

In the middle part of the table the combining results for the combination of distance methods is shown. Here a mapping to probabilities is performed (by equation (5)). Still most often no improvement over the best individual classifier can be observed, only for the product combination rule reliable improvements can be observed. The individual performances on the Zernike dataset are very poor, and almost all combination rules (except for the mean combination rule) can improve these. The good performance of the product combination rule is also somewhat surprising, because the classifiers are trained on identical data, while the mapping from distance to probability might introduce extra noise. Because of the large diversity of the methods however, the errors became uncorrelated and extreme estimates are suppressed by the product combination rule.

Finally the last part of table 2 shows the results of combining both the density and distance based methods. Here the best performance never beats the best individual performance (most often the Parzen density estimator). Again it can be observed that the product combination rule performs the best. In most cases adding the distance methods improves the first three combining rules, but deteriorates the last two.

Table 3. ROC errors obtained by combining the same classifiers trained on the six different feature sets.

	Gauss	MoG	Parzen	SVDD	kmeans	kcenters	autoenc
mv	1.7 (2.5)	0.87 (1.3)	**0.12 (0.07)**	7.5 (2.0)	2.8 (3.7)	**0.38 (0.33)**	**0.13 (0.05)**
mwv	1.72 (2.5)	0.8 (1.5)	**0.12 (0.07)**	7.5 (2.0)	3.1 (3.6)	**0.37 (0.33)**	0.12 (0.05)
pwv	1.84 (2.5)	0.9 (1.2)	**0.12 (0.07)**	7.5 (2.0)	5.4 (4.3)	**0.36 (0.32)**	0.12 (0.05)
mp	1.37 (2.2)	12.0 (1.3)	11.38 (0.82)	2.06 (1.9)	7.2 (4.5)	2.30 (1.12)	**0.43 (0.35)**
pp	**0.41 (0.7)**	0.2 (0.1)	**0.07 (0.05)**	2.1 (1.8)	3.1 (4.0)	1.77 (1.45)	**0.42 (0.34)**

Finally in table 3 the results of combining classifiers on different feature sets are shown. Clearly combining different feature sets is more effective than combining different classifiers. Only in some cases the performance is worse than the best individual classifier. For the density methods it is the mean combination rule, while for the three last methods (kmeans, kcenters and the autoencoder network) both the mean and product combination rule perform worse than the first three rules. Here the results on the different feature sets vary very much. It appears that the majority vote and the weighted versions are robust enough to use that.

4   Conclusions

In this paper we investigated the use of combining one-class classifiers. The best individual one-class classifiers in this problem appears to be the Parzen density estimator on the pixel dataset. Improving the results of the Parzen estimator appears to be hard, because the training sample in this dataset appears to be a representative sample from the "true" distribution. As can be expected, combining classifiers trained in different feature spaces is the most useful. Here the different feature sets contain much independent information which often results in good classification results. In most situations the product combination rule gives the best results. Approximating the probability by just two values does often harm the combination rules, so it is useful to use the complete density, or distance to the model. The mean combination rule suffers from the fact that the area covered by the target set tends to be overestimated, thus more outlier objects are accepted than is necessary.

Acknowledgments. This work was partly supported by the Foundation for Applied Sciences (STW) and the Dutch Organization for Scientific Research (NWO).

References

1. J.A. Benediktsson and P.H. Swain. Consensus theoretic classification methods. *IEEE Transactions on Systems, Man and Cybernetics*, 22(4):688–704, July/August 1992.
2. A.P. Bradley. The use of the area under the ROC curve in the evaluation of machine learning algorithms. *Pattern Recognition*, 30(7):1145–1159, 1997.
3. G.A. Carpenter, S. Grossberg, and D.B. Rosen. ART 2-A: an adaptive resonance algorithm for rapid category learning and recognition. *Neural Networks*, 4(4):493–504, 1991.
4. R.O. Duda and P.E. Hart. *Pattern Classification and Scene Analysis*. John Wiley & Sons, New York, 1973.
5. R.P.W. Duin. UCI dataset, multiple features database. Available from ftp://ftp.ics.uci.edu/pub/machine-learning-databases/mfeat/, 1999.
6. N. Japkowicz. *Concept-Learning in the absence of counter-examples: an autoassociation-based approach to classification*. PhD thesis, New Brunswick Rutgers, The State University of New Jersey, 1999.
7. J. Kittler, R.P.W. Duin, and J. Matas. On combining classifiers. *IEEE Transactions on Pattern Analysis and Machine Intelligence*, 20(4):226–239, 1998.
8. J. Kittler, A. Hojjatoleslami, and T. Windeatt. Weighting factors in multiple expert fusion. In Clark A.F., editor, *Proceedings of the 8th British Machine Vision Conference 1997*, pages 41–50. University of Essex Printing Service, 1997.
9. M.A. Kraaijveld and R.P.W. Duin. A criterion for the smoothing parameter for parzen-estimators of probability density functions. Technical report, Delft University of Technology, September 1991.
10. M.R. Moya, M.W. Koch, and L.D. Hostetler. One-class classifier networks for target recognition applications. In *Proceedings world congress on neural networks*, pages 797–801, Portland, OR, 1993. International Neural Network Society, INNS.
11. M. Tanigushi and V. Tresp. Averaging regularized estimators. *Neural Computation*, 9:1163–1178, 1997.
12. L. Tarassenko, P. Hayton, and M. Brady. Novelty detection for the identification of masses in mammograms. In *Proc. of the Fourth International IEE Conference on Artificial Neural Networks*, volume 409, pages 442–447, 1995.
13. D.M.J. Tax and R.P.W Duin. Data domain description using support vectors. In M. Verleysen, editor, *Proceedings of the European Symposium on Artificial Neural Networks 1999*, pages 251–256. D.Facto, Brussel, April 1999.
14. D.M.J. Tax and R.P.W Duin. Support vector domain description. *Pattern Recognition Letters*, 20(11-13):1191–1199, December 1999.
15. A. Ypma and R.P.W. Duin. Support objects for domain approximation. In *ICANN'98*, Skovde (Sweden), September 1998.

Finding Consistent Clusters in Data Partitions

Ana Fred

Instituto de Telecomunicações
Instituto Superior Técnico, Lisbon, Portugal
afred@lx.it.pt

Abstract. Given an arbitrary data set, to which no particular parametrical, statistical or geometrical structure can be assumed, different clustering algorithms will in general produce different data partitions. In fact, several partitions can also be obtained by using a single clustering algorithm due to dependencies on initialization or the selection of the value of some design parameter. This paper addresses the problem of finding consistent clusters in data partitions, proposing the analysis of the most common associations performed in a majority voting scheme. Combination of clustering results are performed by transforming data partitions into a co-association sample matrix, which maps coherent associations. This matrix is then used to extract the underlying consistent clusters. The proposed methodology is evaluated in the context of k-means clustering, a new clustering algorithm - *voting-k-means*, being presented. Examples, using both simulated and real data, show how this majority voting combination scheme simultaneously handles the problems of selecting the number of clusters, and dependency on initialization. Furthermore, resulting clusters are not constrained to be hyper-spherically shaped.

1 Introduction

Clustering algorithms are valuable tools in exploratory data analysis, data mining and pattern recognition. They provide a means to explore and ascertain structure within the data, by organizing it into groups or clusters. Many clustering algorithms exist in the literature [6,8], from model-based [5,13,16], non-parametric density estimation based methods [15], central clustering [2] and square-error clustering [14], graph theoretical based [4,18], to empirical and hybrid approaches. They all underly some concept about data organization and cluster characteristics. Best fit to some criteria, no single algorithm can adequately handle all sorts of cluster shapes and structures; when considering hybrid structure data sets, different and possibly inconsistent data partitions are produced by different clustering algorithms. In fact, many partitions can also be obtained by using a single clustering algorithm. This phenomena arises due, for instance, to dependency on initialization, such as the k-means algorithm, or by particular selection of some design parameter (such as the number of clusters, or the value of some threshold responsible for cluster separation). Model order selection is sometimes left as a design parameter; in other instances, the selection

J. Kittler and F. Roli (Eds.): MCS 2001, LNCS 2096. pp. 309–318, 2001.

of the optimal number of clusters is incorporated in the clustering procedure [1, 17], either using local or global cluster validity criteria.

Theoretical and practical developments over the last decade have shown that combining classifiers is a valuable approach in supervised learning, in order to produce accurate recognition results. The idea of combining the decisions of clustering algorithms for obtaining better data partitions is thus worth investigating.

In supervised learning, a diversity of techniques for combining classifiers has been developed [7,9,10]. Some make use of the same representation for patterns while others explore different feature sets, resulting from different processing and analysis or by simple split of the feature space for dimensionality reasons. A first aspect in combining classifiers is the production of an ensemble of classifiers. Methods for constructing ensembles include [3]: manipulation of the training samples, such as bootstrapping (*Bagging*), reweighing the data (*boosting*) or using random subspaces; manipulation of the labelling of data, an example of which is *error-correcting output coding*; injection of randomness into the learning algorithm - providing random initialization into a learning algorithm, for instance, a neural network; applying different classification techniques on the same training data set, for instance under a Bayesian framework. Another aspect concerns how the output of the individual classifiers are to be combined. Once again, various combination methods have been proposed [10,11], adopting parallel, sequential or hybrid topologies. The simplest combination method is majority voting. The theoretical foundations and behavior of this technique have been studied [11, 12], proving its validity and providing useful guidelines for designing classifiers; furthermore, this basic combination rule requires no prior training, which makes it well suited for extrapolation to unsupervised classification tasks.

In this paper we address the problem of finding consistent clusters within a set of data partitions. The rational of the approach is to weight associations between sample pairs by the number of times they co-occur in a cluster from the set of data partitions produced by independent runs of clustering algorithms, and propose this co-occurrence matrix as the support for consistent clusters development using a minimum spanning tree like algorithm. The validity of this majority voting scheme (section 2) is tested in the context of k-means based clustering, a new algorithm being presented (section 4). Evaluation of results on application examples (section 5) makes use of a consistency index between a reference data partition (taken as ideal) and the partitions produced by the methods; a procedure for determining matching clusters is hence described in section 3.

2   Majority Voting Combination of Clustering Algorithms

In exploratory data analysis, different clustering algorithms will in general produce different results, no general optimal procedure being available. Given a data set, and without any *a priori* information, how can one decide which clustering algorithm will perform better? Instead of choosing one particular method/algorithm, in this paper we put forward the idea of combining their classification results: since each of them may have different strengths and weaknesses, it is expected that their joint contributions will have a compensatory effect. Having in mind a general framework, not conditioned by any particular clustering technique, a majority voting rule is adopted.

The idea behind majority voting is that the judgment of a group is superior to those of individuals. This concept has been extensively explored in combining classifiers in order to produce accurate recognition results. In this section we extend this concept to the combination of data partitions produced by ensembles of clustering algorithms. The underlying assumption is that neighboring samples within a "natural" cluster are very likely to be co-located in the same group by a clustering algorithm. By considering the partitions of the data produced by different clusterings, pairs of samples are voted for association in each independent run. The results of the clustering methods are thus mapped into an intermediate space: a co-association matrix, where each (i, j) cell represents the number of times the given sample pair has co-occurred in a cluster. Each co-occurrence is therefore a vote towards their gathering in a cluster. Dividing this matrix values by the number of clustering experiments gives a normalized voting. The underlying data partition is devised by majority voting, comparing normalized votes with the fixed threshold 0.5, and joining in the same cluster all the data linked in this way. Table 1 outlines the proposed methodology.

Table 1. Devising consistent data partitions using a majority voting scheme.

Input: N samples; E clustering ensembles of dimension R
Output: Data partitioning.
Initialization: Set the co-association matrix, *co_assoc*, to a null $N \times N$ matrix.
Steps:
  1. Produce data partitions and update the co-association matrix:
    For $i = 1$ to R do
    1.1. Run the ith clustering method in the ensemble E and produce a data
        partition P;
    1.2. Update the co-association matrix accordingly:
        For each sample pair, (i, j), in the same cluster in P set
        $co\_assoc(i, j) = co\_assoc(i, j) + \frac{1}{R}$
  2. Obtain the consistent clusters by thresholding on *co_assoc*
    2.1. Find majority voting associations:
        For each sample pair, (i, j), such that $co\_assoc(i, j) > 0.5$ join the samples in
        the same cluster; if the samples where in distinct previously formed clusters,
        join the clusters;
    2.2. For each remaining sample not included in a cluster, form a single element
        cluster;
  3. Return the clusters thus formed.

Without requiring prior training, this technique can easily cope with a diversity of scenarios: classifiers using the same representation for patterns or making use of different representations (such as different feature sets); combination of classifications produced by a single method or architecture with different parameters or fusion of multiple types of classifiers.

Section 4 integrates this methodology into a k-means based clustering technique. Evaluation of the results makes use of a partitions consistency index, described next.

3   Matching Clusters in Distinct Partitions

Let P_1, P_2 be two data partitions. In what follows, it is assumed that the number of clusters in each partition is arbitrary and samples are enumerated and referenced using the same labels in every partition, $s_i, i = 1, \ldots, n$. Each cluster has an equivalent binary valued vector representation, each position indicating the truth value of the proposition: *sample i belongs to the cluster*. The following notation is used:

$$P_i \equiv partition\ i: \quad (nc_i,\ C_1^i \ldots C_{nc_i}^i)$$
$$nc_i \equiv \text{ number of clusters in partition } i$$
$$C_j^i = \{s_l : s_l \in \text{ cluster} j \text{ of partition } i\}$$
$$\equiv \text{ list of samples in the } j\text{th cluster of partition } i$$
$$X_j^i : \quad X_j^i(k) = \begin{cases} 1 \ if \ s_k \in C_j^i \\ 0 \ otherwise \end{cases} \quad ,k = 1, \ldots, n$$
$$\equiv \text{ binary valued vector representation of cluster } C_j^i$$

We define *pc_idx*, the *partitions consistency index*, as the fraction of shared samples in matching clusters in two data partitions, over the total number of samples:

$$pc\_idx = \frac{1}{n} \sum_{i=1}^{min\{nc_1,nc_2\}} n\_shared_i$$

where it is assumed that clusters occupy the same position in the ordered clusters lists of the partitions, and n_shared_i is the number of samples shared for the ith clusters.

The clusters matching algorithm is an iterative procedure that, in each step, determines the pair of clusters having the highest matching score, given by the fraction of shared samples. It can be described schematically:

Input: Partitions P_1, P_2; n, the total number of samples.

Output: P_2', partition P_2 reordered according to the matching clusters in P_1; *pc_idx*, the partitions consistency index.

Steps:

1. Convert clusters C_j^i into the binary valued vector description X_j^i:

$$C_j^i \rightarrow X_j^i, \ i = 1, 2 \ \ j = 1, \ldots, nc_i$$

2. Set: $P2_{new\_indexes}(i) = 0, \ i = 1, \ldots nc_2$ (clusters new indexes)
   $n\_shared = 0$.

3. Do $min\{nc_1, nc_2\}$ times:

- Determine the best matching pair of clusters, (k, l), between P_1 and P_2 according to the match coefficient:

$$(k, l) = \overset{arg\ max}{i, j} \left\{ \frac{X^1_i{}^T X^2_j}{X^1_i{}^T X^1_i + X^2_j{}^T X^2_j - X^1_i{}^T X^2_j} \right\},$$

- $n\_shared = n\_shared + X^1_i{}^T X^2_j$.
- Rename C^2_l as C^2_k: $P2_{new\_indexes}(l) = k$.
- Remove C^1_k and C^2_l from P_1 and P_2, respectively.

4. If $nc_1 \geq nc_2$ go to step 5; otherwise fill in empty locations in $P2_{new\_indexes}$ (clusters with no correspondence in P_1) with arbitrary labels in the set $\{nc_1 + 1, \ldots, nc_2\}$.
5. Reorder P_2 according to the new clusters labels in $P2_{new\_indexes}$ and put in P'_2; set $pc\_idx = \frac{n\_shared}{n}$
6. Return P'_2 and pc_idx.

4   K-Means Based Clustering

In this section we incorporate the previous methodology in the context of k-means clustering. The resulting clustering algorithm is summarized in table 2, and will be hereafter referred to as *voting-k-means*. It basically proposes to generate clustering partitions ensembles by random initialization of the cluster centers and random pattern presentation.

Table 2. Assessing the underlying number of clusters and structure based on a k-means voting scheme.

Voting-K-Means algorithm.
Input: N samples; k - initial number of clusters (by default: $k = \sqrt{N}$); R - number of iterations.
Output: Data partitioning.
Initialization: Set the co-association matrix to a null $N \times N$ matrix.

Steps:
 1. Do R times:
    1.1. Ramdomly select k cluster centers among the N data samples.
    1.2. Organize the N samples in random order, keeping track of the initial data indexes.
    1.3. Run the k-means algorithm with the reordered data and cluster centers and update the co-association matrix according to the partition thus obtained over the initial data indexes
 2. Detect the consistent clusters though the co-association matrix, using the technique defined previously.

4.1   Known Number of Clusters

One of the difficulties with the k-means algorithm is the dependency of the partitions produced on the initialization. This is illustrated in figure 1 which represents two partitions produced by the k-means algorithm (corresponding to different cluster initializations) on a data set of 1000 samples drawn from a mixture of two Gaussian distributions with unit covariance and Mahalanobis distance between the means equal to 7. Inadequate data partitions, such as the one plotted in figure 1(a), can be obtained even when the correct number of clusters is known *a priori*. These misclassifications of patterns are however overcome by using a majority voting scheme, as outlined in table 2, setting k to the known number of clusters: taking the votes produced by several runs of the k-means algorithm, using randomized cluster center initializations and samples reordering, leads to the correct data partitioning depicted in figure 1(b).

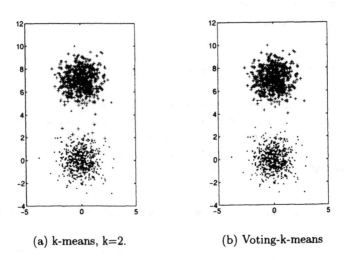

(a) k-means, k=2.   (b) Voting-k-means

Fig. 1. Compensating the dependency of the k-means algorithm on cluster center initialization, k=2. (a)- Data partition obtained with a single run of the k-means algorithm. (b)- Result obtained using another cluster centers initialization and also with the proposed method with 10 iterations.

4.2   Unknown Number of Clusters

Most of the times, the true number of clusters is not known in advance and must be ascertained from the training data set. Based on the k-means algorithm, several heuristic and optimization techniques have both been proposed to select the number of underlying classes [1,17]. Also, it is well known that the k-means algorithm, based on a minimum square error criterium, identifies hyper-spherical clusters, spread around prototype vectors representing cluster centers. Techniques for selecting the number of clusters according to this optimality criterium basically identify an "optimal" number of cluster centers on the data that splits it into the same number of hyper-spherical clusters. When the data exhibits clusters with arbitrary shape, this type of decomposition is not always satisfactory. In this section we propose to use a voting scheme associated with the k-means algorithm to address both issues: selection of the number of clusters; detecting arbitrary shaped clusters.

The basic idea consists of the following: if a large number, k, of clusters is selected, by randomly choosing the initial clusters centers and order of pattern presentation, the k-means algorithm will split the training data into k subsets which reflect high density regions; if k is large in comparison to the number of true clusters, each intrinsic cluster will be split into arbitrary smaller clusters, neighboring patterns having a high probability of being co-located in the same cluster; by averaging over all associations of pattern pairs thus produced over R runs of the k-means algorithm, it is expected to obtain high rates of votes on these pairs of patterns, the true clusters structure being recovered by thresholding the co-association matrix, as proposed before. The method therefore proposed is to apply the algorithm described in table 2 by setting K to a large value, say $\sqrt{N}$, N being the number of patterns in the training set.

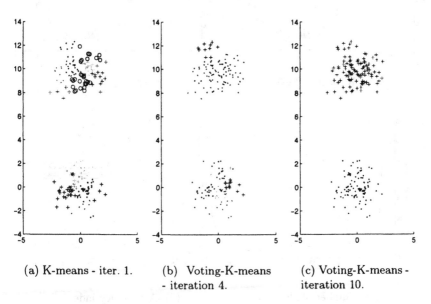

(a) K-means - iter. 1.   (b) Voting-K-means   (c) Voting-K-means -
                          - iteration 4.   iteration 10.

Fig. 2. Partitions produced by the k-means (k=14) and the voting-k-means algorithms.

The method is illustrated in figure 2 concerning the clustering of 200 2-dimensional patterns, randomly generated from a mixture of two Gaussian distributions: unit covariance; Mahalanobis distance between the means – 10. Figure 2(a) shows a data partition produced by the k-means algorithm (k=14); distinct initializations produce different data partitioning. Accounting for persistent pattern associations along the individual runs of the k-means algorithm, the voting-k-means algorithm evolves to a stable partition of the data with two clusters (see figures 2(b) and (c)).

5   Application Examples

5.1   Simulated Data

The proposed method is tested in the classification of data forming two well separated clusters shaped as half rings. The total number of samples is 400, distributed evenly between the two clusters; the voting-k-means is run setting k to 20.

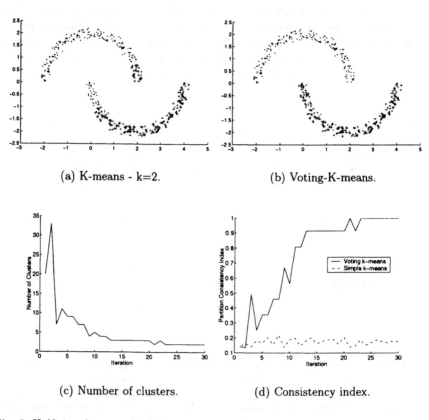

(a) K-means - k=2.

(b) Voting-K-means.

(c) Number of clusters.

(d) Consistency index.

Fig. 3. Half ring data set. (a)-(b) Partitions produced by the k-means and the voting-k-means algorithms. (c)-(d) Convergence of the voting-k-means algorithm.

Figure 3(a) plots a typical result with the standard k-means algorithm when using $k = 2$, showing its inability to handle this type of clusters. By taking the majority voting scheme, however, clusters are correctly identified (figure 3(b)). The convergence of the algorithm to the correct data partitioning is depicted in figures 3(c) and 3(d), according to which a stable solution is obtained after 25 iterations.

5.2   Iris Data Set

The Iris data set consists of three types of Iris plants (Setosa, Versicolor and Virginica), with 50 instances per class, represented by 4 features.

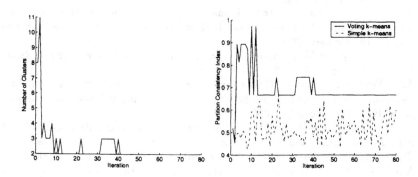

Fig. 4. Iris data set: convergence of the voting-k-means algorithm; $k = 8$.

As shown in figure 4, the proposed algorithm initially alternates between 2 and 3 clusters, with consistency indexes ranging from 0.67 (2 clusters – Setosa *vs* Versicolor + Virginica) and 0.75 (3 clusters). It stabilizes at the two clusters solution, which, although not corresponding to the known number of classes, constitutes a reasonable and intuitive solution as the Setosa class is well separated from the remaining classes, which are intermingled.

6   Conclusions

This paper proposed a general methodology for combining classification results produced by clustering algorithms. Taking an ensemble of clustering algorithms, their individual decisions/partitions are combined by a majority voting rule to derive a consistent data partition.

We have shown how the integration of the proposed methodology in a k-means like algorithm, denoted voting-k-means, can simultaneously handle the problem of initialization dependency and selection of the number of clusters. Furthermore, as illustrated in examples, with this algorithm cluster shapes other than hyper-spherical can be identified.

While explored in this paper under the framework of k-means clustering, the proposed technique does not entail any specificity towards a particular clustering strategy. Ongoing work includes the adoption of the voting type clustering scheme with other clustering algorithms and the extrapolation of this methodology to the combination of multiple classes of clustering algorithms.

References

1. H. Bischof and A. Leonardis. Vector quantization and minimum description length. In Sameer Singh, editor, *International Conference on Advances on Pattern Recognition*, pages 355–364. Springer Verlag, 1999.
2. J. Buhmann and M. Held. Unsupervised learning without overfitting: Empirical risk approximation as an induction principle for reliable clustering. In Sameer Singh, editor, *International Conference on Advances in Pattern Recognition*, pages 167–176. Springer Verlag, 1999.
3. T. Dietterich. Ensemble methods in machine learning. In Kittler and Roli, editors, *Multiple Classifier Systems*, volume 1857 of *Lecture Notes in Computer Science*, pages 1–15. Springer, 2000.
4. Y. El-Sonbaty and M. A. Ismail. On-line hierarchical clustering. *Pattern Recognition Letters*, pages 1285–1291, 1998.
5. A. L. Fred and J. Leitão. Clustering under a hypothesis of smooth dissimilarity increments. In *Proc. of the 15th Int'l Conference on Pattern Recognition*, volume 2, pages 190–194, Barcelona, 2000.
6. A. K. Jain and R. C. Dubes. *Algorithms for Clustering Data*. Prentice Hall, 1988.
7. A.K. Jain, R. Duin, and J. Mao. Statistical pattern recognition: A review. *IEEE Trans. Pattern Analysis and Machine Intelligence*, 22:4–37, January 2000.
8. A.K. Jain, M. N. Murty, and P.J. Flynn. Data clustering: A review. *ACM Computing Surveys*, 31(3):264–323, September 1999.
9. J. Kittler. Pattern classification: Fusion of information. In S. Singh, editor, *Int. Conf. on Advances in Pattern Recognition*, pages 13–22, Plymouth, UK, November 1998. Springer.
10. J. Kittler, M. Hatef, R. P Duin, and J. Matas. On combining classifiers. *IEEE Trans. Pattern Analysis and Machine Intelligence*, 20(3):226–239, 1998.
11. L. Lam. Classifier combinations: Implementations and theoretical issues. In Kittler and Roli, editors, *Multiple Classifier Systems*, volume 1857 of *Lecture Notes in Computer Science*, pages 78–86. Springer, 2000.
12. L. Lam and C. Y. Suen. Application of majority voting to pattern recognition: an analysis of its behavior and performance. *IEEE Trans. Systems, Man, and Cybernetics*, 27(5):553–568, 1997.
13. G. McLachlan and K. Basford. *Mixture Models: Inference and Application to Clustering*. Marcel Dekker, New York, 1988.
14. B. Mirkin. Concept learning and feature selection based on square-error clustering. *Machine Learning*, 35:25–39, 1999.
15. E. J. Pauwels and G. Frederix. Fiding regions of interest for content-extraction. In *Proc. of IS&T/SPIE Conference on Storage and Retrieval for Image and Video Databases VII*, volume SPIE Vol. 3656, pages 501–510, San Jose, January 1999.
16. S. Roberts, D. Husmeier, I. Rezek, and W. Penny. Bayesian approaches to gaussian mixture modelling. *IEEE Trans. Pattern Analysis and Machine Intelligence*, 20(11), November 1998.
17. H. Tenmoto, M. Kudo, and M. Shimbo. Mdl-based selection of the number of components in mixture models for pattern recognition. In Adnan Amin, Dov Dori, Pavel Pudil, and Herbert Freeman, editors, *Advances in Pattern Recognition*, volume 1451 of *Lecture Notes in Computer Science*, pages 831–836. Springer Verlag, 1998.
18. C. Zahn. Graph-theoretical methods for detecting and describing gestalt structures. *IEEE Trans. Computers*, C-20(1):68–86, 1971.

A Self-Organising Approach to Multiple Classifier Fusion*

S.P. Luttrell

DERA
Malvern, Worcestershire, U.K.
luttrell@signal.dera.gov.uk

Abstract. In this paper the theory of unsupervised multi-layer stochastic vector quantiser (SVQ) networks is reviewed, and then extended to the supervised case where the network is to be used as a classifier. This leads to a hybrid approach, in which training is governed both by unsupervised and supervised pieces in the network objective function. The unsupervised piece aims to preserve enough information in the network to be able to accurately reconstruct the input (i.e. the network serves as an encoder), whereas the supervised piece aims to reproduce the classification output supplied by an external teacher (i.e. the network serves as a classifier). The tension between these two pieces of the objective function leads to an optimal network, in which typically the lower layers (near to the input) act as faithful encoders of the input, whereas the higher layers (near to the output) act as faithful classifiers. The results of some simulations are presented to illustrate these properties.

1 Introduction

For a review of the subject of combining classifiers see the introduction to [1], where it is stated that the two main reasons for combining classifiers are efficiency and accuracy. Efficiency gains may be obtained when the classifier is implemented using a network of simple processing operations, and accuracy may be improved when results from two or more classifiers (with different strengths and weaknesses) are combined [2]. Typically, both of these strategies are simultaneously employed. Thus a classifer ensemble is implemented, where each classifier has a different set of simple operations, so each has its own peculiar strengths and weaknesses. Then the classifiers in this ensemble are combined to produce the overall classifier.

The question that will be addressed in this paper is how to simultaneously solve the two problems of designing the separate classifiers and combining them together to produce the overall classifier. A novel approach will be used, in which the overall classifier will be allowed to emerge by a process of self-organisation, that is driven by the minimisation of a suitably chosen objective function. This approach implements the overall classifier as a multi-layer network with full

---

J. Kittler and F. Roli (Eds.): MCS 2001, LNCS 2096, pp. 319–328, 2001.
© Springer-Verlag Berlin Heidelberg 2001

interconnections between adjacent layers. However, self-organisation typically discovers optimal solutions in which the connections implement a set of simple processing operations using only a subset of the connections, followed by combination of their outputs to produce the overall classifier.

The basic unit of computation in the self-organising network is a generalisation of the standard vector quantiser (VQ) [3], called a stochastic vector quantiser (SVQ) [4], [5], in which samples are drawn probabilistically from a codebook. The objective function used to optimise a SVQ is the mean Euclidean error that occurs when using the SVQ to encode an input as multiple probabilistic samples, followed by reconstruction from these samples to estimate the input. If multiple samples are allowed, then an SVQ can use much cleverer coding schemes than a standard VQ. For instance, self-organisation can cause the codebook to split into several smaller codebooks, each of which specialises in encoding only part of the input. This propensity for the codebook to split is the key to using self-organisation to form a classifier ensemble, in which the different classifiers have different strengths and weaknesses.

Thus far the SVQ objective function is unsupervised, because it makes no provision for an external teacher to influence the way in which the SVQ encodes its input. This is easily rectified by adding a term to the SVQ objective function that attempts to steer the SVQ output towards some desired target output. This external supervision is readily put to use in designing a classifier network, where it may be used to force the final output of the network to be the required overall classifier.

In Sect. 2 the underlying theory of SVQs is presented, and in Sect. 3 the results of simulations are presented to demonstrate the potential use of SVQs to classification.

2   Theory

In this section various pieces of the previously published theory of stochastic vector quantisers (SVQ) are unified to establish a coherent framework for modelling SVQs. In Sect. 2.1 the basic theory of SVQs is given (which is equivalent to the theory of FMCs reported in [6]), and in Sect. 2.2 it is extended to the case of high-dimensional input data [4]. In Sect. 2.3 the theory is further generalised to chains of linked SVQs [7], and the use of an external teacher to supervise the chain is explained in Sect. 2.4.

2.1   Stochastic Vector Quantisers

The basic building block of the encoder/decoder model used in this paper is the folded Markov chain (FMC) [6], which is equivalent to the SVQ discussed in Sect. 1. Thus an input vector x is encoded as a code index vector y, which is then subsequently decoded as a reconstruction x' of the input vector. Both the encoding and decoding operations are allowed to be probabilistic, in the sense that y is a sample drawn from $\Pr(y|x)$, and x' is a sample drawn from

$\Pr(x'|y)$, where $\Pr(y|x)$ and $\Pr(x'|y)$ are Bayes' inverses of each other, as given by $\Pr(x'|y) = \frac{\Pr(y|x)\Pr(x)}{\int dx'' \Pr(y|x'')\Pr(x'')}$, and $\Pr(x)$ is the prior probability from which x was sampled. Because the chain of dependences in passing from x to y and then to x' is first order Markov (i.e. it is described by the directed graph $x \to y \to x'$, and because the two ends of this Markov chain (i.e. x and x') live in the same vector space, it is called a *folded* Markov chain [6].

In order to ensure that the SVQ encodes the input vector optimally, a measure of the reconstruction error must be minimised. There are many possible ways to define this measure, but one that is consistent with many previous results, and which also leads to many new results, is the mean Euclidean reconstruction error measure D, which is defined as

$$D \equiv \int dx \, \Pr(x) \sum_{y_1=1}^{M} \sum_{y_2=1}^{M} \cdots \sum_{y_n=1}^{M} \Pr(y|x) \int dx' \, \Pr(x'|y) \, \|x - x'\|^2 \quad (1)$$

where $y = (y_1, y_2, \cdots, y_n)$, $1 \leq y_i \leq M$ is assumed, $\Pr(x)\Pr(y|x)\Pr(x'|y)$ is the joint probability that the SVQ has state (x, y, x'), $\|x - x'\|^2$ is the Euclidean reconstruction error, and $\int dx \sum_{y_1=1}^{M} \sum_{y_2=1}^{M} \cdots \sum_{y_n=1}^{M} \int dx'(\cdots)$ sums over all possible states of the SVQ (weighted by the joint probability).

The Bayes' inverse probability $\Pr(x'|y)$ may be integrated out of this expression for D to yield

$$D = 2 \int dx \, \Pr(x) \sum_{y_1=1}^{M} \sum_{y_2=1}^{M} \cdots \sum_{y_n=1}^{M} \Pr(y|x) \, \|x - x'(y)\|^2 \quad (2)$$

where the reconstruction vector $x'(y)$ is defined as $x'(y) \equiv \int dx \, \Pr(x|y)x$. Because of the quadratic form of the objective function, it turns out that $x'(y)$ may be treated as a free parameter, whose optimum value (i.e. the solution of $\frac{\partial D}{\partial x'(y)} = 0$) is $\int dx \, \Pr(x|y)x$, as required.

2.2   High Dimensional Input Spaces

A problem with the standard VQ is that its code book grows exponentially in size as the dimensionality of the input vector is increased, assuming that the contribution to the reconstruction error from each input dimension is held constant. This means that such VQs are useless for encoding extremely high dimensional input vectors, such as images. The usual solution to this problem is to manually partition the input space into a number of lower dimensional subspaces, and then to encode each of these subspaces separately. However, it would be very useful if this partitioning could be done automatically, in such a way that typically the correlations *within* each subspace were much stronger than the correlations *between* subspaces, so that the subspaces were approximately statistically independent of each other. This is an example of the self-organised discovery of a classifier ensemble, in which each classifier focusses on only a subspace of the input.

The key step in solving this problem is to constrain the minimisation of D in such a way as to encourage the formation of code schemes in which each component of the code vector y codes a different subspace of the input vector x. There are two related constraints that may be imposed on $\Pr(y|x)$ and $x'(y)$ which may be summarised as

$$\Pr(y|x) = \Pr(y_1|x)\Pr(y_2|x) \cdots \Pr(y_n|x), \quad x'(y) = \frac{1}{n}\sum_{i=1}^{n} x'(y_i) \qquad (3)$$

Thus, for $i = 1, 2, \cdots, n$ and $1 \leq y_i \leq M$, each component y_i is an *independent* sample drawn from the codebook using $\Pr(y_i|x)$ (which is assumed to be the same function for all i), and the reconstruction vector $x'(y)$ (vector argument) is assumed to be a *superposition* of n contributions $x'(y_i)$ (scalar argument). Taken together, these constraints encourage the formation of coding schemes in which independent subspaces are separately coded, as required.

The constraints in Eq. 3 prevent the full space of possible values of $\Pr(y|x)$ or $x'(y)$ from being explored as D is minimised, so they lead to an upper bound $D_1 + D_2$ on the SVQ objective function D (i.e. $D \leq D_1 + D_2$), which may be derived as (the details of this derivation, including the derivatives of $D_1 + D_2$, are reported in [4])

$$D_1 \equiv \frac{2}{n} \int dx\, \Pr(x) \sum_{y=1}^{M} \Pr(y|x)\, \|x - x'(y)\|^2$$

$$D_2 \equiv \frac{2(n-1)}{n} \int dx\, \Pr(x) \left\| x - \sum_{y=1}^{M} \Pr(y|x)x'(y) \right\|^2 \qquad (4)$$

Note that M (size of codebook) and n (number of samples drawn from codebook using $\Pr(y|x)$) are effectively model order parameters, whose values need to be chosen appropriately for each encoder optimisation problem. The properties of the optimum encoder depend critically on the interplay between the statistical properties of the training data and the model order parameters M and n.

In numerical simulations it is convenient to parameterise (i.e. constrain) $\Pr(y|x)$ thus

$$\Pr(y|x) = \frac{Q(y|x)}{\sum_{y'=1}^{M} Q(y'|x)}, \quad Q(y|x) \equiv \frac{1}{1 + \exp(-w(y).x - b(y))} \qquad (5)$$

where $Q(y|x)$ is a sigmoid function of x, with weight vector $w(y)$ and bias $b(y)$.

2.3   Chain of Linked Stochastic Vector Quantisers

An SVQ may be generalised to a chain of linked SVQs, and further generalisation to any acyclically linked network of SVQs is also readily achieved. The vector of probabilities (for all values of the code index) computed by each stage in the chain is used as the input vector to the next stage, and the overall objective function is a weighted sum of the SVQ objective functions derived from each stage. There are other ways of linking the stages together and defining an overall objective function, but the above prescription is the simplest possibility. The total number of free parameters in an L stage chain is $3L - 1$, which is the sum of 2 free parameters for each of the L stages, plus $L-1$ weighting coefficients. There are $L - 1$ rather than L weighting coefficients because the overall normalisation of the objective function does not affect the optimum solution.

The chain of linked SVQs will now be expressed mathematically. Firstly, an index l (where $1 \leq l \leq L$) is introduced to allow different stages of the chain to be distinguished thus

$$M \to M^{(l)}, \quad n \to n^{(l)}, \quad x \to x^{(l)}, \quad x' \to x'^{(l)}$$
$$y \to y^{(l)}, \quad D \to D^{(l)}, \quad D_1 \to D_1^{(l)}, \quad D_2 \to D_2^{(l)} \tag{6}$$

Then the stages are then defined and linked together thus

$$x^{(l)} \to y^{(l)} \to x'^{(l)}$$
$$x^{(l+1)} = (x_1^{(l+1)}, x_2^{(l+1)}, \cdots, x_{M^{(l)}}^{(l+1)})$$
$$x_i^{(l+1)} = \Pr(y^{(l)} = i | x^{(l)}), 1 \leq i \leq M^{(l)} \tag{7}$$

Finally, the objective function and its upper bound are given by

$$D = \sum_{l=1}^{L} s^{(l)} D^{(l)} \leq D_1 + D_2 = \sum_{l=1}^{L} s^{(l)} (D_1^{(l)} + D_2^{(l)}) \tag{8}$$

where $s^{(l)} \geq 0$ is the weighting that is applied to the contribution $D_1^{(l)} + D_2^{(l)}$ of stage l of the chain to the overall objective function D.

2.4 Supervision by an External Teacher

The objective function D in Eq. 8 can readiliy be extended to allow an external teacher to supervise the chain of linked SVQs. Thus make the following replacement in Eq. 8

$$D_1^{(l)} + D_2^{(l)} \to D_1^{(l)} + D_2^{(l)} + D_{\text{supervise}}^{(l)} \tag{9}$$

where $D_{\text{supervise}}^{(l)}$ is any convenient objective function that the external teacher wishes to apply to stage l of the chain. For instance $D_{\text{supervise}}^{(l)}$ might measure the Euclidean error between the output of stage l (whose components are $\Pr(y^{(l)} = i | x^{(l)}), 1 \leq i \leq M^{(l)}$) and some externally supplied reference vector.

Note that supervision can be applied to any or all of the stages, and is not limited to only the final stage, as is conventional in supervised training. In the context of combining classifiers, not only the design of the combined classifier, but also the design of the individual classifiers may be supervised.

3   Simulations

In this section the results of several simulations are presented to illustrate the behaviour of SVQs in both unsupervised and supervised training scenarios. Circular (i.e. S^1) and 2-toroidal (i.e. $S^1 \times S^1$) input manifolds are used.

3.1   Circular Input Manifold

The simplest demonstration of a SVQ is to train it (unsupervised) with data that lives on a circular manifold. Fig. 1 shows contour plots of the posterior

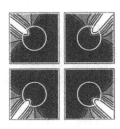

Fig. 1. Contours of $\Pr(y|\boldsymbol{x})$ ($y = 1, 2, 3, 4$) for data lying on a circle (represented by the white circle in each plot), trained using $M = 4$ and $n = 10$

probabilities $\Pr(y|\boldsymbol{x})$ for $y = 1, 2, 3, 4$ in a SVQ with $M = 4$ and $n = 10$. The circular manifold is chopped up by the $\Pr(y|\boldsymbol{x})$ into four softly overlapping arcs.

3.2   2-Toroidal Input Manifold

A more sophisticated demonstration of a SVQ is to train it (unsupervised) with data that lives on a toroidal manifold.

In Fig. 2(a) each of the $\Pr(y|\boldsymbol{x})$ for $M = 8$ and $n = 5$ has a localised response region on the 2-torus, and the 2-torus is thus chopped up into eight softly overlapping regions. This result (2-dimensional manifold) may be compared with the simpler result (1-dimensional manifold) in Fig. 1. In both cases, sampling a single code index from the code book is sufficient to detemine the location of the input vector to an accuracy corresponding to a single localised response region. A major disadvantage of this type of encoder is that the size of the code book that is required to guarantee a given resolution (in each dimension of the input manifold) increases *exponentially* with input manifold dimensionality. This would be completely useless for very high dimensional applications, such as image processing. This general type of encoder will be called a *joint* encoder, because it simultaneously encodes all of the dimensions of the input manifold.

In Fig. 2(b) the results shown are analogous to those shown in Fig. 2(a), except that $M = 8$ and $n = 50$, so 10 times as many samples are now drawn from the code book. There is a marked difference in the shape of the response region of each of the $\Pr(y|x)$. The set of $\Pr(y|x)$ for $y = 1, 2, \cdots, 8$ has split into two subsets. In one subset the response regions are elongated vertically, and in the other subset they are elongated horizontally. In all cases there is approximate invariance of $\Pr(y|x)$ with respect to variations of x along the direction of elongation of the response region. In effect, one subset encodes one of the circular S^1 subspaces of the 2-torus $S^1 \times S^1$, and the other subset encodes the other circular S^1 subspace. In this type of encoder it is necessary to sample many times from the code book in order to guarantee that at least one sample is drawn from each of these subsets, so that both of the circular subspaces are represented in the code. In this case the location of the input vector may be determined to an accuracy corresponding to the region of intersection of an orthogonal pair of elongated response regions.

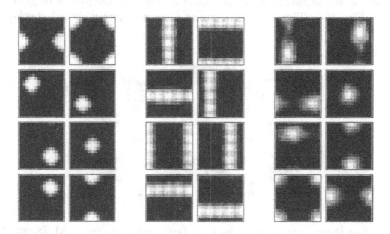

Fig. 2. All of these plots use toroidal boundary conditions. (a) (left) $\Pr(y|x)$ for data lying on a 2-torus, trained using $M = 8$ and $n = 5$. (b) (middle) $\Pr(y|x)$ for data lying on a 2-torus, trained using $M = 8$ and $n = 50$. (c) (right) $\Pr(y|x)$ for data lying on a 2-torus, trained using $M = (8, 2)$ and $n = (50, N/A)$, and using *strong* supervision

A major advantage of this type of encoder is that the size of the code book that is required to guarantee a given resolution (in each dimension of the input manifold) increases *linearly* with input manifold dimensionality, and the price that has to be paid for this is the need to sample many times from the code book. This general type of encoder will be called a *factorial* encoder, because it separately encodes each of the dimensions of the input manifold. This propensity for the codebook to split into a number of smaller code books is the key to using self-organisation to form a classifier ensemble, in which the different classifiers have different strengths and weaknesses.

3.3   2-Toroidal Input Manifold with Supervision

A yet more sophisticated demonstration of an SVQ is to train it with 2-toroidal data (see Sect. 3.2), but this time introduce some supervision by an external teacher.

To allow a reasonable amount of flexibility a 2-stage encoder will be used (see Sect. 2.3), where zero weight will be assigned to the $D_1^{(2)} + D_2^{(2)}$ contribution to the overall objective function D, so that the second stage is devoted entirely to dealing with the supervision that is introduced via the $D_{\text{supervise}}^{(2)}$ contribution. Back-propagation of derivatives of the objective function will ensure that this supervision also influences the first stage of the 2-stage encoder.

The first and second stages will use code books with parameters ($M = 8, n = 50$) and ($M = 8, n = \text{N/A}$), respectively, and the external teacher will attempt to make the pair of outputs from the second stage equal to the pair of target outputs shown in Fig. 3(a). These target outputs form oppositely signed checkerboard

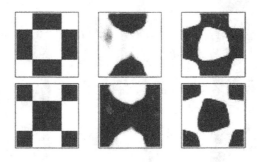

Fig. 3. All of these plots use toroidal boundary conditions. (a) (left) Target outputs used for supervision of a 2-stage encoder. (b) (middle) Output produced when trained using *weak* supervision. (c) (right) Output produced when trained using *strong* supervision

pattern (of 0's and 1's) on the 2-toroidal input manifold, so that they have the properties of a posterior probability (i.e. non-negative and sum to unity at each point on the 2-torus). This particular form of target output has been chosen to be more difficult to produce using a factorial encoder (see Fig. 2(b)) than a joint encoder (see Fig. 2(a)), because the latter uses response regions that are similar in shape to the squares in the checkerboard pattern used by the external teacher (see Fig. 3(a)).

When the 2-stage encoder is trained using supervision that is weak enough not to significantly influence the first stage, the results are the same as those shown in Fig. 2(b). Fig. 3(b) then shows the output of the second stage, which should be compared with the required output shown in Fig. 3(a). The results in Fig. 3(b) are poor because the weak supervision signal cannot produce large enough back-propagated derivatives to override the unsupervised training of the first stage, which insists on producing a factorial code in which the two circular subspaces of the 2-toroidal input manifold are separately encoded (see Fig. 2(b)). In effect, these results are produced by combining the outputs of two badly designed classifiers, each of which concentrates on only one of the S^1 subspaces of the 2-torus.

When the supervision is strong enough to significantly influence the first stage, the results are as shown in Fig. 2(c) and Fig. 3(c) (which are analogous to Fig. 2(b) and Fig. 3(b), respectively). Fig. 2(c) shows that the factorial encoder that arose when weak supervision was used (see Fig. 2(b)) has now been modified by the use of strong supervision (via back-propagation of the correspondingly large derivatives) to resemble a joint encoder (compare Fig. 2(a)). This is as expected, because the response regions of a joint encoder resemble the shape of the squares in the checkerboard pattern used by the supervisor (see Fig. 3(a)). Fig. 3(c) shows the output of the second stage, which now much more closely resembles the required output (see Fig. 3(a)) than when the supervision was weak (see Fig. 3(b)). In effect, these results are produced by a single classifier that makes optimal use of the $S^1 \times S^1$ 2-torus, rather than concentrating on only one of its S^1 subspaces at a time, as was the case in Fig. 3(b).

These results obtained from a 2-stage network of linked SVQs are illustrative of the more general possibilities offered by acyclically linked networks of SVQs.

4 Discussion

A key behaviour of 2-stage encoders is exemplified by the results obtained from a 2-toroidal input manifold with supervision (see Sect. 3.3).

When only weak supervision is used, the first stage optimises itself to encode the input so that it can reconstruct it with minimum distortion (i.e. minimise $D_1 + D_2$ in Eq. 4). There is no guarantee that this encoder will be any good for accurately producing the output required by the weak supervision. Effectively, the first stage preprocesses the input in a way that is heedless of the nature of the task that the second stage has to do. This is analogous to the situation where an overall classifier is constructed by combining the outputs of a set of individual classifiers, that are designed in ignorance of the overall classification problem that is to be solved, so it does not perform very well.

When strong supervision is used, the first stage is forced to heed the requirements of the second stage, and adjusts the way in which it preprocesses the input, so that the second stage is able to accurately produce the output required by the strong supervision. This is analogous to the situation where an overall classifier is constructed by combining the outputs of a set of individual classifiers, that are designed in way that is mindful of the overall classification problem that is to be solved, so it performs very well.

There are many ways in which the results of Sect. 3.3 can be generalised. The multi-stage encoder could have more than two stages, and in general it could be an acyclically linked network of encoders having multiple input and multiple output stages. The basic properties of each encoder are specified by three parameters: size of the code book M, number of samples n drawn from the code book, and objective function weighting s. Supervision by an external teacher could be added to any or all of the encoder outputs.

5   Conclusions

In this paper SVQs have been shown to be a flexible tool for self-organised classifier fusion. The unsupervised part of the network objective function tries to preserve information about the input data as it is processed and passed through the network. The supervised part of the objective function tries to ensure that the required classifier output is produced at the network output, by judiciously discarding irrelevant information and massaging what is left into the required output form. The tension between these two pieces of the objective function leads to an optimal network, in which typically the lower layers (near to the input) act as faithful encoders of the input, whereas the higher layers (near to the output) act as faithful classifiers.

Acknowledgement. This work was carried out as part of Technology Group 10 of the MoD Corporate Research Programme.

References

1. Kittler, J., Duin, R.P.W., Hatef, M., Matas, J.: On combining classifiers, IEEE Transactions on Pattern Analysis and Machine Intelligence, **20** (1998) 226–239
2. Ali, K.M., Pazzani, M.J.: On the link between error correlation and error reduction in decision tree ensembles, Technical Report 95-38, ICS-UCI, (1995)
3. Linde, Y., Buzo, A., Gray, R.M.: An algorithm for vector quantiser design, IEEE Trans. COM, **28**(1) (1980) 84–95
4. Luttrell, S.P.: A theory of self-organising neural networks. In: Ellacott, S.W., Mason, J.C., Anderson, I.J. (eds.) Mathematics of Neural Networks: Models, Algorithms and Applications. Kluwer (1997) 240–244
5. Luttrell, S.P.: A user's guide to stochastic encoder/decoders. DERA Technical Report, DERA/S&P/SPI/TR990290 (1999)
6. Luttrell, S.P.: Bayesian analysis of self-organising maps, Neural Computation, **6**(5) (1994) 767–794
7. Luttrell, S.P.: An adaptive network for encoding data using piecewise linear functions. In: Proceedings of 9th International Conference on Artificial Neural Networks, (1999) 198–203

Error Rejection in Linearly Combined Multiple Classifiers

Giorgio Fumera and Fabio Roli

Dept. of Electrical and Electronic Eng., University of Cagliari
Piazza d'Armi, I-09123 Cagliari, Italy
{fumera, roli}@diee.unica.it

Abstract. In this paper, the error-reject trade-off of linearly combined multiple classifiers is analysed in the framework of the minimum risk theory. Theoretical analysis described in [12,13] is extended for handling reject option and the optimality of the error-reject trade-off is analysed under the assumption of independence among the errors of the individual classifiers. Improvements of the error-reject trade-off obtained by linear classifier combination are quantified. Finally, a method for computing the coefficients of the linear combination and the value of the reject threshold is proposed. Experimental results on four different data sets are reported.

1 Introduction

It is well known that reject option is useful for improving the classification reliability in pattern recognition applications for which the cost of rejecting certain patterns, and handling them with different procedures (e.g., manual classification), is lower than the cost of wrong classifications. In the framework of the minimum risk theory, Chow defined the optimal classification rule with reject option [2]. Let be w_C and w_E the costs for the correct and for the wrong classification of pattern $\mathbf{x}$, and w_R be the cost for reject (obviously, $w_C < w_R < w_E$; usually, $w_C = 0$). The Bayes expected risk is then:

$$w_C P(correct) + w_R P(reject) + w_E P(error) . \tag{1}$$

Accordingly to Chow's rule, the above expected risk is minimised by accepting a pattern $\mathbf{x}$ and assigning it to the class ω_i, if:

$$\max_j P(\omega_j \mid \mathbf{x}) = P(\omega_i \mid \mathbf{x}) \geq T = (w_E - w_R)/(w_E - w_C) , \tag{2}$$

where $P(\omega_i|\mathbf{x})$ is the i-th class posterior probability of $\mathbf{x}$. Otherwise, $\mathbf{x}$ is rejected.

Even in multiple classifier systems (MCSs) there are cases in which the classification of a pattern is poorly reliable. For instance, the majority of classifiers can disagree about the classification of an input pattern; or, when the Bayesian average combination rule is used, more data classes can exhibit comparable values of the posterior probabilities. Therefore, the reject option is useful also for improving classification reliability of MCSs. It is worth noting that Chow's rule can be used only for combination rules which provide estimates of the class posterior probabilities, like the Bayesian average combination rule [15,8] or the linear combination of neural networks [10]. For other kinds of combining rules, the classification reliability must be evaluated using the specific kind of information provided by the combiner. As an

J. Kittler and F. Roli (Eds.): MCS 2001, LNCS 2096, pp. 329–338, 2001.
© Springer-Verlag Berlin Heidelberg 2001

example, for the majority rule and its variations (i.e., weighted voting), the reject option is based on the disagreement among the decisions of the individual classifiers [1]. Therefore, the error-reject trade-off of MCSs strongly depends on the particular combination rule used.

Besides many experimental works that reported the benefits of combining classifiers, some theoretical works investigated the hypotheses under which combination can improve the performances of the individual classifiers, and some papers quantitatively evaluated such improvements. For instance, Lam and Suen provided theoretical results allowing one to understand and quantify the performances of the majority rule [9]. Tumer and Ghosh analysed the performances of linearly combining multiple classifiers in the framework of the Bayes decision theory [12,13]. However, to the best of our knowledge, no theoretical work addressed the problem of the error-reject trade-off for MCSs. Some papers have shown by experiments that classifier combination can improve the error-reject trade-off of individual classifiers [6,10,8]. However, such papers did not analyse the hypotheses under which this can happen and they did not quantify the improvements.

In this paper the error-reject trade-off of linearly combined multiple classifiers is analysed in the framework of the minimum risk theory. Sect. 2 basically extends the work of Tumer and Ghosh, that was confined to the case without reject option [12,13]. In Sect. 3, a method for computing the coefficients ("weights") of the linear combination and the value of the reject threshold is proposed. Experimental results are reported in Sect. 4.

2   Error-Reject Trade-Off for a Linear Combination of Classifiers

The optimal error-reject trade-off is achieved by Chow's rule only if posterior probabilities are exactly known. Unfortunately, this does not happen in practical applications [5]. Therefore, in the following, we will assume that classifiers provide estimates of posterior probabilities, and compare the error-reject trade-off achievable by a linear combination of multiple classifiers with the optimal trade-off that could be obtained if posterior probabilities were exactly known. More precisely, as Chow's rule provides the minimum error probability $P(error)$ for any value of the reject probability $P(reject)$ [3], we compare, for a given value of $P(reject)$, the values of $P(error)$ achieved by a single classifier (Sect. 2.1) and by an MCS (Sect. 2.2) with Chow's optimal value of $P(error)$. The theoretical contribution of this paper is contained in Sect. 2.1, where we show the dependence between $P(error)$ and the estimate errors on posterior probabilities. It is worth noting that this dependence is similar to that found by Tumer and Ghosh [12,13] for the case without reject option. This allows us to extend their results to MCSs with reject option (Sect. 2.2).

2.1   Theoretical Framework

Let us indicate the estimated posterior probability for the i-th class as:

$$\hat{p}_i(\mathbf{x}) = p_i(\mathbf{x}) + \varepsilon_i(\mathbf{x}) \ , \tag{3}$$

where $p_i(\mathbf{x})$ is the "true" posterior probability and $\varepsilon_i(\mathbf{x})$ is the estimation error. In the following, we will consider a simple one-dimensional classification task with two data classes ω_1 and ω_2 characterised by Gaussian distributions. At the end of this section, we will point out that our analysis holds for a general classification task.

Fig. 1 shows the true and the estimated posterior probabilities of classes ω_1 and ω_2.

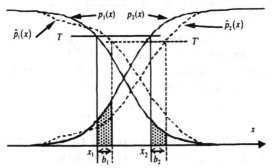

Fig. 1. The true and the estimated posterior probabilities of classes ω_1 and ω_2 are shown

Let us consider values of the reject thresholds T and T' such that the optimal reject region $[x_1, x_2]$ and the estimated one $[x_1+b_1, x_2+b_2]$ provide the same $P(reject)$. We assume that the estimation errors are reasonably small, such that the offsets b_1 and b_2 between the estimated and the optimal decision and reject regions are reasonably small [5]. Due to the estimation errors, patterns belonging to $[x_1, x_1+b_1]$ are accepted and assigned to class ω_1 instead of being rejected. Analogously, patterns belonging to $[x_2, x_2+b_2]$ are rejected instead of being accepted and assigned to ω_2.

Our goal is to compare, for a given $P(reject)$, the $P(error)$ achieved using the estimated and the true posterior probabilities. Following the work of Tumer and Ghosh [12,13], we will first express the offsets b_1 and b_2 as a function of the estimation errors $\varepsilon_1(x)$ and $\varepsilon_2(x)$. Then, we will express and analyse the difference between the error probabilities (shaded areas in Fig. 1) as a function of b_1 and b_2.

The estimated posterior probabilities of classes ω_1 and ω_2 take on the same value (T') at the boundaries of the reject region: $\hat{p}_1(x_1 + b_1) = \hat{p}_2(x_2 + b_2)$. From Eq. (3):

$$p_1(x_1 + b_1) + \varepsilon_1(x_1 + b_1) = p_2(x_2 + b_2) + \varepsilon_2(x_2 + b_2) \cdot$$

Linearly approximating $p_1(x)$ and $p_2(x)$, respectively around x_1 and x_2, and noting that $p_1(x_1) = p_2(x_2)$ (these values are equal to the reject threshold T), we can write:

$$b_1 p_1'(x_1) + \varepsilon_1(x_1 + b_1) = b_2 p_2'(x_2) + \varepsilon_2(x_2 + b_2) \cdot \tag{4}$$

We can now express b_2 as a function of b_1 by exploiting the equality between the reject probabilities of the true and the estimated error regions (see Fig. 1):

$$\int_{x_1}^{x_1+b_1} p(x)dx = \int_{x_2}^{x_2+b_2} p(x)dx \cdot$$

where $p(x)$ is the probability density distribution of x. If we approximate the values of $p(x)$ in the domains of integration $[x_1, x_1 + b_1]$ and $[x_2, x_2 + b_2]$, respectively with the constants terms $p(x_1)$ and $p(x_2)$, we obtain $p(x_1)b_1 = p(x_2)b_2$. Accordingly:

$$b_2 = \left[p(x_1) / p(x_2) \right] b_1 \cdot$$

(5)

By substituting Eq. (5) in Eq. (4), we obtain b_1 as a function of ε_1 and ε_2:

$$b_1 = \frac{\varepsilon_2(x_2 + b_2) - \varepsilon_1(x_1 + b_1)}{\left[p'(x_1) - p(x_1) / p(x_2) \right]} = \frac{\varepsilon_2(x_2 + b_2) - \varepsilon_1(x_1 + b_1)}{s},$$

(6)

where s is a constant term. The above expression is similar to the one obtained by Tumer and Ghosh for the case without reject option [12,13].

Now let us consider the difference ΔE between the error probabilities achieved using the estimated and the true posterior probabilities:

$$\Delta E = \int_{x_1}^{x_1 + b_1} p_2(x) p(x) dx - \int_{x_2}^{x_2 + b_2} p_1(x) p(x) dx \cdot$$

As Chow's rule applied to the estimated posterior probabilities is not optimal, it follows that $\Delta E > 0$. Linearly approximating $p_1(x)$ and $p_2(x)$:

$$p_2(x_1 + b_1) \cong p_2(x_1) + b_1 p_2'(x_1), \quad p_1(x_2 + b_2) \cong p_1(x_2) + b_2 p_1'(x_2),$$

and using the above constant approximation for $p(x)$, the two above integrals coincide with the areas of two trapeziums, as shown in Fig. 2.

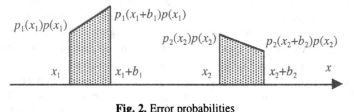

Fig. 2. Error probabilities

Finally, using Eq. (5), it is easy to see that ΔE can be expressed as follows:

$$\Delta E(b_1) = \left[p_2(x_1) - p(x_1) p_1(x_1) \right] b_1 + \frac{1}{2} \left[p_2'(x_1) p(x_1) - p'(x_1) p_1'(x_2) / p(x_2) \right] b_1^2 = c b_1 + d b_1^2,$$

(7)

where c and d represent constant terms. It is worth noting that the expression of ΔE for the case without reject option contains only a second degree term [12,13].

Eqs. (6) and (7) show how the added error probability ΔE, corresponding to a given value of $P(reject)$, depends on the offset b_1, and therefore on the estimation errors $\varepsilon_1(x)$ and $\varepsilon_2(x)$. We pointed out that these expressions are similar to the ones obtained by Tumer and Ghosh [12,13] for the case without reject option. It is then possible to extend their analysis to the case with reject option. More precisely, the expected value E_{add} related to ΔE can be computed as a function of the parameters (mean and variance) of the probability density functions of $\varepsilon_1(x)$ and $\varepsilon_2(x)$. It is then possible to compare the values of E_{add} corresponding to a single classifier and to an MCS. The details of the computations can be found in [4]. The results are summarised in Sect. 2.2.

We conclude this section by discussing briefly the main assumptions we made above. For a problem with more than two classes and more than one decision boundary, the reject region can be made up of several disjoint intervals corresponding to points in which the posterior probabilities of the local dominant classes are lower than the reject threshold. However, it is easy to see that the above analysis would lead to expressions of the offset b and of the error probability ΔE similar to Eqs. (6) and (7). A linear approximation of the distribution $p(x)$, instead of the constant approximation above, would lead to a non linear dependency of b_1 from the estimation errors. But this complicates only the mathematical derivation of the probability distribution of b_1.

2.2 Error-Reject Trade-Off for Linear Combination of Unbiased and Biased Classifiers

In the following, we hypothesise that the estimation errors $\varepsilon_1(x)$ and $\varepsilon_2(x)$ are independent variables with means β_1 and β_2, and variances $\sigma_{r_1}^2$ and $\sigma_{r_2}^2$.

We consider first the unbiased case ($\beta_1 = \beta_2 = 0$). From Eqs. (6) and (7) it turns out that the expected value E_{add} of the added error probability $\Delta E(b_1)$ is $E_{add} = d\sigma_{b_1}^2$, where $\sigma_{b_1}^2$ is the variance of b_1. Let us now consider a constrained linear combination of the outputs of N classifiers. The estimated posterior probabilities, denoted with $\hat{p}_i^{ave}(x)$, can be expressed as follows:

$$\hat{p}_i^{ave}(x) = \sum_{j=1}^{N} \alpha_j \hat{p}_i^j(x) = \sum_{j=1}^{N} \alpha_j p_i(x) + \bar{\varepsilon}_i(x) , \tag{8}$$

where

$$\alpha_j \geq 0, \quad \sum_{j=1}^{N} \alpha_j = 1 , \tag{9}$$

and the estimation error is $\bar{\varepsilon}_i(x) = \sum_{j=1}^{N} \alpha_j \varepsilon_i^j(x)$. In this case, denoting with b_1^{ave} the offset, the expected value E_{add}^{ave} of the added error probability is $E_{add}^{ave} = d\sigma_{b_1^{ave}}^2 = d\sum_{j=1}^{N} \alpha_j^2 \sigma_{b_1^j}^2$. It turns out that the values of the coefficients α_j which minimise E_{add}^{ave}, taking into account the constraints of Eq. (10), are:

$$\alpha_j = \left(\sigma_{b_1^j}^2 \sum_{k=1}^{N} \sigma_{b_1^k}^{-2} \right)^{-1} . \tag{10}$$

Therefore we obtain:

$$E_{add}^{ave} \leq (1/N) \max_{j=1\dots N} E_{add}^j .$$

This shows that the linear combination reduces E_{add}^{ave}, with respect to the worst individual classifier, up to a factor N. If the errors $\varepsilon_i^j(x)$ of the different classifiers exhibit the same variance ($\sigma_{r_j}^2 = \sigma_{r_k}^2$, $\forall j \neq k$), we obtain $\alpha_j = 1/N$ (simple average). In this case the linear combination reduces the added error by a factor $1/N$:

$$E_{add}^{ave} = d\sigma_{b_1^{ave}}^2 = d\sigma_{b_1}^2 / N = E_{add} / N .$$

Let us consider now the biased case ($\beta_j \neq 0$). For a single classifier we obtain:

$$E_{add} = c\beta + d(\sigma_h^2 + \beta^2),$$

where β is the mean of the offset b_1. It is worth noting that this expression differs from the case without reject option for the term proportional to β [12]. Linearly combining N classifiers, the expression of E_{add}^{av} is:

$$E_{add}^{av} = c\bar{\beta} + d(\sigma_{h^{av}}^2 + \bar{\beta}^2) = c\left(\sum_{j=1}^{N} \alpha_j \beta^j\right) + d\left[\sum_{j=1}^{N} \alpha_j^2 \sigma_{h_j}^2 + \left(\sum_{j=1}^{N} \alpha_j \beta^j\right)^2\right], \tag{11}$$

where $\bar{\beta} = \sum_{j=1}^{N} \alpha_j \beta^j$ is the mean of the offset b_1^{av}. In this case the values of the coefficients α_j which minimise E_{add}^{av} depend on the trade-off between the minimisation of the variance and of the mean of b_1^{av}. Therefore the simple average could be not the optimal choice even if the errors $\varepsilon_i^j(x)$ of the different classifiers exhibit the same variance. In this case the simple average reduces by a factor N the variance of b_1^{av}. Let us assume that its mean is reduced by a factor $z \geq 1$ ($\bar{\beta} = \beta/z$). Then, if $z \leq \sqrt{N}$ it turns out that $E_{add}^{av} \leq E_{add}/z$, while if $z > \sqrt{N}$, then $E_{add}^{av} \leq E_{add}/\sqrt{N}$. The improvement of the error-reject trade-off, due to averaging biased classifiers, is then limited by $\min(z, \sqrt{N})$. This is a lower improvement than the one achievable without reject option, which is limited by $\min(z^2, N)$ [13].

Let us now remind that E_{add}^{av} represents, for any given value of $P(reject)$, the difference between the $P(error)$ of the linear classifier combination and the minimum error probability that Chow's rule could provide if posterior probabilities were exactly known (see Sect. 2.1). Accordingly, we can say that, for any given value of $P(reject)$, the value of $P(error)$ achieved by a linear combination of classifiers approximates Chow's minimum value of $P(error)$ as much as the number of classifiers increases.

3   An Algorithm for Computing the Coefficients of the Linear Combination

We showed that linearly combining N classifiers with independent estimation errors, the difference with respect to the optimal error-reject trade-off can decrease up to a factor N. However, theoretical results provided in Sect. 2 cannot be used to determine the values of the coefficients ("weights") of the linear combination, since, in real applications, the probability distribution of the estimation errors is unknown. In particular, Sect. 2 does not provide a method for computing the coefficients in Eq. (10) and the ones that minimise the expected value of the added error probability (Eq. 11). Without reject option, the commonly used approach to evaluate the coefficients relies on the minimisation of the error rate of the MCS on a validation set [10,7,14]. The rationale behind such approach is that, in principle, values of the coefficients such that the corresponding error probability is not higher than the one of the best single classifier always exist. As an example, if we could know that the best classifier on the test set is the i-th one, then a trivial choice of the coefficients would be $\alpha_i = 1$ and $\alpha_j = 0, j \neq i$. When using the reject option, one can find first the coefficients which minimise the error probability without reject, then, using these coefficients, find the value of the reject threshold T that minimises the expected risk. This approach was used in [10]. However, we point out that this approach does not guarantee to effectively minimise the expected risk, since a separate minimisation of the coefficients α_i and the reject threshold T is performed. Accordingly, both the coefficients and the reject threshold should be determined by minimising the expected risk for given values of the costs w_C, w_R and w_E. Let us therefore consider the problem of minimising the expected risk as a function of the coefficients and of the reject threshold, for given values of w_C, w_R, and w_E. Since $P(correct) = 1 - P(error) - P(reject)$, the expected risk (Eq. 1) can be rewritten as follows:

$$\text{risk} = w_C + (w_R - w_C)P(reject) + (w_E - w_C)P(error) . \tag{12}$$

Accordingly, the minimisation problem is:

$$\min_{\alpha_1 \ldots \alpha_N, T} \text{risk}(\alpha_1, \ldots, \alpha_N, T \mid w_C, w_R, w_E) . \tag{13}$$

Since in real applications the $P(error)$ and $P(reject)$ can only be estimated from a finite data set, the corresponding estimate of the expected risk in Eq. (13), called "empirical" risk, is a discrete-valued function and cannot directly be minimised using techniques based on gradient descent. It is also difficult to approximate the empirical risk by a smooth function, as proposed in [14] for the error rate of a classifier (that corresponds to the empirical risk without reject option). We have therefore developed a special purpose algorithm for solving the above minimisation problem. Such algorithm was derived from another proposed by the authors in [5].

Our algorithm iteratively searches for a local minimum of the target function. Starting from a point consisting of given values of the $N + 1$ variables, at each step a neighbourhood of the current point is explored. Such neighbourhood consists of points obtained from the current one by incrementing each variable, one at a time. The amplitude and the number of the increments are predefined. If a point exhibiting a value of the target function lower than the current one is found, then it becomes the new current point; otherwise the algorithm stops, and returns the current point as solution. The solution, for given values of w_C, w_R, and w_E, corresponds to a point in the Error-Rejection (E-R) plane. The E-R curve of the MCS is obtained by varying the value of the costs. We point out that, since minimising function (12) is equivalent to minimise $P(reject) + WP(error)$, where $W = (w_E - w_C) / (w_R - w_C) \in [+1, +\infty]$, then it is more convenient to minimise this last expression, since it depends on only one parameter. Since our algorithm can lead to a local minimum of the target function, the so called "multi-start technique" was used. For the same given values of the costs, the algorithm was run for a predefined number of times, starting from random values of the $N + 1$ variables.

4 Experimental Results

Our experiments were aimed at comparing the error-reject trade-off achievable by a single classifier and by a linear combination of classifiers. The error-reject trade-off is represented here by the Accuracy-Reject (A-R) curve that is equivalent to the E-R curve because minimising the error probability for any given reject probability is equivalent to maximise the accuracy. The accuracy is defined as

$P(correct \mid accept) = P(correct) / [1 - P(reject)]$ and it has been estimated as the ratio between the correctly classified patterns and the accepted patterns. The experiments have been carried out on four different data sets. We used a data set of remote sensing images (the Feltwell data set [11]), two data sets from the ELENA database (Phoneme and Satimage) (ftp://ftp.dice.ucl.ac.be/pub/neural-nets/ELENA/databases), and one from the STATLOG database (Letter) (http://www.ncc.up.pt/liacc/ML/statlog/). Some details about such data sets are given in Table 1.

Four types of classifiers have been used: the linear and quadratic Bayes classifier (indicated in the following with LB and QB), the multilayer perceptron neural networks (MLP), and the k-nearest neighbours classifier (k-NN). Each data set has been subdivided into a training and a test set. After the training phase, the A-R curves

Table 1. Data sets used for experiments

Data Set	Training patterns	Test patterns	Features	Classes
Feltwell	5,820	5,124	15	5
Phoneme (ELENA)	2,702	2,702	5	2
Satimage (ELENA)	3,213	3,216	36	7
Letter (STATLOG)	15,000	5,000	16	26

of the single classifiers have been assessed on the test set. Then, the A-R curve of the linear combination of such classifiers has been computed by the algorithm described in the previous section. We have considered values of the cost parameter W that lead to reject rates between 0 and 20%, since this range is usually the most relevant for application purposes. Figs. 3-6 show the A-R curves of the single classifiers and of the linear combination (denoted with MCS) for the four data sets. For any value of the reject rate, the accuracy achieved by the MCS is always higher than the accuracy of the single classifiers. This means that the method proposed in Sect. 3 allows one to obtain a MCS with a better error-reject trade-off than that of each single classifier. It is worth noting that the linear combination allows a significant improvement of the classification accuracy when the performances of the single classifiers are similar (Feltwell and Satimage data sets). Differently, linear combination accuracy is close to that of the best single classifier if the performance of such classifier is significantly better than that of the others (Phoneme and Letter data sets). In this case, our algorithm assigns a value of the coefficient close to 1 to the best single classifier, that is, the linear combination tends to select the best single classifier.

5 Conclusions

In this paper, we studied the error-reject trade-off of linearly combined multiple classifiers in the framework of the minimum risk theory. We reported a theoretical analysis of the error-reject trade-off under the assumption of independence among the errors of the individual classifiers. We showed that, under the hypotheses made, a linear combination of classifiers can approximate the optimal error-reject trade-off. In addition, we proposed a method for computing the coefficients of the linear combination and the value of the reject threshold. The experimental results reported showed that our method allows designing a linear combination of classifiers that can effectively improve the error-reject trade-off of the individual classifiers.

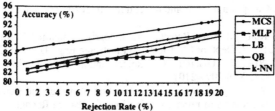

Fig. 3. Results for Feltwell data set

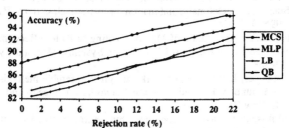

Fig. 4. Results for Satimage data set

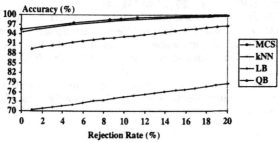

Fig. 5. Results for Letter data set

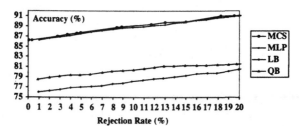

Fig. 6. Results for Phoneme data set

References

1.   Battiti, R., Colla, A.M.: Democracy in neural nets: voting schemes for classification. Neural Networks 7 (1994) 691-707
2.   Chow, C.K.: An optimum character recognition system using decision functions. IRE Trans. on Electronic Computers 6 (1957) 247-254

3. Chow, C.K.: On optimum error and reject tradeoff. IEEE Trans. on Information Theory 16 (1970) 41-46
4. Fumera, G., Roli, F.: Error Rejection in Linearly Combined Multiple Classifiers. Int. Report n. 2001-113, Dept. of Electrical and Electronic Eng., Univ. of Cagliari (2001)
5. Fumera, G., Roli, F., Giacinto, G.: Reject option with multiple thresholds. Pattern Recognition 33 (2000) 2099-2101
6. Giacinto, G., Roli, F., Bruzzone, L.: Combination of neural and statistical algorithms for supervised classification of remote-sensing images. Pattern Recognition Letters 21 (2000) 385-397
7. Hashem, S., Schmeiser, B.: Improving model accuracy using optimal linear combinations of trained neural networks. IEEE Trans. on Neural Networks 6 (1995) 792-794
8. Lam., L., Suen, C.Y.: Optimal combination of pattern classifiers. Pattern Recognition Letters 16 (1995) 945-954
9. Lam, L., Suen, C.Y.: Application of Majority Voting to Pattern Recognition: An Analysis of Its Behavior and Performance. IEEE Trans. on Systems, Man and Cybernetics - Part A 27 (1997) 553-568
10. Perrone, M., Cooper, L.N.: When networks disagree: ensemble methods for hybrid neural networks. In: Mammone, R.J. (ed.): Neural Networks for Speech and Image Processing. Chapman-Hall, New York (1993)
11. Roli, F.: Multisensor image recognition by neural networks with understandable behaviour. Int. Journal of Pattern Recognition and Artificial Intelligence 10 (1996) 887-917
12. Tumer, K., Ghosh, J.: Analysis of decision boundaries in linearly combined neural classifiers. Pattern Recognition 29 (1996) 341-348
13. Tumer, K., Ghosh, J.: Linear and order statistics combiners for pattern classification. In: Sharkey, A.J.C. (ed.): Combining Artificial Neural Nets. Springer, London (1999)
14. Ueda, N.: Optimal linear combination of neural networks for improving classification performance. IEEE Trans. on Pattern Analisys and Machine Intelligence 22 (2000) 207-215
15. Xu, L., Krzyzak, A., Suen, C.Y.: Methods of combining multiple classifiers and their applications to handwriting recognition. IEEE Trans. on Systems, Man, and Cybernetics 22 (1992) 418-435

Relationship of Sum and Vote Fusion Strategies

J. Kittler and F.M. Alkoot

Centre for Vision, Speech and Signal Processing,
School of Electronics, Computing and Mathematics,
University of Surrey, Guildford GU2 7XH, United Kingdom.
{J.Kittler,F.Alkoot}@eim.surrey.ac.uk

Abstract. Amidst the conflicting evidence of superiority of one over the other, we investigate the Sum and majority Vote combining rules for the two class case at a single point. We show analytically that, for Gaussian estimation error distributions, Sum always outperforms Vote, whereas for heavy tail distributions Vote may outperform Sum.

1 Introduction

Among the many combination rules suggested in the literature [1,4,5,6,7,8,9,10, 11,13,16,17] Sum and Vote are used the most frequently. The Sum rule operates directly on the soft outputs of individual experts for each class hypothesis, normally delivered in terms of aposteriori class probabilities. The fused decision is obtained by applying the maximum value selector to the class dependent averages. When fusing by Sum the experts outputs can be treated equally or they could be assigned different weights based on their performance on a validation set. When independent experts are combined, equal weights appear to yield the best performance [1]. The properties of the rule have been widely investigated [7,8,9,11,10,2,3,4,14,15].

Vote, on the other hand, operates on class labels assigned to each pattern by the respective experts by hardening their soft decision outputs using the maximum value selector. The Vote rule output is a function of the votes received for each class in terms of these single expert class labels. Many versions of Vote exist, such as unanimous vote, threshold voting, weighted voting and simple majority voting [13,16]. In addition to these basic rules, the authors in [16] propose two voting methods claimed to outperform the majority voting.

In our theoretical deliberations we focus on the basic Sum and Vote rules. Clearly both the weighted average (see e.g. [12]) and modified voting [16] can outperform the basic rules. However, the advanced strategies require training which is a negative aspect of these approaches. In any case, we believe that the conclusions drawn from the analysis of the simple cases will extend also to the more complex procedures.

Many researchers [2,11,6] have found that Sum outperforms Vote, while a few [6] have demonstrated that Vote can equal or outperform Sum. The aim of this paper is to investigate the relationship between these two rules in more detail. We shall argue that the relative merits of Sum and Vote depend on

J. Kittler and F. Roli (Eds.): MCS 2001, LNCS 2096, pp. 339–348, 2001.

the distribution of estimation errors. We show analytically that, for normally distributed estimation errors, Sum always outperforms Vote, whereas for heavy tail distributions Vote may outperform Sum. We then confirm our theoretical predictions by experiments on 2 class problems.

The paper is organised as follows. In the next section we introduce the necessary formalism and develop the basic theory of classifier combination by averaging and majority voting. The relationship of the two strategies is discussed in Section 3. We draw the paper to conclusion in Section 4.

2   Theoretical Analysis

Consider a two class pattern recognition problem where pattern Z is to be assigned to one of the two possible classes $\{\omega_1, \omega_2\}$. Let us assume that we have N classifiers each representing the given pattern by an identical measurement vector $\mathbf{x}$. In the measurement space each class ω_k is modelled by the probability density function $p(\mathbf{x}|\omega_k)$ and the a priori probability of occurrence denoted by $P(\omega_k)$. We shall consider the models to be mutually exclusive which means that only one model can be associated with each pattern.

Now according to the Bayesian decision theory, given measurements $\mathbf{x}$, the pattern, Z, should be assigned to class ω_j, i.e. its label θ should assume value $\theta = \omega_j$, provided the aposteriori probability of that interpretation is maximum, i.e.

$$assign \quad \theta \to \omega_j \quad if$$

$$P(\theta = \omega_j|\mathbf{x}) = \max_k P(\theta = \omega_k|\mathbf{x}) \tag{1}$$

In practice, the $j - th$ expert will provide only an estimate $P_j(\omega_i|\mathbf{x})$ of the true aposteriori class probability $P(\omega_i|\mathbf{x})$ given pattern $\mathbf{x}$, rather than the true probability. The idea of classifier combination is to obtain a better estimate of the aposteriori class probabilities by combining all the individual expert estimates and thus reducing the classification error. A typical estimator is the averaging estimator

$$\dot{P}(\omega_i|\mathbf{x}) = \frac{1}{N} \sum_{j=1}^{N} P_j(\omega_i|\mathbf{x}) \tag{2}$$

where $\dot{P}(\omega_i|\mathbf{x})$ is the combined estimate based on N observations.

Let us denote the error on the jth estimate of the ith class aposteriori probability at point $\mathbf{x}$ as $e_j(\omega_i|\mathbf{x})$ and let the probability distribution of the errors be $p_{ij}[e_j(\omega_i|\mathbf{x})]$. Then the probability distribution of the unscaled error $e_i(\mathbf{x})$

$$e_i(\mathbf{x}) = \sum_{j=1}^{N} e_j(\omega_i|\mathbf{x}) \tag{3}$$

on the combined estimate will be given by the convolution of the component error densities, i.e.

$$p(e_i(\mathbf{x})) = \int_{-\infty}^{\infty} \dots \int_{-\infty}^{\infty} p_{i1}(\lambda_1)p_{i2}(\lambda_2-\lambda_1)\dots p_{iN}(e_i(\mathbf{x})-\lambda_{N-1})d\lambda_1 d\lambda_2 \dots d\lambda_{N-1}$$

(4)

The distribution of the scaled error $\epsilon_i(\mathbf{x}) = \frac{1}{N}e_i(\mathbf{x})$ is then given by

$$p(\epsilon_i(\mathbf{x})) = p(\frac{1}{N}e_i(\mathbf{x}))$$

(5)

In order to investigate the effect of classifier combination, let us examine the two class aposteriori probabilities at a single point $\mathbf{x}$. Suppose the aposteriori probability of class ω_s is maximum, i.e. $P(\omega_s|\mathbf{x}) = \max_{i=1}^{2} P(\omega_i|\mathbf{x})$ giving the local Bayes error $e_B(\mathbf{x}) = 1 - \max_{i=1}^{2} P(\omega_i|\mathbf{x})$. However, our classifiers only estimate these aposteriori class probabilities and the associated estimation errors may result in suboptimal decisions, and consequently in an additional classification error. In order to quantify this additional error we have to establish what the probability is for the recognition system to make a suboptimal decision. This situation will occur when the aposteriori class probability estimates for the other class becomes maximum. Let us derive the probability of the event occurring for a single expert j for class ω_i, $i \neq s$, i.e. when

$$P_j(\omega_i|\mathbf{x}) - P_j(\omega_s|\mathbf{x}) > 0$$

(6)

Note that the left hand side of (6) can be expressed as

$$P(\omega_i|\mathbf{x}) - P(\omega_s|\mathbf{x}) + e_j(\omega_i|\mathbf{x}) - e_j(\omega_s|\mathbf{x}) > 0$$

(7)

Equation (7) defines a constraint for the two estimation errors $e_j(\omega_k|\mathbf{x})$, $k = 1, 2$, as

$$e_j(\omega_i|\mathbf{x}) - e_j(\omega_s|\mathbf{x}) > P(\omega_s|\mathbf{x}) - P(\omega_i|\mathbf{x})$$

(8)

In a two class case the errors on the left hand side satisfy $e_j(\omega_s|\mathbf{x}) = -e_j(\omega_i|\mathbf{x})$ and thus an additional labelling error will occur if

$$2e_j(\omega_i|\mathbf{x}) > P(\omega_s|\mathbf{x}) - P(\omega_i|\mathbf{x})$$

(9)

The probability $e_A(\mathbf{x})$ of this event occurring will be given by the integral of the error distribution under the tail defined by the margin $\Delta P_{si}(\mathbf{x}) = P(\omega_s|\mathbf{x}) - P(\omega_i|\mathbf{x})$, i.e.

$$e_A(\mathbf{x}) = \int_{\Delta P_{si}(\mathbf{x})}^{\infty} p_{ij}[2e_j(\omega_i|\mathbf{x})]de_j(\omega_i|\mathbf{x})$$

(10)

In contrast, after classifier fusion by averaging, the labelling error with respect to the Bayes decision rule will be given by

$$e_S(\mathbf{x}) = \int_{\Delta P_{si}(\mathbf{x})}^{\infty} p[2\epsilon_i(\mathbf{x})]d\epsilon_i(\mathbf{x})$$

(11)

Now how do these labelling errors translate to classification error probabilities? We know that for the Bayes minimum error decision rule the error probability at point $\mathbf{x}$ will be $e_B(\mathbf{x})$. For the multiple classifier system which averages the expert outputs, the classification error probability is

$$\beta(\mathbf{x}) = e_B(\mathbf{x}) + e_S(\mathbf{x})|\Delta P_{12}(\mathbf{x}))| \tag{12}$$

Thus for a multiple classifier system to achieve a better performance the labelling error after fusion, $e_S(\mathbf{x})$, should be smaller than the labelling error, $e_A(\mathbf{x})$, of a single expert.

Let us now consider fusion by voting. In this strategy all single expert decisions are hardened and therefore each expert will make suboptimal decisions with probability $e_A(\mathbf{x})$. When combined by voting for the most representative class, the probability distribution of k decisions, among a pool of N, being suboptimal is given by the binomial distribution. A switch of labels will occur whenever the majority of individual expert decisions is suboptimal. This will happen with probability

$$e_V(\mathbf{x}) = \sum_{k=\frac{N}{2}+1}^{N} \binom{N}{k} e_A^k(\mathbf{x})[1 - e_A(\mathbf{x})]^{N-k} \tag{13}$$

Provided $e_A(\mathbf{x}) < 0.5$ this probability will decrease with increasing N.

After fusion by Vote, the error probability of the multiple classifier will then be

$$\gamma(\mathbf{x}) = e_B(\mathbf{x}) + e_V(\mathbf{x})|\Delta P_{12}(\mathbf{x}))| \tag{14}$$

Before discussing the relationship between Sum and Vote in the next section, let us pause and consider the formulae (12) and (14). The additional classification error, over and above the Bayesian error, is given by the second term in the expressions. Note that the term depends on the probability $e_X(\mathbf{x})$ of the decision rule being suboptimal and the margin $\Delta P_{12}(\mathbf{x})$. The former is also a function of the margin, the number of experts N and the estimation error distribution. Now, at the boundary $\Delta P_{12}(\mathbf{x}) = 0$ and the multiple classifier system will be Bayes optimal, although at this point $e_X(\mathbf{x})$ is maximum. As we move away from the boundary $\Delta P_{12}(\mathbf{x})$ increases but at the same time $e_X(\mathbf{x})$ decreases. The product of the two nonnegative functions will be zero for $\Delta P_{12}(\mathbf{x}) = 0$ and as $\Delta P_{12}(\mathbf{x})$ increases, it will reach a maximum, followed by a rapid decay to zero. The above behaviour is illustrated in figure 2 for Sum and Vote combination strategies for normally distributed estimation errors with different values of $\sigma(\mathbf{x})$ and N. We note that the additional error injected by the sum rule is always lower than that due to Vote. As the standard deviation of the estimation error distribution increases, the probability of the decision rule being suboptimal increases for all margins. At the same time the peak of the two functions shifts towards the higher margin values. As the number of experts increases the above relationship between $\sigma(\mathbf{x})$ and $\Delta P_{12}(\mathbf{x})$ is preserved. However, the additional experts push the family of curves towards the origin of the graph.

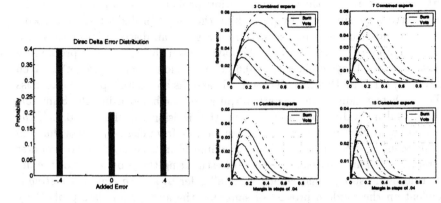

Fig. 1. Dirac delta error distribution

Fig. 2. Sum and Vote switching error for normally distributed estimation errors with $\sigma(\mathbf{x}) = .05, .15, .25$ and $.35$, using 3, 7, 11 and 15 experts

3 Relationship of Sum and Vote

In this section we shall investigate the relationship between the Sum and Vote fusion strategies. Assume that errors $e_j(\omega_i|\mathbf{x})$ are unbiased, i.e. $E\{e_j(\omega_i|\mathbf{x})\} = E\{\hat{P}_j(\omega_i|\mathbf{x}) - P(\omega_i|\mathbf{x})\} = 0$ $\forall i, j, \mathbf{x}$ and their standard derivatives are the same for all the experts, i.e. $\sigma_j(\omega_i|\mathbf{x}) = \sigma(\mathbf{x})$ $\forall i, j$ Then, provided the errors $e_j(\omega_i|\mathbf{x})$ are independent, the variance of the error distribution for the combined estimate $\dot{\sigma}^2(\mathbf{x})$ will be

$$\dot{\sigma}^2(\mathbf{x}) = \frac{\sigma^2(\mathbf{x})}{N} \qquad (15)$$

Let us also assume that the error distributions $p_{ij}[e_j(\omega_i|\mathbf{x})]$ are gaussian. For gaussian error the distribution of the difference of the two errors with equal magnitude but opposite sign will also be gaussian with four times as large variance. The probability of the constraint (8) being satisfied is given by the area under the gaussian tail with a cut off point at $P(\omega_s|\mathbf{x}) - P(\omega_i|\mathbf{x})$. More specifically, this probability, $e_A(\mathbf{x})$, is given by

$$e_A(\mathbf{x}) = 1 - erf(\frac{\Delta P_{si}(\mathbf{x})}{4\dot{\sigma}}) \qquad (16)$$

where $erf(\frac{\Delta P_{si}(\mathbf{x})}{4\dot{\sigma}})$ is the error function defined as

$$erf(\frac{\Delta P_{si}(\mathbf{x})}{4\dot{\sigma}}) = \frac{1}{2\sqrt{2\pi}\dot{\sigma}} \int_0^{\Delta P_{si}(\mathbf{x})} \exp^{-\frac{1}{2}\frac{\gamma^2}{4\dot{\sigma}^2}} d\gamma \qquad (17)$$

In order to compare the performance gains of the Sum and Vote fusion under the gaussian assumption we have designed a simulation experiment involving N

experts, each estimating the same aposteriori probability $P(\omega_i|\mathbf{x})$ $i = 1, 2$. Estimation errors are simulated by perturbing the target probability $P(\omega_i|\mathbf{x})$ with statistically independent errors drawn from a gaussian distribution with a zero mean and standard deviation $\sigma(\mathbf{x})$. We have chosen the aposteriori probability of class ω_1 to be always greater than 0.5. The decision margin $\Delta P_{12}(\mathbf{x})$ is given by $2P(\omega_1|\mathbf{x}) - 1$. The Bayesian decision rule assigns all the test patterns to class ω_1. For each test sample the expert outputs are combined using the Sum rule and the resulting value compared against the decision threshold of 0.5. If the estimated aposteriori probability for a test sample from class ω_1 is less than 0.5 or if the value is greater than 0.5 for a sample from class ω_2 an error counter is incremented. This particular method of estimating the probability of the decision rule being suboptimal, which we shall refer to as *two class set testing* is dependent on the random process of sampling the aposteriori class probability distributions. In order to eliminate the inherent stochasticity of the sampling process and its impact on the estimated error we also ran the same experiment by testing with samples from a single class. The corresponding *one class set testing* method involved samples from class ω_1 only and the switching error was estimated by counting the number of misclassified patterns.

Similarly, the decision errors of the majority vote are estimated by converting the expert outputs into class labels using the pseudo Bayesian decision rule and then counting the support for each class among the N labels. The label of the winning class is then checked against the identity of the test pattern and any errors recorded. The results are averaged over 500 experiments for each combination of $P(\omega_1|\mathbf{x})$ and $\sigma(\mathbf{x})$, the parameters of the simulation experiment.

The empirical results showing the additional error incurred are plotted as a function of the number of experts N in Figure 3. The results were obtained using the *two class set testing* approach. The theoretical values predicted by formulas (11) and (13) are also plotted for comparison. The experimental results mirror closely the theoretically predicted behaviour. All the results shown in Figure 3 indicate that Sum outperforms majority Vote at all error levels and all margins $\Delta P_{12}(\mathbf{x})$ except for the boundary where no improvement is possible. For a large number of experts Vote approaches the performance of Sum. However, for high values of $\sigma(\mathbf{x})$ the initial discrepancy in performance between Sum and Vote is large and the convergence of the two strategies as the number of experts increases is slow. The slight positive bias of the empirical errors as compared with their theoretical predictions is believed to be due to sampling effects. As $\sigma(\mathbf{x})$ increases the additional classification error also increases. In contrast, increasing the margin has the opposite effect.

While under the Gaussian assumption the Sum rule always outperforms Vote it is pertinent to ask whether this relationship holds for other distributions. Intuitively, if the error distribution has heavy tails it is easy to see that fusion by Sum will not result in improvement until the probability mass in the tail of $p_{ij}[e_j(\omega_i|\mathbf{x})]$ moves within the margin $\Delta P_{12}(\mathbf{x})$. In order to gain better understanding of the situation let us consider a specific example with the error distribution $p_{ij}[e_j(\omega_i|\mathbf{x})]$ being defined as a mixture of three Dirac delta func-

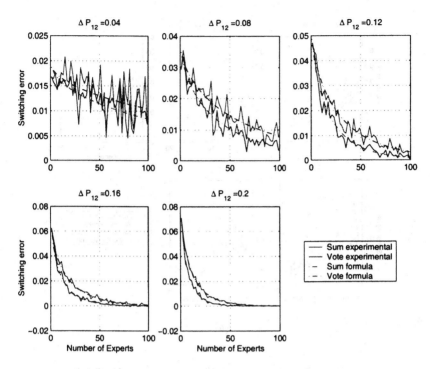

Fig. 3. Comparison of experimental Sum and Vote switching errors with theoretical predictions, for normal noise at $\sigma(\mathbf{x}) = 0.25$, using up to 100 experts.

tions with the weights and positions shown in figure 1. Using the convolution integral in equation (4) and substituting into (11) we can derive the probability, $e_S(\mathbf{x})$ of the decision rule being suboptimal for a given margin $\Delta P_{12}(\mathbf{x})$. Figure 4(a) shows this probability as a function of the number of expert outputs fused. The function has been computed for a range of margins from $\Delta P_{12}(\mathbf{x}) = 0.04$ to $\Delta P_{12}(\mathbf{x}) = 0.2$. The figure shows clearly an oscillating behaviour of $e_S(\mathbf{x})$. It is interesting to note that for small margins, initially (i.e. for a small number of experts) the error probability of the sum combiner has a tendency to grow above the probability of the decision rule being suboptimal for a single expert. First the performance improves when $N = 2$ but as further experts are added the error builds up as the probability mass shifts from the origin to the periphery by the process of convolution. It is also interesting to note that for $N = 2$ Vote degrades in performance. However, this is only an artifact of a vote tie not being randomised in the theoretical formula. Once the first line of the probability distribution of the sum of estimation errors falls below the threshold defined by the margin between the two class aposteriori probabilities the performance dramatically improves. However, by adding further experts the error build up will start all over again, though it will culminate at a lower value than at the previous peak. We can see that for instance for $\Delta P_{12}(\mathbf{x}) = 0.04$ the benefits from

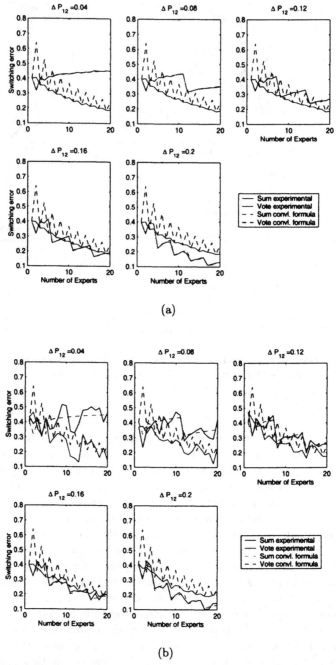

Fig. 4. Sum and Vote switching error: A comparison of (a) single class and (b) two class experimental results and theoretical predictions for delta noise positioned at (1-p), using up to 20 experts

fusion by the sum rule will be very poor and there may be a wide range of N for which fusion would result in performance deterioration. Once the margin reaches 0.16 Sum will generally outperform Vote but there may be specific numbers of experts for which Vote is better than Sum. In both figures 4(a) and 4(b) the position of the Dirac delta components of the error distribution offset from the origin is at $\pm[1 - P(\omega_1|\mathbf{x})]$. Figure 4(b) shows the additional effect of sampling the aposteriori class probability distribution inherent in the *two class set testing* approach.

In contrast the corresponding probability, $e_V(\mathbf{x})$, given for the majority vote by formula (13), diminishes monotonically (also in an oscillating fashion) with the increasing number of experts. Thus there are situations where Vote outperforms Sum. Most importantly, this is likely to happen close to the decision boundary where the margins are small.

By the central limit theorem, as the number of experts increases, the probability distribution of the sum of expert outputs will become more and more gaussian. At the same time the variance of the labelling error distribution will decay with a factor $\frac{1}{\sqrt{N}}$. Thus at some point the result of fusing N expert outputs subject to error distribution in Figure 1 will be indistinguishable from the effect of fusing estimates corrupted by normally distributed noise with the same initial variance. For our distribution in Figure 1 the standard deviation equals $\sigma(\mathbf{x}) = 0.357$. From the experiments presented in Section 2 we already established that for this regime Sum should be better than Vote. As the effective $\sigma(\mathbf{x})$ is quite high it should take relatively long time for the two fusion strategies to converge which is borne out by the plots in Figure 4(a).

In summary, for error distributions with heavy tails we can expect Vote to outperform Sum for small margins. At some point Sum will overtake Vote and build up a significant margin between the two which will eventually diminish as Vote converges to Sum from above.

4   Conclusion

The relationship of the Sum and Vote classifier combination rules was investigated. The main advantage of these rules is their simplicity and their applicability without the need for training the classifier fusion stage. We showed analytically that, for normally distributed estimation errors, Sum always outperforms Vote, whereas for heavy tail distributions Vote may outperform Sum. We then confirmed our theoretical predictions by experiments on synthetic data. We showed for Gaussian error distributions that, as expected, Sum outperforms Vote. The differences in performance are particularly significant at high estimation noise levels. However, for heavy tail distributions the superiority of Sum may be eroded for any number of experts if the margin between the two aposteriori class probabilities is small or for a small number of cooperating experts even when the margin is large. In the latter case, once the number of experts exceeds a certain threshold, Sum tends to be superior to Vote.

Acknowledgements. The support of EPSRC Grant GR/M61320 and EU Framework V Project Banca is gratefully acknowledged. F.Alkoot thanks the Islamic Development bank and the Public Authority for Applied Education and Training of Kuwait for financially supporting his education towards the Ph.D.

References

1. Luis Alexandre, Aurelio Campilho, and Mohamed Kamel. Combining independent and unbiased classifiers using weighted average. In *Proceedings of ICPR15*, volume 2, pages 495–498. IEEE, 2000.
2. F. M. Alkoot and J. Kittler. Experimental evaluation of expert fusion strategies. *Pattern Recognition Letters*, 20(11-13):1361–1369, 1999.
3. F. M. Alkoot and J. Kittler. Multiple expert system design by combined feature selection and probability level fusion. In *Proceedings of the Fusion 2000 conference*, volume II, pages ThC5(9–16), Paris, France, 2000.
4. Fuad M. Alkoot and J. Kittler. Feature selection for an ensemble of classifiers. In *Proceedings of the SCI 2000 conference*, pages 622–627, Orlando, Florida, 2000.
5. E. Bauer and R. Kohavi. An empirical comparison of voting classification algorithms: Bagging, boosting and variants. *Machine Learning*, pages 1–38, 1998.
6. Robert Duin and David Tax. Experiments with classifier combining rules. In Josef Kittler and Fabio Roli, editors, *First International Workshop on Multiple Classifier systems*, pages 16–29. Springer, 2000.
7. L.K. Hansen and P. Salamon. Neural network ensembles. *IEEE Transactions on Pattern Analysis and Machine Intelligence*, 12(10):993–1001, 1990.
8. S. Hashem and B. Schmeiser. Improving model accuracy using optimal linear combination of trained neural networks. *IEEE Transactions on Neural Networks*, 6(3):792–794, 1995.
9. T.K. Ho, J.J. Hull, and S.N. Srihari. Decision combination in multiple classifier systems. *IEEE Transactions on Pattern Analysis and Machine Intelligence*, 16(1):66–75, 1994.
10. J. Kittler. Combining classifiers: A theoretical framework. *Pattern Analysis and Applications*, 1:18–27, 1998.
11. J. Kittler, M. Hatef, R. Duin, and J. Matas. On combining classifiers. *IEEE Transaction on Pattern Analysis and Machine Intelligence*, 20(3):226–239, 1998.
12. J. Kittler, A. Hojjatoleslami, and T. Windeatt. Strategies for combining classifiers employing shared and distinct pattern representations. *Pattern Recognition Letters*, 18:1373–1377, 1997.
13. L. Lam and C. Suen. Application of majority voting to pattern recognition: An analysis of its behaviour and performance. *IEEE Transactions on Systems , Man and Cybernetics, Part A: Systems and Humans*, 27(5):553–568, 1997.
14. David Tax, Martijn van Breukelen, Robert Duin, and Josef Kittler. Combining multiple classifiers by averaging or by multiplying. *Pattern Recognition*, 33(9):1475–1485, 2000.
15. K. Tumer and J. Ghosh. Analysis of decision boundaries in linearly combined neural classifiers. *Pattern Recognition*, 29(2):341–348, 1996.
16. L. Xu, A. Krzyzak, and C.Y. Suen. Methods of combining multiple classifiers and their applications to handwriting recognition. *IEEE Transaction. SMC*, 22(3):418–435, 1992.
17. K. Yu, X. Jiang, and H. Bunke. Lipreading a classifier combination approach. *Pattern Recognition Letters*, 18(11-13):1421–1426, 1997.

Complexity of Data Subsets Generated by the Random Subspace Method: An Experimental Investigation

L.I. Kuncheva[1], F. Roli[2], G.L. Marcialis[2], and C.A. Shipp[1]

[1] School of Informatics, University of Wales, Bangor
Bangor, Gwynedd, LL57 1UT, United Kingdom
{l.i.kuncheva,c.a.shipp}@bangor.ac.uk
[2] Dept. of Electrical and Electronic Eng., University of Cagliari
Piazza d'Armi, I-09123 Cagliari, Italy
{marcialis,roli}@diee.unica.it

Abstract. We report the results from an experimental investigation on the complexity of data subsets generated by the Random Subspace method. The main aim of this study is to analyse the *variability* of the complexity among the generated subsets. Four measures of complexity have been used, three from [4]: the minimal spanning tree (MST), the adherence subsets measure (ADH), the maximal feature efficiency (MFE); and a cluster label consistency measure (CLC) proposed in [7]. Our results with the UCI "wine" data set relate the variability in data complexity to the number of features used and the presence of redundant features.

1 Introduction

Recently, Ho described three measures of complexity of classification tasks and related them to the comparative advantages of two methods for creating multiple classifiers, namely, the Bootstrap method and the Random Subspace method [4]. Here we report the results from a pilot experiment on the complexity of data subsets generated by the Random Subspace method. The main aim was to analyse the *variability* of the complexity among the generated subsets. The rationale behind this objective is the assumption that multiple classifier systems achieve best results when the individual classifiers are *of similar accuracy*. The intuition for this statement is that if the individual classifiers are very different in accuracy (they must be *diverse* in other ways for best performance!), then there will be: (a) at least one classifier which is much better than the rest of the team, and thus using the whole team will hardly improve on the best individual, or (b) at least one classifier which is much worse than the rest of the team, and using it in a combination will only degrade the overall performance. In other words, it is reasonable to expect to gain from using a team of classifiers when the classifiers are of approximately the same accuracy even if this accuracy is not too high [5].

J. Kittler and F. Roli (Eds.): MCS 2001, LNCS 2096, pp. 349–358, 2001.

Another intuitive assumption is that data complexity is straightforwardly related to classification accuracy. Therefore, if the generating method produces subsets of similar complexity, we can expect that classifiers of similar accuracies can be built upon them. However, this does not mean that the classifiers will possess the necessary *diversity* to form a good team.

Note that the individual accuracy and team diversity are different concepts. The members of the team might have the same accuracy and be identical or be as as diverse as the accuracy allows for. For example, let D_1 and D_2 be classifiers of equal accuracies, run on 100 objects. Assume that each classifier recognizes 98 of the 100 objects. The classifiers might be the identical (failing on the same 2 objects), "semi-diverse" (failing simultaneously on 1 object and separately on 1 object each) or diverse (each one failing on a different couple of objects). The individual accuracy is clearly related to the complexity of the problem but diversity is not. Depending on how diversity is defined, it may be bounded from above, and the bound will depend on the magnitude of the accuracy (c.f. [?]). On the other hand, the accuracy *of the team* is related to the diversity among the team members. Thus, we cannot expect a clear-cut relationship between the accuracy of the team and the complexity of the data sets on which the individual classifiers are designed. Therefore we confine the study to finding out about the variability of complexity of the data sets and do not attempt to relate this variability to the team accuracy. An analysis on this matter is out of the scope of this paper.

One approach to enhancing diversity of the individual classifiers is to train them on different subsets of the available labeled data set. Let $Z = \{z_1, \ldots, z_N\}$ be a labeled data set, $z_j \in \Re^n$, $j = 1, \ldots, N$ with N elements. According to the **random subspace method** the individual classifiers are based on different subsets of features, i.e., on different subspaces of the feature space $\Re^n$. Ho [3] shows that random sampling (without repetition) to get a set of $d < n$ features from the integers from 1 to n, is a viable line for building multiple classifier systems.

We applied four measures of complexity: the minimal spanning tree (MST), the adherence subsethood (ADH) based on the ϵ-neighborhood measure, the maximum feature efficiency (MFE), all three from [4], and a measure which we call the *Cluster Label Consistency (CLC)*, introduced in our previous study [7]. In this study we bring in some results from [7] and continue with an additional study on the variability in complexity of the data sets generated by the Random Subspace method.

2   Measures of Complexity

2.1   Minimal Spanning Tree

Given the data set Z and a metric on $\Re^n$, a minimal spanning tree can be constructed which connects all the sample points regardless of their class labels. Here we use the Euclidean distance as the metric throughout this study. Some edges of the MST will connect points from different classes and the count of such edges gives us a measure of the length of the boundary between the classes. Since there are $N - 1$ edges for N sample points, the count can be expressed as a percentage of N [4], leading to a complexity measure

$$MSTcomplexity = \frac{N_e}{N}, \tag{1}$$

where N_e is the number of edges in the minimal spanning tree connecting different classes.

2.2   Adherence Subsets

This method proposed by Ho [4] considers the clustering properties of the data. It is based on a reflexive and symmetric (tolerance) binary relation $\mathcal{R}$ between two points x, y in a set F. $\mathcal{R}$ is defined by $x\mathcal{R}y \Leftrightarrow d(x,y) < \epsilon$, where $d(x,y)$ is a given metric and ϵ is a given non-zero constant. We define $\Gamma(x) = \{y \in F | y\mathcal{R}x\}$ to be the ϵ-neighbourhood of x. An adherence mapping, ad from the power set $\mathcal{P}(F)$ to $\mathcal{P}(F)$ is such that:

$$\begin{cases} ad(\phi) = & \phi \\ ad(x) = & \Gamma(x) \\ ad(A) = \bigcup_{x \in A} ad(x) \ \forall A \subseteq F. \end{cases}$$

The largest possible adherence subsets can be grown for each point by successively expanding the adherence subset at each stage whilst ensuring that all newly included points come from the same class. For example, $ad^0(\{x\}) = \{x\}$, $ad^1(\{x\}) = ad(\{x\})$, $ad^2(\{x\}) = ad(ad(\{x\}))\ldots$, gives us progressively higher order adherence subsets. For each point only the highest order subset is retained such that all elements are from the same class. This procedure defines a partition of the data set where each cluster contains data points with the same class label. The number of such clusters is an indication of the complexity of the problem. If the classes are compact and far from each other, then each class will ideally form a single separate adherence subset. When the classes are overlapping, multiple clusters are likely to appear.

The calculation works by taking a labelled data set Z of size N and for each point growing the largest possible adherence subset such that all elements of the subset are from the same class. The complexity is then given by:

$$ADHcomplexity = \frac{N_s}{N} \tag{2}$$

where N_s is the number of different adherence subsets..

In Ho's paper [4] the choice of ϵ was $\epsilon = 0.55\delta$ where δ was the minimal distance between two points of different classes. In a preliminary experiment we studied the effect of ϵ on the complexity value and found that the relationship between ϵ and $ADHcomplexity$ is not monotonic. Indeed, if ϵ is too small, then each point will be a cluster on its own, and $ADHcomplexity = 1$. On the other hand, if ϵ is too large, then the ϵ-neighbourhood of $\mathbf{x}$ will contain point(s) from a different class. Again, $\mathbf{x}$ will be marked as a cluster on its own, leading to $ADHcomplexity = 1$. Since there seems to be no clear reason for choosing a particular ϵ, we picked $\epsilon = min + 0.1 * (max - min)$, where min and max were the minimum and maximum distances in the data set regardless of class labels.

2.3   Maximum Feature Efficiency

This method is suitable for 2 classes only. The complexity on each feature is assessed separately. All points are projected on that feature axis and the overlap interval is found. The MFE complexity for the i-th feature is

$$MFEcomplexity_i = \frac{N_i}{N},\tag{3}$$

where N_i is the number of points within the overlap interval. The final complexity value is defined as

$$MFEcomplexity = \min_i MFEcomplexity_i.\tag{4}$$

2.4   Cluster Label Consistency

This measure estimates how well the classes match the possible clusters in data. First c clusters are obtained on the whole data set regardless of the class labels and then the labels are used to count the number from each class within each cluster. "Pure" clusters will give low complexity values whereas "contaminated" clusters will give high complexity values. The complexity measure is

$$CLCcomplexity = 1 - \frac{1}{c}\sum_{i=1}^{c} C_i,\tag{5}$$

where C_i is the *cluster label consistency* of cluster i, found as the fraction of the maximal number of points of the same class label in the cluster. In case of a perfect match, i.e., when each class is a cluster on its own, the complexity is 0.

Consider as an example a data set distributed according to a mixture of 5 Gaussians in $\Re^2$ with centers $(0,0),(2,3),(0,4),(3,1)$ and $(2,4)$, respectively, and variance 0.4 along each axis. The left plot in Figure 1 shows the clusters and their centroids. A circular decision boundary is applied on the data set centered at $(1,2)$ with radius 2. All points inside the circle are labeled in class ω_1, and the points outside the circle are labeled in ω_2, as illustrated on the right plot in Figure 1. Thus, the Bayes error for this data model is zero. The peculiar feature about this data set is that the cluster structure of the data is not representative for the true class structure.

The quadratic discriminant classifier gave a 17 % training error on this data set. The following complexity values have been obtained:

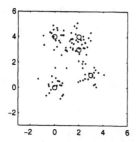 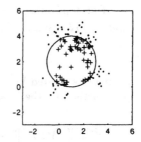

Fig. 1. A 5-clusters example of a problem where perfect separation is possible but the complexity is high because the cluster structure of the data is not representative for the class label structure.

$MST_{complexity}$ 0.1200 $CLC_{complexity}$ ($c = 2$) 0.4782
$ADH_{complexity}$ 1.0000 $CLC_{complexity}$ ($c = 3$) 0.4789
$MFE_{complexity}$ 0.6800 $CLC_{complexity}$ ($c = 4$) 0.4408
                                    $CLC_{complexity}$ ($c = 5$) 0.4632

The purpose of showing this example was to highlight two seemingly discouraging observations. First, the *achievable* accuracy (100 % in this case) is not necessarily related with the measures of complexity. Second, the results give us an early indication of the severe disagreement between the measures of complexity despite the fact that they are all meant to measure the same characteristic of the data set. However, we note that: (1) in real problems, the class-cluster relationship may be less deceiving than in this example, and (2), the difference in the values of the complexity measures shows that the notion "complexity" needs a stricter definition beyond the common intuition.

3 Experiments

3.1 Data

We used the "wine" data set from the UCI Repository of Machine Learning Database[1]. It contains 178 cases labeled in 3 classes, with 13 continuous-valued features and no missing values. From this data set we derived the following 7 problems

Case A: 1 v 2 v 3.
Case B: 1 v (2 and 3).
Case C: 2 v (1 and 3).
Case D: 3 v (1 and 2).
Case E: 1 v 2.
Case F: 1 v 3.
Case G: 2 v 3.

[1] Found at [http://www.ics.uci.edu/ mlearn/MLRepository.html]

Applying the Random Subspace method, we formed 50 subsets by randomly choosing 5 of the $n = 13$ features. The four complexity measures were calculated for each data set.

Table 1. Complexity calculated by MST, ADH, MFE and CLC (in %) with the Random Subspace method for the 7 cases

Case	MST		ADH		MFE		CLC	
	mean	std	mean	std	mean	std	mean	std
A	21	7	100	0	–	–	35	11
B	12	5	99	4	44	14	23	11
C	18	5	100	3	57	15	30	6
D	13	8	95	17	34	12	24	4
E	13	5	99	7	39	17	19	10
F	9	5	98	14	8	17	21	14
G	18	10	97	10	39	18	28	12

3.2 Results

Table 1 shows the means and the standard deviations of the 4 measures and the 7 cases. As in the example at the end of the previous section, the measures give very different values. Knowing that the three of them (except CLC) span approximately the same intervals ($0.01 \leq MSTcomplexity \leq 0.99$, $0.02 \leq ADHcomplexity \leq 1$, and $0 \leq MFEcomplexity \leq 1$), the differences in the complexity values are puzzling.

In [7] we carried out similar experiments for the Bootstrapping and the Data splitting methods too. To compare visually the variability of the Random Subspace method with the other two, we display in Figure 2 the means for the 21 experiments (3 methods × 7 cases) and the minima and maxima as the error bars. (For the MFE, there are (3 methods × 6 cases) because it works for two classes only, and case A is excluded.)

In all 4 subplots, the first 7 (six for MFE) bars are for the Bootstrapping method, the next 7 (6) are for the Data splitting method, and the last 7 (6) correspond with the Random Subspace method in the same order of the cases (A to G).

A common finding of all complexity measures is that the Random Subspace method for creating data subsets offers the highest variability of the complexity of the obtained sets. However, this seems to be the only finding where the four complexity measures agree. For example, while the ADH measure designates the Random Subspace method as producing the least complex data (Figure 2), the MFE measures classes these data set as the hardest.

The Bootstrap method has the lowest standard deviations (on all four measures) indicating that the data sets obtained exhibit complexity of a similar value.

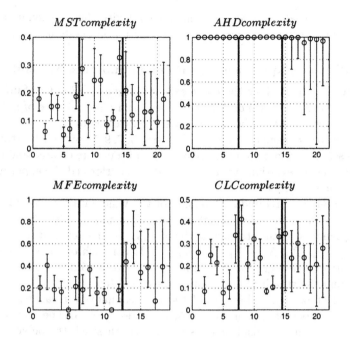

Fig. 2. The mean and limits for the 4 complexities. Bars 1-7: Bootstrapping, 8-14: Data Splitting, 15-21: Random Subspace

These two findings can be explained by the following

1. The Bootstrap method creates data subsets by small variations of the original data set. Consequently, the variations in complexity among such data subsets can be expected to be small. In fact, as pointed out by Breiman [1], unstable classifiers are necessary to exploit effectively the low diversity of the data subsets generated by the Bootstrap method. Neural networks are examples of such unstable classifiers, and, curiously, we rely on their ability to overtrain.

2. Differently, the Random Subspace method usually generates data subsets exhibiting very different complexities because projecting the data set on a subspace may lead to a very different pattern of the classes' disposition. However, it should be noted that such variability in complexity strongly depends on the number of features used. It is easy to argue that variability in complexity among subsets should decrease as the number of randomly picked features increases. In addition, we think that complexity variations also depend on the degree of redundancy among the features. For example, if we have picked a subset of features containing redundant feature X_i, and another subset containing redundant feature X_j on its place, the difference in complexity between the two data sets will not be great. Ho conjectures in [4] that multiple classifier systems based on the Random Subspace method are expected to perform well exactly when there is a certain redundancy in the feature set. This comes in support of our intu-

itive hypothesis that data sets of similar complexity (hence similar individual accuracy) are a better basis for a classifier combination system.

3.3   Additional Experiments on Random Subspace Method

In order to investigate how the complexity variations of Random Subspace depends on the number of random features used and on the degree of redundancy among the features, two experiments have been carried out:

1. We created subsets by randomly choosing 5, 7, 9, 11 of the 13 features of the wine data set. For each number of features, 50 subsets were created and the mean and the standard deviations were computed. We performed the experiments for all seven problems A–G.

2. We created a "redundant" version of the wine data set by adding 13 redundant features to the original feature space. The new 13 features were created by adding the first feature to each of the others, i.e., the new feature set consists of $\{X_1, \ldots, X_{13}, 2X_1, X_2 + X_1, \ldots, X_{13} + X_1\}$. For each of the seven problems A–G, 50 subsets were generated by randomly choosing 5 of the 13 features and the mean and the standard deviations were computed.

Figure 3 shows the behaviour of the four complexity measures as a function of the number of random features, for cases A to G. The means and the standard deviations are displayed. As it was hypothesized, the behaviour of the standard deviation shows that complexity variations among subsets decrease as the number of features increases whereas the mean tends to level off.

Table 2 shows the standard deviations obtained by sampling from the original feature space and the augmented feature space for the seven cases and the 4 complexity measures. The standard deviations for the augmented feature space are lower than the ones for the original feature space in most of the cases: for all 7 cases with MST; for 3 cases with ADH; for 5 cases with CLC; and 2 of the 6 possible cases with MFE. This points out that complexity variation among the generated data sets depends on the degree of redundancy as anticipated: the higher the redundancy, the smaller the variability.

Table 2. Standard deviation (%) of the complexities for the Random Subspace method on the original and redundant feature spaces (augmented with redundant features).

Case	MST		ADH		CLC		MFE	
	orig	redn	orig	redn	orig	redn	orig	redn
A	8.04	4.35	5.45	12.05	11.37	5.68	–	–
B	5.68	2.12	6.88	9.21	10.69	6.85	15.86	13.67
C	6.30	3.48	3.73	8.95	5.81	8.39	17.24	18.61
D	8.01	3.73	14.77	11.40	3.68	4.64	13.17	17.35
E	4.90	3.01	9.44	10.94	10.63	3.42	14.94	14.43
F	6.12	4.50	25.52	21.89	12.19	9.85	15.53	27.80
G	10.86	6.41	16.17	14.42	11.55	8.06	14.06	18.95

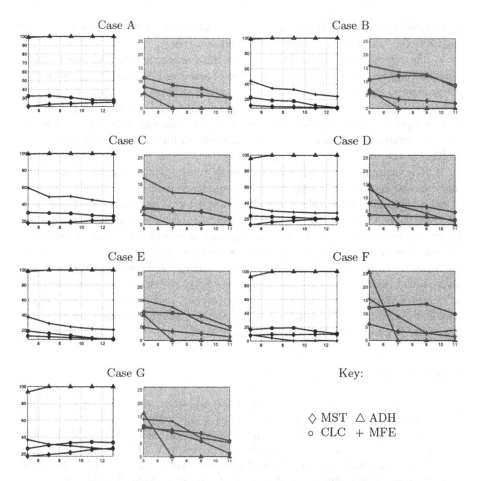

Fig. 3. Plots of the means (left) and standard deviations (right, shaded) of the 4 complexity measures versus the number of features selected at random. 50 experiments have been carried out for each of the cases A-G for each of 5, 7, 9, and 11 features.

4   Conclusions

In this paper, we considered the Random Subspace method for generating data sets for multiple classifier systems. We used 4 measures of complexity: the minimal spanning tree (MST), the adherence subsets measure (ADH), the maximal feature efficiency (MFE); and a cluster label consistency measure (CLC). Our results with the UCI "wine" data set led us to the following conclusions:

1. Random Subspace method usually generates data subsets exhibiting different complexities. The variability in complexity is higher than that for bootstrapping and data splitting (Figure 2). All 4 measures are capable of detecting

this variablity, with ADH failing to distinguish between the complexity of the data sets for 7, 9 and 11 randomly selected features.

2. The variability in complexity of the data sets generated by the Random Subspace method is related to the number of features being selected. Our experiment showed that complexity variations among subsets decrease as the number of features increases whereas the mean complexity tends to level off (Figure 3). This complies with our hypothesis based on the idea that the more feature we use, the greater the chance for getting data sets on highly overlapping subspaces and hence the more similar the complexity.

3. The redundancy in the feature set *generally* leads to generating sets of more similar complexity compared to sets obtained from a feature set with little or no redundancy. While MST and CLC support this intuition (100 % for MST and ~70 % for CLC), ADH and MFE produce dubious results. According to the latter two measures, there is no clear pattern of reduction of the variability of the complexity value when redundant features are used.

Since there is no consensus on a single definition of complexity, we agree with [4] that at this point we can use a (probably restricted) set of measures as a "complexity vector". This vector can be further used to select an appropriate classifier model for a certain data set or to indicate whether a collection of subsets is a suitable basis for a multiple classifier system.

References

1. L. Breiman. Combining predictors. In A.J.C. Sharkey, editor, *Combining Artificial Neural Nets*, pages 31–50. Springer-Verlag, London, 1999.
2. J.H. Friedman and L.C. Rafsky, Multivariate generalisations of the Wald-Wolfowitz and Smirnov two-sample tests *Annals of Statistics*, **7**, 4, 1979, 697-717 In [4]
3. T.K. Ho. The random space method for constructing decision forests. *IEEE Transactions on Pattern Analysis and Machine Intelligence*, 20(8):832–844, 1998.
4. T.K. Ho. Complexity of classification problems and comparative advantages of combined classifiers. In *Proc. First International Workshop on Multiple Classifier Systems*, pages 97–106, Cagliari, Italy, 2000.
5. C. Ji and S. Ma. Combination of weak classifiers. *IEEE Transactions on Neural Networks*, 8(1):32–42, 1997.
6. L.I. Kuncheva, C.J. Whitaker, C.A. Shipp, and R.P.W. Duin. Limits on the majority vote accuracy in classifier fusion. (submitted).
7. B. Littlewood and D.R. Miller. Conceptual modeling of coincident failures in multiversion software. *IEEE Transactions on Software Engineering*, 15(12):1596–1614, 1989.

On Combining Dissimilarity Representations

Elżbieta Pękalska and Robert P. W. Duin

Pattern Recognition Group, Department of Applied Physics,
Faculty of Applied Sciences, Delft University of Technology,
Lorentzweg 1, 2628 CJ Delft, The Netherlands
{ela,duin}@ph.tn.tudelft.nl

Abstract. For learning purposes, representations of real world objects can be built by using the concept of dissimilarity (distance). In such a case, an object is characterized in a relative way, i.e. by its dissimilarities to a set of the selected prototypes. Such dissimilarity representations are found to be more practical for some pattern recognition problems.
When experts cannot decide for a single dissimilarity measure, a number of them may be studied in parallel. We investigate two possibilities of combining either dissimilarity representations themselves or classifiers built on each of them separately. Our experiments conducted on a handwritten digit set demonstrate that when the dissimilarity representations are of different nature, a much better performance can be obtained by their combination than on individual representations.

1 Introduction

An alternative to the feature-based description is a representation based on dissimilarity relations between objects. In general, dissimilarities are built directly on raw or preprocessed measurements, e.g. based on template matching. The use of dissimilarities is especially of interest when features are difficult to obtain or when they have a little discriminative power. Such situations are encountered in practice when there is no straightforward manner to define features, when data is highly dimensional or when features consist of both, continuous and categorical measurements. The choice in favor of dissimilarity representations depends also on the application or the data itself. For instance, some particular characteristics of objects or measurements, like curves or shapes, may naturally lead to such representations, since they make recognition tasks more feasible.

To construct a decision rule on dissimilarities, the training set T of size n and the representation set R [2] of size r will be used. R consists of prototypes which are representatives of all classes present. In the learning process, a classifier is built on the $n \times r$ dissimilarity matrix $D(T, R)$, relating all training objects to all prototypes. The information on a set S of s new objects is provided in terms of their distances to R, i.e. as an $s \times r$ matrix $D(S, R)$.

A conventional way to discriminate between objects represented by dissimilarities is the nearest neighbor rule (NN) [1]. This method suffers, however, either from a potential loss of accuracy when a small set of prototypes is selected or

J. Kittler and F. Roli (Eds.): MCS 2001, LNCS 2096, pp. 359–368, 2001.
© Springer-Verlag Berlin Heidelberg 2001

from its sensitivity to noise. To overcome these limitations, we have proposed an another approach. Our suggestion is to treat the dissimilarity representation $D(T, R)$ as a description of a space where each dimension corresponds to a distance to an object. $D(x, R)$ can be, therefore, seen as a mapping of x onto an r-dimensional dissimilarity space. The advantage of such a representation is that any traditional decision rule operating on feature spaces may be used.

Most of the commonly-used dissimilarity measures, e.g. the Euclidean distance or the Hamming distance, are based on sums of differences between measurements. The choice of Bayesian classifiers [4], assuming normal distributions, is a natural consequence of the central limit theorem applied to them, when a large number of measurements is considered. The LNC (Linear Normal densities based Classifier) [4] is especially of interest because of its simplicity. Such a suggestion is strongly supported by our earlier experiments [7,8].

Selecting a good dissimilarity measure becomes an issue for the classification problem at hand. When considering a number of different possibilities, it may happen that there are no convincing arguments to prefer one measure over another. Therefore, the interesting question is whether combining dissimilarity representations might be beneficial. Two possibilities are here consider to study this problem. In the first one, the base classifiers (the LNC or the NN rule) are found on each dissimilarity representation separately and then combined into one decision rule. If the representations differ in character, a more powerful decision rule may be constructed by combining them. Secondly, instead of combining classifiers, representations are combined to create a new representation for which only one classifier has to be trained.

The paper is organized as follows. Section 2 gives some insight into the dissimilarity representations, classifiers and combining rules used. Section 3 describes the dataset and the experiments conducted. Results are discussed in section 4 and conclusions are summarized in section 5.

2   Combining Dissimilarity Representations

Assume that we are given the representation set R and p different dissimilarity representations $D^{(1)}(T, R)$, $D^{(2)}(T, R)$, ..., $D^{(p)}(T, R)$. Our idea is to combine good base classifiers, but on distinct representations. It is important to emphasize that the distance representations should have different character, otherwise they convey similar information and not much can be gained by their combination.

Two cases are here considered. In the first one, a single LNC is trained on each representation $D^{(i)}(T, R)$ separately and then all of them are combined in the end. In the second case, the NN rule is also included. The NN rule and the LNC differ in their decision-making process and their assignments. The NN method operates on dissimilarity information in a rank-based way, while the LNC approaches it in a feature-based way. Although the recognition accuracy of the NN method is often worse than of the LNC [8], still better results may be obtained when both types of classifiers are included in the combining procedure. Although many possibilities exist for combining classifiers [5], we limit ourselves to fixed rules operating on posterior probabilities. For the LNC, the posterior probabilities are based on normal density estimates, while for the NN method, they are estimated from distances to the nearest neighbor of each class [3].

Another approach to learning from many distinct dissimilarity representations is to combine them into a new one and then train e.g. a single LNC. As a result, a more powerful representation may be obtained, allowing for a better discrimination. The first method for creating a new representation relies on building an extended representation D_{ext}, in a matrix notation given by:

$$D_{ext}(T, R) = \left[D^{(1)}(T, R) \ D^{(2)}(T, R) \ \ldots \ D^{(p)}(T, R) \right] \qquad (1)$$

It means that a single object is now characterized by pr dissimilarities coming from p various representations, but still computed to the same prototypes. The requirement of having the same prototypes is not crucial, however, for the sake of simplicity, the same representation sets are used here.

In the second method, all distances of different representations are first scaled so that they all take values in a similar range. Then, the final representation is created by computing their sum, as shown below:

$$D_{sum}(T, R) = \sum_{i=1}^{p} D_{max}^{(i)}(T, R), \qquad (2)$$

where $D_{max}^{(i)}(T, R) = \alpha_i \, D^{(i)}(T, R)$ and α_i's scale all representations so that their maximum values become equal. (Note that now the representation sets should be identical to perform the sum operation.) The scaling procedure is necessary, otherwise the new representation will copy the character of a representation contributing the most to a sum, i.e. one with the largest distances. Scaling changes the orders of magnitude, but not the rankings, therefore all neighbor information is preserved. More sophisticated possibilities of scaling can be considered, as well, e.g. the weighted sum or the median from a sequence of dissimilarity values of different representations but relating a training object to the same prototype.

3   Dataset and Experiments

To illustrate our point, we investigate a 2-class classification problem between the NIST handwritten digits 3 and 8 [10]. The digits are represented as 128×128 binary images. Since no natural features arise from the application, constructing dissimilarities is an interesting possibility to deal with such a recognition problem. Three dissimilarity measures are considered: Hamming, modified-Hausdorff [6] and 'blurred', resulting in the representations: D_H, D_{MH} and D_B correspondingly. The Hamming distance counts the number of pixels which disagree. The modified-Hausdorff distance is found useful for template matching purposes [6]. It measures the difference between two sets (here two contours) $A = \{a_1, \ldots, a_g\}$ and $B = \{b_1, \ldots, b_h\}$ and is defined as $D_{MH}(A, B) = max(h_M(A, B), h_M(B, A))$, where $h_M(A, B) = \frac{1}{g} \sum_{a \in A} \min_{b \in B} ||a - b||$. To find

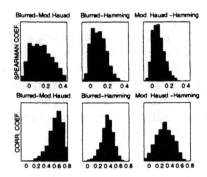

Fig. 1. Spearman coefficients (top) and traditional correlation coefficients (bottom) comparing dissimilarity representations.

D_B, images are first blurred with the Gaussian kernel and the standard deviation of 8 pixels. Then the Euclidean distance is computed between the blurred versions. The resulting distances are referred as to the 'blurred' distances.

Each of the distance measures uses the image information in a particular way: binary information, contours or blurring. From the process of the construction, it follows that our dissimilarity representations differ in properties. To prove, however, their different characteristics, the Spearman rank correlation coefficient is used to rank the distances computed to each prototype. Basically, we want to show that the rankings differ between representations. Therefore, for each pair of representations, the Spearman coefficients between the distance rankings to all prototypes are computed. Histograms of their distributions are presented in Fig. 1. All coefficients are between -0.05 and 0.4, where most of them are smaller than 0.2, which implies that the rankings differ significantly.

The traditional correlation coefficient is used to check whether the dissimilarity spaces of the individual representations (and, therefore, linear classifiers built there) are different. Such correlation values are higher than those given by the Spearman rates. It is to be expected, since now the exact distances are considered, which cannot completely vary from one representation to another, since the representations are descriptions of the same data and the same relations. On average, the correlations are found to be (see Fig. 1): 0.39 between the blurred and modified Hausdorff, 0.56 between the blurred and Hamming and 0.28 between the modified Hausdorff and Hamming. In the end, most coefficients are smaller than 0.6, thereby, they indicate only weak linear dependencies. Consequently, we can say that our dissimilarity representations differ in character.

The experiments are performed 25 times and the results are averaged. In a single experiment, the data, consisting of 1000 objects per class, is randomly split into two equally-sized sets: the design set L and the test set S. Both L and S contain 500 examples per class. The test set is kept constant, while L serves for obtaining the training sets T_1, T_2, T_3 and T_4 (being subsets of L) of the following sizes: 50, 100, 300 and $500 (= L)$. For each training set, the experiments are conducted with varying size of the representation set R. Here, for simplicity, R is chosen to be a random subset of the training set.

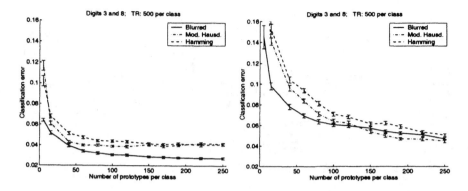

Fig. 2. Averaged classification error of the individual LNC's (left) and NN rules (right) as a function of the representation set size for the training set T_4.

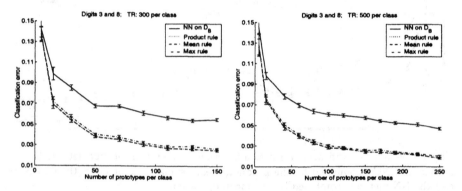

Fig. 3. Averaged classification error as a function of the representation set size for the individual NN rules trained on the sets T_3 (left) and T_4 (right).

4   Discussion

Considering single classifiers, it appears that the LNC consistently outperforms the NN rule for training sets: $T_1 - T_4$. Also, the LNC built on the blurred dissimilarities reaches a higher accuracy than for the other two representations. Since this behavior is repeated over all training sets, only the performance of the individual classifiers for the largest training set T_4 is presented in Fig. 2.

The results of combining either classifiers or representations for different training sets are presented in Fig. 3 – 6. These small, moderate and large training sets are considered to investigate the influence of the training size on our combining results. All plots in Fig. 3 – 6 show curves of averaged classification error (based on 25 runs) together with its standard deviation. Each error curve is a function of the representation set size, where the largest representation set considered is about half of the training set. Since our goal is to improve the performance of single classifiers by combining the information, all the results are presented with respect to the behavior of the LNC on the blurred representation D_B, as to the one that reaches the highest individual accuracy overall.

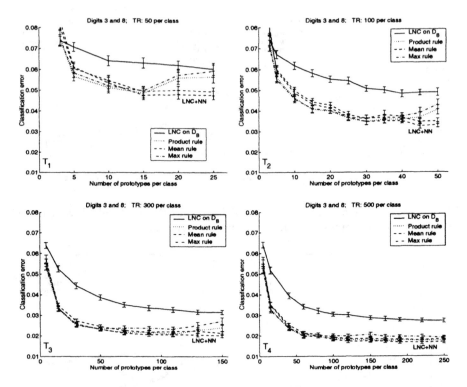

Fig. 4. Averaged classification error as a function of the representation set size for the individual LNC's combined by the product, mean or max rule or for both the LNC's and the NN methods combined by the mean operations.

Fig. 3 presents the generalization errors obtained for combining three individual NN methods by the mean, maximum and product rules. Operating on posterior probabilities is motivated by the intention of combining both the LNC and the NN method further on. Although the estimation of these probabilities is rather crude for the NN method, it still allows for an improvement of the combined rules. In all cases, the combination by the mean, max or product operation gives significantly better results than each individual NN rule. The larger, both training and representation sets, the more indicative gain in accuracy.

Fig. 4 shows the error curves obtained for three individual LNC's combined by the mean, maximum and product rules. For all training sets and small representation sets (in comparison to the training set size) considered, the product and maximum rules give slightly better results than the mean rule. However, for larger representation sets, the mean rule performs better. In addition, the error curve for the mean combiner of both the LNC and NN method is also shown. It can be observed, that incorporating the NN rule to the combiner, lowers somewhat the classification errors for larger representation sets. (This does not hold for small representation sets due to bad performance of each individual NN rule.)

Fig. 5 presents the error curves of a single LNC operating on new dissimilarity representations constructed from the three given: D_B, D_{MH} and D_H. Two

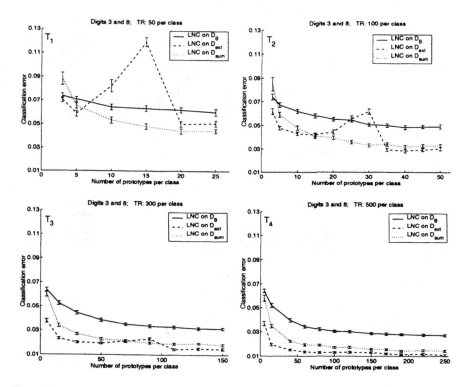

Fig. 5. Averaged classification error of the LNC as a function of the representation set size for the combined representations.

different cases are here considered: an extended representation D_{ext} (1) and the combined representation D_{sum} (2). The LNC on D_{sum} significantly outperforms the individual LNC's (it reaches higher accuracy than the best individual result on D_B), which is observed for all training sets. The LNC on D_{ext} can gain even better accuracy, however, the comparison between the representations D_{sum} and D_{ext} should be explained carefully. If the LNC is trained on D_{sum} using, say, r prototypes per class, then the representation D_{ext} is built from three such representations, each based on r prototypes, thereby the LNC operates in a $3r$-dimensional space. It means that for larger representations sets, the total number of dimensions exceeds the training size. The LNC is then not defined since the sample covariance matrix becomes singular and its inverse cannot be determined. In such cases, a fixed, relatively large regularization is used [4]. For moderate representation sizes (for which the dimensionality of D_{ext} approaches the number of training examples) the error curve of the LNC shows a peaking behavior (characteristic for this classifier). Therefore, worse performance is observed when number of prototypes is close to one third of the training size. For either small or larger representation sets, a very good performance is reached.

Fig. 6 presents the comparison between the mean combiner of individual classifiers and the LNC trained on the combined representation D_{sum}. For larger

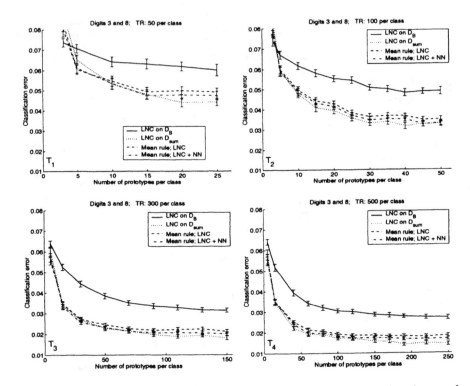

Fig. 6. Comparison between the accuracy of the combined classifiers found on each representation separately and one LNC on the combined representation D_{sum}. The classification error is as a function of the representation set size.

representation sets, the LNC trained on D_{sum} works somewhat better than the combined decision rule consisting of the LNC's and NN methods.

Summarizing, most of the combining rules perform significantly better than the individual classifiers. For small dissimilarity spaces, the representations tend to be independent and, therefore, the product rule based on the LNC's is expected to give better results than the mean rule [9] (here observed only slightly). For larger dissimilarity spaces, the posterior probabilities are not well estimated, and the product rule deteriorates; then the mean com-

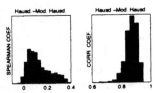

Fig. 8. Spearman and traditional correlation coefficients comparing D_{MH} and D_{HS}.

biner is preferred. For the NN rule, the posterior probabilities are estimated from distances to the nearest neighbor and do not depend on the dimensionality of the problem. Therefore, both combiners perform about the same.

To illustrate the importance of dissimilarity representations of different nature, we present an example where the Hausdorff dissimilarity D_{HS} is used instead of the Hamming distance. Therefore, a triple $\{D_B, D_{MH}, D_{HS}\}$ is considered. The Hausdorff distance and the modified Hausdorff distance are similar,

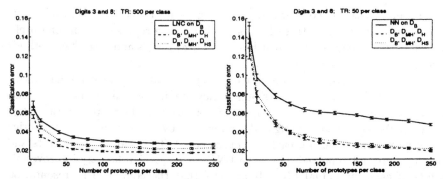

Fig. 7. Comparison of the classification error for the combined LNC's (left) and NN rules (right) and for two representation triples: $\{D_B, D_{MH}, D_H\}$ and $\{D_B, D_{MH}, D_{HS}\}$ and the training set T_4. Combining is done by applying the mean rule.

however, the latter violates the triangle inequality. Therefore, in the modified Hausdorff representation the dissimilarity rankings are changed with respect to the Hausdorff one. However, the dissimilarity spaces D_{MH} and D_{HS} are rather similar. In Fig. 8 histograms of both the Spearman and traditional correlation coefficients for these two representations are plotted. The Spearman values are similar to those obtained before (compare Fig. 1), but the traditional correlations become much higher, on average 0.91, indicating high dependence between those two dissimilarity spaces. It means that although by combining the individual NN rules for D_B, D_{MH} and D_{HS} an essential improvement may be gained, it does not necessarily hold for combining the LNC's. Fig. 7 presents the comparison between the performances of such classifiers combined by the mean rule for the training set T_4. It can be clearly observed that when D_{HS} is used instead of D_H, the performance of the combined LNC's deteriorates. Still, the combined NN rules are behaving only somewhat worse than for the triple $\{D_B, D_{MH}, D_H\}$.

When the Hausdorff representation is added to the original three, the performances of the combined individual classifiers or the LNC on D_{sum} are slightly better or not at all. The only significant improvement is observed for the extended representation D_{ext}.

5   Conclusions

Combining a number of distance representations may be of interest when there is no clear preference for a particular one. It can be beneficial when the dissimilarity representations emphasize different data characteristics. This is illustrated by a 2-class recognition problem between the digits 3 and 8 for three dissimilarity representations: Hamming, modified Hausdorff and blurred.

We have analyzed two possibilities of combining such information, either by combining classifiers or by combining representations themselves. In the first approach, individual classifiers are found for each representation separately and then they are combined into one rule. Our experiments show that the mean combining rule works well, especially for larger representation sets (with respect to the training size). In comparison to the best results of individual classifiers, the mean combiner based on three LNC's (built on each representation separately) or even better, the mean combiner based on three LNC's and three NN methods, performs significantly better.

In the second approach, dissimilarity representations are combined into a new one on which a single LNC is built. They are first scaled so that their maximal values are equal and then summed up, resulting in the representation D_{sum} (see (2)). We have also investigated scaling, e.g. by making the means identical or the maximum values for each prototype equal. They gave worse results and, therefore, are not reported here. The LNC on D_{sum} significantly improves the results of each individual LNC. It appears that the combined representation, built in this way, has a more discriminative power. As a reference, the extended representation D_{ext} is also considered (see (1)). The LNC on such a representation reaches even better results than on D_{sum}, provided that the number of all prototypes is either small or large in comparison with the training set size.

In conclusion, when dissimilarity representations differ in character, combining either individual classifiers or by creating a new representation can be beneficial. In our experiments, we have shown that when distinct representations are combined into D_{sum}, as a result, a representation which allows for a better discrimination can be obtained. This not only improves the classifier, but also it is of interest because of the computational aspect.

Acknowledgments. This work is supported by the Dutch Organization for Scientific Research (NWO).

References

1. R.O. Duda and P.E. Hart. *Pattern Classification and Scene Analysis*. John Wiley & Sons, Inc., 1973.
2. R.P.W. Duin. Classifiers for dissimilarity-based pattern recognition. In *15th Int. Conf. on Pattern Recognition*, volume 2, pages 1–7, Barcelona (Spain), 2000.
3. R.P.W. Duin and D.M.J. Tax. Classifier conditional posterior probabilities. In *Advances in Pattern Recognition, Lecture Notes in Computer Science*, volume 1451, pages 611–619, Sydney, 1998. Proc. Joint IAPR Int. Workshops SSPR and SPR.
4. K. Fukunaga. *Introduction to Statistical Pattern Recognition*. Acad. Press, 1990.
5. Duin, R.P.W. Kittler, J., Hatef M. and Matas, J. On combining classifiers. *IEEE Transactions on Pattern Analysis and Machine Intelligence*, 20(3):226–239, 1998.
6. Dubuisson M. P. and Jain A. K. Modified hausdorff distance for object matching. In *12th Int. Conf. on Pattern Recognition*, volume 1, pages 566–568, 1994.
7. E. Pekalska and R.P.W. Duin. Classifiers for dissimilarity-based pattern recognition. In *15th ICPR*, volume 2, pages 12–16, Barcelona, 2000.
8. E.Pekalska and R.P.W. Duin. Automatic pattern recognition by similarity representations. *Electronic Letters*, 37(3):159–160, 2001.
9. Duin, R.P.W. Tax, D.M.J. and Kittler, J. Combining multiple classifiers by averaging or by multiplying? *Pattern Recognition*, 33(9):1475–1485, 2000.
10. C.L. Wilson and M.D. Garris. Handprinted character database 3. Technical report, National Institute of Standards and Technology, February 1992.

Application of Multiple Classifier Techniques to Subband Speaker Identification with an HMM/ANN System

J.E. Higgins, T.J. Dodd, and R.I. Damper

Image, Speech and Intelligent Systems Research Group,
Department of Electronics and Computer Science,
University of Southampton, Southampton SO17 1BJ, UK.

Abstract. In previous work, we have confirmed the performance gains that can be obtained in speaker recognition by splitting the (clean) wideband speech signal into several subbands, employing separate pattern classifiers for each subband, and then using multiple classifier fusion ('recombination') techniques to produce a final decision. However, our earlier work used fairly rudimentary recognition techniques (dynamic time warping), just sum or product fusion rules and the spoken word *seven* only. The question then arises: Can subband processing still deliver performance gains when using state-of-the-art recognition techniques, more sophisticated recombination, and different spoken digits? To answer this, we have applied hidden Markov modelling and artificial neural network (ANN) recombination to text-dependent speaker identification, for spoken digits *seven* and *nine*. We find that ANN recombination performs about as well as the sum rule operating in log probability space, but the ANN results are not unique. They depend critically on user-specified parameters, initialisation, etc. On clean speech, all classifiers achieve close to 100% identification. Subband techniques offer advantages when the speech signal is significantly degraded by noise.

1 Introduction

Automatic speaker recognition is an important, emerging technology with many potential applications in commerce and business, security, surveillance etc. (Campbell 1997). Recent attention in speaker recognition has focussed on the use of subband processing, whereby the wideband 'signal is fed to a bank of bandpass filters to give a set of time-varying outputs, which are individually processed before using multiple classifier techniques to produce a combined, overall decision (Besacier and Bonastre 1997, 2000; Sivakumaran, Ariyaeeinia, and Hewitt 1998), Higgins, Damper, and Harris 1999. Because the subband signals vary slowly relative to the wideband signal, the problem of representing them by some data model should be simplified (Finan, Damper, and Sapeluk 2001). Although our previous work has demonstrated performance gains from subband processing with clean speech, this

J. Kittler and F. Roli (Eds.): MCS 2001, LNCS 2096, pp. 369–377, 2001.

used fairly rudimentary recognition and fusion (or 'recombination') techniques—dynamic time warping and sum or product fusion rules respectively, as well as a single spoken digit (*seven*). The question which then arises and which is addressed in this paper is: Can subband processing still deliver performance gains when using state-of-the-art recognition and fusion techniques and a wider variety of speech materials? To answer this, we have used hidden Markov models (HMMs) and neural network recombination with spoken digits *seven* and *nine*.

The subband, or multiple classifier, approach has also become popular in recent years in *speech* recognition (Bourlard and Dupont 1996; Tibrewala and Hermansky 1997; Morris, Hagen, and Bourlard 1999). In this related area, the main motivation has been to achieve robust recognition in the face of noise. The key idea is that the recombination process allows the overall decision to be made taking into account any noise contaminating one or more of the partial bands. Hence, as well as investigating subband speaker recognition from clean speech, we also report on work in which narrow-band noise is added to test utterances.

The remainder of this paper is organised as follows. Section 2 gives essential background on the problem of speaker recognition. Section 3 briefly describes the speech database used. Section 4 describes the subband processing system, including details of the feature extraction and data modelling. In Section 5 we detail the various recombination techniques studied, with results presented in Section 6. Finally, Section 7 concludes.

2   The Speaker Recognition Problem

The speaker recognition problem can be divided into *verification* and *identification*, each of which may in turn be *text-dependent* or *text-independent* (Campbell 1997; Furui 1997). In verification, the aim is to determine if a given utterance was produced by a claimed speaker. This is most directly done by testing the utterance against the model of the claimed speaker, comparing the score to a threshold, and deciding on the basis of this comparison whether or not to accept the claimant. In identification, the aim is to determine which speaker from among a known group produced an utterance. The test utterance is scored against all possible speaker models, and that with the best score determines the speaker identity. Of the two tasks, identification is generally accepted to be the harder, especially for large speaker populations (Doddington 1985, p. 1660).

In text-independent recognition, there are no limits on the vocabulary employed by speakers. This is in contrast to text-dependent recognition, where the tested utterance comes from a set of predetermined words or phrases. As text-dependent recognition only models the speaker for a limited set of speech sounds ('phones') in a fixed context, it generally achieves higher performance than text-independent recognition, which must model a speaker for a variety of phones and contexts.

Since identification is simply a matter of selecting among speakers, typically using a minimum distance decision rule, performance is easily quantified by a single measure. There are only two possible outcomes—correct or incorrect—so that the identification error fully specifies the situation. Things are a little more complicated with verification where the system has to accept or reject a claimed speaker identity in the face of potential impersonation. Hence, there are four possible outcomes, of which two—false acceptance and false rejection—are errors. Thus, some decision threshold must be set which effects a balance between the two types of error. Because of the slightly increased difficulty of quantifying error in verification, we focus exclusively on identification in this paper. Also, we restrict attention to text-dependent recognition because of its more obvious applicability (Doddington 1985, p. 1660).

3   Speech Database

We use the text-dependent British Telecom Millar database, specifically designed and recorded for text-dependent speaker recognition research. It consists of 60 (46 male and 14 female) native English speakers saying the digits *one* to *nine*, *zero*, *nought* and *oh* 25 times each. Recordings were made in 5 sessions spaced over 3 months, to capture the variation in speaker's voices over time which is an important aspect of speaker recognition (Furui 1974).

The speech was recorded in a quiet environment using a high-quality microphone and a sampling rate of 20 kHz with 16-bit resolution. The speech data used here were downsampled to 8 kHz sampling rate as this reduces simulation times and is more typical of the data which might be encountered in a real application. For the work reported here, we consider utterances *seven* and *nine*, i.e., text-dependent identification. Data from the first two sessions (i.e., 10 repetitions of each word) were used for training and data from the remaining three sessions (15 repetitions) were used for testing.

In order to achieve good performance, manual editing of the start and end points of each utterance was necessary. This was done by author JEH. This was a time-consuming task: For a fully automatic system, we would obviously need to implement a high performance automatic endpointing algorithm.

As so far described, the speech data are essentially noise-free. However, a major motivation behind subband processing has been the prospect of achieving good recognition performance in the presence of narrowband noise. Such noise affects the entire wideband model but only a small number of subbands. Hence, we have also conducted identification tests with added noise. Following Besacier and Bonastre (2000), Gaussian noise was filtered using a 6th-order Butterworth filter with centre frequency 987 Hz and bandwidth 365 Hz. It was added to the test tokens at a signal-to-noise ratio of 10 dB. Figure 1 shows typical power spectra of the wideband speech signal (Fig. 3) and of the subband signals for the 4 subband case described in the next section (Fig. 3). It can be seen that the middle two bands are affected by the noise whereas the low- and high-frequency bands are relatively clean.

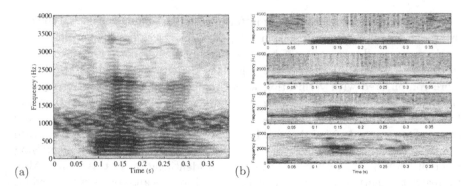

(a)   (b)

Fig. 1. Typical spectra of a test utterance *seven* with added narrowband noise: (a) wideband; (b) subband spectra for $N = 4$. In (b), the two mid-frequency bands are contaminated but the low- and high-frequency bands are relatively clean.

4   Subband Processing

Figure 2 shows a schematic of the subband system used here to model each individual speaker. We use 2, 4, 6, 8 or 10 bandpass filters (6th-order Butterworth). Filter centre frequencies are equally spaced on the psychophysically-motivated mel scale (Stevens and Volkmann 1940), and feature extraction is performed on each subband. The resulting sequences of feature vectors are passed on to each subband's HMM recognition algorithm.

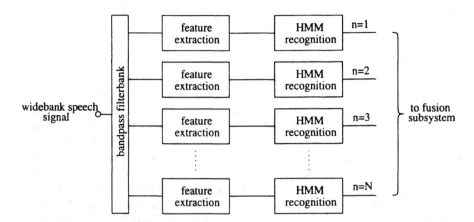

Fig. 2. Schematic diagram of the subband processing subsystem. Each subband (filter) has its own HMM recogniser. In this work, we use either 2, 4, 6, 8 or 10 6th-order Butterworth filters with centre frequencies equally spaced on the mel scale. There is one such subsystem for each speaker.

Here, we model the speech signal by extracting features on a frame-by-frame basis. The features are cepstral coefficients, obtained from linear prediction (Markel and Gray 1976). Cepstral analysis is motivated by, and designed for, problems centred on voiced speech (Deller, Proakis, and Hansen 1993). However, it also works well for unvoiced sounds. Cepstral coefficients have been used extensively in speaker recognition (Furui 1981; Reynolds and Rose 1995), partly because a simple recursive relation exists that approximately transforms the easily-obtained linear prediction coefficients into 'pseudo' cepstral ones (Atal 1974). The analysis frame was 16 ms long, Hamming windowed and overlapping by 50%. The first 12 coefficients were used, excluding the zeroth cepstral coefficient (as is usual).

Subsequently, we have to derive recognition models for the utterances of the different speakers, for which we use the popular hidden Markov models. HMMs are powerful statistical models of sequential data that have been used extensively for many speech applications (Rabiner 1989). They embody an underlying (hidden) stochastic process that can only be observed through a set of stochastic processes that produces an observation sequence. In speech processing applications, this observation sequence is the series of feature vectors that have been extracted from an utterance.

Discrete HMMs were used with 4 states for word *seven* and 3 states for word *nine*, plus a start and end state in each case. This structure was found to give best results in preliminary tests. Apart from self-loops (staying in the same state), only left-to-right transitions are allowed. Speech frames were vector quantised, and each HMM has its own linear codebook of size 32. Therefore, in the wideband case there are 60 codebooks (equal to the number of speakers) and in the subband system there are $60 \times N$ codebooks (where N is the number of subbands), which were constructed using a Euclidean distance metric. HMMs were trained and tested using the HTK software of Young, Kershaw, Odell, Ollason, Valtchev, and Woodland (2000).

5 Subband Recombination

Our earlier work has used the sum and product rules specified by Kittler, Hatef, Duin, and Matas (1998). Here, we explore the use of artificial neural networks (ANNs) for subband recombination. In this work, the HMMs deliver log likelihood values, so that sum-rule fusion corresponds to taking products of likelihoods. Under assumptions of conditional independence and equal priors, this strategy is optimal (e.g. Morris, Hagen, and Bourlard 1999). Using this rule, the identified speaker, i, is that for whom:

$$i = \arg\max_s [y^s] = \arg\max_s \sum_{n=1}^{N} \log L_n^s \qquad 1 \le s \le S = 60 \qquad (1)$$

where N is the number of classifiers (subbands), L_n^s is the likelihood that classifier n and model speaker s produced the observed data sequence, and y^s is the recombined (final) score for speaker s from the set of S speakers.

The formulation in equation (1) is linear with constant (unity) weights. However, according to Bourlard and Dupont (1996) in their work on subband speech recognition: "... it is often argued that the recombination mechanism should be nonlinear" (p. 427). Also, the assumption of conditional independence is unsatisfactory. Accordingly, Bourlard and Dupont used a multilayer perceptron (MLP) trained to estimate posterior probabilities of speech units (HMM states, phones, syllables or words) given the log-likelihoods of all subbands and all speech units. It is also intuitively-attractive for a recombination scheme to have variable weights (Okawa, Nakajima, and Shirai 1999) and the MLP offers this.

Hence, MLPs have been used for the ANN recombination in this work (see Bishop 1995 for relevant background). Various MLP recombination structures were considered initially, namely:

Single 'global' MLP: this structure would have taken each of N subbands from each of 60 speaker models to give $60 \times N$ inputs and would have needed an output layer capable of encoding $S = 60$ speaker labels. We did not believe there were sufficient data available to train such a large ANN, so this option was not pursued.

Single 'local' MLP: this structure has N inputs and only a single output. It is trained on outputs from all 60 speaker subsystems (as in Fig. 2). During test, output from each speaker subsystem is passed in turn to the MLP, and the identified speaker is that producing the largest output activation.

Multiple 'local' MLPs: here, there are again N inputs and a single output, but there are 60 separate ANNs—one per speaker. The decision rule is as for the single local MLP.

Because it performed best in preliminary tests, only the single local structure was used here. This is most likely a consequence of the much larger data set used in training the single global MLP. In particular, the multiple MLPs each 'saw' only 10 positive examples as compared to 590 negative examples.

Each MLP was trained 10 times from different initial points in the search space, with the initial weights drawn from a zero-mean, unit-variance isotropic Gaussian distribution. The single output had a logistic activation function. For the results reported here, all MLPs had a single hidden layer of five tanh nodes. It was found that using either 10 or 15 hidden nodes did not significantly affect the results. Training minimised the cross-entropy error function using a conjugate-gradient algorithm. Outputs were trained to 0 or 1, with the latter indicating that the MLP classified the utterance as belonging to the speaker model. A weight decay scheme (with $\alpha = 0.2$) was used to prevent over-training. The order of the training data was randomised to avoid bias in the learning (in terms of all the positive examples being presented in a single block). Training used noise-free speech data only.

Input data were scaled to be in the unit-interval in each input axis. This was to make the weight initialisation easier (as above) and also to avoid slow convergence of the weights in the presence of highly imbalanced data (less than 2% of the examples were positive). Without this scaling it was found that the weights could not converge in the number of iterations allowed.

6 Results

All systems tested gave approximately 100% correct identification on the clean speech data. Figure 3 shows the results obtained for the noisy speech with the wideband system, with the sum of log likelihood fusion rule, and with the MLP. The latter two are depicted as a function of the number of subbands. Error bars are shown for the MLP, as a measure of the variability of the results starting from different random initial weight settings.

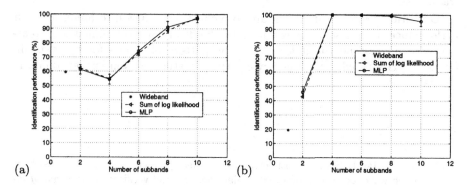

Fig. 3. Results as a function of the number of subbands for test utterances *seven* (a) and *nine* (b).

There are three notable aspects to these results:

1. Subband processing delivers enormous performance advantages, raising identification from just below 60% correct for the wideband system with word *seven* to approximately 95% correct, and from below 20% correct for the wideband system with word *nine* to 100% correct.
2. There is little difference in the performance of the two fusion techniques, suggesting that the conditional independence assumption in equation (1) is reasonable.
3. There is widespread variation in the pattern of results for the two different words. For *seven*, the wideband result is much higher than for *nine*, yet the subband system achieves 100% correct identification for *nine* but not for *seven*. Best results for *seven* are obtained with 10 subbands for both fusion methods whereas best results for *nine* are obtained with 4–10 subbands using equation (1).

7 Conclusions and Future Work

In this paper, we have extended our earlier work on subband speaker recognition using multiple classifier techniques. We have studied speaker identification both in noise-free conditions and with narrowband noise added to the test utterances only (training remained noise-free). By including word *nine* in addition to word *seven* for 60 speakers, we have tested a wider range of speech materials than previously.

For the clean speech, all systems tested achieved either 100% correct identification or very close to 100%. With noisy speech, the sum rule of recombination working on log likelihoods gave comparable results to the MLP fusion. The best MLP in preliminary tests was the single local version, which had the same number of inputs as the number of subbands and was trained on the entire training set.

Our priorities for future work are to include other fusion techniques in our performance comparisons, to explore other kinds of noise contamination, to attempt to understand the difference in the pattern of results for the two different words studied here, and beyond that to study all ten spoken digits in the database.

References

[Atal 1974] Atal, B. S. (1974). Effectiveness of linear prediction characteristics of the speech wave for automatic speaker identification and verification. *Journal of the Acoustical Society of America 55*, 1304–1312.

[Besacier and Bonastre 1997] Besacier, L. and J.-F. Bonastre (1997). Subband approach for automatic speaker recognition: Optimal division of the frequency domain. In *Proceedings of 1st International Conference on Audio- and Visual-Based Biometric Person Authentication (AVBPA)*, Crans-Montana, Switzerland, pp. 195–202.

[Besacier and Bonastre 2000] Besacier, L. and J.-F. Bonastre (2000). Subband architecture for automatic speaker recognition. *Signal Processing 80*, 1245–1259.

[Bishop 1995] Bishop, C. M. (1995). *Neural Networks for Pattern Recognition*. Oxford, UK: Clarendon Press.

[Bourlard and Dupont 1996] Bourlard, H. and S. Dupont (1996). A new ASR approach based on independent processing and recombination of partial frequency bands. In *Proceedings of Fourth International Conference on Spoken Language Processing, ICSLP'96*, Volume 1, Philadelphia, PA, pp. 426–429.

[Campbell 1997] Campbell, J. P. (1997). Speaker recognition: A tutorial. *Proceedings of the IEEE 85*(9), 1437–1462.

[Deller, Proakis, and Hansen 1993] Deller, J. R., J. P. Proakis, and J. H. L. Hansen (1993). *Discrete-Time Processing of Speech Signals*. Englewood Cliffs, NJ: MacMillan.

[Doddington 1985] Doddington, G. (1985). Speaker recognition – identifying people by their voices. *Proceedings of the IEEE 73*(11), 1651–1664.

[Finan, Damper, and Sapeluk 2001] Finan, R. A., R. I. Damper, and A. T. Sapeluk (2001). Text-dependent speaker recognition using sub-band processing. *International Journal of Speech Technology 4*(1), 45–62.

[Furui 1974] Furui, S. (1974). An analysis of long-term variation of feature parameters of speech and its application to talker recognition. *Electronic Communications 57-A*, 34–42.

[Furui 1981] Furui, S. (1981). Cepstral analysis techniques for automatic speaker verification. *IEEE Transactions on Acoustics, Speech and Signal Processing ASSP-29*(2), 254–272.

[Furui 1997] Furui, S. (1997). Recent advances in speaker recognition. *Pattern Recognition Letters 18*, 859–872.

[Higgins, Damper, and Harris 1999] Higgins, J. E., R. I. Damper, and C. J. Harris (1999). A multi-spectral data-fusion approach to speaker recognition. In *Proceedings of 2nd International Conference on Information Fusion, Fusion 99*, Volume II, Sunnyvale, CA, pp. 1136–1143.

[Kittler, Hatef, Duin, and Matas 1998] Kittler, J., M. Hatef, R. P. W. Duin, and J. Matas (1998). On combining classifiers. *IEEE Transactions on Pattern Analysis and Machine Intelligence 20*(3), 226–239.

[Markel and Gray 1976] Markel, J. D. and A. H. Gray (1976). *Linear Prediction of Speech*. Berlin, Germany: Springer-Verlag.

[Morris, Hagen, and Bourlard 1999] Morris, A., A. Hagen, and H. Bourlard (1999). The full-combination sub-bands approach to noise robust HMM/ANN-based ASR. In *Proceedings of 6th European Conference on Speech Communication and Technology, Eurospeech'99*, Volume 2, Budapest, Hungary, pp. 599–602.

[Okawa, Nakajima, and Shirai 1999] Okawa, S., T. Nakajima, and K. Shirai (1999). A recombination strategy for multi-band speech recognition based on mutual information criterion. In *Proceedings of 6th European Conference on Speech Communication and Technology, Eurospeech'99*, Volume 2, Budapest, Hungary, pp. 603–606.

[Rabiner 1989] Rabiner, L. R. (1989). A tutorial on hidden Markov models and selected applications in speech recognition. *Proceedings of the IEEE 77*(2), 257–285.

[Reynolds and Rose 1995] Reynolds, D. A. and R. C. Rose (1995). Robust text-independent speaker identification using Gaussian mixture models. *IEEE Transactions on Speech and Audio Processing 3*(1), 72–83.

[Sivakumaran, Ariyaeeinia, and Hewitt 1998] Sivakumaran, P., A. M. Ariyaeeinia, and J. A. Hewitt (1998). Sub-band speaker verification using dynamic recombination weights. In *Proceedings of 5th International Conference on Spoken Language Processing, ICSLP 98*, Sydney, Australia. Paper 1055 on CD-ROM.

[Stevens and Volkmann 1940] Stevens, S. S. and J. Volkmann (1940). The relation of pitch to frequency: A revised scale. *American Journal of Psychology 53*(3), 329–353.

[Tibrewala and Hermansky 1997] Tibrewala, S. and H. Hermansky (1997). Sub-band based recognition of noisy speech. In *Proceedings of International Conference on Acoustics, Speech and Signal Processing, ICASSP 97*, Volume II, Munich, Germany, pp. 1255–1258.

[Young, Kershaw, Odell, Ollason, Valtchev, and Woodland 2000] Young, S., J. Kershaw, J. Odell, D. Ollason, V. Valtchev, and P. Woodland (2000). The HTK Book. Available from URL http://htk.eng.cam.ac.uk/.

Classification of Time Series Utilizing Temporal and Decision Fusion

C. Dietrich, F. Schwenker, and G. Palm

University of Ulm, D-89069 Ulm, Germany
{dietrich, schwenker, palm}@neuro.informatik.uni-ulm.de

Abstract. In this paper we discuss classifier architectures to categorize time series. Three different architectures for the fusion of local classifier decisions are presented and applied to classify recordings of cricket songs. Different features from local time windows are extracted automatically from the waveform of the sound patterns. These features are used to classify the whole time series. We present results for all three classifier architectures on a data set of 28 different categories.

1 Introduction

The classification of time series is the topic of this paper. In real world applications information or features extracted from time series are used for the categorization. For example, in medical diagnosis a patient may be classified into one of two or more classes using an electrocardiogram (ECG) recording. Another pattern recognition problem may the identification of an individual based on its speech recording. One difficulty with the classification of time series is that the number of measurements is typically large in comparison to the number of objects and varies from recording to recording. To overcome these problems some kind of preprocessing and feature extraction on these time series has to be performed.

In principle there are two approaches of feature extraction for time series:

1. **Global features.** These features based on the information in the whole time series, e.g. the mean frequency, mean energy, etc.
2. **Local features.** These are derived from subsets of the whole time series, which are usually defined through a local time windows W^t. In this type of feature extraction a set of features is calculated within the window W^t. The window is then moved by a time step Δt into $W^{t+\Delta t}$ and the next set of features is calculated. Moving the window over the whole time series leads to a sequence of feature vectors.

In this paper we focus on the classification of time series based on local features, i.e. on sequences of locally derived feature vectors. The paper is organized as follows: In Section 2 we present three different classifier architectures for the fusion of local decisions. For the classification of feature vectors we use the *fuzzy-k-nearest-neighbour* approach, which is described in Section 3. In Section 4 we

J. Kittler and F. Roli (Eds.): MCS 2001, LNCS 2096, pp. 378–387, 2001.

present an application of these classifiers in the domain of bioacoustics (the classification of cricket songs). We present and discuss the classification results for the proposed fusion architectures on this dataset in Section 5.

2   Classification Fusion for Local Features

In this section we propose three different types of classifier architectures for the fusion of local features and decisions based on these local features. This situation is illustrated in Figure 1. Here a window W^t covering a small part of the time series is moved over the whole time series. For each window W^t, $t = 1, ..., T$ a set of p features $F_i^t \in \mathbb{R}^{d_i}$, $i = 1, ..., p$ and $d_i \in \mathbb{N}$, is extracted from the time series. Typically T, the number of time windows varies from time series to time series.

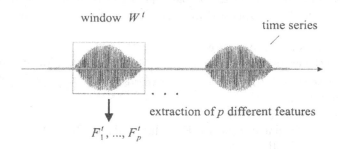

window W^t

time series

extraction of p different features

$F_1^t, ..., F_p^t$

Fig. 1. A set of p features $F_1^t, ..., F_p^t$ is extracted from a local time window W^t located at time t.

A. Architecture **CDT** (see Figure 2a)
In this architecture the classification of the time series is performed in the following three steps:
1.) Classification of single feature vectors (C-step)
For each feature F_i^t, $i = 1, ..., p$ derived from the time window W^t a classifier c_i is given through a mapping (see Section 3)

$$c_i : \mathbb{R}^{d_i} \to \Delta \qquad (1)$$

where the set Δ is defined through

$$\Delta := \{(q_1, ..., q_l) \in [0, 1]^l | \sum_{i=1}^{l} q_i = 1\}. \qquad (2)$$

Here l is the number of classes. Thus for time window W^t, the p classification results are $c_1(F_1^t), ..., c_p(F_p^t)$.

2.) Decision fusion of the local decisions (D-step)
The classification results are combined into a decision $C_A^t \in \Delta$ for the time window W^t through a fusion mapping $\mathcal{F} : \Delta^p \rightarrow \Delta$

$$C_A^t := \mathcal{F}(c_1(F_1^t), ..., c_p(F_p^t)), \quad t = 1, ..., T \tag{3}$$

which calculates the fused classification result of the p different decisions.
3.) Temporal fusion of decisions over the whole time series (T-step)
The classification for the whole set of time windows W^t, $t = 1, ..., T$ is given through

$$C_A^o = \mathcal{F}(C_A^1, ..., C_A^T) \tag{4}$$

again $\mathcal{F} : \Delta^T \rightarrow \Delta$ is a fusion mapping.
B. Architecture **DCT** (see Figure 2b)
Here the classification of the whole time series is determined through the classification of the fused features and decision fusion over the whole time series:
1.) Data fusion of feature vectors (D-step)
Here the extracted features $F_1^t, ..., F_p^t$ in the time window W^t are simply concatenated into a single feature vector $F^t = (F_1^t, ..., F_p^t) \in \mathbb{R}^P$, with $P = \sum_{i=1}^p d_i$.
2.) Classification (C-step)
The combined feature vector F^t is classified into $C_B^t \in \Delta$ using a classifier mapping $c^t : \mathbb{R}^P \rightarrow \Delta$.

$$C_B^t := c^t(F^t) \tag{5}$$

3.) Temporal fusion of decisions over the whole time series (T-step)
Here

$$C_B^o = \mathcal{F}(C_B^1, ..., C_B^T) \tag{6}$$

is the classification result for the whole set of time windows W^t, $t = 1, ..., T$.
C. Architecture **CTD** (see Figure 2c)
Here, the final classification result is determined through temporal fusion followed by decision fusion.
1.) Each of the p feature vectors $F_1^t, ..., F_p^t$ within W^t is classified (C-step)

$$F_i^t \rightarrow c_i(F_i^t) \in \Delta \tag{7}$$

2.) Temporal fusion based on each feature $j = 1, ..., p$ (T-step)

$$C_C^j = \mathcal{F}(c_j(F_j^1), ..., c_j(F_j^T)) \in \Delta \tag{8}$$

again $\mathcal{F}$ is a fusion mapping $\mathcal{F} : \Delta^T \rightarrow \Delta$.

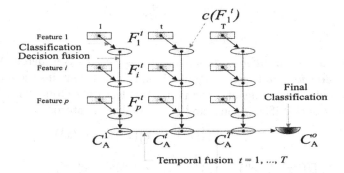

(a) CDT - Classification, Decision fusion, Temporal fusion.

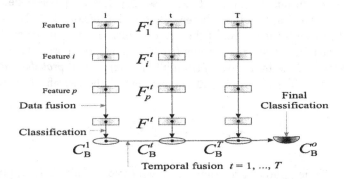

(b) DCT - Data fusion, Classification, Temporal fusion.

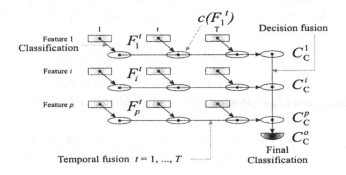

(c) CTD - Classification, Temporal fusion, Decision fusion.

Fig. 2. Classifier architectures for the classification of time series

3.) Decision fusion over all p features C_C^i (D-step)

$$C_C^o = \mathcal{F}(C_C^1, ..., C_C^p) \qquad (9)$$

here $\mathcal{F}$ is a fusion mapping $\mathcal{F} : \Delta^p \to \Delta$.

For the integration different fusion mappings may be considered. We now consider the *decision profile* for an input $x^1, ..., x^n$ which contains the individual classifier outputs. Here n denotes the number of feature vectors which is equal to the number of classifier outputs and l the number of categories.

$$DP(x^1, ..., x^n) = \begin{bmatrix} e_1^1(x^1) & ... & e_j^1(x^1) & ... & e_l^1(x^1) \\ ... & ... & ... & ... & ... \\ e_1^i(x^i) & ... & e_j^i(x^i) & ... & e_l^i(x^i) \\ ... & ... & ... & ... & ... \\ e_1^n(x^n) & ... & e_j^n(x^n) & ... & e_l^n(x^n) \end{bmatrix} \qquad (10)$$

For temporal fusion $e^i \in \Delta$, $i = 1, ..., T$ (see Eq. 4, 6, 8) denotes the classifier output of the i-th time window whereas for decision fusion $e^i \in \Delta$, $i = 1, ..., p$ (see Eq. 3, 9) denotes the output of the i-th classifier. Then e_j^i is the evidence for class j obtained from the i-th classifier/time window. Temporal fusion and the decision fusion is done by *average fusion* [6] or *symmetrical probabilistic fusion*. For n decision vectors $e^1, ..., e^n \in \Delta$ the average of the classification results is given by

$$\mathcal{F}(e^1, ..., e^n) := \frac{1}{n} \sum_{i=1}^{n} e^i. \qquad (11)$$

A probabilistic approach to combine classification results is to apply Bayes' rule [8] under the assumption that the classification results are independent.

For this the posterior probability $P(\omega_j | x^1, ..., x^n)$ for the class ω_j has to be approximated, given the evidence readings (classifications) $e_j^1, ..., e_j^n$ for the class ω_j, which will be interpreted as posterior probabilities $P(\omega_j | x^1), ..., P(\omega_j | x^n)$. Then the classifier output is given by

$$\mathcal{F}(e^1, ..., e^n)_j := P(\omega_j | x^1, ..., x^n) + \epsilon_j(x^1, ..., x^n) \qquad (12)$$

where $\epsilon_j(x^1, ..., x^n)$ is the error made by the classifier ensemble.

Let $O(\omega_j | x^1, ..., x^n)$ be the posterior odds. Then the posterior probability is given by [8]

$$P(\omega_j | x^1, ..., x^n) = \frac{O(\omega_j | x^1, ..., x^n)}{1 + O(\omega | x^1, ..., x^n)} = 1 - (1 + \frac{P(\omega_j | x^1, ..., x^n)}{P(\neg \omega_j | x^1, ..., x^n)})^{-1}. \qquad (13)$$

Assuming that the conditional probabilities $P(x^i | \omega_j)$ for $i \neq i'$ are independent of $P(x^{i'} | \omega_j)$ leads to the product rule

$$P(\omega_j | x^1, ..., x^n) = \alpha \prod_{i=1}^{n} P(\omega_j) P(x^i | \omega_j) \qquad (14)$$

where α is a normalizing constant to be computed by requiring that that Eq. 14 sum to unity (over i) [8]. For a multi class problem the posterior odds are then given by

$$O(\omega_j | x^1, ..., x^n) = \frac{P(\omega_j | x^1, ..., x^n)}{P(\neg\omega_j | x^1, ..., x^n)} = \alpha \frac{P(\omega_j)}{P(\neg\omega_j)} \prod_{i=1}^{n} \frac{P(x^i|\omega_j)}{P(x^i|\neg\omega_j)} \qquad (15)$$

Integrating the posterior odds (Eq. 15) into Eq. 13 and applying the Bayes' rule leads to the symmetrical probabilistic fusion function

$$
\begin{aligned}
P(\omega_j | x^1, ..., x^n) &= 1 - \left(1 + \alpha \frac{P(\omega_j)}{P(\neg\omega_j)} \prod_{i=1}^{n} \frac{P(x^i|\omega_j)}{P(x^i|\neg\omega_j)}\right)^{-1} \\
&= 1 - \left(1 + \alpha \frac{P(\omega_j)}{P(\neg\omega_j)} \prod_{i=1}^{n} \frac{P(\omega_j|x^i)}{P(\neg\omega_j|x^i)} \frac{P(\neg\omega_j)}{P(\omega_j)}\right)^{-1}
\end{aligned}
\qquad (16)
$$

where $P(\omega_j)$ denotes the class probability for the class ω_j which is set to $\frac{1}{l}$ in our numerical experiments.

3   Classification with the k-Nearest-Neighbour Rule

One of the most elegant and simplest classification techniques is the *k-nearest-neighbour rule* [2]. The classifier searches for the k nearest neighbours among a set of m prototypes $\{x^1, ..., x^m\} \in \mathbb{R}^d$ and an input vector $x \in \mathbb{R}^d$. The k nearest neighbours are calculated utilizing the L_p-norm.

$$d_j^p(x, x^j) = ||x - x^j||_p = \left(\sum_{i=1}^{d} |x_i - x_i^j|^p\right)^{\frac{1}{p}} \qquad (17)$$

between x and x^j [11]. The class which occures most often among the k nearest neighbours is the classification result.

Let l be the number of classes. To determine the membership of an input vector x to each class, a *fuzzy-k-nearest-neighbour classifier* is applied [10]. A fuzzy classifier $\mathcal{N}$ is a mapping $\mathcal{N} : \mathbb{R}^d \to [0,1]^l$, with output $\mathcal{N}(x) = (\delta_1(x), ..., \delta_l(x)) \in \Delta$.

For each class $\omega = 1, ..., l$ let m_ω be the number of prototypes with classlabel ω. Then for input x and each class ω there is a sequence $(\tau_i^\omega)_{i=1}^{m_\omega}$ with $||x^{\tau_1^\omega} - x||_p \leq, ..., \leq ||x^{\tau_{m_\omega}^\omega} - x||_p$. Here m_i denotes the number of prototypes of class ω. The k nearest neighbours ($k \leq m_\omega$) of x to class ω are given by

$$\mathcal{N}_k^\omega(x) := \{x^{\tau_1^\omega}, ..., x^{\tau_k^\omega}\}. \qquad (18)$$

Let

$$\tilde{\delta}_\omega(x) = \frac{1}{\sum_{x_i \in \mathcal{N}_k^\omega(x)} \left(\frac{||x - x_i||_p}{\xi} + \alpha\right)}, \quad \alpha > 0 \qquad (19)$$

be the support for the hypothesis that the true label of x is ω. The parameter α is used to determine how to grade low values of $||x - x_i||_p$.

After normalisation by $\delta_j(x) := \tilde{\delta}_j / \sum_{i=1}^l \tilde{\delta}_i$ we call the classifier outputs *soft labels* [5]. For input x the classification result $\mathcal{N}(x) := (\delta_1(x), ..., \delta_l(x)) \in \Delta$ is containing the membership of x for each class.

After normailsation with

$$\Delta_j := \frac{\delta_j}{\sum_{i=1}^l \delta_i} \tag{20}$$

we can restrict $\Delta_j(x)$ without loss of generality within the interval $[0, 1]$ and call the classifier outputs *soft labels* [5].

For input x the classification result $\mathcal{N}(x) = (\Delta_1(x), ..., \Delta_l(x))$ is containing the membership of x for each class. The parameter k determines the fuzzyness of the classification result. In our numerical experiments we set p to 1, α to 0.01, ξ to 100 and k to 3.

4   Application

We present results achieved by testing the algorithms on a dataset which contains sound patterns from 28 different cricket species. The dataset contains recordings of 3 or 4 different individuals per species. The recordings are from Thailand (used by Ingrisch [3,4]) and from Ecuador (used in the doctoral thesis by Nischk [7]). The sound patterns are stored in the standard WAV-format (44.100 Hz sampling frequency, 16 Bit sampling accuracy).

The cricket songs consist of sequences of sound patterns (chirps). Based on these chirps (sequences of so-called pulses) the crickets may be classified [1,7]. Therefore we analyse the structure of single pulses in the cricket songs, and so the first processing step is the pulse detection.

4.1   Pulse Detection

The position of the pulses are located using an modified algorithm of Rabiner and Sambur [9], which uses the signal's energy and two thresholds (see Figure 3b) to detect the onsets (start position) and offsets (stop position) of the signals. A modified algorithm is applied to extract single pulses of the cricket songs [1]. These pulses are used to calculate the features.

4.2   Local Features

The following three local features are extracted from the single pulses and then used as inputs for the classifiers:

1. **Pulse length:** Let n be the amount of pulses. Furthermore let λ_i be the onset of the i-th pulse and μ_i be the offset of the i-th pulse. Then the length L_i is extracted by $\mu_i - \lambda_i$, $i = 1, ..., n - d$, where d is the amount of dimensions used for the pulse distances.

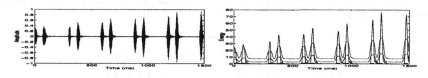

(a) Filtered cricket waveform

(b) The energy functions for signal segmentation

Fig. 3. Waveform and energy of the species *Noctitrella glabra* (time window 1500 ms).

2. **Pulse distances**: Let $\Delta = (\Delta_1, ..., \Delta_{n-1})$ be the distances between two pulses calculated by

$$\Delta_j = \lambda_{j+1} - \lambda_j, \quad j \in \{1, ..., n-1\}. \tag{21}$$

Then the pulse distances are extracted using a d−tuple encoding scheme producing $n - d$ datapoints $T_i \in \mathbb{R}^d$

$$T_i := (\Delta_i, \Delta_{i+1}, ..., \Delta_{i+d-1}) \in \mathbb{R}^d, \quad i = 1, ..., n - d. \tag{22}$$

3. **Pulse frequency**: The pulse frequency F_i, $i = 1, ..., n - d$ is extracted from the spectra of the single pulses. The algoritm searches the frequency band with the highest energy.

5   Results and Discussion

Because of the limited data sets 108 sound recordings (4 records for 24 species and 3 records for 4 species) we utilize the cross validation method to evaluate the classifiers. The training set has been used to design the classifiers, and the test set for testing the performance of the classification task. The test is done in a *k-fold cross validation test* with $k = 4$ cycles using 2-3 records of each species for training and 1 record of each species for the classification test. In the numerical evaluation 25 different cross validation tests have been made. The training and test records are randomly splitted and are always recordings from different individuals. Table 1 shows the cross-validation results for the single features.

The best feature for the classification are the distances between pulses T_i. Including other features into the classification procedure may enhance the classification rate. Table 2 and 3 depicts the classification rates of the previously introduced classifier architectures for the three local features. For the DCT architecture the fusion functions average fusion and symmetrical probabilistic fusion (see Eq. 11, 16) are only be used for the temporal fusion (see Eq. 6), because data fusion is the first fusion step.

The best classification rate (6.924 % error) for the described application is achieved with the DCT architecture and the average function for temporal

Table 1. Classification performance of the single local features after temporal fusion through average fusion.

feature	error %
Pulse length (L_i)	82.068 ± 2.178
Pulse frequency (F_i)	72.879 ± 2.448
Time structure (T_i)	18.396 ± 3.086

Table 2. Classification results of locally fused features for the DCT architecture dependent on the fusion function (AF_T temporal fusion with the average function and SPF_T temporal fusion with the symmetrical probabilistic function).

architecture	AF_T	SPF_T
DCT	6.924 ± 1.655	7.091 ± 1.711

fusion (AF_T). For this architecture the symmetrical probabilistic fusion over time (SPF_T) leads almost to the same results (7.091 %, see Table 2).

For decision fusion and temporal fusion with average fusion (AF_D/AF_T) the CDT architecture is equivalent to the CTD architecture (classification error 8.595 %). For decision fusion with average fusion and temporal fusion with the symmetrical probabilistic function (AF_D/SPF_T) the CDT architecture outperforms the CTD architecture. The reason for that is that the symmetrical probabilistic function is sensitive to errors in the probability estimations $P(\omega_j|x^i)$. These probability estimations may be better if the classifier results are combined through decision fusion (CDT architecture) before temporal fusion is applied (see Table 3). The same effect is observed for the AF_D/SPF_T fusion function combination.

We observed that in our numerical experiments the CTD architecture outperforms the CDT architecture.

It seems that symmetrical probabilistic fusion is sensitive for temporal fusion, because the product $\mathcal{F}(e_1, ..., e_n)$ is equal to zero if just a single decision e_j^i in the

Table 3. Classification results of locally fused features for the CDT and CTD architecture dependent on the fusion function (AF average fusion (see Eq. 11) and SPF symmetrical probabilistic fusion (see Eq. 16)). The indices D and T indicate if the fusion function is used for D decision fusion or T temporal fusion.

architecture	AF_D/AF_T	AF_D/SPF_T	SPF_D/AF_T	SPF_D/SPF_T
CDT	8.595 ± 1.776	8.409 ± 1.975	7.314 ± 1.656	7.073 ± 1.816
CTD	8.595 ± 1.776	15.296 ± 2.737	7.407 ± 1.792	14.424 ± 2.528

sequence is equal to zero (see Eq. 16). But for decision fusion the symmetrical probabilistic function outperforms average fusion in our application (see Table 3).

Acknowledgement. DORSA (www.dorsa.de) forms part of the Entomological Data Information System (EDIS) and is funded by the German Ministry of Science and Education (BMBF). We are greatful to Klaus Riede (ZFMK Bonn, Germany), Sigfrid Ingrisch (ZFMK Bonn, Germany) and Frank Nischk, for providing their sound recordings, suggestions and discussions.

References

1. C. Dietrich, F. Schwenker, K. Riede, and G. Palm. Automated classification of cricket songs utilizing pulse detection, time and frequency features and data fusion. *submitted to Journal of the Acoustical Society of America, 2001.*
2. K. Fukunaga. *Introduction to Statistical Pattern Recognition.* Academic Press, New York, 1990.
3. S. Ingrisch. Taxonomy, stridulation and development of podoscirtinae from thailand. *Senckenbergiana biologica,* 77:47–75, 1997.
4. S. Ingrisch and G. Koehler. *Die Heuschrecken Mitteleuropas.* Westarp Wissenschaften, Magdeburg, 1998.
5. L. I. Kuncheva. Clustering and selection model for classifier combination. In *4th International Conference on Knowledge-Based Intelligent Engineering Systems,* 2000.
6. L. I. Kuncheva and J. C. Bezdek. An integrated framework for generalized nearest prototype classifier design. *Journal of Uncertainty, Fuzziness and Knowledge-Based Systems,* 6(5):437–457, 1998.
7. F. Nischk. *Die Grillengesellschaften zweier neotropischer Waldökosysteme in Ecuador.* PhD thesis, University of Köln in Germany, 1999. Memorandum UCB/ERL–M89/29.
8. J. Pearl. *Probabilistic Reasoning in Intelligent Systems.* Morgan Kaufmann Publishers, San Francisco, 1988.
9. L. R. Rabiner and S. E. Sambur. An algorithm for determining the endpoints of isolated utterances. *Bell Syst. Technical Journal,* 54(2):297–315, 1997.
10. S. Singh. 2D spiral pattern recognition with possibilistic measures. *Pattern Recognition Letters,* 19(2):141–147, 1998.
11. D. B. Skalak. *Prototype Selection for Composite Nearest Neighbour Classifiers.* PhD thesis, University of Massachusetts, 1997.

Use of Positional Information in Sequence Alignment for Multiple Classifier Combination

U.-V. Marti and H. Bunke

Institut für Informatik und angewandte Mathematik
Universität Bern, Neubrückstrasse 10, CH-3012 Bern, Switzerland
email:{marti,bunke}@iam.unibe.ch

Abstract. There are problems in pattern recognition where the output of a system is a sequence of classes rather than a single class. A well-known example is handwritten sentence recognition. In order to make those problems amenable to classifier combination techniques, an algorithm for sequence alignment must be provided. The present paper describes such an algorithm. The algorithm extends an earlier method by including information about the location of each pattern in a sequence. The proposed approach is evaluated in the context of a system for handwritten sentence recognition. It is demonstrated through experiments that by the use of positional information the computationally expensive process of multiple sequence alignment can be significantly sped up without loosing recognition accuracy.

Keywords: multiple classifier combination, multiple sequence alignment, string edit distance, positional information, handwriting recognition.

1 Introduction

Multiple classifier combination has become a very active area of research [1]. The motivation behind the activities in this area is based on the observation that classification errors can be often corrected if an ensemble of classifiers rather than a single classification method is used for a given task. However, most of the approaches to classifier combination aim at the situation where the target of each classifier, and the whole system, is just a single class. For this kind of problem, a multitude of combination techniques have been proposed, including product, sum, median, maximum and minimum of a posteriori probabilities and related quantities [2], as well as voting [3] and trainable combiners [4].

But there are many pattern recognition problems, where the desired result is a sequence of classes, rather than just a single class. An example is handwritten sentence recognition [5,6,7]. Here the goal of the recognizer is to produce a sequence of words, or classes, that represent the handwritten text. A difficult problem in the recognition of handwritten sentences is the segmentation of a line of text into individual words. Such a segmentation can be performed in an explicit way prior to recognition [5,6], or it can be integrated into the recognizer

J. Kittler and F. Roli (Eds.): MCS 2001, LNCS 2096, pp. 388–398, 2001.
© Springer-Verlag Berlin Heidelberg 2001

[7]. In either case, both recognition and segmentation are prone to errors. Therefore, we can neither expect that the identity of a word delivered by a recognizer is correct, nor that the correct number of words is reported. Consequently, given N sequences of words, each delivered by a different recognizer, an alignment of the N sequences needs to be done, before 'conventional' classifier combination techniques, such as the ones mentioned above, can be applied.

A well-known method for sequence alignment is based on the edit distance of sequences [8]. The method reported in [8] can be used for the alignment of two sequences. An extension to the case of $N \geq 2$ sequences is described in [9]. This procedure has been used for the postprocessing of OCR results [10]. A problem with the alignment procedure described in [9] is its high computational complexity. Let N denote the number of sequences and n the maximum sequence length. Then the algorithm described in [9] needs $O(n^N)$ time and space. In [10] a suboptimal version of the procedure described in [9] was used, which explores only part of the N-dimensional search space. However, a drawback is that the portion of the search space that is actually considered has to be specified a priori. I.e., it is independent of the actual input data. In the present paper, another version of the algorithm described in [9] is proposed. It is distinguished by the fact that it uses positional information about the words delivered by the recognizers. If the words in an N-tuple under consideration differ significantly in their spatial location in a line of handwritten text, they are not considered any longer as potential candidates for alignment. This leads to a quite substantial pruning of the search space. But in contrast with defining the part of the space that is actually explored in a fixed manner beforehand, the proposed method dynamically adapts itself to the most promising regions in the search space based on the actual input data.

The present paper is organized as follows. In Section 2 the problem of sequence alignment for multiple classifier combination is stated formally, and the proposed solution is described. Then in Section 3, experimental results obtained with the new method in a system for handwritten text recognition are presented. Finally, the paper is summarized in Section 4, and conclusions are drawn.

2 Problem Statement and Proposed Solution

Assume we have N recognizers, $R_1, \ldots, R_N$, where recognizer R_i yields a sequence of words (or classes)

$$s^i = w_1^i w_2^i \ldots w_{n_i}^i \tag{1}$$

as output; $i = 1, \ldots, N$. If the number of words output by each R_i were the same, i.e., $n_1 = n_2 = \ldots = n_N = n$, then 'traditional' classifier combination techniques, such as the ones referenced in Section 1, could be directly applied. That is, the most plausible word could be determined for each position j based on $(w_j^1, \ldots, w_j^N), j = 1, \ldots, n$. In practice, however, due to segmentation errors, we have to anticipate that all $n_1, \ldots n_N$ may be different from each other. Hence, before any of the combination methods mentioned in Section 1 can be

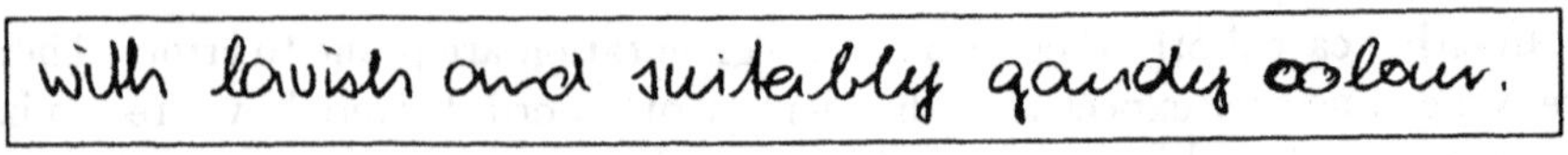

Fig. 1. Example of a text to be recognized.

Table 1. Output for the text of Fig 1, output by three different recognizers.

> with lavish and suitably gaudy colour
> with lavish and suitably gaudy colour .
> with lavish and spite they gaudy about .

Table 2. Alignment for the text of Fig 1, produced by three different recognizers.

	1.	2.	3.	4.	5.	6.	7.	8.
a.)	with	lavish	and	suitably	ϵ	gaudy	colour	ϵ
b.)	with	lavish	and	suitably	ϵ	gaudy	colour	.
c.)	with	lavish	and	spite	they	gaudy	about	.

applied, an alignment between all N sequences $w_1^1 \ldots w_{n_1}^1, \ldots, w_1^N \ldots w_{n_N}^N$ has to be performed.

As an example, Fig. 1 shows an image of a word sequence, for which the recognition result delivered by three different recognizers are listed in Table 1[1]. (Notice that the results of the first and second classifier differ only in the period at the end of the word sequence.) In Table 2 an optimal alignment of the three sequences is shown. The symbol ϵ denotes the empty word that is inserted in the sequence of recognizer R_i, if $R_j, i \neq j$, outputs a word for which no corresponding word is reported by R_i. By an *optimal* alignment we mean an alignment that minimizes the total number of ϵ's as well as the number of word substitutions involved. It can be seen that for the first three positions a perfect alignment with no word substitutions or insertions of the empty word can be found. At the fourth and seventh position word substitutions have to be performed, while the empty word has to be inserted at the fifth position and at the end.

Computing an optimal alignment between word sequences $s^1, \ldots, s^N$ is equivalent to computing a sequence of words, s, that has, among all possible sequences of words from the underlying dictionary V, the minimum average edit distance to $s^1, \ldots, s^N$. Formally, given $s^1, \ldots, s^N$ we want to find a sequence of words, s, that minimizes

$$\frac{1}{N} \sum_{i=1}^{N} d(s, s^i). \tag{2}$$

where $d(s, s^i)$ is the edit distance between s and s^i. A sequence of words with this property is also known as a *generalized median* of set $\{s^1, \ldots, s^N\}$ [11]. Next, we review the algorithm for generalized median computation that was described in [9]. It is an extension of the classical algorithm for string edit distance

---

[1] This example is based on the recognizers described in Section 3.

computation proposed in [8]. In order to model recognition and segmentation errors, three types of edit operations are considered, namely, the deletion, insertion, and substitution of a word. Let $w \to \epsilon$ and $\epsilon \to w$ denote the deletion and insertion of word w, respectively, and $w \to w'$ the substitution of w by w'. Each of these edit operations is assigned a cost, which is a real non-negative number. Let $c(w \to \epsilon)$, $c(\epsilon \to w)$ and $c(w \to w')$ denote the cost of edit operations $w \to \epsilon$, $\epsilon \to w$ and $w \to w'$, respectively. In the remainder of this paper, we'll use the following costs:

$$c(w \to w') = \begin{cases} 0, \text{ if } w = w' \\ 1, \text{ otherwise} \end{cases} \tag{3}$$

Notice that $w \neq w'$ includes, as a special case $w = \epsilon$ or $w' = \epsilon$. Hence the cost of deleting or inserting word w as well as the cost of substituting w by w', where $w \neq w'$, is equal to one. (Note that edit operation $\epsilon \to \epsilon$ will be excluded from our considerations.)

To find an optimal alignment of sequences $s^1, \ldots, s^N$, i.e., to compute their generalized median, for an N-tuple of words $(w^1_{i_1}, \ldots, w^N_{i_N})$ the word $v \in V' = V \cup \{\epsilon\}$ causing the minimal edit costs needs to be determined. Formally, v is defined by means of the following equation:

$$v = \delta(w^1_{i_1}, \ldots, w^N_{i_N}) = \min_{v \in V'} (c(v \to w^1_{i_1}) + c(v \to w^2_{i_2}) + \ldots + c(v \to w^N_{i_N})). \tag{4}$$

Having defined function δ in this way, the optimal alignment of N sequences $s^1, \ldots s^N$ can be computed by means of dynamic programming [9], similarly to string edit distance computation [8] in an N-dimensional array. To simplify the notation in this paper, the following algorithm addresses only the case $N = 3$. But the generalization to arbitrary N is straightforward.

initialization:

$$\begin{aligned} d_{i,0,0} &= i; & i &= 0, 1, \ldots, n_1 \\ d_{0,j,0} &= j; & j &= 0, 1, \ldots, n_2 \\ d_{0,0,k} &= k; & k &= 0, 1, \ldots, n_3 \end{aligned} \tag{5}$$

iteration:

$$d_{i,j,k} = \min \begin{cases} d_{i-1,j-1,k-1} + \delta(w^1_i, w^2_j, w^3_k) \\ d_{i-1,j-1,k} + \delta(w^1_i, w^2_j, \epsilon) \\ d_{i-1,j,k-1} + \delta(w^1_i, \epsilon, w^3_k) \\ d_{i-1,j,k} + \delta(w^1_i, \epsilon, \epsilon) \\ d_{i,j-1,k-1} + \delta(\epsilon, w^2_j, w^3_k) \\ d_{i,j-1,k} + \delta(\epsilon, w^2_j, \epsilon) \\ d_{i,j,k-1} + \delta(\epsilon, \epsilon, w^3_k) \end{cases} \begin{Bmatrix} 1 \le i \le n_1 \\ 1 \le j \le n_2 \\ 1 \le k \le n_3 \end{Bmatrix} \tag{6}$$

end:

$$\text{if } (i = n_1) \wedge (j = n_2) \wedge (k = n_3) \tag{7}$$

Table 3. Minimal edit distance and the corresponding path through the search space for the example in Tabs. 1 and 2, and Fig. 1.

$$
\begin{aligned}
d_{0,0,0} &= 0 \\
d_{1,1,1} &= 0 = d_{0,0,0} + \delta(\text{with, with, with}) \\
d_{2,2,2} &= 0 = d_{1,1,1} + \delta(\text{lavish, lavish, lavish}) \\
d_{3,3,3} &= 0 = d_{2,2,2} + \delta(\text{and, and, and}) \\
d_{4,4,4} &= 1 = d_{3,3,3} + \delta(\text{suitably , suitably, spite}) \longleftarrow \\
d_{4,4,5} &= 2 = d_{4,4,4} + \delta(\epsilon, \epsilon, \text{they}) \qquad\longleftarrow \\
d_{5,5,6} &= 2 = d_{4,4,5} + \delta(\text{gaudy, gaudy, gaudy}) \\
d_{6,6,7} &= 3 = d_{5,5,6} + \delta(\text{colour, colour, about}) \qquad\longleftarrow \\
d_{6,7,8} &= 4 = d_{6,6,7} + \delta(\epsilon, ., .) \qquad\qquad\longleftarrow
\end{aligned}
$$

The path through the search space that leads from $d_{0,0,0}$ to d_{n_1,n_2,n_3} with minimum cost defines both the optimal alignment of s^1, s^2, s^3 and their generalized median. As an example, in Table 3 the optimal path trough the three-dimensional search space for the example given in Table 2 is shown. At the positions marked with an arrow, edit costs are caused. At these positions, word substitutions occur or the empty word is inserted to achieve an optimal alignment.

Obviously it is very unlikely that a word at the beginning of a sequence corresponds to a word at the end of another sequence. More generally, only words that occur at a similar position in a line of text are meaningful candidates for being matched to each other. Therefore positional information about the beginning and the end of the words can be used to reduce the search space of the previous algorithm. For each word w_l^k the starting point s_l^k and ending point e_l^k are considered. Based on this information several distance functions can be defined. In our work three distance functions were used.

In the first distance function the overlap of the words of an N-tuple is considered. If the words have a high degree of overlap, the distance is low. The overlap region between N words $w_{i_1}^1, \ldots, w_{i_N}^N$ that are being matched to each other is computed by means of the following two values max_s and min_e:

$$
max_s = \max_{j=1}^{N}(s_{i_j}^j) \tag{8}
$$

$$
min_e = \min_{j=1}^{N}(e_{i_j}^j) \tag{9}
$$

Then the distance function is computed by summing all parts of the words which do not overlap with all other words. This is done in the following way:

$$
D_{overlap}(w_{i_1}^1, w_{i_2}^2 \ldots w_{i_N}^N) = \sum_{j=1}^{N}(max_s - s_{i_j}^j) + (e_{i_j}^j - min_e). \tag{10}
$$

The second distance function considers the sum of the maximal distance between all starting points and the maximal distance between all ending points of the words. This can be expressed by the following formula:

$$D_{max-min}(w_{i_1}^1, w_{i_2}^2 \ldots w_{i_N}^N) = [max_s - \min_{j=1}^{N} s_{i_j}^j] + [\max_{j=1}^{N} e_{i_j}^j - min_e]. \quad (11)$$

In the third distance function the maximum among all distances between starting points s_l^k and ending points s_l^k is computed. This is done as follows:

$$D_{max-dist}(w_{i_1}^1, w_{i_2}^2 \ldots w_{i_N}^N) = \max_{j,k}(|s_{i_j}^j - s_{i_k}^k|, |e_{i_j}^j - e_{i_k}^k|). \quad (12)$$

In the alignment algorithm, for each N-tuple of words the positional distance is computed using one of the distances defined in eqs. (10-12). If this distance is larger than a predefined threshold θ, the N-tuple of words $(w_{i_1}^1, w_{i_2}^2, \ldots, w_{i_N}^N)$ is not considered as an appropriate candidate for alignment, i.e., the corresponding d-value is not computed. By varying the threshold θ, various degrees of search space reduction can be achieved.

Having computed the optimal alignment of a set of word sequences, each delivered by a different classifier, one can either take the generalized median sequence directly as the recognition result [10], or apply 'conventional' classifier combination techniques to each position in the aligned strings, using, for example, voting or some combination function on the scores of the individual classifiers (see Introduction).

3 Experimental Evaluation

In our earlier work we have developed three different recognition procedures for handwritten sentence recognition, which will be called R_1, R_2 and R_3 in the following. R_1 is a segmentation free recognizer that takes a complete line of handwritten text as input and yields a sequence of words as output. This recognizer is based on hidden Markov models (HMMs). R_2 is similar to R_1, but while R_1 processes lines of text in the normal left-to-right order, R_2 processes them from right to left. As the Viterbi decoding algorithm used in our HMMs is an approximative, non-exhaustive search procedure, it can be expected that R_1 and R_2 yield different results on an input sequence. R_3 is a segmentation based recognizer. It uses a number of heuristic rules to extract the individual words from a line of handwritten text. Classification of these individual words is again based on HMMs. As R_3 is significantly different from R_1 and R_2 regarding the segmentation of a line of text into individual words, it can be expected that the behavior of R_3 is different from R_1 and R_2. For a detailed description of these three classifiers see [12,13,7].

The images of the handwritten texts used for the experiments are a subset (c03-*[a-f]) of the IAM-database [14]. Altogether 59 text pages containing 541 text lines, with a total of 4523 word instances out of a vocabulary of 412 words are used. For an example of a line of Text from this database see Fig. 1. The data are split into five subsets of approximately equal size. Each subset is used once for testing, while the others are taken for training of the HMM-based recognizers.

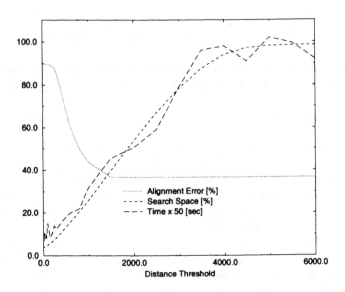

Fig. 2. Error, search space and time behaviour for the distance function $D_{overlap}$.

On this data set a correct alignment rate of 63.64% was achieved on the word level. This means that 63.64% of all handwritten words were aligned in such a way that the words output by R_1, R_2, and R_3 were identical and correct. This result was obtained by using the full search space for the alignment as described in [9].

Note that the correct alignment rate of 63.64% can be regarded as a lower bound on the recognition rate of any classifier combination procedure that is based on the alignment method described in this paper. The lower bound will be produced by a combiner that outputs word w at position j if all three aligned sequences have the same word, w, at position j, and commits an error in all other cases, for example, the case where two or all three words at position j are different.

To simplify the graphical representation, we'll not use the *correct alignment rate* in the following, but the *alignment error*. This quantity is defined as 1-*correct alignment rate*. Hence *alignment error* and *correct alignment rate* are equivalent to each other. In the experiment described above the *alignment error* is 1-63.64%=36.36%.

To test the potential of the three distance functions introduced in Section 2 for search space reduction, three experiments were conducted. In the first experiment we have used the distance function $D_{overlap}$. For different thresholds, the alignment error, the size of the explored search space and the computation time[2] used by the algorithm were measured. The results obtained are shown

---

[2] Computation time was measured on Sun Microsystems Ultra 5/270.

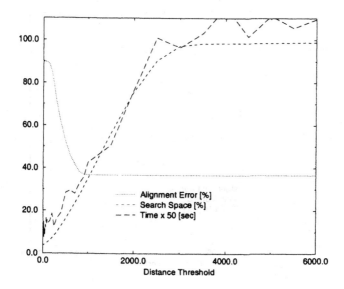

Fig. 3. Error, search space and time behaviour for the distance function $D_{max-min}$.

in Figure 2. It can be seen that if we start with a large value of the distance threshold θ and decrease it (i.e. if we go from right to left along the x-axis in Fig. 2), the alignment error remains stable at the minimum of 36.36% until $\theta \approx 1000$, while the search space and the computation time are getting smaller. By further decreasing θ, search space and computation time are further decreased, but now the alignment error increases rapidly. Hence a threshold $\theta \approx 1000$ is optimal. It leads to a significant speed up of the algorithm without any loss in recognition accuracy.

The second experiment uses the distance function $D_{max-min}$. The alignment error, the size of the search space and the computation time are shown in Figure 3. This distance function behaves similarly to $D_{overlap}$. Again by reducing the distance threshold θ to a certain value, the search space and computation time can be reduced without affecting the alignment error.

Finally for the third experiment the distance function $D_{max-dist}$ is used (see Fig. 4), which again shows a behavior similarly to the previous two experiments. So with all three distance functions it is possible to reduce the search space, and speed up the alignment algorithm, without loosing recognition performance.

It is obvious from Figs. 2 to 4 that there is a trade-off between the alignment error and the reduction of the search space. However, it is difficult to directly compare the three measures $D_{overlap}$, $D_{max-min}$, and $D_{max-dist}$ to each other based on the graphs shown in Figs. 2 to 4. But such a direct comparison is possible if we plot the search space versus the alignment error, see Fig. 5. From this figure it can be concluded that for large values of the threshold θ, i.e. for the

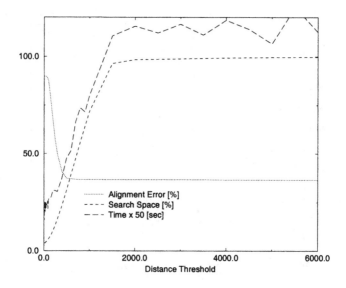

Fig. 4. Error, search space and time behaviour for the distance function $D_{max-dist}$.

case where more than 40% of the search space are explored, all three distance functions behave identically. However, for smaller values of θ, i.e. for the case were 40% or less of the search space is explored, $D_{max-min}$ and $D_{max-dist}$ still exhibit similar performance. But they are both superior to $D_{overlap}$. Clearly $D_{overlap}$ uses a larger portion of the search space in order to achieve the same alignment error as $D_{max-min}$ and $D_{max-dist}$. Equivalently, it produces a lower alignment rate when using the same amount of search space.

4   Conclusion

There are many tasks in pattern recognition where the desired output is a sequence of classes rather than just a single class. To make classifier combination applicable to those tasks, an alignment of the output sequence produced by individual classifiers is needed. Known alignment procedures suffer from a high computational complexity. The main contribution of the present paper is a method for reduction of the search space by using positional information. Three different distance functions were tested to reduce the search space with this positional information. One advantage of the proposed method is that the search space is not reduced in a fixed way but in a dynamic fashion, depending on the actual input, i.e. the word sequences to be aligned.

In a number of experiments three recognizers for handwritten sentence recognition were used, each producing a word sequence with the positional information of the recognized words as output. The experiments show that over a wide range

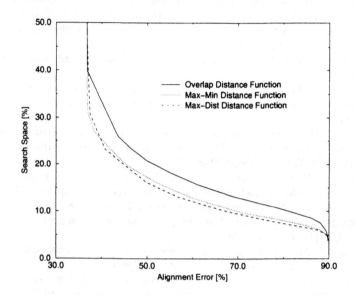

Fig. 5. Comparison of the three metrics in an error-search space graph.

of possible distance thresholds, the search space can be reduced without including additional errors. Corresponding to the reduction of the search space, less computation time is needed. Comparing the three distance functions for search space reduction in a graph that shows search space vs. alignment error, it can be seen that the functions $D_{max-min}$ and $D_{max-dist}$ behave better than $D_{overlap}$.

In the experiments described in this paper only three different recognizers were involved, which means that the proposed alignment procedure was applied to three strings only. Also the length of the considered strings is rather short. But it can be anticipated that the proposed procedure is applicable to problems involving a larger number of longer strings. Moreover, it can be expected that the computational savings achieved through the use of positional information become even more pronounced if longer and/or more sequences are involved. Another potential application of the method proposed in this paper is classifier combination in machine printed OCR, where each classifier outputs positional information about the individual characters or words on a page.

References

1. J. Kittler and F. Roli, editors. *Multiple Classifier Systems, First Int. Workshop, MCS 2000.* Springer, Lecture Notes in Computer Science 1857, 2000.
2. J. Kittler, M. Hatef, R.P.W. Duin, and J. Matas. On combining classifiers. *IEEE Trans. on Pattern Analysis and Machine Intelligence*, 20(3):226–239, 1998.

3. L. Lam, Y.-S. Huang, and C.Y. Suen. Combination of multiple classifier decisions for optical character recognition. In H. Bunke and P.S.P. Wang, editors, *Handbook of Character Recognition and Document Image Analysis*, chapter 3, pages 79–101. World Scientific Publ. Co., 1997.

4. R.P.W. Duin and D.M.J. Tax. Experiments with classifier combining rules. In *[1]*, pages 16–29, 2000.

5. B. Lazzerini, F. Marcelloni, and L.M. Reyneri. Beatrix: A self-learning system for off-line recognition of handwritten texts. *Pattern Recognition Letters*, 18(6):583–594, June 1997.

6. G. Kim, V. Govindaraju, and S.N. Srihari. Architecture for handwritten text recognition systems. In S.-W. Lee, editor, *Advances in Handwriting Recognition*, pages 163–172. World Scientific Publ. Co., 1999.

7. U. Marti and H. Bunke. Using a statistical language model to improve the performance of an HMM-based cursive handwriting recognition system. *To appear in Int. Journal of Pattern Recognition and Artificial Intelligence*, 2001.

8. R.H. Wagner and M. Fischer. The string-to-string correction problem. *Journal of the ACM*, 21(1):168–173, 1974.

9. J.B. Kruskal. An overview of sequence comparison: Time warps, string edits, and macromolecules. *SIAM Review*, 25(2):201–237, 1983.

10. D. Lopresti and J. Zhou. Using consensus sequence voting to correct OCR errors. *Computer Vision and Image Understanding*, 67(1):39–47, July 1997.

11. T. Kohonen. Median strings. *Pattern Recognition Letters*, 3:309–313, 1985.

12. U. Marti and H. Bunke. Handwritten sentence recognition. In *Proc. of the 15th Int. Conf. on Pattern Recognition, Barcelona, Spain*, volume 3, pages 467–470, 2000.

13. U. Marti. *Offline Erkennung handgeschriebener Texte*. PhD thesis, University of Bern, Switzerland, 2000.

14. U.-V. Marti and H. Bunke. A full English sentence database for off-line handwriting recognition. In *Proc. of the 5th Int. Conf. on Document Analysis and Recognition, Bangalore, India*, pages 705–708, 1999.

Application of the Evolutionary Algorithms for Classifier Selection in Multiple Classifier Systems with Majority Voting

Dymitr Ruta and Bogdan Gabrys

Applied Computational Intelligence Research Unit,
Division of Computing and Information Systems, University of Paisley,
High Street, Paisley PA1-2EP, United Kingdom
{ruta-ci0, gabr-ci0}@paisley.ac.uk

Abstract. In many pattern recognition tasks, an approach based on combining classifiers has shown a significant potential gain in comparison to the performance of an individual best classifier. This improvement turned out to be subject to a sufficient level of diversity exhibited among classifiers, which in general can be assumed as a selective property of classifier subsets. Given a large number of classifiers, an intelligent classifier selection process becomes a crucial issue of multiple classifier system design. In this paper, we have investigated three evolutionary optimization methods for the classifier selection task. Based on our previous studies of various diversity measures and their correlation with majority voting error we have adopted majority voting performance computed for the validation set directly as a fitness function guiding the search. To prevent from training data overfitting we extracted a population of best unique classifier combinations, and used them for second stage majority voting. In this work we intend to show empirically, that using efficient evolutionary-based selection leads to the results comparable to absolutely best, found exhaustively. Moreover, as we showed for selected datasets, introducing a second stage combining by majority voting has the potential for both, further improvement of the recognition rate and increase of the reliability of combined outputs.

1 Introduction

A research devoted to pattern recognition proves that no individual method can be shown to be the best for all classification tasks [1]. As a result increasing effort is being directed towards the development of fusion methods hoping to achieve improved and stable classification performance for a wider family of pattern recognition problems. Indeed, recently classifier fusion has been shown to outperform the traditional, single-best classifier approach in many different applications [1-5]. In the safety critical systems, where the decisions taken are of crucial importance, any method offering improvement of the classification rate is invaluable even if it leads to higher complexity of the model. In such cases, the design of a reliable classification

J. Kittler and F. Roli (Eds.): MCS 2001, LNCS 2096, pp. 399–408, 2001.

model should start from pooling of all available classifiers, ensuring that no potentially supporting information is wasted.

Given a large number of different classifiers it is always a question of how many and which ones to select for combining in order to achieve the highest performance of the fusion method. So far, a dominating approach was to pick several best classifiers, which commonly resulted in moderate improvement. As recently shown [4], picking several best classifiers does not necessarily lead to the best or sometimes even good solution. Further analysis revealed that in addition to individual performances, diversity among classifiers has to be taken into account for selection purposes [6,7]. Effectively, only reasonably diverse, and in particular negatively dependent classifiers could offer large improvement of the classification performance [8,9]. This fact imposes the necessity for selecting the most diverse classifiers, which are most likely to produce robust combined results.

Many different scientists tried to apply different measures of diversity to select the best team of classifiers [7,10,11]. As shown in [11] for majority voting diversity measures are particularly good at reduction of system complexity but selection based on the diversity measures appears to be rather imprecise and limited to the lower order dependencies. Moreover, there are problems with consistent evaluation of the diversity for variable number of classifiers involved.

An alternative to imprecise diversity-based selection is a direct search using the performance of combiner as selection criterion. There is no imprecision inflicted by diversity measures and the performance of selection process relies fully on the quality of searching algorithms applied. However this strategy imposes operating on an exponentially complex and rough searching space. Genetic algorithms as well as other evolutionary algorithms have been shown to deal well and efficiently with large, rough searching spaces [12,13,16-18].

In this paper we assume selection from a large number of classifiers and having all available information in the form of hardened binary classifier outputs (correct/incorrect) obtained from classification performed over validation set. We used majority voting (MV) as a combination method relevant for the assumptions mentioned above. Although very simple, MV quite often showed the performance comparable to the much more advanced techniques [14,15]. Moreover, as shown in [8,9] theoretical possibilities of classification improvement using MV are tremendous especially using large number of classifiers. Facing a large and rough searching space, we applied well-known evolutionary algorithms: genetic algorithm (GA) [16], tabu search (TS) [17] and population-based incremental learning (PBIL) [18]. The selected algorithms represent quite different approaches of evolutionary learning. We intend to use these algorithms for efficient searching for a unique population of best classifier combinations and combine them further to improve reliability of obtained solutions.

The remaining of the paper is organized as follows. Section 2 explains the problem of classifier selection for the optimal MV performance. In section 3 we give a detailed analysis of the presented searching algorithms: GA, TS and PBIL and show implementation solutions and adjustments needed to reach a satisfactory selection quality and compatibility with MV. Section 4 provides the results from the experiments with real datasets. Finally, summary and conclusions are given in section 5.

2 Classifier Selection for Majority Voting

Even using simple majority voting the classifier selection process is far from trivial. The first problem is the representation of a single combination of classifiers, which ought to be uniform throughout the searching process regardless of the number of classifiers used. We chose binary strings used in GA's, in which bit in j^{th} position indicated inclusion (1) or exclusion (0) of the jth classifier in the further fusion process. Another problem is designing the fitness function. Based on our previous studies in [11] we decided not to use diversity measures which are vaguely correlated with MV performance. In our case, the searching algorithms account for system simplification and there is no need to use imprecise diversity measures. Therefore, we employed directly MV performance as a fitness function. For smaller number of classifiers, the quality of searching can be always inspected by comparing it with the results of an exhaustive search. For larger systems, due to exponential complexity, the exhaustive search very quickly becomes intractable and taking very rough searching space into account, the global optimum is rarely known.

Given a system of M classifiers: $D = \{D_1,...,D_M\}$, let $\mathbf{y}_i = (y_{1i}, y_{2i},...y_{Mi})$ denote a joint output of a system for i^{th} multidimensional input sample $\mathbf{x}_i$, where $y_{ji} = y_j(\mathbf{x}_i)$ $1 = 1,...,N$ $j = 1,...,M$ denote the hardened output of the jth classifier for data sample $\mathbf{x}_1$. In this work we assume the transformed binary outputs to be $y_{ji} = 1$ for correct classification and $y_{ji} = 0$ for misclassification. Let $\mathbf{v}_k = (v_{k0}, v_{k1},...v_{kM})$ represent a combination of classifiers, where $v_{kj} = \{0,1\}$ indicates inclusion (1) or exclusion (0) of the jth classifier in the decision fusion. Given a combination $\mathbf{v}_k$, the combined decision produced by MV combiner $y_i^{MV}(\mathbf{v}_k)$ can be obtained by:

$$y_i^{MV}(v_k) = \begin{cases} 0 & if \;\; \sum_{j=1}^{M} y_{ji} v_{kj} \leq \left\lfloor \sum_{j=1}^{M} v_{kj}/2 \right\rfloor \\ 1 & if \;\; \sum_{j=1}^{M} y_{ji} v_{kj} > \left\lfloor \sum_{j=1}^{M} v_{kj}/2 \right\rfloor \end{cases} \tag{1}$$

Given a validation set $X_{VA} = (\mathbf{x}_1, \mathbf{x}_2,..., \mathbf{x}_N)$, the selection can be reformulated as a simple optimization process where the object of optimization is $\mathbf{v}_k$ and the fitness function, which we used in this study, is represented by the following formula:

$$y^{MV}(v_k) = \left[\sum_{i=1}^{N} y^{MV}(v_k) \right] / N \tag{2}$$

MV definition shown above imposes further irregularities. Namely, it enforces combining only odd number of classifiers. Otherwise one would have to implement a rejection rule observed for an equal number of contradictory votes, which brings additional complexity to the system. Another problem is that even assuming that the global best validation combination is found, for the testing set it may be no longer the optimal selection. In order to avoid this problem, instead of obtaining single best combination, we intend to extract a population of best solutions and apply them all for the second stage combining process. In the experimental section we illustrate the advantage of the second stage combining, which resulted in improved classification performance and reduced variability of classification performance.

3 Searching Algorithms

The choice of searching algorithms to be used for classifier selection has been dictated by several requirements. On one hand the algorithms should quickly and efficiently explore large searching spaces formed by a number of possible subsets of classifiers. Secondly, as mentioned above, combining at the second stage is to be pursued in this work. Therefore, rather than a single best solution, a population of best combinations found should be returned as an output from a searching process. Furthermore the algorithms should be rather sensitive to searching criterion as due to common high positive correlations among classifiers the differences in combining performance is expected to be small. For the reasons above, we proposed to use evolutionary algorithms operating directly on combining performance. Three examples of such algorithms are here investigated and specifically implemented for the use with majority voting combiner.

3.1 Genetic Algorithms

Genetic algorithms (GA) have been used for a number of pattern recognition problems [12,13,16]. There are several problems in adopting GA to classifier selection for combining with MV. The major problem derives from the constraint of odd number of classifiers that has to be imposed. To keep the number of selected classifiers odd throughout the searching process, crossover and mutation operators have to be specially designed. Mutation is rather easy to implement as assuming already odd number of classifiers set randomly in initialization process, the odd number of selected classifiers can be preserved by mutating a pair of bits or in general any even number of bits. Crossover is much more difficult to control that way. To avoid making GA too complex, crossover is performed traditionally and after that, if the offspring contains even number of classifiers one randomly selected bit is additionally mutated to bring back the odd number of 1's in the chromosome. To increase exploration ability of GA we introduced additional operator of 'pairwise exchange', which simply swaps random pair of bits within the chromosome preserving the same number of classifiers. In order to preserve the best combinations from generation to generation we applied a specific selection rule according to which populations of parents and offsprings are put together and then a number of best chromosomes equal to the size of population is selected for the next generation. Being aware of the potential generalization problems, we have developed a simple diversifying operator. It enforces all chromosomes to be different from each other (unique), by mutating random bits until this requirement is reached. The whole algorithm can be defined as follows:

1. Initialize a random population of n chromosomes
2. Calculate fitness (MV performance) for each chromosome
3. Perform crossover and mutate single bits of offsprings with even number of 1's
4. Mutate all offsprings at randomly selected one or many points
5. Apply one or more pairwise exchanges for each offspring
6. From all offsprings and parents select n best unique chromosomes to the next generation
7. If convergence is reached then finish, else go to step 2

Although this particular version of GA represents hill-climbing algorithm, multiple mutation and pairwise exchange together with diversifying operator substantially extend the exploration abilities of the algorithm. Convergence condition can be associated with the case when no change in the mean MV error is observed for arbitrarily large number of generations. Preliminary experiments with real classification datasets confirmed superiority of the presented version of GA to its standard definition and highlighted the importance of diversifying operator for classifier selection process.

3.2 Tabu Search

Tabu search (TS) in its standard form is not a population-based algorithm yet shares some similarities with GA's particularly in the encoding of the problem [17]. Instead of a population, it uses only single chromosome, mutated randomly at each step. Due to this fact there can be no crossover and the only genetic change is provided by mutation. This limits strongly an ability of the algorithm to jump into different regions of the searching space. Moreover, it represents a hill-climbing algorithm, which reaches convergence much faster than typical GA, but on the other hand, a global optimum may not be found, as it simply may be unreachable from initial conditions. Effectively, the tabu search in its original version quite easily gets trapped in local optima. To prevent from such effects we applied multiple consecutive mutations together with 'pairwise exchange' before the fitness is examined. Similarly to GA we keep the population of unique best chromosomes found during the process. As for the previous algorithm, convergence condition is satisfied if a pool of k best solutions is not changed for a fixed number of generations. The presented version of TS algorithm can be described in the following steps:

1. Create a single random chromosome
2. Mutate the chromosome at randomly selected one or many points
3. Apply one or more pairwise exchanges
4. Test the fitness of the new chromosome: if it is fitter than the changes are accepted
5. Store the new chromosome if it is among k unique best solutions found so far
6. If convergence is reached finish, else go to step 2

3.3 Population-Based Incremental Learning

Due to the lack of crossover operator, even after many adjustments tabu search partially loses the ability to explore the whole searching space. There is a possibility to regain the ability of the algorithm to reach most points of the searching space, while keeping convergence property at the satisfactory level. The algorithm offering these properties is called a population-based incremental learning (PBIL) [18]. It also uses a population of chromosomes, sampled from a special probability vector, which is updated at each step according to the fittest chromosomes.

The update process of the probability vector is performed according to a standard supervised learning method. Given probability vector $\mathbf{p} = (p_1, p_2, ..., p_M)$, and population of chromosomes $G = (\mathbf{v}_1, \mathbf{v}_2, ..., \mathbf{v}_C)$, where $\mathbf{v}_k = (v_{k1}, v_{k2}, ..., v_{kM})$, each probability bit is updated as in the following expression:

$$p_j^{new} = p_j^{old} + \Delta p_j \qquad \Delta p_j = \eta \left[\left(\sum_{k=1}^{C} v_{kj} \right) / C - p_j \right] \qquad (3)$$

where $k = 1, ..., C$ refers to the C fittest chromosomes found and η controls the magnitude of the update. A number of best chromosomes taken to update the probability vector together with the magnitude factor η control a balance between a speed of reaching the convergence and the ability to explore the whole search space. Convergence is reached if the probability vector contains only integer values: 0 or 1. In such a case $\mathbf{p}$ becomes the best combination of classifiers. As we are rather in favor of obtaining a population of best solutions, they are extracted and stored during the process preserving diversity rule as in the previous algorithms. The PBIL algorithm can be described in the following steps:

1. Create probability vector of the same length as the required chromosome and initialize it with values of 0.5 at each bit
2. Sample a number of chromosomes according to the probability vector
3. Update the probability vector by increasing probabilities in positions where the fittest chromosomes had 1's
4. Update the pool of k best unique solutions
5. If all elements in probability vector are 0 or 1 then finish, else go to step 2

Although PBIL algorithm does not use any genetic operators observed in GA, it contains a specific mechanism that allows exploiting beneficial information through generations, and thus preserves the stochastic elements of evolutionary algorithms.

4 Experiments

The experiments have been organized in two groups. In the first part the presented algorithms have been examined for three realistic datasets[1] from UCI Repository[2] and compared against simple alternative strategies: exhaustive search (ES), the single-best classifier (SB) and a random search (RS). Selection was performed from a set of 15 different classifiers available from PRTOOLS 3.1[3]. Finally, in the second part of the experiments we investigated the possibility of combining at the second stage by combining MV outputs from the selections found as best at the first level.

In all experiments, we used the same parameters of the algorithms, for which preliminary experiments showed the best results. Both PBIL and GA used 50 chromo-

---

[1] Datasets: *Iris* – recognition of the types of iris plant: 150 samples, 4 features, 3 classes; *Cancer* – cancer diagnosis: 569 samples, 30 features, 2 classes; *Diabetes* – diabetes diagnosis: 768 samples, 8 features, 2 classes
[2] University of California Repository of Machine Learning Databases and Domain Theories, available free at: ftp.ics.uci.edu/pub/machine-learning-databases
[3] Pattern Recognition Toolbox for Matlab 5.0+, implemented by R.P.W. Duin, available free at: ftp://ftp.ph.tn.tudelft.nl/pub/bob/prtools

somes in the population. In TS and GA single bit mutation has been applied together with single 'pairwise exchange'. The learning rate for PBIL was set to $\eta = 1$. The best validation combinations have been examined also for a testing set to evaluate the generalization ability. To be able to compare the algorithms in terms of efficiency, in all experiments the algorithms finished the run after examining a fixed number of chromosomes, which was used instead of specifying convergence conditions.

Given a pool of M=15 different classifiers has been applied for 3 datasets from UCI Repository. All the datasets have been split into equally sized: training, validation and testing sets. Trained classifiers were then applied for a classification performed over the validation and testing set. Trying to reliably estimate true performances, we repeated this process for many random splits of the dataset, until we obtained binary matrices of size N=5000 containing classification results separately for the validation and testing set. Searching algorithms have been applied for the validation matrix. The searching results for the first stage MV combining are shown in Table 1. For all presented datasets the performances of the best selections found by the proposed searching algorithms were better than those quickly given by SB selection and were very close to the obtainable boundaries determined by the ES. The time of searching was however substantially reduced in comparison with ES. For larger number of classifiers ES starts to be intractable, whilst the searching time for the presented searching algorithms increases slowly. Moreover the balance between searching precision and the time of searching is adjustable and can be controlled by the search method parameters.

Table 1. MV performance (BV) and an average from 50 best (BV50) selections found by the searching algorithms from a validation matrix (5000 ×15) obtained from classification of *Iris*, *Cancer* and *Diabetes* datasets by 15 different classifiers. The last two rows, contain testing matrix (5000 ×15) results: T(BV) and T(BV50) for the same selections. The time of searching corresponds to the time of checking 1000 different selections by each algorithm

IRIS	SB	ES	RS	TS	PBIL	GA
Time [s]	-	219.3	12.69	11.54	34.77	22.00
BV [%]	97.22	97.82	97.62	97.82	97.82	97.82
BV50 [%]	-	97.66	97.14	97.62	97.65	97.62
T(BV) [%]	97.02	97.48	97.46	97.48	**97.48**	97.48
T(BV50) [%]	-	97.38	96.91	97.36	**97.38**	97.37
CANCER	SB	ES	RS	TS	PBIL	GA
Time [s]	-	209.2	12.58	14.45	39.31	23.67
BV [%]	96.33	96.99	96.60	96.93	96.99	96.93
BV50 [%]	-	96.83	96.40	96.77	96.81	96.77
T(BV) [%]	96.64	97.03	96.85	**97.26**	97.03	97.26
T(BV50) [%]	-	97.10	96.67	**97.06**	97.11	97.01
DIABETES	SB	ES	RS	TS	PBIL	GA
Time [s]	-	229.4	13.24	16.11	37.68	24.01
BV [%]	75.97	76.57	76.37	76.53	76.57	76.57
BV50 [%]	-	76.50	76.17	76.45	76.48	76.46
T(BV) [%]	76.77	77.11	76.78	76.86	76.98	**77.11**
T(BV50) [%]	-	77.03	76.72	77.01	77.05	**77.06**

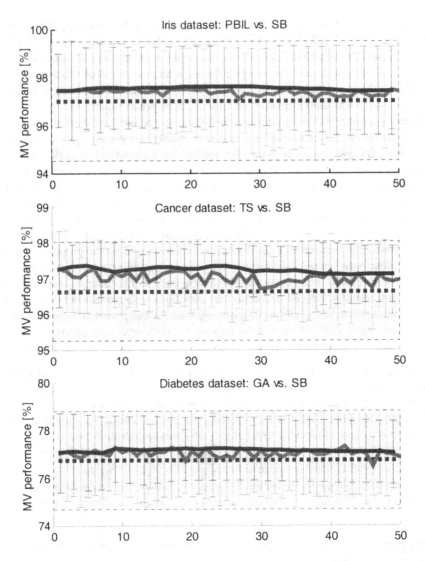

Fig. 1. Performance of the second stage MV combiner compared against mean MV performance of the best 50 validation combinations and single best classifier. supported by the statistics of variability along different random splits of the datasets. The graphs correspond to the datasets from Table 1 and relate to the testing set performance. The shaded area limited by dashed lines together with doted line in the middle represent SB confidence intervals and the mean MV performance of the classifier selected by SB strategy, respectively. Grey solid line shows the mean MV performance of the best 50 validation selections with their confidence intervals. Black solid line represents MV performance of the second stage MV combining shown as a function of the number of the best validation combinations with corresponding confidence intervals. All the confidence intervals have been obtained by calculating the means over different splits and taking 3 times the standard deviation.

4.1 Experiment 2

In this experiment, we looked at generalization ability of analyzed selection algorithms. For that purpose we examined the idea of introducing a second stage of combining and its implications for variability of obtained results. We prepared statistics of MV performances of the best selections obtained over consecutive splits of the examined datasets. Calculating means and standard deviations of MV performance varying along different splits allowed to estimate the reliability of the selected models and compare it against SB approach. The results for the 50 best combinations of classifiers (represented by thick gray lines) and SB (represented by dotted black lines) are illustrated in Fig 1. It can be seen that counting only on the best selection found for validation set is in general risky. This is due to the generalization dilemma especially evident for small amount of training data. A better and more reliable strategy turned out to be taking the MV outputs from a number of best validation selections and obtaining a final decision by second-stage majority voting. The performance of the second stage MV combiner is shown by thick black lines in Fig. 1. The plots show slight improvement in comparison to any individual combination and also prove that this strategy is much more reliable and stable in terms of different number of selections taken. Reliability improvement in comparison to SB results stems from decreased variance imposed by aggregation of outputs.

5 Conclusions

In this paper, we studied the applicability of three evolutionary optimization techniques for the problem of classifier selection for combining by majority voting operating on binary classification outputs. Introducing binary-strings representation of classifier combinations, we proposed specific implementations of genetic algorithm, tabu search and probability-based incremental learning applied for the constrained majority voting rule accepting only odd number of classifiers. Facing a huge and rough searching space we assigned directly majority voting performance as a fitness function and put the main effort to develop searching algorithms with high exploration capabilities and simultaneously working fast to be applicable for a large number of classifiers.

Comparing the efficiency of searching with an exhaustive search we obtained mostly the same best selections while substantially reducing the time of searching. For all experiments we recorded improvement of majority voting performance of the best selections found in comparison with the simple single-best selection strategy. Moreover, due to aggregation applied we observed increased reliability of the best selections evident in the form of reduced variance of the majority voting performance from different splits of datasets. Nevertheless the best validation selection not necessarily has to be the best for the testing set. So can be any individual selection found among the best solutions. To avoid this risk we applied second stage combining applying majority voting for the MV outputs of the best solutions at the first stage. This strategy turned out to be successful and produced the results slightly better than individual selections but more importantly improving also reliability and stability of the output performance. These results allow choosing arbitrarily large number of the best selections for a second-stage fusion without risking dramatic loss of generalization ability, and at the same time preserving the general good performance of the system.

References

1. Bezdek J.C.: Fuzzy Models and Algorithms for Pattern Recognition and Image Processing. Kluwer Academic Boston (1999)
2. Sharkey A.J.C.: Combining Artificial Neural Nets: Ensemble and Modular Multi-net Systems. Springer-Verlag, Berlin Heidelberg New York (1999)
3. Zhilkin P.A., Somorjai R.L.: Application of Several Methods of Classification Fusion to Magnetic Resonance Spectra. Connection Science 8(3,4) (1996) 427-442
4. Rogova G.: Combining the Results of Several Neural Network Classifiers. Neural Networks 7(5) (1994) 777-781
5. Xu L., Krzyzak A.: Methods of Combining Multiple Classifiers and Their Applications to Handwriting Recognition. IEEE Transactions on Systems, Man, and Cybernetics 23(8) (1992) 418-434
6. Partridge D., Griffith N.: Strategies for Improving Neural Net Generalization. Neural Computing and Applications 3 (1995) 27-37
7. Sharkey A.J.C., Sharkey N.E.: Combining Diverse Neural Nets. The Knowledge Engineering Review 12(3) (1997) 231-247
8. Kuncheva L.I., Whitaker C.J., Shipp C.A., Duin R.P.W.: Limits on the Majority Vote Accuracy in Classifier Fusion. Submitted to IEEE Transactions on Pattern Analysis and Machine Intelligence
9. Ruta D., Gabrys B.: A Theoretical Analysis of the Limits of Majority Voting in Multiple Classifier Systems. Technical Report No. 11. University of Paisley (2000)
10. Kuncheva L.I., Whitaker C.J.: Measures of Diversity in Classifier Ensembles. Submitted to Machine Learning
11. Ruta D., Gabrys B.: Analysis of the Correlation Between Majority Voting Errors and the Diversity Measures in Multiple Classifier Systems. Accepted for the International Symposium on Soft Computing SOCO'2001
12. Kuncheva L., Jain L.C.: Designing Classifier Fusion Systems by Genetic Algorithms. To appear in IEEE Transactions on Evolutionary Computation
13. Cho S.B.: Pattern Recognition With Neural Networks Combined by Genetic Algorithms. Fuzzy Sets and Systems 103 (1999) 339-347
14. Cho S.B., Kim J.H.: Combining Multiple Neural Networks by Fuzzy Integral for Robust Classification. IEEE Trans. on Systems, Man, and Cybernetics 25(2) (1995) 380-384
15. Kuncheva L.I., Bezdek J.C.: On Combining Classifiers by Fuzzy Templates. Proc. NAFIPS'98, Pensacola, FL (1998) 193-197
16. Davis L.: Handbook of Genetic Algorithms. Van Nostrand Reinhold New York (1991)
17. Glover F., Laguna M.: Tabu Search. Kluver Academic Publishers Boston (1997)
18. Baluja S.: Population-Based Incremental Learning: A Method for Integrating Genetic Search Based Function Optimization and Competitive Learning. Technical Report No. 163. Carnegie Melon University, Pittsburgh PA (1994)

Tree-Structured Support Vector Machines for Multi-class Pattern Recognition

Friedhelm Schwenker and Günther Palm

University of Ulm
Department of Neural Information Processing
D-89069 Ulm
{schwenker,palm}@informatik.uni-ulm.de

Abstract. Support vector machines (SVM) are learning algorithms derived from statistical learning theory. The SVM approach was originally developed for binary classification problems. In this paper SVM architectures for multi-class classification problems are discussed, in particular we consider binary trees of SVMs to solve the multi-class pattern recognition problem. Numerical results for different classifiers on a benchmark data set handwritten digits are presented.

1 Introduction

Statistical learning theory developed by Vladimir Vapnik formalizes the task of learning from examples and describes it as a problem of statistics with finite sample size [1]. Originally, the SVM approach was developed for two-class or binary classification. The N-class classification problem is defined as follows: Given a set of M training vectors $(x^\mu, y^\mu)_{\mu=1}^M$, with input vector $x^\mu \in \mathbb{R}^d$ and with $y^\mu \in \{1, \dots, N\}$ as the class label of input x^μ. Find a decision function $F : \mathbb{R}^d \to \{1, \dots, N\}$ mapping an input x to a class label y. Multi-class classification problems (where the number of classes N is larger than 2) are often solved using voting schemes based on the combiniation of binary decision functions. One approach is constructing N binary classifiers (e.g. a SVM network), one for each class, together with a maximum detection across the classifier outputs to classifiy an input vector x. This *one-against-rest* strategy is widely used in the pattern recognition literatur. Another classification scheme is the *one-against-one* strategy, where $\binom{N}{2}$ binary classifiers are constructed—separating each pair of classes, together with a majority voting scheme to classify the input vectors. A different approach to solve a N-class pattern recognition problem is to build a hierachy or tree of binary classifiers. Each node of the graph is a classifier performing a predefined classification subtask. In this procedure the hierarchy of subtasks has to be determined before the classifiers are trained.

2 Support Vector Machines

In this section we briefly review the basic ideas of support vector learning and present four multi-class classification techniques which may be applied to SVMs.

J. Kittler and F. Roli (Eds.): MCS 2001, LNCS 2096, pp. 409–417, 2001.
© Springer-Verlag Berlin Heidelberg 2001

SVMs were initially developed to classify data points of linear separable data sets [6,8]. In this case a training set consisting of M examples (x^μ, y^μ), $x^\mu \in \mathbb{R}^d$, and $y^\mu \in \{-1, 1\}$ can be divided up into two sets by a separating hyperplane. Such a hyperplane is determined by a weight vector $b \in \mathbb{R}^d$ and a bias or threshold $\theta \in \mathbb{R}$ satisfying the separating contraints

$$y^\mu(\langle x^\mu, b \rangle + \theta) \geq 1 \quad \mu = 1, \dots, M.$$

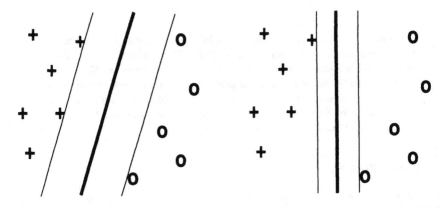

(a) Optimal separating hyper-plane with a large margin.

(b) Separating hyperplane with a smaller margin.

Fig. 1. Binary classification problem. The examples of the two different classes are linear separable.

The distance between the separating hyperplane and the closed data points of the training set is called the margin, see Figure 1. The separating hyperplane with maximal margin is unique and can be expressed by a linear combination of those training examples (so-called support vectors) lying exactly at the margin has the form

$$H(x) = \sum_{\mu=1}^{M} \alpha_\mu^* y^\mu \langle x, x^\mu \rangle + \alpha_0^*.$$

Here $\alpha_1^*, \dots, \alpha_M^*$ is the solution optimizing the functional

$$Q(\alpha) = \sum_{\mu=1}^{M} \alpha_\mu - \frac{1}{2} \sum_{\mu,\nu=1}^{M} \alpha_\mu \alpha_\nu y^\mu y^\nu \langle x^\mu, x^\nu \rangle$$

subject to the constraints $\alpha_\mu \geq 0$ for all $\mu = 1, \dots, M$ and $\sum_{\mu=1}^{M} \alpha_\mu y^\mu = 0$. Then a training vector x^μ is a support vector if the corresponding coefficient

$\alpha_\mu^* > 0$. Then it is $b = \sum_{\mu=1}^M \alpha_\mu x^\mu$ and the bias α_0^* is determined by a single support vector (x^s, y^s): $\alpha_0^* = y^s - \langle x^s, b \rangle$.

The SVM approach can be extended to the nonseparable situation and to the regression problem. In most applications (regression or pattern recognition problems) linear solutions are insufficient, so it is common to define an appropriate set of nonlinear mappings $g := (g_1, g_2, \ldots)$, transforming the input vectors x^μ into a vector $g(x^\mu)$ which is element of a new feature space $\mathcal{H}$. Then the separating hyperplane can be constructed in the feature space $\mathcal{H}$. Provided $\mathcal{H}$ is a Hilbert space, the explicit mapping $g(x)$ does not need to be known since it can implicitly defined by a kernel function $K(x, x^\mu) = \langle g(x), g(x^\mu) \rangle$ representing the inner product of the feature space. Using a kernel function K satisfying the condition of Mercer's theorem (see [8]), the separating hyperplane is given by

$$H(x) = \sum_{\mu=1}^M \alpha_\mu y^\mu K(x, x^\mu) + \alpha_0.$$

The coefficients α_μ can be found by solving the optimization problem

$$Q(\alpha) = \sum_{\mu=1}^M \alpha_\mu - \frac{1}{2} \sum_{\mu,\nu=1}^M \alpha_\mu \alpha_\nu y^\mu y^\nu K(x^\mu, x^\nu)$$

subject to the contraints $0 \le \alpha_\mu \le C$ for all $\mu = 1, \ldots, M$ and $\sum_{\mu=1}^M \alpha_\mu y^\mu = 0$ where C is a predefined positive number. An important kernel function satisfying Mercers condition is the Gaussian kernel function (also used in this paper) $K(x, y) = e^{-\frac{\|x-y\|_2^2}{2\sigma^2}}$.

In many real world applications, e.g. speech recognition, or optical character recognition, a multi-class pattern recognition problem has to be solved. The SVM classifier is a binary classifier. Various approaches have been developed in order to deal with multi-class classification problems. The following strategies can be applied to build N-class classifiers utilizing binary SVM classifiers.

One-against-rest classifiers. In this method N different classifiers are constructed, one classifier for each class. Here the l-th classifier is trained on the whole training data set in order to classify the members of class l against the rest. For this, the training examples have to be re-labeled: Members of the l-th class are labeled to 1; members of the other classes to -1. In the classification phase the classifier with the maximal output defines the estimated class label of the current input vector.

One-against-one classifiers. For each possible pair of classes a binary classifier is calculated. Each classifier is trained on a subset of the training set containing only training examples of the two involved classes. As for the *one-against-rest* strategy the training sets have to be re-labeled. All $N(N-1)/2$ classifiers are combined through a majority voting scheme to estimate the final classification [2,3]. Here the class with the maximal number of votes among all $N(N-1)/2$ classifiers is the estimation.

Hierarchies/trees of binary SVM classifiers. Here the multi-class classification problem is decomposed into a series of binary classification sub-problems organised in a hierarchical scheme; see Figure 2. We discuss this approach in the next section.

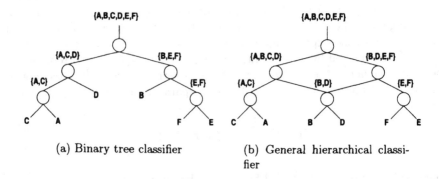

(a) Binary tree classifier

(b) General hierarchical classifier

Fig. 2. Two examples of hierarchical classifiers. The graphs are directed acyclic graphs with a single root node at the top of the graph and with terminal nodes (leaves) at the bottom. Individual classes are represented in the leaves, and the other nodes within the graph are classifiers performing a binary decision task, which is defined through the annotations of the incoming and the outgoing edges.

Weston and Watkins proposed in [9] a natural extension to the binary SVM approch to solve the N-class classification problem directly. Here re-labeling of the training data is not necessary. All the N classes are considered at once, and the separating conditions are integrated into a single optimisation problem. As for the *one-against-rest* classifiers, the result is a N-class classifier with N weight vectors and N threshold values. The recall phase is organized as for the *one-against-rest* classifier strategy.

The goal of this paper is to apply the decomposition shemes *one-against-rest*, *one-against-one*, and *tree-structured* for the SVM classifier in a multi-class pattern recognition problem. Whereas the *one-against-rest* and *one-against-one* classifiers are clearly defined, the hierarchical classifier achritecture needs further explanation.

3   SVM Classifier Hierachies

One of the most important problems in multi-class pattern recognition problems is the existence of confusion classes. A confusion class is a subset of the set of the classes $\{1, \dots, N\}$ where the feature vectors are very similar and a small amount of noise in the measured features may lead to misclassifications. For example, in OCR the measured features for members of the classes o, O, 0 and Q are typically very similar, so usually {o, O, 0, Q} defines a confusion class. The major idea of hierarchical classification is first to make a coarse discrimination between confusion classes and then a finer discrimination within the confusion classes [5].

In Figure 2 examples of hierarchical classifiers are depicted. Each node within the graph represents a binary classifier discriminating feature vectors of a confusion class into one of two smaller confusion classes or possibly into individual classes. The terminal nodes of the graph (leaves) represent these individual classes, and the other nodes are classifiers performing a binary decision task, thus these nodes have exactly two children. Nodes within the graph may have more than one incoming edge. Figure 2a shows a tree-structured classifier, where each node has exactly one incoming edge. In Figure 2b a more general classifier structure defined through a special directed acyclic graph is depicted. In the following we restrict our considerations to tree structured SVMs.

The classification subtask is defined through the annotations of the incoming and outgoing edges of the node. Let us consider for example the SVM classifier at the root of the tree in Figure 2a. The label of the incoming edge is $\{A, \ldots, F\}$, so for this (sub-)tree a 6-class classification task is given. The edges to the children are annotated with $\{A, C, D\}$ (left child) and $\{B, E, F\}$ (right child). This means that this SVM has to classify feature vectors into confusion class $\{A, C, D\}$ or $\{B, E, F\}$. To achieve this, all members of the six classes $\{A, \ldots, F\}$ have to be re-labeled: Feature vectors with class labels A, C, or D get the new label -1 and those with class label B, E, or F get the new label 1. After this re-labeling procedure the SVM is trained as described in the previous section. Note, that re-labeling has to be done for each classifier training.

We have not answered the question how to construct this subset-tree. One approach to construct such a tree is to divide the set of classes K into disjoint subsets K_1 and K_2 utilizing clustering. In clustering and vector quantization a set of representative prototypes $\{c_1, \ldots, c_k\} \subset \mathbb{R}^d$ is determined by unsupervised learning from the feature vectors $x^\mu, \mu = 1, \ldots, M$ of the training set. For each prototype c_j the Voronoi cells R_j and clusters C_j are defined by

$$R_j := \{x \in \mathbb{R}^d \; : \; \|c_j - x\|_2 = \min_i \|c_i - x\|_2\}$$

and

$$C_j := R_j \cap \{x^\mu \; : \; \mu = 1, \ldots, M\}.$$

The relative frequency of members of class i in cluster j is

$$p_{ij} := \frac{|\Omega_i \cap C_j|}{|C_j|}.$$

For class i the set Ω_i is define by

$$\Omega_i = \{x^\mu \; : \; \mu = 1, \ldots, M, \; y^\mu = i\}.$$

The k-means clustering with $k = 2$ cluster centers c_1 and c_2 define hyperplane in the feature space $\mathbb{R}^d$ separating two sets of feature vectors. From the corresponding clusters C_1 and C_2 a partition of the classes K into two subsets K_1

and K_2 can be achieved through the following assignment:

$$K_j := \{i \in K \ : \ j = \mathrm{argmax}\ \{p_{i1}, p_{i2}\}\}, \quad j = 1, 2.$$

Recursively applied, this procedure leads to a binary tree as depicted in Figure 2. This assignment scheme can be extended to the case $k > 2$.

4   Numerical Experiment

The data set used for evaluating the performance of the classifier consists of 20,000 handwritten digits (2,000 samples per class). The digits, normalized in height and width, are represented by a 16×16 matrix (g_{ij}) where $g_{ij} \in \{0, \dots, 255\}$ is a value from a 8 bit gray scale (for details concerning the data set see [4]).

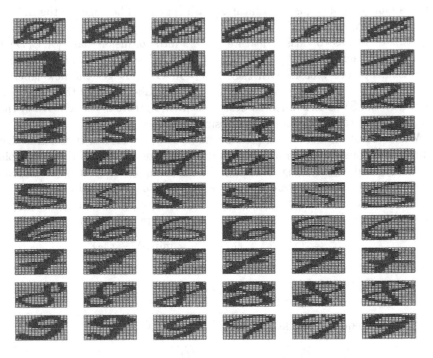

Fig. 3. 60 exampels of the handwritten digits data set.

The whole data set has been divided into a set of 10,000 training samples and a set of 10,000 test samples. The training set has been used to design the classifiers, and the test set for testing the performance of the classifiers.

For this data set we give results for the following classifiers and training procedures:

MLP: Multilayer perceptrons with a single hidden layer of sigmoidal units (Fermi transfer function) trained by standard backpropagation; 100 training epoches; 200 hidden units.

1NN: 1-nearest neighbour classifier.

LVQ: 1-nearest neighbour classifier trained with Kohonen's software package with the OLVQ1 and LVQ3 training procedures each with 50 training epoches; 500 prototypes are used.

RBF: RBF networks with a single hidden layer of Gaussian RBFs trained through three phase learning [7] (first phase: calculating the RBF centers and scaling parameters through Kohonen's learning vector quantization; second phase: learning the output weights by supervized gradient descent optimization of the mean square error function; third phase: backpropagation-like learning of the whole RBF architecture (centers, scaling parameters, and output weights) with 100 training epoches). 200 units each with a single scaling parameter are used in the hidden layer.

SVM-1-R: SVM with the Gaussian kernel function; em one-against-rest strategy; NAG library for optimization has been.

SVM-1-1: As **SVM-1-R** but with the *one-against-one* decomposition scheme.

SVM-TR: Binary tree of SVM networks. The classifier tree has been build by k-means clustering with $k = 2$. In Figure 4 a representative tree is depicted which was found by clustering experiments. The decomposition into subclassification problems which is given in Figure 4 is then used for the training of the singular SVM classifiers.

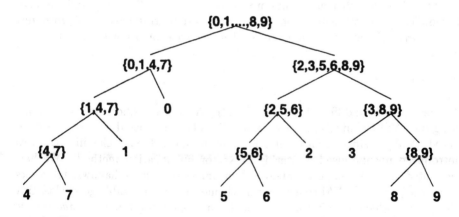

Fig. 4. Tree of subclasses calculated through a 2-means clustering procedure for the handwritten digits data set.

For this data set further results may be found in the final StatLog report (see p. 135-138 in [4]) and in [7]. In the StatLog report the error rate of the best clas-

Table 1. Results for the handwritten digits. Here the medians of three different classification experiments are given.

Classifier	MLP	1NN	LVQ	RBF	SVM-1-R	SVM-1-1	SVM-TR
error [%]	2.41	2.32	3.01	1.51	1.40	1.37	1.39

sifiers (quadratic polynomials, k-nearest neighbours, and multilayer perceptrons) is approximately 2% by using the first 40 principal components of this data. The error rate for the RBF networks is 5.5%, this error issignificantly higher than the 1.5% error rate found here, this is because in the numerical experiments given in [4] two phase RBF learning has been used. In [7] it has been shown that the claasification performance of RBF networks can significantly be improved through a three phase learning scheme, calculating the centers and scaling parameters of the RBF kernels in a first learning step through a clustering or vector quantization algorithm, training the output layer weights separately through a second supervized learning phase, and finally learning the whole architecture (centers, scaling parameters, and output weights) in a third backpropagation-like training phase. The error rates for **1NN**, **LVQ**, and **MLP** classifiers are similar to the results stated in the StatLog report. The **1NN** and **LVQ** classifiers perform well, RBF networks trained through three phase learning scheme and support vector learning show the best classification performance. Each RBF classifier architecture trained through three phase learning or support vector learning has been tested three times. In Tabel 1 the medians of these three experiments are given. The error rates of the three different SVM architectures are very close together all results are in the range of 1.35-1.46%, and therefore a significant difference between the decomposition strategies *one-against-rest*, *one-against-one*, and the binary SVM classifier tree could not be found.

5   Conclusion

We have presented different strategies for the N-class classification problem utilising the SVM classifier approach. In detail we have discussed a novel tree structured SVM classifier architecture. For the design of binary classifier trees we introduced unsupervised clustering or vector quantisation methods. We have presented numerical experiments on a benchmark data set of handwritten digits. Here, the proposed SVM tree classifier scheme shows remarkably good classification results which were in the range of the *one-against-rest* and *one-against-one* classifier architectures. For further evaluation of this tree-structured SVM classifier numerical experiments for different multi-class problems have to be made, particularly on data sets with many different classes.

References

1. C. Cortes and V. Vapnik. Support vector networks. *Machine Learning*, 20:273–297, 1995.
2. J.H. Friedman. Another approach to polychotomous classification. Technical report, Stanford University, Department of Statistics, 1996.
3. U. Kreßel. Pairwise classification and support vector machines. In B. Schölkopf, C. Burges, and A. Smola, editors, *Advances in Kernel Methods*, chapter 15, pages 255–268. The MIT Press, 1999.
4. D. Michie, D.J. Spiegelhalter, and C.C. Taylor. *Machine Learning, Neural and Statistical Classification*. Ellis Horwood, 1994.
5. M. Nadler and E.P. Smith. *Pattern Recognition Engineering*. John Wiley & Sons Inc. 1992.
6. A. Schölkopf, C. Burges, and A. Smola. *Advances in Kernel Methods — Support Vector Learning*. MIT Press, 1998.
7. F. Schwenker, H.K. Kestler, and G. Palm. Three Learning Phases for Radial Basis Function Networks. *Neural Networks*, 2001 (in press).
8. V.N. Vapnik. *Statistical Learning Theory*. John Wiley and Sons, 1998.
9. J. Weston and C. Watkins. Multi-class support vector machines. Technical Report CSD-TR-98-04, Royal Holloway, University of London, Department of Computer Science, 1998.

On the Combination of Different Template Matching Strategies for Fast Face Detection

Bernhard Fröba and Walter Zink

Fraunhofer Institute for Integrated Circuits,
Departement of Applied Electronics
Am Weichselgarten 3, D-91058 Erlangen,Germany
{bdf,zwr}@iis.fhg.de

Abstract. Computer-based face perception is becoming increasingly important for many applications like biometric face recognition, video coding or multi-model human-machine interaction. Fast and robust detection and segmentation of a face in an unconstrained visual scene is a basic requirement for all kinds of face perception. This paper deals with the integration of three simple visual cues for the task of face detection in grey level images. It is achieved by a combination of edge orientation matching, hough transform and an appearance based detection method. The proposed system is computationally efficient and has proved to be robust under a wide range of acquisition conditions like varying lighting, pixel noise and other image distortions. The detection capabilities of the presented algorithm are evaluated on a large database of 13122 images including the frontal-face set of the m2vts database. We achieve a detection rate of over 91% on this database while having only few false detects at the same time.

1 Introduction

Robust and fast face detection for real-world applications such as video coding, multi-modal human machine interaction or biometric face recognition is still an open research field. For many such applications the detection should be possible at more than 10 frames/second which would allow online tracking of the detected faces. Besides that detection should be robust under a wide range of acquisition conditions like variations of lighting and background.

In the past many approaches to the problem of face detection have been made. Most of the fast algorithms use color information for the segmentation of skin-tone-like areas. These areas are usually clustered and searched for facial features. See [1,2,3,4,5] for reference. Another widely-used class of methods for finding faces uses various kinds of grey level correlation approaches. The majority of the approaches [6,7,8,9] use a separate class for each of the faces and non-faces to model the problem domain.

In this paper we will investigate a combination method of three simple matching algorithms. Due to the simple structure of each single method the processing is real-time (12fps for a 320 × 240 video stream). We also will present a fusion

J. Kittler and F. Roli (Eds.): MCS 2001, LNCS 2096, pp. 418–428, 2001.

method based on statistical normalization. The detection capabilities of the presented algorithm are evaluated on a large database of 13122 images each of them containing one or more faces. We achieve a detrection rate of over 91% on this databese while having only few false detects at the same time.

2   Edge Orientation Based Methods

2.1   Edge Orientation Fields

The extraction of edge information (strength and orientation) from a two-dimensional array of pixels $I(x,y)$ (a grey-scale image) is the basic feature calculation in our detection framework. In this work we use the Sobel method (see for example [10]) for edge processing. It is a gradient-based method which needs to convolve the image $I(x,y)$ with two 3×3 filter masks, K_x for horizontal filtering and K_x for vertical filtering. The convolution of the image with the two filter masks gives two edge strength images $G_x(x,y)$ and $G_y(x,y)$,

$$G_x(x,y) = K_x \star I(x,y), \tag{1}$$

$$G_y(x,y) = K_y \star I(x,y). \tag{2}$$

The absolute value $S(x,y)$, referred to as edge strength and the edge direction information $\Phi(x,y)$ are obtained using:

$$S(x,y) = \sqrt{G_x{}^2(x,y) + G_y{}^2(x,y)}, \tag{3}$$

$$\Phi(x,y) = \arctan(\frac{G_y(x,y)}{G_x(x,y)}) + \frac{\pi}{2}. \tag{4}$$

The edge information on homogenous parts of the image where no grey value changes occur is often noisy and bears no useful information for the detection. To exclude this information we apply a threshold T_s to the edge strength $S(x,y)$ generating an edge strength field $S_T(x,y)$,

$$S_T(x,y) = \begin{cases} S(x,y) & if \quad S(x,y) > T_s \\ 0 & else \end{cases}. \tag{5}$$

The edge direction as stated in equation (4) takes on values from 0 to 2π. The direction of an edge depends on whether the grey value changes from dark to bright or vice versa. This information is irrelevant for our purposes. Therefore, we map the direction information to a range of value $[0\ldots\pi]$ obtaining a new field

$$\hat{\Phi}(x,y) = \begin{cases} \Phi(x,y) & if \quad 0 \le \Phi(x,y) < \pi \\ \Phi(x,y) - \pi & if \quad \pi \le \Phi(x,y) < 2\pi \end{cases}, \tag{6}$$

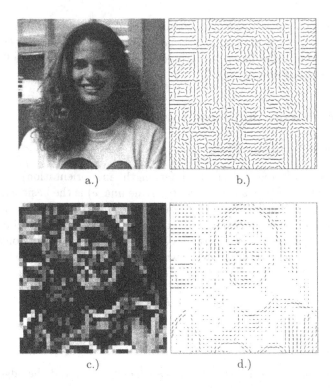

Fig. 1. Example of an image (a), the edge directions (b), edge strength (c), and the thresholded edge orientation field (d), which is used for further processing

which we call the edge orientation field. The edge orientation information can be rewritten using a complex formula

$$\mathbf{V}(x, y) = S_T(x, y)e^{j\hat{\phi}(x,y)}, \tag{7}$$

where $\mathbf{V}(x, y)$ is the complex edge orientation vector field and $j^2 = -1$. $S_T(x, y)$ and $\hat{\phi}(x, y)$ are obtained using equation (5) and (6). The edge orientation vector field can be displayed like shown in figure 1. The elements of $\mathbf{V}$ are referred to as vectors $\mathbf{v}$.

2.2 Edge Orientation Matching

We introduced EOM (edge orientation matching) in an earlier work [11], and will review the main steps here shortly. To build a face model for EOM we use a sample of hand-labeled face images. The faces are cropped, aligned and scaled to the size 32×40 in the grey level domain. From this set of normalized face images an average face is computed. We also add to the average face a vertically mirrored version of each face in the set . Finally the edge orientation vector field $\mathbf{V}_M(x, y)$ is calculated from the average face. This is used as a model for the detection process. For face detection the model $\mathbf{V}_M(x, y)$ is shifted over the image, and at each image position (x, y) the similarity between the model and the underlying image patch is calculated. The image is represented by its orientation field $\mathbf{V}_I(x, y)$. In order to determine the similarity between model and image patch one can think of several distance metrics which either rely on the direction information only or use both edge strength and direction for score calculation. In general the orientation matching process can be described as a convolution-like operation like

$$\mathbf{C}_O(x, y) = \sum_n \sum_m dist(\mathbf{V}_M(m, n), \mathbf{V}_I(x + m, y + n)), \tag{8}$$

where $\mathbf{C}_O(x, y)$ is an image like structure containing the similarity score between a sub-image of size $m \times n$ and the model which is of the same size for each possible model position within the image. The function $dist()$ calculates the local distance between two single orientation vectors. In the present system the function $dist()$ is always designed to give a low value for a high similarity and a high value for poor similarity.

The local distance function $dist()$ is defined as a mapping of two 2-dimensional vectors $\mathbf{v}_m$ and $\mathbf{v}_i$ to $[0 \ldots s_{max}]$. In our case they stem from an edge orientation field of the image $\mathbf{V}_I$ and of the model $\mathbf{V}_M$. They have the property $\arg\{\mathbf{v}\} = [0 \ldots \pi]$. The upper bound of the distance s_{max} occurs when these vectors are perpendicular and both of maximal length. The value of s_{max} depends on the normalization of the vectors $\mathbf{v}_i, \mathbf{v}_m$. As we use 8-bit grey level-coded images we normalize the vectors and so we get $s_{max} = 255$.

If one only wants to regard the edge direction information the local distance can be written as follows:

$$dist = \begin{cases} \sin(|\arg\{\mathbf{v}_i\} - \arg\{\mathbf{v}_m\}|) \cdot s_{max} & \text{if } |\mathbf{v}_i|, |\mathbf{v}_m| > 0 \\ s_{max} & \text{else} \end{cases} \tag{9}$$

This means that only directional information is used, no matter how reliable it is because noisy edges usually fall below the threshold and are set to zero. In [11] we introduce more ways to compute the function $dist()$. There we also propose an elastic matching method.

2.3   Generalized Hough Transform for Face Shape Detection

A technique based on the generalized Hough Transform, published in [12], is used for the detection of the elliptical outline of the frontal face shape. This method is capable of detecting the approximate position of all the ellipses within a certain range of variation in scale and rotation. The main idea is to perform a generalized Hough Transform by using an elliptical annulus as template. Actually, the directional information allows the transformation to be implemented very efficiently, since the template used to update the accumulator array can be reduced to only

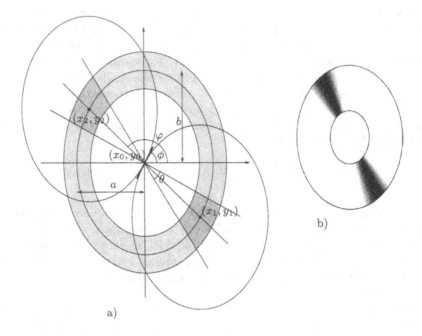

a)

b)

Fig. 2. Geometric construction of the templates. (a) The two possible positions of the center point of the ellipses depends on the direction of the vector **v**. (b) Representation of an ideal weighted template **T** for a $\phi = 33°$.

two sectors of the elliptical annulus. Then the technique can be described as follows. We assume that a and b are the lengths of the semi-axes of an ellipse used as a reference, and that ρ_r and ρ_e are, respectively, the reduction and expansion coefficients defining the scale range: $a_{min} = \rho_r \cdot a$, $b_{min} = \rho_r \cdot b$, $a_{max} = \rho_e \cdot a$ and $b_{max} = \rho_e \cdot b$. As well we assume that V is the edge orientation field obtained in the section 2.1 and that C_H is the accumulator array or similarity map. The template **T** is a function of the angle ϕ at the point (x_0, y_0). The points (x_1, y_1) and (x_2, y_2) in figure 2 are the only two points where an ellipse tangent to **v** in (x_0, y_0) with semi-axes a, b could be centered. Finally, if an angular variation θ is introduced in the directional information, the geometric locus **T** of the possible centers becomes:

$$\mathbf{T} = \left\{ (x, y) \,\middle|\, \rho_r^2 \le \left(\frac{x - x_0}{a} \right)^2 + \left(\frac{y - y_0}{b} \right)^2 \le \rho_e^2, \right.$$

$$\left. \Delta_{angle} \left(\arctan \left(\frac{y - y_0}{x - x_0} \right), \varphi \right) \le \frac{\theta}{2} \right\}, \tag{10}$$

where $\Delta_{angle} (\alpha, \beta)$ returns the smaller angle determined by α, β.

Figure 3 shows an example of an image and the accumulator array C_H generated by the hough transform.

3   Appearance Based Matching

In the third branch we use an appearance based matching method for face detection first published by Yang et al. [9]. Compared to similar methods like neural network based, histogram based or SVM based methods, it is computationally efficient. This algorithm models the problem domain as a two-class problem consisting of a face class and a non-face class. Each class is trained from small 20×20 grey value image-patches. Each image-patch $I_s(u, v)$ is histogram equalized before training or classification. After this it is transformed into a feature-vector using

$$F_s = 256 * (u * 20 + v) + I_s(u, v). \tag{11}$$

Thereby we assume that the values of $I_s(u, v)$ in the grey level domain are restricted to $0 \leq I_s(u, v) \leq 256$. The classification method is the so called SNoW (Sparse Network of Winnows) method. It is a network of linear units which is close related to the perceptron [13]. The similarity map produced by this method is called $\mathbf{C_C}$.

For this system we do not adopt the expensive bootstrapping training like proposed in [6] and [14]. Instead a set of 10000 manually cropped face images and 50000 randomly generated non-face images are used for training. This results in considerably higher number of false positives as for example reported in [9], but we can show that the number of false positives of each individual method does not play a key role in our fusion framework.

4   Fusion Method

As the similarity maps are produced by different matching algorithms they cannot be compared in that form. Figure 3 shows an example of such a similarity map of the Hough Transform (called accumulator array there). Therefore we want to estimate a statistical description of each matching algorithm that gives

 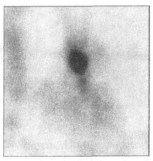

Fig. 3. Example of an image and the corresponding accumulator array $\mathbf{C_H}$ after processing the hough transform. Dark areas are good candidates for ellipse centers.

probability for a successful detection at a certain image location. This probabilities can be combined by using simple fusion strategies as shown in the next paragraph.

4.1 Similarity Map Normalization

We assume that $\mathbf{C}$ is a similarity map from the set $[\mathbf{C}_C, \mathbf{C}_O, \mathbf{C}_H]$. In addition we assume that c is an element of this map at position (x, y) , $c = \mathbf{C}(x, y)$ and $c \leq T_{m_i}$, where T_{m_i} is a predefined matching threshold for each cue. We can now define a binary event ω, which describes whether c belongs to a true face position or a false detect. We are especially interested in the two probability density functions $p(c \mid \omega_0)$, which describe the probability for a similarity value c being associated with the correct face detection and $p(c \mid \omega_1)$ for the opposite event.

The PDF (probability density function) for c can be written as

$$p(c) = p(c \mid \omega_0)p(\omega_0) + p(c \mid \omega_1)p(\omega_1); \qquad (12)$$

where the a-priory probability $p(\omega_0)$ is the recognition rate or ground truth of the classifier and $p(\omega_1) = 1 - p(\omega_0)$ is the miss classification rate. This probabilities are estimated from a training data set. We use the detection results from the single branches as an estimate for this probabilities.

The PDF is calculated from histograms which are obtained from a training data set. Figure 4 shows an example of such a histogram generated from the typical scores of the EOM branch. The probability of assigning the right class label to a measurement is according to Bayes' theorem:

$$p(\omega_0 \mid c) = \frac{p(c \mid \omega_0)}{p(c)} p(\omega_0); \qquad (13)$$

The PDF $p(c \mid \omega_0)$ and $p(c \mid \omega_1)$ are estimated on the training database.

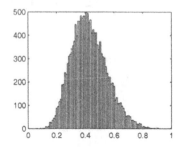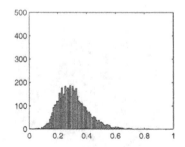

Fig. 4. Example for a measured histogram of the OEM obtained from 6000 test images. The first histogram shows the distribution for correctly matched face locations while the second was obtained from false matches.

4.2   Decision Fusion

The final step in our fusion approach is the combination of the results obtained from the normalized template matchers. In order to do so simple fusion approaches are used. We evaluate the sum rule (SUM) which is defined as

$$\hat{c} = \frac{1}{3} \sum_i p(\omega_0 \mid c_i) \tag{14}$$

and the product rule (PROD)

$$\hat{c} = \sqrt[3]{\prod_i p(\omega_0 \mid c_i)}, \tag{15}$$

where i addresses the three matching methods. To obtain a final decision we combine the whole similarity maps to a final similarity map which is illustrated in figure 5. The similarity maps from the OEM and Hough Transform are fully computed and fused for each pixel resulting in a new similarity map $\mathbf{C}_{OH}$. The values of $\mathbf{C}_C$ are only computed an fused if $\mathbf{C}_{OH}$ is above a certain threshold. This is done for efficiency reasons, because the appearance based alogorthm is computationally rather demanding compared to the EOM and Hough Transformation. In order to find a face position the combined similarity map $\hat{\mathbf{C}}(x, y)$ is searched for all values that are above a predefined matching threshold T_f. Appropriate values for T_f can only be found heuristically.

5   Experiments and Results

5.1   Database

We used a database of 13122 images mostly with a resolution of 384×288 pixels encoded in 256 grey levels, each of them showing one or more persons for the test of our system. The database also includes 2352 images from the frontal face

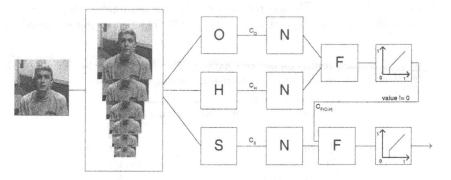

Fig. 5. Fusion principle of the three proposed matching methods.

Fig. 6. Example images from the database used for detection tests.

set of the m2vts database [15]. All persons are displayed in frontal views with considerable variations in size and illumination. Figure (6) shows some examples.

5.2   Results

The detection capabilities of the proposed algorithm is shown in table 1. We regard a face as detected if the found face position and size do not deviate from the true values for more than a predefined small tolerance . The face position and size are defined by the position of the two eyes. In this work we count a face as detected if the eye position and eye distance do not deviate from the true values more than 30% in terms of the true eye distance.

All the results reported in table 1 are obtained using a resolution pyramid with 8 resolution levels. The size ratio of two adjacent pyramid levels is $R_p = 1.25$ and the level size of the biggest level is 384×288. The processing is carried out

Table 1. Detection results on our test dataset. The number of false detects can be lowered significantly by the fusion compared to the single methods.

Method	Detection	#False Detects
EOM	97.7%	18341
Hough	96.0%	92866
Appearance	91.5%	141489
PROD - fusion	91.0%	540
SUM - fusion	90.8%	567

in less than $100msec$ on a Pentium II 500Mhz, using an efficient coarse-to-fine search method described in [11]. The size of the OEM template was 32×40 and it was created from a training sample of 200 hand labeled and normalized face images. The ellipse size for the Hough transform was slightly bigger than 26×34. The classifier of the appearance based method was trained from a set of 10000 face images an 100000 non-face images of size 20×20 pixel. As one can see from table 1, the number of false detects is reduced considerably by combining the three classifiers. The detection rate reaches a good 91% which is in between the rates of the best and worst single algorithm.

6   Related Work

There are several face processing algorithms that use edge orientation information or some kind of fusion for face processing. Bichsel [16] uses dot products of orientation maps for purposes of face recognition. Burl et al. [17] utilize shape statistics of the facial feature (eyes, nose, mouth) configuration learnd from a training sample. The feature candidates are detected by Orientation Template Correlation. Another algorithm which was partly used in this work is proposed by Maio and Maltoni [12]. They use the hough transform (see Sect. 2.3) with a subsequent matching of a manual generated orientation models for verification. Their results are obtained by a small database of 70 images and they do not use a full multi-resolution analysis and therefore can only detect faces of a certain size. Recently Feraud et al.[18] published their work on the combination of appearance based face detection with motion and color analysis for speed-up. The system is reported to have a good detection performance but it is still not real-time.

7   Conclusions and Future Work

We have shown that a fusion of simple template matchers is a powerful method for unconstraint face detection in natural scenes. Especially the number of false detects is considerably lower compared to each single method. This novel combination for face detection yields a very good recognition rate of more than 91% on a large database of 13122 images and can be carried out in real-time on a standard PC. We plan to incorporate more sophisticated matching algorithms for further improvement of the detection capabilities. We also plan to test the fusion algorithm for the task of human body detection.

Acknowledgments. The work described here was supported by the German Federal Ministry of Education and Research (BMBF) under the project EM-BASSI.

References

1. J.-C. Terrillon, M. David, and S. Akamatsu, "Automatic detection of human faces in natural scene images by use of a skin color model and of invariant moments," in *International Conference on Face and Gesture Recognition*, pp. 112–117, 1998.
2. J. Yang, W. Lu, and A. Waibel, "Skin-color modelling and adaption," in *ACCV'98*, 1998.
3. Q. Sun, W. Huang, and J. Wu, "Face detection based on color and local symmetry information," in *International Conference on Face and Gesture Recognition*, pp. 130–135, 1998.
4. D. Chai and K. N. Ngan, "Locating facial region of a head-and-shoulder color image," in *International Conference on Face and Gesture Recognition*, pp. 124–129, 1998.
5. S. McKenna, S. Gong, and Y. Raja, "Face recognition in dynamic scenes," in *British Machine Vision Conference*, no. 12, 1997.
6. H. A. Rowley, S. Baluja, , and T. Kanade, "Neural network-based face detection," *IEEE Transactions on Pattern Analysis and Machine Intelligence*, vol. 20, no. 1, pp. 23–38, 1998.
7. B. Fasel, "Fast multi-scale face detection," IDIAP-COM 4, IDIAP, 1998.
8. H. Schneiderman, *A Statistical Approach to 3D Object Detection Applied to Faces and Cars*. PhD thesis, Robotics Institute, Carnegie Mellon University, Pittsburgh, PA, May 2000.
9. M.-H. Yang, D. Roth, and N. Ahuja, "A snow-based face detector," in *Advances in Neural Information Processing Systems 12 (NIPS 12)*, pp. 855–861, MIT Press, 2000.
10. K. R. Castleman, *Digital Image Processing*. Prentice Hall, 1996.
11. B. Fröba and C. Küblbeck, "Face detection and tracking using edge orientation information," in *SPIE Photonics West*, 2001.
12. D. Maio and D. Maltoni, "Real-time face location on gray-scale static images," *Pattern Recognition*, vol. 33, pp. 1525–1539, September 2000.
13. R. O. Duda, P. E. Hart, and D. G. Stork, *Pattern Classufucation*. New York: John Wiley & Sons, 2001.
14. K. K. Sung, *Learning and Example Seletion for Object and Pattern Detection*. PhD thesis, Massachusetts Institute of Technology, January 1996.
15. K. Messer, J. Matas, J. Kittler, J. Luettin, and G. Maitre, "Xm2vtsdb: The extended m2vts database," in *Second International Conference on Audio- and Video-based Biometric Person Authentication*, pp. 71–77, 1999.
16. M. Bichsel, *Strategies of Robust Object Recognition for the Automatic Identification of Human Faces*. PhD thesis, Eidgenössische Technische Hochschule Zürich, Zürich, 1991.
17. M. Burl and P. Perona, "Recognition of planar object classes," in *Proc. CVPR'96*, 1996.
18. R. Feraud, O. J. Bernier, J.-E. Viallet, and M. Collobert, "A fast and accurate face detector based on neural networks," *IEEE Transactions on Pattern Analysis and Machine Intelligence*, vol. 23, pp. 42–53, January 2001.

Improving Product by Moderating k-NN Classifiers

F.M. Alkoot and J. Kittler

Centre for Vision, Speech and Signal Processing,
School of Electronics, Computing and Mathematics,
University of Surrey, Guildford GU2 5XH, United Kingdom.
email: {F.Alkoot,J.Kittler}@eim.surrey.ac.uk

Abstract. The veto effect caused by contradicting experts outputting zero probability estimates leads to fusion strategies performing sub optimally. This can be resolved using Moderation. The Moderation formula is derived for the k-NN classifier using a bayesian prior. The merits of moderation are examined on real data sets.

1 Introduction

Recently, the use of classifier fusion to improve accuracy of classification has become increasingly popular [4,5,6,7,10,12,13,14,15,16]. Although many diverse and sophisticated strategies have been developed, there is still a considerable interest in simple fusion methods that do not require any training. Such methods can either perform at the decision level or operate directly on the soft decision probability outputs of the respective experts, as in Sum and Product.

In the following we shall focus on the decision probability level fusion in general and on the product rule in particular. The product rule, which combines the multiple expert outputs by multiplication plays a prominent role because of its theoretically sound basis in probability calculus [9,8]. It is the proper fusion strategy when combining the outputs of experts utilising distinct (statistically independent) signal representations. It is also the optimal operator for combining the outputs of experts responding to an identical stimulus, under the assumption that the experts have been designed using statistically independent training sets. In spite of its theoretical underpinning, in many experimental studies Product has been shown to be outperformed by the less rigorously founded sum rule [1]. The inferior performance is attributed to the veto effect. If estimation errors drive one of the class aposteriori probability estimates to zero, the output of the product fusion will also be zero, even if other experts provide a lot of support for the class. This severity of the product fusion strategy has motivated our previous research which led to the development of a heuristic modification of the classifier outputs before the product fusion is carried out [2]. The advocated MProduct which stands for Modified Product was demonstrated to be superior not only to Product but also to the sum rule.

In this paper we argue that estimation errors are often caused by small sample problems. We show that by taking small sample effects into account we can

J. Kittler and F. Roli (Eds.): MCS 2001, LNCS 2096, pp. 429–439, 2001.

develop a formula for correcting the outputs of individual experts, provided the sampling distribution is known and can be incorporated as a Bayes prior. We develop such a correction formula for the k Nearest Neighbour $(k-NN)$ decision rule. Incidentally, this rule is affected by small sample problems even when the size of the training set is large, as each decision is made by drawing a small number of samples from the training set. We then validate our correction formula experimentally on synthetic and real data sets. We demonstrate that Product using moderated outputs of multiple $k-NN$ classifiers strongly outperforms the product fusion of raw classifier outputs. Finally, we compare the proposed scheme with the heuristic MProduct and show that they are quite similar in performance. The former has the advantage that the modification formula is very simple and adaptive to the number of nearest neighbours used by the decision rule.

The paper is organised as follows. In the next section we shall introduce the concept of classifier output moderation. In Section 3 we focus on the $k-NN$ decision rule and derive the formula for correcting the outputs of $k-NN$ experts. Experiments and experimental results are presented in Sections 4 and 5. The paper is drawn to conclusion in Section 6.

2   Theory

Given R experts and m classes, the product rule assigns an input pattern vector $\mathbf{x}$ to class ω_j if

$$\Pi_{i=1}^{R} P_i(\omega_j|\mathbf{x}) = max_{k=1}^{m} \Pi_{i=1}^{R} P_i(\omega_k|\mathbf{x}) \qquad (1)$$

where $P_i(\omega_k|\mathbf{x})$ is an estimate of the kth class aposteriori probability $P(\omega_k|\mathbf{x})$ delivered by expert i. Note that the estimate will be influenced by a training set, X_i, used for the design of expert i. Once the form of the classifier is chosen, the training set is then deployed to estimate the underlying model parameters denoted by vector γ_i. A particular value of the parameter vector obtained through training will then define the ith expert output. This can be made explicit by denoting the output by $P(\omega_k|\mathbf{x}, X_i, \gamma_i)$. However, γ_i is only an estimate of the true model parameters. The estimate will be just a single realisation of the random variable drawn from the sampling distribution $P(\gamma_i)$. If the sampling distribution is known a priori, then the raw estimate

$$P_i(\omega_k|\mathbf{x}) = P(\omega_k|\mathbf{x}, X_i, \gamma_i) \qquad (2)$$

can be moderated by taking the prior into consideration. In other words, a new estimate is obtained by integrating parameter dependent estimates over the model parameter space as

$$\dot{P}_i(\omega_k|\mathbf{x}) = \int P_i(\omega_k|\mathbf{x}, X_i, \gamma_i)p(\gamma_{ij})d\gamma_i \qquad (3)$$

This is known as marginalization in Bayesian estimation.

3   k-NN Classifier Output Moderation

In Section 2 we argued for a moderation of raw expert outputs. The moderation is warranted for pragmatic reasons, namely to minimise the veto effect of overconfident erroneous classifiers.

It is perhaps true to say that for training sets of reasonable size there should not be any appreciable difference between moderated and raw expert outputs. However, for some types of classifiers, moderation is pertinent even for sample sets of respectable size. An important case is the $k - NN$ classifier. Even if the training set is relatively large, say hundreds of samples or more, the need for moderation is determined by the value of k, which may be as low as $k = 1$. Considering just the simplest case, a two class problem, it is perfectly possible to draw all k-Nearest Neighbours from the same class which means that one of the classes will have the expert output set to zero. In the subsequent (product) fusion this will then dominate the fused output and may impose a veto on the class even if other experts are supportive of that particular hypothesis.

We shall now consider this situation in more detail. Suppose that we draw k-Nearest Neighbours and find that κ of these belong to class ω. Then the unbiased estimate $P_i(\omega|\mathbf{x})$ of the aposteriori probability $P(\omega|\mathbf{x})$ is given by

$$P_i(\omega|\mathbf{x}) = \frac{\kappa}{k} \qquad (4)$$

It should be noted that the actual observation κ out of k could arise for any value of $P(\omega|\mathbf{x})$ with the probability

$$q(\kappa) = \binom{k}{\kappa} P^\kappa(\omega|\mathbf{x})[1 - P(\omega|\mathbf{x})]^{k-\kappa} \qquad (5)$$

Assuming that a priori the probability $P(\omega|\mathbf{x})$ taking any value between zero and one is equally likely, we can find an aposteriori estimate of the aposteriori class probability $P(\omega|\mathbf{x})$ as

$$\dot{P}_i(\omega|\mathbf{x}) = \frac{\int_0^1 P(\omega|\mathbf{x})P^\kappa(\omega|\mathbf{x})[1 - P(\omega|\mathbf{x})]^{k-\kappa} dP(\omega|\mathbf{x})}{\int_0^1 P^\kappa(\omega|\mathbf{x})[1 - P(\omega|\mathbf{x})]^{k-\kappa} dP(\omega|\mathbf{x})} \qquad (6)$$

where the denominator is a normalising factor ensuring that the total probability mass equals to one. By expanding the term $[1 - P(\omega|\mathbf{x})]^{k-\kappa}$ and integrating, it can be easily verified that the right hand side of (6) becomes

$$\dot{P}_i(\omega|\mathbf{x}) = \frac{\kappa + 1}{k + 2} \qquad (7)$$

which is the beta distribution. Thus the moderated equivalent of $\frac{\kappa}{k}$ is $\frac{\kappa+1}{k+2}$. Clearly our estimates of aposteriori class probabilities will never reach zero which could cause a veto effect. For instance, for the Nearest Neighbour classifier with $k = 1$ the smallest expert output will be $\frac{1}{3}$. As k increases the smallest estimate will approach zero as $\frac{1}{k+2}$ and will assume zero only when $k = \infty$.

For m class problems equation (7) can be extended to become

$$\dot{P}_i(\omega|\mathbf{x}) = \frac{\kappa + 1}{k + m} \qquad (8)$$

4   Experiments

The aim of the experiments described in this section is to confirm the theoretically predicted benefits of $k - NN$ classifier output moderation. As the moderation of aposteriori class probabilities eliminates the veto effect, we would expect the performance of the product rule on moderated outputs to surpass the success rate obtained with raw class aposteriori probability estimates.

The multiple classifiers used in the experiments are designed using training sets obtained by bootstrapping. Bootstrapping is a re-sampling procedure routinely used in bagging. Each bootstrap set is derived from the original training set by sampling with replacement. The size of the bootstrap set is normally equivalent to the cardinality of the original training set. When a training data set is small, the proportions of training patterns from the different classes may be unrepresentative. The probability of drawing a training set with samples from some class completely missing becomes non negligible. When this occurs, bagging may even become counterproductive. In our earlier work [3] we investigated the effect of different control mechanisms over sampling to minimise the imbalance in the representation of the class populations in the resulting bootstrap sets. Three modifications of the standard bagging method were considered. The same sampling strategies have been adopted in the following experiments to demonstrate the merits of moderation. We refer to the standard procedure as method 1 and its modified versions as methods 2-4. The methods which exploit increasing amounts of prior knowledge can be summarised as follows.

- **Method 1.** This is the standard bagging method outlined above.
- **Method 2.** When bootstrap sets are created from the learning set we check the ratio of the number of samples per class in the bootstrap set. This ratio is compared to the ratio of samples per class in the learning set. If the difference between the compared ratios is larger than a certain class population bias tolerance threshold we reject the bootstrap set. We set the bias tolerance threshold to 10%.
- **Method 3.** This method is similar to method 2 except that the bootstrap set ratio is compared to the ratio in the full set. By full set we mean the set containing all samples, learning and test samples. This full set ratio simulates a prior knowledge of the class distribution in the sample space.
- **Method 4.** Here we only require that all classes be represented in the bootstrap set, without enforcing a certain ratio of samples per class. This is done by rejecting any bootstrap set that does not represent all classes.

4.1   Experimental Methodology

A single training set is randomly taken from the original sample space represented by the full data set. The $k - NN$ classifier built using this original learning set is referred to as the single expert. The remaining samples are used as a test set. Using the learning set, 25 boot sets are generated by bootstrapping. The decision of the 25 boot sets are aggregated to classify the test set. These results are referred to as the bagged expert results. We compare these results to those obtained from the single expert, and to those obtained from other bagging methods. The above is repeated for three training set sizes. The sizes used were 20, 40, and 80 samples. We concentrate on this range of training set sizes for the following reasons. For the data sets used in our experiments the upper cardinality corresponds to a sufficiently large data set for which the $k - NN$ classifier becomes stable. The lower end of the spectrum represents the case when the main assumption underpinning the $k - NN$ decision rule, i.e. that the aposteriori class probability $P(\omega|\mathbf{x})$ at all k Nearest Neighbours is the same, breaks down. Thus the focus of our experimentation is on the range between these two limiting values.

We measure the performance of the four methods of creating bootstrap sets for two types of learning sets. In the first case the learning set is created by randomly taking samples from the full data set. This results in a set that may contain samples from all classes with a population bias towards a certain class. The second type of learning set is referred to as a modified learning set. It is constructed using Method 3 which was mentioned as a technique to create unbiased bootstrap sets at the beginning of Section 4. This results in a set that is representative of all the classes, with the class population ratios similar to those of the full set. The modified learning set simulates an unbiased sample space.

All experiments are repeated 100 times and we average the error rates by dividing by the number of repetitions. We compare the moderation results with the results obtained using non-moderated $k - NN$ experts. We also compare the moderation results with results obtained using the modified product fusion strategy proposed in [2].

To find the misclassification error rate of a single expert, a test sample is presented to the $k - NN$ classifier. The class posterior probabilities for each test sample are estimated in the non-moderated and moderated case using formulas 4 and 8 respectively.

The test sample is assigned a class label that corresponds to the largest posterior probability. If the original label of the sample is found to be different from the assigned label the error counter is incremented. This is repeated for all samples in the test set. After presenting all test samples the error counter is divided by the number of test samples used, in order to get the misclassification rate.

In order to see the effect of Moderation we adopt a simple relative performance measure defined in equation 9. It relates the difference between two results, for example results obtained using moderated and non-moderated systems, to the classification rate of the latter. In this way we will be able to reflect any improvements or degradations in performance even if the baseline classification rates are quite high. The relative performance measure s is given as

$$s = \frac{c_m - c_u}{c_u} \times 100 \tag{9}$$

where c_m is the moderated classification rate, or the new result, and c_u is the unmoderated classification rate, or the baseline result. If the improvement or degradation exceeds 5 % we consider it as significant. This value is calculated for all four bagging methods and each of the two learning set types under varying set sizes.

Both synthetic and real data sets were used in our experiments. Synthetic data was chosen to carry out controlled experiments for which the achievable recognition rate is known. The computer generated data is two dimensional involving two classes. The two class densities have an overlap area which was designed to achieve an instability of the class boundary. The theoretical Bayes error of this data set is 6.67%. Most of the real data used were the standard sets obtained from the UCI repository [11]. The exception is the seismic data set made available by Shell. Table 1 summarises the essential information about these data sets.

Table 1. Data sets used and the number of samples available in each data set.

Data Name	No. of samples	No. of features	No. of classes	Data Name	No. of samples	No. of features	No. of classes
Synthetic	1231	2	2	BCW	699	9	2
Seismic	300	25	3	Ionosphere	351	34	2
Wine	178	13	3	Iris	150	4	3

5   Results

Table 2 displays the baseline classification rates of the single expert and bagging using the product rule with raw aposteriori class probability estimates. These results have been analysed and discussed in detail elsewhere [3]. For the purpose of this paper we only note the main points, namely that

- bagging does not improve the $k - NN$ rule performance for sufficiently large training sets (in excess of 80 samples)
- for smaller sample sets, bootstrapping and aggregation of moderated estimates of aposteriori class probabilities via product can be useful
- for very small training and bootstrap sets created by means of regular sampling, bagging can lead to degradation in performance

The benefits of moderating the $k - NN$ classifier outputs can be gleaned from Figures 1(a) and 1(b) which plot the relative performance measure defined in 9. In Figure 1(a) we show the improvement gained over the single expert whereas Figure 1(b) relates the product aggregation of moderated $k - NN$ outputs to the product of raw outputs. We note that for training sets of size less than 80 samples the performance improves significantly. The gains are inversely proportional to the training set size. Bagging with moderation can largely compensate for the lack of training data.

The method for moderating the outputs of the $k - NN$ classifier advocated in this paper is based on the principles of sampling with a Bayesian prior. The Modified Product (MProduct) proposed in [2], has the same motivation, i.e. eliminating the veto effect of the product fusion rule that can be caused by raw aposteriori class probability estimates. However, MProduct is heuristic and it

Table 2. Classification rate of the single expert and bagging using Product of non-moderated aposteriori class probability estimates

Data set	Learn set type	Bagging method	Learning samples 20	40	80	Data set	Learn set type	Bagging method	Learning samples 20	40	80
Seis.	Regular	1	89.87	98.16	99.17	BCW	Regular	1	90.05	94.63	95.35
		2	95.29	98.12	99.13			2	91.69	94.68	95.35
		3	96.56	98.62	99.16			3	92.70	94.78	95.44
		4	94.73	98.13	99.17			4	91.43	94.62	95.42
		Single xp	96.41	98.08	99.16			Single xp	92.66	94.47	95.44
	Modified	1	94.83	98.03	99.08		Modified	1	90.89	94.79	95.38
		2	96.41	98.16	99.09			2	92.01	94.86	95.41
		3	96.34	98.37	99.15			3	92.43	94.88	95.49
		4	95.50	97.96	99.10			4	91.50	94.76	95.42
		Single xp	96.90	97.91	99.10			Single xp	93.32	94.65	95.48
Wine	Regular	1	76.05	91.39	93.54	Iris	Regular	1	81.42	93.46	96.13
		2	83.20	92.09	93.65			2	87.00	93.71	95.93
		3	86.07	92.37	93.84			3	88.76	94.30	96.06
		4	81.04	91.80	93.78			4	84.33	93.05	96.11
		Single xp	85.14	91.75	93.56			Single xp	91.35	94.07	96.27
	Modified	1	79.54	91.22	94.28		Modified	1	83.45	93.78	95.86
		2	85.84	91.74	93.95			2	88.75	94.46	95.96
		3	86.43	92.01	94.26			3	89.22	94.68	96.03
		4	82.72	91.09	94.16			4	84.52	93.59	95.93
		Single xp	88.27	91.34	94.02			Single xp	92.15	94.54	96.13
Iono.	Regular	1	68.28	71.97	76.00	Synth	Regular	1	88.76	91.12	92.28
		2	68.24	72.63	75.86			2	89.23	91.07	92.27
		3	68.31	72.99	75.62			3	89.85	91.52	92.36
		4	67.40	72.31	75.85			4	88.72	91.30	92.29
		Single xp	68.60	70.25	75.93			Single xp	89.34	91.02	92.28
	Modified	1	67.21	71.76	75.62		Modified	1	89.35	91.54	92.23
		2	68.10	71.90	75.56			2	90.03	91.86	92.27
		3	67.68	72.36	76.15			3	90.06	91.91	92.42
		4	66.97	71.70	75.48			4	89.32	91.58	92.28
		Single xp	67.55	70.22	75.61			Single xp	89.97	91.59	92.30

is of interest to compare its performance with the moderated output scheme based on theoretical foundations. In MProduct the jth expert output $P_j(\omega_i|x)$, which estimates the a posteriori probability for class ω_i given pattern vector x, is modified before entering the product fusion rule as follows:

$$\hat{P}_j(\omega_i|x) = t \quad \text{if} \quad P_j(\omega_i|x) \leq t$$
$$\hat{P}_j(\omega_i|x) = P_j(\omega_i|x) \quad \text{if} \quad P_j(\omega_i|x) > t \tag{10}$$

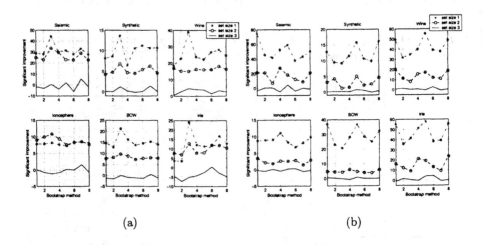

(a)   (b)

Fig. 1. (a) Moderated Product significant improvement over the single expert. (b)Moderated Product significant improvement over the unmoderated Product. Numbers 1 to 4 on the x-axis represent bagging methods 1 to 4 using regular learning set, while numbers 5 to 8 represent the same bagging methods using modified learning set.

The respective transfer functions between the raw inputs and outputs delivered by moderation and MProduct are shown in Figure 2. The posterior probability estimates of MProduct cover almost the full range 0 to 1, regardless of the value of k. In contrast, the range of moderated posterior probability estimates reduces as k decreases. However, these differences in transfer functions do not seem to translate to any significant differences in performance. In all the above experiments the value of k for a particular training set size was automatically chosen using the usual square root rule, i.e. $k = \sqrt{N}$ where N is the size of the training set. This leads to using an odd value for k at the largest set size and even k for the smaller two sizes. We wanted to check the consistency of the above results as k varies. We repeated the same experiments for the number of Nearest Neighbours varying from 2 to N. Typical results are shown in Figure 3. Figure 3(a) gives the classification error rates for the Seismic data for a single expert, and a product fusion combining raw, moderated and heuristically modified $k-NN$ classifier outputs respectively. Note that the performance of Product of $k - NN$ raw outputs improves with

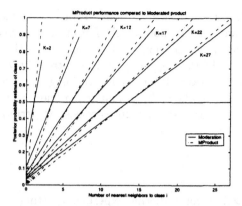

Fig. 2. Comparison of posterior probability estimates when using Moderation to when using Modified Product

increasing k. Clearly the probability of the veto effect occurring will be highest for the smallest k and will go down as k increases. However, the improvement in performance of this fusion method is undermined by the general downward trend of the $k - NN$ classifier as a function of k for small training sets. Thus the performance curve of Product of raw outputs will peak at some point and then monotonically decay with increasing k.

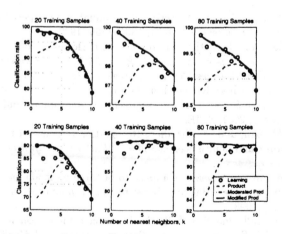

Fig. 3. Comparison of classification rates of Product when expert outputs are raw, Moderated or Modified, all compared to the single expert. Results are for bagging method four using regular learning set for Seismic data (top row), and Wine data (bottom row)

The product of moderated outputs and MProduct peak at the lowest value of k i.e. at $k = 2$ and then monotonically fall off as k increases. On average, MProduct is marginally better than moderation, but at the peak ($k = 2$) the curves meet. Interestingly, the single expert does extremely well for odd numbers of k and larger sets, but less well for smaller training sets. Most importantly, it does not do well for $k = 2$ where the probability of indecision is high. Thus one of the benefits of bagging is that it produces consistent performance for odd and even values of k.

6   Conclusions

The veto effect caused by contradicting experts outputting zero probability estimates leads to fusion strategies performing sub optimally. This can be resolved using Moderation. The Moderation formula has been derived for the k-NN classifier using the bayesian prior. The merits of moderation are examined on real data sets. Tests with different bagging methods indicate that the proposed moderation method improves the performance of Product significantly, especially when the size of the training set leads to sever sampling problems.

Acknowledgements. The support of EPSRC Grant GR/M61320 and EU Framework V Project Banca is gratefully acknowledged. F.Alkoot thanks the Islamic Development bank and the Public Authority for Applied Education and Training of Kuwait for financially supporting his education towards the Ph.D.

References

1. F. M. Alkoot and J. Kittler. Experimental evaluation of expert fusion strategies. *Pattern Recognition Letters*, 20(11-13):1361–1369, 1999.
2. Fuad M. Alkoot and J. Kittler. Improving the performance of the product fusion strategy. In *Proceedings of the 15th IAPR International Conference on Pattern Recognition*, volume 2, pages 164–167, Barcelona, Spain, 2000.
3. Fuad M. Alkoot and Josef Kittler. Population bias control for bagging knn experts. In *In proceedings of Sensor Fusion: Architectures, Algorithms, and Applications V*, Orlando, Fl, USA, 2001. SPIE.
4. J. Cao, M. Ahmadi, and M. Shridhar. Recognition of handwritten numerals with multiple feature and multistage classifier. *Pattern Recognition*, 28(2):153–160, 1995.
5. T. Dietterich. An experimental comparison of three methods for constructing ensembles of decision trees: Bagging, boosting, and randomization. *Machine Learning*, pages 1–22, 1998.
6. T.K. Ho, J.J. Hull, and S.N. Srihari. Decision combination in multiple classifier systems. *IEEE Transactions on Pattern Analysis and Machine Intelligence*, 16(1):66–75, 1994.
7. M I Jordan and R A Jacobs. Hierarchical mixture of experts and the em algorithm. *Neural Computation*, 6:181–214, 1994.
8. J. Kittler. Combining classifiers: A theoretical framework. *Pattern Analysis and Applications*, 1:18–27, 1998.

9. J. Kittler, M. Hatef, R. Duin, and J. Matas. On combining classifiers. *IEEE Transaction on Pattern Analysis and Machine Intelligence*, 20(3):226–239, 1998.
10. D. Lee and S.Srihari. Dynamic classifier combination using neural networks. *SPIE*, 2422:26–37, 1995.
11. P. Murphy. Repository of machine learning databases and domain theories. ftp://ftp.ics.uci.edu/pub/machine-learning-databases, 1999.
12. G. Rogova. Combining the results of several neural network classifiers. *Neural Networks*, 7(5):777–781, 1994.
13. K. Tumer and J. Ghosh. Order statistics combiners for neural classifiers. In *Proceedings of the World Congress on Neural Networks*, volume I, pages 31–34, Washington, DC., 1995.
14. D.H. Wolpert. Stacked generalisation. *Neural Networks*, 5(2):241–260, 1992.
15. K Woods, W P Kegelmeyer, and K Bowyer. Combination of multiple experts using local accuracy estimates. *IEEE Transaction Pattern Analysis and Machine Intelligence*, 19:405–410, 1997.
16. L. Xu, A. Krzyzak, and C.Y. Suen. Methods of combining multiple classifiers and their applications to handwriting recognition. *IEEE Transaction. SMC*, 22(3):418–435, 1992.

Automatic Model Selection in a Hybrid Perceptron/Radial Network

Shimon Cohen and Nathan Intrator

Computer Science Department,
Tel-Aviv University,
email: www.math.tau.ac.il/~nin

Abstract. We introduce an algorithm for incrementaly constructing a hybrid network fo radial and perceptron hidden units. The algorithm determins if a radial or a perceptron unit is required at a given region of input space. Given an error target, the algorithm also determins the number of hidden units. This results in a final architecture which is often much smaller than an RBF network or a MLP. A benchmark on four classification problems and three regression problems is given. The most striking performance improvement is achieved on the vowel data set [4]. [1]

1 Introduction

The construction of a network architecture which contains units of different types at the same hidden layer is not commonly done. One reason is that such construction makes model selection more challenging, as it requires the determination of each unit type in addition to the determination of network size. A more common approach to achieving higher architexture flexibility is via the use of more flexible units [17,8]. The potential problem of such a construction is over flexibility which leads to overfitting.

We have introduced a training methodology for a hybrid MLP/RBF network [3]. This architecture, produced far better classification and regression results compared with advanced RBF methods or with MLP architectures. In this work, we further introduce a novel training methodology, which evaluates the need for additional hidden units, chooses optimaly their nature – MLP or RBF – and determines their optimal initial weight values. The determination of additional hidden units is based on an incremental strategy which searches for regions in input space for which the input/output function approximation leads to highest residual (error in case of classification). This approach, coupled with optimal determination of initial weight values for the additional hidden units, constructs

---

[1] This work was partially supported by the Israeli Ministry of Science and by the Israel Academy of Sciences and Humanities – Center of Excellence Program. Part of this work was done while N. I. was affiliated with the Institute for Brain and Neural Systems at Brown University and supported in part by ONR grants N00014-98-1-0663 and N00014-99-1-0009.

J. Kittler and F. Roli (Eds.): MCS 2001, LNCS 2096, pp. 440–454, 2001.

a computationaly efficient training algorithm which appears to scale up with the complexity of the data, better than regular MLP or RBF methods.

2   Motivation for Incremental Methods and the Use of a Hybrid MLP/RBF Networks

There are many ways to decompose a function into a set of basis functions. The challenging task is to use a complete set which converges fast to the desired function (chosen from a sufficiently wide family of functions.) For example, while it is well known that MLP with as little as a single hidden layer is a universal approximator, namely, it can approximate any L^2 function, it is also known that the approximation may be very greedy, namely the number of hidden units may grow very large as a function of the desired approximation error.

Analysing cases where convergence of the architecture (as a function of number of hidden units) is slow, reveals that oten there is at least one region in input space where an attempt is being made to approximate a function that is radially symmetric (such as a donut) with projection units or vice versa. This suggests that an incremental architecture which chooses the appropriate hidden unit for different regions in input space can lead to a far smaller architecture. Earlier approaches, attempted to construct a small network approximation to the desired function at different regions of input space. This approach which was called "divide and concur", has been studied since the eighties in the machine learning and connectionists community. Rather than reviwing the vast literature on that, we shall point out some approaches which indicate some of the highlights that had motivated our work. Work on trees is reviewed in [1] where the goal is to reach a good division of the input space and use a very simple architecture at the terminating nodes. That work suggested some criteria for splitting the input space and provided a cost complexity method for comparing the performance of architectures with different size. An approach which constructs more sophisticated architectures at the terminating nodes was proposed in [20,14], where a gating network performs the division of the input space and small neural networks perform the function approximation at each region separately. Nowlan's many experiments with such architecture led him to the conclusion that it is better to have different type of architectures for the gating network and for the networks that perform the function approximation at the different regions. He suggested to use RBF for the gating network, and MLP for the function approximation, and thus constructed the first hybrid architecture between MLP and RBF. A tree approach with neural networks as terminating nodes was proposed by [15]. The boosting algorithm [6] is another variant of the space division approach, where the division is done based on the error performance of the given architecture. In contrast to previous work, this approach takes into accounts the geometric structure of the input data only indirectly. A remote family of architectures where the function approximation is constructed incrementally is projection pursuit [10] and additive models [11,12].

If one accepts the idea of constructing a local simple architecture to different regions in input space, then the questions becomes, which architcture family should be used. The local architecture should be as simple as possible in order to avoid overfitting to the smaller portion of regional training data. Motivated by theoretical work that have studied the duality between projection-based approximation and radial kernel methods [5], we have decided to use RBF or perceptron units. Donoho's work has shown that a function can be decomposed into two parts, the radial part and the ridge (projection based) part and that the two parts are mutually exclusive. It is difficult however, to separate the radial portion of a function from its projection based portion before they are estimated, but a sequential approach which decides on the fly, which unit to use for different regions in input space, has a potential to find a useful subdivision.

The most relevant statistical framework to our proposal is Generalized Additive Models (GAM) [11,12]. In that framework, the hidden units (the components of the additive model) have some parametric form, usually polynomial, which is estimated from the data. While this model has nice statistical properties [25], the additional degrees of freedom, require strong regularization to avoid over-fitting. Higher order networks have at least a quadratic terms in addition to the linear term of the projections [17] as a special case of GAM.

$$y = \sum_i w_i g(\sum_j w_{ij}x_j + \sum_k \sum_l w_{ikl}x_k x_l + a_i) + w_0 \qquad (1)$$

While they present a powerful extension of MLPs, and can form local or global features, they do so at the cost of squaring the number of input weights to the the hidden nodes. Flake [8] has suggested an architecture similar to GAM where each hidden unit has a parametric activation function which can change from a projection based to a radial function in a continuous way [8]. This architecture uses a squared activation function, thus called Squared MLP (SMLP) and only doubles the input dimension of the input patterns.

Our proposed hybrid extends both MLP and RBF networks by combining RBF and Perceptron units in the same hidden layer. Unlike the previously described methods, this does not increase the number of parameters in the model, at the cost of predetermining the number of RBF and Perceptron units in the network. The hybrid network is useful especially in cases where the data includes some regions that contain hill-plateau and other regions that contain Gaussian bumps, as demonstrated in figure 1. The hybrid architecture [3], which we call Perceptron Radial Basis Net (PRBFN), automatically finds the relevant functional parts from the data concurrently, thus avoiding possible local minima that result from sequential methods. The first training step in the previous approach [3] was to clusterized the data. In the next step, we tested two hypotheses for each cluster. If a cluster was far from radial Gaussian we rejected this hypothesis and accepted the null hypothesis. However, we had to use a threshold for rejecting the normal distribution hypothesis. When it was decided that a data cluster is likely to be normal, an RBF unit was used and otherwise a Perceptron (projection) unit was used. The last step was to train the hybrid network with full gradient descent on the full parameters.

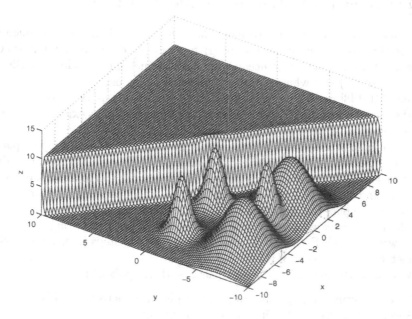

Fig. 1. Data that is composed of five clusters and a sigmoidal surface.

However, the selection based on a simple hypothesis test could be improved and suffered from an unclear way of estimating the hypothesis rejection threshold. Another problem with the old approach is that the number of hidden units has to be given to the algorithm in advance. In this paper we introduce a new algorithm that automatically selects the type of hidden units as well as the number of units.

There are several approaches to set the structure of a Neural Network. The first one is forward selection. This approach starts with a small [19,7] network and add units until an error goal is reached. Another approach is to start with a large network and [21] and prune un necessary units, until a given criteria is met.

In this paper we use the first approach. We start with a small network and expand it until a given error goal is met. Thus, the algorithm determines the number of hidden units automatically. As noted above, a very difficult task in training an hybrid neural network is to find the radial and projection parts automatically. This problem in amplified for high dimension data, where the data cannot be visualized very well. We purpose a novel way to select the type of hidden unit automatically for regression and classification. This algorithm leads to smaller networks while maintaining good generalization of the resulting network.

3   Paramter Estimation and Model Selection

An incremental architecture with more than one type of building components, requires three decisions at each step; (i) find the next region in input space where a hidden unit might be needed; (ii) decide which unit to add, an RBF or a perceptron; (iii) test whether the new unit is actually useful.

The SMLP [8] network uses both RBF and Perceptron units at each cluster. In higher order networks [17] quadratic and linear terms always exists and strong regularization must be used to avoid over-fitting.

We prefer to attempt to select the proper unit for each region in input space. Thus, the number of hidden units is minimal and over-fitting is reduced. In order to select the type of units in a high dimensional space, one has to divide the space to regions and then to select the type of hidden unit for each region. During the division of the space into small region we can estimate the overall error and stop the splitting process when an error goal is reached. Thus, monitoring the size of the network as well. For these reasons there are several steps in estimating the parameters and structure of the hybrid network.

We outline the algorithm's steps to achieve these goals as follows:

- Data clustering and splitting to reduce an error objective function.
- Automatic selection of unit type for each cluster.
- Full gradient descent.

In subsequent sections we describe each step of the algorithm in more details.

3.1   Data Clustering

We start by clustering the data and reducing an objective error function on the data. The objective function can be the Entropy, for classification, or the Sum of Square Errors (SSE) for regression problems. The entropy serves as a measure of information or surprise. The less entropy a cluster has the more uniform in class tags are the its patterns. The SSE is equivalent to the maximum likelihood under Gaussian assumption about the noise. Thus, reducing the SSE is equivalent to the maximization of the data likelihood.

The algorithm, that is described here, splits the cluster with the largest objective function (error value) into two clusters as follows. We feel that more work is needed in the theoretical justification of the splitting rule. This is subject for future work.

- Start with the whole data as one cluster.
- Find the cluster with the largest error.
- For regression problems use regression split and otherwise classification split.
- The splitting is continued until an error goal is reached or maximum number of clusters are achieved.

The splitting for regression divides each cluster into two regions. One region is where the target function is approximated rather good, the other one where there is still a large error. This is done as follows:

- Find the pattern with the largest error in the above cluster.
- Sort the patterns by distance to the pattern with the largest error value.
- Split the current cluster by considering $(n-1)$ ways to divide the cluster by forming a division on the sorted patterns.
- Choose the split with the largest reduction in the SSE.

The splitting procedure for classification problems minimizes the Entropy criterion. Thus, splitting the cluster with the largest Entropy split the cluster with maximum impurity. Breiman [1] has used the Gini criterion for splitting nodes in the CART algorithm. He has found that the two criterions are equivalents. We purpose the following splitting procedure for a given cluster:

- Select the two classes with the maximum number of patterns.
- Compute their mean and form two new clusters of these means.
- For each pattern associate it with the nearest mean and its cluster.

The above splitting procedures are simple and there is no need to work through every coordinate as done in the CART [1] algorithm.

3.2   Unit Selection

Several authors have used the Bayesian approach for model selection. Mackay[18] uses the evidence to select a model out of a set of models. Kass and Raftery [16] consider the Bayes Factors, for given models $M1, M2$ and data set D. We follow this approach here by starting with the Bayesian formulation which computes the most probable model by integrating over the model parameters:

$$p(D|M) = \int_w p(D, w|M)dw = \int_w p(D|w, M)p(w|M)dw. \tag{2}$$

The Bayes Factors are then defined as:

$$\frac{p(M1|D)}{p(M2|D)} = \frac{p(D|M1)p(M1)}{p(D|M2)p(M2)}. \tag{3}$$

The integration of 2 can be performed by using Laplace integral. That is, approximating the integrand by a quadratic function. Thus, the value of the integral becomes:

$$p(m|D) \cong (2\pi)^d |H|^{-1|2} p(D|W_{m_0}, M)p(W_{m_0}|H), \tag{4}$$

Where H is the Hessian matrix of the approximation and W_{m_0} is the most probable value of the likelihood $p(D|M)$. Note that this calculation takes into account the performance of the model in the vicinicty of the parameter vector m_0 and is thus much more informative than a simple likelihood at m_0.

With the lack of a-priori knowledge we assume that a model with an RBF or a perceptron as a hidden unit is equally likely, thus:

$$p(M1) = p(M2).$$

This leads to the likelihood ratio:

$$\frac{p(D|M1)}{p(D|M2)}.$$

The purposed algorithm selects the type of hidden unit automatically by using likelihood ratio. The maximum likelihood is computed for each cluster and unit type. The unit type with the higher likelihood is selected. The maximum likelihood is defined differently for classification and regression problems and it is described in the next sub-sections.

Regression unit type selection. In the regression context the maximum likelihood is defined as follows:

$$L = \exp(-\frac{\sum_{i=n}^{N}(y_n - t_n)^2}{2\sigma^2}). \tag{5}$$

Where t_n are the target values and y_n is the output the neural network. Maximization of the likelihood is equivalent to the minimization of the sum of squares, if one assumes that the function values are corrupted with a noise that is normally distributed with given variance σ^2. This assumption is plausible when the noise is a sum of signals from independents source according to the Central Limit Theorem.

As noted above, the selection of the unit type is done for each cluster and the above computation is repeated for each cluster.

To decide between the two possible units, we project the data eigher using an RBF or a ridge, thus consider two 1-D data fiting problems; The ridge projection is a monotonic increasing with the correlation between its weight vector and the data points. It achieves its maximum value when the correlation is maximized (for a unit projection vector). Therefore, the weight vector should be proportional to the average over all patterns in the cluster (there is a strong assumption here about the lack of effect of the sigmoidal term on the optimization, but remember that this is only to choos optimal initial conditions, and perform model selection.)

The RBF function, on the other hand, is monotonic decreasing with the distance from the maximum point. Thus, the center of the RBF is located at the function maximum point. Selection of the value that maximizes the likelihood in this case is trivial. Finally, the unit type with the higher likelihood is selected for the current cluster.

The above calculation did not take into account the sign of the forward parameter that connects the hidden unit to the ouput layer. In order to take it into account, we need to calculate the values that maximze and minimize the likelihood for each unit, and then calculate the sign of the forward connection (using the simple inverse procedure of the hidden unit activity matrix) and choose the values which are consistent with the sign of the forward connection. In other words, if the forward connection turns out to be positive, the value which maximized the likelihood should be chosen and vice versa.

Thus, the above procedure is repeated with the above transformation on each of the target function values. Finally, the most probable unit type of both cases is chosen.

Classification unit type selection. In classification, the target function has multiple values for each pattern. Thus, the previous technique can not be directly applied. For simplicity, we assume that the clustering which has been performed in the previous step, has purified the clusters, namely, each cluster mostly contains patterns from a single class. Under this assumption, it is reasonable to use the likelihood of the data points within the cluster as an indication of the fit of different unit types. Note, that this assumption may be too strong, especially in the early stages of incrementaly constructing an architecture. Relaxing this assumption is a subject for future work.

To derive the most probable value of the weights, a linear approximation for the weights of the ridge function is used. Thus, the ridge function is approximated by $w^T x$. Hence, we wish to maximize the scalar product of w and the sum of the patterns in the current cluster. Since this is an unconstrained optimization, a Lagrange multiplier is introduced to enforce the following constrain:

$$w^T w = 1,$$

arriving at the following objective function:

$$L(w, \alpha) = \sum_{i=1}^{N} w^T x_i + \alpha(w^T w - 1), \tag{6}$$

where N is the number of patterns in the current cluster. The partial derivative with respect to the weight vector is:

$$\frac{\partial L}{\partial w} = \sum_{i=1}^{N} x_i + 2\alpha w, \tag{7}$$

and the partial derivative with respect to α is

$$\frac{\partial L}{\partial \alpha} = \sum_{i=1}^{d} w_i^2 - 1. \tag{8}$$

For convenience, let $Z = \sum_{i=1}^{N} x_i$. Setting Equation 7 to zero gives:

$$Z = -2\alpha w.$$

Squaring both sides and using (8) gives:

$$\| Z \|^2 = 4\alpha^2.$$

Thus, we obtain:

$$2\alpha = \pm \| Z \|,$$

or,

$$w = \pm \frac{Z}{\| Z \|}. \tag{9}$$

The Hessian, which is derived from Equation 7, provides the correct sign of w_j and ensures the maximization procedure:

$$\frac{\partial^2 J}{\partial w^2} = 2\alpha I. \tag{10}$$

Thus, the Hessian is a diagonal matrix, and it is negative when α is negative, leading to setting w as follows:

$$w = \frac{Z}{\| Z \|}. \tag{11}$$

The response of an RBF unit is proportional to the distance of patterns from its center. Thus, we seek to minimize the the sum of distances of the patterns from an unknown vector. Let us define the following objective function:

$$L(m) = \sum_{i=n}^{N} (x_n - m)^2, \tag{12}$$

where x_n is a pattern vector in the current cluster and m is an unknown vector. The partial derivative with respect to m is

$$\frac{\partial L}{\partial m} = -2 \sum_{i=1}^{N} (x_i - m). \tag{13}$$

Equating to zero we arrive at:

$$m = \frac{1}{N} \sum_{i=1}^{N} x_i. \tag{14}$$

Thus, we have the most probable values of the center of the RBF and weight of the Ridge function. We, now compute the likelihood of the cluster data for the two models and select the most likely model. The likelihood is defined as

$$p(D/M) = \prod_{i=1}^{N} p(xi|C), \tag{15}$$

where

$$p(xi|C) = \frac{1}{1 + \exp(-w^T x)}$$

for ridge function, and

$$p(xi|C) = \exp(\frac{- \| x - m \|^2}{2\sigma^2})$$

for RBF function. However, since the ridge function is an improper probability density function, that is:

$$\int_{-\infty}^{\infty} p(x|C)dx \neq 1$$

We normalize it by the factor:

$$\sum_{i=1}^{N} p(x_i|C),$$

Where N is the number of the patterns in the data set.

4 Experimental Results

This section describes regression and classification results of several variants of RBF and the proposed PRBFN architecture on several data sets. Since this paper extends our first extension into hybrid MLP/RBF network [3], we shall denote the architecture resulting from the previous work as PRBFN and results from the construction presented in this work as PRBFN2. The following results are given on the test portion of each data set (full details are in [3]). They represent are an average over 100 runs and include standard error.

4.1 Regression

The LogGaus data set is a composition of one ridge function and three Gaussian-s as follows 1:

$$f(x) = \frac{1}{1 + exp(-w^T x)} + \sum_{i=1}^{3} exp(-\frac{\| x - m_i \|^2}{2\sigma^2}),$$

Where $w = (1,1)$, the centers of the Gaussian functions are at $(1,1),(1,-5),(-4,-2)$ and $\sigma = 1$. A random normally distributed noise with zero mean and 0.1 variance is added to the function. The whole data is composed of 441 points and it is divided randomly into two sets of 221 and 220 points each. The first set is served as the train set and the second one is the test set. All the regressors, that we have tested did not reveal the true structure of the data, only PRBFN2 revealed the three Gaussian-s and the ridge function. This fact is amplified from the results on this data set. Thus, we make the observation that PRBFN has high performance when the data is composed from ridge and Gaussian-s. If the data is composed either from Gaussian-s of ridge function it can reach the performance of other regressors.

The second data-set is a 2D sine wave,

$$y = 0. \sin(x_1/4) \sin(x_2/2),$$

with 200 training patterns sampled at random from an input range $x_1 \in [0, \; 10]$ and $x_2 \in [-5, \; 5]$. The clean data was corrupted by additive Gaussian noise with

$\sigma = 0.1$. The test set contains 400 noiseless samples arranged as a 20 by 20 grid pattern, covering the same input ranges. Orr measured the error as the total squared error over the 400 samples. We follow Orr and report the error as the SSE on the test set.

The third data-set is a simulated alternating current circuit with four input dimensions (resistance R, frequency ω, inductance L and capacitance C and one output impedance $Z = \sqrt{R^2 + (\omega L - 1/\omega C)^2}$. Each training set contained 200 points sampled at random from a certain region [21, for further details]. Again, additive noise was added to the outputs. The experimental design is the same as the one used by Friedman in the evaluation of MARS [9]. Friedman's results include a division by the variance of the test set targets. We follow Friedman and report the normalized MSE on the test set. Orr's regression trees method [21] outperforms the other methods on this data set. However, the PRBFN neural network achieves similar results to Orr's method.

Table 1. Comparison of Mean squared error results on three data sets (see [21] for details). Results on the test set are given for several variants of RBF networks which were used also by Orr to asses RBFs. MSE Results of an average over 100 runs including standard deviation are presented.

	LogGauss	2D Sine	Friedman
Rbf-Orr	0.02 ±0.14	0.91 ±0.19	0.12±0.03
Rbf-Matlab	-	0.74±0.4	0.2 ±0.03
Rbf-Bishop	0.02 ±0.02	0.53 ±0.19	0.18 ±0.02
PRBFN	0.02 ±0.02	0.53 ±0.19	0.15 ±0.03
PRBFN2	0.01±0.01	0.49 ±0.23	0.118±0.03

4.2   Classification

We have used several data sets to compare the classification performance of the proposed methods to other RBF networks. The sonar data set attempts to distinguish between a mine and a rock. It was used by Gorman and Sejnowski [22] in their study of the classification of sonar signals using neural networks. The data has 60 continuous inputs and one binary output for the two classes. It is divided into 104 training patterns and 104 test patterns. The task is to train a network to discriminate between sonar signals that are reflected from a metal cylinder and those that are reflected from a similar shaped rock. There are no results for Bishop's algorithm as we were not able to get it to reduce the output error. Gorman and Sejnowski report on results with feed-forward architectures [24] using 12 hidden units. They achieved 90.4%

correct classification on the test data with the angle dependent task. This result outperforms the results obtained by the different RBF methods, and is only surpassed by the proposed hybrid RBF—FF network.

The Deterding vowel recognition data [4,8] is a widely studied benchmark. This problem may be more indicative of the type of problems that a real neural network could be faced with. The data consists of auditory features of steady state vowels spoken by British English speakers. There are 528 training patterns and 462 test patterns. Each pattern consists of 10 features and it belongs to one of 11 classes that correspond to the spoken vowel. The speakers are of both genders. The best score so far was reported by Flake using his SMLP units. His average best score was 60.6% [8] and was achieved with 44 hidden units. Our algorithm achieved 68% correct classification with only 27 hidden units. As far as we know, it is the best result that was achieved on this data set. The waveform data set is a three class problem which was constructed by Brieman to demonstrate the performance of the Classification and Regression Trees method [1]. Each class consists of a random convex combination of two out of three waveforms sampled discretely with added Gaussian noise. The data set contains 5000 instance, and 300 are used for training. Recent reports on this data-set can be found in [13,2]. Each used a different size training set. We used the smaller training set size as in [13] who report best result of 19.1% error. The Optimal Bayes classification rate is 86% accuracy, the CART decision tree algorithm achieved 72% accuracy, and Nearest Neighbor Algorithm achieved 38% accuracy. PRBFN has achieved 85.8% accuracy on this data set. There is not much room for improvement over the PRBFN classifier, in this example.

Table 2 summarizes the percent correct classification results on the different data sets for the different RBF classifiers and the proposed hybrid architecture. As in the regression case, the STD is also given however, on the seismic data, due to the use of a single test set (as we wanted to see the performance on this particular data set only) the STD is often zero as only a single classification of the data was obtained in all 100 runs.

Table 2. Percent classification results of different classifiers variants on three data sets.

Algorithm	Sonar	Vowel	waveform
RBF-Orr	71.7±0.5	–	–
RBF-Matlab	82.3±2.4	51.6±2.9	83.8±0.2
RBF-Bishop	–	48.4±2.4	83.5±0.2
PRBFN	91±2	67±2	85.8±0.2
PRBFN2	91.3±2	68±2	85±0.3

The Protein data set imposes a difficult classification problem since originally the number of instance of each class diverse significantly. The input dimension of the patterns is 20 and there are 2255 patterns and two classes. The data set is divided to 1579 patterns in the train set and 676 patterns in the test set. The first class in the train set has only 340 instance and the second one has 1239 instances. Thus, the a-priori probability of the first class is 0.2153 while the a-priori probability of the second class is 0.7847. To overcome this problem we re-sample the first class patterns with normally distributed noise with mean zero and 0.01 variance. This data was not used in [3].

Table 3. Percent classification results of different classifiers variants on the Protein data sets.

Algorithm	OKProb class1	OKProb class2	Total OKProb
RBF-Orr	– ± – –	–	–
RBF-Matlab	– ± – –	– ± – –	– ± – –
RBF-Bishop	75.18±3	79.49±1.5	78.6±2
PRBFN2	77.4±5	80.11±2	79.56±3

5   Discussion

The work presented in this paper represent a major step in constructing an incremental hybrid architecture. It was motivated by the success of the original hybrid architecture which was introduced in [3]. Several assumptions were made in various parts of the architecture construction. Some of them are more justified and some require further refinement which is the subject of future work. Our aim was to show that even under these assumptions, an architecture that is smaller in size and better in generalization performance can already be achieved. Furthermore, while this architexture is particularly useful when the data contain ridge and Gaussian parts, its performance were not below the performance of the best known MLP or RBF networks when data that contains only one type of strucutre was used.

In previous work [3] we used hard threshold for unit type selection. The previous algorithm also accepted the number of hidden units in advance. This paper introduces an algorithm that reveals automatically the relevant parts of the data and maps these parts onto RBF or Ridge functions respectively. The algorithm also finds the number of hidden units for the network given only an error target. The automatic unit type detection uses the maximum likelihood principle in different manner for regression and classification. In regression the connection between the likelihood to the SSE is long known and used. In the classification case the output target function is not continuous and not scalar. The ridge function is an improper probability density function (PDF) and a normalization is made to transfer it into a PDF like function.

We have tested the new architecture construction on three regression problems and four classification problems. There are three cases where better results were obtained. In the extensively studied vowel data set, the proposed hybrid architecture achieved average results which are superior to the best known results [23] and uses a smaller number of hidden units. On the waveform classification problem [1], our results are close to the Bayes limit for the data and are better than the current known results. In the LogGaus data set, which is composed of Ridge and Gaussian parts – an excellent example for our hybrid – results were again improved with our proposed architecture construction. We are excited about the ability to better model extensively studied, nonlinear data, in particular, demonstrate increased generalization, while keeping the number of the estimated parameters smaller.

References

1. L. Breiman, J. H. Friedman, R. A. Olshen, and C. J. Stone. *Classification and Regression Trees*. The Wadsworth Statistics/Probability Series, Belmont, CA, 1984.
2. J. Buckheit and D. L. Donoho. Improved linear discrimination using time-frequency dictionaries. Technical Report, Stanford University, 1995.
3. S. Cohen and N. Intrator. A hybrid projection based and radial basis function architecture. In J. Kittler and F. Roli, editors, *Proc. Int. Workshop on Multiple Classifier Systems (LNCS1857)*, pages 147–156, Sardingia, June 2000. Springer.
4. D. H. Deterding. *Speaker Normalisation for Automatic Speech Recognition*. PhD thesis, University of Cambridge, 1989.
5. D. L. Donoho and I. M. Johnstone. Projection-based approximation and a duality with kernel methods. *Annals of Statistics*, 17:58–106, 1989.
6. H. Drucker, R. Schapire, and P. Simard. Improving performance in neural networks using a boosting algorithm. In Steven J. Hanson, Jack D. Cowan, and C. Lee Giles, editors, *Advances in Neural Information Processing Systems*, volume 5, pages 42–49. Morgan Kaufmann, 1993.
7. S. E. Fahlman and C. Lebiere. The cascade–correlation learning architecture. CMU-CS-90-100, Carnegie Mellon University, 1990.
8. G. W. Flake. Square unit augmented, radially extended, multilayer percpetrons. In G. B. Orr and K. Müller, editors, *Neural Networks: Tricks of the Trade*, pages 145–163. Springer, 1998.
9. J. H. Friedman. Mutltivariate adaptive regression splines. *The Annals of Statistics*, 19:1–141, 1991.
10. J. H. Friedman and W. Stuetzle. Projection pursuit regression. *Journal of the American Statistical Association*, 76:817–823, 1981.
11. T. Hastie and R. Tibshirani. Generalized additive models. *Statistical Science*, 1:297–318, 1986.
12. T. Hastie and R. Tibshirani. *Generalized Additive Models*. Chapman and Hall, London, 1990.
13. T. Hastie, R. Tibshirani, and A. Buja. Flexible discriminant analysis by optimal scoring. *Journal of the American Statistical Association*, 89:1255–1270, 1994.
14. R. A. Jacobs, M. I. Jordan, S. J. Nowlan, and G. E. Hinton. Adaptive mixtures of local experts. *Neural Computation*, 3(1):79–87, 1991.
15. M. I. Jordan and R. A. Jacobs. Hierarchies of adaptive experts. In J. E. Moody, S. J. Hanson, and R. P. Lippmann, editors, *Advances in Neural Information Processing Systems*, volume 4, pages 985–992. Morgan Kaufmann, San Mateo, CA, 1992.
16. R. E. Kass and A. E. Raftery. Bayes factors. *Journal of The American Statistical Association*, 90:773–795, 1995.
17. Y. C. Lee, G. Doolen, H. H. Chen, G. Z.Sun, T. Maxwell, H.Y. Lee, and C. L. Giles. Machine learning using higher order correlation networks. *Physica D,*, 22:276–306, 1986.

18. D. J. C. MacKay. Bayesian interpolation. *Neural Computation*, 4(3):415–447, 1992.
19. John Moody. Prediction risk and architecture selection for neural networks. In V. Cherkassky, J. H. Friedman, and H. Wechsler, editors, *From Statistics to Neural Networks: Theory and Pattern Recognition Applications*. Springer, NATO ASI Series F, 1994.
20. S. J. Nowlan. Soft competitive adaptation: Neural network learning algorithms basd on fitting statistical mixtures. Ph.D. dissertation, Carnegie Mellon University, 1991.
21. M. J. Orr, J. Hallman, K. Takezawa, A. Murray, S. Ninomiya, M. Oide, and T. Leonard. Combining regression trees and radial basis functions. Division of informatics, Edinburgh University, 1999. Submitted to IJNS.
22. Gorman R. P. and Sejnowski T. J. Analysis of hidden units in a layered network trained to classify sonar targets. *Neural Network*, pages 75–89, 1988. Vol. 1.
23. A. J. Robinson. *Dynamic Error Propogation Networks*. PhD thesis, University of Cambridge, 1989.
24. D. E. Rumelhart, G. E. Hinton, and R. J. Williams. Learning internal representations by error propagation. In D. E. Rumelhart and J. L. McClelland, editors, *Parallel Distributed Processing*, volume 1, pages 318–362. MIT Press, Cambridge, MA, 1986.
25. C. J. Stone. The dimensionality reduction principle for generalized additive models. *The Annals of Statistics*, 14:590–606, 1986.

Author Index

Lecture Notes in Computer Science

For information about Vols. 1–1998
please contact your bookseller or Springer-Verlag